discover LOS
ANGELES

An Informed Guide
to L.A.'s Rich and
Varied Cultural Life

by Letitia Burns O'Connor

introduction by Kevin Starr

with contributions by
Robin Dunitz
Sharon K. Emanuelli
René Engel and Jason Martin
Noriko Fujinami
Peter Henné
Ellen Krout-Hasegawa
Mary Jane O'Donnell
Tom Provenzano
Margaret Trumbull Nash

THE J. PAUL GETTY TRUST

discover LOS

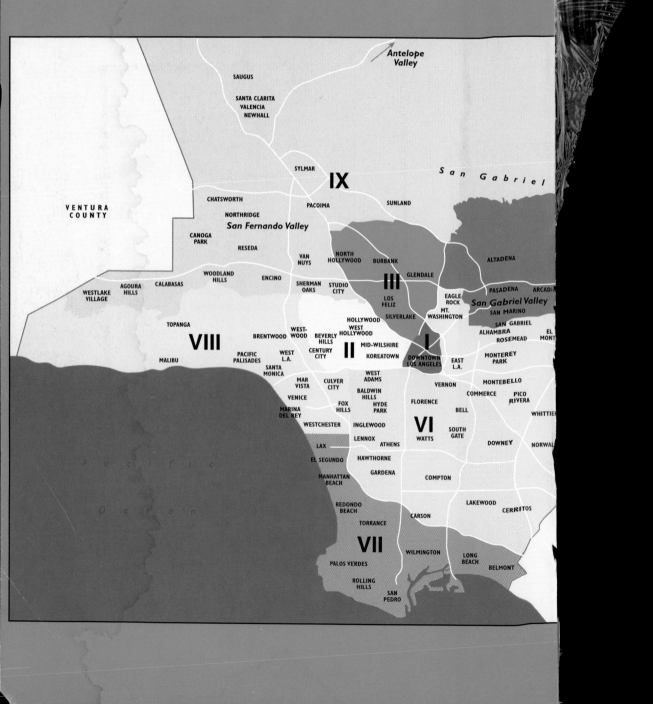

Antelope Valley

SAUGUS

SANTA CLARITA
VALENCIA
NEWHALL

San Gabriel

SYLMAR

IX

VENTURA
COUNTY

CHATSWORTH   PACOIMA   SUNLAND

NORTHRIDGE
San Fernando Valley

CANOGA
PARK

RESEDA

ALTADENA

VAN
NUYS

NORTH
HOLLYWOOD   BURBANK

WOODLAND
HILLS   ENCINO

AGOURA   CALABASAS
HILLS

SHERMAN
OAKS   STUDIO
CITY

GLENDALE

PASADENA   ARCADIA

WESTLAKE
VILLAGE

LOS
FELIZ

EAGLE
ROCK   SAN MARINO
MT.   *San Gabriel Valley*
WASHINGTON   SAN GABRIEL

TOPANGA

HOLLYWOOD
WEST-   WEST
WOOD   HOLLYWOOD

SILVERLAKE

ALHAMBRA   EL
ROSEMEAD   MONT

VIII

BRENTWOOD   BEVERLY
HILLS

II   MID-WILSHIRE

I

MALIBU

PACIFIC
PALISADES

WEST
L.A.   CENTURY
CITY   KOREATOWN

DOWNTOWN
LOS ANGELES   EAST
L.A.

MONTEREY
PARK

SANTA
MONICA

MAR
VISTA   CULVER
CITY

WEST
ADAMS

VERNON

MONTEBELLO

VENICE

BALDWIN
HILLS

FLORENCE   COMMERCE   PICO
RIVERA

MARINA
DEL REY   FOX
HILLS   HYDE
PARK   BELL

WHITTIER

WESTCHESTER   INGLEWOOD

VI
WATTS   SOUTH
GATE

DOWNEY   NORWAL

LAX   LENNOX   ATHENS

EL SEGUNDO   HAWTHORNE

MANHATTAN
BEACH   GARDENA

COMPTON

LAKEWOOD   CERRITOS

REDONDO
BEACH   CARSON

TORRANCE

VII

PALOS VERDES   WILMINGTON   LONG
BEACH   BELMONT

ROLLING
HILLS   SAN
PEDRO

Pacific   Ocean

ANGELES

by Letitia Burns O'Connor

suits are available in the region's many parks and preserves. It takes two full pages of fine print to inventory the sites and activities within the six-square-mile Griffith Park, in the center of the city proper—its zoological gardens, its four golf courses, its twenty-four tennis courts, its merry-go-round and cycling paths, and its hiking trails that lead into the high chaparral and offer a stunning 360-degree view of Los Angeles. Numerous regional parks, many of them centered on the great canyons — Eaton Canyon, Franklin Canyon, Marshall Canyon —which crisscross the region, preserve near-wilderness environments similar to what Native-Americans and Spanish pioneers must have experienced in times past.

Each park is, of course, in its own way a garden, but the region is famous as well for its more formal public gardens. The Huntington Botanical Gardens in San Marino, especially its famous cactus collection, recapitulates the flora of the entire region. The Arboretum of Los Angeles County includes historic buildings as well as specimen trees and landscaped environments. Descanso Gardens in La Cañada-Flintridge, developed by publisher E. Manchester Boddy and purchased by Los Angeles County in 1953, features 100,000 camellias beneath a canopy of ancient live oaks. The Rancho Santa Ana Botanic Garden in Claremont (now affiliated with the university) has one of the finest native plant environments in the region. Even Forest Lawn Memorial Parks, among the most famous cemeteries in the world, are gardens of sorts, and the Rose Hills Memorial Park in Whittier, which won a national award for its rose garden, also features a Japanese-theme garden. Henry Huntington built a garden in the Japanese style for his new wife in 1913, and the format is still favored by landscape architects, who have used it to transform a water-reclamation plant in the San Fernando Valley and enhance the campus of California State University, Long Beach.

In 1769 Alta California came into the possession of the Spanish crown, which used four key institutions—missions, presidios, pueblos, and ranchos—to Hispanicize its new colony. Miraculously, the "queen of the California missions"—Mission San Gabriel Arcángel, founded in 1771—still survives and recently underwent a $3-million restoration. Here, for more than 225 years, men and women of Native-American, Spanish, and Mexican descent have gathered with others for worship in a building that predates the founding of the American republic and that—like the Mission San Fernando Rey de España and Our Lady, Queen of the Angels (La

Placita), the city's oldest church—continues to link metropolitan Los Angeles to living history.

Recognizing that this city, for all its worldliness and engagement with the present, has not ceased its collective and individual search for the transcendent, this volume devotes eight pages to churches, synagogues, and temples, wherein the great religious traditions of the world flourish, together with a number of other, newer variations on humankind's continuing search for meaning. "Finding God in the City of Angels"—along with inventories of the region's extraordinary offerings in music, theater and dance, film and video, public art and murals, commercial art galleries and auction houses, and essays on its literary life and that most modern forum of human exchange, the Internet—is evidence that *Discover Los Angeles* has redefined the guidebook format.

The Hispanic past that survives in the adobes of El Pueblo de Los Angeles Historical Monument, a forty-four-acre state historic park near the Civic Center, adjacent to the spot where Los Angeles was founded in September 1781, is an instance of living history; for the crowded life of El Pueblo—its Mexican restaurants and shops, the throngs of shoppers up and down Olvera Street, the worshipers at La Placita —represent a living link between present-day Los Angeles and its Spanish and Mexican foundations. Survivors of the rancho era, when longhorn cattle roamed a thousand hills, include La Casa Primera and Adobe de Palomares in Pomona, the Dominguez Ranch Adobe in the southern district of the city, and Rancho los Cerritos and Rancho los Alamitos in Long Beach.

Turn-of-the-century Angelenos rediscovered the Spanish and Mexican past and appropriated it as their own. They introduced Hispanic themes in the architecture of the developing city, dubbed streets with Spanish names, and in general romanticized the mission, pueblo, and rancho era. No one was more committed to this historicizing effort than the turn-of-the-century writer Charles Fletcher Lummis. His home, El Alisal, named for the sycamores growing nearby, still graces the Arroyo running through Highland Park and serves as the headquarters for the Historical Society of Southern California, which takes as its special province the Spanish, Mexican, American frontier, and American Victorian eras of the region.

The military brought California into American possession during the Mexican War. The Drum Barracks Civil War Museum in Wilmington is the closest we can come to that pioneering military presence. Established in 1862, Camp Drum supported at its height some 7,000 Union soldiers, whose presence in California continued an army occupation unbroken since 1846. The nearby Fort MacArthur Military Museum in San Pedro, named after the father of General Douglas MacArthur, brings the story of Southern California and the military up through World War II, as does the SS *Lane Victory*, berthed in San Pedro Harbor next to the World Cruise Center, one of the few surviving Liberty ships of the hundreds built in this area during that era, when metropolitan Los Angeles emerged as a Gibraltar on the Pacific, an identity it maintained through the end of the Cold War.

The Workman and Temple Family Homestead Museum (in today's City of Industry) recalls the first phase of the American frontier in this region: the years when Yankees and Southerners came to California, married Mexican women, became (before the conquest of 1846) Mexican citizens, and lived as lords of land and cattle. The Banning Residence Museum in Wilmington, built in 1864 in the Greek revival style, keeps alive the memory of the most dynamic entrepreneur of the American frontier era. Phineas Banning arrived in San Pedro in 1851 at the age of twenty-one, dreaming of developing the region, and proceeded to do exactly that— as rancher, shipper, lumberman, hotelman, railroad developer, and real-estate magnate. The home he built re-created as closely as possible a house he had seen on a hill outside Wilmington, Delaware, as a fourteen-year-old boy. He vowed that he, too, would one day have a home like that, and he did, albeit on the other side of the continent.

Banning was first and foremost an entrepreneur of shipping and transportation. In the first phase of its American existence, Los Angeles was a hard place to get to. A railroad connection to the East did not arrive until 1876, and that was via San Francisco. The Travel Town Museum in Griffith Park addresses the transportation history of Los Angeles, as do the Los Angeles Maritime Museum in San Pedro and artifacts scattered in collections throughout the county. Not surprisingly, given the region's longtime love affair with cars, the automobile has its own museum. The Petersen Automotive Museum, affiliated with the Natural History Museum of Los Angeles County in Exposition Park, not only preserves superb specimens but also explores the impact of the car on the urban landscape— in the evolution of its freeways and the architecture of its streetscapes.

The Autry Museum of Western Heritage, in Griffith Park, takes as its domain the frontier era of fact and the mythopoetic West of a thousand films, paperback westerns, and cowboy songs. Built with a $54-million gift from the Autry Foundation, the museum celebrates this region's *vaquero* and cowboy past—although it is actually devoted to the entire West in its frontier phases—while reveling in the vivid and colorful part that singing cowboy

and entrepreneur Gene Autry and his cohorts played in developing its mythology.

Little of the Victorian past that succeeded the frontier has survived in metropolitan Los Angeles, which is not surprising in a region surging so relentlessly toward the future. However, surviving Victorians, dating from 1865 to 1914, have been brought together in the Heritage Square Museum in Highland Park, and the Los Angeles Conservancy, which over the past two decades has coaxed the citizens of Los Angeles to value the architectural heritage of the metropolitan area, has recently inaugurated monthly walking tours of Angelino Heights, a suburban development of that era that still exists as a living neighborhood and repository of Victorian residential buildings. Architecture, the Conservancy has argued, is one of the primary means through which the city has stored its past and thereby created an arsenal of visual and design references for an eclectic postmodernist future.

Of special interest to the Conservancy, which is headquartered downtown, are the great 1920s movie palaces lining Broadway and such art deco treasures as the Oviatt Building. *Discover Los Angeles* lists many of the tours offered by the Conservancy, which, together with many other buildings described in this guide, take the metropolitan region through its successive architectural eras: Craftsman, "City Beautiful," early modernism, art deco, the International Style, modernism, and postmodernist contemporary.

The Craftsman (bungalow) era, which flourished at the turn of the century, is most vividly represented in the magnificent Gamble House in Pasadena, designed by Charles S. and Henry M. Greene in 1908 for the heirs to the Procter and Gamble fortune. Its fastidiously worked wood, magnificent art glass, and colorful tile unite the artisanal traditions of the Arroyo School, which gave the Arts and Crafts movement expression in Southern California. Early modernism—indeed, a modernism ahead of its time, inspired by the stark simplicities of North Africa and the Spanish Southwest—characterizes the country home built in 1920 by Irving Gill for Chauncey and Marie Clarke on their sixty-acre citrus ranch in Santa Fe Springs. Constructed from poured-in-place concrete, this 8,000-square-foot structure expresses, as only the buildings of Irving Gill can, the sense of new beginnings in dialogue with tradition which pervaded early twentieth-century Southern California.

Frank Lloyd Wright was, of course, an architect unto himself in terms of school or style, yet his Hollyhock House in Los Feliz also exudes the innovative hopefulness of metropolitan Southern

California in that era. Built between 1917 and 1920 for oil heiress and art patron Aline Barnsdall, Hollyhock House now stands at the center of the buildings and programs of Barnsdall Art Park, which include the Municipal Art Gallery, a public institution where Barnsdall's interest in the arts survives in a score of arts-oriented exhibitions and programs.

The City Beautiful movement, against which Wright struggled so vociferously, survives dramatically in both the Civic Center of Pasadena and the stately pathways, formal gardens, and beaux-arts revival architecture of Exposition Park, south of downtown. Within Exposition Park is the Los Angeles Memorial Coliseum, built a full decade in advance for the Summer Olympic Games of 1932, which Los Angeles used as a spur to civic self-improvement and development. On the nearby University of Southern California campus are a number of fine buildings from the 1920s—the Mudd Hall of Philosophy, the Doheny Memorial Library, the Bovard Administration Building, and the Wilson Student Union Building. Founded in 1880, USC experienced quantitative and qualitative growth in the 1920s, propelled in part by its nationally prominent football team, but also by the sheer exuberance of metropolitan Los Angeles in that decade, which saw more than three million new residents pour into Southern California.

Dedicated in the early 1930s, the Doheny Memorial Library—built in honor of Edward Laurence Doheny Jr., who was murdered in February 1929—is linked to another great building of this era: Greystone in Beverly Hills, a fifty-five-room, 46,000-square-foot English Gothic mansion designed by Gordon Kaufmann for oil magnate Edward Doheny, who hoped to establish an oil-based dynasty in this stupendous edifice. Greystone and its gardens represent the absolute high point of a lavish architectural decade.

*D*iscover Los Angeles begins appropriately with what is perhaps the single greatest building in the city and one of its most impressive cultural resources: the Los Angeles Public Library's Central Library. Designed by Bertram Goodhue and Carleton Winslow in 1922 and completed at the foot of Bunker Hill downtown in 1926, the Central Library is, like Los Angeles itself, sui generis, one of a kind. If the question "Where is Los Angeles localized?" can be answered—because Los Angeles is everywhere—the one place that encapsulates it might very well be the Central Library, which, since its restoration and expansion by Hardy Holzman Pfeiffer Associates after severe damage caused by two arson fires in 1986, has regained its rightful place in the city's fabric. Another candidate for L.A.'s signature icon is City Hall (1928), a modernist shaft sur-

mounted by an Halicarnassian ziggurat, which, through the long decades of the 150-foot height limit, floated above the city like a survivor from the set of D. W. Griffith's *Intolerance*. City Hall anchors the Civic Center, the second-largest governmental complex in the United States. (The number of independent municipalities in the region has created other impressive civic centers; Beverly Hills Civic Center, smaller in scale, Spanish in style, is especially notable for a $120-million renovation and expansion by the noted postmodernist architect Charles Moore.)

The Central Library is the flagship of only one of the three systems that provide public library services to the citizens of Los Angeles County. The Metropolitan Cooperative Library System unites the resources of the many independent communities in a cooperative network; and the county libraries not only offer services in unincorporated districts but have created four resource centers that house collections relevant to significant ethnic groups (Asian Pacific, African-American, Chicano, and Native-American Resource Centers). *Discover Los Angeles* thoroughly documents that metropolitan Los Angeles is one of the great library cities of the nation, listing public libraries that are significant for their holdings, as well as their history and architecture, and the main branch of each independent system. The Huntington Library, Art Collections, and Botanical Gardens in San Marino is especially notable among the private libraries because its founder successfully realized the almost ferocious determination of the turn-of-the-century generation—which continued through the 1920s—to make Los Angeles a world center of culture and art. The Spanish Romanesque quadrangle of the University of California, Los Angeles, radiates the same spirit; like the Huntington, the William Andrews Clark Memorial Library, built in 1926 in the West Adams district of the city and donated to UCLA in 1934, houses a world-class collection of British and Irish literature. The Southwest Museum encompasses the richly endowed Braun Research Library, with particular strength in early California cultures and history.

In the 1930s, when the City of Los Angeles reversed its north-south axis of expansion and moved westward toward Santa Monica Bay, it also embraced the art deco style, which became another of the eclectic metropolis's signatures. The Bullocks-Wilshire Department Store Building (1929), designed by John and Donald Parkinson, led this westward parade down Wilshire Boulevard through the Miracle Mile. Today, restored as the Southwestern University School of Law Library, the building remains the commanding point of reference for art deco Los Angeles. Also in this category is Kaufmann's astonishing Los Angeles Times Building near the Civic Center, designed in 1931, and Union Station (1939), yet another Parkinson creation and the last great masterpiece of the art deco era. Today the station has been integrated into the Gateway Transit Center, a convergence and departure point for Amtrak, Metro Rail, and MTA buses: another instance of recycling and continuance in the surviving historic fabric of the city. Union Station can be described as Spanish revival, but it also looks back to the Hispanic minimalism of Irving Gill and is linked laterally to the cool, clean lines of the moderne.

Los Angeles's chief exponents of the International Style were Viennese émigrés Rudolf Schindler and Richard Neutra. Two of these influential architects' masterpieces survive in the public domain: the R. M. Schindler House in West Hollywood has since 1994 been administered by the Austrian Museum of Applied Arts (MAK) as a center for visiting scholars in art and architecture; the School of Environmental Design at California Polytechnic University, Pomona, has more recently become the custodian of Richard Neutra's Silverlake home.

The rise of metropolitan Los Angeles cannot be considered outside the context of entertainment, the single industry that, above all others, has given Los Angeles its signature identity, most notably in motion pictures, television, and recorded music. Three of the best-known motion picture studios—Paramount Pictures Studios (which incorporates RKO Studios), Universal Studios, and Warner Bros.—offer widely differing access to the public. Other aspects of the cultural and economic forces that have led this region since the 1920s are explored in the Hollywood Studio Museum (currently undergoing reorganization) which is housed in the barn where Cecil B. DeMille launched his filmmaking career, and the new Hollywood Entertainment Museum, funded by the Community Redevelopment Agency as part of its efforts to restore the luster of Hollywood Boulevard. The Academy of Motion Picture Arts and Sciences, with its Center for Motion Picture Study, the American Cinémathèque, and the American Film Institute, as well as UCLA and LACMA, are included in an ambitious listing of the many ongoing film programs in the metropolitan region.

So, too, do institutions of music, dance, drama, and the other performing arts pervade this guide, for Los Angeles is a performing arts–oriented town. The Hollywood Bowl, after all, and the Music Center (the Dorothy Chandler Pavilion, the Mark Taper Forum, the Ahmanson Theater) helped the city define itself at critical stages of its development through great public works devoted to the performing arts. Somewhat surprisingly, given the overwhelming presence of motion pictures and television, *Discover Los Angeles* demonstrates through dozens and dozens of listings that Los Angeles is a music town and a dance town and a theater town as well as a city enamored of cinema.

In the first era of national radio, Los Angeles was king, and the city has been a center for the television industry since it was inaugurated. The Museum of Television & Radio, which has existed in New York since 1975, recently opened a branch in Beverly Hills—in a stunning building designed by Richard Meier, architect of the Getty Center—to bring that media story back where it began. NBC Television offers 75-minute tours of its gigantic Burbank facility, made famous by Johnny Carson, who each evening announced to millions that he was broadcasting from "beautiful downtown Burbank." Burbank, one of the most vibrant cities in the region, documents its role in the entertainment industry in a museum complex run by the Burbank Historical Society, where the city's predominance as a center of aircraft manufacture, home of the Lockheed plant during World War II, is also celebrated. Aviation, like entertainment, has historically been one of the leading elements in the economy, and hence the physical fabric, of this metropolitan region.

Aviation was both a cause and an effect of the area's longtime connection to science: the Mount Wilson Observatory, established in 1904 by astronomer George Ellery Hale in the San Gabriel Mountains overlooking Pasadena, led to the revitalization of the Throop Polytechnic Institute into a new and soon-to-be-awesome entity called the California Institute of Technology (Caltech), where the winning of Nobel Prizes soon seemed an annual, or at least biannual, occurrence. Planned by Bertram Goodhue, with its first quadrangle designed by Myron Hunt, the 124-acre Caltech campus in Pasadena superbly evokes the culture of science in the Southland. The landmark Griffith Observatory continues to advance the cause of astronomical education from a more popular and accessible platform. Los Angeles County maintains an outstanding Natural History Museum in Exposition Park, adjacent to the state-run California Science Center, which is the focus of a multimillion-dollar redevelopment, evidence of the continuing importance of science education in the region's future.

The metropolitan region is also a world center of higher education. USC, UCLA, and Caltech have already been mentioned. Occidental College in Highland Park is an integrated architectural masterpiece by Myron Hunt, and the Claremont Colleges, clustered on the eastern edge of Los Angeles County, celebrate sheer architectural variety within their Oxbridge-style quadrangles. The region's various California State University campuses—in Los Angeles, Pomona, Dominguez Hills, Northridge, and Long Beach—each provide an intellectual focus for their communities, with art galleries, theaters, and performing arts programs.

Ethnicity is fundamental to any definition of Los Angeles: this most diverse city has been that way since its founding in September 1781. For several ethnic groups, it is the largest population center outside the homeland: the second-largest Mexican population, after Mexico City; the second-largest Korean population, after Seoul. Here, after all, is being carried on—sometimes successfully, sometimes catastrophically—a global-level experiment in multicultural, multiethnic living.

The Southwest Museum, in the Highland Park–Mount Washington district, is committed to the appreciation and presentation of the Native-American past, not only of the Los Angeles region but of the entire Southwest as well. Stored and displayed here, in an elegant Spanish revival building that opened in 1914, are the art and artifacts of the Native-American centuries, which form not only the prologue to the Spanish, Mexican, and U.S. history of metropolitan Los Angeles but a paradigm of the future as well, for today the region supports the nation's largest urban enclave of Native-Americans. Their living traditions, as well as their history and present concerns, are an important focus of the Southwest Museum's programs.

The connection of metropolitan Los Angeles to Mexico and its people is of no mere antiquarian interest. It is, rather, part of the vital present and future of the city; for Latinos are surging toward demographic dominance of both Los Angeles and the state. The many Latino organizations and programs listed in this guide bespeak the importance, numerically and culturally, of this heritage; and the creation of new institutions, like the Museum of Latin American Art in Long Beach—half of whose collection consists of contemporary Mexican art—and new programs—including the Los Angeles County Museum of Art's plans to celebrate the recent donation of a collection of Mexican modernist paintings—suggests the ongoing cross-cultural assimilation.

Metropolitan Los Angeles is also one of the world centers of Jewish civilization: within the Jewish Federation Building, headquarters of one of the region's oldest social service organizations, is the Martyrs Memorial and Museum of the Holocaust; bus tours of sites associated with the city's Jewish heritage depart monthly from the building. The Museum of Tolerance at the Simon Wiesenthal Center for Holocaust Studies and the Skirball Cultural Center are new centers of Jewish life created by institutions with a long history in the area. Yiddish language and culture is enjoying a revival at Workman's Circle, especially through exhibitions at *A Shenere Velt* Gallery, dedicated to creating a "better and more beautiful world."

The Los Angeles area is one of the planet's most vital centers of Asian culture and economic enterprise. The "new Chinatown," north of downtown, has carried on the Chinese tradition in Los Angeles since the mid-nineteenth century and has been the first stopping-off point for many Asian peoples; more recently it has been supplanted by other, less central communities of immigrants. The experience of the Japanese, including the tragic events of their internment during World War II, are movingly portrayed at the Japanese American National Museum in Little Tokyo, with wide-ranging cultural programs available at the nearby Japanese American Cultural and Community Center. With its large Korean population, Los Angeles is naturally an outpost for the government-sponsored Korean Cultural Center, but in the aftermath of the 1992 civil disturbances, the history of Korean immigrants to America found a poignant voice in the new Korean American Museum of Art. The Pacific Asia Museum in Pasadena reflects the multifaceted fine arts of Asia in its collections and programs.

The African-American experience structures and animates a variety of established and new institutions; its arts and history are explored at the California African-American Museum in Exposition Park, the Museum of African American Art in the Baldwin Hills area, and the Western States Black Research Center. Leimert Park has become the locus of a renaissance in African-American life, which is galvanized by the music that emanates from the World Stage. William Grant Still set the standard for musical achievement in the black comunity, and the center that bears his name honors that legacy; the new partnership of the Theolonious Monk Institute of Jazz with the Music Center brings an important forum for African-American excellence to one of the city's most prestigious and prominent cultural venues. African-Americans came to metropolitan Los Angeles, slowly at first, then in larger numbers during World War II for the same reasons everyone else came: the chance for better jobs, home ownership, and a better education and other opportunities for their children. Today metropolitan Los Angeles is one of the most active centers of African-American urbanism in the country. No phase of regional life—whether politics, business, athletics, or entertainment —is without its influence.

Metropolitan Los Angeles is, in short, a great museum town. *Discover Los Angeles* includes entries on many of its unusual (even odd) collections: the Museum of Ancient Art, currently searching for exhibition space for its 2,000 artifacts; the Carole and Barry Kaye Museum of Miniatures on Wilshire Boulevard; and the Museum of Jurassic Technology. Every organization in Los Angeles seems to want a museum. The Los Angeles Sheriffs Department has its own museum in Whittier; firefighters have one in Long Beach. Scheduled to open in 1998 is the Los Angeles Police History and Community Education Center on York Avenue, designed to usher in a new era of understanding between the LAPD and the public. Even Frederick's of Hollywood maintains a lingerie museum on Hollywood Boulevard.

The region is especially rich in museums oriented toward children: the Los Angeles Children's Museum in downtown and Kidspace in Pasadena, which emphasize hands-on exhibits and the Children's Museum in La Habra, in northern Orange County. Older students are well served on the region's college campuses, notably by the Vincent Price Gallery at East Los Angeles College and the Fisher Art Gallery at the University of Southern California, which maintain interesting collections and ambitious exhibition programs in academic settings.

Discover Los Angeles reveals its author's fascination with how traditional fine art museums have evolved in the young city. The history of patronage at the Los Angeles County Museum of Art and the Museum of Contemporary Art is examined; the quirky benevolence that created the J. Paul Getty Museum and the collections of Norton Simon, Armand Hammer, and Henry Edwards Huntington are recalled. Collectively, these major museums—in terms of their holdings, exhibitions, research and teaching programs, as well as such popular events as free concerts—are transforming metropolitan Los Angeles into an art Alexandria on the Pacific Coast. The Getty Center, which published this guidebook on the occasion of its opening to share the expected, inevitable limelight with hundreds of other, less well-endowed institutions that enhance the cultural life of Los Angeles, should not itself be overlooked. It is a magnificent crown for a city that, through its consistent inventiveness, has come to deserve (and even demand) one.

A listing of commercial art galleries and auction houses fills eight pages in this book. Murals and public art are everywhere: in the lobbies of great buildings, alongside freeway overpasses, in post offices, terminals, and other public spaces. Contributors to this volume document the innovative tithing for public art that has created many places where murals and other installations, many of them of considerable artistic merit, might be enjoyed.

Here, then, in hundreds of listings of hundreds of cultural institutions, great and small, is proof positive that metropolitan Los Angeles, despite its well-known proclivity for private life, nevertheless sustains a commitment to public life, especially as it relates to the preservation and enjoyment of the many, many things human beings do as they seek to understand and to celebrate imaginatively the world around them and the mystery of human life. Men and women come together in cities, the ancient Greek philosopher Aristotle noted, so that they might become more human. That is what each of these institutions, grand and unpretentious alike, is all about: the struggle for humanity in an urban context. From this perspective the most significant listing in this guide is the whole metropolitan region itself, centered on the City of Angels: a community in time, where for the past 200 years people have come together (and, it can be hoped, will continue to do so for hundreds and hundreds of years to come) in institutions such as those listed here so that they might become more human, so that they might experience—in art, culture, and education—the enduring gifts of urban civilization.

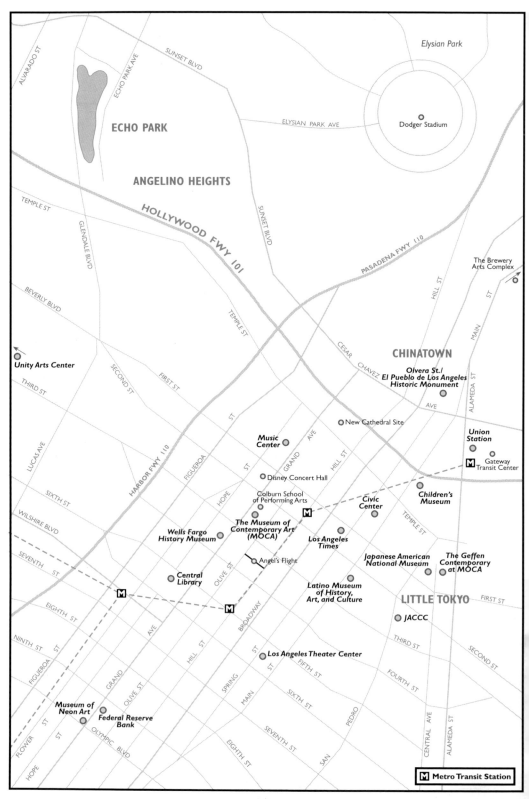

Elysian Park

ECHO PARK

Dodger Stadium

ANGELINO HEIGHTS

The Brewery
Arts Complex

CHINATOWN

Olvera St./
El Pueblo de Los Angeles
Historic Monument

Unity Arts Center

New Cathedral Site

Union
Station

Music
Center

Gateway
Transit Center

Disney Concert Hall

Colburn School
of Performing Arts

Civic
Center

Children's
Museum

The Museum of
Contemporary Art
(MOCA)

Wells Fargo
History Museum

Los Angeles
Times

Japanese American
National Museum

The Geffen
Contemporary
at MOCA

Angel's Flight

Central
Library

Latino Museum
of History,
Art, and Culture

LITTLE TOKYO

JACCC

Los Angeles Theater Center

Museum of
Neon Art

Federal Reserve
Bank

M Metro Transit Station

ALVARADO ST
ECHO PARK AVE
SUNSET BLVD
ELYSIAN PARK AVE
TEMPLE ST
GLENDALE BLVD
HOLLYWOOD FWY 101
SUNSET BLVD
PASADENA FWY 110
HILL ST
MAIN ST
BEVERLY BLVD
SECOND ST
FIRST ST
TEMPLE ST
CESAR CHAVEZ
ALAMEDA ST
THIRD ST
ST
AVE
LUCAS AVE
FIGUEROA
ST
GRAND
AVE
HILL ST
HARBOR FWY 110
HOPE
SIXTH ST
TEMPLE ST
WILSHIRE BLVD
SEVENTH ST
OLIVE ST
EIGHTH ST
BROADWAY
FIRST ST
THIRD ST
SECOND ST
NINTH ST
ST
AVE
HILL ST
FIFTH ST
FOURTH ST
FIGUEROA
GRAND
OLIVE ST
SPRING
MAIN
SIXTH ST
PEDRO
CENTRAL AVE
ALAMEDA ST
FLOWER ST
HOPE
OLYMPIC BLVD
SEVENTH ST
EIGHTH ST
SAN

Los Angeles Public Library
Central Library

630 W. Fifth Street
Los Angeles 90071
Mon., Thurs.–Sat. 10 a.m.–5:30 p.m., Tues.–Wed.
noon–8 p.m., Sun. 1–5 p.m.
213-228-7000

Two arson fires—the first in April 1986, the second the following September—badly damaged the Central Library, the administrative headquarters for the Los Angeles Public Library, which serves the city with sixty-seven branch libraries. The fate of the building, designed by Bertram Goodhue in 1922, had been the subject of intense debate for more than a decade: it was crammed with twice as many books as it was designed to hold and so inadequately wired that modern communication and retrieval systems could not be installed. A plan had been adopted by the Community Redevelopment Agency in 1983 to transfer the unused air rights above the library's five-acre site to a nearby location and sell those rights to a commercial developer, which would fund the expansion of the Central Library at little cost to the city. The architectural firm of Hardy Holzman Pfeiffer Associates, then engaged in developing a new master plan for the Los Angeles County Museum of Art, was selected in June 1983 to design an expanded library that would incorporate the historic building. When the fire alarm rang on the morning of April 29, 1986, architect Norman Pfeiffer and Central Library Director Elizabeth Gay, who were discussing the plans for the new library, were among those evacuated from the building.

When the smoke cleared, it was found that the building itself had fared better

than the collections: 600,000 books had been destroyed, and 700,000 water-soaked books had to be flash-frozen within forty-eight hours and later freeze-dried. A $10-million campaign to replace books lost in the fires was realized in twenty-two months, kicked off by a $2-million grant from the J. Paul Getty Trust and $500,000 from ARCO.

Closed for almost seven years, and sorely missed, the Central Library still incorporates the 1926 structure as the centerpiece of a state-of-the-art information complex. Free docent-led tours of the building, offered daily (Mon.–Fri. 12:30 p.m., Sat. 11 a.m. and 2 p.m., Sun. 2 p.m.), are a good introduction to library services as well as to the architecture of its flagship. A library card, good at all branches, is delivered immediately on completion of a simple application and allows the bearer access to the two million books organized in eleven subject departments.

When the Central Library reopened in October 1993, a reproduction of its finial torch topped the signature pyramidal tower, again holding the Light of Learning above Los Angeles. The pyramid and other Egyptian motifs in the decorative scheme, like the sphinxes flanking the original main staircase, were inspired by the discovery of King Tut's tomb in 1922. Limestone figures of Saint John, Homer, Shakespeare, David, Milton, Goethe, Plato, and Dante on its exterior were restored, revealing the true art deco style given them by artist Lee Lawrie (who also sculpted the main entry to the RCA building in Manhattan's Rockefeller Center). Lawrie's one-ton chandelier, incorporating forty-eight lights (for each state then in the Union) and zodiac symbols, is again suspended in the Loderick M. Cook Rotunda.

Murals and wall stencils, found to have escaped irreversible smoke damage thanks to sixty years of surface buildup, were cleaned by teams from the Getty Conservation Institute. The rotunda murals, painted in 1933 by Dean Cornwall, are elaborate, romantic tableaux including 300 figures and depicting four eras in California's past: the arrival of Spanish galleons off the coast, the building of the missions, the founding of Los Angeles, and the advent of the railroad. The historical theme continues in the murals by Albert Herter in what is now the children's department, off the rotunda, because this area previously housed the history collections. Open stacks in the children's department put most of its books within reach of young people, and ample seating, just the right size, invites

kids to curl up with a good book. There is also a multimedia center and the KLOS Story Theater, which presents free performances most Saturdays and Sundays at 2 p.m. Call 213-228-7250 for children's programs at the Central Library. The space formerly occupied by the children's wing—identified by the murals of Ivanhoe, painted by Julian Garnsey (who also stenciled the ceilings of the rotunda and main reading room) and A. W. Parsons—now houses the Fletcher Jones International Language Center, which offers computer databases in forty languages.

The new Tom Bradley Wing, which extends the building east along Fifth Street and more than doubles the library's space, respected the profile of Goodhue's structure, submerging half of the addition underground to continue the horizontal lines of the original plan. To illuminate the lower floors and create a focal point equivalent to the rotunda of the old building, the architects designed an eight-story glass-roofed atrium with paired escalators that transport visitors through the soaring, sunlit space. One percent of the construction costs (or $500,000) was earmarked for art, with the commission divided among several artists, who designed chandeliers and lanterns for the new atrium, a fence and gate with multilingual texts along Fifth Street, and even the elevator, which incorporates old catalogue cards whose subject headings identify the nature of the collections on each floor. Those really familiar with the Dewey decimal system can get their bearings just from the call numbers. Because ceiling heights in the addition are lower than those in the original structure, the architects inverted the ornamentation plan, adding interest underfoot with carpets that incorporate motifs from the murals and stencils that draw the eye toward the ceilings of the old building.

The Central Library sponsors a monthly roundtable, which examines issues facing the community through panel discussions and questions from the audience, as well as regular classes on new technology and literary events. Call 213-228-7040 for a bimonthly program that lists events at all branch libraries in the city system.

Robert F. Maguire III—who, with his firm, Maguire Thomas Partners, played a central role in the 1983 redevelopment plan for the library site—has been honored for his long and generous patronage as the named benefactor of the renovated

gardens. The 1.5-acre park sits atop the new parking garage, but unlike Pershing Square, which did not have enough ground covering its garage to support full-sized trees, this urban oasis is shaded by 160 imported trees. Replicas of the pools from the old West Lawn, as well as two new fountains, add motion and sound to the garden; artwork includes a staircase by Jud Fine with risers inscribed in the many languages and with the various typologies found in the library collections.

The Central Library is the hub of a network of branches that, since November 1996, have been linked by an electronic network that allows patrons to place a hold on any book in the collection. This has increased transshipment requests sixfold. The need for branch libraries in order to "relieve congestion" and "save patrons time and carfare" was first articulated by Mary Jones, city librarian from 1900 to 1905. A successor convinced Andrew Carnegie to include Los Angeles in his library philanthropy, and in 1911 his contribution of $210,000 was used to build the first permanent branch buildings. Bond measures in 1921—used primarily to finance construction of the Central Library—and 1925 funded the expansion of the system: $500,000 from each bond was used to construct twelve to fourteen new buildings! The nucleus of the system was in place by the end of the 1920s, with thirty-four branches providing citizens access to library services within their own neighborhoods. In 1989 the voters authorized $53.4 million to renovate, replace, and build new branch libraries throughout Los Angeles. Branches notable for their architecture or collections are called out in each geographic section of this book.

Shades of L. A. is an ongoing effort to enhance the historical photo collection donated to the library by Security Pacific Bank by copying photographs from family albums (8,000 to date) to reflect more accurately the city's cultural diversity and community histories. Part of this collection is often displayed in one of the Central Library's gallery areas.

The Bunker Hill Steps includes an escalator and sweeping stairway surrounding a monumental watercourse, which some liken to Rome's Spanish Steps. It is a stylish link between the renovated Central Library and cultural institutions along Grand Avenue.

Music Center of Los Angeles County
Dorothy Chandler Pavilion
Mark Taper Forum
Ahmanson Theater

135 N. Grand Ave.
Los Angeles 90012
213-972-7483

To celebrate the thirtieth anniversary of the Taper, Judy Baca and SPARC painted a mural that depicts some of the theater's landmark productions on the south wall of the Music Center's administrative offices at Temple and Grand. A companion mural, featuring highlights of the Ahmanson Theater, is planned for the east wall of that building.

Free guided tours of the Music Center are offered Tuesday through Saturday; call 213-972-7483 to make reservations, required for groups of ten or more.

This three-theater, seven-acre white marble complex sits atop the northern edge of Bunker Hill. Its elevated site creates the atmosphere of a place apart—the world of great performances—especially if the visitor enters by the bronze gate with emerging figures designed by Robert Graham. That exhilarating feeling is not reinforced by the glacial architecture, but the playful, mesmerizing fountain surrounding Jacques Lipchitz's sculpture has become a tourist attraction, especially in summer, when some can't resist running through it.

The Dorothy Chandler Pavilion, named for the civic leader who spearheaded the drive to finance and build the complex, is the largest theater (3,197 seats) and was the first to open (in December 1964). It is home to the Los Angeles Philharmonic, Los Angeles Opera, and the Los Angeles Master Chorale and boasts one of the largest multipurpose stages in the country. The Thelonious Monk Institute of Jazz recently formed a partnership with the Music Center; among the first of its programs is a History of Jazz performance and lecture series, and the existing Jazz Sports L.A. an educational program in the public schools, will also be expanded. The round building in the center of the complex has a thrust stage and a 750-seat, steeply pitched auditorium that is home to the Mark Taper Forum, which for almost three decades has produced adventurous theater. The newly renovated proscenium-stage Ahmanson Theater can be

configured to seat from 1,300 to 2,000 patrons; it is often booked with long-running theatrical extravaganzas.

Symphonies for Youth introduces children ages six to twelve to the joys of music appreciation. The five concerts by the Los Angeles Philharmonic, held on Saturday mornings at the Dorothy Chandler Pavilion, are preceded by an hour-long interactive demonstration or workshop. Tickets, which cannot be refunded or exchanged, cost $6 to $10 for each performance. Call 213-972-0703 for more information on this program.

P.L.A.Y. (Performing for Los Angeles Youth) is a new acronym for the Mark Taper Forum's high-energy, multicultural theater program, which has been delighting young audiences for twenty-five years. Check listings for community cultural centers, or call Music Center on Tour (213-977-9555) to book P.L.A.Y. for your own school or organization. Through **Young Audiences** 3,000 high school students enjoy free tickets to a main-stage performance at the Taper or Ahmanson. Call 213-972-7662 for details.

Spotlight Awards is a recognition and scholarship program for performing artists in grades nine to twelve. Hundreds of students compete for twelve scholarships awarding $5,000 to finalists and $2,500 to runners-up in six categories: ballet, modern dance, classical voice, musical theater voice, classical instrumental music, and jazz instrumental music. Finalists perform at the Dorothy Chandler Pavilion in April; tickets are $10. Write to the Education Division for an application, available in September, or call 213-202-2245.

More than 2,000 schools in the Southland are already members of the Music Center's Education Division, which produces an extraordinary array of in-school performances, teacher training programs, master classes, awards programs, and more. The free **Showcase of Artists**, held each May on the plaza at the Music Center, is an inspiring event. Call 213-977-9555 for information.

Construction of the 2,380-seat Disney Concert Hall, designed by Frank Gehry, has proceeded no further than the parking garage, halted by L.A. County's requirement that funding be secured. The con-

troversial design, viewed as too costly by some, has won support in the arts community, including an exhibition at MOCA intended to familiarize the public with the plan. As the final addition to the Music Center, Disney Hall is being pitched by supporters as the linchpin of downtown revitalization, and that seems to have started the fund-raising campaign rolling along again. In the first months of 1997, $75 million was added to the project's coffers; with contributions from The ARCO Foundation, Bank of America, Ralphs, Times Mirror, Wells Fargo, and $5 million each from Mayor Richard Riordan and fund-raising chairman Eli Broad, a successful resolution of the project seemed feasible. When Gehry—who had been commissioned to design a residence for Broad that the client chose to have completed by another construction firm—threatened to withdraw his plans for Disney Hall unless he was allowed to oversee its construction, Disney's daughter, Diane Miller, assumed an active role, assigning the balance of her family's pledge to fund completion of the architect's working drawings. If the project gets off the drawing board, it is expected to open in 2001.

Colburn School of Performing Arts

200 S. Grand Ave.
Los Angeles 90012
213-621-2200

Started in 1950 as the USC School of Music's prep division, the Colburn School adopted its current name in 1980 and, without altering its commitment to train gifted musicians of every age, broadened its scope to include the full range of performing arts. It had long outgrown the warehouse building on Figueroa that it shared with USC's television studio whose warren of rehearsal rooms teemed with energy and activity, but limited space and lack of amenities like air-conditioning curtailed the school's curriculum.

For more than a decade Colburn administrators explored various options to relocate, finally approaching the Community Redevelopment Agency in 1993 and requesting a lease on the empty site adjacent to the Museum of Contemporary Art (MOCA). With a ninety-nine-year lease signed in October 1996, Colburn promptly broke ground for a new 55,000-square-foot facility—eight times the size of its USC building—which will include a 420-seat hall for chamber music performances. Its classes will be conducted there from summer 1998.

The design by Hardy Holzman Pfeiffer Associates—also the architects of the addition to the Central Library and the Robert O. Anderson Building at the Los Angeles County Museum of Art—features a sloping zinc-clad roof on one side of a glass-walled entrance and lobby and, on the other side, a striated brick cube topped with three pyramid-shaped skylights. A multistory parking garage under the building, accessible from Olive Street, aligns the structure with MOCA along the Grand Avenue side.

Colburn's **Early Childhood Curriculum** (ages three to seven) is a yearlong introduction to the performing arts that allows parents and children to explore music, dance, and drama together. The classes—Rhythm and Music, Music, Movement and Mime, Storytelling, Pre-Tap, and Introduction to Music Theory—are offered on Saturday mornings in two sixteen-week semesters and an eight-week summer program. Tuition ranges from $140 to $190 per semester. Introduction to the Piano uses the Suzuki method, which teaches music as if it were a language, with imitation and repetition; it costs $350 per semester. Registration takes place in late August, mid-January, and mid-May.

Music instruction is central to the Colburn School's methodology, so its offerings in this area are particularly rich, including both individual instruction and classes. Classes and clinics, intended either to supplement or precede private lessons, may be the best way to test a child's interest. Private lessons for virtually any string, wind, brass, or percussion instrument are available, and the school rents instruments at reasonable fees. Five styles of guitar are taught: classical, jazz, folk, pop, and rock. Children may begin classes in guitar, which cost about $185 per semester, at age eight. The Colburn School has a comprehensive **instrumental ensemble** program, including chamber music and orchestras. The orchestras range from a string ensemble to the highly acclaimed Colburn Chamber Orchestra.

At the earliest level, **dance instruction** helps build strong, coordinated, and expressive bodies; technique and performance skills are developed as the student progresses. Students' class levels are determined by interviews and auditions, and they are evaluated and promoted as appropriate at the end of each semester. Classes in ballet, modern dance, jazz, and tap are offered for children seven and up. Tuition is $170 per semester for one one-hour class a week and $260 for two one-hour classes a week; ninety-minute classes are a bit more expensive.

Drama classes for kids ages eight to fifteen use theater games, improvisation, body movement, and voice training to develop basic acting skills. Colburn recommends that students begin drama studies in the Early Childhood Curriculum. Tuition is about $140 for sixteen hour-long classes.

Participants in the **Voice Institute** may start by joining the **Saturday Morning Pre-Teen Singers** or **Young People's Chorus**, for which no audition is required. The **Honor Choir** requires audition and rehearses on Friday evenings and Saturday afternoons. Both programs cost about $250 a semester, but the fee is reduced if the student is also studying an instrument. Financial aid is also available.

The excellent programs at the Colburn School require an early commitment from students, but they offer new incentives at each level—like the popular (and maybe unique) **Jazz Program**, which students may begin at about age twelve. Jazz/commercial piano and guitar are available, and students are urged to join a weekly performance seminar that meets on Saturdays.

Angels Walk, a walking tour of the historic core of downtown and Bunker Hill, was patterned on Boston's Freedom Trail but the permanent markers that provide historical information about sites on that route have not been installed on L.A.'s itinerary. Visitors can pick up a colorful, free brochure, in which author Sam Hall Kaplan provides lore and architectural commentary, at the Central Library and other downtown sites.

The Museum of Contemporary Art (MOCA)

MOCA at California Plaza
250 S. Grand Ave.
Los Angeles 90012

The Geffen Contemporary at MOCA

152 N. Central Ave.
Los Angeles 90013
213-626-6222
www.Moca-LA.org
Tues.–Sun. 11 a.m.–5 p.m., Thurs. until 8 p.m.
Entry (good for admission to both facilities on date purchased): adults $6, seniors/students $4, children under 12 free

In 1979 civic leaders decided that the Los Angeles cultural scene should include a museum devoted to contemporary art, and funding from a progressive initiative of the Community Redevelopment Agency, stipulating that 1 to 1.5 percent of the total budget for developments must be spent for public art, allowed them to realize this goal. That funding also creating certain stipulations for the building design, which had to incorporate a prominent open space that would connect it to other public walkways at California Plaza. Japanese architect Arata Isozaki created two pavilions faced in rough red sandstone: one with a barrel roof is poised above the required open plaza; the other is topped with pyramidal skylights, which illuminate the galleries that have been pushed beneath street level. Art produced since 1940 is now displayed in two facilities administered by MOCA, which has accumulated an extensive and important permanent collection in relatively few years.

In 1983, during the protracted design and construction of the building at California Plaza, MOCA began presenting exhibitions in a warehouse space eight blocks away (off First Street at the edge of Little Tokyo), which was renovated by Frank Gehry and dubbed the Temporary Contemporary. Recognizing that it would be almost impossible to expand Isozaki's design and that Gehry's open plan worked well for sprawling exhibitions filled with oversized pieces, MOCA decided to retain the "tem-

porary" facility. The two venues are separate parts of one museum, with complementary programming: your entrance fee at either location allows you to visit the other on the same day.

The confusion over the relationship of the two venues was compounded when MOCA was forced to suspend operations for three years at the Temporary Contemporary site to accommodate a city construction project. When it reopened late in 1995, MOCA used large parts of the building to display its remarkable permanent collection, which had not often been seen because of its size and the restricted space. Because the open gallery space is easily reconfigured and particularly well suited to large artworks or exhibitions, like those of "Helter Skelter: L.A. Art in the 1990s" or "Blueprints for Modern Living: The History and Legacy of the Case Study Houses," it will regularly be used for large traveling exhibitions. The building's clever moniker was changed in 1996, when it was renamed the Geffen Contemporary to recognize a $5-million gift from the Geffen Foundation to MOCA's endowment campaign, but by then the Temporary had long since become a permanent and welcome part of the Museum of Contemporary Art and L.A.'s cultural life.

MOCA continues to build the permanent collection it started, even before the California Plaza site opened, with the purchase of eighty abstract expressionist and pop works from the Italian collector Count Giuseppe Panza. Bequests from Rita and Taft Schreiber added more important abstract expressionist and modern works, and Marcia Simon Weisman donated a signature painting by Jasper Johns, *Map* (1962), and eighty-three works on paper. Artist Sam Francis, a founding member of MOCA's board, gave ten paintings spanning the last forty years of his career, which will be included in the retrospective

MOCA began organizing before his death in 1994.

Television executive Barry Lowen inaugurated the emphasis on works from the 1960s to the present with the gift in 1985 of sixty-seven works by forty artists, many of them local. A major grant received that year was designated specifically for acquisition of works by emerging California artists, also the focus of the Spiegel collection. Ten years later Panza donated seventy works created since 1982 by artists associated with Los Angeles. The dispersal of the Lannan Foundation collection in 1997 brought MOCA a windfall of 105 works by fifty-three artists, many already associated with the museum—including Robert Irwin, a seminal figure in the light and space movement and the subject of a 1993 retrospective organized by MOCA—and two dozen of them not previously represented in the collection.

Refusing to cede hegemony in the field of photography to the J. Paul Getty Museum, in 1995 MOCA purchased more than 2,000 prints from a New York dealer, which chronicle the careers of ten critical figures, primarily American, in postwar documentary photography.

MOCA has presented a remarkable series of exhibitions on modern architecture, focusing on both solo practitioners—Gehry, Isozaki, Frank Israel, and Louis Kahn—and landmark programs like the Case Study Houses and contemporary strategies in urban planning ("Urban Revisions: Current Projects for the Public Realm"). It continues this investigation with "End of the Century," an exploration of world architecture through the twentieth century.

All visitors are welcome at two free programs presented regularly in the galleries: **Art Talks** (selected Thursdays at 6:30 p.m. and Sundays at 3 p.m.) are led by artists and critics who explore various issues in contemporary art; **Gallery Tours,** docent-

California Plaza is a happening place, especially during the summer months. There is eclectic programming on Friday and Saturday evenings, designed to lure office workers from the financial district, as well as free noontime concerts and Sunday afternoon events. The setting is pretty spectacular too, with all the splash and cool of the Water Court (between Third and Fourth Streets, east of Grand) as a backdrop. Call California Plaza Presents, Inc. (213-687-2159) for the schedule of this festival, which the Downtown News called "too good to be free."

led introductions to current exhibitions, take place daily in the early afternoon. Schedules of both programs are included in membership mailings and are available at information desks.

Together at MOCA is a free program, offered five times per year, designed to help families discover contemporary art. The workshops, for children ages six through thirteen accompanied by an adult, include a guided exhibition tour and a related studio art project. Reservations are required, so call the museum's education department (213-621-1751) for a schedule.

Wells Fargo History Museum
333 S. Grand Ave.
Los Angeles 90071
213-253-7166
Mon.–Fri. 9 a.m.–5 p.m.
Entry: free

Within five years after gold was discovered at Sutter's Mill in January 1848, a quarter of a million people had poured into the frontier territories in hopes of securing their fortunes. Many had left families behind and wanted to exchange news, money, and goods with communities back east. Henry Wells (1805–78) and William G. Fargo (1818–81), cofounders in 1850 of the American Express Company, went into business in 1852 to service the communication and banking needs of the pioneers, opening their first branch in a mother lode town. Wells Fargo financed the construction of stagecoach routes through the western territories and expanded its involvement in transporting people and mail.

Artifacts of this colorful history, as well as a replica of the Concord stagecoaches used in the trek across the country, are displayed in well-designed exhibits on the plaza level of the Wells Fargo headquarters downtown. A seventeen-minute video recounts the history of western settlement and Wells Fargo's role in it. An audiotape in the stagecoach presents portions of the journal of a twenty-one-year-old Englishman who in 1859 paid $200 to travel from Saint Louis to San Francisco and gives an animated account of the trip west. Certain to appeal to students of California history, this underutilized small museum welcomes school groups.

Los Angeles Conservancy
523 W. Sixth St.
Los Angeles 90014
213-623-CITY
Tours: $5

The Los Angeles Conservancy, founded in 1978, supports the preservation and revitalization of historic architecture and is especially identified with downtown. It is a membership organization, with some 5,000 supporters, who pay a minimum of $35 per year to receive its newsletter and be kept abreast of the organization's role in development and preservation issues. Recently it led a successful effort to halt demolition of one of the oldest buildings in downtown, Saint Vibiana's cathedral (1876), which was badly damaged in the January 1994 earthquake. This victory did not dissuade Cardinal Mahony from closing the site (its congregation had shrunk to 100 members) or building a new cathedral elsewhere, but it did allow professionals in the fields of architecture and planning an opportunity to propose plans for adaptive reuse of the historic build-

ing. The Conservancy commissioned University of Southern California's School of Architecture to coordinate the reuse study, which produced nine plans for viable developments on the two-acre downtown site that would incorporate the former cathedral. While the imaginative schemes, all prepared pro bono by some of the region's most creative teams, were intriguing, none has so far attracted a developer with financing, but Conservancy officials remain hopeful.

The Last Remaining Seats, a June film series held in the historic downtown movie theaters, is another of the Conservancy's most popular programs. Call 213-623-CITY for more information.

Broadway is still swarmed with Saturday shoppers, as lively as any street market in Hong Kong or Mexico City, and retains the Grand Central Public Market (315 S. Broadway), with forty-eight stalls that sell all kinds of produce and other vendors who offer prepared foods, including Mexican specialties. The street really draws a crowd—more than 100,000—to its Cinco de Mayo celebration. Latin music sets the beat for Fiesta Broadway, with five stages erected in a thirty-block area.

Other site-specific tours—including City Hall, Little Tokyo, and the Conservancy's newest tour, to Angelino Heights—are described in the relevant sections of this book.

The Conservancy's walking tours are one of its most popular and least controversial programs and a good way to begin exploring downtown. Trained docents lead groups of about fifteen people, which meet Saturday mornings at 10 a.m. at the entrance of the Biltmore Hotel (515 S. Olive St.), on routes that feature different aspects of downtown's past as seen in its buildings. Reservations are required; call 213-623-CITY.

Pershing Square Landmarks, the benchmark of Conservancy tours, meets every Saturday at the Biltmore, which was designed in 1923 by the same team responsible for New York's Waldorf Astoria, and focuses attention on the most-often renovated central public space in the city. From 1866, when it was first identified as a public square until 1918, when "in a fit of Armistice Day fever," its name was changed to Pershing Square, this park had had three names and at least as many landscaping designs. Most of the buildings on or near the square were built in the 1920s, when a tropical motif was introduced to its planting scheme. The construction of a parking garage under the site in the 1950s reduced Pershing Square to a roof of grass; the ground was too shallow to support full-size trees, and access ramps for cars isolated the park from pedestrians. After other failed attempts to revitalize Pershing Square, the park was given its most successful redesign in 1994 (see photo, page 19) by Mexican architect Ricardo Legoretta and landscape architect Laurie Olin, who introduced walkways into the space, and added color in structures and shade in multilevel, seasonally changing plantings. Look for Barbara McCarren's artwork of an earthquake fissure. Some of the city's most famous buildings are visited on this tour, including the 1893 Bradbury Building (304 S. Broadway), with its cast-iron staircase and balconies ringing a skylit atrium court (photo at left).

Of the dozen lavish movie palaces that the Conservancy featured in its 1992 brochure on the **Broadway Historic Theater District,** only three still show films and two now house churches. But weekly tours still showcase what was once the most important public venue for the film industry, where dozens of elaborate theaters were constructed between 1910 and 1931. The now-closed Los Angeles Theater (615 S. Broadway), inaugurated with the premiere of Charlie Chaplin's *City Lights,* simulates the opulent decor of Louis XIV's palace at Versailles. The Orpheum (842 S. Broadway) has retained its great three-rank, three-manual Wurlitzer theater organ, which is kept operational by the dedicated Los Angeles Theater Organ Society, who exercise its metal and wood pipes—often on Saturday mornings, allowing the Conservancy tour to enjoy music in a glorious architectural setting. The Spanish Gothic style of the United Artists Theater (933 S. Broadway) was selected by Mary Pickford to memorialize her Iberian honeymoon with Douglas Fairbanks, but it also seems appropriate to the church that now occupies it.

The Conservancy's weekly **Art Deco** tour features architecture built in the late 1920s, when downtown was booming and jazzy geometric ornamentation became the hallmark of some of the city's greatest buildings, notably the 1927 Oviatt Building (617 S. Olive), with its treasure of art deco Lalique glass.

Other tours, offered monthly, spotlight Los Angeles's historical development. **Palaces of Finance** explores the substantial architectural style that characterized the Wall Street of the West; **Mecca for Merchants** strolls through what was the city's premier shopping district from 1909 to 1929, visiting the palatial Fine Arts Building (811 W. Seventh St.) and Engine Co. 28, which now houses a restaurant. Many of the retail buildings—Brooks Brothers (1912), Coulter's Dry Goods (1917), Robinson's (1934)—are now (ominously) closed, and the former Bullocks is now the Jewelry Mart. **Marble Masterpieces** features some of downtown's most sumptuous lobbies. The **Terra-Cotta** tour spotlights buildings that used "baked earth," which was cheaper than carved stone but could produce the same Gothic motifs.

A new cathedral for Los Angeles has been designed by Spanish architect José Rafael Moneo for a 5.8-acre site on Temple Street, adjacent to the Hollywood Freeway. A grand plaza, which will sit atop a parking garage, will link the 43,000-square-foot cathedral (which can seat 2,600 worshipers) with the rectory and parish meeting center. A 120-foot-high freestanding bell tower, designed to be visible from the adjacent freeways, is the dominant feature of a meditation garden at the northwest corner of the site. A mission-style covered colonnade forms the perimeter of the three-acre plaza, which will be used for processions and holiday celebrations.

El Pueblo de Los Angeles Historic Monument

125 Paseo de la Plaza
Los Angeles 90012
213-628-1274

American Tropical, a mural by David Alfaro Siqueiros that had been obscured soon after it was painted in 1932, has been uncovered and stabilized by the Getty Conservation Institute, which plans a permanent display on the mural tradition, with particular reference to this work.

Self-Help Graphics has opened a gallery, named for its founder, the late Sister Karen Boccalero, which will bring the works of East L.A. artists to Olvera Street.

El Pueblo de Los Angeles is a forty-four-acre state historic park that was developed in one of the oldest sections of the city "to preserve and present the customs, trades, and traditions of early California." It includes the oldest building in the city, Avila Adobe (1818), and several other historic buildings as well as a thriving Mexican open market along Olvera Street. The Instituto Cultural Mexicano, housed at the top of Olvera Street, facing the Plaza, is a binational, bilingual programming body dedicated to keeping alive the Mexican culture represented by the first settlers to the pueblo, a group of families who migrated from New Spain in 1781. Visitors to the historic Biscailuz Building pass a mural depicting the Blessing of the Animals, an event held each spring on the plaza since 1938, and find a noncirculating library and a bookstore filled with Spanish-language books imported from Mexico, as well as a gallery shop filled with traditional crafts. But the park celebrates the historic presence of many different ethnic groups on this site. To commemorate old Chinatown, which occupied nearby land reclaimed to build Union Station, a museum of Chinese-American history has been planned for the Garnier block, built in 1890 for Chinese commercial use and occupied by Chinese merchants until 1950, when they were displaced by freeway construction.

Firehouse #1, built in 1884, is also located on the south side of the plaza and may be visited (Mon.–Fri. 10 a.m.–3 p.m., Sat. and Sun. 10 a.m.–4:30 p.m.). Free walking tours of the park, conducted by Los Angelinas del Pueblo, depart from next door, 130 Paseo de la Plaza (Tues.–Sat. 10 a.m.–1 p.m. on the hour). Call 213-628-1274 for group reservations since they are especially popular with school groups. Fronting Main Street are Pico House, a first-class hotel built in 1870 by the last Mexican governor of California in hopes of revitalizing the declining pueblo, and the Merced Theater. Although both are beautiful buildings, they enjoyed financial success only briefly and remain vacant today awaiting development.

Across Main Street stands La Iglesia de Nuestra Señora la Reina de Los Angeles (Church of Our Lady, Queen of Angels) on a spot that has been occupied by a church since 1818, although the building has been continually renovated and rebuilt. It serves the largest Roman Catholic congregation of Latinos in North America with a dozen masses celebrated in Spanish each Sunday and nuptials and baptisms in record numbers. After church, families promenade along Olvera Street, stopping for sweets and visiting its historic buildings.

At the entrance to the Old Plaza is a map, and brochures for a self-guided tour are on sale at Sepulveda House , the park's visitor center (Mon.–Sat. 10 a.m.–3 p.m.), which presents interpretive displays on the history and the culture of the pueblo; a twenty-minute film on the history of Los Angeles is offered free of charge on request. Visitors can tour the Avila Adobe (daily 9 a.m.–5 p.m.), which reflects the lifestyle of a wealthy ranchero family circa 1850. Thick walls insulate the family room, office, and parlor, which front on Olvera Street and are furnished with period reproductions and antiques, including an 1881 Steinway square piano. The domestic rooms face a courtyard, which was also used as kitchen and garden. Plantings, typical of what might have grown here in the 1840s, include citrus and fig trees, cacti, and a grape arbor. In a separate building across the courtyard are displays on water procurement and management in Los Angeles and a tribute to Christine Sterling, who spearheaded the drive to refurbish Olvera Street as a Latin American cultural and commercial center.

"New Chinatown" was settled in 1938, when Chinese residents, who could not hold citizenship and therefore could not own land, were forced to evacuate the settlement near the old pueblo they had occupied for more than fifty years. Old Chinatown was torn down, and the land was used for train tracks leading into Union Station.

The area surrounding the present 900 block of North Broadway was the first planned urban Chinatown in the United States. Gates to the east and west (Hill Street) define the original business district, and the residential area stretched up the hill to the west. That Sun Yat-sen was honored with the statue that dominates the square must reveal something of its historic character. The surrounding buildings are embellished with sweeping tile roofs and topped with animal statues, traditional protective talismans. The fanciful wishing-well fountain, which encompasses a six-foot mountain and an eclectic assortment of statues and plants surrounded by a gold-fish pond, is the pièce-de-résistance in this environment of fake chinoiserie, albeit innocently designed.

Union Station, built in 1939 at a cost of
$13 million, was the last of the great rail-
road stations constructed in the United
States and instantly became a Los Angeles
landmark. Its west facade and bell tower
evoke the style of the early California missions, with streamline moderne modifica-
tions. The interior features tilework in
muted earth tones with patterns borrowed
from Navajo rugs; most of the original,
heavy wooden furniture is still in place.
The east side of the building has been
transformed into the Gateway Transit
Center, a well-designed concourse for bus
and subway access that incorporates $3
million in public art.

Los Angeles Historical offers free two-hour
bus tours of downtown on the first and
third Wednesday of each month at 10 a.m.
Reservations are required: 213-628-1274 or
213-628-0605. The docent-led tours, which
depart from the Los Angeles Street side of
the Old Plaza, near the old firehouse, identify many historic buildings and sites, as well
as modern developments. At the
Bradbury Building and Carroll
Avenue in Angelino
Heights (the Victorian
enclave that was the
site of Los Angeles first
suburb), the bus stops
to allow the group to
disembark for a more
leisurely look.

Gateway Transit Center

At the east end of Chinatown, this tall
building, completed in 1995, is the
headquarters of the Metropolitan Transportation Authority; the artworks described below were all completed in
1995. The railings and grilles facing
Cesar E. Chavez Avenue are by Michael
Amescua and are entitled *Guardians of
the Track,* and the fountains and seating
areas—*Paseo Cesar Chavez*—are collaborative projects by Elsa Flores,
Roberto Gil de Montes, and Peter Shire.
Within the semipublic lobbies of the
building are murals by three artists who
have interpreted the themes of Southern
California, transportation, and time. In
the lobby area, James Doolin's mural
panels, *Los Angeles Circa 1870, 1910,
1960 and after 2000,* depict Los Angeles
in the four time periods of the title; on
the third floor are Margaret Nielson' s
collage-murals *L.A. Dialogs,* which use
images of L.A. from antique postcards
and souvenir items, and Patrick
Nagatani' s *Epoch,* which traces the evolution of transportation, beginning with
an image of Eadweard Muybridge's photomontage of a running man.

The building connects with the east
portal of Union Station. This multilevel
area is the transportation hub for trains,
buses, and subways. The white-canopied
bus shelters—a work called *ReUnion*—
were designed by a team of artists:
Torgen Johnson, Noel Korten, Matthew
Vanderborgh, and Kim Yasuda. In a pas-
sageway there is a ceramic tile mural by
East Los Streetscapers entitled *La
sombra del arroyo.*

City of Dreams/River of History is a
collaborative project by three artists
(photo above). Large train stations are
often like airports—dull and monoto-
nous—but here it's startling to encounter live fish swimming in a large
aquarium and a stone sculpture with a
water channel containing found objects
from the L.A. River. These are elements
of a collaborative work by May Sun and
Paul Diez; completing the work is a mural by Richard Wyatt painted inside the
glass dome of the east portal. In addition, artist Bill Bell has installed
A TRAIN, twelve vertical "light sticks"
that produce light patterns and mes-
sages; by speaking into a hidden micro-
phone, a sound system is activated.

— *Noriko Fujinami*

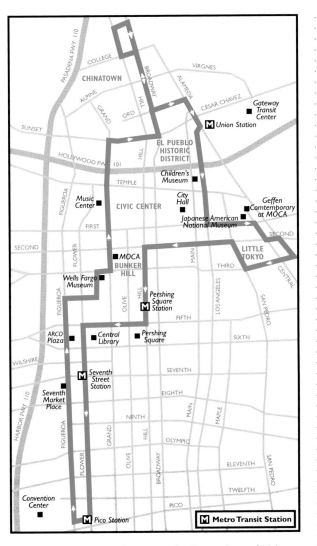

The Downtown Discovery Route (above) of the DASH buses operates on weekends only.

With a seed grant from the National Endowment for the Arts, the bureau is developing a pilot project called the **California Cultural Tourism Initiative,** which it hopes will increase the length of time (and therefore money) that the average tourist spends in our city (as well as San Francisco and San Diego, partners in the project). Although tourism is already a booming segment of the local economy, generating about $10 billion annually, the average visitor only stays three days, and so may never grasp the nature of this sprawling, complex urban structure. Visitors most often request help organizing L.A.'s many possibilities into a doable plan, according to bureau staff, who suggest itineraries that match particular interests (as well as the area of town where they are lodged, amount of time they plan to spend, and so forth).

The California Cultural Tourism Initiative has had input from many community and arts activists in devising thematic itineraries that will help visitors and residents alike structure routes through the city's past and present and identify the cultural possibilities in the diverse ethnic neighborhoods of the region. The itineraries—covering heritage sites for various ethnic groups as well as thematic tours on topics including jazz and blues, car culture, natural history and science, and Western heritage—will be compiled in a Web site (www.californiasedge.com), which is described in Virtual L.A., p. 259.

The bureau, which has never been successful in booking enough shows to make the Convention Center self-supporting, much less profitable, has given its support to a plan to build a new sports and entertainment arena on a site at 11th Street and Figueroa. The mayor and other proponents in the downtown business community view the project as a linchpin in the redevelopment of this section of downtown, and one that could attract enough nonresidents to justify construction of a large hotel, which would also benefit the Convention Center. (Taxpayers continue to fund the Convention Center, which ran a deficit of $19 million in 1996.)

The new arena, with 20,000 seats in a $240-million complex, would be home base for the Los Angeles Lakers and Kings, and is expected to book another 200 events per year. Because the arena project is backed with $58 million in municipal bonds, which the developers are required to pay back, approval by the City Council was delayed until the public

The Los Angeles Convention and Visitors Bureau operates a twenty-four-hour, up-to-date information hotline (213-689-8822) that includes information in six categories (seasonal/special events; music/dance; theater; sports; special exhibitions at museums; TV/studio tapings). The recorded information can be accessed in four languages—Japanese, German, Spanish, and French—besides English. There is a separate line (800-228-2452 or CATCH-LA) for those who want to order a printed vacation planning kit.

The bureau also operates two walk-in information sites: downtown at 685 S. Figueroa (Mon.–Sat. 8 a.m.–5 p.m.) and in Hollywood, 6541 Hollywood Boulevard in Janes House Square (Mon.–Sat. 9 a.m.–5 p.m.). Drop by to pick up some of the promotional materials on Southern California that the bureau produces with tax dollars.

The Metropolitan Transportation Authority (MTA) is the agency in charge of all public transportation for Los Angeles County; the MTA runs the buses that serve one million daily riders and is responsible for the planning, design, and implementation of the rail lines that currently stretch from Union Station downtown west to Wilshire Boulevard and Western Avenue (the "Red Line," a subway); from downtown south to Long Beach (the "Blue Line," an above-ground line); and from Redondo Beach stretching east to Norwalk (the "Green Line," which runs both above and below ground). When the lines are complete, the Red Line will stretch east to west from East Los Angeles to the Wilshire district, and all the way north through Hollywood to North Hollywood, and the Blue Line will go as far north as Pasadena. In addition, the Metrolink light rail system (administered by the Southern California Regional Rail Authority) runs from Union Station outward to points north (Lancaster, Oxnard), east (San Bernadino, Riverside), and south (Orange County), and Metro Art has been responsible for art projects at those stations as well.

The MTA's Metro Art program brings together artists, designers, architects, and engineers to create art works that expose a broad spectrum of Southern California's diverse communities to art during their daily commutes, thus enhancing the public transit experience. To that end, each of the Metro Rail stations contains commissioned artworks that reflect the uniqueness and history of the communities in which they are located and which often involved neighborhood residents in planning and design. For more information about Metro Art and its many programs, call 213-922-2727; a map with brief descriptions of all MTA art projects is available upon request.

THE RED LINE

The Red Line begins at Union Station (see page 22); Terry Schoonhoven's tile mural *Traveler* (1993) is a time-travel fantasy featuring references to Spanish galleons, nearby Olvera Street, and actress Carole Lombard. Two other works enliven this station: Cynthia Carlson's 1993 *L.A.: City of Angels* consists of eleven sets of hovering wings representing the eleven families who founded the city as well as eleven angels from different religions; *Union Chairs* (1993) by Christopher Sproat makes historical reference to the elegance of Union Station while giving commuters comfortable seating. At the Civic Center station Jonathan

Borofsky's *I Dreamed I Could Fly* (1993) features six fiberglass figures that hover overhead, while recorded bird trills accompany their flights. At the Pershing Square station, neon artist Stephen Antonakos's *Neons for Pershing Square* (1993) uses twelve sculptures to commemorate the first installation of a neon sign in the U.S. at a business once located near the station. Traveling west, at the Seventh Street/Metro Center station, Joyce Kozloff's 1993 hand-painted ceramic murals entitled *The Movies: Fantasies* and *The Movies: Spectacles* resemble unfolding film strips, the artist's tribute to the movies and our shared culture; at the same station, Roberto Gil de Montes created *Heaven to Earth* (1993), a ceramic tile triptych alluding to the heavens, to the sky, and to the terrestrial. Therman Statom's 1993 *Into the Light*—five everyday objects suspended in a skylight, casting changing shadows—is installed at the Westlake/MacArthur Park station, as are Francisco Letelier's *El Sol* and *La Luna* (both 1993), two ceramic tile murals that use images of the community of

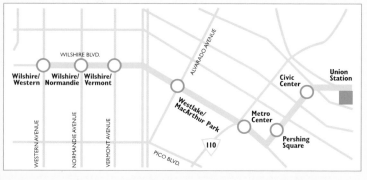

MacArthur Park to reference the past and reflect the future. Peter Shire's *Los Angeles Seen* (1996) is installed at the Wilshire/Vermont station: a series of sculptures floats throughout the entrance, and a mechanical acrobat on a unicycle travels to and fro; Shire also helped design the station's skylights, benches, and paving patterns. *Festival of Masks Parade* (1996) by Frank Romero, at the Wilshire/Normandie station, is a sixty-foot curved mural depicting the annual parade of masks along Wilshire Boulevard—Chinese dragons, African masks, Native-American dancers, and the scarecrow from *The Wizard of Oz* are among the figures depicted dancing along in front of various Miracle Mile architectural landmarks. The Wilshire/Western station has two 52-foot-long ceramic murals by Richard Wyatt—*People Coming* and *People Going* (both 1996)—showing members of the community doing just that, coming and going. There are fourteen additional stations planned along the Red Line, and the artists are working closely with the architectural teams to integrate their artworks into a total station design. —*Sherri Schottlaender*

was satisfied that all terms of the deal had been disclosed and that the project would be self-supporting. That approval (in October 1997) coincided with the announcement that Staples, the office supply company, had bid $100 million for twenty-year naming rights to the new arena, which is expected to be completed by fall 1999.

Civic Center
200 N. Spring St.
Los Angeles 90012

As the population of Los Angeles nearly doubled between 1910 and 1920 and then increased nearly threefold, to 1,416,000 within the next decade, the demand for city services grew commensurately. The need for a municipal building that could serve as a symbol for the new city was recognized by Mayor George E. Cryer (elected in 1921) who promised that the design would be "in keeping, architecturally, with the dignity and community idealism of America's most rapidly growing city." A special ordinance not only allowed it to exceed the height of other structures downtown, at 452 feet the pinnacle of the twenty-eight-story City Hall tower (where there is still an observation deck, open daily) was three times the size of neighboring buildings; it literally towered over the landscape until 1957 when the height restriction (to thirteen stories) was repealed from the building code.

Some of the region's most esteemed architects collaborated on the City Hall project, which was completed in April 1928: John C. Austin (who also designed the Moorish Shrine Auditorium (1926) and later (1935) the Griffith Observatory); Albert C. Martin (who used the Spanish Rococo style called Churrigueresque for both St. Vincent de Paul Church (1925) and Broadway's Million Dollar Theater

Composite map of the DASH routes introduced in 1996

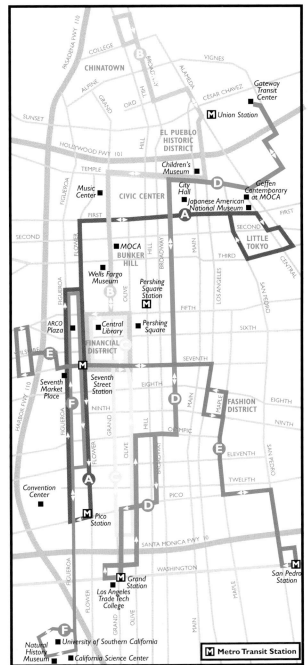

(1918), now also a church); and John Parkinson (whose 1928 zigzag moderne design for Bullocks-Wilshire and 1939 adaptation of Spanish mission style for Union Station became beloved landmarks). Whether the eclectic style was the result of such collaboration or an intentional effort to create a new hybrid, the design incorporates elements of Byzantine, Romanesque, Renaissance, and art deco, all rendered in California materials, including granite cladding on the lower four stories.

The interior spaces were designed by Austin Whittlesey, who had worked with Bertram Goodhue, architect of L.A.'s Central Library (completed a few years earlier), on the State Capitol in Lincoln, Nebraska. The hallways and chambers are embellished with marble columns and floor tiles and coffered and painted ceilings in a Spanish-Byzantine style. The circular floor of the rotunda, 135 feet in diameter, is inlaid with more than 4,000 pieces of marble depicting a Spanish caravel, the type of ship that plied the California waters from 1542 to 1800. The tiled ceiling represents the various attributes of municipal government: public service, health, trust, art, protection, education, law, and government. The City Council meets regularly (Tues., Wed., Fri. 10 a.m.) in wood-paneled chambers decorated with flags that represent the various powers in this region through its history. To give citizens access to council proceedings, the meetings are broadcast by audio (213-621-CITY) and on cable television channel 35.

Las Angelenas, the Mayor's volunteer corps, leads tours for schoolchildren and other groups (reservations required: 213-485-4423), explaining the functions of city officials and pointing out features of the building. On the fourth Saturday of each month, the L.A. Conservancy (213-623-CITY) offers a more architectural view of the complex, which has been continually expanded, beginning with the construction of City Hall South in 1964. Most of the additions reflect basic needs—like office space for some 33,000 government employees—but recently the Civic Center Authority, which had not met for more than a decade, convened to coordinate the government facilities with a master plan and reduce redundancies (such as eleven government-owned maintenance yards within a mile of City Hall). Its recommendations, summarized as the "Ten-Minute Diamond" plan, includes using landscaping, signage, and pedestrian-oriented services to create four quadrants, each a ten-minute walk from the central point at City Hall, that enhance the historical character of these districts.

SEAL OF THE CITY OF LOS ANGELES

The lion of León and the castle of Castile are from the Arms of Spain and represent Los Angeles under Spanish control from 1542 to 1821.

The eagle holding a serpent is from the Arms of Mexico and represents the period of Mexican sovereignty from 1822 to 1846.

The bear flag typifies the California Republic of 1846.

The stars and stripes indicate the present status of Los Angeles as an American city.

The sprays of olive, grape, and orange suggest the location of Los Angeles as a city set in a garden. The beaded circle surrounding the shield represents a rosary and suggests the part played by the mission padres in founding the city.

Los Angeles Children's Museum

310 N. Main St.
Los Angeles 90012
213-687-8800
Sat. and Sun. 10 a.m–5 p.m.; open additional hours
during school holidays and summer
Entry: adults and children over 2 $5
Groups with prepaid reservations, Tues.–Fri.:
213-687-8825

No organization can endure such uncertainty for a long time and remain fresh and vital. Resolving the issue of its long-term location could relight the spark that has made this place so special to many kids and their grown-ups. Let your council representative know whether you think keeping the Children's Museum downtown is important enough to justify limiting its public access to weekends and holidays.

Museums dedicated to children are a fairly recent phenomenon in this city's cultural life. The oldest and most comprehensive of them, the Los Angeles Children's Museum, opened in 1979 for a two-month trial in a city-owned building in the heart of downtown, attracting more than 40,000 visitors and therefore winning support from the mayor and City Council. That support garnered the fledgling museum a long-term lease on the 17,000-square-foot building a block from City Hall, and architect Frank Gehry was engaged to design a "Discovery Ramp" linking the exhibits, many of which were popular enough to remain there still.

But the Children's Museum to this day receives no other public funding for its programs, relying on earned income (half of its annual budget of about $1 million comes from admissions, membership fees, and sales of museum products and services) and private contributions. Within a few years the size and location of its downtown building hampered its ability to service the number of interested visitors it anticipated, and in 1984 its trustees voted to seek a much larger facility of 100,000 square feet. Where such a museum will be constructed has become a politically charged issue, with proponents of a site in the downtown core protesting a move elsewhere, even to other central-city locations like Griffith Park. So for now the Children's Museum remains downtown and open to the public only on weekends, except during school holidays and summer vacation, when weekday hours are added.

Like many facilities dedicated to kids, the museum has to remind its visitors that children must be accompanied by an adult, whose job is to help the youngsters discover the many stimulating, interactive exhibits at fifteen spaces within the museum. By its own definition this is a "hands-on educational facility," not a place where unsupervised kids are allowed to roam free, and its mission is to create a supportive environment in which children ages two to twelve can learn about the world around them. Here the modus of learning is play, and the exhibits are designed to elicit positive, progressive, and creative responses on a variety of levels, depending on the child's

age and interests. Trained facilitators help children utilize each exhibit, but they are there to supplement, not replace, parental interaction.

Young children will find **Sticky City** well suited to their abilities, attaching large, soft shapes with Velcro to create structures for crawling, climbing, and playacting. The walls of **Shadow Box** are made of a photosensitive material that records the body positions of kids in the room when a light flashes, making a continually evolving mural of overlapping images. **City Streets** is an installation that demonstrates how traffic signals work, presents different types of maps, and allows kids to experience the operation of a bus from the driver's seat and to climb onto an LAPD motorcycle. **Cave of the Dinosaurs** is a secret spot with dinosaur footprints, bones, and holograms to discover. **LEGO L.A.** would inspire any budding architect to participate in the cityscape constantly evolving in its carpeted space.

The exhibits are cleverly designed to incorporate educational concepts but connect with kids as fun places, "where children touch the world." It must be the principles of engineering, biology, and physics embedded in H_2O: **The Story of Water** that cause my four-year-old such delight in watching me pedal a bike hard enough to create a water turbine. This is an environment where getting wet is part of the fun, as kids discover how water recirculates by floating things through a maze of channels and watch fish in a tank and other marine life on an adjacent video monitor. **Take Care of Yourself** teaches children about health and safety. Panels on the parts of the human body and the functions of the five senses feature attractive graphics, and foods kids really eat are analyzed in the section on nutrition. Exhibits in **Club Eco** teach the importance of the environment and recycling, concepts made engaging through creative craft projects that use recycled materials to create toys, masks, jewelry, and stationery. Other materials can be purchased in bulk at the **Recycled Art Studio** or in cleverly packaged kits with clear instructions and great ideas.

Appearances are transformed in the face-painting studio, and would-be actors can proceed, makeup in place, to put on a talent show in **VideoZone**. Older children can provide technical support in the interactive video and sound recording studios, in the process developing appreciation for technology and visual arts, as well as practicing teamwork and cooperation. **Zoetropes** demonstrate how the separate frames of a cartoon strip are integrated into a moving picture; kids can color in the blank frames of strips stacked nearby with crayons and magic markers, then test their creations on a spinning drum like those used by pioneers of animation. **Kaleidoscope** uses light tables, colored materials, and mirrors to produce these fascinating visual toys on a huge scale.

The highlight of many visits to the Children's Museum is catching one of the excellent performances by storytellers, musicians, dancers, actors, and visual artists in **The Louis B. Mayer Performance Space**. These programs, free with museum admission and regularly scheduled from 11:30 a.m. to 3:30 p.m. on Saturdays and Sundays, make every visit to the museum a different experience. Becoming a member ($50 a year gives a family of six unlimited free admission, plus a quarterly newsletter with a schedule of special projects and performances) allows visitors to select a weekend when the theme or performance particularly interests their children.

The Children's Museum is heavily utilized on weekday mornings by schoolchildren and other groups with advance reservations; it offers reduced fees for groups who book early in the school year and visit before December. The museum fulfills its mission as an educational resource for parents with seminars led by child development specialists and a special program for teenage parents.

The Children's Museum is located at the Los Angeles Mall, built in 1974 to link the surrounding civic buildings with parking and an adjacent park. The most convenient parking is in the city garage underneath the museum, at 225 North Los Angeles Street. Rates are steep during the week ($1.20 for twenty minutes), but a flat rate of $3.30 per day on weekends allows museum visitors to walk or use public transportation to explore other sites in the downtown area. DASH buses, which cost just $.25, stop outside the door and offer a great overview of all the cultural attractions downtown. See DASH route maps on pages 23, 25.

Los Angeles Theater Center (LATC)

514 S. Spring St.
Los Angeles 90013
213-627-6500

The remodeling of a bank on a rather grim stretch of Spring Street was part of a larger redevelopment plan, implemented sporadically, which left the Los Angeles Theater Center somewhat stranded in an area that does not draw nighttime crowds. The Cultural Affairs Department took over when the original repertory producer bailed out in late 1991, and it has slowly found creative ways to utilize the four theaters (numbered one through four and seating 499, 296, 320, and 90, respectively). Cultural Affairs also rents the theaters at LATC—as well as at Barnsdall Art Park, the Warner Grand in San Pedro, and at the Ebony Showcase and the Madrid Theater in Canoga Park—to performing arts groups, and so sponsored a conference/workshop about producing theater to help develop new presenting organizations. By providing a technically superior venue—which also includes a spacious and stylish lobby created from the old banking floor—at reasonable fees, Cultural Affairs hopes to encourage low ticket prices and a broad spectrum of performances. Its own increasingly active program includes music arts—even opera instruction, a playwrights' workshop, and conferences, like one on folk and traditional arts held in 1997.

Los Angeles Times
202 W. First St.
Los Angeles 90053
Plant tours: 213-237-5757

Harry Chandler's directions to architect Gordon Kaufmann were to design a building that is "fireproof and earthquake proof and . . . a monument to the progress of our city and of Southern California." The commission, undertaken in 1931, was executed in the prevailing art deco style, but it is less flamboyant and decorative than the zigzag buildings constructed in that idiom before the Wall Street crash in 1929 and more in keeping with the neighboring Civic Center buildings. It has been enlarged continually to accommodate the growing staff of the paper, which has its principal editorial and advertising offices here.

The circular lobby features a revolving globe and two ten-by-twenty-seven-foot murals by Hugo Ballin entitled *The Newspaper*, which were obscured by aluminum paneling when the building was remodeled in the 1960s and only brought into view again twenty years later. A display of the first century of the *Times* (1881–1981) will occupy visitors waiting for a tour; those who'd just like to get a peek inside the newspaper headquarters may enjoy just visiting this lobby.

Tours for individuals and groups of fewer than ten are offered without charge at 11:15 a.m. and 3 p.m. from Monday through Friday (except holidays). Reservations are not necessary; just inform the guard in the lobby that you've come for a plant tour. Guides answer questions and interject prepared facts about the paper, its history, circulation, and manufacturing. More than fifty people staff the research library, or "morgue," where some fifteen million clippings and photos are stored. Staff photographers shoot about 300 rolls of film each day and process and print both color and monochrome pictures in twelve darkrooms. The *Times* subscribes to fifteen wire services, including Reuters and AP, which are monitored on silent video display terminals, which have replaced clattering ticker tapes in the war room. Laser photo machines inscribe images transmitted by audio frequency, allowing the paper to illustrate stories soon after they occur. Visitors are surprised by the prevailing quiet on the editorial floor, where journalists sit at computer terminals to write and do research using an extensive network of databases. About 500,000 words are typeset each day on the electronic editing and composing system, which transmits the journalists' copy directly from their computers into print.

The cost of materials—paper and ink—used to print an issue of the daily paper is higher than its purchase price, but revenues from advertising, which occupy 65 percent of the average page, make up the difference. A cast-metal printing plate is displayed as a relic; today the paper is printed from photosensitive aluminum plates, which are cheaper to produce and more easily replaced. The *Times* is manufactured in two satellite facilities, in the San Fernando Valley and in Orange County; the original plant in the bowels of Times Mirror Square was replaced by a new plant that opened in 1990 on a twenty-six-acre site at Alameda and Eighth Streets, where each printing press can produce 70,000 ninety-six-page papers in an hour.

Latino Museum of History, Art, and Culture
112 S. Main St.
Los Angeles 90012
213-626-4534
Mon.–Sat. 10 a.m.–4 p.m., Sun. 11 a.m.–5 p.m., closed Wed.
Entry: free

With a fifteen-year lease on a small Bank of America building, the museum began renovation in 1996 to transform itself from a resource center offering teacher training and other outreach programs to a destination museum celebrating the artistic and cultural contributions of Latinos in the United States and throughout the Americas. It plans to organize exhibitions, starting with "Los Four," devoted to the founders of the East Los Angeles school of painting and the Chicano art movement, as well as film festivals and celebrations of such traditional events as the Day of the Dead.

Little Tokyo, the heart and soul of the largest Japanese-American community in the mainland United States, almost ceased to exist during the dark days of World War II when Americans—both citizens and legal residents—of Japanese ancestry had to evacuate the West Coast or were forced by Executive Order 9066 into internment camps throughout the western states. Before revised quotas were introduced with 1965 immigration reforms, which increased the number of Asians who were allowed to emigrate to the U.S. from a total of 100 to about 20,000 per annum per country, the Japanese community in America was quite small; now the Japanese-American population of Little Tokyo numbers 200,000. When Japanese businesses took the leading role in Pacific Rim trade, the local community prospered enough to reclaim the historic Little Tokyo neighborhood from Skid Row. Shopping and entertainment arcades that simulate all components of an authentic Tokyo experience (except the jet lag) sprang up following construction of the luxurious New Otani Hotel (First and Los Angeles Sts.), which has a lovely Japanese-style garden on its rooftop. (To reach this garden, take the hotel elevator to the restaurant level or use the staircases that connect it to the top level of adjacent Weller Court, but don't miss this secluded spot with a scenic vista of downtown.)

One block of the nineteenth-century community has been preserved (along First Street between San Pedro and Central), with the Japanese American National Museum, in a renovated Buddhist temple, as its anchor. Now a nearby stretch of San Pedro Street (renamed Asio Street in honor of a local judge) is being reclaimed. The long-vacant Union Church—the first Christian house of worship in Little Tokyo when it was built in 1922—is being renovated with $3.4 million in public and private grants as a theater for the East West Players; an art gallery and multimedia production group will also become tenants of the building. A fund-raising campaign to construct a memorial on Central Avenue to the 15,000 Japanese-American soldiers who fought in World War II (while their families were being held in camps at home) is in the final phase; groundbreaking is projected for spring 1998. City Councilwoman Maxine Waters has advocated creating another Japanese-style garden above a subterranean park-

PUBLIC ART IN LITTLE TOKYO

In 1983 sculptor **Isamu Noguchi,** who was born in Los Angeles, designed a plaza in front of the Japanese American Cultural and Community Center (244 S. San Pedro St.) and the Japan America Theater. This plaza is now the focal point of the community, with Noguchi's stone sculpture *To the Issei* (1983), dedicated to the first generation of Japanese-Americans. The plaza also features seating areas and fountains shaded by graceful trees. Conceived by the artist to be used as an active center of the community, the plaza is the site of numerous events throughout the year.

The north side of First Street, between San Pedro and Central, is preserved as a historic site, with several notable public art pieces. In front of the Japanese American National Museum, there is a replica of a camera used by Toyo Miyatake when he was interned at Manzanar during World War II. Miyatake, a photographer, was not allowed to bring his camera equipment, so he made a box camera with a lens he smuggled into the camp. This work is part of a proposed series of thirteen sculptures conceived by artist **Nobuho Nagasawa** to document events in the Japanese-American community's history; unfortunately *Toyo Miyatake's Camera* (1993) is the only piece that has been realized to date. The bronze camera contains slide images of photographs taken by Miyatake during his internment. The photographs are projected onto the facade of the museum at night, and during the day they can be seen by looking into the lens.

On San Pedro Street near First, in front of what was once the Japanese Union Church of Los Angeles, there is a work completed in 1996 by **Sheila Levrant de Bretteville,** *Omoide no Sho-Tokyo (Remembering Little Tokyo)*. The brass inscriptions on a series of time-line bands embedded in the sidewalk identify the uses of each historic building, along with events relating to Japanese-American history from 1890 to 1940. In addition, inscriptions in both English and Japanese contain thoughtful and poignant recollections and quotations from three generations of individuals.

In Weller Court, at the corner of Second Street and Astronaut Ellison S. Onizuka Street, there is a tall white sculpture by **Shinkichi Tajiri,** *Friendship Knot* (1972). Another cast of this sculpture is installed in Berlin, Los Angeles's sister city. Farther north on the street is a memorial to Japanese-American astronaut Ellison Onizuka, who died in the space shuttle *Challenger* explosion in 1986.

Tucked behind the Union Bank building (120 S. San Pedro St.) is a black granite sculpture by **Seiji Kunishima** entitled *Stonerise* (1984). The massive granite slabs are separated by small, round stones that appear to float above their surface. Around the corner, **Michihiro Kosuge** created three bronze poles entitled *Towers of Peace, Prosperity, and Hope* (1989).

—*Noriko Fujinami*

Nearby are two artists' live/work complexes, which are open to the public once or twice a year:

The Brewery (680 S. Ave. 21, Los Angeles 90031), the world's largest art studio complex, houses hundreds of artists and art-related businesses in the former Pabst Blue Ribbon brewery. It's open to the public for the annual spring Art Walk and Open Studio Tours; call 213-694-2911 for event information.

The studios of the Santa Fe Art Colony are located not in the New Mexico desert, but on the fringes of downtown L.A. These artists also open their doors to the public during a spring festival that features music and food in the courtyard of the renovated bathrobe factory (2401 S. Santa Fe Ave.; *213-587-6381).

ing structure to be constructed further down First Street, and the Little Tokyo Service Center has plans for a community gymnasium.

The Los Angeles Conservancy offers a walking tour of Little Tokyo, which meets on the plaza of the Japanese American Cultural and Community Center at 10 a.m. on the first Saturday of each month. Docents provide information on the cultural history of the neighborhood; the tour visits Higashi Hongwangji Temple (505 E. Third St.) and discusses the fate of nearby (now closed) Saint Vibiana's Cathedral. The Little Tokyo Business Association will also lead guided tours for groups of more than fifteen people; call 213-620-0570 to schedule.

Japanese Village Plaza, built in 1979 as the commercial hub of the community, incorporates blue-tile roofs and white-washed walls, and a fireman's lookout tower stands sentinel over the modern, urban re-creation of a traditional small-town shopping district. More recent developments, like enormous Yaohan Plaza (333 S. Alameda) and Honda Plaza (between Central and Alameda on Second), offer many restaurants that deliver a cultural experience along with the food, or for a mind-boggling immersion in Japanese cuisine, check out Yaohan's sprawling food hall with hundreds of pickles and *sembei* (crackers); this is where I acquired a live *shiso* plant, which has since reseeded itself to assume a larger corner of my vegetable garden every year.

Japanese American National Museum

369 E. First St.
Los Angeles 90012
213-625-0414
www.lausd.k12.ca.us
Tues.–Sun. 10 a.m.–5 p.m., Thurs. until 8 p.m.
Entry: adults $4, seniors/students/children 6–17 $3

The incarceration of Japanese-Americans during World War II is an often overlooked fact of history, yet it is especially wrenching because it was perpetrated by our own government, in large part against its own citizens, who were singled out not for their actions but because of their ethnicity. The emotional anguish and financial scars suffered by the more than 100,000 internees had profound social ramifications in the Japanese-American community, which were explored in "America's Concentration Camps," one of the first exhibitions mounted by the then-new museum.

The internment is only one sad chapter in the time line of Japanese immigration and assimilation in the United States displayed at the museum, which opened in 1992. There are no permanent exhibitions at the museum, not (as I had assumed) because space within the former Nishi Hongwangji Temple was too limited, but to attract repeat visits from its core audience with each new installation. The chronology of its exhibitions thus defines the museum's mission to an unusual extent, but the large space dedicated to the Legacy Center, which allow visitors to research

The garment district
draws fashion hounds
who love bargains to
the Cooper Building and
the monthly sales at
the California Mart
(1933 S. Broadway).

Otis Art Institute, which
moved its main campus
from the MacArthur
Park area to
Westchester in 1996
(see p. 245), offers
classes in fashion design
at a downtown site in
the California Mart.

family internment files in the U.S. National Archives via computer, reveals the importance of such programs. Both the changing exhibition program and an expanded Legacy Center (to be called the National Resource Center) will be featured in an 85,000-square-foot addition currently under construction on a city-owned lot across First Street from the historic 1925 building that was renovated to create the museum's original space (photo, p. 31).

Also on the lower level of the old temple is "Moving Memories," a continuous video presentation of home movies; a small temporary exhibition gallery; and space for such educational programs as classes in samisen and piano taught by the museum's musicians-in-residence. The second floor contains more traditional gallery space, which was inaugurated with "Issei Pioneers," an exhibition that explored the role of early Japanese immigrants to Hawaii in developing the islands' agriculture and the different experience of immigrants to California, where agriculture was based on migrant labor. "Fighting for Tomorrow," an exhibition on the heroic wartime service of Japanese-Americans in the U.S. armed forces, occupied the main gallery for more than a year. The last two exhibitions, each on view for six months, were "Kona Coffee Story," which had a specific regional focus and reflected the input of the Japanese-American population in that locale, and "Sumo USA," which examined how "wrestling in the grand tradition" had been adapted to American sports culture.

Together with the UCLA Film and Television Archive, the museum has produced a CD-ROM, *Executive Order 9066: The Incarceration of Japanese Americans During World War II*, which builds upon the museum's exhibition on this event.

Japanese American Cultural and Community Center (JACCC)

244 S. San Pedro St.
Los Angeles 90012
213-628-2725
Daily 9 a.m.–6 p.m.

The plaza and rock sculpture designed by Isamu Noguchi and the James Irvine Garden, named for its major benefactor but built by 200 volunteers, anchor the Japanese American Cultural and Community Center buildings to their site. The Seiryuen, or the Garden of the Clear Stream, includes rocks from Mount Baldy and both local and traditional Japanese plants—azaleas, various kinds of bamboo, and pittosporum. The rushing stream at the top of the garden, which signifies the turbulent life of the *Issei* (first-generation Japanese-Americans), ends in a quiet pool, suggesting that subsequent generations will live in peace. The sunken garden is visible from the JACCC Plaza, but take the elevator in the main building down to the lowest level to enter it. There are few nicer spots for a stroll anywhere in Los Angeles.

The JACCC preserves Japanese cultural traditions and encourages the appreciation of this heritage in those born in America. The community center offers its own programming—especially during twice-yearly workshops, in July and December—and leases space to other organizations that offer classes in such traditional activities as Kabuki dancing, flower arranging, and the tea ceremony. A Calligraphy Center has been established at the JACCC with support from teachers in Japan, and the North American Taiko Conference (held for the first time in 1997 but expected to become a regular event) showcased the explosive drumming of Japanese and American practitioners of this art. Contact the education department (213-628-2725) for information. The annual calendar includes many events celebrated with community festivals, starting with Oshogatsu (New Year); Hanamatsuri, honoring Buddha's birthday, and the Cherry Blossom Festival in April; Children's Day in May; Obon, the feast of the dead in June and July; and Nisei Week in August.

The 841-seat Japan America Theater presents traditional and contemporary performing arts (often Japanese) in an exceptional space. Call the box office (213-680-3700) for the current schedule. Exhibitions in the George J. Doizaki Gallery (Tues.–Fri. noon–5 p.m., Sat. and Sun. 11 a.m.–4 p.m.) are changed frequently; they feature both traditional and contemporary aspects of Japanese culture.

Mark Taper Center/Inner City Arts

720 S. Kohler St.
Los Angeles 90021
213-627-9621

Inner City Arts filled a need with its first programs—studio art classes for students at the nearby Ninth Street Elementary School during the day and classes for neighborhood latchkey kids after school. It was a creative social center for teenagers on several weeknights and catered to gifted students on Saturdays. By 1991, when it was forced to close its studio because of potentially toxic fumes from an adjacent business, it had enough advocates to keep the programs functioning in temporary quarters and to help it find a long-term solution. The Mark Taper Foundation generously funded its purchase of an auto-body shop and adjacent yard, and some of the area's best architecture and design firms donated their services to transform the building into a state-of-the-art complex worthy of Inner City Arts's fine programs. This is a model of community collaboration that assists at-risk inner-city kids and helps a few public schools restore the arts to their curriculums. Although it has limited opportunities for the general public, more than 8,000 public school students benefit each year from its classes in visual arts, music, ceramics, dance, drama, and animation.

Museum of Neon Art (MONA)

501 W. Olympic Blvd.
Los Angeles 90015
213-489-9918
Tues.–Sat. 11 a.m.–6 p.m.
Entry: adults $3.50, children under 12 free
Free parking in Renaissance Tower; enter from
Grand just north of Olympic

For more than ten years artist Lili Lakich shared her loft east of downtown with a growing collection of vintage signs that she had rescued. She also dedicated space to a gallery exhibiting contemporary works of neon, electric, and kinetic art, including some vintage signs (although many were too large to be shown in this space). She was ready to push her fledgling museum into the public domain, and then the civil disturbances of 1992 so drastically reduced the number of casual visitors to the Traction Avenue site that the museum took a gamble, accepting retail space at Universal CityWalk in exchange for allowing some of its vintage signs to be installed there.

This unlikely partnership between an artist-based museum and an entertainment-retailing conglomerate lasted only a few years. Twenty-two signs from the MONA collection, which were restored with funding from CityWalk's developer, will remain in the streetscape at Universal City, including the famous twenty-foot neon swimmer performing a five-part somersault-pike dive, which once advertised Steele's Motel in the San Fernando Valley.

In 1996, with support from the Community Redevelopment Agency, "the only museum in the world dedicated to electric art" reopened in downtown Los Angeles, with street-level display windows on Olympic Boulevard and frontage on Grand Hope Park. It's a handsome space, identified on the outside by the museum's signature logo, a neon rendition of the Mona Lisa, based on MONA's moniker. A witty donor's wall—your name in lights—and a wedge-shaped ceiling perforated with lights link the entry to the principal gallery, where light-infused materials such as painted-glass ceiling panels and translucent fiberglass dividers contrast nicely with the natural concrete walls. New exhibitions are mounted three or four times each year, continuing the tradition of showcasing new work to bring fine-art status to a genre that was tainted by neon's commercial use.

In its first fifteen years the museum has exhibited works by some 400 artists, many of whom learned or refined their technique in the eight-week classes that MONA offers each spring and fall. MONA periodically conducts double-decker bus cruises highlighting the neon signs and bright lights of Hollywood; call 213-617-0274 for a schedule and reservations.

Fashion Institute of Design and Merchandising (FIDM), a handsome building designed in 1990 by the Jerde Partnership, offers degree and continuing-education classes in fashion design and includes a small gallery that shows student work and, occasionally, more ambitious thematic displays. It fronts two-acre Grand Hope Park, designed by Lawrence Halprin with outdoor rooms (one defined by a wisteria-bearing pergola), a great playground, and a fifty-three-foot yellow and red clock tower that is everything the *Triforium*, at Main and Temple (see Public Art, page 37) failed to achieve.

Federal Reserve Bank

950 S. Grand Ave.
Los Angeles 90013
213-683-2904
Mon.–Fri. 8:30 a.m.–5 p.m.
Entry: free

The hands-on computer exhibits at the Federal Reserve Branch in downtown Los Angeles allow visitors to participate in managing the money supply and setting fiscal policy. Devising tax and spending policies that "promote low unemployment, low inflation, and steady growth" will certainly present challenges to all players, but it won't bore anyone.

Understanding the concepts of supply and demand is crucial to the success of many businesses. These principles are demonstrated in user-friendly exhibits geared to kids aged twelve and up, like the Muffin Mogul game, which simulates the experience of running a bakery. The computer evaluates the player's business skills at the end of the game. Free tours of the Fed are offered Tuesdays, Wednesdays, and Thursdays at 10 a.m. and 1 p.m., but reservations are required (213-683-2900).

Unity Arts Center

At the William Reagh Los Angeles Photography Center
412 S. Park View
Los Angeles 90057
213-833-0650
Tues.–Fri. 3–10 p.m., Sat. 10 a.m.–4 p.m.,
Sun. 11 a.m.–4 p.m.

This center, formerly operated by the Cultural Affairs Department, is now a public-private partnership. Under the direction of U.P., Inc., which was formed in the wake of the 1992 L.A. riots to help resolve those issues that precipitated the civil disorder, a consortium of four arts organizations now offers a wide range of programming at the former photography center. Grupo de Teatro Sinergia, State of the Arts, and the Korean Classical Music and Dance Company produce bilingual theater, art workshops and exhibitions, and cultural festivals. Low-fee photography classes and darkroom facilities are available.

At more than 600 acres **Elysian Park** is the second-largest park in Los Angeles, after Griffith Park, which it predates by a century. Most of its slopes, crisscrossed by hiking trails, are cloaked in native chaparral, but Chavez Ravine Arboretum (Stadium Way, from Scott Ave. to Academy Rd.) was planted in the nineteenth century with rare trees, now mature specimens. The Los Angeles Police Academy (1880 N. Academy Rd.), which has been a park resident since 1925, features a rock garden where streams trickle into a tranquil pool; the law-abiding public is welcome to share this lovely space with police officers.

Bob Baker Marionette Theater (1345 W. First St.; 213-250-9995) has been entertaining Los Angeles audiences, young and old, for thirty-five years. Performances (Saturdays and Sundays at 2:30 p.m.) incorporate many of the hundreds of marionettes that Baker has crafted by hand over the years, bringing the characters of literature and the products of his vivid imagination to life. The show changes about twice a year, and birthday parties are happily accommodated.

PUBLIC ART TOUR

In 1983, when Al Nodal was hired as director of exhibitions at Otis Art Institute/Parsons School of Design, then located adjacent to MacArthur Park, the park and the surrounding neighborhood were in decline. The college proposed to revitalize the area through an active public arts program that involved not only the college and artists but nearby businesses, community organizations, and neighbors as well. Through the creation of an active neighborhood association, it established cultural activities in an underserved area and united the community. Through this program several artists were commissioned to create public art in the park. There is an entry arch by **R. M. Fischer**, murals by **Willie Herron** and **Patssi Valdez**, ceramic tile pyramids by **Judy Simonian**, a poetry bench by **Doug Hollis** and **Richard Turner**, **George Herms's** *Clocktower: A Monument to the Unknown*, and a series of mini-monuments by **Alexis Smith**.

One of the most interesting projects was proposed by Smith. Inspired by Raymond Chandler novels set in Los Angeles, she suggested a restoration and relighting of the neon signs on top of the buildings that surround the park. From the 1920s through the 1940s this once-fashionable residential and hotel district was seen as an urban resort, and its buildings bore romantic names like Westlake, Ansonia, and Asbury. This period was also the heyday of elegant, colorful neon signs, but during the blackouts of World War II the use of the signs was prohibited, and they fell into disuse. Through an effort spearheaded by Nodal, involving various city departments, the neon signs around the park were restored in 1996, and they again illuminate the night sky.

Unfortunately the park today suffers from neglect once again. The changing neighborhood and the closure of the park for Metro construction have contributed to an increase in vandalism and crime in the 1990s. The recent departure of Otis to the new Westchester campus leaves the once-vital MacArthur Park public arts program lacking in leadership.
— *Noriko Fujinami*

The heyday of evangelist Aimee Semple McPherson (see Finding God in the City of Angels, p. 143) is commemorated in the quarter-round, 5,000-seat Angelus Temple built in 1923 at the northwest end of Echo Park.

Carroll Avenue is the centerpiece of an enclave of Victorian architecture in Angelino Heights, the first suburb constructed in L.A.'s relentless westward march. A mile-and-a-half west of downtown, on a knoll linked by trolleys to downtown offices, Angelino Heights became a dense concentration of shingled Eastlake and Queen Anne homes; a restoration foundation, begun in the 1970s, has reintroduced globed street lamps that illuminate an earlier era in Los Angeles. Call the L.A. Conservancy (213-623-CITY) for reservations for its monthly tour of this neighborhood, or wear walking shoes and give yourself an extra hour for a self-guided exploration before a baseball game at nearby Dodger Stadium.

Nearby **Echo Park** (Glendale Blvd., one block south of Sunset) has a fifteen-acre lake that during the 1870s was used to irrigate area farms. Donated to the city in 1891 for a public park, the 26-acre lot was landscaped with semitropical plants, rows of palm trees, and a lotus pond as its defining element. The lotus has been celebrated in an annual festival that dates to 1972 and has become a celebration of Asian cultures, in which the flower signifies rebirth, beauty, and purity. During the summer months the lotus blossoms transform the lake, which is used for dragon-boat races in the Chinese tradition during the July festival and for rides in paddleboats (available for rental) at other times.

The Echo Park neighborhood is a multi-ethnic community; since 1995 it has been a primary site in a Cultural Affairs Department–sponsored festival of Cuban culture, whose contribution to the area's Latino heritage has often been overlooked. Originally a two-day outdoor event, it has grown into a two-month festival (May–June) at venues throughout the county. For scheduling information, check out

the Web site (www.CubaFestLA.com) or call Cultural Affairs (213-485-2433).

Artists have also congregated in Echo Park, where a fall studio tour (modeled on the Venice Art Walk) and arts festival, centered on a block of Lemoyne Avenue (near the Echo Park Recreation Center), have celebrated this part of the local population and raised funds for community arts organizations.

Sunset Junction, as the southern edge of Silverlake is called, celebrates with a street fair each August; during the rest of the year, locals head to Millie's Coffee Shop to find out what's going on. A lot of what's happening for teenagers takes place at the Sunset Junction Neighborhood Alliance (4019 W. Sunset Blvd; 213-661-7771), where free acting classes and art instruction produce neighborhood theater and murals. Drums of Passion (1523 Griffith Park Blvd.; 213-644-1457) offers instruction on traditional West African percussion instruments, including the *djembe,* or talking drum. Professional dancers teach (and take) classes at Studio A (2306 Hyperion; 213-661-8311), where impressive physiques are matched by good-natured enthusiasm.

Jóvenes' Inc., which offers art programs for homeless and at-risk youths, has begun mounting seasonal shows in an outdoor gallery designed to be seen by pedestrians or from passing cars. Sunset Art Park, at 1478 Sunset Boulevard, two blocks east of Echo Park Boulevard, was once just an empty lot, but you never

know what you'll find there now. Works by professional artists and the students in Jóvenes' Inc.'s classes are sometimes commingled; the site may be dedicated to a performance, like a recent slide show with music that displayed images that reflect the lives of inner-city kids.

PUBLIC ART

Noriko Fujinami

For descriptions of public art in other parts of the county, see pages 24, 30, 34, 122, 207, and 245.

When the National Endowment for the Arts launched the Art in Public Places program in the late 1960s, its requirement for matching funds resulted in the growth of complementary programs on the state and city levels. Today Los Angeles and several surrounding cities mandate that a percentage of development costs for public and private buildings be set aside for art. Led by the city's Community Redevelopment Agency (CRA) and Cultural Affairs Department, Los Angeles requires that 1 percent of development costs be dedicated to public art or cultural programs. This requirement has produced a collection of imaginative public art and innovative cultural programs. Perhaps the most unusual use of these funds is the building of the Museum of Contemporary Art. When a group of citizens proposed the creation of a museum to showcase contemporary art to then-mayor Tom Bradley, the CRA conceived a plan to set aside 1 percent of the California Plaza development budget for the construction of a museum, which opened in 1986. The process of public artmaking has also matured, and today placing a ready-made sculpture in the middle of a plaza will not satisfy the requirement. Artists are asked to collaborate with architects and designers, meet with members of the community, learn about its history, and create environments that engage the public in an experience that

is unexpected and meaningful. Numerous successful public art projects are found in Los Angeles and surrounding communities, and a few are highlighted on these pages.

As part of the expansion of the Los Angeles Convention Center (1201 S. Figueroa St.), which was completed in 1993, James Ingo Freed designed a soaring, light-filled entrance space. The architect worked with artists Alexis Smith and Matt Mullican. Smith designed the floors of the twin lobby spaces. The first lobby features *Pacific Rim*, a map in multicolored terrazzo tile, with bronze medallions marking different cultures; the second lobby has the blue *Constellations*. It is best to view these massive works from the balconies. The connecting bridge between the two Convention Center buildings contains inverted archways by Mullican; the series of carved granite squares illustrates the history of Los Angeles from prehistoric times to the present.

In an outdoor plaza a ten-foot-high sculpture by Pat Ward Williams (1995) commemorates the life of Councilman Gilbert Lindsay. Instead of the usual commemorative bust, the artist has etched images and narratives chronicling the councilman's life and achievements on three granite columns, creating a multifaceted portrait of Los Angeles's first African-American councilman who served the city for twenty-seven years, until his death in 1990. All three works are wonderful pieces to discover with children, and a refreshing break from the crowds at the Convention Center.

When the Los Angeles Central Library (630 W. Fifth St.) was rebuilt after

the 1986 fires, the west lawn, turned into a parking lot in the 1940s, was transformed into a garden by landscape architect Lawrence Halprin. The main feature of this garden, which faces Flower Street, is *Wells of Scribes* by artist Jud Fine, who has created works that symbolize the stages of human evolution and the development of language and science on the steps and pools in front of the library. There are fountains by Laddie John Dill and Mineo Mizuno and, along Fifth Street, a fence designed by Reis Niemi. The interior of the new Tom Bradley Wing, which was completed in 1993, incorporates a ceiling mural by Renee Petropoulos entitled *Painting with Multiple Centers*, sculptural chandeliers by Therman Statom, and wall torches by Ann Preston. Inside the elevators artist David Bunn has lined the walls with now-obsolete Dewey Decimal System catalogue cards. By selecting the cards that begin with the words *complete* and *comprehensive,* the artist makes a wry joke about the notion of the library as the center of absolute knowledge.

The First Interstate World Center (633 W. Fifth St.), a white tower designed by I. M. Pei, is currently the tallest skyscraper in downtown Los Angeles. Within the geometrically shaped walls above the entrance lobby, artists Vitaly Komar and Alexander Melamid have painted a pair of angels (1992). Outside, grand steps connect Fifth Street to Hope Avenue. A person in good physical shape can sprint up these steps, but there is an escalator for the not-so-athletic. At the top, on Hope Street, is a lovely fountain with Robert Graham's *Source Figure* (1991), a serene female

nude whose cupped hands overflow with water that cascades down the steps. At this height, the figure is nearly at eye level with the pyramid on top of the Central Library.

For many years a large neon sign atop a church on Hope Street, which read "Jesus Saves," was a downtown landmark. When the church was razed and replaced with a high-rise (550 S. Hope St.), artist Lita Albuquerque memorialized it in a work entitled *Site/ Memory/Reflection* (1993). In addition to the numerous sculptural works that are symbolically situated in an L-shaped corridor surrounding the building, there is an artist-designed meditation room at the entrance on Hope Street.

At 333 South Grand Avenue is a large, colorful bronze sculpture by Nancy Graves entitled *Sequi* (1993), and inside the lobby there are additional sculptures by Jean Dubuffet (1982), Joan Miró (1967), and Louise Nevelson (1985). Among the fountains and pools that define the interior lobby are Robert Graham's four *Fountain Figures* (1983).

Artist Barbara McCarren undertook a remarkable transformation of Pershing Square (Fifth St., between Olive and Hill), a square park surrounded by tall buildings, as part of its redesign in 1992 by Mexican architect Ricardo Legorreta. Beginning with an earthquake fault line that marks the central pond, McCarren created constellations, telescopes, postcard-inlaid benches, and walkways through orange groves. Various monuments that date back to the original Pershing Square of the 1920s have been grouped in one section of the park, and here we find statues of Beethoven, a Spanish-American War soldier, a World War I doughboy, and a cannon from the USS *Constitution* sharing space among the palm trees.

Born a slave in Georgia, Biddy Mason arrived in California in the 1830s by walking behind a wagon train. In 1856 she won her freedom in court and settled in Los Angeles. She earned her living as a nurse and midwife, becoming the first black woman to own property. She established a home for herself and her family at 331 South Spring Street, now **Biddy Mason Park**. Situated behind a parking garage, but next to the historic Bradbury Building, *Biddy Mason: Time and Place* (1990) was designed by **Sheila Levrant de Bretteville**. The wall of time lines—marked with images, historical annotations, and narrative texts about Mason's accomplishments—is heartfelt and inspiring. Nearby there is an assemblage by artist **Betye Saar**, *Biddy Mason's House of the Open Hand* (1990).

At the entrance to the **Fashion Institute of Design and Merchandising** (919 S. Grand Ave.) stands a bronze angel, a collaborative work created by **Tony Berlant** and **Gwynn Murrill** in 1990. Inside, Berlant has created an environment in the rotunda by covering its columns in colorful metal.

Grand Hope Park (at Ninth and Hope), designed by **Lawrence Halprin** and completed in 1993, is situated behind the Fashion Institute, and it features a children's playground with fountains, walls, and benches designed by **Raul Guerrero**. There is also a poet's walk, with pergolas stenciled with poetry by **Kate Braverman** and **Wanda Coleman**. On a grass berm there are life-size bronze coyotes by **Gwynn Murrill**. Hawks and snakes by the same artist also grace the pergolas. *Clocktower*, designed by

Halprin, plays contemporary music by **John Carter, Michael McNabb,** and **Ushio Torikai.**

The **Museum of Neon Art** (501 W. Olympic Blvd.), which moved to the first floor of the Renaissance Tower in 1996, conducts nighttime bus tours of neon signs, movie marquees, and permanent installations of contemporary neon art in the city. Call 213-489-9918.

At the **Sanwa Bank Building** (601 S. Figueroa St.), at the corner of Figueroa and Wilshire, is a large sculpture by **Eric Orr** entitled *L.A. Prime Matter* (1991), a bronze rectangular column sheathed in cascading water. A lucky pedestrian or motorist caught at this signal might see fire erupt from the top of the sculpture, an event that occurs for a few seconds at each hour.

A massive sculpture protrudes from the interior of the lobby of the **ManuLife Tower** (865 S. Figueroa St., at Eighth Pl.) to the street. Entitled *Lithos* (1991), the environmental sculpture of stone and water was designed by **Elyn Zimmerman.**

At the corner of Flower and Fifth Streets (444 S. Flower St.), tucked behind the neatly planted palm trees, there are geometric sculptures by **Michael Heizer** entitled *North, East, South, West* (1982). Farther behind this plaza are additional works by **Mark di Suvero, Bruce Nauman, Robert Rauschenberg,** and **Frank Stella.**

On the rear perimeter of the building at 801 Figueroa Street, artist **Andrew Leicester** created *Zaja Madre* (1992), a garden plaza modeled after the early aqueduct that carried water to Los Angeles from the Los Angeles River. There are beautifully designed cactus gardens and playful animals and images throughout this garden oasis.

At **Citicorp I** (725 S. Figueroa St.) is a sculpture by **Terry Allen**, *Corporate Head* (1991), at the corner of Figueroa and Seventh. This life-size sculpture, which is often reproduced in books, seems to epitomize the life of a corporate executive, its head having disappeared into an office building. The public art project of which it is a part was conceived as a poet's walk, a collaboration between artists and poets, and each project includes poetry specifically commissioned with the art. **Terry Allen** is teamed with **Philip Levine**; other artist-poet teams include **George Herms** and **Charles Simic, James Surls** and **Robert Creeley, Joe Fay** and **Gary Soto, David Gilhooly** and **Robert Mezey, Lawrence Weiner** and **Carolyn Kizer, April Greiman** and **Lucille Clifton**. Most of the projects are located on the upper levels of the Seventh Street Marketplace, a shopping mall.

In keeping with **Home Savings of America**'s tradition of using mosaic tiles to decorate the exterior of nearly all its buildings, the bank commissioned **Joyce Kozloff** to do the same for its corporate headquarters (660 S. Figueroa St.) in 1989. The artworks in the lobby include glass panels by **Patsy Norvell** and interior murals by **Richard Haas, Tony Berlant,** and **Carlos Almaraz**. This project was completed in 1989. The underground of this building also serves as the **Seventh Street/Metro Center Station**, and additional artworks, completed in 1993, include a ceiling mural by **Terry Schoonhoven**, fiber-optic work by **Tom Eatherton**, and ceramic tile murals by **Roberto Gil de Montes** and Kozloff.

A large steel sculpture by **Jonathan Borofsky**, *Molecule Man* (1991), marks

the front of the **Edward Roybal Federal Building** (255 E. Temple St., at San Pedro). The building's main feature is a fountain, colonnade, and sculpture by **Tom Otterness**, entitled *The New World*. When this project was completed in 1991, Congressman Edward Roybal objected to the nudity found in Otterness's work—in particular, to the naked baby placed in the center of the fountain. After much public debate the controversy was settled by installing a railing around the figure. The colonnade features a whimsical and humorous interpretation of the creation of a new world. There is also an untitled bronze sculpture by **Joel Shapiro** (1990).

Perhaps the most controversial unveiling of public art in recent L.A. history occurred in 1975, when *Triforium*, a sixty-foot sculpture by **Joseph Young**, was installed at the corner of Temple and Main Streets. A mass of concrete with computerized winking colored lights, it played piped-in music at specific times. Arts professionals were offended to learn that the city had spent $900,000 on a commission that was not subject to review. Numerous public meetings followed, and on one occasion an outraged arts patron offered to commission the artist Christo to wrap the sculpture . . . permanently.

The **Community Redevelopment Agency** has published a set of public art walking tours of six different areas: Los Angeles Civic Center, South Park Area of Downtown, Historic Core to Bunker Hill, Heart of Downtown, Chinatown, and Little Tokyo Area. The maps are available at the front desk of the Central Library or from the CRA (213-977-1600).

ART GALLERIES AND AUCTION HOUSES

Sharon K. Emanuelli

A new area code will be introduced in 1998, replacing some 213 numbers with 323. Those phone numbers that will be affected are marked with an asterisk.

There are more than 120 commercial art galleries in Los Angeles, primarily on the Westside—in Santa Monica, West Hollywood, and Hancock Park. Smaller numbers operate in Venice, Beverly Hills, and downtown, and a few more are scattered across the county. This selection is limited to those neighborhoods where clusters of galleries can be visited. Galleries are great places to see changing displays of up-to-the-minute work and provide opportunities to learn more. Most dealers and their staffs are willing to be engaged. Though an attempt has been made to represent the range of subjects available from the viewpoint of the casual gallery-goer (rather than the collector or professional), many worthwhile galleries could not be included. Other lists can be found in the *Los Angeles Times* (Thursday and Sunday Calendar sections), the *L.A. Weekly* (free at many locations), *Art Scene* (by paid subscription or free at galleries, museum shops, and online [artscenecal.com]), and *Gallery Guide* (free in participating galleries).

With some exceptions, the galleries listed here are primarily in the business of selling art. They all maintain regular public hours and mount changing exhibitions. Like other entrepreneurial endeavors (the restaurant business is a good analogy), the art market is volatile and sensitive to economic fluctua-

tions. Galleries can come and go, change locations, or remain for years in the same spot. Many didn't survive the recession of the early 1990s. There does appear to be more confidence in the market now, and it seems that there are more galleries opening than closing.

Downtown has an energetic and unique art scene. The Museum of Contemporary Art is always worth a trip, but there is a whole different art universe beyond it. Since the 1970s, when downtown revitalization plans were initiated and zoning restrictions were relaxed to permit live/work spaces, the area has attracted elements from every stratum of the local art world. What now survives is a young, experimental art crowd; impromptu exhibitions and site installations; artist-run alternative galleries; and nonprofit arts centers. There has been a lot of talk and print in recent years—from influential people who don't even live here—about the emergence of Los Angeles as one of the world's most important centers for art making (and, not coincidentally, art education). Yet, in terms of the art market and exhibition venues, the city lags far behind New York in the volume of activity. So artists all over L.A. County have created other opportunities, opening artist-run nonprofit "alternative" spaces, artist cooperatives, and "experimental" or "project" galleries—hybrids of alternative and commercial spaces—owned by individual artists. This sometimes underground, very "happening" scene is characteristic of downtown, existing among warehouses and wholesale markets and overlaying long-standing and vibrant (but more traditional) Jap-

anese, Chinese, and Hispanic commercial districts. The suggested tour of these sites is for the open-minded and adventurous; the art is often challenging, the atmosphere is iconoclastic, and the galleries may be located in isolated industrial districts. One or two of the more traditional nonprofit spaces, as well as corporate and commercial galleries, round out the mix.

DOWNTOWN TOUR

(Note: Wednesday through Saturday are the most common open days, but Deep River is open only on weekends, and RTKL is open weekdays only. Listings of the individual galleries featured here follow the tour instructions.)

I like to start with the **Brewery Arts Complex** on North Main Street (take the Alameda exit off the 5 Freeway; go north past Union Station to North Main and bear right at the fork; at Avenue 21, turn right into the complex). An early weekday lunch under patio umbrellas at Café Berlin (Mon.–Fri. 8 a.m.–3 p.m.) is a great way to get a sense of this working artists' community housed in refurbished industrial buildings (see also Artists' Studio Tours, below). Someone will steer you to **SITE Gallery** and the **L.A. Artcore Annex**, both on Brewery grounds. From there, go back to Alameda and head south over the freeway, stopping at **Spanish Kitchen Studios** on Third Street east of Alameda. Don't let the grunge deter you. Go around the corner on Traction to brand-new **Deep River Gallery** (near the legendary Al's Bar). Continue south on Alameda to **Cirrus Gallery**, at Factory Place, and then to **Post** by turning left off Alameda onto Seventh Street, right on Mateo, and left on Seventh Place. Post has tiny signage, so

be persistent. Go back to Alameda, head north (right turn off Seventh) to Third Street, and park near San Pedro Street to visit the main gallery of **L.A. Artcore**. The last stop is the new **RTKL International Exhibition Gallery** on the concourse level (one below street level) of the building at 333 S. Hope Street (some street parking and underground lot). This will be a sentimental journey for those who remember Security Pacific National Bank's Plaza Gallery in the building lobby.

SITE Gallery (Seeking It Through Exhibitions)
Brewery Arts Complex
2100 N. Main St., #A-9
Los Angeles 90031
*213-221-9039
Wed.–Sat. 11 a.m.–4 p.m.

This nonprofit artists' organization with an open membership emphasizes emerging and underrepresented artists, especially those whose mediums—performance, installation, video, or poetry—receive limited exhibition opportunities. There are small members' critique groups, public programs, and annual open and juried shows. A peer committee reviews members' exhibition proposals, which can be pretty venturesome.

L.A. Artcore Brewery Annex
650A S. Ave. 21
Los Angeles 90031
*213-276-9320
Wed.–Sun. noon–4 p.m.

This is one of two satellite spaces operated by L.A. Artcore, a not-for-profit exhibiting organization that emphasizes underrecognized and emerging artists, although fairly prominent ones appear here as well. Director-founder Lydia Takeshita oversees the programming, which includes solid exhibitions, education programs, and annual competitions.

Spanish Kitchen Studios
734 E. Third St.
Los Angeles 90013
*213-680-4237
Tues.–Sat. 11 a.m.–4 p.m.

Multimedia artists Voychek Szaszor and Paul Oberman have maintained this multidisciplinary gallery and production facility since 1992 as "a for social profit transcultural urban organism," to make art independent of institutional or corporate sponsorship. They accommodate as many collaborative proposals in art, design, film, video, theater, poetry, and music as possible. Artists share expenses and responsibilities. There are regular film screenings and weekend performances by Wolfskill Theater.

Deep River Gallery
716 Traction Ave.
Los Angeles 90013
213-625-2715
Sat.–Sun. noon–6 p.m.

Set to open in December 1997, so not seen at press time, the gallery is operated by artists Rolo Castillo, Glen Kaino, and Daniel J. Martinez. It's a bit of a political experiment in providing a well-appointed, neutral space for artists who submit proposals for review. The gallery expects to use word-of-mouth rather than standard publicity and will ban critics. Martinez is known for the confrontational situations he has created for visitors to New York's Whitney Biennial and other exhibitions.

Cirrus Gallery/Cirrus Editions
542 S. Alameda St.
Los Angeles 90013
213-680-3473
Tues.–Sat. 10 a.m.–5 p.m.

A print workshop, publisher, and gallery, Cirrus was founded by Jean Milant in 1969 in Hollywood but moved downtown in 1979. Milant happily remains, running the

only real commercial gallery in the area. He was the first publisher to focus on California artists, and many produced their first editions at Cirrus. Early on, he offered options to experiment (Ed Ruscha printed with food) and promoted Californians in international venues. In recent years Cirrus has published Lita Albuquerque, Kyoko Asano, John Baldessari, Jill Giegerich, Joe Goode, Gronk, Sabina Ott, Lari Pittman, and Sarah Seager.

Post
1904 E. Seventh Pl.
Los Angeles 90013
213-488-3379
Wed.–Sat. 11 a.m.–6 p.m.

Artist Habib Kheradyar sells the art he shows but runs this more as a project space to serve artists' other needs: experimentation, exposure, and interaction. He does not represent artists, but his taste is widely respected. Others with similar operations cite him as a mentor.

L.A. Artcore
420 E. Third St., #110
Los Angeles 90013
213-617-3274
Wed.–Sun. 11 a.m.–4 p.m.

This is L.A. Artcore's main gallery and headquarters (see listing above).

RTKL International Exhibition Gallery
Concourse Level, #C200
333 S. Hope St.
Los Angeles 90071
213-627-7373
Mon.–Fri. 9 a.m.–4 p.m.

RTKL International is a multifaceted urban planning and architecture firm based in Baltimore. The storefront office is unorthodox for such a firm, situated across from the snack bar and fronted by the high glass walls of a former bank lobby. Staff architect (and artist) LeRad Darrell Nilles is the curator of this public-service program. A huge stu-

dio full of busy designers is visible from the public area used for exhibitions, a glass-walled conference room is on another side, and executive offices open into it. The public can see architecture being made, changing aesthetic views stimulate the designers, and everyone can muse on the significance of art in human environments. It's worth the effort to park, but call ahead; there's generally a month of downtime between shows.

ARTISTS' STUDIO TOURS
Santa Fe Art Colony Open Studios and Silent Auction
2401 S. Santa Fe Ave.
Los Angeles 90058
*213-587-6381
One weekend each spring
Free

A renovated robe factory houses fifty-seven artists' live/work spaces. Opened for occupancy in 1988, the four-building compound (including a garden) has been fully occupied ever since. Artists who apply to rent the below-market-rate studios are screened by the owners for their commitment to art careers and, as of this writing, work in the usual media plus design, architecture, computer graphics, calligraphy, and art education. Most residents participate in the Open Studios event, which includes music, food, and a silent auction to benefit a different charity each year. Dawn Arrowsmith, Pamela Blackwell, Mac McClain, Michael Barton Miller, Trevor Norris, Laurel Paley, Sharon Ryan, and Therman Statom are among the current residents.

The Brewery Art Walks
Brewery Arts Complex
688 S. Ave. 21 (enter on Moulton Ave.)
Los Angeles 90031
213-694-2911 (Art Walk information and directions)
Two weekends a year, usually in April and November
Free

This impressive reuse of the old Pabst Brewery (built in 1888 for the Eastside Brewery) is the largest contained art community in the world, with nearly 400 artists (including Lynn Aldrich, Rod Baer, Eugenia Butler, Brad Durham, Bruce Gray, Christian Munger, John O'Brien, and Roland Reiss), commercial photographers, designers (April Greiman, James Suelflow), and architects (Annie Chu, Michael Rotondi) in more than 300 live/work spaces.

It was bought and renovated by Carlson and Sons in 1980 for industrial use. Instead it was offered for artists' studios in 1982. Two exhibition spaces are here—L.A. Artcore's Brewery Annex and SITE Gallery (see above)—along with related enterprises such as Coagula Art Journal and the Los Angeles Opera Costume Shop. Café Berlin is open on Art Walk weekends.

DOWNTOWN LIVES
Location varies from year to year
Organized by the Downtown Arts Development Association (DADA)
213-625-3232
Three to four weeks each fall
Entry: $2–$3

DADA is a nonprofit, all-volunteer organization made up of artists and businesspeople which aims to improve the quality of life and promote the arts in downtown L.A., home to approximately 500 artists, probably the largest concentration on the West Coast. Each year DADA celebrates this with a series of events, usually centered on a huge exhibition in which any downtown artist can participate. In addition to visual art, dance, poetry, and music are included.

Hancock Park and West Hollywood

This was L.A.'s first cohesive gallery district, and the galleries are still sprinkled among a concentration of interior design businesses, antique dealers, and vintage goods stores. West Hollywood and Hancock Park have competed for decades with Santa Monica, Venice, and, for a while, downtown as the most desirable location for commercial galleries. While there are a number who show fresh new work here, the atmosphere is different from that of downtown, with its underground/alternative sensibility, or of Santa Monica, where the excitement of being stylishly at the edge prevails. It's tempered by the presence of respected galleries that deal in earlier twentieth-century art and the resale market, as well as the fact that a number of galleries have been around for more than twenty years. Members of the Los Angeles Art Galleries are indicated with ❖.

❖ Newspace Gallery
5241 Melrose Ave.
Los Angeles 90028
*213-469-9353
Tues.–Sat. 11 a.m.–4 p.m.

When Joni Gordon bought this gallery in 1975, she was already an important collector of Los Angeles art. Profoundly affected by the light-and-space group, she champions emerging and established artists who explore the effects of light, along with conceptual formalists. Special interests are photographs by painters and sculptors, public sculpture, and the resale of rare twentieth-century art. Artists include L.A.-based Martha Alf, Emilio Cueto, Kristin Leachman, Marcos Lutyens, Tiffanie Morrow, and Timothy Nolan as well as German Isabell Heimerdinger.

❖ Jack Rutberg Fine Arts
357 N. La Brea Ave.
Los Angeles 90036
*213-938-5222
Tues.–Fri. 10 a.m.–6 p.m.,
  Sat. 10 a.m.–5 p.m.

Rutberg handles modern and contemporary American and European art, with a special interest in expressionist styles. He has organized historical shows such as "Contrasting Expressions: Käthe Kollwitz and Georges Roualt," "On the Edge of America: California Modernist Art," and "Max Weber's Women" and sometimes publishes scholarly catalogues. He represents allegorical figure painter Ruth Weisberg and the estate of Hans Burkhardt.

❖ Tobey C. Moss Gallery
7321 Beverly Blvd.
Los Angeles 90036
*213-933-5523
Tues.–Sat. 11 a.m.–4 p.m.

Moss, unequaled in pre-1960 California modernism, is one catalyst for recent scholarly interest in this subject. She represents Jules Engel, Helen Lundeberg, the estates of Lorser Feitelson and Peter Krasnow, and Jim Hueter and Ynez Johnston, artists of a later generation. A rare showing by ninety-five-year-old early surrealist Dorr Bothwell was an important recent event.

❖ Richard Telles Fine Art
7380 Beverly Blvd.
Los Angeles 90036
*213-965-5578
Tues.–Sat. 11 a.m.–5 p.m.

Telles's refreshing, low-key endeavor showcases the hippest young (and some older) photographers and artists, many of whom have a neo-assemblage approach, including Liz Craft, Jeanne Dunning, Jim Isermann, Jorge Pardo, and B. Wurtz.

❖ Stephen Cohen Gallery
7358 Beverly Blvd.
Los Angeles 90036
*213-937-5525
Tues.–Sat. 11 a.m.–5 p.m.

A range of international historic and contemporary photography, especially journalism, is shown in this beautifully designed space. Lauren Greenfield's series on L.A. youth was a recent hit.

❖ Jan Kesner Gallery
164 N. La Brea Ave.
Los Angeles 90036
*213-938-6834
Tues.–Sat. 11 a.m.–5 p.m.

I visit this photography gallery (one of three on the block) often for contemporaries Richard Misrach, Ruben Ortiz Torres, and collaborators Erik Otsea and Jan Tumlir. Kesner's twentieth-century inventory features focused collections of Ansel Adams and Robert Frank; she also represents the estates of Max Yavno and W. Eugene Smith.

❖ Iturralde Gallery
154 N. La Brea Ave.
Los Angeles 90036
*213-937-4267
Tues.–Fri. 10 a.m.–5 p.m., Sat. 11 a.m.–5 p.m.

Current Latin-American art is the specialty here, particularly the magical realist and psychologically charged modes that are common in that region.

❖ Jan Baum Gallery
170 S. La Brea Ave.
Los Angeles 90036
*213-932-0170
Tues.–Sat. 10 a.m.–5:30 p.m.

A venerable dealer—and proprietor of a handsome building—Baum has exhibited contemporary painting and sculpture and has sold tribal art since 1977. Though international in scope, she is known for her attention to L.A. art, particularly current forms of assemblage (Bruce Houston, Betye Saar) and painting in many modes (Roberto Gil de Montes, Milano Kay, Peter Plagens).

Ace Contemporary Exhibitions
5514 Wilshire Blvd., 2nd Fl.
Los Angeles 90036
*213-935-4411
Tues.–Sat. 10 a.m.–6 p.m.

Doug Chrismas established himself with a spacious 1970s Venice gallery. This extravagant space, in the historic Desmond's building since 1987, accommodates some of the most spectacular art since the 1960s with extraordinary installations of large-scale and more intimate work. I have heard the space variously described as a cathedral and a mausoleum, but Chrismas's taste remains unquestioned.

6150 Wilshire Blvd.
Los Angeles 90048
Call information for phone numbers
Tues.–Sat. 11 a.m.–6 p.m.

Three cutting-edge galleries, displaced from their Santa Monica "Little Bergamot" location, have cast their fortunes together again, opening here in January 1998. ACME (space 1) owners Robert Gunderman and Randy Sommers, veterans of the alternative scene, show challenging but engaging work by experimental, emerging, and underrecognized artists: Chris Finley's mechanized constructions, Joyce Lightbody's music-related collages, Carlos Mollura's huge inflatables, Monique Prieto's computer-designed paintings, and Jennifer Steinkamp's abstract computer animation. Dan Bernier Gallery (space 3; *213-936-1021) shows "conceptually based" work about "ordinary experience" but avoids abstraction. For a while Bernier showed only L.A. artists, such as Russell Crotty, Tamara Fites, Martin Kersels, John Sonsini, and Patty Wickman, but he is now searching out international artists such as the multidimensional team of Fischli and Weiss. Although **Marc Foxx Gallery** (space 5) represents a diverse group of youngish locals (Robert Blanchon, T. Kelly Mason, Frances Stark), he also has a track record for importing new art, including work by Olafur Eliasson (Iceland), Udomsak Krisanamis (Thailand, New York), Hiroshi Sugito (Japan), and New Yorkers Jim Hodges and Joe Mama-Nitzberg. Established Californians such as sculptor Robert Therrien and artist-designer Roy McMaken illustrate his attraction to work that is "formally interesting *and* conceptually weighted."

The West Hollywood Galleries Consortium holds simultaneous opening receptions reminiscent of the old Gallery Walks, when the nearby section of La Cienega was Gallery Row and the locus of much art world socializing from the late 1950s to the early 1970s. Openings are usually the first Thursday of the month, from 6 to 9 p.m., although some galleries have longer reception hours and not all participate every month. They are located along six longish blocks of Melrose, between Almont Drive and Flores Street. It is possible to walk from one end to the other, including side-street detours, but probably not to see all the exhibitions within a three-hour period. Consortium members listed here are marked with a ‡, and there are others as well. Parking is available at the Pacific Design Center, the EPI public lot on Melrose at Almont, and on the street. For reception information, call Daniel Saxon Gallery (310-657-6033).

‡ **Margo Leavin Gallery**
812 N. Robertson Blvd.
Los Angeles 90069
310-273-0603
Tues.–Fri. 10 a.m.–5 p.m.,
  Sat. 11 a.m.–5 p.m.

An icon among dealers, Leavin opened in this spot in 1970, first working with New York galleries to show blue-chip contemporaries such as Dan Flavin, Jasper Johns, Claes Oldenburg, and Robert Rauschenberg. With the rise in respect for local artists, she has become the representative for prominent Angelenos such as John Baldessari, Roy Dowell, Maria Nordman, and Alexis Smith.

‡ **Regen Projects**
629 N. Almont Dr.
Los Angeles 90069
310-276-5424
Tues.–Sat. 11 a.m.–5 p.m.

Owner Stuart Regen and gallery director Shaun Caley are often touted as *the* dealers to watch for cutting-edge new and established artists. They present a fascinating group in their unassuming, open-to-the-outdoors space, including On Kawara, Toba Khedoori, Sol LeWitt, Catherine Opie, Raymond Pettibon, Lari Pittman, Charles Ray, and Rosemarie Trockel.

‡ **Manny Silverman Gallery**
619 N. Almont Dr.
Los Angeles 90069
310-659-8256
Tues.–Sat. 10 a.m.–5 p.m.

The Silvermans are important dealers in post–World War II American abstract art, especially the New York school. Here the origins of the creative spirit that sparked the many movements of the 1960s—and led to today's stylistic pluralism—can be seen. The gallery represents Michael Goldberg and Emerson Woelffer and the estates of Hannelore Baron, Edward Dugmore, Sam Francis, and Adolph Gottlieb.

Chac-mool Gallery
8920 Melrose Ave.
Los Angeles 90069
310-550-6792
Mon.–Fri. 10 a.m.–6 p.m.,
  Sat. 11 a.m.–6 p.m.

Although the focus of this gallery has been established Mexican and South American contemporary artists, Esthella Provas has recently begun mixing in some American and European art. She also coordinates several exchange projects each year with Mexican institutions.

‡ **George Stern Fine Arts**
8920 Melrose Ave.
Los Angeles 90069
310-276-2600
Mon.–Fri. 10 a.m.–6 p.m.,
  Sat. 11 a.m.–5 p.m.

George Stern exhibits early California (nineteenth- and early twentieth-century) paintings and, occasionally, other American art in a lovely, very genteel showroom. Landscapes and still lifes are the dominant genres.

‡ **William Karges Fine Art**
9001 Melrose Ave.
Los Angeles 90069
310-276-8551
Mon.–Sat. 10 a.m.–5 p.m.

One of the largest dealers in early California painting, Karges also stocks midcentury Soviet impressionism. The gallery, known for publishing scholarly catalogues, recently began representing three contemporary artists.

‡ **Tasende Gallery**
8808 Melrose Ave.
West Hollywood 90069
310-276-8686
Tues.–Sat. 10 a.m.–6 p.m.

This La Jolla–based gallery specializes in monumental sculpture but shows paintings as well. The space accommodates big pieces but still feels intimate. The gallery represents Eduardo Chillida, Mark di Suvero, Roberto Matta, and others.

‡ **De Ville Galleries**
8751 Melrose Ave.
Los Angeles 90069
310-652-0525
Tues.–Fri. 10 a.m.–5 p.m.,
  Sat. 10 a.m.–4 p.m.

A dealer for more than forty years, Christian Title draws his exhibitions from an extensive inventory of American paintings of circa 1870 to 1930, including works by William Merritt Chase, Bernhard Gutmann, George Luks, Edgar Payne, Carl Peters, and Mary B. Titcomb, plus some contemporary "impressionists."

‡ **Koplin Gallery**
464 N. Robertson Blvd.
Los Angeles 90048
310-657-9843
Tues.–Fri. 10 a.m.–5:30 p.m.,
  Sat. 11 a.m.–5:30 p.m.

Marti Koplin shows contemporary representational art spanning several generations. Though in fairly traditional modes, there is highly individual work to be seen here by Theophilus Brown, Robbie Conal, James Doolin, Kerry James Marshall, Len Paschoal, Sarah Perry, and others.

‡ **Remba Gallery/ Mixografía**
462 N. Robertson Blvd.
Los Angeles 90048
310-657-1101
Tues.–Fri. 10 a.m.–5:30 p.m.,
  Sat. 11 a.m.–5:30 p.m.

One of three major publishers of limited-edition multiples in L.A., Mixografía is a Remba family enterprise begun in Mexico City and moved here in 1984. A unique printing process is used to create deep relief on the paper's surface or fully three-dimensional paper or metal forms, with incredibly nuanced coloration.

‡ **Kohn Turner Gallery**
454 N. Robertson Blvd.
Los Angeles 90048
310-854-5400
Tues.–Fri. 10 a.m.–5:30 p.m.,
  Sat. 11 a.m.–5:30 p.m.

I have long admired Jan Turner-Colburn, who specializes in post–World War II California art, and her 1994 merger with Michael Kohn, who handles New

York artists, was felicitous. A terrific recent show featured beat-era assemblagist Bruce Conner's new work. Also look for Jay DeFeo, John Frame, Peter Halley, Mark Innerst, and Astrid Preston.

Daniel Saxon Gallery
552 Norwich Dr.
West Hollywood 90048
310-657-6033
Tues.–Fri. 11 a.m.–5 p.m.,
  Sat. noon–4 p.m.

Saxon limits his enthusiastic representation to Chicano-identified artists, most of them from Los Angeles. Among others, the de la Torre brothers, Gronk, Delilah Montoya, John Valadez, and Patssi Valdez are shown here.

Heritage Gallery
718 N. La Cienega Blvd.
Los Angeles 90069
310-652-7738
Tues.–Sat. 11 a.m.–5 p.m.

Benjamin Horowitz opened this space in 1962—showing socially conscious American figurative artists such as William Glackens (of the Eight), William Gropper, and Reginald Marsh—and may not have recarpeted it since. As president of the Art Dealers Association of California, he oversaw the inauguration of the 1960s and 1970s Monday Gallery Walks on La Cienega. This rumpled but friendly space has also been home to African-American modern realists, including Charles S. White.

Kiyo Higashi Gallery
8332 Melrose Ave.
Los Angeles 90069
*213-655-2482
Tues.–Sat. 11 a.m.–6 p.m.

Higashi is committed to minimalist and other reductive abstract art with a contemplative tone. This is a great place to see it, too. Artists include Perry Araeipour, Larry Bell, Max Cole, William Dwyer, Lies Kraal, Penelope Krebs,

Ted Kurahara, Carolee Toon, and Guy Williams.

Gemini G.E.L. (Graphic Editions Limited)
8365 Melrose Ave.
Los Angeles 90069
*213-651-0513
Mon.–Fri. 9:30 a.m.–5:30 p.m.

An internationally respected workshop, Gemini has issued more than 1,700 print and sculpture editions since 1966. The gallery displays its recent publications. Founders Sidney Felsen, Stanley Grinstein, and Kenneth Tyler (who later established Tyler Graphics in Westchester County, New York) first worked with "mature master" Josef Albers, though prominent midcareer artists were soon added. Their collaborators have included Vija Celmins, Richard Diebenkorn, Sam Francis, David Hockney, Jasper Johns, Roy Lichtenstein, Elizabeth Murray, Bruce Nauman, Ken Price, Dorothea Rockburne, and Susan Rothenberg.

Beverly Hills

In 1995 when two of New York's most powerful galleries—Gagosian and PaceWildenstein—opened branches here, pledging to originate shows instead of sending watered-down versions from home, Beverly Hills seriously entered the art scene. The galleries listed here fall within the Wilshire/ Little Santa Monica Boulevard/Cañon Drive triangle and are within walking distance of one another.

Gagosian Gallery
456 N. Camden Dr.
Beverly Hills 90210
310-271-9400
Tues.–Sat. 10 a.m.–5:30 p.m.

Hometown boy moves gallery to New York and returns a success! This is the high-status Beverly Hills branch of Larry Gagosian's two New York galleries. The stunning space, de-

signed by Getty Center architect Richard Meier, can accommodate the large work of important American sculptors such as Chris Burden, Richard Serra, and Elyn Zimmerman. Gagosian also represents Americans Jennifer Bartlett, Andrew Lord, and Frank Stella; French artists Annette Messager and Yves Klein (estate); and Italian Francesco Clemente.

Latin American Masters
264 N. Beverly Dr.
Beverly Hills 90210
310-271-4847, 310-271-4913
Tues.–Sat. 11 a.m.–6 p.m.

Works by blue-chip midcentury Latins Wifredo Lam, Armando Morales, Diego Rivera, Rufino Tamayo, and Francisco Toledo are in the inventory here. A museum-quality show of surrealist Roberto Matta's paintings and drawings was mounted in 1997.

PaceWildenstein
9540 Wilshire Blvd.
Beverly Hills 90212
310-205-5522
Tues.–Sat. 10 a.m.–6 p.m.

In 1993 New York's oldest gallery, Wildenstein & Co. (founded in 1875), merged with Pace (1961) and made major news. Wildenstein's inventory spanned continents and five centuries; the gallery had sold much of the lifework of Cézanne, van Gogh, Picasso, and Renoir. Pace dealt with big-ticket contemporaries like Chuck Close, Robert Irwin, Agnes Martin, Henry Moore, and Claes Oldenburg. More recent art and photography dominate programming in this understated, expansive Charles Gwathmey–designed gallery.

West Los Angeles

Del Mano Gallery
11981 San Vicente Blvd.
Los Angeles 90049
310-476-8508
Tues.–Sat. 10 a.m.–6 p.m.,
  Sun. noon–5 p.m.

The most prominent local contemporary craft and decorative arts gallery, Del Mano deals internationally in ceramics, glass, wood, fiber, and metal objects. The gallery is rather shoplike, though there is a changing exhibition space. Large-scale work and handmade furniture are handled in the Pasadena gallery (33 E. Colorado Blvd.; 626-793-6648).

Santa Monica/Venice

Santa Monica has the county's largest concentration of commercial art galleries. This is helped by arts-friendly civic policies, including a very active arts commission. The addition of Bergamot Station Arts Center solidified a process of gallery migration from Hollywood and downtown that began in the 1980s. Venice, by contrast, is not the center of gallery activity it was in the 1970s (there was never enough parking). Its position as an artists' enclave and generally artsy community is an important part of local folklore, however, and remains a fact, even as the residents' cultural diversity increases.

Fred Hoffman Fine Art
1721 Stewart St.
Santa Monica 90404
310-453-3330
Tues.–Sat. 10 a.m.–5:30 p.m.

This soaring warehouse space is the most recent of several Fred Hoffman galleries, which always seem lacking in friendliness. Hoffman shows "underexposed important postwar art" in museum-style presentations. Exhibitions have included George Segal's new sculpture, retrospectives for pop painters Tom Wesselmann and Alex Katz, abstract work by Charles Arnoldi, and photographs by Dennis Hopper.

BROADWAY GALLERY COMPLEX

Park in the free lot between the buildings and enter the galleries from there.

Mark Moore Gallery

2032-A Broadway
Santa Monica 90404
310-453-3031
Tues.–Fri. 10 a.m.–5 p.m.,
   Sat. 11 a.m.–5 p.m.

After running the Works, a highly visible gallery in Long Beach and, later, Costa Mesa, where competition was nil, Moore has joined the crowd in Santa Monica. He has a fancy mix of artists—from "cool school" types Tony DeLap and Jay McCafferty to campy Carole Caroompas and Tom of Finland, as well as Mark Bennett, Deborah Brown, Vernon Fisher, and Ken Kelly.

Blum & Poe

2042 Broadway
Santa Monica 90404
310-453-8311
Tues.–Sat. 10:30 a.m.–6 p.m.

This is one gallery that admits being interested *only* in rigorous conceptualism, or "idea art," rather than formal concerns. It shows all mediums—including photography, video, and installation—and represents prominent practitioners of the genre, including Jennifer Bornstein, Kim Dingle, Dave Muller, Bruce and Norman Yonemoto (all local), Anya Gallaccio (England), Yoshitomo Nara (Japan), and Andrei Roiter (Russia).

Ruth Bachofner Gallery

2046 Broadway
Santa Monica 90404
310-829-3300
Tues.–Sat. 10:30 a.m.–5:30 p.m.

Bachofner prefers traditional media, especially formal painting; she eschews conceptualism. She represents Karl Benjamin, Southern California's influential geometric abstractionist, and New Yorkers Michel Alexis,

Stephen Greene, Robert Kingston, Selina Trieff, and Patrick Wilson. She was early in the late-1980s migration from Hollywood to Santa Monica.

COLORADO AVENUE

G. Ray Hawkins Gallery

908 Colorado Ave.
Santa Monica 90401
310-394-5558
Tues.–Sat. 9:30 a.m.–5:30 p.m.

This is a prominent, long-lived, fairly traditional photography gallery. Hawkins does stock work by contemporaries such as Nan Goldin, Robert Mapplethorpe, Cindy Sherman, and William Wegman—well, almost anyone you can think of—plus a large inventory of historic and vintage photography. He hosts regular auctions periodically.

Christopher Grimes Gallery

916 Colorado Ave.
Santa Monica 90401
310-587-3373
Tues.–Sat. 9:30 a.m.–5:30 p.m.

Grimes shows challenging work by emerging and midcareer artists, focusing on "dialogue between aesthetic seduction and conceptual premise." Much of the work is formally reductive, though more eccentric than meditative. He represents Linda Burnham, Jaccui Den Hartog, Tom Friedman, and Tony Tasset.

Merging One Gallery

1547 Sixth St.
Santa Monica 90401
310-395-0033
Tues.–Sat. 11 a.m.–5 p.m.
   (Oct.–Apr.), noon–6 p.m.
   (May–Sept.)

Formal and pictorial concerns seem to interest Rachele Lozzi, a veteran of art businesses in Italy and New York. She shows an international array of accomplished, fairly accessible art, which has included Richard Beckman's abstract sculpture, Gary Bukovnik's photorealist

watercolors, Patrick Gourley's geometric abstractions, and Diana Wong's impressionistic installations.

BERGAMOT STATION ARTS CENTER

2525 Michigan Ave.
Santa Monica 90404
310-829-5854 (for directions)

This 5.5-acre compound—with more than twenty galleries, plus architectural and design firms, other art services, and a charity boutique—is the most accommodating place in L.A. for gallery-hopping. There is a big parking lot and a café with outdoor seating for light lunches. Bergamot Station is the historic name for the site, dating to 1875, when bergamot flowers flourished there and it was a stop for the Red Line trolley. After the trolley's demise in 1953, the warehouses were used for industry and eventually abandoned. The city purchased the property and, when plans for a light-rail line were shelved, instigated its redevelopment as an arts complex, which opened in September 1994. The architect was Frederick Fisher, who has designed some of the most architecturally interesting galleries over the years.

You will find twentieth-century art and photography here, with an emphasis on the contemporary. A representative group of galleries is listed here. The buildings in the complex are designated by a letter and a number (e.g., A1), which follows the name of the gallery.

Gallery Luisotti (RAM)/RAM Publications, USA (A2)

310-453-0043
Tues.–Sat. 10:30 a.m.–5:30 p.m.

Many first knew Theresa Luisotti's work from MIN Gallery in Japan. Featuring primarily California photographers, MIN publications are particularly im-

pressive. RAM Publications distributes its own art books and those of California and Japanese organizations. The gallery shows historical figures Imogen Cunningham and Jacques-Henri Lartigue and contemporaries Lewis Baltz, Barbara Kasten, and Toshio Shibata.

Shoshana Wayne Gallery (B1)

310-453-7535
Tues.–Fri. 10 a.m.–5:30 p.m.,
   Sat. 11 a.m.–5:30 p.m.

Shoshana Blank, with her husband, Wayne (Bergamot Station's developer), specializes in conceptual sculpture and installations. In addition to Yoko Ono, an éminence grise who barely makes objects, the gallery represents younger, more materially based object-makers who respond to Ono's generation, including Nicole Eisenman, Victor Estrada, Rachel Lachowicz, Kiki Smith, and Pae White.

Craig Krull Gallery (B3)

310-828-6410
Tues.–Fri. 10 a.m.–5:30 p.m.,
   Sat. 11 a.m.–6 p.m.

This may be my favorite photography gallery. (Other media are also shown.) Krull takes an inquisitive approach to the purposes of photography, with exhibitions such as "Action/Performance and the Photograph" (which spanned the century and toured internationally) and "Photographing the L.A. Art Scene: 1955–1975." He has an eye for the meeting of formal beauty and content, representing Terry Braunstein, Anthony Hernandez, and Michael Kenna. This is one of the few galleries that provides museum-style text panels.

Rosamund Felsen Gallery (B4)

310-828-8488
Tues.–Sat. 10 a.m.–5:30 p.m.

Over the years Felsen has

shown and probably advanced the careers of some of Southern California's most individual and influential artists. I first saw Chris Burden's ambitious performance installations in her garden-shed-like La Cienega space in the 1970s, along with Alexis Smith's story collages. She currently shows Marc Pally's abstract paintings, M. A. Peers's dog paintings, Erika Rothenberg's social commentary, and Jeffrey Vallance's cultural send-ups.

Gail Harvey Gallery (B5)
310-829-9125
Tues.–Sat. 11 a.m.–5 p.m.

Serving as an advocate for lesser-known but established Americans (mostly based out of state), Harvey emphasizes pure painting in the form of nonobjective abstraction (Allen Cox, Keiko Hara, Stephanie Weber) and some abstracted landscape (Susan Hall).

Frank Lloyd Gallery (B5b)
310-264-3866
Tues.–Sat. 11 a.m.–5 p.m.

Frank Lloyd inherited artists formerly represented by ceramics historian, author, and dealer Garth Clark, now in New York. Lloyd emphasizes artists who transcend the functional associations of ceramics, even while many make vessel forms. The roster has some of our most important ceramists: Californians Ralph Bacerra, Philip Cornelius, Roseline Delisle, Viola Frey, Harrison McIntosh, John Mason, Adrian Saxe, Akio Takamori, and Beatrice Wood and Midwesterner Ken Ferguson.

Bobbie Greenfield Gallery (B6)
310-264-0640
Tues.–Fri. 10 a.m.–5 p.m.,
  Sat. 11 a.m.–5 p.m.

Greenfield shows only works on paper (drawings, paintings, and monoprints) and multiples (including prints and sculptural media), mostly by prominent contemporary artists such as Richard Diebenkorn, Sam Francis, Helen Frankenthaler, David Hockney, Ed Moses, and Frank Stella.

Patricia Faure Gallery (B7)
310-449-1479
Tues.–Sat. 11 a.m.–5 p.m.

Faure has a long association with important Southern California artists. Before she opened her first gallery with the late Betty Asher, she was director of the venerated James Corcoran Gallery. She represents Llyn Foulkes, Craig Kauffman, and Margaret Nielsen, along with John Coplans, Judy Fiskin, Wade Hoefer, Gwynn Murrill, Elsa Rady, and David Reed.

Track 16 Gallery (C1)
310-264-4678
Tues.–Sat. 11 a.m.–6 p.m.

As a financial partner in the development of Bergamot, comedy writer Tom Patchett seemed set to showcase his unbelievable collection of billboards, neon, decorative arts, and Americana. In fact, Track 16 hosts an eccentric but significant mix of everything from American popular culture to important art. A collaboration with Robert Berman produced a museum-quality Man Ray show. He also owns Smart Art Press and produces catalogues for his own and others' gallery exhibitions.

Patricia Correia Gallery (E2)
310-264-1760
Tues.–Fri. 10 a.m.–6 p.m.,
  Sat. 11 a.m.–6 p.m.

Correia's hallmark—aside from her exuberant personality—is art by emerging and midcareer Californians such as Richard Godfrey, Pam Goldblum, Samantha Harrison, Jeff Kaisershot, Bari Kumar, Joseph Maruska, and Norton

Wisdom. She also handles some notable glass sculpture, including the light-bending crystalline forms of Steven V. Correia, John Luebtow's plate glass and industrial metal constructions, and the multimedia work of Steven Schauer.

Gallery of Functional Art (E3)
310-829-6990
Tues.–Sat. 11 a.m.–6 p.m.,
  Sun. noon–5 p.m.

This is an exuberant collection of unique artists' furniture and other useful objects.

MAIN STREET
Angles Gallery
2222 and 2230 Main St.
Santa Monica 90405
310-396-5019
Tues.–Sat. 10 a.m.–6 p.m.

David McAuliffe has shown such a clear preference for a minimalist aesthetic, an almost Zen-like asceticism, that other dealers often describe their own styles in relationship to his. The elegant work that made me fall in love with this gallery is now augmented by the extroverted art of younger artists such as Greg Bogin, Pauline Stella Sanchez, and Linda Stark. Look for Claudia Matzko, Carter Potter, Ross Rudel, and Buzz Spector; Brits Anish Kapoor and Richard Long; and Canadians Rodney Graham and Geoffrey James.

Bryce Bannatyne Gallery
2439 Main St., #B-2 (in the Edgemar Complex)
Santa Monica 90401
310-396-9668
Tues.–Sat. noon–5 p.m.

Bannatyne brings together a harmonious grouping of early American modernist work, Arts and Crafts–era decorative arts, midcentury master ceramics, American and Latin-American paintings from 1900 to 1960, architecture, and design.

L.A. Louver Gallery
45 N. Venice Blvd.
Venice 90291
310-821-4955
Tues.–Sat. 10 a.m.–5 p.m.

Founded in 1975, this is by far the most important gallery in Venice and should be included on any dedicated art follower's regular rounds. Owner Peter Goulds has developed steady relationships with artists, mostly Californian, who came to prominence in the 1960s and early 1970s. They include Terry Allen, Tony Berlant, Wallace Berman (estate), William Brice, Joe Goode, George Herms, David Hockney, Edward and Nancy Reddin Kienholz, Michael C. McMillen, Ed Moses, Ken Price, and Peter Shelton. Now in a spiffy new building, Goulds has begun to show a younger group, many of whom are influenced by the older artists. Parking is validated for the lot across the street.

Auction Houses

The primary goal of auction houses is, of course, to sell the rarest art and artifacts at the highest possible prices. Along the way, however, they sell objects of varying value and type, sometimes at (relatively) bargain prices. They also provide up-close previews of objects that are rarely seen by the public, information about art and the marketplace in their catalogues, and some real-life theater during the bidding.

Auction-house sales are open to the public free of charge. There is lots of activity during the proceedings, and observers come and go as they please, but potential buyers must register on the day of the sale in order to bid. Three major international art houses maintain Los Angeles operations. To be on their mailing lists, one simply has to ask. Catalogues for specific auctions may be purchased singly or by subscription; actual sale prices are published later. Preview exhibitions, with staff experts present to answer questions, are held for three to five days before locally conducted sales or to show the highlights of upcoming sales in other cities. All three houses publish brochures explaining the auction process.

In addition, these auction houses each have long histories of community service. They support the fund-raising efforts of cultural, social service, and educational organizations by providing auctioneers and appraisers pro bono and by hosting exhibitions, meetings, and other events.

Butterfield & Butterfield Auctioneers and Appraisers
7601 Sunset Blvd.
Los Angeles 90046
*213-850-7500
Appraisal clinics: first and third
  Tuesdays of the month,
  9:30 a.m.–12:30 p.m. (free)

William Butterfield founded his auction house in 1865, during the Gold Rush era, to sell surplus goods consigned by merchant ships anchored in San Francisco Bay. Generations of family members have since remained active in the business, still based in San Francisco. In 1988 a full-service branch was opened in Los Angeles, and in 1997 expanded exhibition space was acquired at 7575 Sunset Boulevard. Major auctions are simulcast between the two cities. The company maintains an international network

of regional offices and partnerships.

Butterfield's is especially noted for handling early California paintings. Specialty departments in L.A. also include American paintings, modern and contemporary paintings, manuscripts, prints, furniture and decorative arts, Asian art, silver, coins and stamps, entertainment memorabilia, and jewelry and timepieces. In addition to its sales of art and antiques, Butterfield's monthly estate sales offer intermediately priced items.

Staff experts are available to the public on the first and third Tuesdays of the month for free appraisal clinics. Objects are reviewed on a first-come, first-served basis. You may bring up to five objects and/or photographs for a verbal estimate of auction value. Possessions can be consigned to Butterfield's at that time, if it is appropriate.

Sotheby's
9665 Wilshire Blvd.
Beverly Hills 90210
310-274-0340
Mon.–Fri. 9 a.m.–5 p.m.; preview hours (when applicable): 11 a.m.–4 p.m.

Sotheby's began in 1744 as a bookseller in London, eventually expanding into other areas. Between 1971 and 1982 Sotheby's had a full-scale operation in L.A., with about 100 employees, and owned the land it occupied between CBS Television City and the landmark Pan Pacific Auditorium (later destroyed by fire). When London management

wanted to generate some cash to shore up hemorrhaging European operations, the property was sold and the bustling office reduced to a bare presence—just before the 1980s boom in the art and real estate markets. With a current staff of twenty, in elegant new offices occupied since 1995, there are plans to expand, but the major auctions and senior experts will remain in New York. The Beverly Hills office now houses departments of contemporary and impressionist painting, prints and photographs, American and old master paintings, jewelry, entertainment memorabilia, wine, and decorative arts, and senior experts in those and other fields often make their way here from New York.

Along with October and April previews for New York sales, the local office now plans six to ten auctions annually for various types of collectibles. Some types of art, such as limited-edition prints and photographs, may be auctioned here in the future.

.

Christie's Fine Art Auctioneers
360 N. Camden Dr.
Beverly Hills 90210
310-385-2600
Mon.–Fri. 9 a.m.–5 p.m.

The world's oldest auctioneer of fine art, Christie's was founded in London in 1766 by James Christie, whose portrait by Thomas Gainsborough now hangs in the Getty Museum. From the beginning, it provided a gathering place for artists, collectors, and deal-

ers and conducted some of the most famous eighteenth- and nineteenth-century sales, including Catherine the Great's purchase of Sir Robert Walpole's painting collection (which became the basis of the Hermitage's holdings), Madame du Barry's jewelry auction, and the forty-day auction of the Duke of Buckingham's collection at Stowe House. Christie's literature states, however, that 80 percent of the items it auctioned in 1995 sold for under $5,000.

There are now more than 100 offices worldwide. After maintaining an office in Beverly Hills for fifteen years, mainly to service the New York auctions, Christie's inaugurated a full-service operation in May 1997, "a testimony to the growing importance of this market," with resident specialists in motor cars, jewelry, American and contemporary paintings, and European decorative arts. Staff specialists from other cities make periodic appearances here as well. The posh new quarters are designed to reflect a blend of mission revival and other regional architectural styles and will host auctions of California art, jewelry, cars, celebrity memorabilia, wine, and perhaps more. Plans include an extensive education program, with free talks preceding each sale and two-day study seminars. The 1997 seminar topics were animation, contemporary art, jewelry, and opera.

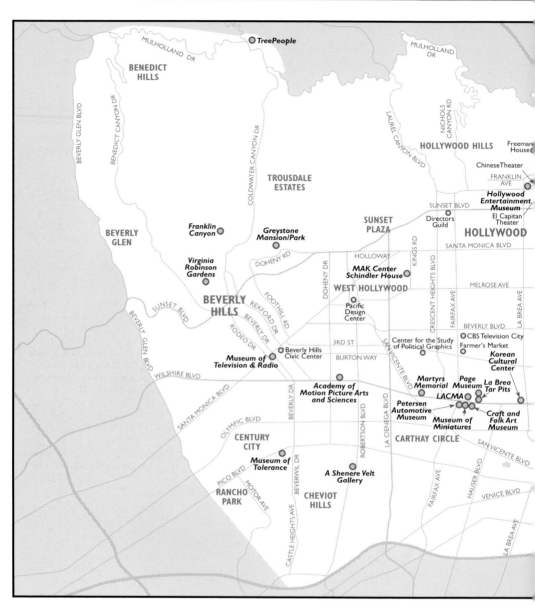

MULHOLLAND DR

○ **TreePeople**

MULHOLLAND DR

BENEDICT HILLS

BEVERLY GLEN BLVD

BENEDICT CANYON DR

NICHOLS CANYON RD

LAUREL CANYON BLVD

HOLLYWOOD HILLS Freeman House

ChineseTheater

FRANKLIN AVE

COLDWATER CANYON DR

TROUSDALE ESTATES

Hollywood Entertainment Museum ○

SUNSET BLVD

Directors Guild ○

El Capitan Theater

SUNSET PLAZA

KINGS RD

HOLLYWOOD

SANTA MONICA BLVD

BEVERLY GLEN

Franklin Canyon ○

Greystone Mansion/Park ○

HOLLOWAY

DOHENY RD

DOHENY DR

MAK Center Schindler House ○

CRESCENT HEIGHTS BLVD

MELROSE AVE

FAIRFAX AVE

LA BREA AVE

Virginia Robinson Gardens ○

SUNSET BLVD

FOOTHILL RD

WEST HOLLYWOOD

BEVERLY HILLS

REXFORD DR

BEVERLY DR

Pacific Design Center ○

BEVERLY BLVD

○ CBS Television City

BEVERLY GLEN BLVD

RODEO DR

3RD ST

Center for the Study of Political Graphics ○

Farmer's Market ○

Korean Cultural Center

WILSHIRE BLVD

Museum of Television & Radio ○

Beverly Hills ○ Civic Center

BURTON WAY

SAN VICENTE BLVD

Martyrs Memorial ○

Page Museum

La Brea Tar Pits

SANTA MONICA BLVD

BEVERLY DR

Academy of Motion Picture Arts and Sciences ○

ROBERTSON BLVD

LA CIENEGA BLVD

LACMA ○

Petersen Automotive Museum ○

○○○○ ○

Craft and Folk Art Museum

OLYMPIC BLVD

CENTURY CITY

BEVERWIL DR

Museum of Tolerance ○

Museum of Miniatures

CARTHAY CIRCLE

SAN VICENTE BLVD

PICO BLVD

MOTOR AVE

A Shenere Velt Gallery ○

FAIRFAX AVE

HAUSER BLVD

VENICE BLVD

RANCHO PARK

CASTLE HEIGHTS AVE

CHEVIOT HILLS

LA BREA AVE

* indicates area code that changes in 1998

Hollywood Bowl and Museum

2301 Highland Ave.
Los Angeles 90068
Bowl information: *213-850-2000
www.hollywoodbowl.org
Box office: daily 10 a.m.–6 p.m. from mid-May, or call Ticketmaster (213-480-3232)

Museum: *213-850-2058
Tues.–Sat. 10 a.m.–8:30 p.m. in summer; 10 a.m.–4:30 p.m. the rest of the year
Entry: free

"As the sky turns first pink, then purple, then midnight blue, and the music rises to meet the first stars of the night, you'll realize there is only one place on earth to expe-

rience such magic." This unattributed assessment, inscribed at the entrance to the new museum at the Hollywood Bowl, is what the administration hopes its audiences will conclude.

Like any long-term love affair, the relationship of Angelenos to the once-natural amphitheater that has become the city's primary venue for music during the summer has had its ups and downs. From its inaugural season in 1922 the Hollywood Bowl has been the summer home of the Los Angeles Philharmonic, and almost every famous classical and popular musician

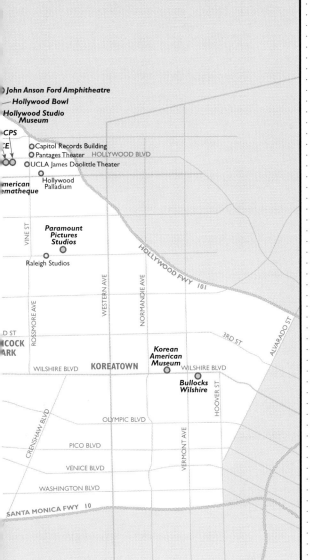

three concerts per week were scheduled for a season that never exceeded ten weeks, but in 1969 Ernest Fleischmann became general director of the Hollywood Bowl and inaugurated a new era. Nearly thirty years later, more than a million tickets were sold, and the Bowl has again claimed its role as a centerpiece of summer in Southern California.

The history of the Hollywood Bowl's transition is the focus of the long-term exhibits in the new museum, which opened in 1996 and is named for former County Supervisor Edmund D. Edelman, who saw the enjoyment of "the cultural opportunities and recreation that come with population density" as the primary rationale for people to live in cities. Curators accepted the challenge to reveal this jewel in the city's fabric, assembling a fascinating collection of historical artifacts—film, recordings, photographs, and vintage graphics—that reveal the Bowl's history. A handsome new building designed by Skidmore, Owings & Merrill, which occupies no more space than the "footprint" of a former teahouse, is filled with well-mounted exhibits that chronicle the great performances that have brought renown to the Hollywood Bowl and joy to Los Angeles.

"The music is what it's all about," wrote museum director Carol Merrill-Mirsky, revealing her plan for the exhibition's structure. Visitors may put on headsets at each of the five chronological exhibit areas to experience great performances of the past while enjoying such film clips as silent footage of great conductors taken by a member of the orchestra, Judy Garland gamely performing in pouring rain, and swooning fans during the Beatles' 1964 concert. A slide show reveals the development of the physical space, which attracted some of the region's best architects: Lloyd Wright designed two shells for the Bowl, which still retains the arched proscenium of his 1928 structure; in 1926, Myron Hunt, who also designed Pasadena's Rose Bowl, added seating that balloons up the hillside; and Frank Gehry created fiberglass spheres that hover inside the shell to improve acoustics. The entrance fountain and a fifteen-foot statue, *The Muse of Music*, designed by George Stanley (who also sculpted the Oscar statuette), were added in 1940.

Patrons, burdened with picnic baskets and pressed for time, too often pass by the museum without entering, but don't make that mistake! Admission is free, and the exhibits whet the musical appetite and deepen the appreciation for this magical spot in the city's history. Even a half hour

of the twentieth century has performed there. During its first quarter-century, audiences flocked to the hills south of the Cahuenga Pass—then virtually uninhabited—to enjoy open-air concerts, and the natural amphitheater was transformed with permanent seating to accommodate the crowds and a series of shells—designed to improve the carrying power of sound in the vast space—was added. By the end of the war years, changing musical tastes introduced popular performers (Frank Sinatra made a controversial appearance in 1943), and audiences for classical music declined. From 1946 to 1968 in the museum will enhance the experience of the Hollywood Bowl, whether a symphony under the stars, a jazz concert, or a performance of popular music is your final destination.

Get there early—the shuttle buses are convenient, but on-site parking can be chaotic and gets worse as the hour of the concert approaches. The picnic area was expanded to about 1,500 spaces during the recent renovations, and the information

kiosk, box office, and gift shop were remodeled. Sitting in the boxes is a treat, but these are often sold out by subscription; to snare tickets to box seats that become available because of cancellations, sign up for the waiting list that was inaugurated in 1997. Tickets at the top of the Bowl sell for only a few dollars and are almost always available.

Listening to music in an outdoor space with almost 18,000 seats depends on the quiet and cooperation of all: crying babies, talking patrons, and bottles bouncing beneath the tiered seats can ruin the experience for everyone. Remember the words of the great conductor Bruno Walter, who credited the quiet of the crowd with overcoming his fear of this performance venue: "There was the splendor of the California night, of the starry sky, and of the dark mountains surrounding us; there was the touching silence of the immense throng. For once my musical conscience, stunned by so much beauty, yielded, and I felt overcome by a mood of happy exaltation, renewed at every future visit to the magic valley" (*Theme and Variations*, Knopf, 1946).

Rehearsals at the Hollywood Bowl are open to the public free of charge. The Los Angeles Philharmonic—or whatever performers are on the stage that night—can use the stage to rehearse from 10 a.m. on. They don't always rehearse, but you may be lucky enough to hear a great performance from great seats you couldn't get at the box office. Visitors are asked to respect the rehearsal with quiet, but picnics are permitted.

Open House at the Hollywood Bowl is one of the nicest ways to spend a summer morning with a child. The performances are held in a flat, shaded area adjacent to the box office, rather than the Bowl itself, which is reserved for rehearsals of the evening's performances. Two acts share the hour of performance time, presenting a wide variety of artists—puppeteers, folk dancers, musicians, storytellers—who explore different areas of the day's theme. This is one of the great bargains in L.A.'s cultural life: admission to the performance still costs $3, just as it did a decade ago. Immediately after each show the audience goes down to the shaded parking lot for a hands-on workshop ($1 per child, free for parents to watch) keyed to each performance; the participants are divided into three age groups so each can work to their own level. For more information call *213-850-2000.

As daylight faded at the Bowl or when a sea of taillights filled the Hollywood Freeway, you may have gazed at a ridge on the east side of the Cahuenga Pass and wondered, "What is that cross doing there?" The radio evangelist who rebuilt this landmark in 1993 sees it as a rebuke to the reputation of Hollywood: "louder than the freeways' din, greater than the city's sin . . . radiating the world's one abiding hope where pain and loss have brought shame and ruin," wrote the pastor of the Church of the Way in Van Nuys when raising funds to acquire and protect this Christian symbol. There was a lot less bluster associated with the cross when it was erected in 1922 as a memorial to Christine Wetherell Stevenson, an heir to the Pittsburgh Paint fortune who had supported construction of the Hollywood Bowl. In 1920 she purchased twenty-nine acres on the hillside opposite the Bowl for an open-air theater in which *The Pilgrimage Play*, a story about Jesus Christ written by her, would be performed. Although she died two years later, the play ran for forty years before lawsuits challenged that it violated the constitutional separation of church and state because the theater had been given to the county in 1941 (and is now the John Anson Ford Amphitheater). The cross, however, remained, and was even replaced by the county when it was damaged by fire, although a successful lawsuit in 1980 contended that it was illegal to maintain this religious symbol at public expense. Hollywood Heritage became proprietor of the site in 1984, but its volunteers only sporadically maintained the cross. The Church of the Way, which raised $50,000 as an endowment for maintenance, has invited other Christian ministries and churches to become trustees of the monument to ensure its survival.

John Anson Ford Amphitheater

2580 Cahuenga Blvd.
Los Angeles 90068
213-974-1396
Box office: *213-466-1767

A decade ago this delightful outdoor amphi-theater across the freeway from the Holly-wood Bowl was operated as a rental facility by L.A. County, which owns it, and patrons never knew what kind of programming to expect or received enough notice to include it in their long-range summer plans. Recently the county got its act together and packaged a festival, Summer Nights at the Ford, which has in its first few seasons won loyal subscribers and sold out many of its events. More than twenty local arts groups are included in each season's calendar, many in thematic series like Dance, Dance, Dance!, Global Rhythms, All That Jazz, and Chamber Music Under the Stars, which are available by subscription.

The fun at the Ford actually begins before nightfall, with two series especially for families: Saturdays at 10 a.m. from mid-June to Labor Day, there are wide-ranging multiethnic performances in dance, music, and theater, which will appeal to kids from age seven; popular music for kids, with some of the best contemporary performers, is scheduled late on a few Sunday after-noons. Ford Family Fun discount cards offer savings on each ticket and give families the flexibility they need: they are passes, rather than reservations for specific events, and can be used for any number of admissions for any performance in the family series.

As the Ford continues to grow in popu-larity, the shuttle service from a parking lot farther up the Cahuenga Pass may become as essential as that to the Bowl, but its ar-chitecture will not permit the large-scale expansion that has transformed its neigh-bor across the freeway. The chaparral-cov-ered hillside behind the stage can be seen from each seat, a view little changed since performances began here back in the 1920s. This little gem has been polished up and renewed: it's time to rediscover it.

Hollywood Heritage (*213-874-4005) is an advocacy group that fights for the preserva-tion of culturally and architecturally signifi-cant properties in Hollywood, including film studios and production lots. At present, much of its efforts have been dedicated to the **Hollywood Studio Museum**, which was closed in 1996 when a fire set by transients damaged the landmark building that housed its collections. The Barn, in which Cecil B. DeMille filmed the first feature pro-duced in Hollywood, *The Squaw Man* (1913), had helped to create the aura of the fabled crossroads of Hollywood and Vine, where it stood until the sentimental director moved it in 1926 to the production lot he had founded with partners Jesse Lasky and Samuel Goldwyn. The first California State Landmark associated with the film industry when it was designated in 1956, the Barn had since 1983 stood on the edge of a park-ing lot across from the Hollywood Bowl where it housed a museum dedicated to the era of silent films. Despite quick action by the fire department, the Barn was badly damaged by the pre-dawn blaze in Septem-ber 1996, but the museum's collections were salvaged. When it reopens in 1998, the mu-seum (2100 N. Highland Ave., Los Angeles 90068) will be called the Hollywood Heri-tage Museum; although its focus will re-main the earliest era of Hollywood film his-tory, plans for actual exhibits had not been completed when this guide was published.

The original **Hollywood sign** was erected in 1923 to draw attention to a housing devel-opment called Hollywoodland, located in the bucolic canyon on the east side of Hol-lywood that is today called Beachwood. By 1978 the sign had become a landmark, per-haps the most visible pop icon in the world, but it had deteriorated structurally and was replaced in a campaign funded by some of the stars who earned their fame in its shadow. Gene Autry, Alice Cooper, Hugh Hefner, and the Warner Bros. Studios each contributed funds to reconstruct one letter in the famous sign. The canyons and hills above Hollywood are still leafy refuges from the city sprawl, but the east side of Holly-wood is a district that earns Los Angeles its designation as the most ethnically diverse city in America; new immigrants fill the apartment complexes on side streets, and ethnic markets and restaurants line the main thoroughfares.

The Freeman House (1962 Glencoe Way, L.A. 90068), a textile-block house designed by Frank Lloyd Wright, has been owned by the University of Southern California since1986. Inside, two-story walls of mitered glass enclose a dramatic space that incorporates a vast urban view. Many of the original furnishings, which were designed by R. M. Schindler (then in Wright's employ), have been preserved because the house was continuously occu-

pied by the couple that commissioned it.

Damage from the 1994 Northridge earthquake and the departure of its resident curator forced the university to suspend public tours in late 1997. Little progress has been made in restoring the fragile structure; securing the necessary funding remains a prerequisite because USC maintains that it should not initiate the repairs until it is convinced that the project can be completed. Solid and perforated concrete blocks, which were cast on site with materials found there, have proven unstable, and the house's foundations may never have been sufficient for the steep slope. Although FEMA has offered a grant of more than $800,000 for the restoration, that sum is one-quarter of USC's original request. It remains uncertain, as this book goes to press, whether the Freeman House will become the cultural center that the architect and his clients envisioned or face the wrecking ball.

Tours of the **Ennis-Brown House**, the last of the four textile-block houses Wright built in Los Angeles, are offered with advance prepaid reservations on the second Saturday of odd-numbered months. Tours are available to groups (three person minimum) or to out-of-town visitors by special arrangement; call *213-668-0234.

The circular **Capitol Records Building** (1750 Vine St.), designed in 1956 by Welton Becket, takes the form of a stack of records with a stylus on top. Will the generations raised on CDs understand the programmatic form of this Hollywood landmark? A mural on the south side of the building, painted in 1972 by Los Angeles artist Richard Wyatt, pays tribute to the artists and clubs that made Hollywood a center for innovative jazz.

Hollywood Farmers Market
Ivar Ave. (between Sunset and Hollywood Blvds.)
Sun. 8:30 a.m.–I p.m.

Ivar Intermission is a piece of public art that uses stars—those motifs people find underfoot elsewhere in Hollywood—and bits of colored glass to mark the entrance to the Frank Gehry–designed Frances Howard Goldwyn Hollywood Library on Ivar Avenue, a half block south of Hollywood Boulevard, which has an extensive collection of film memorabilia and scripts.

At the turn of the century Fort Lee, New Jersey, was the capital of fledgling film industry. But when Thomas Edison and others formed a trust to control use of their technology in film production, independent filmmakers moved west to escape the East Coast's realm of influence. In 1913 Cecil B. DeMille went to inspect a film laboratory in Hollywood, a town of 5,000 people that had been incorporated only six years earlier. DeMille rented a barn a few blocks south of Hollywood's main thoroughfare—a dirt road called Sunset Boulevard—on Jacob Stern's ranch at Vine and Selma, to use as a production studio. By 1914 DeMille and his partners, Jesse Lasky and Samuel Goldwyn, employed a stock company of eighty players, as well as five cameramen and five directors, and their headquarters near Hollywood and Vine became the center of the young industry.

The **Cinerama Dome**, the only geodesic dome in the world built entirely of concrete, has been one of Hollywood's most recognizable landmarks since it was constructed in 1963 on Sunset between Vine and Ivar. A proposed development would add fifteen more theaters to the 5.75-acre site, along with restaurants, retail shops, and a health club.

The offices of **Hollywood Heritage** are located in the **Wattles Mansion**, a historic residence built in 1907 by Myron Hunt and Elmer Grey, architects of the Huntington Art Gallery and the Pasadena Library, as the winter home of an Omaha banker and his family. The Wattles Mansion (1824 N. Curson Ave.) can be rented for parties, but otherwise can be seen only by appointment (Mon., Wed., Fri. noon–5 p.m.). Tours also visit the rose garden, which has been replanted with pre-1920 vintage roses.

Wattles Farm and Neighborhood Gardens, Inc., occupies five acres south of the mansion, between Curson and Sierra Bonita, north of Hollywood Boulevard. The avocado trees that line the south end of the lot were planted by Wattles when his family lived there. By the 1970s the land was used for love-ins and community feasts from the "hippie plots" tended, erratically, by neighborhood free spirits. In an attempt to get funding for irrigation systems from such government programs as Metro Farms, the group incorporated in 1972, got the funding, developed an infrastructure, and became a model in community gardening. Twenty-five years later several dozen plots are tended by people in the neighborhood, under the supervision of garden masters who ensure that they perform the required community service—like donating excess produce to Project Angel Food. Gates are usually open on Saturdays and Sundays from about 10 a.m.–2 p.m., when the public is welcome, or call board member and head garden master Charles Ruiz at *213-876-5066 for more information.

North of the Wattles Mansion is a five-acre city park with hiking trails to the crest of the hill, where there are panoramic city views and access to Runyon Canyon and its trail system. **Runyon Canyon** was made a city park in 1984 after a colorful history of failed developments—including plans by millionaire Huntington Hartford, who purchased the acreage in 1942, to develop a futuristic resort designed by Frank Lloyd Wright—and remains a natural area. Hikers can access trails (daily, dusk to dawn) from Fuller Street, north of Franklin Avenue.

Paramount Pictures Studios

Melrose Ave. between Gower St. and Van Ness Ave.; entrance at 5555 Melrose Ave.
*213-956-1777
Tours: Mon.–Fri. on the hour, 9 a.m.–2 p.m.
Entry: adults $15; no children under 10 allowed

Although the term Hollywood is commonly used to designate the film industry, there is only one film studio still located in Hollywood: Paramount. Both Hollywood history and current productions are covered in two-hour walking tours of the lot, which incorporates the former RKO Studios (where Fred and Ginger made musicals during the Depression and Desilu Productions revolutionized sitcoms by filming each episode of *I Love Lucy* so they could be broadcast again and again). Although the tour brochure cautions that there is no guarantee that guests will view actual film production, the backlot sets—which include realistic New York streets—are used constantly. A huge globe marks the southwestern corner of this historic lot, and behind its gates there are some fine buildings whose lore and current function the guide will explain.

The world's most famous sidewalk, the **Walk of Fame,** has grown since 1960 to five acres of pink terrazzo stars set in gray terrazzo squares; these plaques celebrate some 2,500 entertainers. The stars, which are awarded in five categories—motion picture, television, recorded music, radio, and live theater—now line both sides of Hollywood Boulevard (from Sycamore to Gower) and Vine (from Yucca to Sunset); about fifteen new stars are added each year.

Los Angeles Contemporary Exhibitions (LACE)

6522 Hollywood Blvd.
Los Angeles 90028
*213-957-1777
Wed.–Sun. noon–5 p.m., Thurs. until 8 p.m.
Entry: free

One of the first artist-run spaces, LACE has, since it was founded in 1978, been strongly identified with video and performance art. It has garnered such broad respect in the mainstream arts community that in 1994 it was rewarded with low-cost space, becoming part of the Community Redevelopment Association's effort to revitalize Hollywood Boulevard. Its unfailingly hip and trendy image—LACE may hold the endurance record for remaining on the cutting edge—is, in fact, well suited to a neighborhood that attracts teenagers but offers them few constructive outlets. Because its programming has always been determined by a panel of artists, LACE keeps its finger on the pulse of the arts community and its art-as-social-commentary current. Its 2,500-square-foot storefront gallery presents a continuous cycle of conceptual and site-specific art, often exploring new media, as well as performance art and other multidisciplinary work. Weekly programs of video art, coproduced with Filmforum (*213-466-4143), are screened on Sundays at 7 p.m. at LACE. An annual fall art auction benefits LACE's programming, and its "Annuale" exhibition, which celebrated its tenth anniversary in 1996, provides a critical survey of emerging trends and figures in the L.A. art scene. For the rest of the year, you can expect that most of what you'll see at LACE, you wouldn't find elsewhere.

As public funds for the arts decrease and with a membership of fewer than 500, LACE hopes to build support for its activities in its new location. The Hollywood Boulevard site is a crossroads for the local community and attracts lots of transient visitors; it is also a convenient destination for those who work in the film industry and others involved in the arts. LACE, which prides itself on staging events that provoke a conversation, hopes to get a broad cross-section of that potential community engaged in a conversation about contemporary art and the art-making process.

The Los Angeles Convention and Visitors Bureau operates a drop-in information center located at 6501 Hollywood Boulevard, in Janes House Square (Mon.–Sat. 9 a.m.–5 p.m.)

Los Angeles Center for Photographic Studies (LACPS)

6518 Hollywood Blvd.
Los Angeles 90028
*213-466-6232
Wed.–Sat. 11 a.m.–6 p.m.
Entry: free

HOLLYWOOD BOULEVARD TOURIST TRAPS

L. Ron Hubbard Life
Exhibition
6331 Hollywood Blvd.
*213-960-3511
Daily 10 a.m.–9 p.m.
Entry: adults $5, children 12
and under free

Frederick's of Hollywood
Lingerie Museum
6608 Hollywood Blvd.
*213-466-8506
Daily 10 a.m.–6 p.m.
Entry: free

Guinness World of
Records Museum
6764 Hollywood Blvd.
*213-463-6433
Daily 10 a.m.–midnight
Entry: adults $8.95, seniors
$7.50, children 6–12 $6.95

Hollywood Wax Museum
6767 Hollywood Blvd.
*213-462-8860
Sun.–Thurs. 10 a.m.–
midnight, Fri.–Sat.
10 a.m.–2 a.m.
Same entry fees as Guinness
World of Records, or
purchase a combination
pass (adults $12.95,
children 6-12 $8.95).

Ripley's Believe It or Not!
6780 Hollywood Blvd.
*213-466-6335
Daily 10 a.m.–11 p.m.
Entry: adults $8.95, children
5–12 $5.95

Founded by artists and educators in 1974 to "disseminate photography as a fine art," LACPS established a downtown gallery to exhibit work by emerging and established artists and became a forum that encourages and celebrates creative communication in light-generated media. In 1994 the Community Redevelopment Agency offered LACPS a small building on Hollywood Boulevard as part of its effort to upgrade the entertainment facilities in the central Hollywood district.

LACPS's most accessible public program is an exhibition space that occupies 2,300 square feet on the ground floor of the building. To entice more foot traffic to enter the gallery, LACPS held a design competition to renovate its facade and uses its storefront windows for installations. Its schedule of six full-scale exhibitions each year presents challenging work intended to "expand the vocabulary of photography and address contemporary social, political, and cultural issues." One highlight of the exhibition program is the annual fund-raising show each fall, at which upper-level members (who contribute at least $300 per year) are invited to select a print of one of the exhibited works to add to their personal collections.

In a Community Arts Partnership between faculty from California Institute of the Arts and LACPS, inner-city high-school students engage in a year-long program to learn photographic techniques and produce large-scale public art; the remarkable photographic billboards and bus-shelter posters they produced in 1996, the fourth year of the program, were displayed throughout the neighborhoods surrounding LACPS's new site. LACPS sponsors other programs and workshops for youth, as well as community-oriented events.

Frame-Work, the journal LACPS publishes biannually, is a collaboration between guest editors and designers, so each issue offers a fresh perspective on the issues confronting photographers. They also publish a calendar (three times a year) of photo-related events and exhibitions throughout Southern California. One of LACPS's goals is to make the journal available on a Web site to foster conversations within the online community; public readings from the journal are intended to foster an interactive dialogue with its audience.

The **American Cinematheque** (*213-466-FILM), established in 1985 to "honor and promote America's indigenous art form, the moving picture," is a membership organization that fulfills its mandate by presenting weekly screenings, which are also open to the general public, as well as seminars with filmmakers and other special programs. Its film series were originally presented at the Directors Guild, then moved to Raleigh Studios (5300 Melrose Ave.) to accommodate a more ambitious weekly program, and will move in 1998 to the landmark **Egyptian Theater** (6712 Hollywood Blvd.), restored to its 1920s glamour with $2 million in loans and grants from the Community Redevelopment Agency. The inventive team of Hodgetts + Fung has designed a modern theater with state-of-the art equipment to

be inserted within the old building, which had poor sight lines and had deteriorated structurally while it sat unused and suffered further damage in the 1994 earthquake. Its forecourt and kitschy decor have been restored; they create an interesting juxtaposition with the modern style of the interior.

American Cinematheque's film series feature retrospective tributes to a director or actor's work, showcase new films from various world cinemas, and present the newest technological innovations. The Saturday matinee series for children—which screened classics as well as youth-oriented new releases—has been suspended, but it will return at the Egyptian Theater. Memberships start at $35 for students and seniors, which includes a subscription to the publication *Cinegram*, invitations to private screenings of new releases, and discount tickets to the ongoing film series. For programming information, call the twenty-four-hour hotline at *213-466-FILM or check out the online schedule (www.americancinematheque.com).

The Spanish revival facade and opulent decor of the El Capitan (6838 Hollywood Blvd.), built in 1926 as a legitimate theater, were recently refurbished by Disney, which uses this venue in the original center of Hollywood to launch its blockbuster family feature films. The cavernous lobby houses an arcade of related games and activities, making the experience of seeing such films as *Hercules* there different from that available at other area movie houses. It may simply be a clever marketing strategy—our family felt that the additional charge was not justified by the quality of the activities—but it sells out every performance and so attracts a large family audience to Hollywood Boulevard.

The **Chinese Theater** (6925 Hollywood Blvd.), built by movie magnate Sid Grauman in 1927, is famous not for its fantasy Chinese decor but for the hand- and footprints of celebrities in its forecourt.

Today the **Pantages Theater** is one of the top-grossing music and entertainment venues with fewer than 3,000 seats, grossing $3.6 million from twenty-two shows in 1996, but in the 1950s it was the site of the Academy Awards. See Theater and Dance (pp. 76–83) for information on this and other live-theater venues.

Hollywood Entertainment Museum

7021 Hollywood Blvd.
Los Angeles 90028
*213-465-7900
Tues.–Sun. 10 a.m.–6 p.m.
Entry: adults $7.50, seniors/students $4.50, children 5–12 $4

The entertainment industry employs more than a half-million people, pumping $16 billion annually into the local economy and fueling the recovery from the deep recession that gripped the region as the aerospace and defense industries downsized. It not only deserves to be celebrated, but tourists demand access to this most public of professions and expect to find it in Hollywood. Although this simple truth is widely acknowledged, none of the many projects that have been floated over the years had been realized until the Hollywood Entertainment Museum opened at the end of 1996. Its 33,000-square-foot subterranean space, previously occupied by a failed food court at the Galaxy Multiplex Cinemas, is less than fifty stars down Hollywood Boulevard from the Chinese Theater, and so it occupies a central position in the 1,000 acres of Hollywood that is the focus of the Community Redevelopment Agency's thirty-year, $1-billion plan—

which is beginning to restore luster to the tarnished image of the place synonymous with the entertainment industry.

The number of politicians involved in the museum's genesis may be the reason why, when it opened, the place seemed half-empty and lacking soul, more of a concocted solution to a technical problem than a place driven by the passion and spirit of the entertainment business that it seeks to capture. But by its first anniversary, the Hollywood Entertainment Museum had garnered a $2-million state grant to develop education programs and was actively seeking support from the creative community. New artifacts had been donated and new exhibits were in development.

Visitors begin their tour in the rotunda gallery, where there is plenty to see and do while awaiting the scripted tour that begins every half hour and features the highlights of the collection, including sets and other memorabilia from *Star Trek* and *Cheers*. One of the most appealing exhibits in the rotunda is a twelve-by-twelve-foot model, built as a hobby in the 1930s by Joe Pellkofer, a local cabinetmaker, of some 450 detailed miniature buildings in central Hollywood. A time line chronicles the area's 100-year history with the industry; visitors can listen to audio clips—with words of wisdom from Katharine Hepburn on star quality, Orson Welles on money, Bill Cosby on comedy, and Tom Cruise on collaboration—or peruse exhibits on costume and makeup. For seven minutes each half hour the rotunda is transformed into a multiscreen, multimedia theater with famous faces and scenes from early films and TV compiled into a Hollywood retrospective.

More technical exhibits, of an interactive nature, have been installed in the east wing, where the guide explains how the art of editing has evolved, along with the equipment that supports it. The technology that Jack Foley invented for sound effects is described in a video presentation and experienced in a hands-on demonstration. The Samsung Electronic Library isn't on the tour, but it is being developed as an entertainment career-resource center. Two 50-seat screening rooms regularly show films that complement the exhibits, free with admission.

A huge development, above the Metro stop at Highland Ave. and Hollywood Blvd., will bring the Academy Award ceremonies back to Hollywood by the year 2000. A theater that can seat as many as 3,000 people will be the centerpiece of a $350-million complex on which developer TrizecHahn expects to break ground in 1998.

The district known as **Koreatown** began along Olympic Boulevard near Vermont and grew to cover a 500-block area in Mid-Wilshire and Hollywood. Many of the developments that line its streets were torched and targeted by looters during the 1992 civil disturbances, but most of the businesses have risen from the ashes in modern strip malls and new buildings. The scars of that wrenching experience have not healed as easily for some sectors of this community, despite some well-publicized efforts to form alliances and organizations to foster understanding and communication between the Koreans and their neighbors from other ethnic groups. The rate of Koreans leaving Southern California to resettle in Korea has increased sharply since 1992.

In the twenty-five years since U.S. immigration laws were changed, the population of Koreans in America has increased from 20,000 to 500,000, and two-thirds of the new immigrants have settled in Southern California. Unlike the Chinese and Japanese, who had established immigrant populations in the United States by the early years of this century, most Korean immigrants are first received into newly formed communities based on familiar Korean models that are modified little by American experience.

The Confucian societal structure is reinforced with modern affiliations, such as business organizations and school alumni groups. The success of Christian missionaries is evident in the nearly 600 Korean Christian churches in Southern California; ten Korean Roman Catholic congregations and twelve Korean Buddhist temples also serve the population. Three daily Korean-language newspapers are published, and about four hours of Korean news, films, and popular entertainment are broadcast daily on KSCI (channel 18).

The unusually large number of children born in Korea who immigrated to the United States with their parents—38 percent of recent Korean immigrants are under the age of twenty—has created a phenomenon known in the Korean-American community as *itchomose*, or "1.5 generation." The term designates those young immigrants who become bilingual and bicultural, and it differentiates them from their parents, who are also first-generation Americans but who adapt less rapidly to their new country. The "1.5 generation" now

entering the labor force adds to the culturally complex America that will participate in the Pacific Rim economy in the years ahead.

The only natural alkaline mineral hot springs in Los Angeles, discovered by an oil wildcatter at the turn of the century, today supply **Beverly Hot Springs** (308 N. Oxford Ave.; *213-734-7000). Residents of the Koreatown neighborhood, perhaps homesick for the communal bathhouses of their homeland, join studio execs looking to unwind; there are separate spas for men and women, which feature giant tiled pools of hot water, steam baths perfumed with eucalyptus branches, and saunas. The spa is open daily (9 a.m.–9 p.m.); use of spa facilities is $30 Monday through Thursday, $40 Friday through Sunday; massages and other treatments are available for an additional fee in the salon (*213-962-2771).

Korean American Museum of Art and Cultural Center

3333 Wilshire Blvd.
Los Angeles 90010
213-388-4229
Tues.–Sat. 11 a.m.–4 p.m.
Entry: free

Only 1,100 Korean immigrants were admitted to the United States between 1903 and 1924; our country had not yet fully assimilated the West, much less turned its sights (or opened its heart) to our neighbors across the Pacific. But the stories of eight of those pioneer families are the subject of the inaugural, long-term exhibition at the Korean American Museum, which opened in temporary quarters in 1995 after four years of planning. These histories are evoked by objects passed down within families and recounted by members of more recent generations in a video that complements the exhibits.

Although the immigrants who are profiled married within their own ethnic group, the patterns of their lives reveal that they felt it necessary to develop a hybrid culture, distinct from the traditions of their homeland. Even the narrators' relationships to the people in the historical account reveal how the American experience altered the immigrants' perspectives: although at the time the first family member left Korea women transferred their kinship solely to their husbands' families (and so were essentially erased from the records of their natal family), the female descendants interviewed for this project only would recount the history of their natal families, not those with which they had become affiliated by marriage. For Korean-Americans, natal family is the primary kin structure, whereas in Korea that relationship is different for men and women.

The routes that each family took to overcoming racial discrimination, as well as the linguistic and cultural barriers they faced in forging an American life, are fascinating; the photographs and memorabilia are touching; and the geography of the Korean-American experience sheds new light on our city's history.

A Korean-style garden and a sculpture will transform **Ardmore Park** (3250 San Marino St. at Ardmore Ave.), the first site chosen by the Social and Public Art Resource Center (SPARC) for a three-part series of monuments in communities affected by the 1992 riots.

Korean Cultural Center

5505 Wilshire Blvd.
Los Angeles 90036
*213-936-7141
www.kccla.org
Mon.–Fri. 9 a.m.–5 p.m., Sat. 10 a.m.–1 p.m.
Entry: free

The Korean Cultural Center, located since 1980 in an Egyptian revival–style bank building on the Miracle Mile, is an affiliate of the consulate of the Republic of Korea. All of its programs, which include monthly showings of subtitled Korean-language films as well as evening language courses, are presented to the public free of charge. Lectures and exhibitions have explored many aspects of traditional Korean culture, as well as the concerns of contemporary Korean-Americans. Photographs from the Korean War and of American Koreatowns have been presented in its second-floor gallery, along with juried art exhibitions.

The center is a resource for area universities and museums, supplying experts in many fields through its outreach program. It has a 13,000-volume library and publishes *Korean Culture*, an illustrated quarterly English-language magazine.

Wilshire Boulevard was named for a Harvard-educated publisher of socialist newspapers, who counted George Bernard Shaw and Upton Sinclair among his friends. Gaylord Wilshire was a social reformer and inventor who made a lucky real-estate investment when he purchased land between Sixth and Seventh Streets west of downtown in the 1880s and developed it as a fashionable residential district.

When the sumptuous building at 3050 Wilshire Boulevard was designed in 1929, the car was king and Wilshire was the city's premier thoroughfare. Bullocks-Wilshire, the most elegant shopping emporium in town, welcomed motorists at an elaborate porte cochere, complete with murals, situated on the back of the building; its copper-clad 240-foot tower was a beacon to pedestrians on the stylish boulevard. When this landmark was looted during the 1992 riots, its corporate parent, which lacked sentimental ties to the building, closed it. In a neighborhood no longer fashionable enough to sustain a profitable department store, the magnificent building stood boarded up and unoccupied for nearly five years.

Southwestern University has given this paradigm of art deco architecture new life as headquarters for its law school, and those who remember fondly such lavish details as the rose-colored marble walls of the two-story foyer may peek through the tall windows to see for themselves that the old gal is once again doing just fine. The ground floor spaces now accommodate the library, with bookshelves occupying the eight feet of walls above floor level that were once filled with racks and retailing displays, and the decorative murals and other details have been left intact above. The school eventually plans to restore the fifth-floor tea room—an environment that formerly made me hanker for my grandmother and white gloves—as its cafeteria. Southwestern University School of Law plans to offer building tours, but has not yet determined the schedule; call 213-738-6731 for information.

Miracle Mile, the stretch of Wilshire Boulevard between Fairfax and La Brea, was purchased by A. W. Ross for $54,000 in 1920—a sum met with derision by his contemporaries. Wilshire Boulevard had been paved only as far west as La Brea, but Ross planned his retail development around the automobile. Wilshire became the principal bus route, which made it more accessible to shoppers. Because the area was zoned as residential, plans for each commercial building had to be individually approved, prolonging development for more than a decade. The strip is dense with distinctive art deco structures in the streamline moderne and zigzag moderne modes. The area between La Brea and Burnside, listed on the National Register as a historic district, includes a black and gold terra-cotta facade decorated with zigzag patterns (5209 Wilshire); two large developments that combine streamline moderne–style street-level shopping areas and zigzag towers (5217–31 and 5514 Wilshire); and the programmatic facade of the Darkroom (5362–66 Wilshire), the body of a camera rendered in black and burgundy glass.

George C. Page Museum of La Brea Discoveries

La Brea Tar Pits
5801 Wilshire Blvd.
Los Angeles 90036
*213-934-PAGE
www.tarpits.org
Tues.–Sun. 10 a.m.–5 p.m.
Entry: adults $6, seniors/students $3.50, children 5–10 $2

What was discovered in the La Brea Tar Pits was a comprehensive fossil record of plant and animal life in Los Angeles in the Pleistocene Ice Age, 10,000 to 40,000 years ago. The natural asphalt deposits on the Hancock Park site which gave the ranch its modern name—*brea* means "tar" in Spanish—had created a perfect trap for animals who became stuck in the muck. But the fossil treasures that had been embedded in the asphalt pit were not systematically uncovered until the turn of the century.

Since 1913 excavations have proceeded under direction of the Natural History Museum staff, who continue to catalogue the collection in glass-walled laboratories of the Page Museum. "Chock-full of bones" was one paleontologist's description of the tar pits, from which fossils of 140 species of plants and 420 species of animals, many of them extinct, were recovered. Many of the bones are displayed in reconstructed skeletons in the Page Museum, an unusual building designed to make the scientific material visually appealing and accessible to children.

The galleries surround an interior garden, whose bright-green foliage complements the stark brown bones, stained from exposure to asphalt, in the principal exhibits. The skeleton of an imperial mammoth, one of the largest elephants in North America during the Ice Age, stands twelve feet tall. Nearby an animated two-thirds-scale model of a woolly mammoth shakes its head and periodically lets out a healthy roar, which provoked the little girl next to me to ask, "Is that thing alive?" The display of the only human skull found among the three million mammal fossils uses

A joint ticketing package for two satellites of the Natural History Museum, the Page and Petersen, will allow people to visit both sites on one day for a reduced price; adults $9, seniors/students $4.50, children 5–12 $3.

modern technology to project an image of the 9,000-year-old La Brea Woman in the flesh on the skeleton. A California saber-toothed cat, the second most common find in the pits, is displayed behind Plexiglas, with a silkscreen silhouette of this "hunting machine" and labels to explain how each body part earned the animal this description.

Ground sloths, the extinct western horse, three types of bear, two now-extinct species of camel, bison (including two extinct species larger than the modern buffalo), lots of wolves and coyotes, the extinct American lion, pumas, bobcats, and jaguars were all found in the La Brea Tar Pits, and many of these animals are reconstructed in skeleton form. The largest collection of

bird fossils ever found was recovered at this site because asphalt preserved the fragile bones; several skeletons are displayed in front of colorful illustrations showing the birds' appearance when alive. A startling montage of 404 dire wolf skulls on an illuminated yellow background represents the dog family (*Canidae*)—the most abundant find—perhaps because packs of dire wolves fed on other animals mired in the asphalt and so became entrapped themselves.

Two audiovisual presentations run continuously: the fourteen-minute "La Brea Story" orients first-time visitors, and the ongoing film in the dinosaur theater poses that perennial question—"Why did the dinosaur become extinct?"—and introduces paleontology and the process of fossil microsorting, preparation identification, and cataloguing, explaining the activities of the scientists visible in the adjacent fishbowl laboratories. An audiotape on evolution accompanies a time-ribbon mural depicting the 4.5-billion-year history of the earth.

Free guided tours of the Page Museum are offered Wednesday to Sunday at 2 p.m.; free tours of the tar pits in surrounding Hancock Park, held Wednesday to Sunday at 1 p.m., meet at the Observation Pit, an independent structure in the park. The museum regularly schedules lectures for adults and more hands-on children's programs; call 213-763-3534 for current schedule.

Petersen Automotive Museum

6060 Wilshire Blvd.
Los Angeles 90036
*213-930-CARS
www.petersen.org
Tues.–Sun. 10 a.m.–6 p.m.
Entry: adults $7, seniors/students $5, children 5–12 $3

It is only one spoke in the wheel of culture that has the Natural History Museum as its hub (and thus is a sister organization to the nearby Page Museum), but the Petersen Automotive Museum is a unique destination in a region inextricably linked with the evolution of car culture. Many of its artifacts were conserved, logically enough, in the history department of the Natural History Museum, but the Exposition Park building lacked sufficient space to exhibit many of its larger pieces—and early automobiles were certainly large! Size is only one of the striking qualities of the vintage cars now displayed in the cavernous space of the former department store that the museum renovated and named for its primary donor, Robert E. Petersen, whose publishing empire includes such automotive standards as *Road and Track*.

When the museum opened in June 1994, an interactive history of the automobile and its impact on the fabric of the city was installed in its ground-floor galleries. Visitors are invited to walk through—not by—exhibits that simulate Los Angeles in the 1920s and 1930s, with cars of that vintage parked along a streetscape. Changing designs of gas pumps, as well as the advertising and paraphernalia used to make customers loyal to certain brands of gasoline, fill one nook of a gallery that also displays the programmatic architecture designed to catch the eye of the passing motorist. The fad of customizing cars, which seems to have permanently taken hold in Southern California, is presented in a loving historical montage that attracts fiftyish guys reminiscing, "When I was in high school . . ." A car crumpled in a collision, statistics on traffic accidents, and a chronology of freeway construction and the volume of cars that use them evoke less fond responses.

When visitors reach the second floor, where "Little Deuce Coupe" is among the tunes on the boppy soundtrack, they've arrived in guy territory. Little guys race straight for the real Indy car beneath a photomural of a race pit stop, where they can put on a helmet, climb behind the wheel, then rev and grunt through this fantasy. Big guys can't get so up close and personal with the changing display of racing specimens like the 1995 Bernstein/Budweiser King, the first dragster to reach 300 MPH. A red and yellow neon motorcycle beckons visitors to the Otis Chandler Gallery, where fifteen choice models—from a 1903 Orient to a 1969 Harley—are displayed.

A survey of the earliest motorcars now shares a large gallery with the rather hokey exhibit Celebrity Cars (complete with awful cardboard cutouts of movie stars). The design of such "high-wheelers" as the

1906 Black Stanhope evolved from horse-drawn carriages; its familiar silhouette was expected to encourage rural motorists to view it as reliable transportation. The elevated chassis and high wheels of the Ford Model T touring car were designed to withstand rough rural roads. Fifteen million of these "Tin Lizzies" were built from 1909 to 1927. The 1907 Franklin Model G Roadster, the most popular air-cooled car built in the U.S., was touted as best for extreme climates because its engine would neither freeze nor boil over. The 1908 Pierce was a luxury vehicle, with a six-cylinder engine, "gum-dipped" three-foot-tall white Firestone tires, a detachable hood for open touring, brass headlamps and lanterns, and three rows of leather seats.

There's a spacious 1925 Lincoln limousine that shuttled Greta Garbo about, and a 1953 Cadillac Series 62 coupe, originally owned by Rita Hayworth, which has sinuous Jaguar-like lines. In comparison, Dick Van Dyke's 1963 Studebaker Avanti looks like a Ford Rambler that's grown a beak. A 1927 Kissel Model 75 "Gold Bug" Speedster—with cut-down doors, a "bumble bee" rear deck, and golf bags mounted on its running board—was driven by Amelia Earhart, Al Jolson, and Fatty Arbuckle.

Mrs. Ahmanson got one of the last of the hand-built, high-performance Facel Vega IIs—a French car with long, sleek lines, a six-gear stick, and wood-paneled interior—because the company went bankrupt in 1964. The walls are lined with vintage movie posters—*Red Hot Wheels* with Clark Gable and Barbara Stanwyck, *Bullitt* with Steve McQueen, and *American Graffiti*—and a chronology of drive-in movie theaters, which were first built in 1933 and accounted for one-quarter of film profits between 1954 and 1973.

Things got a bit sparse on the third floor during the first years that the museum occupied the huge Wilshire Boulevard site. Along with such interesting exhibits as the original artwork commissioned for *Westway* magazine's covers, there were galleries filled with paintings that displayed more enthusiasm for their subject than artistic talent. But thanks to a million-dollar gift from the May Family Foundation, the third floor is being transformed into a Discovery Center with interactive exhibits and hands-on activities targeted to kids ages six to sixteen. Teenagers can enter an automobile simulator that uses driver's education software to encounter such driving conditions as congested freeways and oncoming emergency vehicles. Other exhibits demonstrate not just how a car works but the principles of engineering and physics that explain why it does. A see-through car, miniature wind tunnel, and giant combustion engines are among the twenty interactive exhibits planned for the Discovery Center, which was developed to incorporate the educational guidelines of the California Public Schools Science Framework. Bottles on a Sparkletts water truck will hold educational toys that young children and their parents can check out together. People who are phobic about noise may want to skip the Vroom Room, where kids can activate fire and police sirens to learn about the Doppler effect. The Discovery Center, which debuted in November 1997, is a welcome addition to the Petersen Automotive Museum. It will certainly enhance the experience of the museum's younger visitors and is expected to attract 250,000 children each year.

One parental gripe is the AM-PM Minimart that serves as the museum's only food outlet. Couldn't such a popular destination support a theme restaurant like the Harley-Davidson Café my son wants to include in every visit to New York City?

Writing a guidebook is a humbling experience, especially perhaps for an editor who—whether suffering from what the French call "la deformation professionelle" or compelled by her own innate characteristics of precision and organization—struggles continually to perfect written communication. If I truly believed that writing a guidebook is like taking a picture of a cloud—a statement with which I attempted to console and encourage my editors on this project—I could not have undertaken this assignment. The challenge for me was to create a format that allowed the reader to see the cloud in the landscape. Although the ephemeral manifestations of culture are sometimes its most vibrant expression and therefore essential to any accurate picture of contemporary civilization, they can be more efficiently chronicled on the Internet or in periodicals and newspapers. A book can instead reveal the context for such temporal phenomena, by celebrating the history of our culture, which has fostered the dynamic present.

I am an editor, but I have written two guides to the cultural life of Los Angeles: the first, commissioned by the *Los Angeles Times* in 1989, focused specifically on offerings for children and school groups; the second, which you are reading, was commissioned by the J. Paul Getty Trust and published on the occasion of the opening of the Getty Center in Brentwood. Its purpose was to share the expected limelight with the hundreds of other less prominent, less well-funded institutions throughout L.A. County that contribute to the rich cultural life of our community. My publisher not only provided professional support throughout the process of compiling this volume, it allowed me a luxurious amount of space for each entry. Thus readers can not only evaluate the merits of visiting any particular place or anticipate what they would experience at each site but also understand how the institutions that are the pillars of L.A. culture have evolved, what challenges they face in the present, and the goals they have set for the future.

Change is the only constant in a dynamic place like Los Angeles, and as soon as the ink had dried on the first printing of this guidebook, the inevitable outdating of its text began. In December 1997, the **Craft and Folk Art Museum**, a cultural institution well loved in our community, closed its doors. Its demise presented me with a dilemma: how to reallocate the space occupied in the first printing by a description of CAFAM. It had been such a vibrant place, a labor of love to which Edith Wyle and her husband Frank had dedicated their energy, creativity, and funding for more than two decades. No cultural history of Los Angeles could be complete without celebrating the contributions of individuals like these. How CAFAM foundered, in the stormy seas of L.A. real estate, is a cautionary tale that reflects a critical reality for other cultural organizations in the city. Perhaps, like the teenager who is never ready to leave home, the museum hadn't successfully completed its transition to a professionally run public institution and continued instead to rely on the Wyles's generosity. Each of those aspects is worthy of consideration and, we hope, may in good time be examined because CAFAM's history has not ended: the City of Los Angeles Cultural Affairs Department and CAFAM's board of trustees are presently exploring how its programs might be ressurected under their auspices.

Although plans are, at this writing, still in the formative stage and will require approval of the City Council, the Cultural Affairs Department hopes to build upon the success of an annual, national folk and traditional arts conference, called Living Roots, which it has sponsored, and to renew CAFAM's original mission with annual curated exhibitions in both contemporary craft and folk art. Because most of CAFAM's collection has been sold at auction (with a few pieces given to LACMA and the Fowler) and its library and archives were donated, to LACMA and UCLA, respectively, in its new incarnation, it will operate more like the Municipal Gallery at Barnsdall Art Park (another outpost of the Cultural Affairs Department). The Festival of Masks, which had drawn as many as 75,000 costumed marchers representing L.A.'s many cultures, is also slated to return. When these activities will resume at the 1930s Georgian-style brick building on Wilshire Boulevard across the street from LACMA is unknown, but we hope that the Cultural Affairs Department's sponsorship of CAFAM will be the beginning of a new era for an institution that fills an important niche in Los Angeles.

Carole and Barry Kaye Museum of Miniatures

5900 Wilshire Blvd.
Los Angeles 90036
*213-937-MINI
Tues.–Sat. 10 a.m.–5 p.m., Sun. 11 a.m.–5 p.m.
Entry: adults $7.50, seniors $6.50, students $5, children 3–11 $3

If the passion of the collector is a measure of the collection, then the Museum of Miniatures, which was single-handedly established and funded by Carole and Barry Kaye, must be among the finest presentations of the art of miniaturization anywhere. Mrs. Kaye's enthusiasm for miniatures began with her attempt to entertain a grandchild with a building project back in 1989. Research on miniature building resources revealed many dedicated practitioners of the craft and finally led her to establish a showcase for the wealth of models she found. To bring this art the attention she feels it deserves, a prime site on Museum Row, across from the Los Angeles County Museum of Art and between the Craft and Folk Art Museum and the Petersen, was selected for the museum, which opened in June 1994.

Her passion had been shared by Walt Disney, whose personal collection of some 2,000 pieces, including some made by him, was made available by a granddaughter for rotating display in the fledgling museum. He described this "hobby" as a lifesaver: "When I work with these small objects, I become so absorbed that the cares of the studio fade away." He was so convinced of the efficacy of the wonderful world to which he could escape that exhibits for Disneyland were first developed in miniature. Some of those, displayed here in wall vitrines as they had been in Disney's own office, include the *Mark Twain,* the riverboat from Frontierland.

Historic sites and period interiors are projects that motivate the most dedicated and skilled craftsmen: it took one couple in England eighteen months to fabricate the shell for the Chateau de Fontainebleau, and other teams spent years researching the interior furnishings for accuracy and detail. The King's Apartments at Hampton Court have been lovingly reconstructed following Sir Christopher Wren's 1689 design, along with his plan for Christ Church, built in the form of a Greek cross in Virginia in 1732. Carter's Grove, an eighteenth-century Virginia plantation home, is one of the largest models: with some thirty-five rooms, it took a master miniature builder, Charles Holcomb, 2,700 hours to assemble. Another vitrine assembles about eighty specimens of fine furniture, from all periods and styles, including one five-by-two-by-three-inch chest that incorporates 6,000 pieces of inlaid wood. Another highlight with mind-boggling statistics is the ten-foot replica of the *Titanic,* which was made from 75,000 toothpicks and two gallons of Elmer's glue.

Inspired by the Thorne collection of miniature rooms at the Art Institute of Chicago, Tom Roberts assembled "room boxes" that transform one gallery: included are a Dutch interior, called *Homage to Vermeer,* and a French streetscape with wallpaper store, boulangerie, and tea salon. Local and contemporary sites include the Hollywood Bowl, shown with jazz performers on stage and enlivened by a musical track, and four boxed dioramas of Venice Beach, at 1:25 scale, built by Roy Anderson, who applied to this labor of love skills refined by thirty years working as a mechanical engineer.

A natural complement to these small-scaled worlds is a miniature population that one would be tempted to call dolls were they not such elaborate and detailed renditions. Those on display include personable, lifelike babies by Anne Mitrani, big-eyed stylized fantasy figures (like a frog in Colonial dress) by John Friedericy, and forty-four First Ladies at one-inch-to-one-foot scale wearing period gowns by Galia Bazylko.

Visitors smitten with the urge to create their own Lilliputian worlds will find lots of intriguing items in the Petite Elite gift shop, from simple paper-doll and building kits to exquisite (and expensive) pieces of miniature furniture, porcelain, silver, and dolls.

Los Angeles County Museum of Art (LACMA)

5905 Wilshire Blvd.
Los Angeles 90036
*213-857-6000
Mon., Tues., Thurs. noon–8 p.m., Fri. noon–9 p.m.,
Sat.–Sun. 11 a.m.–8 p.m.; closed Wed.
Entry: adults $6, seniors/students $4,
children 6–17 $1

The Los Angeles County Museum of Art is one of our young city's oldest cultural institutions. Originally it was part of the hybrid museum in Exposition Park (now the Natural History Museum) that in 1913 began to present exhibitions on natural science, history, and art; by the 1960s, the arts demanded a more focused venue, and the county and civic leaders funded construction of a separate art museum in Hancock Park. But its original role within a broader cultural complex seems to have manifested itself in its latest incarnation: LACMA has recently (and successfully) developed its programs in music, film, and education to offer more incentives for a broader segment of the local population to venture more often onto its expanded campus—whether they choose to enter the galleries

to look at art or not. In a radical move that is intended to make the museum more accessible to the public, LACMA altered its hours, remaining open until 8 p.m. five nights a week and until 9 p.m. on Fridays (when it also hosts free jazz concerts that regularly draw an audience of up to 1,000 people); the museum is now open on Mondays, which allows locals and out-of-town visitors enjoying a long holiday weekend to include LACMA on their itineraries and gives the museum little competition for attracting visitors on that day.

A demoralizing few years followed the 1992 departure of director Rusty Powell (for the National Gallery in Washington, D.C.). It became clear that the acknowledged leaders in the field were not clamoring for the top position at LACMA, especially after Powell's successor departed after less than a year on the job. LACMA's board of trustees (who had been more obstreperous than productive during some periods in the past) restructured the administration, hiring Andrea Rich, then executive vice chancellor at UCLA,

for the top position, and Graham Beal, who had served as chief curator and director at several major institutions in the west, to oversee the museum's collections, programs, and staff. Although naysayers still mutter that such a division of labor has had little success at other U.S. museums that have tried it, LACMA's team looks plucky. Within its first year on the job, revenues from the museum's shop and restaurant have doubled and visitation has increased 15 percent. The backlog of issues that needed prompt attention when the new team came on board has been prioritized, and with the announcement that a MoMA-organized Picasso exhibition would be shown at LACMA, which in 1999 will also host a landmark Van Gogh exhibition organized by the National Gallery, the new administration has scored a lineup of blockbuster shows, certain to foster popular support.

The acquisition of 8.6 acres in Hancock Park and the historic building that had been designed by Albert C. Martin in 1940 as the flagship of the May Company department stores gave LACMA the opportunity to schedule more exhibitions like these, as well as showcase new initiatives by its own curators. When Otis Art Institute pulled out of a deal to renovate the landmark May Company building for its campus headquarters, LACMA had to reformulate how to best use this vast space, but its deliberations have involved other less spacious and well-situated institutions, that may be allowed to present exhibitions in this prime location. Its plan now includes using the ground floor primarily as exhibition space, with an experimental gallery dedicated to small installations from the permanent collection organized by theme, medium, or cultural context. A second cafe and a new museum shop in this building will increase these revenue-producing areas of the museum complex. On the upper floors will be classrooms for LACMA's expanded educational offerings; a reception area, available for rental, will retain the art deco ambience of the old tearoom and its rooftop terrace.

Within thirty years of relocating to the Hancock Park site in 1965 LACMA had expanded its campus east to Fairfax and to a total of eighteen acres. Two of the three original buildings had been renovated and expanded, and two new buildings, constructed during the booming 1980s, brought LACMA's exhibition and work space to 415,000 square feet. An ambitious $12-million plan to improve the expanded territory of Hancock Park has been funded from Proposition A and a $7-million gift from LACMA trustee Dorothy Collins Brown. Times Mirror Court is also slated for renovation, which entails moving the information kiosk down to a new Welcome Center at the Wilshire Boulevard entrance and constructing a new shop at the head of the long stairway, to permit again opening up the breezeway beneath the Hammer Bridge, which will link the plaza with the refurbished park beyond.

LACMA has carved a difficult role for itself by attempting to represent all cultures throughout time, although as a relatively young and precariously funded institution it was forced to piece together a general art collection by relying on donors and limited acquisition budgets in a period of escalating prices. It has not yet (and may never) become "the only encyclopedic museum on the West Coast," as its press office has asserted, because forming a collection of that magnitude demands either resources of a similar magnitude or a large and extremely well-heeled group of patrons with singular loyalty to the institution. Whether the many competing and worthy causes in our global society will permit such single-minded devotion again in our time is a conundrum. With that thought in mind, I paid attention to the donor information on wall labels when I revisited its permanent collection galleries. That focus revealed the enduring value of gifts made by the fledgling institution's earliest benefactors (like the George Gard de Sylva Collection, given to the museum in 1948); the consistent generosity of others, including Anna Bing Arnold and the Ahmanson Foundation; the unfortunate association of arts patronage with self-aggrandizement; and a heartening number of recent and important gifts. In the latter category, the $25-million collection of Mexican modernist art, which was donated in 1997 by art dealers Bernard and Edith Lewin, builds upon such early acquisitions as *Flower Day* by Diego Rivera (photo, p. 63) and gives LACMA the premier U.S. holdings in recent art created by our nearest neighbors.

LACMA's collections comprise more than 150,000 works organized into ten curatorial departments—American Art; Ancient and Islamic Art; Costumes and Textiles; Decorative Arts; European Paintings and Sculpture; Far Eastern Art; Indian and Southeast Asian Art; Photography; Prints and Drawings; and Twentieth-Century Art. The reinstallation of many permanent collection galleries reflects the role of a new generation of curators in the continuing evaluation of its collections. The mosaics and gold and silver objects that former trustee Arthur Gilbert withdrew in 1996 have not left perceptible gaps in the decorative arts galleries where they were something of a collection anomaly. That space has been supplanted by a new focus on the Arts and Crafts movement in America and its antecedents in England, Scotland, and Vienna, which curator Leslie Greene Bowman has also explored in special exhibitions. A substantial collection of these works, largely acquired by LACMA within the past decade through the patronage of Ellen and Max Palevsky, has been handsomely installed in ground-floor galleries of the Ahmanson Building. Many of the interior fixtures and furnishings designed by brothers Charles and Henry Greene for their 1906 Blacker House in Pasadena surround one entrance to these galleries, which also showcase representative pieces by Gustav Stickley, the Roycrofters, Fulper Pottery, and the Shop of the Crafters in Cincinnati. In 1997 LACMA began offering a flexible audio tour ($3 per adult) that supplements (rather than repeats) wall texts, so I gave it a try—not once, but three times: it's that good. The CD-ROM tour examines how a 1912 sideboard exemplifies Stickley's design philosophy of honesty and simplicity by emphasizing the lively grain of the white oak and the functional quality of the drawer pulls and nailheads, and notes that it was offered for $84 in the sales catalogue. Representing the English tradition, there are silver and pewter pieces encrusted with stones and enamel from Liberty & Co., speckle-glazed pottery by Ruskin, and elaborate bookbindings by Riviere and Sons.

Renowned curator Pratapaditya Pal built a comprehensive 5,000-piece collection of Indian and Southeast Asian art during his LACMA career and trained many scholars in this field. This treasure trove is beautifully displayed on the top floor of the Ahmanson Building, along with Islamic art and changing displays from the museum's broad holdings in costumes and textiles. I virtually had the place to myself one summer evening, strolling past vitrines filled with the portable, largely utilitarian art that was created primarily for use in mosques after the religion of Islam was founded in the ninth century A.D. Although interpretive labels were sorely

lacking in some galleries, the repetition of certain names on the donor labels was hard to miss: Hans Cohn's encyclopedic collection of glassware and the Nasli M. Heeramaneck Collection, some 3,000 pieces of ancient Near Eastern, Islamic, and Indian works, acquired over many years through the generous patronage of Joan Palevsky and others. A scale model of a mosque, created as a souvenir of some Englishman's tour of duty in the colonies, was accompanied by an informative label that identified the religious function and meaning of architectural elements. My son was not with me when I encountered the case filled with bejeweled daggers and Byzantine metalwork from Mughal India, but on another visit I'll be able to lead him right to artwork he'll find fascinating. An ornately carved wooden doorway, with an Arabic inscription that identifies it as the house of a Muslim, frames cases filled with Indian works on paper, from elaborately illustrated pre-

Mughal paintings to contemporary prints.

Parables of noteworthy deeds form an important part of Sanskrit Buddhist literature, according to the label on the *Story of the Golden Horn,* a late eighteenth-century scroll that shares a gallery filled with Tibetan and Nepalese sculpture. A monumental tenth-century Cambodian sculpture of the Hindu god Vishnu, a gift from Anna Bing Arnold, has been protected by a seismic base that can accommodate eight inches of ground displacement. A tympanum of frolicking monkeys, carved in Laos or northern Thailand in the nineteenth century, is a charming work found in the same gallery.

Down on the second level, ample exhibition space is given to show the evolution of glass art, featuring pieces from the collection of Hans Cohn. One case is devoted to the changing form of drinking glasses created 1550–1650 in Venice and identified as the "highest achievement" of artisans in a city still known for that craft. William Randolph Hearst had a strange passion for "pass glasses," large tubes of Bohemian glass divided by enamel rings *("pässe")* that were used for drinking games. Another alcove is occupied by the colorful, frivolous art nouveau glass produced in turn-of-the-century Parisian ateliers like Galle and Daum.

On the lower level of the Ahmanson Building, the galleries of Far Eastern art have also been redesigned by curator Keith Wilson, who replaced George Kuwayama (whose tenure was the longest in LACMA's history when he retired in 1996). Five galleries of early Chinese art and Southeast Asian ceramics were unveiled in June 1997, and the process will continue with the department's other holdings. More Asian art is found in the $13.6-million Pavilion for Japanese Art, an unusual green stone-and-glass structure with a flying roofline designed by Bruce Goff and constructed after his death under the supervision of architect Bart Prince. It houses the extraordinary Shin'enkan Collection of some 300 Edo-period (1615–1868) screens and scroll paintings amassed by Etsuko and Joe Price, important collectors and donors who have since bitterly severed their relationship with LACMA. The Frances and Raymond Bushell Collection of 550 *netsuke,* miniature sculptures that originally served as toggles in traditional Japanese dress, are displayed in innovative cases on the ground floor; woodblock prints and Japanese ceramics are displayed in rotating exhibitions on the top floor of the pavilion.

The Anderson Building, a hulking $40-million structure that in 1986 extended

LACMA's original campus to Wilshire Boulevard, is dedicated to modern art. LACMA's growing collection of twentieth-century art is installed on the third floor: artists who worked in Paris just after the turn of the century are shown in one gallery, which includes Picasso's portrait of fellow artist Sebastian Juner-Vidal from his early Blue Period, while adjacent still lifes by Diego Rivera (1914) and Georges Braque (1917) reveal different interpreta-

tions of the evolving cubist style. Five Matisse bronzes, *Jeannette I–V*, are all portraits of the same person, which the artist wanted displayed together. The Russian avant-garde, which flourished in the first decades after the Revolution (when artists had the role of defining the new society), includes works by Alexandr Rodchenko and Wassily Kandinsky, as well as Natalia Goncharova's *Archangel Michael*, whose simplified forms were inspired by folk art. A Giacometti bronze stands sentinel by the bridge to the Hammer Building, along with other modern sculptures—a form in which LACMA is particularly well endowed. Rodins from the Iris and B. Gerald Cantor bequest are installed in the outdoor sculpture garden, which will be revamped during improvements to Hancock Park.

Spacious plaza-level galleries are reserved for special exhibitions, allowing LACMA to focus on contemporary art, both local and international. Curator Stephanie Barron has mounted several landmark exhibitions of German Expressionist art, starting with sculpture and continuing with "Degener-

ate Art," which re-created the infamous show of 1937, a virulent attack on modern art organized by the Nazi regime. "Exiles and Emigrés," which examined the diaspora of European artists and intellectuals created by World War II, precipitated a citywide pageant of related cultural events that was an inspiring example of cooperation among local institutions.

Escalators from the plaza bring visitors to galleries for photography, prints, and drawings within the Hammer Building. The collection of drawings was given an early boost by William Preston Harrison, who in 1918 became the first donor to the fledgling Exposition Park museum with a gift of 28 paintings; his generosity and interest in modern drawings from the 20th-century School of Paris helped establish a collection that today includes a comprehensive selection of the modern prints produced at the local Gemini G.E.L. studio and exceptional holdings in German expressionist prints and drawings, donated, in part, by collector Robert Gore Rifkind in a complex acquisition also funded by Anna Bing Arnold. The crucial role of the Ralph M. Parsons Foundation in establishing LACMA's photography collection was recognized in a recent exhibition.

Late nineteenth-century and impressionist paintings occupy the galleries constructed in 1984 to link the Hammer and Ahmanson Buildings, allowing the visitor to stroll progressively through European painting. A huge canvas by Edouard Vuillard, which shows the influence of Japanese woodblocks in its composition, shares the first gallery with a rare work by Swiss artist Ferdinand Hodler and canvases by Emile Bernard, Mary Cassatt, and Henri Toulouse-Lautrec. In the next room are some magnificent paintings that are new to the LACMA collection: a shimmering landscape painted near Cézanne's studio at Aix, a 1992 gift of the Hal Wallis Foundation, is hung between a still life and portrait by the same artist; the latter is from the George Gard de Sylva Collection, given to the museum in 1948. The same two donors contributed paintings by Gauguin, and in honor of LACMA's twenty-fifth anniversary in 1992 Lucille Simon made a gift of Gauguin's *Swineherd, Brittany,* which had been on long-term loan. Degas is represented by a portrait of two sisters (from the Gard de Sylva Collection), a pastel drawing, *Woman Drying Herself,* and four small bronzes. A version of the audio tour especially designed for children's use ("unique among U.S. museums," they say) uses Camille Pissarro's *La Place du Théâtre*

Française to define impressionism ("little dabs of paint with blurry edges"). In the next gallery are several paintings by Claude Monet, including *Beach at Honfleur,* a depiction of a rocky beach on a sunny, windy day painted by the young artist; a waterlily study; and landscapes showing a seaside town and a route through a village. The most compelling work by this artist, *Le Havre: Fishing Boats Leaving Port* (1874), is an anonymous loan.

The Ahmanson Foundation has been the most generous and consistent benefactor of LACMA's collections of European art. In the gallery of eighteenth-century French art are two paintings acquired with Ahmanson funds: Jean-Siméon Chardin's deceptively simple genre painting *Soap Bubbles,* and Hubert Robert's huge 1775 landscape with stairs and fountains, which the audio guide informs us must be a fantasy garden because the small pool could never contain the enormous volume of water splashing into it. *Magdalen with Smoking Flame* by Georges de La Tour is another legacy of the Ahmanson Foundation, which provided funds for more than ten large seventeenth-century Spanish and Italian works that hang together in one grand gallery.

Docents lead special tours of temporary exhibitions; the schedule is available at the information desk and is published in the magazine sent to members. One-hour Gallery Tours on some aspect of the collection are offered on weekdays and most weekends at 1, 2, and 3 p.m. Spotlight Tours are short (fifteen to twenty minute) lectures on masterworks in the collection and are offered at 12:30 p.m. daily. The Education Department sponsors monthly Family Days on Sundays, along with many enrollment classes on weekends for children of different age groups. There are special classes for teenagers and adults, as well as some for "students ages 5–105," that include both studio instruction and lectures on art history, with ample time for in-gallery exploration. For information on all of LACMA's educational programs and classes, call *213-857-6512.

LACMA has recently instituted some of its most popular programs—for instance, the free jazz concerts that fill its plaza (if not its galleries) every Friday night—and continues to mount excellent temporary exhibitions, both those that its curators originate and traveling shows. Its film programs, known for both quality and frequency, have continued to run the gamut from classics at the $2 matinees (which moved from Wednesdays to Tuesdays when LACMA changed its hours) to ambitious retrospectives and thematic programs, often mounted with other film organizations in town. Its music programs have been expanded from the Monday evening concerts that have drawn a small but loyal audience for thirty years to include more varied offerings and, in partnership with the city's Cultural Affairs Department and KUSC (91.5 FM), Sunday afternoon concerts have attracted a wider audience through broadcasting. LACMA was among the first local institutions to establish a well-designed and informative presence on the World Wide Web and has embraced other evolving technology, such as the excellent audio tours referenced above. These efforts reflect the new administration's dedication to revitalizing its educational programs to better reflect and attract the diverse ethnic groups in our community. About 65,000 Angelenos renew their memberships at LACMA annually, testament to its popularity and its role as a multipurpose cultural center. Things are happening at LACMA: go by for a relaxing and stimulating Friday night date and check it out.

At its northern end **Fairfax Avenue** is the site of a lively ethnic neighborhood with a high concentration of elderly Jewish residents. A landmark twenty-four-hour delicatessen, a well-stocked newsstand, kosher meat markets, and produce stands line the commercial strip. The attractive surrounding residential area, between La Brea and La Cienega, is home to a fast-growing young Jewish population, including many Orthodox Jews. Two museums farther west commemorate the Holocaust and the destruction of the European Jewish communities during World War II.

Farther south, near Olympic Boulevard, Fairfax has become the commercial center of the Ethiopian community, which numbers about 30,000, mainly recent immigrants who've fled political upheaval in their homeland since the late 1970s. The coffee plant (*Coffea arabica*) is native to Ethiopia, which may explain why elaborate rituals involving the beverage have evolved in this culture. The fragrance of roasting coffee beans and the rich scent of frankincense, which is placed on a charcoal brazier, lure strollers into coffee houses, where live music or a billiards-like game called *carambola* might also be enjoyed. Hansen's Bakery (1070 S. Fairfax) commemorates the era when this area was largely Danish. Since 1947 Hansen's has been baking and decorating cakes to celebrate weddings, birthdays, and *quinceañeras*. Watch the frosting wizards at work or ogle masterpieces in display cases and photo-filled books.

Every Picture Tells a Story

7525 Beverly Blvd.
Los Angeles 90038
*213-932-6070
Tues.–Sat. 10 a.m.–6 p.m.

This gallery-cum-bookstore exhibits original art from children's books and is well-stocked with the best illustrated works for young readers. Artwork that has been published is displayed with the final book, which is available for purchase in the bookstore. When this gallery opened a decade ago, it signaled a new collecting interest of the baby-boom generation, which had already made children's books one of the strongest segments of the publishing industry. Unlike some other stores, which use the art mainly as fancy decoration, Every Picture Tells a Story has kept the gallery as its focus. Its programs elucidate the synthesis of illustration and text that produces successful children's books, and they celebrate a genre that continues to attract great artists.

The Los Angeles Art Galleries (LAAG) comprise about a dozen galleries clustered around La Brea and Beverly, which are marked with street banners. Located not far from Museum Row, they create another destination for art lovers, and visitors will find it's a pleasant stroll between galleries with good window shopping and cafes for a refreshing pause along the way. See page 40 for descriptions of some of these galleries.

Martyrs Memorial and Museum of the Holocaust

6505 Wilshire Blvd.
Los Angeles 90048
*213-852-3242
Mon.–Thurs. 9 a.m.–5 p.m., Fri. 9 a.m.–3 p.m., Sun. 1–3 p.m.
Entry: free

Stepping into the Martyrs Memorial and Museum of the Holocaust is like opening up a family picture album and discovering a tragic history. Galleries on the street level of the Jewish Federation Council building extend the museum district a few blocks down the boulevard from Hancock Park. Cases are filled with personal papers and memorabilia, including illustrations of the concentration camps re-created by an artist who survived his internment. Didactic labels stressing the historical context of the displays accompany many of the photographic murals. One room dedicated to children of the Holocaust contains a model of Terezin, a concentration camp through which 15,000 kids under the age of twelve passed from 1942 to 1944. Other photos show human captives, including children forced to endure starvation under Josef Mengele at Auschwitz. The museum continues its active affiliation with local schools and offers other educational programs for all age groups.

The Southern California Jewish Historical Society offers two different guided bus tours to sites that reflect the evolution of the Jewish community in Los Angeles. One tour starts in Boyle Heights, whose population was once 90 percent immigrant Jews, visits Hollywood sites that reflect Jewish contributions to the film industry, and tours the majestic Wilshire Boulevard Temple. Another visits South L.A., where seven synagogues south of 21st Street and east of Figueroa once marked a vibrant center of Jewish culture. The tours are offered on the second Sunday of each month from September through June and leave at 10 a.m. from the Jewish Federation Building (6505 Wilshire Blvd.). Reservations are required (213-653-7740), and the fee is $20 for members or for groups of ten or more, $25 for nonmembers.

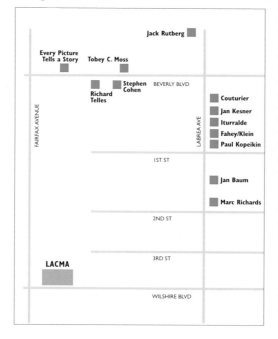

Museum of Tolerance at the Simon Wiesenthal Center for Holocaust Studies

9786 W. Pico Blvd.
Los Angeles 90035
310-553-8403
Mon.–Thurs. 10 a.m.–4 p.m. (last tour departs);
Fri. 10 a.m.–1 p.m.(last tour) from Nov.–Mar., and 10
a.m.–3 p.m. from Apr.–Oct.; Sun. 10:30 a.m.–5 p.m.
Entry: adults $8, seniors $6, students $5, children
under 10 $3

Simon Wiesenthal is a crusader whose mission is to keep alive the memory of atrocities committed in World War II not only by honoring the millions of Jewish people slaughtered during the Holocaust but also by teaching humans to practice tolerance. To that end, the Wiesenthal Center mounted a fund-raising campaign in the 1980s to build a museum that would both document the events of the Holocaust and also force people of all races, creeds, and ages to confront their own prejudices. By the time the $50-million Museum of Tolerance opened in 1993, the 1992 uprising that expressed profound distrust and deep divisions among this city's various ethnic communities seemed to validate its goals, and exhibits that explore the underlying causes of the uprising were incorporated into the displays. In its first year 250,000 people visited the museum, many of them schoolchildren.

The museum encompasses two themes—the dynamics of racism and prejudice in America and the history of the Holocaust—each presented in tightly scripted, docent-led tours of about two hours' duration. Self-guided and paced tours are not permitted: all visitors are escorted in groups, like the ninth-graders from Sun Valley Middle School that I joined. Shepherded down the spiral staircase, the group then stands in a small room while a slide show is projected on the walls. A "greeter" on a video monitor assures the group that our belief in equality is obvious, then challenges us to enter the "Tolerancenter" through one of two doors: one marked "prejudiced" in red neon, the other "unprejudiced" in green. The green door won't open, because we must confront the fact that we're all guilty of some bias. Properly chastened, we are greeted in the first gallery with a catalogue of "images that stay with us," including "women are helpless, fat men are jolly, and Indians are savages," and a video entitled "Me . . . a bigot?" in which "normal people" express concerns about such topics as the effect of ethnic diversity on real-estate values or intermarriage on social standing. We are invited to "try changing places" with a group of cardboard cutouts—policemen, bikers, construction workers, whose faces have been replaced with mirrors—"because you might think differently."

To access the exhibit Understanding the Los Angeles Riots, visitors enter information about their age, gender, and ethnicity, so the computer can "challenge them accordingly on questions of social justice and responsible citizenship." Various viewpoints about the causes and events of this troubling moment in Los Angeles history are expressed by its citizens.

"In Our Time" is a ten-minute video that chronicles the death of twenty-five million soldiers and twenty-five million civilians in World War II, asking "where is there not fear and hatred?" The "ethnic cleansing" of Bosnia and the intertribal slaughter in Rwanda are more recent examples of the "easy readiness to believe the worst of each other."

The struggle to achieve universal civil rights in America is outlined on a trilevel time line captioned Historic Milestones, Intolerance Persists, and In Pursuit of Tolerance. A seven-minute film on the civil rights movement of the 1960s, projected on sixteen screens, expresses one white man's belief that "if you are born into a system, you come to believe it," and another's view that "I am fighting for my own freedom, because if another man is not free then I am not free."

A "light- and sound-paced tour" of Berlin in the 1920s inaugurates the visit to the Holocaust section of the museum, where displays and text reveal how the selection of facts and the context in which they are presented affects perception. Before Germany had recovered from an economic depression in 1923 that rendered savings worthless, the U.S. stock market crash of 1929 exacerbated the situation. The growing panic found an easy scapegoat—"The Jews are our misfortune" screams a banner headline on *Der Stern*, which is mounted on a newsstand with other examples of propaganda. *Mein Kampf*, which Hitler wrote while imprisoned in the early 1920s, was becoming a bestseller by the 1932 election in which he was narrowly defeated by Hindenburg. At a monochromatic cafe scene in prewar Berlin, parties at five tables discuss the impending Nazi takeover of Germany, then the narrator reveals their fates: the publisher became a propagandist; a Jewish-Christian couple commits double suicide; and the waiter, a part-time journalist, is deported to Dachau for distributing anti-Nazi literature.

The growing isolation of the Jews—the edict banning them from German citizenship was unopposed even by the Vatican; most nations sent delegations to the 1936 Olympics as planned; and the 1938 Evian Conference offered no refuge for Jews who wanted to flee—gave the Nazis confidence

to attack. The events of *Kristallnacht*, the pogrom in November 1938 that included the destruction of many synagogues and initiated the mass deportations, begins a three-screen video presentation.

A tableaux vivant of the Wannsee Conference, at which Nazi leaders decide on "the Final Solution of the Jewish Question," introduces the horrible statistics of the Holocaust. Graphs illustrate how much of European Jewry was eliminated: 315,000 of 360,000 Jews in Czechoslovakia; 1,252,000 of 2,850,000 in the Soviet Union; 40,000 of 200,000 in Austria. Most of the installation effects are dramatic: bombed-out brick cases hold red-tinted photographs, and visitors are led into a concrete bunker to experience the deprivation and humiliation of processing at the Nazi death camps. In the Hall of Testimony, many who survived the Holocaust recount stories of courage and sacrifice.

The Multimedia Learning Center has extensive documentation on the Holocaust and World War II available at thirty computer work stations. Artifacts and documents from the Holocaust and an exhibit highlighting Simon Wiesenthal's efforts to bring to justice the perpetrators of the Holocaust are displayed here. An active program of lectures, concerts, and films continues at the Museum of Tolerance,

along with monthly performances on Sunday afternoons geared especially to kids: Lenny and Lori, the lion and lamb who learn to get along, alternate with storytellers recounting tales from around the globe.

Tools for Tolerance, a diversity-awareness program designed to help civil servants and professional groups develop such communication skills as team-building and conflict resolution through community awareness, benefited local corporations and more than 2,500 police officers in its first three years. The California state budget allocates $2 million annually to underwrite the program.

A *Shenere Velt* Gallery Workmen's Circle/*Arbeter Ring*

1525 S. Robertson Blvd.
Los Angeles 90035
310-552-2007
Mon.–Fri. 1–4 p.m., and by appt.

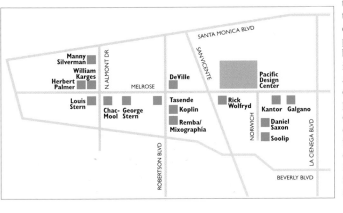

West Hollywood Farmers Market Plummer Park (7377 Santa Monica Blvd.) Mon. 9 a.m.–2 p.m.

Workmen's Circle, or *Arbeter Ring* in Yiddish, was organized a century ago to aid Jewish immigrants in creating a better life in the New World and to maintain the secular Jewish traditions of *Yidishkayt*. The gallery, whose name means "a more beautiful world" in Yiddish, has recently begun mounting exhibitions to further the goals of its parent organization to integrate the arts into a vision of a more humane social order. It displays creative work by artists whose themes express social justice, including posters on racism and anti-Semitism from the collection of the Center for the Study of Political Graphics. There are photographs documenting the sixty-year history of Los Angeles's Vanguard Branch 1016 (established in 1937), which illustrate the westward movement of the Jewish community from Boyle Heights to the Pico-Robertson area. The Workmen's Circle held an open competition for a mural to be painted on the south wall of its building, which will celebrate secular Jewish culture and highlight the organization's campaigns on behalf of labor, universal healthcare, and immigrant rights.

The Yiddish language is central to the preservation of Jewish culture, so evening classes from beginning to advanced levels are held throughout the year in low-fee, ten-week sessions. A Yiddish discussion group and a chorus interpreting Yiddish and Israeli songs meet regularly, and an active program of concerts, lectures, and events helps further the creation of *"a shenere un besere velt"*: a more beautiful and better world.

Center for the Study of Political Graphics

8124 W. Third St., Ste. 211
Los Angeles 90048
*213-653-4662

This collection of some 30,000 political posters evolved from a personal passion to become a unique "activist archive," the term its founder/director prefers to describe the use of the collection in educational exhibitions. Although the collection is open only to researchers by appointment, the general public can view its holdings in thematic exhibitions that are mounted regularly (including at Track 16 Gallery at Bergamot Station in Santa Monica), and circulated to school and university galleries.

During a trip to Central America in 1981, director Carol Wells was impressed by the power of graphics to communicate, even to a largely illiterate population. Drawing on her background as an art historian, she began ferreting out the works of local Southern California graphics and poster studios, many of which disappeared without any other repository. The women's movement, the United Farm Workers, the Vietnam War, the worldwide protest movement of 1968, and the history of protests in L.A. are among the themes that have been explored in past cullings from the collection.

The **Pacific Design Center** (8687 Melrose Ave.), the blue- and green-glass-clad structures designed by Cesar Pelli and Gruen Associates, is the center of interior design in Los Angeles. More than 200 showrooms are incorporated within the mammoth buildings, which now welcome the public to browse (though the services of a licensed interior designer are required for all purchases). An intermittent gallery program, which has featured small exhibitions of decorative arts from LACMA's collection, as well as architecture and contemporary design, is unpredictable but can be interesting. An active special events program addresses concerns of contemporary designers. Call 310-657-0800 for the schedule of events.

An affiliated group of West Hollywood galleries presents joint openings on a regular basis which allow art lovers to stroll among the fifteen sites and explore their wide-ranging offerings. For more information about art galleries in Los Angeles, see pages 38–44.

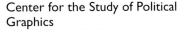

MAK Center for Art and Architecture at the R. M. Schindler House

835 N. Kings Rd.
West Hollywood 90069
*213-651-1510
Wed.–Sun. 11 a.m.–6 p.m.
Entry: adults $5

Until 1969, when the Irving Gill–designed Dodge House was demolished, there were two great modernist buildings on Kings Road. Preservationists then mobilized to protect the Schindler House, a center of the avant-garde intellectual community since its construction in the 1920s.

The structure had been continually modified during the thirty years since Austrian architect Rudolf M. Schindler's death in 1953. Using grants from the city of West Hollywood and the California Office of Historic Preservation, the Friends of the Schindler House (FOSH) lovingly restored the building and grounds to reflect its original scheme. Photographs from the 1920s were consulted to reconstruct the furniture originally in the Schindler studios; paint was stripped from the concrete walls; and sleeping baskets that had been walled in as permanent rooms were rebuilt in their original form. The landscaping plan had incorporated sunken beds of native grasses to create privacy for the individual studio spaces, and tall perimeter plantings served the same purpose: these have been re-created, making this again a quiet enclave in the city fabric.

The cost of maintaining this site exceeded the revenues generated by admission and rental fees, and the Friends of the Schindler House struggled for a decade to support it. But architects from around the world flock to Los Angeles to see the concentration of modernist design constructed here from the 1920s to the 1940s and Schindler's buildings are well known in his native Austria, so in 1994 a partnership between the Austrian Museum of Applied Arts (MAK), Vienna, and FOSH brought new life to the great California building that is a prototype of Schindler's designs. It is now the centerpiece of a program that allows European artists and architects to spend six months in residence at the Mackey Apartments, designed by Schindler in 1939; exhibitions, symposia, lectures, and performances organized by the visiting scholars are presented at the Kings Road site, which also features a bookstore that sells architecture books and publications of the MAK Center.

Schindler, who was born in 1887 in Vienna and studied architecture there with Otto Wagner, left Europe for good in 1914. He came to Los Angeles in 1920 to work for America's most influential architect, Frank Lloyd Wright, supervising construction of Wright's commission for Aline Barnsdall on Olive Hill. By October 1921, when his work on the Barnsdall commission was completed, Schindler and his wife (Sophie Pauline, née Gibling), had decided to remain in Los Angeles, where R. M. would establish an independent architectural practice.

With another couple, Clyde and Marian Chace, the Schindlers purchased a 100-by-200-foot lot on Kings Road from Walter

Dodge. In a letter to his in-laws dated November 26, 1921, Schindler described his plan for a communal living structure on Kings Road and asked for financial assistance: "The basic idea was to give each person his own room—instead of the usual distribution—and to do most of the cooking right on the table—making it more a social 'campfire' affair. . . . The rooms are large studio-rooms—with concrete walls on three sides, the front

Beverly Hills
Farmers Market
200 block of N.
Cañon Dr. (north of
Wilshire Blvd.)
Sun. 9 a.m.–1 p.m.

open (glass) to the outdoors—a real California scheme. On the roof two 'sleeping baskets' are provided—for open-air sleeping—with temporary cover for rainy nights."

This unconventional plan was Schindler's response to California's climate and lifestyle, and many of its elements—flat roof, sliding doors, integration of indoor and outdoor spaces—were later incorporated into much housing typical of the region; it also utilized new construction techniques, such as concrete poured on the site and lifted into position. Schindler acknowledged in a 1932 article his radical approach to materials: "The traditional building scheme, by which the structure members of the house are covered onion-like with layers of finishing materials—lathe, plaster, paint, paper, hanging, etc.—is abandoned. The house is a simple weave of few structural materials, which retain their natural color and texture throughout."

Within a few years of completing construction at Kings Road, the Chaces moved out of state and were replaced in the cooperative residence by a Viennese friend from Schindler's youth, Richard Neutra, who lived with his family in the house from 1925 until 1930. Schindler and Neutra formed an architectural partnership during these years, but it ended bitterly in 1930. The Schindlers' marriage also failed, and Pauline moved elsewhere for several years, though she returned in the mid-1930s to live apart from her former husband in the Chace Studio until her death in 1977. The building never worked well as a home—every tenant complained about its impracticality and structural imperfections—and as the MAK Center, it no longer strives to provide basic creature comforts but instead serves as a meeting place, stripped of the accoutrements of daily life, that again shines in its stark beauty and inspires a new generation of artists.

The Pearl M. Mackey
Apartments (1137–41 S.
Cochran Ave., Los
Angeles 90019) were
acquired by the
Republic of Austria in
1995 to house students
from the MAK Center
during their sojourn in
L.A. Inquire at the
Schindler house about
public tours or events
scheduled at the
Mackey Apartments.

The California Museum of Ancient Art has a post office box (#10515, Beverly Hills 90213) but so far no exhibition space for the 2,000 ancient artifacts it has collected, largely by donation. It has mounted an ambitious lecture series by noted scholars, who have elucidated many of the mysteries surrounding the cataclysmic ending to the Bronze Age in the twelfth century B.C., and also leads educational tours to the Middle East. For more information on museum programs, call 818-762-5500.

Beverly Hills, primarily a residential and commercial area, until recently lacked any museums, concert halls, or cultural centers, but it offers both residents and visitors attractions formed from its greatest resource: real estate. Franklin Canyon, Wilacre, and Coldwater Canyon Parks are preserved tracts of natural land straddling the mountain crest on either side of Mulholland Drive. Greystone Park and Robinson Gardens are cultivated gardens in the city's posh residential districts, and beautifully landscaped Beverly Gardens Park along Santa Monica Boulevard gives the city a central greenbelt.

The Beverly Hills Civic Center, anchored by the landmark Spanish baroque City Hall, was the focus of the city's most ambitious public works project in the late 1980s. The $120-million renovation and construction project, designed by postmodern architect Charles Moore, centralized the municipal services—fire and police departments—in new buildings and nearly tripled the size of the public library (to 92,000 square feet) in a construction that retains the original 1965 structure. Gold leaf applied to the cupola atop the eight-story tower of City Hall was only the most visible part of its renovation; modernization of its operating systems and revamping the offices in space vacated by the police department were the core of the project. Moore respectfully acknowledged the architecture of City Hall in his design, adapting the height and spacing of its window bays to the entire complex and finding inspiration in the decorative elements of the 1932 building, reinterpreting them in a modern vernacular.

A sequence of three oval courtyards surrounded by covered pedestrian arcades links the buildings, with its north-south axis cutting diagonally across Rexford Drive. The colored tiles and landscaping—flowering vines and shrubs were selected to extend the colors of the tile into the plantings—were the architect's way of adding "pizzazz" to these central public spaces. "Architecture is a choreography of the familiar and the surprising," Moore wrote. "To be successful, a place must lure people in; then, when they are in the middle, it must astonish them." He called the Civic Center, "one of my best examples of this theory."

Museum of Television & Radio

465 N. Beverly Dr.
Beverly Hills 90210
310-786-1000
www.mtr.org
Wed.–Sun. noon–5 p.m., Thurs. until 9 p.m.
Entry: adults $6, students and seniors $4,
children 12 and under $3

The Directors Guild (7920 Sunset Blvd.) is a professional organization that, according to a spokesperson, is generally used for membership events, not public programs. Its large (650 seat) and well-equipped theater, which was once used for American Cinematheque screenings, is now the site of the annual television festival organized by the Museum of Television & Radio.

The Museum of Television & Radio has existed in New York since 1975, when CBS founder William S. Paley spearheaded the effort to collect media that, especially in the earliest years of their development, had been ephemeral. Preserved in its collections are both the historical record of the twentieth century—Roosevelt's "Fireside Chats," the struggle for civil rights in the U.S. in the 1960s and at Tienanmen Square in 1989; the war in Vietnam, which lost public support because it was broadcast into living rooms throughout America—and the evolution of an art form—performances, often live, by Orson Welles and Laurence Olivier, Lucille Ball, and Mary Tyler Moore. The collection that had been accumulated was again sorted and cataloged in preparation for moving to a new site in New York; when that process was completed in 1991, 75,000 hours of programming had been reproduced in Hi-8 format—much of it converted from older VHS tape. The process continues—90,000 hours of tape were duplicated to stock the Beverly Hills facility that opened in 1996—and each year the museum adds hundreds of programs, contributed by the commercial networks, studios, the Public Broadcasting Service, and other producers around the world.

Architect Richard Meier, commissioned by the New York museum to remodel a Beverly Hills bank as its West Coast headquarters, used materials that also figure prominently in his design for the Getty Center—which may invite unfair comparisons, but the budgets of the two projects weren't comparable either. Here the travertine marble is polished, and many of the building's features are inscribed with donors' names. Each of the museum's primary functions has a purpose-designed space: a 150-seat theater has state-of-the-art equipment, unobstructed sight lines, and wood paneling. In the radio listening room, visitors, ensconced in comfortable leather chairs, may select from five different one- to two-hour programs, changed several times each year, to be played on their headsets. The 500 most-requested programs are already loaded in consoles at each of the sixty-four carrels in the library, but visitors can access the entire collection at computer terminals and order a custom selection. An adjacent Scholar's Room has fourteen units, which researchers can reserve for $25 per day, with access to the entire database. A small lobby gallery holds rotating exhibits, which have included *Star Trek* costumes and drawings for animated Peanuts specials; other objects from the collection—including a treasure trove of Hirschfeld drawings—line the corridors and library walls. On weekday mornings, before its doors open to the public, the museum's center is the educational projection room, which is booked with special classes (for students from kindergarten up) on animation, science fiction, planet earth, advertising, the presidency, and the civil rights movement. These classes, designed to teach critical viewing skills and reveal how television and radio inform, persuade, and entertain, cost $50 and require advance reservations (call 310-786-1034). There's a well-stocked museum shop with books, videos, and souvenirs from current TV shows.

No attempt has been made to replicate the infrastructure of the New York museum in Beverly Hills; instead, its programs, like its collections, are presented for a new audience. The Museum of Television & Radio has clearly addressed a need in the Entertainment Capital: in the first year it enrolled 3,000 members (memberships start at $50, $35 for seniors/students). Its annual two-week television festival in the spring regularly sells out the 650-seat theater at the Directors Guild (7920 Sunset Blvd.). The museum draws from its collections to organize exhibitions and screening series on such subjects as Stand-up Comedians on Television; Murder in the Living Room; Hitchcock by Hitchcock; and The Artist at Work. The Seminars Program is a forum for industry professionals and the public to explore, in bimonthly events, such diverse topics as comedy writing, children's programming, sports, and a look behind-the-scenes at the making of prime-time television.

Each year in mid-November some of the best children's programs from around the globe have been presented in the annual International Children's Television Festival, showcasing such familiar characters as Ms. Frizzle, Snoopy, and Madeline, as well as those who've won children's hearts in twenty-five other nations, like music professor Plinket E. Plonk from Ireland and the Swiss-German Pingu. Families also enjoy the Saturday-morning Re-creating Radio Workshops (tickets $5, reservations required; 310-

La Cienega Park (325 S. La Cienega, at the corner of La Cienega and Olympic) has good playground equipment and playing fields that are heavily subscribed but always provide spectators with lots of exciting games.

See Film and Video (pages 106–10) for information on programs sponsored by the Academy, both at this location and at other venues like the James Bridges Theater at UCLA.

786-1014), which uses special scripts and sound effects to enact such classics as *Superman* and *The Lone Ranger*, and an audiocassette of their performance is sent to participants.

Academy of Motion Picture Arts and Sciences

8949 Wilshire Blvd.
Beverly Hills 90211
310-247-3900
Tues.–Fri. 10 a.m.–5 p.m., Sat.–Sun. noon–6 p.m.

Two spaces within the Academy's headquarters are dedicated to exhibitions of a wide range of art and artifacts created in conjunction with moviemaking. Recently striking and stylish portraits of stars, which established the reputation of photographer John Engstead (his collection was donated to the Academy's library), filled both spaces with the glamour of Hollywood portraiture. Eight decades of great designs from the collection amassed by costume historians Larry McQueen and Bill Thomas included outfits worn by Jessica Lange in *King Kong* (1976) and Christopher Reeve in *Superman* (1978), as well as classic Adrian-designed gowns from the 1930s for *Marie Antoinette* and *Queen Christina*. The little-known film craft of glass-title paintings, vintage and contemporary posters for sports-themed films, and detailed presentations on animation art with working drawings as well as video clips are among recent exhibitions that pay tribute to the art and science of filmmaking throughout its history.

Beverly Hills Public Library

444 N. Rexford Dr. (in Civic Center complex)
310-288-2200
Mon.–Thurs. 10 a.m.–9 p.m., Fri.–Sat. 10 a.m.–6 p.m., Sun. noon–5

First-time visitors may find the pamphlet at the information desk, which outlines a self-guided walking tour of library, a useful introduction to its services. Families must sign up in advance for each ten-week session in the storytelling and reading program offered fall/winter/spring; drop-in participation is not allowed. There are no such restrictions—and no fee—for the monthly Storytelling Festival, where professional actors interpret classic tales in one-hour performances.

Programs for adults include a musical recital series, Sundays at 2 p.m.; screenplays and theatrical plays are presented monthly in readings; other workshops include the ongoing "comedy tonight" group that has helped some launch writing careers in the entertainment industry.

Center for Motion Picture Study

Academy of Motion Picture Arts and Sciences
333 S. La Cienega Blvd.
Beverly Hills 90211
Reference desk: 310-247-3020 (Mon.–Tues., Thurs. 9 a.m.–3 p.m.)
Library hours: Mon.–Tues., Thurs.–Fri. 10 a.m.–5:30 p.m.
Film archive: by appt., 310-247-3000

The Academy of Motion Picture Arts and Sciences won the affection of preservationists by leasing and renovating the Italian Romanesque Beverly Hills waterworks, which had been vacant and plagued by vandals since 1976, for use as the Center for Motion Picture

Study, with a library and film archive. The noncirculating library is named for Margaret Herrick, former librarian and executive director of the Academy, but the present staff is tight-lipped about the legend that she gave the Oscar its name by remarking that the statue looked like her Uncle Oscar. The collection includes 20,000 books, 6,000,000 still photographs, 17,000 posters, and 60,000 scripts, as well as 1,400 periodicals and files of clippings from seventy-five years of trade publications.

The Academy Archive contains 12,000 films (stored in former water-filtration vaults) from the silent-film era to the present, with special emphasis on the Academy Awards and documentary films. Production and costume sketches, music scores, and sound recordings are also preserved. Researchers (with valid photo ID) may utilize the library collections at the site, and the film archive by prior appointment.

Virginia Robinson Gardens
1008 Elden Way
Beverly Hills 90210
310-276-5367
Guided tours by appt. only: Tues.–Thurs. 10 a.m.,
1 p.m.; Fri. 1 p.m.
Entry: adults $5, seniors/students/children over 5 $3

In 1903 Harry Robinson, heir to the J. W. Robinson department store chain, and his new wife, Virginia, departed on a four-year, around-the-world honeymoon. She became enamored of European gardens during their travels and on their return began to transform the fifteen-acre site they purchased in Beverly Hills with extensive landscaping.

Beverly Hills supported cattle ranching and bean fields until 1905, when part of the Rancho de las Aguas land grant was purchased by investors hoping to discover oil. Their drilling was largely unproductive, but they did find water, a rare resource that later permitted the area to remain an independent city rather than be incorporated into the city of Los Angeles. The land was developed as a residential district, and in 1912 developers built the Beverly Hills Hotel hoping to lure affluent visitors who might become permanent residents in the area. When "America's sweethearts," Douglas Fairbanks and Mary Pickford, chose Beverly Hills as the site of their home, Pickfair, it became a most fashionable residential address.

The Robinsons built a 6,000-square-foot beaux arts–style residence that featured mirrored walls to reflect the gardens, which Virginia cultivated with the assistance of twelve gardeners. A Palladian poolhouse built at the end of the grassy front terrace helped to enclose the outdoor space; it was the preferred site of the Robinson's lavish parties, which tour docents describe in great detail. Mrs. Robinson, who outlived her husband by fifty years, left the estate, which is listed on the National Register of Historic Places, to Los Angeles County as a botanical garden.

The lovely gardens are connected with brick stairs and walkways: in the shade of towering specimen trees, an environment of camellias, kafir lilies, impatiens, and azaleas flourishes. The fifty types of camellias include one named for Virginia Robinson, but her greatest horticultural legacy must be the two-acre palm garden, which includes the largest stand of king palms outside Australia and myriad examples of California fan, paradise, and lady palms. Cycads, which look a bit like sego palms but are actually conifers that have existed since the Pleistocene era, and gingko biloba, another ancient plant form, are also featured in the plantings.

TreePeople
Coldwater Canyon Park
12601 Mulholland Dr.
Beverly Hills 90210
818-753-4600
Daily, sunrise to sunset
Entry: free

The average American consumes the equivalent of seven trees each year in newspaper and paper products, most of which is not recycled. TreePeople, an organization dedicated to replenishing the supply of trees and encouraging recycling to prevent further destruction, engages the public in its cause through the very simple act of planting trees. At its headquarters in Coldwater Canyon Park, TreePeople maintains a nursery of rooted seedlings and conducts frequent planting workshops for the public and school groups, teaching conservation and gardening techniques while encouraging a commitment to protect the environment. TreePeople frequently schedules nature walks for families on weekends and participates in school programs. Drought- and smog-tolerant plants are sold in their nursery in Coldwater Canyon (Tues. and Sat. 2–4 p.m.).

A lovely nature trail leading down the chaparral-covered canyon identifies plants and animal habitats. A recycling center presents the staggering statistics of waste management and a step-by-step guide to initiating a thorough recycling system in your own household.

Greystone Mansion and Park
905 Loma Vista Dr.
Beverly Hills 90210
310-550-4796
Grounds: daily 10 a.m.–5 p.m.

Edward Doheny, who made the first oil strike in the city of Los Angeles, purchased a 415-acre tract in Beverly Hills on which his only son, Ned, built a fifty-five-room residence for his family. The mansion, designed by Gordon Kaufmann, was faced in Indiana limestone and roofed in Welsh slate, a somber color scheme that gave the residence its name: Greystone. More than $3 million was spent in developing the estate, with $1.24 million to construct the 46,054-square-foot house, setting a record in Beverly Hills in 1927 and perhaps establishing a trend for the future.

In the mid-1950s the family sold 410 acres to a developer, Paul Trousdale, who lent his name to the opulent subdivision that still defines the northeast corner of Beverly Hills. Ten years later, the city of Beverly Hills purchased the remaining property to build a nineteen-million-gal-

Franklin Canyon

2600 Franklin Canyon Rd.
Beverly Hills 90210
310-858-3090
Daily, sunrise to sunset
Entry: free

This steep canyon, owned by the family of Edward Doheny until 1977, is one of the most accessible tracts in the Santa Monica Mountains National Recreation Area. More than 100 acres in the lower canyon are available to the public for hiking on several miles of easy, marked trails or playing and picnicking on the wide-open, grassy fields. This oasis within the urban sprawl, located only ten miles from the Ventura Freeway, boasts trails climbing the canyon walls that reward the hiker with surprising views of the city and the ocean.

Upper Franklin Canyon is now also operated by the Santa Monica Mountains Conservancy (the Department of Water and Power had previously kept this reservoir site closed to the public). The pond and lake have been left in their wild state as a habitat for ducks and other birds, fish, amphibians, coyote, deer, and rabbits, and for hikers to enjoy. The **William O. Douglas Outdoor Classroom**, named for the Supreme Court Justice and conservationist, is a nonprofit environmental education agency that operates an active program of nature walks, such as Incredible Edibles, Evening Birds, and Canyon Tykes. Interpretive hikes for school groups are heavily subscribed, and its after-school program for kids in grades three to six demonstrates how the chaparral environment supports plant and animal life. The schedule of hikes—weekend walks through the ranch for all ages, and parent-child walks on weekday mornings—is included in *Outdoors,* the National Park Service quarterly calendar of events in the Santa Monica Mountains; call 818-597-9192, ext. 201.

The **Sooky Goldman Nature Center** (Mon.–Fri. 9 a.m.–5:30 p.m. and in conjunction with weekend programs) includes hands-on exhibits and interpretive programs on the local ecosystem. The rustic outdoor amphitheater with bench seating for 150 behind the Nature Center is used for storytelling and education programs, and is available to rent for special events.

lon reservoir. The grounds, which include a formal garden that is a popular wedding site, are open as a public park, but picnicking and ball-playing are not allowed. The site affords spectacular views of the city, and the wonderfully manicured and quiet garden makes the visitor feel like a landowner in this exclusive neighborhood.

The use of the mansion has been hotly debated by civic leaders and nearby residents, resulting in a stalemate that has endured for more than thirty years. The mansion was leased to the American Film Institute as its headquarters for more than a decade, and it is often used for filming— *The Bodyguard* and *Nixon* both include scenes shot in this recognizable location. Attempts to convert the building into a cultural center have repeatedly failed. Two collectors of contemporary art, Joseph Hirshhorn and Frederick Weisman, negotiated, at different times, with the city to renovate the mansion as a museum, but each was dissuaded by public controversies, including the argument that modern art is inappropriate for Beverly Hills! While other plans are being considered to allow Greystone to become a cultural resource for the community, a summer concert series—Beverly Hills Live!—is held in the courtyard of the mansion; call Beverly Hills Recreation and Parks Department (310-285-2537) for information on programs in the park.

THEATER AND DANCE

Tom Provenzano

THEATER

No longer stepchild to the film industry, theater has become a vital contributor to the cultural life of Los Angeles. On any given week approximately twenty live productions open, ranging from extravagant touring musicals and some of the most influential new works in world theater to hundreds of more modest offerings at small venues spread across the county. **Theatre L.A.** is a nonprofit association of more than 100 Southern California theaters and theatrical producers. It maintains calendar listings, provides a twenty-four-hour information hotline (213-688-ARTS), gives out the annual Ovation awards for local theater excellence, and maintains a Web site (www.TheatreLA.org).

The Presenters

These theaters and organizations sponsor touring shows and artists.

Nederlander Organization

The largest owner and operator of legitimate theaters in the world had been slipping in recent years, but the management of the Nederlander Organization is currently in the process of reclaiming its prestige. Los Angeles is one of its most important showplaces, and the Nederlander's Pantages, Wilshire, and Henry Fonda Theaters are three of the county's most

important theater venues. Though all have been dark more than they have been open through the 1990s, Nederlander Concerts and Broadway L.A. are taking steps to keep the venues alight as much as possible. Broadway L.A. replaces the old L.A. Civic Light Opera, which boasted some 80,000 subscribers in 1964 but was down to 4,500 in 1996. Expensive new productions of *The Phantom of the Opera, West Side Story,* and *The King and I* are expected to swell the subscription base.

Impresario Alexander Pantages opened the landmark **Pantages Theater** (6233 Hollywood Blvd., Los Angeles; *213-468-1700) near Hollywood and Vine in 1930 as a movie-vaudeville palace, the crown jewel of his Fox Studio chain. In 1949 Howard Hughes acquired the theater through RKO Pictures, and for ten years it served as the glittering home of the Academy Awards. The 1959 premiere of *Spartacus* demanded a reduction in seats, and the theater lost the Oscars. In 1963 a star-studded screening of *Cleopatra* commanded $250 per seat, with proceeds going to the construction of the new Music Center downtown. The theater remained one of the West Coast's finest movie houses until 1977, when the screen went dark and the Nederlander Organization stepped in to turn the Pantages into Los Angeles's premier legitimate theater. Though subway construction darkened the theater for more than a year, it has reopened, and the Nederlander expects it to serve Los Angeles with Broadway-style theater for years to come.

One of Los Angeles's first live theaters, the

Henry Fonda Theater

(6126 Hollywood Blvd., Los Angeles; *213-468-1700) opened in 1926 as the Carter DeHaven Music Box Theater, presenting performers like Fannie Brice in elaborate revues designed to rival the Ziegfeld Follies. Legitimate theater soon replaced revues, with productions such as *Chicago,* starring Clark Gable, and *Dracula,* with Bela Lugosi. By the 1930s the theater, simply known as the Music Box, played host to the popular weekly radio series "The Lux Radio Theater," boasting stars like Joan Crawford, Marlene Dietrich, and Al Jolson. Through the late 1940s and beyond, the theater went through several owners and name changes and finally became a Spanish-language movie house called the Pix. In the mid-1980s the Nederlander Organization, in an effort to redevelop Hollywood as a legitimate theater hub, restored the building to its original purpose, with 863 seats, and named it for Henry Fonda, the movie star also known for a distinguished stage career. Nederlander Concerts books in scores of comedians and musicians but also reserves the theater for important theatrical productions, from Athol Fugard's *My Children! My Africa!* to the musical-comedy phenomenon *Nunsense.*

Though the **Wilshire Theater** (8440 Wilshire Blvd., Beverly Hills; 310-939-1128) lacks the colorful histories of the Pantages and the Henry Fonda, its location in Beverly Hills and large size (1,800 seats) made it the best choice for the West Los Angeles site of the Nederlander's push to revive large-scale commercial theater in Southern California. Broadway L.A.

uses the Wilshire for smaller-scale musical revivals like *Grease* and *Dreamgirls.*

Shubert Organization

800-233-3123

The powerful Shubert Organization has battled the Nederlander through the century for primacy in legitimate theater. The **Shubert Theater** (2020 Avenue of the Stars, Los Angeles; 800-447-7400), the last of the great theaters built by the organization, is a centerpiece of Century City's ABC Entertainment Center. The theater was designed for one purpose: to play host to the biggest, most expensive, and popular first-class musical theater productions available. In 1997 the Shubert added the American premiere of *Ragtime* to its list of multimillion-dollar productions, which have included Disney's *Beauty and the Beast,* Glenn Close's debut in Andrew Lloyd Webber's *Sunset Boulevard,* and a record run of *Les Miserables.*

Alex Theater

216 N. Brand Blvd.
Glendale 91203
818-243-ALEX

New Year's Eve 1993 marked the grand reopening of the Alex Theater. The original Alexander Theater, a vaudeville and motion picture house decorated with Greek and Egyptian motifs, opened in 1925. Through the 1950s the theater served as a preview house for major studio releases, making it a glamorous host to movie stars from neighboring Hollywood. Its newly refurbished auditorium has 1,460 seats and state-of-the-art technical operation. The theater is designed as an "atmospherium"—with an illusion of being open-air. The mission of the Alex is to preserve its historically and architecturally significant site while serving as home to a wide array of performing arts organizations. Music and dance are well represented, along with the Los Angeles Theater League's Best of Broadway series. The City of Glendale plans to expand the Alex's event schedule to at least 275 evenings of performing arts each year by the turn of the century.

Cañon Theater
205 N. Cañon Dr.
Beverly Hills 90210
310-859-8001

Mostly a commercial rental house, this 382-seat theater has played host to many big successes. Beatrice Arthur played a long run of *Bermuda Avenue Triangle*—costarring its playwrights, Rene Taylor and Joseph Bologna—before the play moved off-Broadway. The theater has also had phenomenal recent successes, such as A. R. Gurney's *Love Letters* and the musical sensation *Forever Plaid*.

Cerritos Center for the Performing Arts
12700 Center Court Dr.
Cerritos 90703
800-300-4345

Since opening in 1993, the Cerritos Center has become a dominant force in Southern California theater, music, and dance. In the early 1980s the City of Cerritos sought to distinguish itself from the mass of L.A. County municipalities and create its own personality. Swimming against the current of reduction in government expenditure for the arts, the city committed the funds to create this $60 million performing arts center, with a 17,000-square-foot auditorium designed for flexibility. The theater's innovative design, by architects Barton Myers Associates, won the 1994 honor award for excellence in design

from the United States Institute of Theater Technology; it was one of only five U.S. theaters so honored. The center has become one of California's highest-grossing performance venues, with average attendance above 80 percent capacity. An annual season is carefully designed to deliver a wide variety of performing arts and pull in diverse audiences from throughout Los Angeles and Orange Counties. The most popular attractions are big Broadway musicals like *A Chorus Line* and country music stars, but the center is also committed to short runs of theatrical tours, such as its highly successful *Death of a Salesman*.

Geffen Playhouse
10886 Le Conte Ave.
Los Angeles 90024
310-208-6500
Box office: 310-208-5454

Across the street from UCLA, the 498-seat Westwood Playhouse long lived with rumors of a curse because so few of the very ambitious productions that booked the theater succeeded. Hoping to develop the venue to showcase its newly revamped theater department, UCLA purchased the property. Then, in the mid-1990s, multimillionaire record producer and philanthropist David Geffen bestowed $5 million to refurbish the theater. UCLA gratefully renamed it the Geffen Playhouse and quickly leased it, at a very low rate, to its current resident company. Critically acclaimed shows from New York and Chicago offering West Coast premieres, in addition to original plays developed at the playhouse, make for an eclectic season expected to have an imprint on theater worldwide and offer competition to the long-established Mark Taper Forum.

La Mirada Theater for the Performing Arts
14900 La Mirada Blvd.
La Mirada 90638
714-994-6150

Just inside Los Angeles County, on the border of Orange County, is one of the region's busiest and most popular theaters. In 1977 the city of La Mirada converted its old movie palace into a 1,264-seat proscenium theater. In subsequent decades the once-isolated theater has become the centerpiece of the community's bustling economy, surrounded by packed restaurants and shopping centers. Operated by the city, it offers an eclectic variety of theatrical events. Most popular is the annual series of celebrity-cast Broadway musicals. When not filled with musical comedy, the theater is rented to community groups such as the semiprofessional La Mirada Symphony and the highly popular Golden State Children's Theater.

Pepperdine University
Smothers Theater
24255 Pacific Coast Hwy.
Malibu 90263
310-456-4522

L.A.'s northern beach and valley communities are well served theatrically by this tenaciously active 450-seat house ensconced in the gorgeous hillside campus of Pepperdine University. Though the theater hosts many of the college's own productions, most of the year there is a constant flurry of local and touring productions, from dance and chorales to family theater. As part of a religious school, the theater is committed to offering uncontroversial but highly professional plays and musicals that appeal to theater lovers who wish not to be assaulted by nudity or profanity. The biggest hits have been musi-

cal comedies and revues like *Ain't Misbehavin'* and *All Night Strut*.

Redondo Beach Performing Arts Center
1925 Manhattan Beach Blvd.
Redondo Beach 90278
310-372-1171, ext. 2213

The South Bay is home to one of the county's most beautiful and active theaters. This venue is owned and operated by the city and has 1,425 seats as well as a large outdoor facility. Though many of its events are local in nature, the center does boast one of the last surviving examples of a California tradition: the civic light opera companies that once provided musical theater to communities throughout the state. The Civic Light Opera of South Bay Cities has implemented a program of popular musical titles, supported by extremely high production values, which has allowed it to thrive in an era of shrinking government support. Eschewing experimental or controversial productions, the Civic Light Opera sticks to audience-pleasing shows, packing in crowds for such performances as *Cabaret, Joseph and the Amazing Technicolor Dreamcoat*, and *My Fair Lady*.

The Producers

These theaters and organizations create their own new and revival productions.

Center Theater Group
Music Center of Los Angeles County
135 N. Grand Ave.
Los Angeles 90012
213-972-0700

Poised above downtown Los Angeles, atop Bunker Hill, this seven-acre theatrical complex, developed through the efforts of civic leader and philanthropist Dorothy Chandler, is the county's world-class performing arts venue.

Once a showcase for plays hot from Broadway, the **Mark Taper Forum** is now a chief supplier of productions to New York. Three of 1994's four Tony nominees for best play were developed at the Taper: *Angels in America— Perestroika, The Kentucky Cycle,* and *Twilight: Los Angeles— 1992.* The Taper's position in American theater was underscored when two of its productions, *Angels in America—Millennium Approaches* and *The Kentucky Cycle,* won back-to-back Pulitzers. The theater's loyal subscription audience of more than 22,000 vies for places in the 760-seat auditorium, originally built for public meetings, but now a model for newly built thrust theaters nationwide. For more than three decades the Taper has been under the guidance of producer-director Gordon Davidson, lauded by many for his commitment to new and experimental work and criticized by some for diluting his strength by taking over responsibility for running Center Theater Group's productions at the neighboring Ahmanson. Nevertheless, Davidson's partnership with talented directors and producers, such as George Wolfe (artistic director of the Joseph Papp Public Theater in New York) and Robert Egan (the Taper's current producing director), has helped the theater retain its position as one of the most influential regional theaters in the United States. For several years the experimental Taper Too inhabited a small space in the John Anson Ford Amphitheater, but recently the company has searched for a new home. As of this writing, an agreement has been signed with the Culver City Redevelopment Agency for the Taper to take over the Culver Theater, a landmark 1940s movie palace, as part of that city's redevelopment plans.

For years the large proscenium-stage **Ahmanson Theater** was the premier venue for large commercial plays produced by the Ahmanson and starring Hollywood notables like Charlton Heston. Then a record-breaking run of the Andrew Lloyd Webber phenomenon *Phantom of the Opera* forced the producers to move the Ahmanson's annual subscription play series to Hollywood's Doolittle Theater. When the final curtain came down on *Phantom,* the Ahmanson received an architectural reconfiguration, leaving it with a variable seating plan that accommodates between 1,300 and 2,000 depending on the production. Though the Ahmanson series of Broadway-style shows is still the theater's mainstay, the new seating plan has opened up a world of choices, including a new experiment with intimate dance performances (see below).

East West Players
The Union Center for the Arts
120 N. San Pedro St.
Los Angeles 90012
213-625-7000

In 1965 famed Japanese stage and film actor Mako (Tony-nominated for *Pacific Overtures* and Oscar-nominated for *The Sand Pebbles*) was named artistic director of a new small theater for Asian-Pacific performers, located in an isolated area near downtown. The original concept was to give Asian actors a chance to play Western roles they wouldn't ordinarily be offered. In the mid-1970s its mission was expanded to encourage Asian playwrights, and the theater season was subsequently divided between well-known Western drama and new Asian plays. The company's David Henry Hwang Writers Institute, named for America's best-known playwright of Asian descent, offers opportunities to aspiring writers. Three decades of fine work led the city of Los Angeles to offer extraordinary support, which has allowed East West Players to move to the gorgeously appointed, refurbished Union Center downtown, where it is the sole theater company, operating year-round under artistic director Tim Dang. The opening production at the new theater, *Pacific Overtures,* was chosen to reflect both the company's affection for Broadway genius Stephen Sondheim and its mission to celebrate Asian theater. The musical depicts the first contact between a very closed nineteenth-century Japan and an even more insistent American military.

A Noise Within
234 S. Brand Blvd.
Glendale 91204
818-546-1449

In the mid-1990s an upstart troupe of classically trained actors from San Francisco's legendary American Conservatory Theater, tired of the diet of contemporary realistic drama favored by small theater in Los Angeles, began mounting small, elegant productions of works by Shakespeare, Molière, Shaw, Ibsen, and other venerated playwrights. The unusually high quality of these productions quickly captured the imagination of the press, and the public responded, filling the theater to an astounding 97 percent capacity (a rare feat in L.A.'s small-theater community). Limited production values gave way to full-scale presentations as the theater's reputation began to attract major artists. The city of Glendale recognized the jewel in its midst and offered to help support the company's growth into a larger space. By 1997 the company had boosted its seating from 99 to 144, with plans to renovate its space in an old Masonic temple to accommodate a much larger theater—all part of Glendale's generous and astute redevelopment plans. A Noise Within has few peers among L.A. County's small to mid-sized theaters.

Pasadena Playhouse
39 S. El Molino Ave.
Pasadena 91101
626-356-7529

Officially recognized as the State Theater of California by proclamation of the state legislature in 1937, this elegant 686-seat proscenium theater has a rich history reaching back to its founding in 1917. The present structure was built in 1924. From the 1930s through the 1950s the playhouse was known as Hollywood's talent factory because of its renowned training program, which launched the careers of such stars as William Holden, Dustin Hoffman, and Gene Hackman. During its golden age the playhouse presented hundreds of plays, including 477 world premieres. It was also the first American venue to present all of Shakespeare's plays. Through the 1970s and into the 1980s the Pasadena Playhouse saw a steady decline in its prestige as USC and UCLA developed training programs attached to full-scale university degree programs. Its building also fell into disrepair. In 1986 the once-stately theater was restored. It now operates year-round, producing a season of classics, contemporary revivals, and new plays. Many of its original productions have gone on to Broadway (*Mail, Accomplice, Twilight of the Golds*), and others have become Hollywood films or are in development (*David's Mother, Sisterella*).

Big-Little Theaters

Thanks to an arrangement with the actors' union Equity, small theaters have been able to operate in Los Angeles County while providing only a very modest remuneration to actors who desire simply to create theater. The idea was to provide performance opportunities to showcase acting talent for industry producers. While showcasing continues to be a major impetus, small theater also thrives because of a renewed commitment by artists to fine theater and exciting treatments of revivals as well as new plays.

Actors' Gang
6209 Santa Monica Blvd.
Los Angeles 90038
*213-465-0566

Once most famous for its founding artistic director, Tim Robbins, the Actors' Gang has quickly become one of L.A.'s most intriguing companies. From audacious new adaptations of Aeschylus and Molière to starkly confrontational original work, the Gang consistently offers extremely lively, emotionally packed drama and comedy that invariably surprise audiences and captivate critics.

Bilingual Foundation of the Arts (BFA)
421 N. Ave. 19
Los Angeles 90031
*213-225-4044

As the West Coast's most influential Spanish-English theater company, the BFA presents an annual season of plays with rotating Spanish- and English-

speaking casts. The company was founded in 1973 by Mexican-American film, stage, and television star Carmen Zapata; Cuban actress Margarita Galban; and Argentine playwright and scenic designer Estela Scarlata. Its mission is to present Hispanic world drama to English and Spanish speakers alike through school tours and public performances. After seven years of moving from space to space throughout Los Angeles, Zapata found a permanent home for the troupe in 1980, at the old Lincoln Heights Jail. The company, seen annually by more than 180,000 audience members through its various programs, is Southern California's largest employer of Latino theater artists. Through its critically acclaimed and popular performances, the BFA has become one of the county's most important cultural forces. Since 1980 it has consistently been in the vanguard of L.A.'s growing small-theater movement, winning scores of theater awards and government citations for its varied programming. Like a few other well-placed small theaters, the BFA plans to move into a mid-sized space.

Celebration Theater
7051-B Santa Monica Blvd.
West Hollywood 90038
*213-658-4044

L.A.'s long-established gay and lesbian theater concentrates on developing new plays, originating such works as Tom Jacobson's *Cyberqueer*, Guillermo Reyes's *Men on the Verge of a His-panic Breakdown*, and Chay Yew's *A Language of Their Own*, which were all subsequently produced in New York. In addition to emotionally wrenching dramas and uplifting comedies, the company is famed for its

splashy production of *The Gay Nineties Musical: Looking Back, Moving On*.

Colony Studio Theater
1944 Riverside Dr.
Los Angeles 90039
*213-665-3011

The Colony has one of the oldest and most respected small theater troupes in Los Angeles. The highly professional productions boast a vast and loyal subscription audience, and its season of musicals and classic American plays consistently sells out. The group is in the last round of negotiations with the city of Burbank for a new theater, so this should be the next small theater to move to a larger space.

Cornerstone Theater
1653 18th St. #6
Santa Monica 90404
310-453-4347

This extraordinary collective of theater artists uses theater as a social tool to build better understanding between different racial and cultural communities. For its first five years the company worked in diverse communities across the United States, creating musical productions combining drama and social activism. Since 1992 Cornerstone has been based in Los Angeles, where it has become recognized as one of the most original and important theater organizations in the country. The company has no permanent space but performs in venues throughout the city.

Groundlings Theater
7307 Melrose Ave.
Los Angeles 90046
*213-934-9700

This the home of L.A.'s champion improv-sketch comedy troupe. The consistently bright antics of the group has produced stars such as Pee-wee Herman, Laraine Newman, Phil Hartman, and Julia

Sweeney. In addition to its popular headlining sketch comedy, the troupe offers Sunday shows with fresh new faces, late-night improv jams, and year-round classes for actors and comedians.

Group Repertory Theater
10900 Burbank Blvd.
North Hollywood 91601
818-769-7529

Since the early 1970s artistic director Lonny Chapman has guided this theater through seasons split between new plays and revivals. Approximately 150 playwrights, actors, and technicians make up a volunteer company that has kept the organization at the forefront of Los Angeles theater, with a penchant for bold, highly individual new productions.

Highways Performance Space
1651 18th St.
Santa Monica 90404
310-453-1755

Located in the 18th Street Arts Complex, this thorn in the side of Senator Jesse Helms and the religious right is home to highly controversial performance art from nationally known artists like Tim Miller and Michael Kearns. Alternative dance, drama, poetry, and self-revelatory monologues dealing with gay and lesbian themes, multiculturalism, and other community-based issues draw huge crowds to this artistic arena that has so often been pilloried by those who wish to undo the National Endowment for the Arts.

Hudson Theater
6539 Santa Monica Blvd.
Los Angeles 90038
*213-856-4249

This extremely elegant space shines amid Santa Monica Boulevard's self-proclaimed Theater Row, a strip of several run-down but highly popular small theaters. The Hudson is home to the Hudson Guild, which produces high-quality new works.

Matrix Theater

7657 Melrose Ave.
Los Angeles 90046
*213-852-3279

Under the direction of Joe Stern, this graceful space on the Melrose strip has been one of the most innovative theaters in Los Angeles. Through an experiment with double casting, Stern has been able to produce high-quality revivals of important plays, using well-known actors from film and television. (The double casting allows them to easily walk away from a production should a film job come up—and makes it just as easy to return when the job is over.)

Odyssey Theater

2055 S. Sepulveda Blvd.
Los Angeles 90025
310-477-2055

Under the direction of Ron Sossi, the Odyssey is one of the oldest and most successful small theaters in the county. Three ninety-nine-seat auditoriums operate year-round, mostly filled with new plays or fresh approaches to the classics. Literary manager Jan Lewis is constantly looking for new works, and many productions originating at the Odyssey move on to larger venues and regional theaters.

Pacific Resident Theater Ensemble

705½ Venice Blvd.
Venice 90291
310-301-3971

Pacific Resident Theater Ensemble offers the beach city of Venice a fine venue for classy revivals, especially of Chekhov and the modern masterworks of mid-twentieth-century American theater. The company prides itself on some of the best acting in Los Angeles, under the artistic direction of award-

winning actress and director Marilyn Fox.

Theater/Theatre

1713 N. Cahuenga Blvd.
Hollywood 90028
*213-871-0210

This ramshackle theater sits in the center of the never-quite-revitalized Hollywood Walk-of-Fame district. Ever-active artistic director Jeff Murray holds the theater together with talented artists like playwright Del Shores, who has launched his television career with a series of uproarious Texas comedies at the theater. One of them— *Daddy's Dyin'* . . . *Who's Got the Will?*—has become a major motion picture.

Tiffany Theater

8532 Sunset Blvd.
West Hollywood 90069
310-289-2999

In 1984, during the Los Angeles Summer Olympics, France's minister of culture declared that L.A. would be the capital of the twenty-first century. Producer Paula Holt heard his prediction and knew she had to take part in making it come true. Soon after, her new two-auditorium theater complex on the Sunset Strip became the jewel of the vital small-theater movement and helped build L.A. into a thriving theater town. The old Tiffany movie palace became the new Tiffany Theater, a high-priced small stage that has offered some of the finest new plays produced locally since 1986. Famed for its legendary location, its gorgeously appointed lobby and house, and state-of-the art technical facilities, the Tiffany has attracted major theater, film, and television talent. Holt's production of *Nite Club Confidential* became an international sensation and launched Scott Bakula's career. She also co-produces another eight to eleven plays each year, always taking an active interest.

West Coast Ensemble

522 N. La Brea Ave.
Los Angeles 90036
*213-525-0022

Since 1981 the West Coast Ensemble has been one of L.A.'s premier producers of solid theater work. Whether revivals of Shakespeare or American classics, Sondheim musicals or contemporary plays, this ensemble of more than 150 actors, directors, and technicians creates consistently high-quality productions under the artistic direction of founder Les Hanson. In addition to a fine season of major plays, the company provides readings, workshops, and an annual celebration of new one-acts.

Children's Theater

Though Los Angeles sorely lacks a major children's theater company, a few venues offer popular, high-quality work for young audiences. **Glendale Centre Theater** (324 N. Orange St., Glendale; 818-244-8481) presents musical retellings of fairy tales, which don't play well to adults but are incredibly popular with the hundreds of children who flock to the theater every Saturday. The **Los Angeles Children's Museum** (310 N. Main St., Los Angeles; 213-687-8800) provides the flexible Louis B. Mayer performance space to children's theater performers throughout Los Angeles for public performances on weekends and school groups during the week. **Santa Monica Playhouse** (1211 Fourth St., Santa Monica; 310-394-9779) is a cramped but beautiful theater concentrating on family fare. Its highly popular children's matinees are often silly, but the remarkably clever musicals delight without condescending to young audi-

ences. **Serendipity Theater Co.** (at the Burbank Little Theater, 1100 W. Clark St., Burbank; 818-557-0505) is most impressive, operating under the actors' union contract for youth theater. The company concentrates on well-known titles to attract crowds and buses school-children to the theater on a regular basis. **Storybook Theater** (at Theater West, 3333 Cahuenga Blvd. West, Los Angeles; 818-761-2203), a professional company under the direction of Barbara Mallory Schwartz, creates its own brand of "nonviolent" children's theater, offering watered-down but amusing versions of fairy tales for very young children.

Theater Festivals

Common Grounds Festival
Audrey Skirball Kenis (A.S.K.) Theater Projects

310-478-9ASK

One of the most influential theater organizations in Southern California, Audrey Skirball Kenis Theater Projects was founded in 1989 as "a force for new plays for a new theater." Each June A.S.K. presents its yearly Common Grounds Festival on the UCLA campus. For six days and nights the organization invites L.A. to this "annual array of audacious and original theater." Spend afternoons at theater labs exploring the craft of playmaking. Spend evenings at eye-popping works-in-progress by some of the most innovative theater ensembles and playwrights around." Theater labs provide multidisciplinary forums for playwrights to test their ideas and for audiences to expand their knowledge of the theatrical process. Workshop productions allow audiences a first glimpse of a new play that has undergone a rigorous development and rehearsal process on its way to being fully realized. Company presentations showcase some of the most exciting theater troupes around in the midst of creating avant-garde works. Throughout the weeklong event, artist workshops, lecture-demos, and seminars underscore the amazing vitality of the Los Angeles theater community. All events at the Common Grounds Festival are free to the public, but reservations must be made, and tickets go very quickly. Obtain a brochure by calling A.S.K., or visit the organization online at www.primenet.com/~askplay. In addition to the festival, A.S.K. sponsors young playwrights through a Playwrights-in-the-Schools program in Los Angeles and programs at summer camps. The organization provides many playwriting awards and fosters the art form year-round through playwrights' exchanges with London's Royal Court and New York's Lincoln Center and ties with other theaters. A.S.K. also publishes *Parabasis*, a biannual journal of American theater, and sponsors symposia throughout the year.

Shakespeare Festival/L.A.
213-489-1121

Since 1986 Shakespeare Festival/L.A. has provided free summer performances of highly professional, union-cast productions of the Bard's immortal works. In lieu of paid admission, the company has adopted a "food for thought" policy, accepting donations of canned food for entrance. This program has helped provide well over $1 million worth of food for the needy. The extraordinarily talented production staff and actors, as well as an environment always distinct from that of conventional theater, lend a bright, contemporary feel to the classic plays. The company prefers outdoor settings and has taken its movable theater cart to

such diverse locations as the Veterans Administration Grounds' Japanese Gardens, the California Plaza Water Court in downtown L.A., the Ambassador Auditorium grounds in Pasadena, and the South Coast Botanical Gardens in Palos Verdes.

Taper Too: New Works Festival
213-972-0700

For years the Mark Taper Forum's experimental wing, the Taper Too, has been in the forefront of creating new plays for the American theater. The New Works Festival commissions new plays, in addition to developing plays that have gone through a careful screening process by the Taper literary staff, led by Frank Dwyer (submissions are usually in the form of a one-page synopsis sent to the Mark Taper Forum literary department). The selection, refinement, and development of material is a year-round process, but the culminating festival each fall is one of Los Angeles's most cherished theatrical events. During the fall festival between sixteen and twenty plays are produced with the playwright in residence. Paid professional directors and actors staff these productions, whose production values range from minimal to sophisticated. Readings of an additional eight to ten plays are presented with some degree of staging. This festival has seen some extraordinary results: about 80 percent of the plays produced in the festival have gone on to full-scale productions, in venues ranging from regional theaters to Broadway. The biggest single success in recent years was the development of Tony Kushner's *Millennium Approaches*, the first half of *Angels in America*, which

won the Pulitzer prize and the Tony award for best new play on Broadway. *Angels in America*, which began as a commissioned twenty-minute play in San Francisco, grew to an eight-hour marathon through its development at the Taper. Other recent Broadway successes from the festival have included *The Kentucky Cycle* and *Jelly's Last Jam*. For several years the festival was held in the small auditorium at the John Anson Ford Amphitheater, but it is currently looking for a new home. Admission to all plays is free, but reservations are required.

Will Geer Theatricum Botanicum Summer Repertory Season
1419 N. Topanga Canyon Blvd.
Los Angeles 90290
310-455-3723

In the 1950s Will Geer, one of the many actors victimized by the McCarthy-era blacklists, opened his large Topanga Canyon backyard to blacklisted actors and folk singers. When he was able to resume his career, Geer found new fame on television, including his final role as Grampa in the long-running *Waltons*. For relaxation and company, Geer and his family invited actors to their home to rehearse and perform Shakespeare's plays in an outdoor amphitheater. Upon Geer's death in 1978 his daughter Ellen set about creating a professional Shakespeare company to celebrate her father's life on stage. Each summer, from early June through Labor Day, the theater presents a season of plays, to great critical acclaim. Shakespeare's plays are always among the offerings, but Tennessee Williams's works have also become a mainstay, along with a variety of plays representing other styles and genres. The

once-wild outdoor theater was recently tamed, with new seats replacing the quaint but uncomfortable wooden benches that required patrons to bring pillows. Though the renovations changed the look of the theater, the high quality of the under-the-stars productions remains unaltered, reflecting the commitment of one of America's leading theatrical families to the memory of its patriarch. Tickets range from $8 to $15 and are available from the theater.

DANCE

Venues and Presenters

California State University, Los Angeles Harriet and Charles Luckman Fine Arts Complex
5151 State University Dr.
Los Angeles 90032
*213-343-5121

Designed for flexibility, this beautiful theater moves between 1,175 and a more intimate 500 seats depending on the production. Under the guidance of Clifford Harper, former chair of Cal State L.A.'s Department of Theater and Dance, the Luckman has chosen to underscore its commitment to dance above all other performing arts, with the intention of becoming the dance venue of choice for local as well as touring companies. Foremost in planning a season of dance is diversity—not simply multiculturalism, but artistic diversity. Significantly, Harper's mission is to enhance education, bringing together artists, community, and children to interact in dance. The Luckman is the home base for the prestigious annual Dance Kaleidoscope festival (see below). Tickets are handled through Ticket-master (213-343-6423).

California State University, Northridge
The New Performing Arts Center
18111 Nordhoff St.
Northridge 91330
818-677-3943

As part of a $16-million expansion of its student union facilities, Cal State Northridge elected to build a new performing arts center. Entirely funded by students, the center boasts a seating design that leaves no patron more than fifty feet from the stage. The center was totally operational by February 1996, and offered 225 events in its first season. Among the most impressive performances to grace the new state-of-the-art theater have been internationally known dance troupes, from Argentina's Ritmo Tango to Brigham Young University's Theater Ballet.

John Anson Ford Amphitheater
2580 Cahuenga Blvd.
Los Angeles 90068
213-974-1396

Nestled in the hills between Hollywood and the San Fernando Valley, this charming venue presents many of L.A.'s top performing organizations. The Ford's 1,230-seat amphitheater offers summer concerts in an environment a bit more intimate than that of its across-the-street neighbor, the Hollywood Bowl. Summer Nights at the Ford, sponsored by the Los Angeles County Music and Performing Arts Commission, was inaugurated in 1993 to provide a multidisciplinary performance series. Groups whose proposals are accepted must meet their own staffing expenses, but the county provides a generous in-kind donation of the facility, house management, lighting and sound, and publicity. Among the

summer's biggest draws are the yearly visits from Dance Kaleidoscope and the Brazilian Summer Festival (see below).

Occidental College
Keck Theater
1600 Campus Rd.
Los Angeles 90041
*213-259-2922

Highly advanced theatrical technology, combined with an intimate 400-seat capacity, helps make the Keck Theater one of the most important dance venues in Los Angeles. The Keck, which also supports many theatrical productions, has long been committed to dance events, playing host to local and national dance companies. In the summer of 1997 it inaugurated a new dance festival called Feet Speak, featuring cutting-edge choreographers from Europe as well as home-grown talent. The festival also includes postperformance discussions with the choreographers.

Southern California Theater Association
Dorothy Chandler Pavilion and the Ahmanson
135 N. Grand Ave.
Los Angeles 90012
213-972-7211

The Southern California Theater Association's 1997 season at the Ahmanson, dedicated to the memory of late impresario James A. Doolittle, ushered in a new commitment to ballet companies. This inaugural season was intended to be the first of many that celebrate dance by bringing in important companies from throughout North America. The program opened with the Joffrey Ballet of Chicago's enormous production of *Legends,* followed by tours from the Cleveland/San Jose Ballet, the Houston Ballet, American Ballet Theater, and finally Ballet Folklorico de México of

Amalia Hernandez. The plan is to continue this celebration of American dance each summer. Call for brochures and information.

UCLA Center for the Performing Arts
310-825-2101

Since the late 1930s the UCLA Center for the Performing Arts has been one of the most important presenting organizations for music and dance. The Freud Playhouse and Schoenberg Hall, both on the UCLA campus, and the Veterans Wadsworth Theater in West Los Angeles and the Wiltern Theater in the Mid-Wilshire area provide venues for major performance groups from throughout the world. Alvin Ailey American Dance, the Whirling Dervishes, the Bella Lewitzky Dance Company, and Twyla Tharp are just a few of the world-renowned troupes presented by the center. The organization also works closely with other groups and theaters, including the Luckman Fine Arts Complex (see above), to provide venues that keep dance a vital part of Los Angeles's cultural scene.

Special Events
Brazilian Summer Festival
John Anson Ford Amphitheater

This annual celebration of Brazilian music, dance, food, and crafts grows tremendously each year to accommodate its swelling legions of Southland fans. Brazilian musicians and dancers provide a carnival of colors, sights, and sounds in this extravaganza of jazz, samba, and other delights. Created to increase awareness of Brazilian culture, music, art, and dance in Southern California, the festival always sells out. Past perfor-

mances have included a tribute to brilliant Brazilian jazz artist Moacir Santos, led by Rique Pantoja and his quintet. Some of the top Brazilian dance companies to participate in the event have been Josias and Sambrasil with samba feather dancers; Lula and Afro Brazil, with martial arts dancers; and Meia Noite and the Midnight Drums, featuring dancers demonstrating Bahian rhythms.

Dance Kaleidoscope
*213-343-6600

Though Los Angeles is not home to a major dance company, there are scores of smaller companies creating extraordinary work. As with theater performers, many dancers flock to Los Angeles to work in film and television, but their true pleasure in the art is often expressed through their work for the amazing array of dance troupes throughout the county. A most delightful experience in local dance is the annual Dance Kaleidoscope, a festival showcasing works of choreographers from Southern California. Up to forty local companies are represented in at least five different thematic programs at various locations each summer. The John Anson Ford Amphitheater and the Luckman Fine Arts Complex are the most frequent hosts of this major dance event. The program presents a bounty of distinct styles: from international folk and traditional dance to fine and popular arts programs of ballet, modern, and jazz. Every year choreographers and dancers from across the county vie for a spot in the festival's lineup. Dance Kaleidoscope was created in 1979 by the Los Angeles Area Dance Alliance. In 1989 the Cal State L.A. Department of Theater and

Dance took over responsibility for the festival in co-operation with the Los Angeles Department of Cultural Affairs.

Notable L.A. Dance Troupes

Diavolo Dance Theater
818-906-3343

Under the direction of Jacques Heim, Diavolo Dance Theater has received enormous praise from every segment of the dance community for its energetic, highly original take on movement. The company's name refers to its puckish, daredevil attitude as the dancers surge through Heim's surrealistic choreography. Their risk-taking antics instill awe in the audience but are always underscored by a sense of humor. Physically challenging scenic elements such as a giant staircase with trap doors, a ten-foot steel tunnel, and a large metal cage with pipes, ramps, and platforms help Diavolo create dynamic, dangerous movement.

Helios Dance Theater
310-454-0990

Helios is a modern company with a unique approach. Images of women in their everyday lives are embellished by strong gestures and soaring ballet techniques, combined with sultry modern styles. Pas-sages of stunning grace are interrupted momentarily by common, even crude, movements, ultimately creating a synthesis of fine technique and mundane activity.

JazzAntiqua
310-271-0789

JazzAntiqua (a seven-member dance ensemble and a jazz quintet) was formed in 1992 to celebrate and continue the development of jazz. The company strives to honor the art form it describes as "a major thread in the cultural fabric of African-American history and heritage." With performances in nontraditional venues, JazzAntiqua's goal is to take jazz music and dance to new and diverse audiences. Its artistic concept is to fuse dance with musical composition; the musicians interact with the dancers through a musical conversation, creating a collage of sound and movement. Choreographer Pat Taylor and composer Mark Shelby team up to move beyond "the stereotypical limitations of jazz dance and explore its capabilities to be as flexible, expressive, and communicative as the music from which it springs." Dance and music compositions are based on the works of Duke Ellington, John Coltrane, Miles Davis, and many other great names from the world of jazz. The company provides outreach through schools and workshops as well as clinics, master classes, and free public performances.

Loretta Livingston and Dancers
213-627-4684

Livingston and her troupe take over from the much-loved Bella Lewitsky Dance Company (Lewitsky retired with great fanfare in 1996), with which Livingston danced for fifteen years. This company has garnered numerous awards for its wild and unpredictable power and sensibility. There is no room for timidity or pre-ciousness here.

Los Angeles Choreographers and Dancers
*213-665-5628

Variety has called Los Angeles Choreographers and Dancers "one of the granddaddies of Los Angeles dance." This organization, consisting of modern troupe Louise Reichlin and Dancers and tap dancers Zapped Taps/Alfred Desio, has been at the forefront of the local dance community since 1979. The companies not only perform but also try to link dancers throughout Southern California through Web sites and other means to create cohesion between disparate dance communities.

The two units generally perform and tour separately but occasionally work in collaboration as they travel throughout Los Angeles and the West Coast. Critical acclaim has followed both troupes. Reichlin is best known for her works *The Tennis Dances* and *Urban and Tribal Dances,* in which she draws movement and musical source material from a multiplicity of cultures, underscoring the similarities between peoples around the world. Desio brings to his company a Broadway energy and stylish edge, highlighting broad entertainment, even in some highly experimental concepts involving Tap-Tronics, "an interactive electronic system, which allows [him] to play musical instruments through his taps." As an NEA grant recipient, Desio performed his Tap-Tronics by invitation of the Smithsonian Institution at the opening of its new Experimental Gallery.

Naomi Goldberg's Los Angeles Modern Dance and Ballet
*213-655-6812

Goldberg is known for a fusion of classical traditions and modern energy. A welcome sight at schools throughout the county, the company is also recognized for its klezmer program, which fills the John Anson Ford Amphitheater.

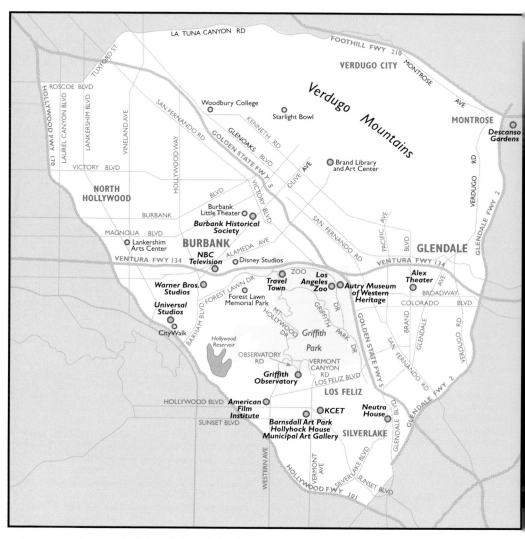

* indicates area code
that changes in 1998

Griffith Park, bounded today by the Golden State (5) Freeway to the east, the Ventura (134) Freeway to the north, and the Hollywood (101) Freeway to the west, had no such boundaries when Colonel G. J. Griffith donated five square miles to the city in 1896. In fact, there was no access route to the land, which then lay a mile outside the city's limits until 1910. It has since become, as Griffith intended, a "place of recreation and rest for the masses, a resort for the rank and file," with an estimated ten million visitors annually. It has also grown (to six square miles) and changed during its first 100 years, affected by natural forces—drought, fire, flood—and surviving such assaults as the use of its core as a dump for 1,200 tons of trash daily for almost thirty years. Its 4,044-acre terrain includes the peak of Mount Hollywood (1,625 feet) and the incredible topography of canyons so untouched they suggest a remote wilderness area. It is the largest park within a city in the United States—it is five times the size of New York's Central Park—but in this most suburban of American cities, it has always had to compete with the wide-open spaces of the San Gabriel and Santa Monica mountains, the recreational opportunities of the beach, and even the convenient pleasures of one's own backyard, and has never enjoyed a budget sufficient for its needs or commensurate to its size.

Miles of scenic drives exist within its boundaries, but when the cost of road repairs and fire danger forced the closure of transmountain routes, the dog-walkers, cyclists, bird-watchers, and hikers found new uses for the abandoned roadways. The Sierra Club has recently established a chapter in the park to make better use of its fifty-three miles of hiking trails. (The Sierra Club publishes a four-month calendar with 300 monthly events listed, which is free to members; call 213-387-4287.) The Los Angeles Equestrian Center (480 Riverside Drive; 818-840-9063), built on the Burbank side of the 134 Freeway for the 1984 Olympics, rents saddle horses for trail rides and supplies a map of forty-three miles of bridle paths in Griffith Park. There are several commercial stables that rent horses on the Atwater edge of the park, and the famous Friday-night trail rides from Sunset Ranch (*213-464-9612) at the top of Beachwood Canyon into the San Fernando Valley are another introduction to the park's horse trails. The park roads are favorite routes for joggers and cyclists; two-wheeled vehicles and rollerblades can be rented at a concession in the parking lot near Los Feliz Boulevard and Riverside Drive.

Sports facilities include twenty-four tennis courts—twelve lighted for night play—at three locations in the park; an Olympic-size pool (operated during the summer months only), soccer fields, and a well-equipped playground are found in the Griffith Recreation Area. The city maintains four golf courses in Griffith Park—two eighteen-hole plus two nine-hole—part of an inexpensive citywide system that is most easily utilized by purchasing a golf registration card ($25, valid for three years) from the Recreation and Parks Department (213-485-5566). Reservations from card-carrying members are accepted one week prior to date of play; eighteen holes cost $17 on weekdays and $22 on weekends. A proposal to transform a ten-acre site at Los Feliz and Riverside, once a pitch-and-putt course that has not been utilized since 1981, into a golf-training facility for youths ages seven to seventeen is testimony to how one young player, Tiger Woods, has redefined the popular image of the game. The city's Recreation and Parks commissioner is seeking financial support for building a new 175-yard driving range with putting and chipping greens, which would improve the flow at the city's thirteen public courses by removing slow beginners.

Among the park's man-made attractions, the Observatory, Zoo, and Equestrian Center attract the largest audiences. An extended season of popular music concerts is offered at the open-air, 6,000-seat Greek Theater on the south edge of the park, which was constructed in 1930 with the proceeds of a trust fund left by Colonel Griffith to make civic and cultural additions to the park bearing his name. The Autry Museum of Western Heritage, the most recent addition to the park's cultural facilities, is a destination for school groups studying California history and has established a following for its programs. A consortium of children's groups has been negotiating for a lease on a piece of land adjacent to the parking lot shared by the zoo and the Autry, which promises to make that corner of the park even more kid friendly—but not before the year 2000.

In July 1997 Mayor Richard Riordan and 150 cyclists inaugurated the first lighted bike path in Los Angeles, a three-mile stretch along the Los Angeles River on the eastern edge of Griffith Park. It is not simply lighted: there are ten different lighting systems because this is a prototype of a proposed bike route from downtown to Canoga Park, in the San Fernando Valley. The next leg to be built will link the existing pathway to downtown but will not be completed before the year 2000.

The merry-go-round (off Crystal Springs Dr. near the park's eastern edge), built in 1926 and well-preserved, affords a peek at a true slice of L.A.'s ethnic mix set in motion before your eyes. Miniature-train rides, a flight simulator, and pony rides make the southeast corner of the park a favorite family destination. Travel Town attracts families to the northwest corner of the park, especially on Sunday mornings when a visit there can be combined with a ride on a miniature steam-powered train at the adjacent Live Steamers. Sadly, maintaining and improving playground equipment seems not to be a priority, but the best children's play areas are along the eastern perimeter—Riverside Drive Recreation Center, Crystal Springs, and within the Zoo. In the western spur of the park is a playground with the best view and decent equipment, adjacent to Lake Hollywood (which is surrounded by a flat roadway for running and cycling) at one end of a flat ridge of land where dogs are allowed to run free, and right beneath the Hollywood sign (from Beachwood Dr., left on Ledgewood Dr. to its terminus at Mulholland Hwy., then left again).

Ferndell, entered near Western Avenue and Los Feliz Boulevard at the southwestern corner of the park, is a shady green glen cooled by a brook—which lures deer from the dry hills for a drink—and filled with flowers and 140 different species of ferns, making it a lovely place to stroll on a summer day.

Griffith Observatory

2800 E. Observatory Rd.
Los Angeles 90027
*213-664-1181
www.griffithobs.org
Tues.–Fri. 2–10 p.m., Sat.–Sun. 12:30–10 p.m.
Entry: free
Planetarium shows: Tues.–Sun. 3 and 7:30 p.m.;
Sat.–Sun. 3, 4:30, 7:30 p.m.
Entry: adults $4, seniors $3, children 5–12 $2
Laserium shows: Tues.–Thurs., Sun. 3 and 7:30 p.m.;
Fri.–Sat. 6, 8:45, 9:45 p.m.
Entry: adults $7, seniors, kids 5–12 $6
Children under 5 are only admitted to
the planetarium show Voyage to the Planets,
Sat.–Sun. 1:30 p.m.; they are not admitted
to any other planetarium or laserium shows

The image of Los Angeles on the cover of this book was shot from the terrace of the Griffith Observatory using a panoramic camera.

It's a landmark recognizable to anyone who has ever approached LAX by air on a clear day, the bulbous white building set on an undeveloped mountain at the northern edge of the heavily built-up L.A. basin. The view from the terrace of the Griffith Observatory can also be awe-inspiring—not for a panorama of the heavens, as its planners envisioned in the era before electricity dimmed the vista of stars from urban areas—but because it encompasses the whole built landscape and the context in which it has grown. From the hills east of downtown to the high-rise towers of downtown, through the developed commercial corridor along Wilshire Boulevard to the business center of Santa Monica and the shining Pacific beyond, the sprawling city is laid out below. The landscape can be examined in more detail with coin telescopes around the Observatory grounds—unless the view is hidden, as it too often is, by a white haze.

Colonel J. W. Eddy, who built Angels Flight to transport people up Bunker Hill in downtown Los Angeles, in 1902 proposed a similar funicular to transport visitors to an observatory and other developments on the highest peak in Griffith Park (now known as Mount Hollywood). His plan included a 2,000-foot-long street railroad up Vermont Avenue, where people would board the funicular; this plan pleased the other colonel, G. J. Griffith, who had given the land for the park and impatiently waited for the city to build roads that would allow people access to this open space. A decade later, with Eddy's plan still on the drawing board, Griffith pledged $100,000 for construction of the observatory, but he wouldn't fund the funicular or other commercial attractions at the peak. Griffith's interest in the observatory was metaphysical as much as scientific: viewing the heavens through the telescope at Mt. Wilson had given him a new perspective. "Man's sense of values

ought to be revised. If all mankind could look through that telescope, it would revolutionize the world," he is reported to have exclaimed. But at his death in 1919, construction had not yet begun, and certain provisions of his will would have to be overturned before it could commence. The public was first invited to view the night sky on May 14, 1935.

The three domes that define the Observatory's silhouette also reveal its main functions: at the west end is a triple-beam solar telescope, at the east, the twelve-inch Zeiss refracting telescope, and in between, the large central dome that forms the planetarium. The Hall of Science Museum, which Griffith had included in his proposals for the Observatory, fills the corridors with exhibits that popularize scientific principles but reflect technological advances he never could have imagined. There are two interactive computer stations where the visitor can explore files on the moon, solar eclipses, galaxies, radio astronomy, the nature of light, and many other topics; challenging multiple-choice quizzes evaluate what's been learned. Less-sophisticated games, which allow children to match descriptions of constellations or other astronomical features with images of them, are very popular. A globe six-feet-three-inches in diameter—a scale of 106 miles

The Sky Report (*213-663-8174) is a three-minute recorded message, changed every Wednesday, with enough information to stimulate an excursion to view the night sky.

The art deco Griffith Observatory starred in its first movie, *Rebel Without a Cause*, in 1955, and now about sixty productions film there annually.

to the inch—completes its rotation in three minutes. My son enjoys the exhibits on meteorites, with samples and guides for recognizing them and information on Leonid meteor showers, which pelt the earth with debris every thirty-three years—140 meteors per second were recorded in 1966. Mark your calendars: the next event is predicted for November 18, 1999.

The problems with the Hubble space telescope during its shakedown phase are dwarfed by its potential: it can see seven times farther into the depth of space, detect objects fifty times fainter, and view them ten times more clearly than ground observation, thus expanding the universe available to man by 350 times. The high points of *Voyager*'s twelve-year odyssey through the solar system are chronicled in startling photographs it recorded before it passed Neptune in 1989 and headed off into the stars. Other exhibits include a camera obscura, which views the Observatory's lawn—on this night crowded with people sharing various telescopic devices to get a better view of the Hale-Bopp comet—and an explanation of the Aztec calendar stone, which reflects the sophisticated understanding of astronomy that enabled this early civilization to predict solar events.

Griffith had proposed a motion-picture theater in the Observatory plans, and some historians have asserted that he anticipated the popular planetarium shows; that technology had not been developed during his lifetime, but it was a centerpiece when the Observatory opened in 1935. My husband claims the show is little changed from his childhood visits, but it may just be the simple wooden folding chairs and all the faces lifted toward the illuminated dome that makes you remember the kid who heard this astounding information way back when. Whatever the reason, the planetarium show is a great way to recover something we've lost: not just personal memories but a clear view of the starry expanse that surrounds our planet. There's a charge for planetarium and laser-light-and-music shows (twice daily on weekdays, four times daily on weekends), and be aware that children under five are admitted only to a special show (Sat., Sun., 1:30 p.m.) geared to this age group.

Travel Town Museum

5200 Zoo Dr.
Los Angeles 90027
*213-662-5874
Mon.–Fri. 10 a.m.–5 p.m., Sat.–Sun. 10 a.m.–6 p.m.
(closes 1 hr. later in the summer)
Entry: free

The main entrance to this transportation museum at the northwest corner of Griffith Park is a train station where visitors can board a miniature train that runs around the perimeter of the site, giving riders an overview of the collection of railroad locomotives and cars. Kids are welcome to climb into the equipment (wherever stairs have been installed for access) and imagine themselves the engineer of a steam locomotive or passenger in a parlor car.

While the oldest artifact is a circus wagon built in 1850 and there is also a horse-drawn Carnation milk-delivery truck, railroad equipment is the heart of the collection. Travel Town has fourteen steam locomotives and two operating diesel locomotives, along with many other pieces that document the role of the railways in developing the West. A super-luxurious club car, "The Little Nugget," from Union Pacific's City of Los Angeles, and a gas-powered rail motorcar from the Atchison, Topeka and Santa Fe are slowly being restored. On the first Sunday of each month, Travel Town's preservation groups offer docent-led tours of the passenger cars or rides on a caboose pulled by diesel locomotives.

The building in the center of the museum park houses a great collection of fire engines and historical exhibits on fighting fires in Los Angeles. It is also home to East Valley Railroad (*213–662–2311), whose N-gauge model trains run in a complex environment of bridges and track through mountains and villages; they are maintained by a group of serious train buffs. In exchange for space at the museum, the East Valley Railroad agreed that members will be present on weekends so visitors can see the model trains in operation. Dedicated in 1952, Travel Town was refurbished a decade ago by the Department of Recreation and Parks.

The airplanes, cars, and trucks (and even a ship model) that had been crammed into the museum building and grounds were dispersed to other institutions throughout the state in order to achieve a cohesive collection. The full-scale two-mile railroad that was envisioned to link Travel Town to the zoo and Autry Museum has not progressed, stymied by the estimated $500,000 needed to construct it.

The line forms early on Sunday mornings at **Live Steamers**, small-scale steam trains operated by another group of rail fans who built a two-mile, elevated track on park land just east of Travel Town (5202 Zoo Dr.; *213-669-9729); it's worth the wait to get a free ride on these lovingly maintained trains (Sun. only, 11 a.m.–3 p.m.).

Los Angeles Zoo

5333 Zoo Dr.
Los Angeles 90027
*213-666-4090
www.lazoo.org
Daily 10 a.m.–5 p.m.
Entry: adults $8.25, seniors $5.25, children 2–12 $3.25

Nearly fifty thousand families support the zoo's activities as members of the Greater Los Angeles Zoo Association (GLAZA) and every year 1.4 million people visit the eighty-acre park near the confluence of the Golden State (5) and Ventura (134) Freeways at the northeast corner of Griffith Park. Voters approved $23 million for zoo improvements in a bond measure, which will go a long way toward making this a zoological park that fulfills its educational mission and becomes a point of pride for the city. The first phase of construction on the **Great Ape Forest,** estimated to cost $12 million, has already begun; the gunite cliffs where the chimpanzees have lived since the zoo opened in 1966 will be replaced with grass and wooden climbing structures. Exhibits will be designed to encourage interaction between human visitors and their cousins: chimps will be able to shower visitors with a cool mist by

Los Angeles Equestrian Center (480 Riverside Dr., Burbank; 818-840-9063) is the site of the annual San Fernando Valley Fair. This four-day event, which just celebrated its fiftieth anniversary, displays winning entries in several pavilions—farming, gardening and floral, and "home arts," which encompasses everything from baked goods to crafts—and has all the elements of an old-time country fair, with livestock exhibits, carnival rides, and rodeo performances.

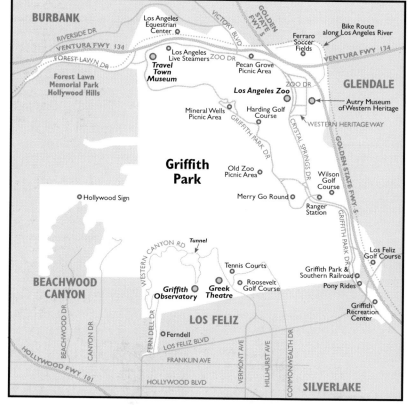

pulling a cord. The animal collection is being reduced, enabling fewer species to share a larger space, and veterinary facilities are being upgraded.

The zoo is a living museum, with more than 1,200 mammals, birds, amphibians, and reptiles representing 400 species in its exhibits, and it participates in forty different Species Survival Plans to bring animals like the California condor back from the brink of extinction. Winding pathways—perfect for pushing a stroller—lead through grounds landscaped with plants from around the world; the zoo has applied for status as a botanical garden. There is an inexpensive shuttle bus that circulates around the grounds so visitors can target a particular area to explore or avoid tiring walks from one area to another.

In many sections, only barriers of water or space separate visitors from animals. Flamingos, monkeys, and meerkats greet visitors along the entrance walkway. Aquatic animals—penguins, polar bears, gray seals, California sea otters—are displayed in one section; an enclosed tree-filled environment serves as a huge aviary, with hundreds of birds hopping and flying overhead, while hill-dwelling animals live in the steep perimeter of the exhibits.

The Ahmanson Koala House, a habitat that replicates a coastal eucalyptus forest, was unique when it opened in 1983 and has recently been refurbished with a mural depicting these animals' native habitat in Australia. The darkened environment simulates dusk or dawn, when koalas are most active; human visitors relax in the mentholated air and cool quiet space. As eyes adjust to the dim light, motion betrays the presence of nocturnal natives. The koalas stay high in the trees, while squirrel gliders and high-flying possums flit quietly past. Bettongs (brush-tailed rat kangaroos) and echidnas (spiny anteaters) rustle among fallen leaves on the ground.

Adventure Island is a zoo environment for small children, with animal displays sited specifically for their eye level. There is a cave with blind fish and a spelunking display, as well as the animal nursery, where recent arrivals from the breeding programs are on view. A recently refurbished play-

Zoo Camp, offered six times each summer, is a popular week-long day camp. Kids in grades one to six can choose between two themes for their sessions (daily 9 a.m.–3 p.m.). Two weeks of morning sessions (daily 9 a.m.–noon) for kids from age four to kindergarten have been added, and more advanced programs are offered for kids in grades seven and eight. Animals and conservation are the focus of the activities, which include sports, arts and crafts projects, and interactive visits to zoo exhibits and behind-the-scenes facilities. Call *213-666-4650 for an application and information about fees.

ground in the Eurasian sector is a favorite destination for little ones, and the trek to it allows kids to view tigers, rhinoceroses, and baboons, or visit the reptile house. Animals and You and The World of Birds are shows held daily at the zoo, and wardens share their experiences and answer questions in daily talks (schedules are posted at the information kiosk).

Education is the primary function of the zoo, and its low-cost field trips are among the most popular destinations for school groups (reservations are required: *213-663-4819). Wild About Science workshops for teachers are offered throughout the year, and award-winning Zoo Discovery Kits help educators prepare for a visit. Every month, weekday programs especially for preschoolers are offered, as well as Saturday programs that allow older kids to learn more about one type of animal in each session or to deepen their knowledge by attending regularly throughout the year. The Curator's Series, two-hour programs for adults only, allows grown-ups to learn more about the different categories of animals that share our world.

Special events include: family sleepovers called Sundown Safaris, Zoo Snooze (which allows seven- to ten-year-olds to experience how animals are cared for after the grounds close), as well as family camp-

ing trips to places like Leo Carrillo Beach and Sequoia National Forest. Art classes use the animals as models, even teaching cartooning techniques, and photo safaris offer tips for creative use of camera equipment. Music in the Zoo is part of the summertime fun: gates open at 6 p.m. and picnic suppers can be preordered; after the music has stopped, take a twilight stroll through the exhibits (flashlights come in handy). On Wild Weekends during the summer, the zoo is open until 7 p.m., with food, music, puppets, performances, and extra shows of The World of Birds as added attractions.

Autry Museum of Western Heritage

4700 Western Heritage Way
Los Angeles 90027
*213-667-2000
Tues.–Sun. 10 a.m.–5 p.m.
Entry: adults $7.50, seniors/students $5,
children 2–12 $3.50

When it opened in 1989, the museum had a difficult time establishing its identity. The museum, which celebrates the changing culture of the lands west of the Mississippi, would not exist without Gene Autry's generosity—it was built with a $54-million gift from the Autry Foundation—but with his name, many visitors expected that the museum would focus on the cowboy ethos or would exhibit Autry's personal collection. The permanent exhibits were developed to support the California history curriculum in school. They are well-thought out and nicely displayed—Walt Disney Imagineering did the design and painted large murals on canvas throughout the galleries. Those who took the time to visit the new museum were quickly convinced of its educational value, and for many families it tops the list of cultural activities that their kids really enjoy. The Autry has continued to define Western heritage with excellent changing exhibitions, both those that it originates and those organized by other institutions.

INDEPENDENT SPIRITS
Women Painters of the American West, 1890–1945
Edited by
Patricia Trenton

Its name remained a stumbling block, so it was altered in 1996 to emphasize "Western Heritage," which is the museum's real focus; however, a cowboy on horseback with lasso is still the museum's logo and is emblazoned on stickers worn by every visitor, which seems to suggest that its image might need still more retooling. Or so I thought until the day my son learned that there was a nearby museum with a lot of cowboy stuff and insisted that we visit that afternoon. Pausing just long enough to view a temporary exhibition on California Indian baskets, we headed straight for the **Spirit of the Cowboy Gallery**, then worked our way backward through the galleries on the lower level. I began to appreciate the educational structure of the exhibits as I responded to his questions. The gallery that holds the matchless Colt collection of 160 guns—purchased from the firm whose founder, Samuel C. Colt, invented the first commercially successful revolver in 1834—was the right environment to correct his

assumption that the cowboys won the West "because they were stronger." Modern technology and better equipment gave them the advantage, Mom explained, but it also bred a climate of violence, a point reinforced by a reenactment of the shootout at O.K. Corral that drove the Earp brothers from Tombstone, Arizona. Displays in a rogue's gallery of infamous outlaws ask whether there was a "gun that won the West" and concludes that the 1873 Colt revolver was the most popular weapon.

The Anheuser-Busch Gallery not only contains a massive carved wood bar built in 1880 for a saloon in Wilbaux, Montana, but its exhibits demonstrate the wild lifestyles that evolved in the virtual absence of family life. There are Tiffany poker chips from the 1880s, a whole collection of cheating devices, like reflector rings that could be used to identify face-down cards, and a circa 1905 wheel of fortune made by an Illinois firm that specialized in making rigged gambling devices. Oscar Berninghaus's painting of a mule train carrying cases of beer was an advertisement for Anheuser-Busch; it once hung in a Saint Louis men's club.

The newly designed **Spirit of Community** exhibit includes an original ornate 1873 fire engine, making the point that a settlement had reached a crucial stage in its development when it organized a volunteer fire brigade. There is a collection of signs advertising essential services (hotels, dentists, pawnshops) and products (sewing machines, plows, stoves). The role played by Mormons in settling the west is examined in a display that explains their journey along the Oregon Trail to the Utah desert and the communities they founded there.

The evolution of Western culture over time is chronicled in galleries dedicated to native populations, Spanish settlers, and American pioneers who colonized the new territories. Although settlers, who needed to haul a ton of seeds and farm equipment to establish a ranch, quickly disposed of almost everything extraneous, the museum has assembled an impressive collection of early artifacts, including a spectacular Saltillo serape, a haunting stone figure, and beaded umbilical cord amulets made by Native-Americans. A replica of a stagecoach is displayed on a rutted unpaved road to evoke the arduous journeys undertaken by settlers; it will soon be replaced with the last remaining Concord stagecoach, newly restored with funds from a private donor. The view from the main stairway includes the **Trails West Garden**, which depicts with different rock installations and plants the various routes pioneers followed to the West; beyond the garden one can see the intersection of the Golden State and Ventura Freeways, a reminder of contemporary transportation problems.

Having completed the circuit of downstairs galleries, we returned to the Spirit of the Cowboy Gallery, where I enjoyed Maynard Dixon's pencil sketches and N. C. Wyeth's painting *Bucking Bronco,* which was the cover illustration for the *Saturday Evening Post* in February 1903; my son ogled the fine boots, spurs, and saddles used mainly for rodeo competitions. One sequence of displays presents an annual chronology of ranching activities, with heavy fur costumes to ward off the winter winds, beat-up boots caked in mud, and a chuckwagon. Then we were ready to explore the **Los Angeles Times Children's Discovery Gallery,** where my son donned miniature leather chaps, red boots with silver spurs, a bandanna, and felt hat, then climbed into the saddle to swing his lasso and live out a little boy's fantasy—with a clearer understanding of the historical reality that inspired it. In the Discovery Gallery children can also pick up old-fashioned toys, scrub clothes on a corrugated metal washboard and run them through a wringer, and get a kid's perspective on life in the frontier.

Thomas Moran's 1875 painting *Mountain of the Holy Cross* hangs at the entrance to the **Spirit of Romance Gallery;** other images suggest how the harsh reality of frontier life was transformed by such beliefs as Manifest Destiny and by the artists' awe at the natural beauty of the West. Exhibits trace the myth and reality of cowboy imagery, from its first use in Wild West shows, to its pervasive presence in film and television, and finally to its place as popular-culture icon. Here you'll find an exhibit devoted to Gene Autry, as well as other highlights of the cowboy genre, including a child's bedroom from the 1950s entirely decorated in a Hopalong Cassidy motif. In the theater, a ten-minute video recapitulates the history of the West; Classic Western films and serials are screened nearly every weekend (members $1, nonmembers $3) in the **Wells Fargo Theater** on the plaza.

The 7,000-square-foot **George Montgomery Gallery** on the upper floor is reserved for changing exhibitions; these expand upon the museum's own holdings and allow it to examine other themes relating to the heritage of the West. "Independent Spirits" (1995) identified women artists throughout the western states; "Western Wonderlands" (1997) explored

Free arts and crafts workshops for children are held on the first Saturday of every month (1:30–3:30 p.m.). On both Saturdays and Sundays of each month's first weekend, a film series, like California's Chronicle: Through the Lens of Hollywood, is screened at 2 p.m. in the Wells Fargo Theater. Classes for children and adults are offered year-round, and week-long summer programs for kids explore different themes with hands-on activities; for education department programming, call *213-667-2000, extension 341.

the history of national parks in the West and their role in the tourist trade; and "Powerful Images," a collaborative effort by a consortium of ten museums, will examine how Native-American people have been portrayed since the time of Columbus and will debunk stereotypes that have been promulgated by such imagery.

KCET, Channel 28

4401 Sunset Blvd.
Los Angeles 90028
*213-666-6500
Tours by appt. only
Entry: free

Few cultural institutions have the potential impact of KCET, which is present in every home with a television set. There is no charge for its programming (although contributions from its subscribers and benefactors are essential), nor is there any effort (beyond changing the channel) required to experience how good our culture's most popular medium can be. You can experience what KCET has to offer without leaving your home, so why travel to the east side of Hollywood to see its headquarters? Perhaps your time would be better spent enjoying KCET's fine programming. The centerpiece of its morning Ready-to-Learn schedule of children's programming is *Storytime,* which features some fine actors reading to a small, live audience and discussing books with the kids. KCET produces the program, which reaches a national audience through the enthusiastic support of other public television stations, and it is one example of KCET realizing its goal to act as PBS's gateway to Hollywood. The weeknight series *Life and Times,* which uses different formats—talking heads who span the political spectrum, mini-documentaries, and live broadcasts— to survey the sociopolitical structure of Southern California life, gets the largest chunk of the station's production budget and has garnered an Emmy in return. Huell Howser's *California Gold* series continues to reveal nuggets of charm and history throughout the state and commands a large and loyal audience.

Today, the center of KCET's existence is a huge satellite dish and a modern three-story administration building, but it is located on a motion-picture studio lot that has been little altered since it was constructed (circa 1912–20). The old red-brick buildings are separated by narrow passageways; many were originally covered with glass roofs because sunlight was needed to supplement the electric lights in the studios. In the 1920s Charles Ray built an enormous studio-cum-pool in which two full-size

The Thai community is well established in this part of Hollywood—check out Thai Plaza and Food Court (a few blocks west of Barnsdall just before Western Ave.), which has an ethnic supermarket on the ground floor and offers food service from a dozen vendors; tables provide a view of a stage where there are live performances in the evenings and of a large screen where music videos are often projected. For the past five years Barnsdall Park has been the site of a September festival celebrating Thai culture which is coordinated by the Thai Community Arts and Cultural Center of Los Angeles (310-827-2910). Despite its name, the Thai Cultural Center has no public facility, just an office in Marina del Rey, but it hopes one day to have a permanent showcase in this community for Thai culture.

galleons were floated for the filming of *The Courtship of Miles Standish.* Unfortunately the picture bombed at the box office and bankrupted Ray, who subsequently sold the lot.

The only production set, Studio A, is used for the filming of *Life and Times.* The entire studio is wrapped in a seamless cyclorama that provides a neutral backdrop, and no expense has been spared to create flooring that is smooth and level so cameras glide, not lurch. The tour guide explained the functions of the sound studio and the control room and the process by which a satellite transmission is monitored and broadcast. This is a low-key, no-frills tour of a small facility that may not interest youngsters accustomed to amusement parks, but volunteers hope to increase community awareness of KCET through the program—a noble goal.

At Wat Thai Temple in North Hollywood (8225 Coldwater Canyon; 818-780-4200) Buddhists from various denominations gather to celebrate Buddha's birthday around the time of the full moon in May (see Finding God, p. 145).

especially important in a time of decreased federal funding—has grown to 135,000 nationally; member benefits include discounts on local workshops plus notification of ongoing programs and screenings.

AFI presents films locally during the annual AFI Los Angeles Film Festival—two busy weeks, variously scheduled in spring and fall—and hosts an annual International Filmfest early in the summer; call *213-856-7707 for information about submitting films or for screening schedules. In 1997 AFI inaugurated online screenings of film classics on its Web site with Buster Keaton's 1921 feature *The Boat,* which was replaced after six weeks with Harold Lloyd's 1920 classic, *High and Dizzy;* there are lots of other reasons to check out the Web site. The Louis B. Mayer library, a noncirculating reading and reference facility on campus, is dedicated to the history of film, television, video, and motion-picture technology. The public is welcome to use this resource (Mon.–Thurs. 10 a.m.–5 p.m.; Fri. 1–5 p.m., Sat. 10 a.m.–4 p.m.; *213-856-7654), but hours may be limited during summer months.

As a national organization, AFI maintains a presence in Washington, D.C., where it offers film programs at the AFI Theater at the Kennedy Center and maintains archives and databases at the Library of Congress. The annual AFI Life Achievement Awards, one of the most prestigious awards given to honor a career in film, is also one of the Institute's highest-profile events, broadcast nationally in a star-studded TV gala.

American Film Institute (AFI)

2021 N. Western Ave.
Los Angeles 90027
*213-856-7600
www.afionline.org

The nonprofit American Film Institute was created in 1967 as part of the same legislation that established the National Endowment for the Arts, and its funding has been sorely affected by Congressional assaults on that agency. It is charged with advancing the arts of film, television, and other forms of the moving image, a goal it satisfies by "training the next generation of filmmakers, presenting the moving image in its many forms, preserving the American film heritage, and redefining the moving image in the digital era." AFI's professional training seminars are modeled on a European-style conservancy and include such programs as the Directing Workshop for Women and the Television Writers Workshop held at the Los Feliz campus. Other programs explore the newest technologies, such as digital graphics and online media, at its state-of-the art labs; call 800-999-4AF1 for more information. Membership in AFI (800-347-6868)—which provides financial support for its programs,

Barnsdall Art Park

4800 Hollywood Blvd.
Los Angeles 90027

Aline Barnsdall (1882–1946) was an heiress who used the fortune her grandfather built after drilling the second oil-producing well in the United States to finance her extensive philanthropy. Her primary artistic interests were poetry and theater, which led her to Chicago, where she served as codirector of an experimental theater and met Frank Lloyd Wright. Following a trip to California in 1915, she commissioned Wright to design a house for her, as well as a theater, a movie house, residences for directors and actors, and studios, and shops for artists on a thirty-six-acre site known as Olive Hill, at the eastern edge of Hollywood. Financial and artistic differences between architect and client reduced the scope of the arts park that she intended to foster, but today Barnsdall's **Hollyhock House** is the centerpiece of one of the most active outposts of the Los Angeles Department of Cultural Affairs, which offers inexpensive art classes for kids at the **Junior Arts Center** and for adults at the **Barnsdall Art Center,** schedules events at three cultural facilities and in the park itself, and organizes exhibitions at the **Municipal Art Gallery.** The construction of a Metro Rail stop has obscured the entrance to the Art Park, but it will eventually make the facility more accessible, and funding to restore the park's landscaping is included in the budget for Metro construction.

Hollyhock House

4800 Hollywood Blvd.
Los Angeles 90027
*213-662-7272
By guided tour only: Wed.–Sun., on the hour,
noon–3 p.m. Reservations for groups of 10 or more:
213-913-4157
Entry: adults $2, seniors/students over 12 $1,
children under 12 free; purchase tickets at
Municipal Art Gallery

Frank Lloyd Wright's first commission in Los Angeles was to realize Aline Barnsdall's vision of an artists' community in the young city. The opportunity led Wright away from the Midwest and allowed him to adapt his distinctive style to a new geography and climate. He in-

tended to create a house unlike any other, and he seemed to have felt that he met that goal, writing in his autobiography, "In any expression of the human spirit it is principle, manifest as character, that alone endures. Individuality is the true property of character. Hollyhock House is such a house." Hollyhock House (1917–20) has a dramatic plan that incorporates gardens in generous proportion to interior spaces, and uses changes in ceiling height to signal transitions from room to room. Such theatrical spaces as an interior courtyard with a stage at one end and rooftops to elevate performers (or audiences) may have been inspired by the original plan for Barnsdall's commission.

Its sobriquet, Hollyhock House, is derived from the principal decorative motif Wright used—stylized stalks of the flower that grew wild and in abundance on the property before it was developed. The flower also decorates the straight-back dining chairs, the only original Wright furnishings in the house. Reproductions of Wright's furniture which now fill the main rooms of the house were installed during a recent renovation. It has been scarred (most recently by the 1994 earthquake) but remains a great house with spectacular city views, a fitting centerpiece to the community Aline Barnsdall started but abandoned.

The heiress blamed Wright for the failure of her plan because he was increasingly occupied with building the Imperial Hotel in Tokyo and rarely at the site of her job in Los Angeles. Her pique at the treatment she received from the great man inspired Wright to import a suitable surrogate to oversee the construction at Olive Hill and appease the client: R. M. Schindler came to Los Angeles to help the Wright studio fulfill the Barnsdall commission. His design influence is most evident in Residence A (1920), now the Barnsdall Art Center. Wright's son Lloyd was also instrumental in completing the commission, and his grandson Eric participated in the recent renovation.

Wright's June birthday is the occasion of an annual festival that has included photography seminars with the Hollyhock House as subject, architectural workshops, and a treasure hunt. One-act plays written by local kids are performed in the Gallery Theater, and musical performances animate the lawns. The annual Children's Festival of the Arts on an August weekend features the hands-on activities kids like best—face-painting, making silly hats and scary masks—as well as storytelling and music; and in December the annual Open House includes offerings for all ages, with a sale of ceramics, crafts, jewelry, and paintings, as well as performances and special exhibitions in both the Municipal Gallery and the Junior Arts Center Gallery.

Junior Arts Center
4814 Hollywood Blvd.
Los Angeles 90027
213-485-4474

For thirty years the Junior Arts Center has nurtured potential artists from age three with an extensive and excellent program of studio classes taught by professional artists and some of the best art educators in the city. The ambitious schedule includes four sessions, each about two months long (beginning in Oct., Jan., Apr., and July), along with a special month-long holiday session in December. Registration for these extremely popular classes starts six weeks before each session. The youngest children can take parent/child classes, which often involve making different kinds of puppets or simple musical instruments. Beginning photography for kids eight and older, more advanced labs for teenagers, and filming music videos are popular classes; the urge to build is channeled productively to making model planes and cars or designing furniture and other usable objects; and basic skills are developed in

---

The relentless march of private housing, from the fledgling city's downtown core toward the west, reached the Los Feliz-Silverlake area by the 1920s, coincident with the arrival or maturation of some of the finest architects working in the modernist aesthetic, leaving this area with a legacy of historic architecture. Most of these buildings are privately owned and should be viewed from the street without disturbing residents. Some of the most spectacular houses were built on canyon ridges in the foothills of Griffith Park (off map), including Richard Neutra's 1929 Lovell House (4616 Dundee Dr.), which was recently featured in the film *L.A. Confidential,* and Frank Lloyd Wright's 1924 Ennis-Brown House (2607 Glendower Ave.), a monumental example of the four cast-block houses Wright built in Southern California (to visit it, write for reservations or call *213-668-0234).

Lloyd Wright

1. **Taggart House** (1922–24) 5423 Black Oak Drive
2. **Carr House** (1925) southeast corner of Lowry Road and Rowena Avenue
3. **Farrell House** (1926) 3209 Lowry Road
4. **Sowden House** (1926) 5121 Franklin Avenue
5. **Samuels-Novarro House** (1926–28) 5522 Verde Oak Drive

R. M. Schindler

6. **Howe House** (1925) 2422 Silver Ridge Avenue
7. **Sachs Apts.** (1926–40) 1811-30 Edgecliffe Drive

8. **Elliot House** (1930) 4237 Newdale Drive
9. **Falk Apts.** (1939–40) 3631 Carnation Avenue
10. **Bubeshko Apts.** (1938, 1941) 2036 Griffith Park Boulevard
11. **Oliver House** (1933–34) 2236 Micheltorena Street
12. **Van Patten House** (1934–35) 2320 Moreno Drive
13. **McAlmon House** (1935) 2717-21 Waverly Drive
14. **Walker House** (1935–36) 2100 Kenilworth Avenue
15. **Wilson House** (1935–39) 2090 Redcliffe Street
16. **Droste House** (1940) 2025 Kenilworth Avenue

On Waverly Drive, along with Schindler's McAlmon House, is one of the rare Southern California homes built by Bernard Maybeck, who is better known for the 1915 Palace of Fine Arts in San Francisco and a wide range of domestic and public buildings he designed in Berkeley, starting with Christian Science Church (1910). The Anthony House (1927), 3412 Waverly Drive, was an unusually flamboyant design, purposefully eclectic, so it would appear that the structure reflected many generations of alterations, like an old European family seat. The client, a very successful Packard dealer, compiled photographs of Gothic castles on his European trips and purchased stone in Caen and roof tiles in Barcelona, which Maybeck incorporated in the building, which cost half a million dollars to construct.

Raphael Soriano

17. **Lipetz House** (1935) 1843 N. Dillon Street
18. **Gogol House** (1938–39) 2190 Talmadge Street
19. **Schrage House** (1951) 2648 Commonwealth Avenue

life drawing, illustration, nature, and landscape painting. During the summer session, "art camp" combines morning and afternoon classes with a supervised lunch and is offered several days each week, and the array of art classes is even more extensive. Most classes for children five and up are held from 3 to 5 p.m. on weekdays (with a few early evening classes that allow working parents to participate), and all day on Saturdays; the cost of an eight-week session ranges from $18 to $40. Call 213-485-4474 for information about schedules and registration.

The Ragan Art Academy, an intensive two-year art program for teenagers, offers students a strong foundation in visual arts. In four eight-week classes per year, students learn art history, explore various studio art skills, and are taught how to develop a portfolio. Call Friends of the Junior Arts Center (*213-660-3362) for more information.

The Junior Arts Center Gallery (Wed.–Sun. 12:30–5 p.m.; free), formerly a venue for children's art, now also presents exhibitions curated by the Municipal Art Gallery staff. Selections from the International Child Art Collection and student work are often featured in one of its spaces; other exhibitions have included entries for the annual Billboard Project or fine children's books for suggested summer reading.

Sunday Open Sunday, free family workshops that originated years ago at the Junior Arts Center, are still frequently held here, but the program has been expanded citywide to other centers managed by the Cultural Affairs Department and in community sites throughout the county. The schedule of programs—which are held from 2 to 4 p.m. on thirty-five weekends throughout the year—is available at Barnsdall Park, or call the Friends of the Junior Arts Center (*213-660-3362) to receive it by mail.

Free storytelling and children's films are scheduled periodically at the Gallery Theater, usually at noon on Saturdays during the school year. Performances are often followed by a hands-on activity, and juice and cookies are served. Call 213-485-0709 for the storytelling schedule, and 213-485-4581 for the Children's Film Series.

John Lautner

20. Lautner House (1939) 2007 Micheltorena Street

21. Silvertop (1957) 2138 Micheltorena Street

Gregory Ain

22. Edwards House (1936) 5642 Holly Oak Drive

23. Ernest House (1937) 5670 Holly Oak Drive

24. Daniels House (1939) 1856 Micheltorena Street

25. Tierman House (1939) 2323 Micheltorena Street

26. Orans House (1940) 2404 Micheltorena Street

Harwell H. Harris

27. Alexander House (1940) 2265 Micheltorena Street

28. Hansen House (1951) 2305 W. Silver Lake Drive

Richard Neutra developed the area adjacent to his own home (see p. 96) from 1948 to 1962, creating a small colony (all denoted **29**) that expressed his vision of urban life.

Treweek House (1948) 2250 E. Silver Lake Boulevard

Sokol House (1948) 2242 E. Silver Lake Boulevard

Reunion House (1949) 2440 Earl Street

Yew House (1957) 2226 E. Silver Lake Boulevard

Flavin House (1958) 2218 Neutra Place

Inadomi House (1960) 2238 E. Silver Lake Boulevard

Kambara House (1960) 2232 E. Silver Lake Boulevard

O'Hara House (1961) 2210 Neutra Place

Akai House (1962) 2200 Neutra Place

30. Mosk House (1933) 2742 Hollyridge Drive

31. McIntosh House (1937) 1317 Maltman Avenue

Barnsdall Art Center

4800 Hollywood Blvd.
Los Angeles 90027
213-485-2116

Older students and adults attend studio classes in a structure designed by Frank Lloyd Wright in 1919 as the Director's House and often identifed as Residence A on the architect's plans. Quarterly sessions, comprising eight or nine classes, are so popular that registration is held one Saturday at the beginning of each quarter, when 90 percent of the available spaces will be filled in a lottery. The low fees (about $60 per class) are one reason for their popularity, but the range of classes—jewelry, printmaking, ceramics, design, weaving, life drawing, and photography—taught by talented professionals inspires a loyal group of students who return to explore a new medium or repeat a favorite class semester after semester. Call 213-485-2116 to be placed on the mailing list.

Municipal Art Gallery
Gallery Theater

4804 Hollywood Blvd.
Los Angeles 90027
213-485-4581
Wed.–Sun. 12:30–5 p.m., Fri. 12:30–8:30 p.m.
Entry: adults $1.50, children under 12 free

The Municipal Art Gallery presents exhibitions of community interest as well as contemporary art in a flexible 10,000-square-foot space. The gallery, which has no permanent collection, faces the continual challenge of discovering the fresh and topical—a daunting task—and is often the first venue to exhibit work by local artists. A joint exhibition of works by the dozen individual artists chosen as COLA award recipients (the acronym refers to City of Los Angeles and to the revamped city grant program) is a new feature of the gallery schedule. The biennial juried exhibition of Southern California artists is the primary summer exhibition in odd-numbered years at four of the art centers run by the City of Los Angeles Cultural Affairs Department, including the Municipal Gallery.

Conversations with the Artists and Walkthroughs with the Curator (Fri. 7 p.m.) permit visitors a more in-depth understanding of an exhibition and give featured artists an informal forum. Night Readings, also held on Friday nights in the Gallery Theater, present poets and writers whose themes intersect those of the current art exhibition. Barnsdall Artists Cafe: Up on Mondays (Mon. 8 p.m.) are more-or-less monthly performances that draw on various arts disciplines and groups to explore different themes; local dance companies and musicians have been featured, as well as films and readings.

A summer internship in museum administration is offered for graduate and undergraduate students majoring in art history, studio art, or general education. The interns work closely with education department staff members to formulate and execute an innovative gallery education program that is designed to build confidence and the perceptual skills to experience and enjoy art. After an initial training period, interns work on an assigned project and participate in weekly group meetings. The Museum Internship and Education Program also introduces students to career opportunities in art institutions; call 213-485-4581 for information about the program.

Neutra House
VDL Research House

2300 E. Silver Lake Blvd.
Los Angeles 90039
By appt. only: 909-869-2667

The house Richard Neutra built for his own family in 1933 was named for the Dutch patron C. H. Van der Leeuw, whose largesse allowed the young architect who had lived in Rudolph Schindler's communal studio/living space on King's Road to attempt his own version. Neutra put the main living space, sleeping porches, and a roof deck on the upper floor of the structure, which permitted a view of the reservoir and flooded it with light reflected from the water; he dedicated the lower level to an open workshop and some rather monastic guest quarters.

When a fire destroyed Neutra's house in 1963, the architect's son Dion, who knew every inch of the original structure from his childhood investigations, designed a new house on the footprint of the original which experimented with new materials to convey the elements of healthful living—water, air, and light—that had defined the previous building. He introduced shallow reflecting pools that bring water right into the house, an aesthetically satisfying idea that is structurally rather dangerous. Mirrored walls and steel stairs and framing (rather than the less-expensive wood dictated by the original budget) reflect light. The house, which was recently granted landmark status, is owned by the School of Environmental Design at California Polytechnic University, Pomona.

Universal Studios Hollywood

100 Universal City Plaza
Universal City 91608
818-508-9600
Daily 9 a.m.–7 p.m. (with extended summer hours);
Memorial Day to Labor Day 7 a.m.–11 p.m

Entry: adults $36, seniors $29, children 3–11 $26

In eighty years these 400 acres at the east end of the San Fernando Valley have gone from chicken ranch to film studio to theme park, and now it's a city, self-proclaimed in letters several stories high intended to be visible from the Hollywood Freeway. Many other cities in the county would envy its economy: a record 43,000 visitors bought tickets to the theme park on one day during a holiday weekend in 1996; at an average of $30 each, that day's gate was $1.3 million—before any of those visitors ate or bought souvenirs. **Universal Amphitheater**, which celebrated its twenty-fifth season in 1997, ranked second among indoor music venues in the United States with 5,000 to 6,999 seats, grossing $13.5 million from eighty-nine shows. Universal City has a huge labor force at both the theme park and working studio, but no residents—only transient guests at its hotels. Without paying for admission to the theme park, the public may only access Universal City's main street, **CityWalk**, an ersatz urban environment isolated at the top of a hill and behind a huge paid-parking garage, where even the "street artists" are screened by management. Security is absolute and abundant creature comforts—from a computer-controlled spouting fountain to bookstores, ice cream shops, and sunny cafe patios—lure five million visitors annually to this pedestrian-friendly zone and the adjacent theme park. The Amphitheater and an eighteen-screen multiplex cinema would certainly attract enough people to support the two blocks of restaurants and shops along CityWalk, even without the overflow from the theme park and hotels, but MCA (the parent company of Universal) has no plans to stop the development that has transformed the Cahuenga Pass in the past decade. Its $2-billion, twenty-five-year plan to create a twenty-four-hour destination

resort was opposed by the two councilmen representing the district, who suggested that doubling the size of the theme park would not add quality jobs to the local economy, but they did approve additions of low-rise hotels and high-quality film-production studios—if they are phased in and their impact on traffic monitored.

Universal Studios Hollywood, the theme park on movie-making, has become the number-two tourist attraction in Southern California (following Disneyland) and is credited by some with fueling a resurgence in that all-important sector of the state's economy. Its budget dwarfs the combined resources of most of the cultural institutions in the county, but as the most accessible view of the film industry that we refer to as "Hollywood," Universal holds a pivotal place in the cultural complex of Los Angeles.

Carl Laemmle charged visitors only 25¢ for a box lunch and access to bleachers overlooking the film lots he built in 1915 on a former chicken ranch, but the presence of visitors on the set became problematic with the advent of sound and tours of Universal Studios ceased until 1964. Now the Backlot Tram Tour is only one option among many offered to visitors, who pass from the entrance through the upper plaza, where thematic streetscapes—including New York, Paris, Cape Cod, and the Western frontier—house retail spaces and restaurants as well as performance spaces. Shows include Animal Actors, Wild West Stunt Show, Waterworld, Beetlejuice's rock revue, and Totally Nickelodeon's just-for-kids audience participation show. At the back of the upper plaza, between two monumental escalators—leading to the newest attractions on the lower lot at one side or to the Backlot Tram Tour on the other—is Back to the Future, The Ride, a roller coaster-cum-time travel machine that allows those not susceptible to motion

sickness to experience (rather than watch) state-of-the-art special effects.

The Backlot Tram Tour is the most sedate choice available, although in the course of visiting many sets and soundstages visitors experience a volcanic eruption and survive an 8.3 earthquake in the San Francisco subway. King Kong and Bruce, the mechanical shark from *Jaws*, make an appearance during the tightly scripted tour, while guides well versed in film lore and trivia interject facts about the many films and TV series produced at Universal. (Visitors not so knowledgeable about American film and TV may be less enthralled; French friends of mine found three-quarters of the references incomprehensible.) Meanwhile the tram passes through graveyards of props and environments that can be adapted to the style and period of particular projects. Among the tour's architectural highlights: the Cleavers' suburban tract house from *Leave It to Beaver;* the fraternity house from *Animal House;* Bates' Motel and the spooky Victorian from *Psycho;* and a Colonial mansion from *Uncle Tom's Cabin.* The largest set is a freestanding backdrop at Fall's Lake, which was painted with water and sky for the splashdown in *Apollo 13* and used as a "green screen" to project special volcanic effects for *Dante's Peak.*

Three flights of escalators scale the other side of the hill and descend to the true theme park plaza, which is anchored by three blockbuster rides: E.T., Jurassic Park, and Backdraft. The first is the only one suitable for the youngest visitors, with lovable little aliens viewed from the safety of a bicycle flying through a misty forest and over the twinkling lights of the city, and out into a star-filled galaxy. Exploding firestorms and pumping adrenaline characterize the experience of Backdraft. Jurassic Park's leafy green world, entered in a twenty-five-passenger raft, rapidly becomes more sinister as rustlings in the bushes become enormous, carnivorous dinosaurs rampaging toward the craft, which almost mercifully goes crashing down an eighty-foot slide to a safe (but wet) landing. A lot more time is spent waiting in long lines than on the actual rides, but they are crammed with special effects to compensate visitors for their patience. Other exhibits include a tribute to Lucille Ball, a show on special effects called the World of Cinemagic, the musical Blues Brothers, and AT&T at the Movies, an interactive video arcade. Like kids who've spent too many hours watching television, the visitor may emerge overstimulated but not sated.

Campo de Cahuenga (3919 Lankershim Blvd., North Hollywood 91602; 818-763-7651; Mon.–Fri. 8 a.m.–2 p.m.; free) is the site where an 1847 treaty was signed to formally end the war between the United States and Mexico, allowing the territory that now includes California and six other states from New Mexico to Wyoming and west to petition for statehood. In a building that simulates the adobe where this document was signed, an exhibit reconstructs this historical moment.

In 1990 a handsome art deco building (5108 Lankershim Blvd., North Hollywood 91601) became the **Lankershim Arts Center**, a community art center that is a linchpin of the fledgling NoHo arts district (Lankershim Blvd. between Magnolia and Chandler Blvds.). Originally sponsored by the Cultural Affairs Department, the Lankershim Arts Center is now operated as a private-public partnership. Call 818-989-8066 or 818-756-8066 for information on current programming. Every June the district celebrates with a weekend theater and arts festival, presenting live theater in several of the twenty local stages and offering music, dance, and performances for kids. The Universal City-North Hollywood Chamber of Commerce (818-508-5155) can provide information and reservations for vendors.

Disney Studios can be glimpsed from the Ventura (134) Freeway; the new headquarters of the animation department (designed by Robert A. M. Stern in 1995) has a wizard's hat over the CEO's office and an eye-catching striated exterior with supergraphics that spell out the facility's function, reminding commuters of its presence in the community. Michael Graves's 1991 administration building has been ridiculed by some architectural critics: "Crowned with a joke pediment—the Seven Dwarfs on steroids," wrote Michael Webb. The general public can form its own opinion as the structure is clearly visible from the street (2100–2300 W. Alameda Blvd., Burbank). There is no public access to the studio lot "for reasons of security," according to a company official, who also acknowledged that the number of paying customers to the Anaheim theme park suggests that business on the lot would be overwhelmed if it were also used as a tourism venue.

Storybook Theater produces quality audience-interactive performances for kids at Theater West (3333 Cahuenga Blvd. W., North Hollywood); call 818-761-2203.

Burbank public libraries offer story times and songs and craft projects on a regular schedule:

Central Library
(110 N. Glenoaks Ave.)
Tuesday 10 a.m.

Northwest Library
(3323 W. Victory Blvd.)
Wednesday 10 a.m

Buena Vista Library
(401 N. Buena Vista St.)
Thursday 10 a.m.

Burbank Farmers Market
Third St. and Orange Grove Ave.
Sat. 8 a.m.–1 p.m.

Woodbury University Art Gallery
(7500 Glenoaks Blvd., Burbank 91510; 818-767-0888) supports the college's programs in architecture and design with changing exhibitions organized by the gallery director, who is also an artist.

Gordon R. Howard Museum Complex

115 N. Lomita St.
Burbank 91506
818-841-6333
Sun. 1–4 p.m.
Entry: free, donations welcomed

Burbank was named for a New Hampshire dentist who in 1871 bought seventy-two acres in the present town; in 1911 it became the Valley's first independent city, with a population of 500. The movie industry has provided an economic base for the city since the 1920s, when production companies began shooting in its wide-open spaces, and the importance of film and entertainment industries in the local economy continues today. Beginning in the late 1930s Lockheed Aircraft created a wartime industrial boom with construction of the Hudson bomber, the P-38, and the PV-1 Ventura; exhibits on these giants of the Burbank economy are displayed in the Gordon R. Howard Museum Complex, named for the local businessman who supported efforts by the Burbank Historical Society (1015 W. Olive Ave.; 818-841-6333) to create a permanent exhibition space. Dioramas with audio highlight daily life in the area, and historic photographs show how the city has changed.

Another building in the complex houses a large collection of antique dolls and dresses, cameras (mostly Kodaks), and some old cars in very fine condition: a 1921 Model T, 1922 Moreland bus, 1934 Packard, and a Mercedes and Rolls-Royce from 1937. Along the main street (Olive Ave.), behind a white picket fence and a colorful flower garden, is the Mentzer House, a "boom house" built in 1887 by Providencia Land, Water, and Development Company, which undertook the first commercial development of the area. The Eastlake-style house, built of redwood, has been lovingly restored and filled with period furniture.

In the adjacent George Izay Park is the city-run **Creative Arts Center Gallery** (Mon.–Thurs. 9 a.m.–9 p.m., Fri. 9 a.m.–5 p.m., weekends for scheduled classes only; call 818-238-5397 for a schedule). The gallery displays contemporary art, including an annual exhibition of works by children in the Burbank schools, and offers studio-art classes. Dance classes at the Olive Recreation Center next door and at two other city parks are administered by the Creative Arts Center.

The Burbank Little Theater (1100 W. Clark Ave.) has been home since 1995 to the Serendipity Theater Co., which stages first-rate productions of children's classics in an ambitious schedule. The professional troupe launched its children's theater productions in 1990 at the Coronet Theater, but chose to program their family-oriented fare in Burbank when the Little Theater's lease became available. Professional actors and technical staff lead the company's repertory troupe of twenty-five young actors, ages seven to seventeen, who become members by invited audition only and are usually drawn from classes offered by Serendipity. Call 818-557-0505 for class information and the annual calendar of productions.

Starlight Bowl (1249 Lockheed View Dr.) is the scene of low-cost concerts on Sunday afternoons in summer, presented by Burbank's Department of Parks and Recreation. A fireworks concert on July 4th kicks off the season, which extends through Labor Day, with all varieties of popular music styles from swing to reggae presented. The outdoor amphitheater holds about 4,000 people, with stadium seating for 3,000 and room for more on a grassy area. Call the Park and Recreation Department (818-238-5300) for the concert schedule at Starlight Bowl and information on the parks and playground areas it maintains.

Lundigan Park (2701 Thornton Ave.—the street that leads from the 5 Fwy. to the main entrance of Burbank Airport) has a new playground and climbing equipment. Next door is a fire station, so kids can inspect the shiny red engines ready to roll to any emergency; overhead are planes on approach to the airport; and every weekend, a city truck brings bats, balls, and other equipment for the kids to use. **The Play Mobile Recreation Van** also makes weekly visits to these Burbank parks: Vickroy Park (2300 Monterey Pl.); **Permanent Charities Park** (1922 Grismer St.); **Elmwood Avenue cul-de-sac** (at Lake St.); and the **Santa Anita Playlot** (250 W. Santa Anita Ave.). Call 818-238-5390 for more information.

The city of Burbank spent $4 million on the four-year renovation of **McCambridge Park** (bounded by Glenoaks Blvd. and Amherst Dr., and San Fernando Blvd. and Scott Rd.). The centerpiece of the 17-acre site is its tennis facilities—ten lighted concrete courts and two clay courts, plus a sunken championship court with seating for 300—but it also offers two baseball diamonds, basketball and bocci courts, and two playgrounds with newly designed climbing structures.

NBC Television

3000 W. Alameda Ave.
Burbank 91523
818-840-3537
Mon.–Fri. 9 a.m.–3 p.m.
Entry: adults $7, children 5–12 $3.75

Bungalows built in the 1920s with boulders collected from a nearby wash are clustered near Olive Avenue and Ninth Street.

The 1941 City Hall (at 275 E. Olive) is a moderne classic in the idiom of the Public Works Administration which includes a mural of DC-3s and other references to the aerospace industry in its elaborate decor.

The People of Burbank, a two-panel fresco painted in 1940 by Barse Miller, is one of the distinguishing elements that earned the Burbank Post Office (E. Olive at First) a listing on the National Register of Historic Places.

When about twenty people have assembled at the NBC office (where tickets to tapings of shows are also dispensed), the seventy-five-minute studio tour begins with a short video on the history of NBC in radio and television. Two television cameras focus on the group to demonstrate zooms, fade-ins, dissolves, wipes, and other feats of video technology, which are visible on monitors.

First stop is the scenery department, where sets for shows filmed at NBC are constructed. Displays on makeup and wardrobe include a video showing how an actor is "aged" by about thirty years; the studio keeps a library of plaster molds of each actor's facial parts so they can construct chins, noses, or cheekbones as needed. Mannequins accurately representing actors' figures are displayed in the costume department, without labels to spare the person so exposed any embarrassment.

Five tapings of game shows are produced back-to-back during one long day, then broadcast over the course of a week. To maintain the illusion of a daily program, returning contestants must bring several changes of clothing—and a lot of stamina! Illusion also affects perception in the newsroom: to make the presentation of soft news more informal, the height of the desk is lowered to reveal the anchor's hands gesturing and shuffling papers, but for headline news, anchors are positioned behind a higher desk.

Kids on the tour enjoy participating in demonstrations of technical effects. They particularly like being positioned in front of a blue screen and then, using a process called chromakey, being inserted into different backgrounds that make it appear as if they're flying over the L.A. basin or interpreting weather maps on the evening news.

Complimentary tickets to watch the filming of shows at the NBC Studios are available most weekdays, including those to *The Tonight Show* with Jay Leno, which tapes at 5 p.m. The schedule of tapings is included in the menu on the automated telephone system (818-840-3537), and tickets are offered on a first-come, first-served basis beginning when the NBC box office opens at 8 a.m. Tickets can be requested in advance by sending a self-addressed, stamped envelope along with a letter stating the name of the show, number of tickets, and desired date to: NBC Tickets, 3000 West Alameda Avenue, Burbank 91523.

Warner Bros. Studios VIP Tour

4000 Warner Blvd.
Burbank 91522
818-972-8687
Tours: Mon.–Fri., on the half-hour 9 a.m.–4:30 p.m.; reservations recommended; no children under 10
Entry: $30

Warner Bros. Studios occupies 110 acres in the southwest corner of Burbank. Along Olive Avenue, a dozen huge billboards mounted on the high perimeter wall advertise films and TV shows produced by the resident companies; these have transformed the area, designated the Burbank Media District, into the Sunset Strip of the Valley. The Warner brothers acquired this property in 1929, two years after they revolutionized the film industry with the first "talkie," Al Jolson's *The Jazz Singer,* and the studio churned out eighty-six features during its first year on the lot. Busby Berkeley filmed frothy musicals here in the 1930s, and in 1937 the studio scored its first Best Picture Oscar for *The Life of Émile Zola.* In the 1950s, the animation department of Tex Avery, Chuck Jones, and Friz Freleng brought its zany cartoon characters—Bugs Bunny, Daffy Duck, Yosemite Sam, Tweety, and Sylvester—to Burbank, and Warner Bros. brought home its second Best Picture Oscar for 1943's *Casablanca.* By the late 1950s, the studio's decision to embrace the new medium of television was vindicated by the success of such series as *Maverick, 77 Sunset Strip,* and *Hawaiian Eye. My Fair Lady* got the Academy's nod for Best Picture in 1964, during a decade in which the studio produced such notable films as *Bonnie and Clyde, Who's Afraid of Virginia Woolf?* and *Camelot.* In 1972 Warner Bros. agreed to share the facilities with Columbia Pictures, and the lot was renamed the Burbank Studios. The 1980s saw a decade of mergers and acquisitions, although Warner Bros. scored two more Best Picture awards, for *Chariots of Fire* in 1981 and *Driving Miss Daisy* in 1989. Warner Bros. purchased the Samuel Goldwyn Studios in Hollywood in 1980 and Lorimar Productions in 1988; in 1989 Warner Bros. merged with Time-Life, forming the Time Warner Inc. communications conglomerate, and Columbia was sold to Sony and moved to its Culver City facility in 1990. The entire lot was jubilantly rededicated as Warner Bros. Studios, and new construction and renovation brought state-of-the-art facilities to the historic site.

For twenty-five years this behind-the-scenes tour has been knowledgeable Angelenos' top pick for treating themselves or visitors to a real "Hollywood" experience. With the addition of a museum (only available to those on the tour) that showcases studio artifacts such as film and TV props and costumes, plus documents from legendary figures in the entertainment business, storyboards, and animation cels from its cartoon favorites, the Warner Bros. Studios VIP Tour has outclassed all competitors. Although reservations are not mandatory, they may be prudent: the number of visitors has swelled tenfold over the past decade. Tour visitors enter the lot from Gate 4 at the intersection of Hollywood Way and Olive Avenue (where parking is available), and sign up for the next available seat on the twelve-passenger trams. There are exhibits in the reception area and a fifteen-minute film collage of Warner Bros. movies—from vintage ones starring Errol Flynn, James Cagney, and James Dean to those featuring Denzel Washington and Kevin Costner—to whet the appetite while you wait.

Once on board the open-air trams, visitors get a spontaneous view of the technical processes involved in creating films and television shows by visiting a rehearsal of a weekly TV series, touring some of the technical facilities, and wandering through the backlot sets. Even if you hit a slow day on the lot—and the long hiatus means that fans of shows like *Friends* and *ER* should not expect to see those series taping in summer—the guides possess an encyclopedic knowledge of film, and they enthrall visitors with the glorious history of the silent sets.

Today the thirty-three soundstages are the most active production areas. "Red eyes"—lights positioned at each corner of the looming, windowless soundstage buildings—are illuminated when recording is in process to warn those in the vicinity not to make noise that could ruin the take. Stage

16 was raised to ninety-eight feet (the tallest such structure in the world) to accommodate filming of a movie starring Marion Davies and Clark Gable, which was so bad it was never released, but the height has been adapted as a water well: maritime scenes like those in *The Old Man and the Sea* and *PT 109* were filmed there. Most soundstages are set up for one particular show that rehearses and records in that space all week. Candace Bergen tapes the series *Murphy Brown* on Stage 4 where Bette Davis once filmed *Now, Voyager*. The huge spaces are divided into permanent and temporary sets, with miles of wiring, lighting, and beams overhead, and many stages include a gallery of seats from which an audience can watch weekly filming; tickets for these sessions can be obtained by calling Audiences Unlimited at 818-753-3470.

The backlot set called Laramie Street, a Western town, was created in 1957 for the TV show *Lawman* and is still used. The 1994 earthquake provided the impetus to renovate and rebuild many older sections of the lot. Most of the Georgian-style buildings along Brownstone Street seem to be faced with brick, but that is an illusion: most of the building materials were fabricated from plastic sheets on a Variform machine in Building 44, where 10,000 molds in every possible architectural style—from rough adobe to gingerbread shingle to roof tiles encrusted with Japanese crests and ornately figured "pressed-tin" ceilings—are stored. The streets are routinely altered with signage or props to suggest urban areas around the globe and throughout history because such camouflage avoids costly location shooting. New York Street is lined with large commercial buildings, including a grand movie house, but it assumes a more sinister air as Gotham City in the *Batman* movies. With the addition of a piece of elevated railroad track, that location becomes Chicago and the hospital entrance in *ER*. A Midwestern residential street of clapboard houses and tree-shaded lawns was featured in *Kings Row*, starring Ronald Reagan, but it also served as the locale for *Mayberry RFD, The Dukes of Hazzard, Sisters,* and *East of Eden.*

More than fifty unions represent workers at Warner Bros. Studios, and thirty-five of them have jurisdiction in the crafts divisions, which fabricate sets and props. Cavernous carpentry and metalworking shops are most active during morning hours; another group builds detailed miniatures—aircraft, cityscapes—which must convincingly suggest a full scale environment in the finished film. Backdrops and the huge billboards along Olive Avenue are painted

in the Scenic Department, where sheets of canvas up to 200 feet long are raised and lowered on a three-story elevator; the artists in this division reproduced all the paintings in the Oval Office and the view from its windows for the set of *Dave*. Props and antique furniture, huge crystal chandeliers, a long hallway filled with mirrors of every style and size, and bibelots and gewgaws galore are crammed in the prop buildings, the wonderful attic in the house of illusion. In a separate shed are cars, trains, planes, boats, and a whole fleet of *Batman* vehicles.

The costume department was consolidated from five locations and is now stored in a state-of-the-art building constructed in 1996, which includes eight miles of hanging racks with one million articles of clothing, four miles of shelves storing every style and size of footwear, and tiers of hats, including an entire wall of headgear from *Camelot*; there is enough chain mail to outfit every knight who ever lived, but it is all knitted from yarn and painted silver so it isn't heavy and won't clank when actors walk. Motion sensors throughout the costume department illuminate the aisles as needed so fabrics don't deteriorate from unnecessary exposure to light, and the whole department is on the lowest level of the building with exterior walls that open up to permit huge wardrobe units to be wheeled out to a truck dock.

We ended our tour at the Warner Bros. Museum, but the installation, which opened in June 1996, has proven so popular that tours now begin here. The museum building also contains the Steven J. Ross Theater, used for gala premieres that spill out to the adjacent city-block set (and can be covered by a retractable canopy). The museum's inaugural exhibition features the first fifty years of production at the studio, which celebrates its seventy-fifth anniversary in 1998. Here are treasures to make any movie fan giddy: Errol Flynn's bow and arrow from *Robin Hood*; John Wayne's chaps, saddle, and rifle; the piano Sam played again in *Casablanca*; the real forty-seven-pound statue of the Maltese Falcon; forty-one lobby cards from all the films featuring Ronald Reagan produced by Warner Bros.; six flamboyant hats from *My Fair Lady*; and James Dean's boots and 1955 Triumph Trophy 500 motorcycle. Visitors can sit on a bench that Dean and Natalie Wood occupied in *Rebel without a Cause* to review his entire career: he made only three films—all of them for Warner Bros.—and they are shown on the exhibit's video monitors. The Women in Film display includes photos of Marilyn Monroe in *The Prince and the Showgirl*, her only film for Warner Bros., and some pretty bitchy memos penned by Bette Davis. Jack Warner didn't pull many punches in his missives either, referring to Warren Beatty as "that bum" during filming of *Bonnie and Clyde*; Warner's own handwritten phone book is open to the page that includes Salvador Dali, Olivia de Havilland, Cecil B. DeMille, and Walt Disney.

On the second floor, it's time for Looney Tunes. Most of the characters in the popular animated cartoons produced by Warner Bros. get their own exhibit: the irrepressible bunny was based on sketches by animator Ben Hardaway, whose nickname was "Bugs"; the consensus among the animators was "we like Bugs' Bunny best"—and you can guess the rest. Chuck Jones and Ted Geisel (better known as Dr. Seuss) collaborated on cartoon propaganda: the exploits of Private Snafu helped save lives of soldiers serving in World War II by preparing them for wartime situations in a comic way. Cartoons were also a less expensive way to fulfill length requirements demanded by the new and eager-to-please theater owners. The genre continues through the modern period: Steven Spielberg's *Tiny Toons, Animaniacs,* and *Batman* series—all drawn on black backgrounds, which makes alteration difficult—have won several Emmys. Monitors in this section screen the history of Warner Bros. animation by director.

During 1998 the entire museum will be devoted to a new anniversary exhibition, "75 Years of Warner Bros. Films, 1923–1998."

Forest Lawn Park accommodates mourning families and the deceased in two beautifully landscaped cemeteries, one on the north side of Griffith Park (6300 Forest Lawn Dr., Los Angeles; *213-254-3131), the other on a Glendale hillside (1712 S. Glendale Ave., Glendale; 800-204-3131). Both facilities include art displays, but the exhibits are mainly oddities—a mosaic composed of ten million pieces of Venetian glass which highlights sentimental favorites of America's colonial past, and "the largest painting in the world," a 195-by-45-foot image of the Crucifixion—and replicas. You should not strike a visit to Old North Church from your itinerary in Boston because you've seen the reproduction of it here, any more than you should skip Paris once you've seen Universal's theme-park version of its cafes and cobblestoned streets.

The state of California is now home to half of the one million Armenians in the United States, and about 400,000 of these immigrants reside in Southern California. Immigration has boosted Armenian above Spanish as the most common non-English native tongue in the Glendale school district and made it one of the fastest-growing segments

Brand Library and Art Center

1601 W. Mountain St.
Glendale 91201
Library: 818-548-2051
Tues., Thurs. 1–9 p.m., Wed. 1–6 p.m., Fri.-Sat. 1–5 p.m.
Brand Studios: 818-548-3782
Park, teahouse, Doctors' House: 818-548-2147
Entry: free

within the Los Angeles Unified School District. Community colleges in Glendale, Pasadena, and Los Angeles offer Armenian language classes, and Cal State Northridge and UCLA both offer degree programs that incorporate history and culture as well as language. The Central Library of the Los Angeles city system has a large collection of books in various languages on Armenian history and culture. Heroyan Legal Services (827 E. Colorado Blvd. Glendale; 818-549-1591) offers free or low-fee classes in Arabic, Armenian, Farsi, and other languages.

This is not a monolithic community—the immigrants are refugees from different countries, fleeing a variety of problems at different points throughout history—but for the past decade *Armenian International Magazine* (AIM) has given voice to its concerns in the local media. The monthly magazine (call 818-246-7979 for subscription) provides information, in English, that it hopes will form links between the various communities of the diaspora. The publishers chose the lingua franca of American journalism so they can become a source for information on Armenian issues to the public and the western media.

Ethnic enclaves in commercial districts throughout L.A. County offer traditional Armenian foods, products, and services: Santa Monica Boulevard in Hollywood, Washington Boulevard in Pasadena, and the south side of Glendale, near Central and Brand. Karabagh and Jon's Markets, both in Hollywood and Van Nuys, offer a sense of community as well as specialty foods.

Turn-of-the-century civic booster and real estate tycoon Leslie C. Brand—he owned 1,000 acres in the foothills of the Verdugo Mountains that mark the east end of the San Fernando Valley—wanted Glendale to be a prominent, prosperous community in the evolving Los Angeles landscape. He placed full-page advertisements in the local Sunday newspapers that asked, "Have you been to Glendale?" and listed reasons why interested citizens should make the twelve-mile trek from downtown. Inspired by the East Indian Pavilion at the 1893 Columbian Exposition in Chicago, he built as his residence a Saracenic architectural fancy that combines Spanish, Moorish, and Indian elements.

On the death of his widow in 1945, the unusual home, called El Miradero, and the surrounding park were left to the city of Glendale, which installed in it an extraordinary collection of 40,000 volumes on art and music history, technique, and theory. Materials in the Brand Library may be used only by high school students or adults, but the adjacent Art Center, built in 1969, offers studio art, dance, and drama programs for all ages. Music students perform in its recital hall, where an annual chamber music series is held (818-548-2051). The city of Glendale offers a lively program of classes in fine arts, ballet, music, and performing arts throughout the year at the Brand Studios (and at other community centers). Weekly classes for children and teenagers include crafts, drawing and painting, and acting. Call 818-548-3782 for class schedules and applications. The Glendale Theater Troupe meets weekly (Wed. 7–10 p.m.) and

Glendale Farmers Market
100 N. Brand. Blvd.
Thurs. 9:30 a.m.–1:30 p.m.

auditions teens for its productions of original one-act plays.

An 1880s Queen Anne home, called the Doctors' House because it was the residence of four physicians from 1895 to 1914, was saved from destruction and moved to Brand Park, where it may be visited (guided tours only, Sun. 2–4 p.m.). A loving restoration has made the turn of the century come alive in this residence, where a "speaking tube," or primitive intercom, was used to link the stained-glass front door with the doctor's office, still fixtured with period medical equipment. Canary Island pines, palm trees, and tropical shrubs are the remnants of the fairy-tale landscaping that Brand had designed. Today the flat areas of the park are used for sporting fields; a fairly steep 3.5-mile hike into the rugged terrain leads to an overlook with a spectacular view across the San Fernando Valley and to downtown Los Angeles.

Its sister-city relationship with one of the outlying suburbs of Osaka has given Glendale a new addition to Brand Park. A traditional stroll garden, surrounding a large pond where colorful koi swim, is open Monday to Friday 8 a.m. to 5 p.m.; on weekends it can be rented for weddings and other events. Within the garden is a traditional teahouse called Whispering Pines, which may be viewed from the outside but not entered.

Two other historic residences are preserved within Glendale parks; call 818-548-2147 for information.

■ **Verdugo Adobe** (2211 Bonita Dr., Glendale; 818-548-3795) was built in 1828 and is listed on the National Register of Historic Places. A collection of dolls and Indian artifacts is displayed within the house, which is now used as a station for park rangers, who may be willing to show interested parties around. The grounds are open daily from 8 a.m. to 4 p.m.

■ **Casa Adobe de San Rafael** (1330 Dorothy Dr.) was built in 1871 by a Los Angeles County sheriff and still retains some nineteenth-century furnishings. Tours of the interior are offered (first Sun. of month, 1–3 p.m.); the grounds are open daily from 8 a.m. to dusk.

A three-acre park tucked along the 2 Freeway at Loma Vista Drive and Sherer Lane is an arboretum with a tree dedicated to each of the forty-three former mayors of Glendale. The native chaparral was preserved and the addition of drought-tolerant plants creates a harmonious landscape.

Alex Theater

216 N. Brand Blvd.
Glendale 91203
818-243-ALEX
Box office: Tues.–Sun. noon–6 p.m.

The art deco marquee of the Alex Theater, built in 1925 as a silent movie and vaudeville house and renovated by S. Charles Lee in 1940, has long been a landmark on Brand Boulevard, Glendale's central thoroughfare. More recently it has become a symbol of the city's commitment to its core neighborhood. When construction of the Glendale Galleria and other destination malls altered traffic patterns on the old main street, the Alex and retail venues in the area suffered. The city of Glendale purchased the building, and in 1994 hired the Ratkovich Company to remodel the 1,450-seat theater. With its spacious open-air forecourt and lobby, it was hoped that the Alex would become an evening destination for upscale audiences who would also patronize area businesses. The investment paid off. Excellent, eclectic programming that supplements the offerings of the Alex's resident companies—Glendale Symphony Orchestra, Los Angeles Chamber Orchestra, Alex Film Society, and Gay Men's Chorus—has lured area residents back downtown after dark.

Glendale still contributes $225,000 annually to subsidize theater operations, and the number of events has been scaled back to make them self-supporting, but the range and quality of the offerings should continue to build committed audiences and subscribers. Some of the best contemporary dance troupes have been featured in the Alex's subscription series, and musical performances include classical series, wide-ranging world music offerings, and concerts presented by the Playboy Jazz Festival. Special children's performances and travelogues complete the season.

The city of Glendale is one of the communities that offers independent library services and is a member of the Metropolitan Cooperative Library System. The Central Library (222 E. Harvard St.; 818-548-2020) hosts a family storytime (Sat. 2–3 p.m.), and grandparent volunteers will read to the kids from 3 to 4:30 p.m. on Saturdays and many weekdays too. Wow! It's Wednesday is a program of stories and crafts for ages six and up, held on, you guessed it, Wednesdays (4–5 p.m.). On Thursdays preschoolers are invited to Toddlertime (10:30–11 a.m.) for stories and songs. An eclectic film program on Tuesdays at 2 p.m. screens travelogues, vintage comedies, and nature films. Call to confirm schedules of these programs and others offered in the six-branch library system.

Descanso Gardens

1418 Descanso Dr.
La Cañada-Flintridge 91011
818-952-4401
Daily 9 a.m.–4:30 p.m.; tram tours at 1, 2, and 3 p.m.
Entry: adults $5, seniors/students $3, children 5–12
$1; tram tours $1.50

Montrose is not a community that many Angelenos could place with certainty on a map (and it is indeed a very small one), but its old downtown section retains many nice small shops in a pedestrian-friendly zone—more like Larchmont Village than Old Town Pasadena.

A fifteen-acre recreational park at Sparr Boulevard and North Verdugo Road provides the community of Montrose with basketball courts, baseball diamonds, and trails for walking and biking. It took the place of a dump and won the state's environmental design award in 1988.

That strange little snippet of freeway, CA 2, climbs northward into the foothills with a perceptible change in elevation and topography. From the Foothill Boulevard exit, it is a short drive to Rancho del Descanso, or "Ranch of Rest," which is one of the most peaceful enclaves in this area. E. Manchester Boddy, then the owner and editor of the *Los Angeles Daily News*, developed the 165-acre garden from 1939 until it was purchased by the county of Los Angeles in 1953. In the shade of a thirty-acre forest of towering California oaks are more than 100,000 camellias, with 600 different varieties represented; from November to March, their bright blossoms illuminate the cool woodland, and colorful petals are strewn on the pathways. This is the most renowned aspect of Descanso Gardens, but not its only attraction.

A Japanese-style garden, inspired by the Asian origin of the camellia plant, features a landscape of water and rock; it surrounds a teahouse pavilion where refreshments are served. In March and April, a one-acre grove of lilacs—cultivars developed by Descanso botanists for the Southern California climate—perfumes the air, iris brighten the Japanese garden, and spring bulbs, azaleas, and flowering trees lend riotous color to the beautiful setting. From May through autumn, the five-acre International Rosarium, which includes many unusual historic varieties, is at its best. We were by no means the only family to celebrate Mother's Day with a picnic at the dozen tables shaded by thousand-year-old oaks, a photo session in the colorful and fragrant rose garden,

and a long walk uphill past the native plants (including those Mantilja poppies I covet), but it sure was fun.

The Bird Observation Station is a rather staid name for a very lively spot: visitors can purchase seed to feed the wild ducks and geese who inhabit the scenic pond, and the animals often reciprocate with antic behavior that captivates bird lovers of all ages. More than 150 species of birds have been sighted in the area, including osprey during the winter months. The chortle of hummingbirds animates nearby gardens landscaped with California native plants, and a network of hiking trails leads into the chaparral-covered hills, where the beauty of untouched nature completes this great garden.

Seasonal events include a Spring Festival of Flowers with thousands of tulips and other flowering bulbs brightening demonstration landscapes; workshops offer gardeners tips for transforming their own plots. The Holiday Celebration in December offers good cheer in abundance, with spectacularly decorated Christmas trees in Hospitality House, a small steam-powered train circling Santa's workshop (with stick-figure reindeer ready to pose with toddlers for photos), musical entertainment, and crafts for sale. During summer months, Descanso is open for longer hours to host twilight events, including concerts by the Pasadena Pops Orchestra (818-792-7677) on the first Saturday of each month and Shakespeare under the Oaks most weeknights in July.

First Saturday Talks, held at 10 a.m. on the first Saturday of each month, are free with paid admission and address gardening concerns like pruning roses, creating an edible landscape or a water garden, and fall planting. Special plant sales and flower shows are also regular features of Descanso's programming.

FILM AND VIDEO

Peter Henné

* indicates an area code that changes in 1998

Universities, Colleges, and Archives

Academy of Motion Picture Arts and Sciences
Center for Motion Picture Study
333 S. La Cienega Blvd.
Beverly Hills 90211
310-247-3020
Mon.–Tues.,Thurs.–Fri.
10 a.m.–6 p.m.

The noncirculating Margaret Herrick Library possesses several million film stills, 20,000 books, and extensive files of clippings containing production and biographical information. Access to the academy's special collections of the papers and photographs of hallowed Hollywood figures such as Alfred Hitchcock and Cary Grant is by appointment only.

The academy boasts a plush, enormous theater at 8949 Wilshire Boulevard, often used for awards ceremonies and gala premieres. The academy holds about a half-dozen general-admission screenings each year, and the films are usually drawn from its own holdings. Call for admission prices; parking is available in the public lot south of Wilshire.

California State University, Long Beach
Carpenter Performing Arts Center
6200 Atherton St.
Long Beach 90840
562-985-4274
Box Office: 562-985-7000

For two weekends each October, the Carpenter puts on the WideScreen Festival, featuring 70mm and 35mm prints. Most of the films are of the Hollywood epic variety *(Ben-Hur, Bridge on the River Kwai, Apocalypse Now)*. The 1,100-seat facility has state-of-the-art equipment, delivering every last ripple of explosive sound and sliver of flashing light. The festival includes symposia with technicians who worked on the films—and occasionally with their directors and cinematographers as well. Tickets are $7 for each screening. Parking is $3 in the Carpenter Center lot.

Claremont Colleges
Mudd Theater, Claremont School of Theology
NW corner of Foothill Blvd. and Harvard Ave.
Claremont 91711
909-626-3521, ext. 275

Claremont has a long history of public screenings and specializes in Hollywood and foreign classics such as *The Kid* and *The Last Laugh*. An added boon is the college's access to archival prints, which it draws on for its comprehensive Classic Film Series. Films screen the first and third Fridays of the month throughout the school year, September through May. The suggested donation is $3; $2 for seniors and children. Parking is free on campus.

UCLA
James Bridges Theater
405 Hilgard Ave.
(NE corner of campus)
Los Angeles 90024
310-206-3456, 310-206-8014

As the video market continues to knock off movie-repertory businesses, UCLA's James Bridges Theater (formerly the Melnitz Theater) has emerged as the royalty of revival houses in L.A. County. Its year-round screenings, intelligent and often provocative programming, and outstanding prints and projection make its 275-seat theater a reliable and exciting haven for movie buffs.

The Bridges programs both revivals and nontheatrical contemporary films. Series vary widely, focusing on internationally renowned directors (John Ford, Jean Renoir), critically hailed auteurs (R. W. Fassbinder, Kenji Mizoguchi), nations (Iran, Italy), studios (United Artists, France's Gaumont), and themes (film and painting, film and photography, film and fashion).

This venue hosts a popular yearly restoration showcase, the Festival of Film Preservation. The monthly Archive Treasure series, which features an obscure Hollywood classic culled from the university's renowned archive, is also a lot of fun. The archive itself is available for use by scholars and researchers. For updated information on programs, call or check the theater's Web site: www.cinema.ucla.edu.

Admission is $6; $4 for seniors and students with ID. The one downside to seeing films at UCLA is the campus's steep public parking fees ($5). Carpool, or hunt for parking on nearby streets.

If you live in the southern part of Los Angeles County, UC Irvine's eclectic film series is well worth investigating. Call 714-824-5588.

Museums and Cultural Centers

Autry Museum of Western Heritage
4700 Western Heritage Way
Los Angeles 90027
*213-667-2000

It's no secret that the Autry programs a lot of westerns. But it also shows films that address the history and culture of the western United States; for example, a recent series included John Ford's *The Grapes of Wrath*. Programming at the Autry is unique; ten films are shown per year, on the first weekend of each month from February through November, and all revolve around a central theme. The Saturday screenings are preceded by a lecture by a guest scholar. On selected national holidays, the museum also plays films starring its famous founder, the "Singing Cowboy." There is a nominal fee for screenings, in addition to the museum admission. Parking is free in the museums lot.

Goethe-Institut
5700 Wilshire Blvd., Ste. 110
Los Angeles 90036
*213-525-3388

The Goethe-Institut has placed itself on the screening-room map by cosponsoring with the American Cinematheque and UCLA extensive retrospectives of films by R. W. Fassbinder, Werner Herzog, and Wim Wenders. The Goethe-Institut also has year-round screenings of old and new German films; many are free, and almost all are subtitled in English. It is often the place to go to see a rare Fritz Lang or F. W. Murnau. Filmforum also screens its regular lineup of experimental films here. The institute has a fine library of film books in German and English, and the staff could not be friendlier or more helpful. The single drawback to seeing films here is the theater's poor sight lines. Arrive early; to ensure an unobstructed view, you'll need to sit in one of the first two rows. Park in the institute's garage or on nearby residential streets.

Long Beach Museum of Art
2300 E. Ocean Blvd.
Long Beach 90803
562-439-2119

The museum hosts a "Video Salon" the third Thursday of every month, year-round, at its Video Annex. Programs are drawn from its collection of 3,500 tapes, which includes experimental videos, independent documentaries, and works of historical interest. Addressing social issues through unique personal perspectives is one of the salon's specialties. Many of the videos screened were funded by the production grants the museum offers to video artists. Shows are free with museum admission; parking is $3 in the museum's lot.

Los Angeles County Museum of Art
Bing Theater
5905 Wilshire Blvd.
Los Angeles 90036
*213-857-6010

A spacious theater, large screen, and reliable prints and projection make LACMA a prime spot for viewing older American and foreign films. If you find yourself with a Tuesday afternoon to kill, you might want to try the Bing's unbeatably priced weekly 1 p.m. matinee, featuring Hollywood classics such as *Shadow of a Doubt* or *The Pirate*. Film series, screened on Saturday evenings, are typically constructed around an engaging theme (twentieth-century French society) or concept (artistic use of the Cinemascope format). Sometimes programs are linked to a concurrent exhibition at the museum. Although LACMA tends to stay away from retrospectives on film personalities, in recent years it has staged valuable career overviews on actor Jimmy Stewart and director Luchino Visconti. The Bing also runs programs in conjunction with the American Film Institute's International Film Festival and with some of UCLA's series. Ian Birnie, director of the film department, who joined the museum in 1996, has added

some interesting twists, such as a series on up-and-coming Russian director Sergei Bodrov.

Guests are sometimes invited to introduce films. Past speakers have included film director Richard Fleischer, actor Harry Carey Jr., and film historian Joseph McBride. Screenings are $6; $4 for museum and AFI members, seniors, and students with ID. Parking is free in the evening in the lot at Wilshire and Spaulding.

Museum of Television & Radio
465 N. Beverly Dr.
Beverly Hills 90210
310-786-1000

In addition to an annual festival held at the Directors Guild theater in March, the Museum of Television & Radio offers programming, Wednesday through Sunday, at its Beverly Drive location. You may be picturing endless hours of *Peyton Place* episodes, but the museum's collection includes international as well as American material. If you are looking for the serious television work of Dennis Potter, for example, stop here; the museum has all of the productions associated with this British scriptwriter. Two theaters run continuously during the museum's regular hours; call ahead to receive a schedule of programs for the day you wish to attend. Seating is on a first-come, first-served basis. Admission is $6; $4 for seniors and students with ID. Park in the museum's garage; the first two hours are free with validation.

Skirball Cultural Center
2701 N. Sepulveda Blvd.
Los Angeles 90049
310-440-4500

This complex nestled in the Santa Monica Mountains is dedicated to the preservation and study of

Jewish culture. Films screen once a week, on Sundays at 2 p.m. The Skirball's programming is commendably thorough, lending depth to the selected subjects. Past series have included an American Jewish comedy film festival and A Nation of Strangers: Immigration in Film. Films are drawn from around the globe; most are subtitled. Admission is $5; $4 for members; $3 for students. Free parking in the museum lot.

Revival Houses
New Beverly Cinema
7165 Beverly Blvd.
Los Angeles 90036
*213-938-4038

This established revival house has survived the home-videotape revolution, dingy but intact. A central location and affordable double bills ($5) have helped to keep the New Beverly attractive, in spite of its crumbling seats; an inadequately slanted floor, which makes viewing the screen from many rows nearly impossible; and prints that are often second-rate. The New Beverly programs a mix of modern-day crime films (fans of directors Quentin Tarantino and John Woo are well served), camp from the 1960s and 1970s, noir from the 1940s, vintage Hollywood comedies (movies by Preston Sturges and Billy Wilder are perennials), and standard foreign fare (*Diabolique, Hiroshima Mon Amour, La Dolce Vita*, etc.). The New Beverly is a good place to get some grounding in film history, yet its lineups are redundant. It's a safe bet that this establishment will pair *The Conformist* with *Last Tango in Paris* at least once a year well into the next century. Unexpected gems grace its schedule now and then, however, such as Robert Bresson's *The Trial of Joan of Arc*.

A rare 35mm print of Orson Welles's *The Trial* has also played at the theater several times. Tickets are $5. Street parking.

Old Town Music Hall
140 Richmond St.
El Segundo 90245
310-322-2592

The Old Town Music Hall specializes in pre-World War II American films. It strives to recapture an era of optimism and innocence in Hollywood movies through its programming, consisting primarily of giddy musicals. Patrons will find well-known ones here (*Top Hat*), but buffs will be pleased to find some obscure ones (*Sun Valley Serenade*) as well. Programs run on weekends only. Tickets are $5; parking is free.

Tales Bookshop
667 S. La Brea Ave.
Los Angeles 90036
*213-933-2640

Tales is a delightful hole-in-the-wall: a used-book shop, coffee bar, and basement-style projection room ensconced in one tidy setting. In spirit it is the closest thing to an old-fashioned cinema club that Los Angeles has to offer. In fact, the film programming is organized by the former owner of the now-defunct Vagabond, a legendary L.A. art house.

Practically all films at Tales are selected from the glory days of American cinema, and a heavy accent is placed on obscure film noir titles. Although the theater possesses only 16mm equipment, the projection is impeccable, and the prints are generally good. The comfortable, homey environment makes one easily forgive any viewing deficiencies. Tales started with weekend-only programming but now screens nightly. Bills change twice weekly. Admission is $5; street parking.

Theaters for Contemporary, Revival, Foreign, and Independent Films

American Cinematheque
*213-466-FILM

The American Cinematheque has cultivated a diverse but well-defined range of programming, emphasizing the forgotten, the censored, and the subversive. In the spirit of its Parisian forerunner, the Cinémathèque, its primary niche is retrospectives of films by overlooked but important auteurs. Budd Boetticher, Nicholas Ray, Roberto Rossellini, and the French gangster-film director Jean-Pierre Melville have all been given their due here, along with more recent outcasts like Werner Herzog and Ken Russell. Whenever possible, a director attends his or her retrospective and takes questions from the audience after film screenings.

The American Cinematheque abides by no strict rules in planning its events. It has offered interesting insights into the American experimental scene through its Alternate Screen programs. Responding to popular demand, it has made its saucy New Spanish Cinema lineup an annual event. Since 1996 the Cinematheque has increased its focus on work made for television, such as banned music videos, golden-era dramas that have a noir angle, and new British television. At present films are shown at Raleigh Studios (5300 Melrose Ave.), but in 1998 the Cinematheque will move to the newly restored Egyptian Theater (6712 Hollywood Blvd.). Call for ticket and membership information.

Filmforum
6522 Hollywood Blvd.
Los Angeles 90028
*213-526-2911

An underground institution for twenty years, Filmforum screens video, Super 8, and 16mm works at LACE on Sunday evenings, and 35mm films at the Nuart one weekend a month at noon only. Filmforum specializes in presenting films and videos that have unconventional narratives and no other commercial outlets. It programs a crafty mix of renowned and younger filmmakers and of historically neglected and contemporary films. Two of the most noteworthy events it has held of late were the Los Angeles premiere of Jean-Luc Godard's gorgeous *Germany Year 90 Nine Zero* and a retrospective on the just-surfacing experimental director Nina Menkes. Admission prices for events vary.

Los Angeles Contemporary Exhibitions (LACE)
6522 Hollywood Blvd.
Los Angeles 90028
*213-957-1777

LACE prides itself on blurring the boundaries between traditional categories such as film, theater, sculpture, and painting. It hosted its first Super 8 Film Festival in March 1997, includes a video program in its yearly "Annuale" exhibition of work by Los Angeles County artists, and, whenever the spirit moves the curators, presents "Video Windows," nightlong video displays in its storefront window. As with many of LACE's events, emphasis falls upon the semantically mischievous, the socially outré, and the sexually outrageous. Most film and video events are free; parking is available behind the building.

Laemmle Theaters
Colorado, 2588 E. Colorado
Blvd., Pasadena; 626-796-9704
Esquire, 2670 E. Colorado
Blvd., Pasadena; 626-793-6149
Monica, 1332 Second St.,
Santa Monica; 310-394-9741
Music Hall, 9036 Wilshire
Blvd., Los Angeles;
310-274-6869
Royal, 11523 Santa Monica
Blvd., Los Angeles;
310-477-5581
Sunset 5, 8000 Sunset Blvd.,
Los Angeles; *213-848-3500
Town Center 5, 17200
Ventura Blvd., Encino;
818-981-9811

Laemmle Theaters provides an invaluable venue for independent and foreign films in Los Angeles County. Owner Bob Laemmle makes a special effort to keep as many films as possible in extended engagements. On the downside, however, the seating, sound, and projection quality in some theaters leave much to be desired.

The Laemmle chain offers more than current art films. As the number of movie repertory theaters has declined, it has played a crucial role in keeping revival programming alive in Los Angeles through its innovative weekend morning programs, screened only at the Sunset 5 and Monica. Patrons have a wide variety of film series to choose from, such as the Summer Western Round-Up, retrospectives on film directors, and festivals that spotlight recent films from nations producing world-class work (Hungary, Greece, Argentina). Laemmle also selects films for its annual Cinema Judaica series and sponsors the independently programmed Israeli Film Festival. Admission prices for events vary; call individual theaters for ticket and parking information.

Landmark Theaters
Goldwyn Pavilion Cinemas
Westside Pavilion, 10800
Pico Blvd., Los Angeles;
310-475-0202
Nuart (see separate listing below)
NuWilshire, 1314 Wilshire
Blvd., Santa Monica;
310-394-8099
Rialto, 1023 Fair Oaks Ave.,
South Pasadena;
626-799-9567

Landmark is a national theater chain that specializes in first-run independent and foreign films. Like Laemmle, it is an invaluable resource for the art-film crowd. The types of films screened at Landmark's Los Angeles–area venues and the lengths of their runs vary from theater to theater. The Goldwyn Pavilion has a fairly quick turnover of risky films (some play special limited-run engagements), while the more conservative Rialto keeps films such as *Il Postino* going for many months. Every serious Angeleno filmgoer should attend South Pasadena's Rialto at least once, just to see the ornate original 1920s fixtures in the lobby and theater hall. Call individual theaters for ticket and parking information.

Nuart
11272 Santa Monica Blvd.
Los Angeles 90025
310-478-6379

A Landmark theater distinct from the others, the Nuart is a landmark, having started operation as a revival house twenty years ago. Over the years it has become a beloved spot for movie fans. Many Angelenos can remember having discovered there some wonderful, long-lost film that never surfaced elsewhere. The Nuart now programs a smorgasbord of American independent, vintage, experimental, documentary, animated, and obscure foreign films. These days the venue is as committed to putting on retrospectives on camp figures such as Ed Wood as it is to showing the latest works of East European auteurs such as Jan Svankmajer. It bravely champions critically applauded domestic and foreign films that distributors regard as uncommercial. Many of the Nuart's contemporary films address issues of gender equality and identity, while others chronicle spiritual quests, bring to light underground cultural trends, and document political and legal controversies in the U.S. and abroad. The theater puts on the annual Tourné of Animation, still has occasional revival runs, and also offers weekend midnight shows. Tickets for most events are $7.50; park in the lot one block south of Santa Monica Boulevard, off Sawtelle.

Festivals and Annual Events

American Film Institute (AFI) International Film Festival
2021 N. Western Ave.
Los Angeles 90068
*213-856-7600

After a long history of venue-hopping, the AFI International Film Festival has finally settled into a three-site home: the Galaxy and Chinese Theaters in Hollywood and the Monica Four-Plex in Santa Monica. Its size, too, has undergone some changes. Over the last five years it has been gradually pared down from a sprawling 140-plus events to a less intimidating program of about fifty. AFI, in conjunction with Los Angeles Contemporary Exhibitions, also sponsors a three-day video festival that runs during the ten-day film festival.

The AFI Fest's stated mission is to pick up the slack for the dwindling number of screens that exhibit international and independent films. Although the festival has surely missed the boat on some important films, overall it does its job better than the press it receives would suggest. Premiering films by European masters is its enduring specialty, as is presenting blocks of new films from Latin America and Asia. The themes

change each year; recent engagements spotlighted the careers of directors (Mike Leigh, Paul Morrissey, Manuel de Oliveira) and chronicled Eastern Europe's political changes.

The festival also includes several interactive events. Panel discussions, for example, are a regular feature. Many directors appear at the screenings of their films, where they take questions from the audience. Additionally, AFI hosts glamorous tributes to film stars; Holly Hunter, Anjelica Huston, and Gena Rowlands have been feted. Call AFI for information on tickets, festival passes, and parking at individual sites.

AFI also has a state-of-the-art Web site, at www.afionline.org/cinema. You can actually see some complete classic short films here (it runs best with a 28.8 Kbps or faster modem).

Cinecon Annual Film Festival
Alex Theater
216 N. Brand Blvd.
Glendale 91203
Reservations: 760-770-9533

This annual one-weekend film memorabilia convention, held in late summer, was established in 1965. In 1997 Cinecon moved to the Alex Theater. A pass buys you admission to a dealers room, where you can purchase anything from lobby cards of movies of the 1930s and 1940s to the complete set of *Cahiers du cinéma* in English. But Cinecon is much more than a film buff's shopping bonanza. The same pass is also your movie ticket for any of more than two dozen screenings of restored and rare films at the Alex. Most of these pictures attract serious aficionados of the silent film and early talkie eras; the latest Cinecon included such

little-seen gems as Carl Dreyer's *The Parsons Widow* (1920) and Frank Borzages's *Little Man, What Now?* (1934). Cinecon also hosts awards ceremonies for some of the stars of yesteryear; past recipients have included actress Sylvia Sidney and controversial director Leni Riefenstahl.

L.A. Freewaves
2151 Lake Shore Ave.
Los Angeles 90039
*213-664-1510

Every two years this video festival appears throughout metropolitan Los Angeles. It kicks off at the Museum of Contemporary Art but takes place in more than a dozen additional locations, from the Downey Art Museum to Cal State Northridge, and also on several public-access television stations. Programs are put into categories, but not traditional ones. Rather, L.A. Freewaves blends viewpoints in an effort to bring together diverse audiences; each program contains a variety of narrative forms (including animation, documentary, fiction, and experimental work). It is a multicultural event, focusing primarily on the work of L.A. County artists; more than 120 videos are included. L.A. Freewaves has also set up an informative Web site: www.pixels.filmtv.ucla.edu/communityLA_Freewaves/

Los Angeles Asian Pacific Film and Video Festival
UCLA, James Bridges Theater, Los Angeles; 310-206-3456
Pacific Asia Museum, 46 N. Los Robles Ave., Pasadena; 626-449-2742
Additional festival sites vary from year to year. For further information on locations and scheduling, call 310-206-3456 or 213-680-3004.

Possibly the most creative filmmaking in the 1990s has come from places like mainland China, Taiwan,

Hong Kong, and Vietnam. And the Asian Pacific Festival, held annually in June, has been right on top of this new wave of films emanating from the other side of the Pacific. The festival premiered the critically acclaimed, modernist fantasy *Chunking Express* two years before its commercial release; other brilliant films, like *Women from the Lake of Scented Souls* and *Ermo,* played here even prior to their engagements at other local festivals. The event has also been responsible for debuting cutting-edge works like *Cyclo, Vive L'Amour, The Wooden Man's Bride . . .* the list of quality films seems practically endless. It can be counted on to screen at least a half-dozen essential titles every year. If you could go to only one place to catch up with what's new and bold in world cinema, this festival would probably be your best bet.

Los Angeles Gay and Lesbian Film Festival
Directors Guild
7920 Sunset Blvd.
Los Angeles 90046
310-289-5300

This festival, which runs for a week and a half each July, is notable both for its exponential growth and consistent quality. Long before British director Derek Jarman's esteemed final films gained theatrical release, the L.A. Gay and Lesbian Festival premiered them. The festival programs more than 150 films and video works from around the world and features panel discussions with directors and critics about the intersections between Hollywood, independent film, and gay and lesbian filmmakers. Ordering tickets ahead of time is a good idea; most events sell out quickly. Parking is free in the Directors Guild garage.

Los Angeles Independent Film Festival

5455 Wilshire Blvd., Ste. 1500
Los Angeles 90036
*213-937-9155

So slick, so cool, so angsty, the Independent Film Festival might be speaking for a young generation, spelled with a capital X. The annual festival—which places a heavy accent on disillusioned love stories, dysfunctional family dramas, and road movies—has turned out to be wildly popular. Presenting more than twenty features and forty shorts, the festival takes place for five days each April at multiple sites. Its programming is nothing if not thematically consistent, and in 1997 alternative-rock bands were added to the program of outsider films. To its great credit, the festival also offers seminars that cover from A to Z the business of how to make a film, as well as a new media/new technologies forum. Even if the Independent Festival isn't your cup of tea, it can nonetheless provide you with the skills to make films that you would rather see. Tickets are $30 for seminars and $7.50 for most screenings. Call for information on locations, dates, times, and parking.

Los Angeles International Latino Film Festival

213-960-2419

The first Los Angeles International Latino Film Festival took place in October 1997. Ever since the American Film Institute discontinued its Americas Film Festival in 1994, a spotlight on Latino cinema has been woefully lacking. While AFI has maintained a small "Cine Latino" category in its annual international festival, and UCLA and the Laemmle Theaters have each offered series focusing on the films of selected Latin American countries, a first-class festival is an obvious necessity for a city so rich in Latino culture. The 1997 festival included fifty films from throughout Latin America, many in their first U.S. showing.

Pan-African Film Festival
Magic Johnson Theaters

4020 Marlton Ave.
Los Angeles 90008
*213-290-5900, 213-896-8221

This yearly festival has grown rapidly and now exhibits more than fifty films. It takes place in January, with the Magic Johnson Theaters as its permanent home.

From the start, coordinator Ayuko Babu, has lent the festival's programming a personal touch, and his accents on formal cinematic excellence, progressive politics, and breezy comedy still prevail. The festival's geographical scope has widened, now encompassing films from Africa, equatorial regions in Asia, the U.S., and communities of African immigrants throughout the world. The growth of this quality festival has been very rewarding for Los Angeles. Call for ticket information; parking is free in the theater complex's lot.

On the Web

Cinemachine (www/.cinemachine.com) is a much-respected Web site that links to other sites that contain movie reviews. It is *not* the be-all-and-end-all place for finding a definitive word on every film, because many independent publications—which are usually the ones that carry the bravest opinions—are not online. And having at your disposal two or three dozen reviews of the newest Hollywood action flick may not seem all that useful. Added into those numbers, of course, are the many reviews by self-styled critics who chat about the movies they have seen, rather than analyzing them in depth. Nevertheless, Cinemachine usually carries a few reviews of even the most obscure contemporary films. It has articles on some classics, too.

Video Stores

If you've never been to Eddie Brandt's **Saturday Matinee** (6310 Colfax Ave., North Hollywood; 818-506-4242), expect to feel a tad disoriented on your first visit. The moment you walk in, your eyes are hit with 40,000 videotapes lining the walls. The store does have *everything*—even that unbelievably hard-to-find copy of Luchino Visconti's *Ludwig*—but a drawback is that it stocks only out-of-date, pre-letterbox versions of some titles.

Laser Blazer (2518 Overland Ave., Los Angeles; 310-558-3773) is a laser-disc-only rental and sales outlet that delivers what its picky, videophile patrons want. The laser market is always flooded with reissues, and Laser Blazer conscientiously keeps its rental sections up-to-date, restocking with new and letterbox versions of old titles. Its foreign rental section is superb. The large used and cutout bins are worth thumbing through regularly. Rentals are $3.

The silly, postmodern facade of **Rocket Video** (726 N. La Brea Ave., Los Angeles; *213-965-1100) may tempt some to snub this store, but inside is an impressive collection of videotapes. It houses thirty shelves of French cinema alone. Rocket doesn't have a weakness in any area of film, but the sheer size of its collection calls out for the store's classification system (by Hollywood classics, westerns, documentaries, television, etc.) to be further subdivided for easier browsing. In addition to its amazing volume of tapes, Rocket also features an eclectic selection of laser discs for rent, ranging from cult sci-fi to classics from the Janus Collection. Call about membership discounts on rentals.

Videoactive (2522 Hyperion Ave., Los Angeles; *213-669-8544) boasts creative filing and some campy sections. Expect, for instance, to find *Christopher Columbus: The Legend* in the "True Crime" section at this fun Silverlake store. There are hundreds of titles on the "Gay Theme" shelf and a couple of hard-to-track-down Jean-Luc Godard films in the "Great Directors" section.

Vidiots (302 Pico Blvd., Santa Monica; 310-392-8508) prides itself on its diverse selection, reaching deep into European, documentary, and experimental film. The scope is impressive, including works by leading as well as obscure auteurs, and films are grouped by director, which makes browsing easy. If you are searching for hard-to-find tapes of Robert Bresson's *Pickpocket* or Roberto Rossellini's *Fear*, you need shop no further. Vidiots frequently replenishes its stock with exciting new arrivals. Its American classics section is, however, disappointing; many chains, including Tower, are superior in this category. The store recently added floor space, opening up its previous cramped quarters. Call about membership discounts on rentals.

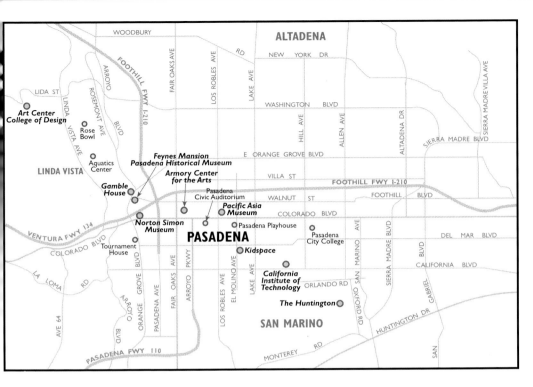

Pasadena, bedecked with flowers and blessed with blue skies, is beamed across America every New Year's Day during the five-mile Tournament of Roses Parade. This image of Pasadena as a bucolic retreat from winter was first created in the 1880s when the Southern Pacific and Santa Fe railroads developed the area as a winter resort and linked it to the frozen heartland. The warm winter air was already scented with flowers—in 1874 a group of Midwestern farmers had planted the land east of the Arroyo with citrus groves, an area that is today traversed by Orange Grove Boulevard.

What began in the 1890s as an annual Battle of the Flowers—those legendary little old ladies pelting each other with sweet-smelling missiles while their consorts engaged in chariot races—was grafted in 1902 to a football game (in which Stanford was trounced by Michigan, 0-49), which has since been known as the Rose Bowl. The event has become an industry—even the description "The Granddaddy of Them All" is a registered trademark—but that doesn't deter thousands of fans from spending New Year's Eve camped on a cold sidewalk to get a good view of the parade, which will pass by them within two hours of the 8 a.m. start. The festival that extends the parade and football game into a three-day event grows more complex year by year, so check out the Web site (www.tournamentofroses.com) or call 626-449-ROSE for information. The Family Festival begins on December 28 and includes opportunities to view the float-decorating in progress; there is a bandfest and a variety of other live entertainment. At the Tournament of Roses Equestrian Festival, held at Santa Anita Racetrack a few days before New Year's, those equestrian parade units that can only plod along Colorado Boulevard get to really strut their stuff: look for the jousting demonstration by the Medieval Times knights and rope tricks by the Roy Rogers and Dale Evans Riders. After the parade the floats are parked at Victory Park (2575 Paloma St.; 626-798-0865) on Sierra Madre Boulevard (between Washington Blvd. and Sierra Madre Villa), where for two days the public can scrutinize the elaborate designs and floral decorations up close.

The resort of Pasadena flourished and the wealthy easterners seeking refuge from the cold helped to give the emerging city its character; many built substantial homes along Orange Grove Boulevard, which had earned the nickname Millionaire's Row by the turn of the century. Visitors can tour the former Wrigley mansion (391 S. Orange Grove Blvd., 626-449-4100; Wed. 2–4 p.m., Feb.–Aug.), since 1959 the headquarters for the Tournament of Roses. The great hotels built during the resort era—the Raymond in South Pasadena, which entertained 35,000 visitors in 1886; the Green Hotel, near the railroad depot; and the Vista del Arroyo, overlooking the canyon—have been destroyed by developers, done in by earthquakes, or converted to other uses; fortunately the

graceful 160-foot-high Colorado Street Bridge, built in 1912 for $200,000 and celebrated as "one of the few bridges that can be classified as a work of art," still marks the principal western entrance to Pasadena. This structure, located where the Ventura (134) Freeway crosses the Arroyo Seco, was once the highest and longest bridge on Route 66, and is now the site of a public party every summer.

A successful City Beautiful development, Pasadena's civic center (along Garfield Ave. between Walnut St. and Colorado Blvd.) includes three masterful buildings: the Italian Renaissance Post Office (1913) established the refined style of the area; Pasadena City Hall (100 N. Garfield), with its domed tower and central courtyard, was designed and built from 1925 to 1927 by John Blakewell and Arthur Brown Jr. (who had earlier designed San Francisco's City Hall); and the

Pasadena Public Library (285 E. Walnut, 626-405-5052; Mon.–Thurs. 9 a.m.–9 p.m., Fri.–Sat. 9 a.m.–6 p.m., Sun. 1–5 p.m.), which is a superb 1927 design by Myron Hunt and H. C. Chambers. The YWCA (78 N. Marengo Ave.) is a 1921 design by architect Julia Morgan.

The Arroyo Seco is a deep canyon that stretches from high in the San Gabriel Mountains—above the site of the present Jet Propulsion Laboratories—through South Pasadena, where the river that carved the canyon joined the Los Angeles River; the extreme southern end of the Arroyo was destroyed in 1942 when the region's first freeway was cut through the canyon to link Pasadena with downtown Los Angeles. The first residents of this area, the Gabrielino Indians, sought food, water, and shelter in the Arroyo Seco; it was given its name—"dry wash"—by Spanish explorers during the late 1700s. Early settlers had woodlots in the Arroyo, and some used it as a convenient dump. By 1885, when Charles Lummis was elected as the first president of the Arroyo Seco Foundation, efforts were underway to preserve it as a natural area. During the tourist boom, the Arroyo was used for recreational activities: hiking and trail riding, fishing and hunting; the residential community along its banks was later populated by writers and artists who celebrated the Arroyo as a symbol of wild California. In 1909 tilemaker Ernest Batchelder began to build his home and first production kiln at 626 South Arroyo Boulevard, one of the buildings that make the eastern edge of the Arroyo an extraordinary enclave of Craftsman architecture.

The Arroyo began to lose its integrity by the turn of the century: a city-owned incinerator was operating at the northern end by 1902 and in 1922 the Rose Bowl stadium was built in the central portion. In 1917 landscape architect Emil Mische, with sponsorship from the Pasadena Garden Club, drew a plan for the preservation of the lower Arroyo; Charles Lummis organized the Arroyo Seco Foundation in support of the plan, and citizens passed a bond ordinance to fund the purchase of private land in the Arroyo. Much of the land still belongs to private organizations: an archery range stretches along the western edge of the lower Arroyo, and the Casting Club and the Garden Club control other sections of the park. A Nature Discovery Trail, reached from a parking lot at Norwood Drive and Arroyo Boulevard, is one way to begin exploring the Arroyo—declared a cultural landmark in 1982—which will always symbolize the native California environment and those who celebrate it.

The worst degradation of the landscape has resulted from attempts to control regional water flow. In a WPA project of the late 1930s, a concrete barrier intended as a flood-control channel divided the canyon and destroyed the riparian environment that once flourished there. In the early 1990s the city of Pasadena granted Browning-Ferris Industries (BFI), a huge waste-hauling contractor, the right to expand its local landfill operations on the condition that it invest in reviving the natural ecosystems of the Arroyo. BFI spent $5 million to remove fifteen-foot cement walls from the old stream bank and re-create a broad, cobbled streambed that flows, at the rate of five to ten cubic feet per second, through more than twenty-five acres of new plantings. Stream-zone species and those that flourish in associated woodlands and meadows had been carefully chosen by naturalists who reviewed archival photographs of the Arroyo. In April 1997 a valve beneath the Colorado Street Bridge was opened, bringing close-to-natural irrigation back to the lower Arroyo; within a few months, naturalists reported not just success, but a near-miraculous surge in the fauna and flora found in the habitat.

Devil's Gate Dam and Reservoir, located at the northern end of the Arroyo, which hadn't been used to store water since the 1971 earthquake, has become a 250-acre Watershed Park labeled with the Gabrielino Indian name for this area, *Hahamongna,* which is variously translated as "fruitful valley" and "flowing waters." A smaller tract along Oak Grove Drive has more citified park amenities.

Brookside Park (Arroyo Blvd. and Park Rdwy. A), which includes the Rose Bowl and Aquatics Center, covers sixty-one acres. Among the facilities are tennis, badminton, handball, and horseshoe courts; a golf course; two lighted softball stadiums; and a regulation baseball diamond with grandstand seating for 4,200. A network of hiking and equestrian trails leads from the park into the surrounding hills.

Gamble House

4 Westmoreland Pl.
(300 block of N. Orange Grove Blvd.)
Pasadena 91103
626-793-3334
By guided tour only: Thurs.–Sun. noon–3 p.m.
Entry: adults $5, seniors $4, students $3, children under 12 free

The extraordinary house built by Charles and Henry Greene for David and Mary Gamble combines the elements that defined early Pasadena culture: the wealthy Gambles, scions of Procter and Gamble, fled the cold Midwestern winters for the restorative climate of Pasadena, and in 1908 built a house near—but not on—Millionaire's Row. They chose as architects the brothers whose style exemplified the Arts and Crafts movement and whose designs celebrated the unique Southern California climate. (The Greenes had developed much of nearby Arroyo Terrace, on which Charles Greene had his own house.)

The Gambles commissioned Greene and Greene to build the ultimate California bungalow instead of a beaux-arts marble residence like some others along Orange Grove Boulevard. The ground-floor perimeter of the house is extended by terraces, and the bedrooms on the second story are supplemented with sleeping porches in the open air: Pasadena was at that time renowned, not infamous, for its air quality. Dark woods—teak, redwood, Port Orford cedar, maple, oak—glow in the interior rooms made even darker by overhanging eaves that give protection from the bright California sun. The light is also filtered by art-glass windows: the magnificent front entry features a sprawling California oak designed by Charles Greene and executed by Emil Lange in leaded art glass. The house, designated a National Historic Landmark in 1978, barely escaped desecra-

their designs to include a porte cochere on the front elevation and is flanked on either side by large chimneys that incorporate boulders and clinker bricks. Other noteworthy residences on Westmoreland Place include the **Ayers House** (C) at #5, designed in 1913 by Edwin Bergstrom (who would later collaborate on the Italian Renaissance design of the Pasadena Civic Auditorium), and the **Jesse Hoyt Smith House** (D) at #6, designed in 1911 by Myron Hunt and Elmer Grey, who were also engaged during that period on the Huntington mansion in San Marino. In 1917 the Greenes designed the gate at the north end of Westmoreland Place to insulate this enclave of superb residential architecture from tour buses.

Charles Greene began building a home for his own family in 1901 at 368 Arroyo Terrace (E), adding characteristic Craftsman details in subsequent renovations of 1906, 1914, 1916. The plan of the house he built in 1903 for his sisters-in-law was dictated by the shape of the lot at 370 Arroyo Terrace (F); the original shingled exterior was stuccoed by later owners.

Josephine Van Rossem commissioned the house at 400 Arroyo Terrace (G) in 1903 and another one at 210 North Grand Avenue (H) in 1904, both as speculative real estate ventures. The **Hawks House** (I) of 1906 (408 Arroyo Terrace) is a variation of the house the Greenes built that same year for John C. Bentz, who developed a thirty-two-acre tract called Prospect Park that is marked by boulder and clinker brick portals on Prospect Boulevard at Orange Grove. In addition to Bentz's own home at 657 Prospect Blvd (J), Prospect Park included "La Miniatura," or **Millard House** (K), a Frank Lloyd Wright–designed textile-block house with a pre-Columbian motif (1923) and its studio, added in 1926 by his son Lloyd, at 654 Prospect Crescent. Shrubbery obscured most views of the property before it changed hands in 1997, but it was best seen from below from Rosemont Avenue.

The Greenes' 1905 design for the **Willett House** (L) at 424 Arroyo Terrace was obscured by a later remodel in the Spanish colonial style. The 1907 **Ranney House** (M) at 440 Arroyo Terrace reflects an unusual amount of input from the client, who worked as a draughtsman in the Greenes' office. Only the section to the left of the front door is

tion when, its style out of fashion, it was placed on the market in the 1950s. Although the Gamble heirs chose not to live year-round in Southern California, they allegedly decided to donate the house instead of selling it when they overheard a prospective buyer's comment that a coat of white paint would brighten the place up; since 1966 the Gamble House has been administered jointly by the city of Pasadena and the University of Southern California. Its spirit still shines brightly. This showplace of Craftsman style is both somewhat Victorian and simultaneously avant-garde, and it recalls the era when Easterners came to Pasadena to sleep in the orange-blossom-scented open air. Docent-led one-hour tours are offered between noon and 3 p.m. Thursday through Sunday. Larger groups need reservations one month in advance; call 626-793-3334.

The research library, previously located in the Gamble House garage, has been transferred to the care of the Huntington Library; selections from the Gamble House collection—eighty pieces of furniture and decorative arts designed by the Greenes for other clients—are on permanent view in the Virginia Steele Scott Gallery at the Huntington, where they are displayed in the broader context of American art. The Gamble House bookstore, which carries an excellent selection of books and research materials on the Arts and Crafts movement, has been greatly expanded into the space formerly occupied by the library.

The Greene Brothers designed many houses in the adjacent area, starting with the **Cole House** (B), built two years before the **Gamble House** (A) on the lot next door (2 Westmoreland Place). It was the first of original. Several noteworthy residences are to be found on North Grand Avenue, including the **Hutchins House** (N), a Queen Anne cottage at #206, built in 1895, and Myron Hunt's own residence (O) of 1905 at #200. The first house designed by Greenes in this neighborhood, at #240, was commissioned by Katherine Duncan in 1900 and expanded by the architects for Theodore Irwin in 1906. The **Duncan-Irwin House** (P) incorporates the wide overhanging eaves, clinker-brick walls, and exposed joinery that became hallmarks of Greene and Greene architecture. Their work was largely obliterated from the **Culbertson House** (Q) at #235 by a remodel in the 1950s, but an art glass door, pergola, and clinker-brick wall remain. To add a second story to the **Halsted House** (R), which they had designed in 1905 at #90, the Greenes moved the entrance to face the side driveway.

A map of interesting local architecture is available at the Gamble House bookstore, or look for the pamphlet *Ten Tours of Pasadena* produced by the city's cultural heritage commission, which notes estimated times to walk or bicycle each route.

The Aquatics Center (360 N. Arroyo Blvd.; 626-564-0330), built by the Amateur Athletic Foundation with surplus funds from the 1984 Olympics, has world-class facilities that are available free to Pasadena residents and for a small fee ($3–5 per day or $45 per month) to others. One of the fifty-meter pools is always reserved for lap swimming, while free-swim sessions and classes are scheduled in the other.

Pasadena Historical Museum at Feynes Mansion

470 W. Walnut St.
Pasadena 91103
626-577-1660
Thurs.–Sun. 1–4 p.m.
Entry: adults $4, seniors/students $3,
children under 12 free

The Pasadena Historical Museum calls the Feynes House in which it is located its "largest artifact"; docents call it "the mansion" in recognition of the opulence befitting its position on Millionaire's Row. Designed in 1906 by Robert Farquhar (who later built the Clark Library in the West Adams area and the California Club downtown), its neoclassical style is exemplified in the entrance hall, which has fat mahogany columns, Oriental rugs, and silk damask covering the walls. The eighteen-room mansion was expanded in 1912 with a solarium—which has a stairwell that can be covered for use as a buffet table—and a studio that incorporates a stagelike balcony and stairs used for performances; an eclectic mix of period furniture fills the downstairs rooms. Although the Feynes Mansion was not the greatest house on Millionaire's Row, it is one of the last and recalls that gilded moment in Pasadena's history.

The gardens are still lovely, filled with ferns, camellias, bamboo, redwoods, and fruit trees. A Swiss-style chalet was moved from another Pasadena estate to house a collection of Finnish folk art formed by Consul Paloheimo, who married one of the Feynes daughters; these specimens of snow country are certainly unique in Southern California, and may be viewed on request (although hours are erratic).

In recent years the mission of the Pasadena Historical Museum has been expanded to include collecting oral, written, and photographic records of Pasadena and the San Gabriel Valley, and its name was changed to Museum to reflect its status as a repository of these collections. One million photographs, bound volumes of the Pasadena *Star News* and earlier local newspapers, as well as postcards, stereographs, and maps, document local history (with a special focus on events such as the Tournament of Roses).

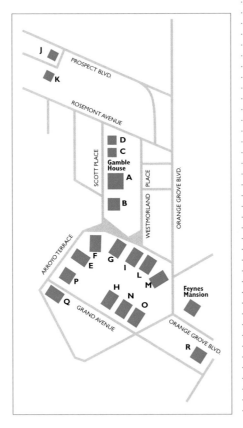

Norton Simon Museum

411 W. Colorado Blvd.
Pasadena 91105
626-449-6840
www.citycent.com/CCC/nsmuseum.html
Thurs.–Sun. noon–6 p.m.
Entry: adults $4, seniors/students $2,
children under 12 free

Norton Simon built a multinational corporation (Hunt-Wesson Foods, *McCalls*, Canada Dry) that secured his fortune. He also formed one of the last great private

art collections: in the 1950s he began acquiring European paintings and sculpture, starting with Degas, Renoir, Gauguin, and Cézanne, and in the 1960s he added a comprehensive selection of Old Masters. He toured the collection and loaned it to other institutions before settling it in Pasadena in 1974, when he took over the financially troubled Pasadena Museum of Modern Art (which had supplanted the Pasadena Art Institute, founded in 1924 as an outgrowth of the Arroyo avant-garde culture). Norton Simon transformed that institution into a home for the 12,000 works in his collection and renamed it in his honor.

Simon was so intimately involved in forming the collection and even in the day-to-day operations of the museum that the art world wondered what would happen to it after his death. In 1996 the late collector's wife, actress Jennifer Jones Simon—who is now president of the museum's board—announced a $3-million plan to renovate the galleries and gardens. Architect Frank Gehry was commissioned to replace cluttered lighting and increase usable wall space; long hallways were broken up to provide more intimate viewing areas and to establish a chronological sequence through the galleries. Gehry realized that charge with a surprisingly subdued and elegant renova-

tion that includes light-colored wide-board flooring and travertine pavers that continue up the walls as baseboards. Landscape architect Nancy Goslee Powers was asked to redesign the gardens in a style more compatible with the late nineteenth-century focus of one of its most renowned collections: the *spirit* of Giverny—not a *copy* of Monet's famous gardens—inspired her to replace rectangular reflecting pools with meandering ponds and create informal plantings as settings for sculpture. Gehry's design for a 2,000-square-foot teahouse, which will be a focal point of the new outdoor spaces, has not been revealed.

The previous configuration of the galleries included a few oddities: the collection of Indian and Southeast Asian art was divided between two spaces—on the upper and lower levels—now it will all be brought together in a redesigned open space divided by columns rather than walls. The comprehensive Degas collection—more than 100 paintings, pastels, monotypes, and drawings, plus a unique, complete group of Degas bronzes cast from the artist's wax masters—has been moved to galleries filled with other nineteenth- and twentieth-century art. Now visitors will find the Old Master collections to the right of the entrance, the nineteenth-century, impressionist, and modern works to the left, and South Asian art on the lower level.

The Renaissance galleries display early Italian altarpieces and panel paintings on gold ground, along with a Madonna and Child (c. 1468) by Botticelli and a circa 1502 version by Raphael. A dog so large it intersects all four edges of a large composition by Il Guercino and an image of the martyred Cecilia (patron saint of music) by Guido Reni are highlights of the Italian baroque. Among the Spanish paintings are de Ribera's masterful image of a blind man, *The Sense of Touch* (1616), and the only signed still life by Zurbarán (see photo, right), along with his more typical paintings depicting saints and monastic life. Dutch paintings include portraits by Frans Hals; Rembrandt's image of himself at age thirty (ca. 1636–38) and *The Artist's Son Titus* (ca. 1645–50); and Rubens's rendition of *David Slaying Goliath* (1630) and *The Holy Women at the Sepulchre*. The genres of still life and landscape are well represented by paintings from the northern European schools.

Across the hall is one of the most appealing and intelligent selections of modern European art found in America. This collection has been shuffled and reinstalled, with more emphasis given to chronology and artistic affiliations than to nationality. Two of Picasso's signature portraits—a colorful image of his mistress Marie-Thérèse Walter daydreaming, and a more classical *Bust of a Woman* from 1923, rendered in oil and fixed black chalk on canvas—hang opposite the gallery entrance and firmly identify it as being filled with works from the twentieth century. Up the north hallway are later works—anchored at each corner with more works by Picasso—including two of the draped and exotic female figures that master colorist Henri Matisse began to paint when he moved to Nice. Georges Braque is represented with a large painting

of the artist and his model rendered in oil and sand on canvas, as well as some of the still lifes in which he explored the shifting planes of cubism.

The sightline to the left terminates at a handsome terra-cotta-colored wall where *The Ragpicker* (1865–69), one of the series of monumental figures that Manet called the "Four Philosophers," draws the eye down a long corridor and back in time. A still life of fruit by Gustave Courbet and a pensive portrait of a young woman in a red bodice by Jean-Baptiste Corot now flank *The Ragpicker* to one side; Manet's deceptively simple still life of a fish is on the other. I was surprised to find Goya's *Saint Jerome in Penitence* (1798) in this gallery, but the juxtaposition reveals Manet's admiration for the painters of Spain's golden age.

One of the new galleries along the southwest corridor contains works that predate Manet by a century. There are light-filled images of Venice by Canaletto and Guardi and works by the French painters Hubert Robert and Fragonard, who were both drawn to the classical landscape of Rome and became lifelong friends. The work of Tiepolo, who has been called the "purest exponent of Italian rococo," dominates the room with *The Triumph of Virtue and Nobility Over Ignorance*, painted for a Venetian palazzo, and a pair of smaller oval works. Portraits by Ingres, Goya, and Vigée-Lebrun, and still lifes by Chardin

and his student, Thomas Germain Duvivier (who later became the director of the Royal Tapestry Works at les Gobelins), complete this survey of the eighteenth century.

Artists whose works prefigure impressionism and very early works by artists identified with that movement are juxtaposed in one large square gallery. A Normandy coast seascape with brooding clouds above a narrow strip of beach—a genre that earned Eugène-Louis Boudin the nickname "king of skies" from fellow artist Corot—hangs above a striking square pastel, *Marine* by Gustave Courbet. A comparison of that artist's *Cliffs at Etretat, La Porte d'Aval* (1869) and his traditional Barbizon school landscapes in the adjacent gallery reveals the rapid evolution of the modern aesthetic. Twenty-seven-year-old Renoir sold several early works that sound the major chords of his oeuvre to the influential dealer Durand-Ruel. They are: a view of the Ponts des Arts, Paris; a small portrait of artist friends gathered in his studio in 1876; and a straightforward depiction of a bouquet of lilacs—so lush and inviting that I found myself sniffing for their scent. There are three early works by Monet: two dark-toned seascapes and a sunny view of his garden at Vetheuil, where he lived years before he began the famous plantings around his house at Giverny. Berthe Morisot's depiction of two languid figures on a porch overlooking a limpid green sea is a memento of the summer holiday she shared in 1874 with the Manet family, during which she accepted the marriage proposal of the painter's younger brother Eugène.

Selections from the Norton Simon's extensive collection of works by Degas appear in several galleries throughout the museum. Other spaces are devoted exclusively to them; one closet-sized gallery is so tiny that viewers inevitably find their noses only inches from the eight drawings and pastels on view there. Degas' sculptures are scattered throughout the suite of galleries, and his paintings line two walls in one narrow space, acting as transition to the modern works at the large gallery located at the entrance.

Two still lifes by Cézanne and one by Paul Serusier illustrate the evolution of cubism as naturalism was discarded and the three-dimensional verisimilitude of the picture plane shattered. Van Gogh believed that his 1888 portrait of the old gardener and shepherd Patience Escalier marked his break with the principles of impressionism, and in the explosive *Mulberry Tree*, painted a year before his death in 1890, color is used freely to express emotion. Gauguin also moved from naturalistic renderings of the world to imaginative compositions painted in symbolic colors, like *Tahitian Woman and Boy* (1899). *Exotic Landscape*, painted by Henri Rousseau in 1910, and Diego Rivera's *Flower Vendor* (1941) flank the entrance to this gallery.

Works by Puvis de Chavannes, Vuillard, Bonnard, and the Nabis painters, as well as decorative arts created by them (such as the cupboard on which Emile Bernard painted figures wearing traditional Breton *coiffes* or lace bonnets), are alongside those of their German contemporaries, the Blue Four—Lyonel Feininger, Alexei Jawlensky, Wassily Kandinsky, and Paul Klee. The German works were bequeathed to the Pasadena Art Institute by the artists' American representative, Galka Scheyer. The museum's extensive holdings of prints, including works on paper by Rembrandt, Goya, and Picasso, as well as Japanese *ukiyo-e*, will be displayed in changing exhibitions.

Sculpture, a medium in which many museum collections seem lacking, is a conspicuous presence at the Norton Simon: Rodin's *The Burghers of Calais* marks the front walk; just inside the entrance in the glass-walled atrium are modern works including three pieces by Henry Moore. Other works by Moore and Brancusi are found in the modern galleries. The surprise here is the large group of South Asian sculptures, a highly regarded collection that Simon formed—under the tutelage of then-LACMA curator Pratapaditya Pal—following his first trip in 1971 to that part of the world. Serene monumental Thai and Cambodian figures, small animated bronzes from the Himalayan nations, and sculptures from all regions of India are dispersed throughout the galleries; they also can be seen outdoors in natural light, set against lush green foliage.

Before the museum opens to the public on Thursday and Friday mornings, it is reserved for free guided tours to school groups from grades seven to twelve; the students are also give free admission to the museum for the rest of the day to continue their exploration. Adults may also book private tours of the museum, but it isn't free: before noon, Thursday through Sunday, tours (including museum admission) cost $250 per twenty-five people; in the afternoon, when the galleries are open to other visitors, the rate drops to $200 per twenty-five people. Call 626-844-6923 for tour reservations, which are essential.

Its long tradition of excellence in book arts is maintained at Art Center's off-campus facility: Archetype Press (40 Mills Pl.) is a traditional typography lab with a large collection of letterpress equipment on which students produce limited-edition books. There is no drop-in visitation, but the facility can be seen by appointment (626-396-2411), and special exhibitions are open to the public.

Art Center College of Design

1700 Lida St.
Pasadena 91103
626-396-2200
Tours of sculpture garden and building: Mon.–Thurs. 2 p.m., Fri. 10:30 a.m. (during school sessions)
Entry: free

Art Center was founded in 1930 to educate students for professional careers in design and the visual arts. It continues to adapt its programs to new technologies and the changing needs of society so that its graduates "are ready and able to work, to make both a living and a life in art and design." It now offers nine majors—advertising, environmental design, film, fine art, graphic design, illustration, photography, product design, and transportation design—that allow its 1,200 students (drawn from thirty-seven foreign countries) to pursue a wide range of careers.

Art Center relocated in 1977 to the northwestern section of Pasadena, choosing a spectacular 175-acre canyon-rim site with a panoramic view of the San Gabriel Valley. Craig Ellwood's design—spare, black, with exposed engineering elements—bridges the road and houses classrooms, art laboratories, and a gallery. In 1992 James Tyler Architects (who had worked with Ellwood on the original structure), added the 47,000-square-foot south wing filled with studio space and a new $17-million computer lab; the entire campus was retrofitted with technological upgrades that allow Art Center to remain on the cutting edge of design, and the layout was revamped to allow for more collaboration and sequential assignments among departments.

The Alyce de Roulet Williamson Gallery (Tues.–Sun. noon–5 p.m., Thurs. noon–9 p.m.), a 4,600-square-foot space for changing exhibitions, was among the new programs facilitated by construction of the new building. Topics of recent exhibitions have included: Czechoslovakian book design from 1920 to the 1940s; the first quarter-century of video art; and masterworks of Italian design, 1960–1994. The gallery's curator has designed a Web site (www.artcenter.edu/exhibit/williamson.html); Internet users can see a 360-degree view of current and past exhibitions and critique them interactively, and there is a virtual wing with art made specifically for the Internet.

Leading to the new formal gallery is a space dedicated to student work (Mon.–Thurs. 9 a.m.–10 p.m., Fri.–Sun. 9 a.m.–5 p.m., Sun. noon–5 p.m.). Students' best solutions to assigned design problems are displayed here and changed at the end of each semester.

The public is welcome at many of Art Center's programs: there are lectures (Tues. or Thurs., noon) by prominent figures in the art and design community, and film screenings are regular features on Friday nights. Among the public events on its annual calendar is the Arts Center 100, an October art sale that includes furniture, fashion, and photography, as well as painting and sculpture; 80 percent of the proceeds of each sale go to the artist and the rest to the scholarship fund. The children's book festival in April showcases Art Center grads who are authors and illustrators with readings, book signings, and reading-related crafts. Call the public relations office (626-396-2338) to be notified of future programs and events.

Most visitors will experience Art Center through its on-campus galleries or its space downtown in the Del Mar Building (10–30 Del Mar Blvd.; Fri.–Sat. 10 a.m.–10 p.m., Sun. noon–5 p.m.), where work by graduate students is exhibited. But adults seeking to facilitate a career change or learn new technology and motivated high school students can take advantage of the college's fine staff and facilities through special programs. Check out the Web site for Art Center at Night (acan@artcenter.edu) or call 626-396-2319 for catalogue of classes. Steep fees don't deter dedicated adults from acquiring new skills; in fact, the computer-based courses are so popular that admission is by lottery. The courses for high school students are much less expensive ($150) but equally demanding; morning and afternoon classes are offered, so motivated students can enroll in more than one subject. In addition to the artist's basic skills—painting, still life and figure drawing, photography, and film—classes in advertising, graphic design, industrial design, and interior and environmental design are taught by the same top-notch staff that draws students from around the world to this campus. Scholarships are offered to talented students (who must submit a portfolio for review) on the basis of need. Call 626-396-2319 for information.

Pacific Asia Museum

46 N. Los Robles Ave.
Pasadena 91101
626-449-2742
Wed.–Sun. 10 a.m.–5 p.m.
Entry: adults $4, seniors/students $2

Grace Nicholson was an interesting woman who, with wit and determination, created a successful career as an art dealer; she traded for the first fifteen years in Native-American art (see the Southwest Museum), then developed a passion for the arts of Asia. Within a decade she could afford to build a palatial showplace—a Chinese imperial-style home and shop designed to her specifications in 1924—which she called the Chinese Treasure House; she lived in the building until her death in 1948 and bequeathed it to the city of Pasadena. It is listed on the National Register of Historic Places as "an outstanding example of 1920s Period Revival architectural design" for such elements as the upturned roofline of green tiles surmounted by ceramic guard dogs and the courtyard garden with koi ponds and specimen rocks.

In the early 1960s the building housed the Pasadena Art Museum; during that time, it was the site of an important Marcel Duchamp retrospective organized by Walter Hopps, a legendary curator who also showcased the emerging generation of contemporary L.A. artists in the space. When that institution moved to a new building (now the Norton Simon Museum), a group called the PacifiCulture Foundation, which for a decade had been organizing Asian cultural events, petitioned the city for a lease on the Pasadena landmark.

No reservations are required for the Pacific Asia Museum's Family Free Day programs (3rd Sat. of the month); the museum also waives its admission charge on these days.

The Pacific Asia Museum, which celebrated its twenty-fifth anniversary in 1996, continues the tradition of the PacifiCulture Foundation by presenting such events as the monthly Family Free Days, which combine performances with participatory workshops to explore many aspects of a particular culture. The museum strives for pan-Asian coverage in its programming to reflect the influx of trans-Pacific immigration in Southern California's ethnic mix: the arts of Korea, Afghanistan, Vietnam, and Myanmar (Burma) were featured in Family Free Day programs during the past year, and various art forms of Thailand, Indonesia, the Philippines, Australia, Tibet, and India were the focus of lectures and classes. Workshops in mah-jongg (one of the oldest Chinese games) and ikebana (the Japanese art of flower arranging) are offered frequently, along with ongoing classes in Chinese language (beginning and intermediate), tai chi, brush painting, and taiko drumming. The museum store, well stocked with books on Asian subjects, and gift and souvenir items, also hosts book signings and lectures by authors.

Selections from the museum's permanent collection—little known because it has never been published—are generally displayed in several galleries on the lower level. Among the 17,000 objects preserved by the museum are important collections of Chinese textiles, Ming and Ching dynasty porcelains, carved jade, and Japanese paintings of the Edo period; furniture from the permanent collection will be featured in a renovated space on the second floor. Across the courtyard garden are galleries devoted to changing exhibitions: for its quarter-century anniversary, the Pacific Asia Museum paid tribute to Grace Nicholson, mounting a long-term exhibition of the Asian art she collected and sold. The eclectic ensemble of objects—Chinese furniture and embroidered tapestries, Japanese fan paintings, and Tibetan *tanka*, for example—revealed Nicholson's appreciation of these exotic cultures and her business acumen, for she had an instinct about which artifacts could be most readily assimilated into American homes. Recent exhibitions examined the influence of the Japanese woodblock tradition on western artists Paul Jacoulet and Lilian Miller and showcased the works of Fu Baoshi, an influential modern master of Chinese ink painting. In the Foyer Gallery, works by contemporary Asian and Asian-American artists are featured.

Kidspace

390 S. El Molino Ave.
Pasadena 91101
626-449-9143
Tues. 1:30–5 p.m., Wed.–Thurs. 1–5 p.m.,
Sat. 10 a.m.–5 p.m., Sun. 1–5 p.m.;
(hours vary with seasons, so call ahead)
Entry: adults and children over 2 $5, seniors $3.50,
children 1–2 $2.50, children under 1 free

My five-year-old son whoops with delight whenever a visit to Kidspace is proposed. Although the major hands-on exhibits usually are unchanged, they invite repeated exploration, and Kidspace reinvents itself with a new theme each week during the summer and each month during the rest of the year; projects in the art space, live animal shows, and workshops—all included in the admission price—will reflect the special focus. Nature dominates the spring calendar: build a butterfly bungalow and adopt a pupa to nurture; meet California's own critters—the desert tortoise (state reptile) and California quail (state bird)—and find out what lives in Southern California's oceans with Save the Whales; make a Mother's Day gift from pressed flowers.

Three very simple environments flank the entrance—a supermarket, post office, and fire station—but the details of each are refined to maximize educational potential: kids can dress in boots and oilcloth and dangle from a fire engine and slide down a pole, as well as attach long hoses to a real hydrant and find the fire site on an illuminated map. **Eco-beach** is a sand pit that can be explored with sieves, shovels, and buckets; there are wave-creation devices in the porthole windows, a mural of undersea life, and aquariums. **Critter Caverns** is a treehouse/climbing labyrinth with a mural that depicts the underground habitats of such burrowing animals as ants and mice. In one of the terrariums in an adjacent display there is a kangaroo rat in its burrow, and other desert dwellers, like scorpions—did you know Southern California is blessed with the largest variety of scorpions in the world and that Kidspace has a live specimen of the world's largest? There are iridescent Morpho butterflies and a tiny hummingbird in the terrarium containing tropical titans, as well as a Goliath bird-eating tarantula.

Mouse House—a four-station computer lab stocked with lots of educational games—and an interactive TV news set are more high-tech exhibits. Costume closets and a mirrored performance stage share one section with musical instruments.

There are lots of puppets and a curtained

Pasadena Heritage (651 St. John Ave., Pasadena 91105; 626-441-6333) conducts walking tours of Old Town on the second Saturday of the month.

stage for performances, and a shadowbox with photosensitive walls records an evolving mural of kids' antics. Different kinds of manipulatives or building blocks are featured in one carpeted area, and simple games, like checkers, in another. **Toddler Territory** has padded floors and walls that are often filled with large, soft balls for rolling around.

On the last Monday of every month, Kidspace stays open late (until 8 p.m.; free admission after 5 p.m.), and in addition to the regular exhibits, there is always an in-

teresting program: a Chinese New Year celebration, storytellers spinning tales from around the globe, or Brazilian music and martial arts. A few events are regular highlights of the annual schedule: for the Halloween Haunted House, the whole museum is transformed into a special installation and the open field in front is filled with game booths, a bounce house, a crawl-through maze, and musicians. The Rosebud Parade (mid-Nov.) has been a Pasadena tradition for the past decade: in the morning kids decorate their bikes, tricycles, and wagons with donated flowers and greenery, then march with live music and drill teams. The Eco-Arts festival coincides with Earth Day (Mar.); Critter Expo (Aug.)—which features an assortment of reptiles, from simple box turtles to a seventeen-foot banana python, as well as face-painting and origami folding—is held at One Colorado, the event sponsor. Kamp Kidspace offers week-long summer sessions, recommended for children ages six to ten, with different activities for the three-hour morning and afternoon classes that can be combined for a full day.

Pasadena Civic Center (300 E. Green St.) is a 1931 Italian Renaissance structure that is listed on the National Register of Historic Places. It includes the **Civic Auditorium**, a multipurpose rental facility that also hosts concerts by the **Pasadena Symphony** and a **Distinguished Speakers** series, inaugurated in 1996 and featuring Maya Angelou, Colin Powell, and Tommy Lasorda on the current roster (call 800-508-9301 for subscription information). A 17,000-square-foot ballroom within the building was converted in the 1960s to an ice-skating rink; call the

The Pasadena Symphony's Musical Circus is a series of free workshops for families offered on the morning of its scheduled concerts at the Pasadena Civic Center. There are eight concerts on its annual schedule, about monthly from October to June, each accompanied by this popular program, which consists of three elements. Starting at 8:30 a.m., kids can sample musical instruments, with assistance from musicians, often of their own age; the guest conductor and soloists then offer a performance suited to the young audience; finally, participants are welcome to remain for an open rehearsal of that evening's concert. Call 626-793-7172 for the schedule.

Pasadena Ice-Skating Center (626-578-0800) for information on classes and schedule of public skating.

For forty years following its opening night in May 1925, the 700-seat **Pasadena Playhouse** (39 S. El Molino Ave.) received critical and popular acclaim and also distinguished itself as the only center west of the Mississippi for training classical actors which rivaled the prestigious Juilliard School in New York. In 1937 it was designated a State Theater in recognition of founder Glinor Brown's innovative and exciting programming, but competition from television and the new Music Center downtown caused declining revenues, and in 1966 the theater closed its doors. Twenty years and $1.5 million later, the Pasadena Playhouse reopened and began rebuilding its reputation for well-produced, intelligent theater. Call 626-356-7529 for season brochure or tickets; see Theater and Dance, pp 78–79.

Armory Center for the Arts

145 N. Raymond Ave.
Pasadena 91103
626-792-5101
Gallery: Wed.–Sun. noon–5 p.m., Thurs.–Fri. 6:30–9 p.m.
Entry: free

The Pasadena Art Workshops, which provided innovative arts education programs to local children for many decades, began the latest chapter of their community service in 1989 when the city gave the program a home in a renovated National Guard Armory. At the new Armory Center for the Arts, educators rededicated themselves to goals that had characterized their earlier efforts: encouraging individual expression in both the creation and interpretation of art; revealing the connection between the visual arts and other disciplines, including music, the sciences, and literature; and fostering collaboration with other cultural, educational, and civic institutions to integrate the arts into community life.

The main gallery at the Armory Center holds exhibitions of contemporary art, and is used for performances. The Community Room displays student work and can be rented for shows by other organizations and artists in the community. For an intellectually stimulating start to your weekend, check out Friday Nights at the Armory, programs that engage audiences in conversations with artists, curators, and writers; these alternate with the performance series Breaking the Code of Contemporary Music, informal concerts by the Southwest Chamber Music Society.

Pasadena Farmers Market
Victory Park
(between Altadena Dr.
and Sierra Madre Blvd.
at Paloma St.)
Sat. 8:30 a.m.–1 p.m.

The most well known and well loved of the Armory Center's programs are its art classes for all ages, which are taught by professional artists. Classes for preschoolers are offered every weekday morning at the Armory: four-to six-year-olds bring a sack lunch from home to join the Lunch Bunch and enjoy a class like Ooey Gooey, which uses fingerpaints, paper pulp, and clay, or Fairytale Friends, which combines reading and the creation of fanciful artworks. The joint really gets jumping after school when a half dozen classes for ages three to thirteen explore drama, dance, mime, magic, and juggling, as well as more traditional studio art subjects and contemporary styles of animation. Saturday classes and special short sessions during school holidays ensure that there is something for every child on the Armory's schedule.

Most of the classes for adults are held in the evening (Tues.-Thurs.); they make use of the Armory Center's letterpress facilities to explore book arts, the darkroom for specialized photographic printing, or the ceramics studio. The Armory reluctantly raised its rates in 1998: fees for kids' classes are now $140, but tuition assistance is available; fees for adults range from $160 to $190 for each ten-class session. Register by mail or by phone (626-792-5101).

During the school year older students (ages 11–18) are recommended by teachers for inclusion in Art Mentorships for Youth—a free semester-long course taught by an artist-in-residence—where they can study photography, letterpress, video, music, painting, and sculpture. During the summer months, any talented teenager can apply to an equivalent program called Art High, which is offered free of charge but requires regular attendance.

Neighborhood children—6,000 each year—discover the joys of art through the Armory Center's extensive outreach program Walk to Art, which are free classes for children (grades 3–5) conducted after school in local libraries, parks, and schools; before each quarterly series begins, parents must come to the Armory Center to register kids for the full program. Educators and artists from the Armory Center contract with local schools from elementary to high school for art-viewing and art-making programs—Children Investigate the Environment; Cultural Traditions/New Visions; Project FLARE: Fun with Language, Arts and Reading.

The Pasadena Art Alliance (PAA) fosters appreciation for contemporary art by offering grants to area arts organizations and presenting a biennial exhibition program. Pasadena-based organizations receive most of the $100,000 distributed annually: Art Center, Kidspace, Pasadena City College, Pacific Asia Museum, the Armory Center, and the Huntington are regularly awarded funding. Institutions interested in applying for grants (individuals are not eligible), can contact the PAA's administrative offices, 626-795-9276.

Pasadena Public Art Tour

In addition to redevelopment projects initiated by the city's 1% for Public Art Program, Pasadena has a new municipal visual and performing arts center, the **Pasadena Art Space** (155 E. Holly St.; 626-744-6770). Open since the fall of 1996, it offers changing exhibitions and performances.

Inside the **Plaza Pasadena** shopping mall (300 E. Colorado Blvd.), *Pasadena Painting*, a 6,000-square-foot mural painted in 1981 by **Terry Schoonhoven**, covers the walls and ceiling. On the Green Street side, facing the Pasadena Civic Auditorium, there are sculptures by **Jay Willis** and **Christopher Georgesco.**

Plaza la Fuentes, on the northeast side of Colorado and Los Robles Avenues, was designed by **Lawrence Halprin** to evoke the atmosphere of a Mediterranean town square. A tile mural by **Joyce Kozloff** covers a series of freestanding walls. Early Pasadena artist **Ernest Batchelder** created the tile fountain in the central garden, and **Michael Lucaro** has installed eight bronze animal sculptures throughout the plaza, as well as creating *Dreamer with Fish Fountain* for the plaza.

At **California Institute of Technology** (1201 E. California Blvd.), Lloyd Hamrol has installed an earthwork entitled *Moore's Stone Volute*, commissioned in conjunction with the building of Moore Hall, which houses the engineering department and is named for its benefactor, Caltech alumnus Gordon Moore. The work is located on the west side of campus; take the paved walkway about fifty yards from the corner of Wilson Avenue and San Pasqual Street. Completed in 1995, the work appears to grow out of the ground in a spiral form, spanning fifty feet in diameter and rising six feet in height. It offers not only a visual experience but a physical one, as viewers walk in and out of its interior and exterior spaces.

The City of Pasadena Arts Commission has maps and descriptions of public art walking tours, which include historically significant buildings, museums, and exhibition spaces, and public art projects; call 626-744-6770 for information.
—*Noriko Fujinami*

California Institute of Technology (Caltech)

1201 E. California Blvd.
Pasadena 91125
626-395-6811

On the third Wednesday of every month, KPCC (89.3 FM) broadcasts AirTalk, a program that features interviews with Caltech researchers working on the cutting edge of science and technology.

Caltech is one of the world's major research centers, and nearly half of its annual budget ($289 million) comes from federal grants. Its faculty and alumni have been awarded the Nobel Prize twenty-three times to date, the National Medal of Science thirty-eight times, and the National Medal of Technology nine times. About 2,000 students, half of them undergraduates, enroll in this prestigious independent university to study engineering and science; women, first admitted in 1970, today make up 25 percent of the student body.

Caltech played a key role in the aerospace industry—the principles of flight and aircraft design were developed in the 1930s by Theodore von Karman and his students in Caltech's Graduate Aeronautical Laboratory (GALCIT)—and today it manages the Jet Propulsion Laboratory (JPL) for NASA. (JPL is the area's leading employer, with a work force of 6,000; another 2,500 people are employed on the Caltech campus, making it the third largest employer in Pasadena.)

During the 1920s and 1930s scientists in the seismological laboratory invented the first instrument capable of recording vibrations from distant earthquakes; they devised a logarithmic scale to measure quake magnitude, a system still identified with theoretical physicist Charles Richter. More recently the U.S. Geological Survey has joined forces with Caltech to establish and monitor more than 200 seismic stations, and when a temblor rattles Southern California, residents turn to seismologists Kate Hutton and Lucy Jones for information and reassurance (626-395-3003). Caltech also operates an Earthquake Hotline at 626-395-6977.

The campus of the California Institute of Technology, which today occupies 124 acres (between Del Mar and California Blvds. at north and south, Hill and Wilson Aves. at east and west), has been systematically developed using harmonious architectural master plans and a Spanish Renaissance style chosen for its compat-

Among Caltech's off-campus attractions are the Palomar Observatory in San Diego County, which houses the 200-inch Hale Telescope and includes displays of astronomical photographs and video on modern developments in astronomy in the Greenfield Museum.

ibility with the California landscape.

Bertram Grosvenor Goodhue, who had used this style for the 1915–16 Panama-California International Exposition in San Diego, was hired by administrators in 1917 to design the first master plan for the campus; an east-west axis along Olive Walk and a north-south axis from California Boulevard (terminated with the construction of Beckman Auditorium in

ARNOLD AND MABEL BECKMAN LABORATORY OF CHEMICAL SYNTHESIS

1964) grouped academic buildings by discipline and established a specific sector for residential and social life.

At the intersection of the axes is a central court modeled after Spanish city plazas; today it is defined by the Millikan Library pond. Columned arcades with vaulted ceilings and terra-cotta floor tiles establish a continuous line connecting the buildings and provide shaded walkways, and homogeneous cast-stone decoration around doors and windows accents the walls of the plain rectilinear buildings. The decorative elements in the West Court, completed by his firm after Goodhue's death in 1924, reveal the academic affiliation of each building: sea horses, lobsters, octopuses, and a chain of monkeys for biology; cacti, corn, and sunflowers for genetic research; a Tree of Life, volcanoes, and waterfalls for historical geology; and a symbol of the sun for astronomy.

In 1930 British architect Gordon Kaufmann, a Pasadena resident, was selected to design the Athenaeum, which was modeled on the faculty clubs at Oxford and Cambridge Universities; he also designed the complex of student housing south of Olive Walk, which—following the model of Oxford's residences—is subdivided into "alleys" intended to foster loyalty among students and lessen the appeal of fraternities. Kaufmann used eclectic Mediterranean elements to create harmonious and elegant buildings with open courtyards surrounded by loggias. The capitals along the Olive Walk arcade take the form of athletes, aviators, scientists, and musicians.

Architectural walking tours of the Caltech campus are offered (4th Tues. of month at 11 a.m., Sept.-June); call 626-395-6327 for reservations. More general campus tours leave from the Visitors Center (315 S. Hill Ave.) and are offered weekdays at 2 p.m. when the university is in session.

The Beckman Institute, which unites scientists of varied disciplines with similar research interests within the largest building on campus, also houses a small museum (Mon.–Thurs. noon–4 p.m., Fri. noon–2 p.m.; 626-395-2704; free) which celebrates the innovations in scientific instrumentation designed by Caltech alumnus Arnold O. Beckman, who invented the pH meter in 1934. An illustrated time line chronicling scientific discoveries from the seventeenth century forward features the work of Caltech scientists, and a re-creation of a 1920s-era chemistry lab includes an intricate system of glass tubes created by Beckman as a student.

Caltech Presents is the public events program at Caltech, which includes the Watson Caltech Lecture Series (Wed. 8 p.m.; free; call 626-395-4652 for upcoming topics) and Family Faire, events held about once a month (Sat. 2 p.m.) in Beckman Auditorium. Order tickets or the season brochure at the Caltech Ticket Office (332 S. Michigan Ave., Pasadena 91125) or by phone (800-423-8849 or 626-395-4652). Sundays with Coleman is the oldest chamber music series in the U.S. and has been a staple of Caltech's public programming since 1965; the six-concert series, held in the Beckman Auditorium, culminates with an annual competition (free to the public) in the spring. Individual tickets are available from the Caltech ticket office (800-423-8849 or 626-395-4652; season tickets can be ordered only from the Coleman Chamber Music Association (626-793-4191).

Free Sunday-afternoon chamber music concerts have been held for nearly fifty years in the lounge of Dabney Hall, a building designed in 1928 for the Division of Humanities; the well-loved concert series was renamed in honor of late Caltech professor Paco A. Lagerstrom, who guided them for twenty years. Call the Caltech Music Program (626-395-4652) for a schedule of musical events by student groups, including glee clubs, the symphony orchestra, jazz bands, and chamber ensembles.

Jet Propulsion Laboratory (JPL)

4800 Oak Grove Dr.
Pasadena 91109
Information: 818-354-5011
Tours: 818-354-2180

The Jet Propulsion Laboratory, operated by Caltech as one of nine NASA field centers, is the nerve center of America's unmanned space program. When JPL was established in 1944, it was staffed by some of Caltech professor Theodore von Karman's best graduate students from the Institute's renowned aeronautical lab, known as GALCIT; the pioneering research this group undertook in the 1930s defined the principles of modern aviation and is credited with establishing the aerospace industry in Southern California. Von Karman's students applied those aeronautic principles to the space program, and within its first thirty years all of the planets in our solar system with the exception of Pluto—the subject of a mission to be launched early in the next century—were visited by space vehicles designed at JPL. From the first U.S. satellite sent into space, *Explorer I* (a puny fourteen-pound missile), to *Viking, Mariner, Voyager, Galileo,* and *Sojourner,* JPL employees have designed, built, and tracked the spacecraft that allow NASA to explore our solar system. Some departments participate in NASA's Mission to Planet Earth, which studies how our global environment is changing, and the Technology and Applications Program conducts research for NASA and other sponsors and transfers JPL-developed technology to U.S. industry.

JPL maintains a public presence on its Web sites and by hosting an annual open house, both efficient and information-rich ways to access the contributions that JPL makes to local culture, but if these whet your curiosity rather than satiate it, as a last resort you can make arrangements to tour the facilities. JPL is certainly not open to the public in a general sense, and you should not try to wander onto the 176-acre campus unannounced, but JPL does accommodate about 1,000 members of the general public each year: call several months in advance for reservations (up to nine persons) for a Visitors Day tour (818-354-9314). These two-hour tours are offered about twice each month (generally the first and third weeks) and include a video on JPL's activities and accomplishments, entitled "Welcome to Outer Space," and visits to the Spacecraft Museum, mission control, and the facility where spacecraft are assembled.

Start exploring the technological expertise that allows humans to access the heavens by logging onto www.jpl.nasa.gov. Public interest in this research facility was overwhelming following such missions as *Voyager* and *Galileo*, but when the *Pathfinder* expedition dropped the little *Sojourner* onto Mars on the Fourth of July, 1997, all hell broke loose. JPL Webmasters anticipated twenty-five million hits a day on the Web site so they set up twenty mirror sites, but they received almost twice that number; Web site visitors were entranced by astonishing details of the Red Planet's landscapes, the weather conditions on Mars, and live audio and video feeds from NASA-TV. Teachers praised the sites both for the quality of the immediately available information and for such kid-friendly features as the ability to download and build *Pathfinder* models. (A public installation with these features is offered at the Aerospace Museum in Exposition Park for those without Internet access.

Ten percent of JPL's employees volunteer to staff its annual Open House during a June weekend. A twenty-two-minute video on JPL is shown continuously in von Karman Auditorium; a half-hour talk on the research facility's activities draws crowds all day long to another site. Guides are stationed at several other buildings to explain their functions to visitors: animation 3-D imaging, remote sensing, and data-processing systems; demonstrations of computer-based tools for designing future missions; levitating magnets and superconducting instruments in a wind tunnel. A video of present and future missions is shown in the Space Flight Operations Facility, and works in progress can be viewed in the Spacecraft Assembly Facility.

Learn how to access JPL homepages and other public online facilities at a bank of computer workstations, or follow the special circuit of activities just for kids: see yourself flying in space in the JPL television studio, experience reduced gravity, build an Estes rocket, and collect lithographs of images captured by the Hubble telescope or fact-filled summaries of various missions. About twenty-five booths set up on JPL's mall contain exhibits and handouts on various JPL missions—among the most popular in 1997 was the "MarsYard," where two full-scale replicas of the micro-rover cruised a simulated Martian landscape while engineers explained the ingenious bubble packaging that cushioned the landing on Mars and the mundane floral foam that allows the launch to right itself from any position. A thirty-foot replica of the *Cassini* spacecraft, destined to expand our knowledge of Saturn, was displayed, along with a CD-ROM the flight will carry, which contains 600,000 signatures of people around the globe.

If your kids have made regular forays onto the Internet to see what JPL is doing, enjoyed a full weekend at the Open House, and still haven't had enough, be persistent and patient and you'll eventually get reservations for the Visitors Day tour (818-354-9314). The visit begins in an auditorium dominated by a full-size replica of *Voyager*, which in 1977 sent back photographs of the outer planets; there a captivating film on the history of U.S. space exploration (and JPL's significant role in it) is screened. A guide explains the lab's primary missions: to develop advanced technology and build robotic spacecraft; to operate the Deep Space Network that tracks all satellites in the solar system; to conduct studies for NASA's Mission to Planet Earth and develop instruments for the Earth-observing satellites to be launched in the late 1990s; and to continue research in astronomy, astrophysics, and engineering. The guide diligently answers all questions, and visitors are even allowed to take photographs.

The structure of a spacecraft like *Voyager* is deceptively simple: three canisters (each about the size of a five-pound bag of sugar) comprise the thirty-year power supply and electricity is produced from energy generated by deteriorating plutonium-238 pellets; its long arms put magnetometers, which measure the magnetic field of planets, outside the interference of the craft itself. *Voyager* also carries a record of civilization on Earth in case it encounters any intelligent life forms after leaving our solar system; the contents of the record include greetings in fifty languages, and recordings of classical, folk, jazz, and rock music plus the sounds of cities, jungles, and beaches. A photomural of the 116 images encoded on *Voyager*'s disk is on view at the Spacecraft Museum; other displays include a full-size model of the *Galileo* spacecraft, which was launched in 1989, began orbiting Jupiter in December 1995, and is sending back a steady stream of information on the solar system's largest planet and its moons. Many other prototypes of space vehicles are displayed with concise, fact-filled labels.

Next stop is Space Flight Operations, an earthquake-safe structure where scientists monitor eighteen space vehicles now orbiting the earth or journeying through the galaxy. The two-hour tour ends at the Spacecraft Assembly Facility where the two-story-tall robotic spacecraft that will be sent to explore Saturn and its moon Titan during the international *Cassini* mission sits behind glass in a clean, dust-free environment. This fascinating tour could rival Disneyland in popularity, and while no one wants to divert the JPL scientists from productive research, to encourage public interest in the taxpayer-supported space program and influence some young visitors to join the next generation of its scientists JPL needs to make its facility somewhat accessible and its welcome a bit more cordial.

JPL's Teaching Resource Center (818-354-6916) offers a variety of booklets, posters, and curriculum materials, as well as eight videotapes (each about two hours long); written requests for this material should be sent (on school letterhead) to Mail Stop 601-244 at JPL. The Best of JPL, Travels of *Voyager* and *Galileo*, JPL Computer Graphics, The Shuttle Collection, The *Apollo* Collection, and Elementary Science from Space can be utilized by elementary schools; two Project Mathematics! tapes are designed for high schools.

Eaton Canyon County Park and Nature Center
1750 N. Altadena Dr.
Pasadena 91107
626-398-5420
Park: dawn to dusk
Nature Center: daily 9 a.m.–5 p.m.

At the first stop on the self-guided nature trail at Eaton Canyon, the visitor is informed that "poison oak is one of the most common plants in the park." Most writers wouldn't choose such information to begin a description, but this is a plain sort of a place, untainted by public relations, and it hopes to prevent unnecessary pain or injury to its visitors. There are lots of other plants and animals in Eaton Canyon's 189 acres; its site—at the base of Mount Wilson on the edge of the Angeles National Forest—gives it a dramatic setting and a feeling of spaciousness that's rare in Pasadena.

The activities at Eaton Canyon Nature Center make the joys of exploring this natural wilderness area accessible to those of all ages and levels of fitness. A monthly newsletter is sent to its members ($30 per year), but anyone can participate in the regularly scheduled programs. Its location inspires an active hiking program: there are family nature walks (Sat. 9 a.m.); more strenuous exercise hikes take place several times a month. One weekend per month a docent leads a bird walk, and near the night of the full moon you can stroll with other nocturnal critters on the moonlight hike. Free printed guides allow visitors to identify the plant and animal ecology found on the short trails north of the parking lot.

The Altadena fire of October 1993 burned 6,000 acres in the foothills, destroyed the nature center building, and scorched two-thirds of the Eaton Canyon Natural Area. Fire ecology—how native plants and animals respond to fire, a natural factor in their ecosystem—is the subject of a new trail at Eaton Canyon and an informative brochure that accompanies it. The population of coast live oak (called "live" because it doesn't shed its leaves in winter) was burned severely, but due to the plants' thick bark, 95 percent of these specimens have recovered. A miniature botanical garden featuring fire-safe native plants will surround the new 7,500-square-foot Nature Center, expected to begin welcoming visitors by summer 1998. The 200-seat multipurpose room and two classrooms will be used for events and educational programs, and the Naturalist's Room will contain live exhibits of small animals that

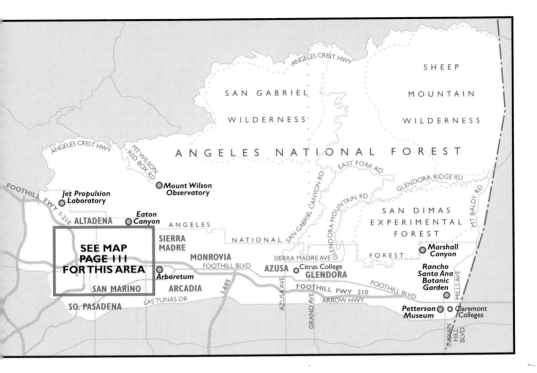

live in the area. Displays that define ecosystems and identify the characteristics of the Eaton Canyon system are also planned, along with a three-dimensional relief map of the area.

The Angeles National Forest consists of 694,000 acres, most of which is in the San Gabriel Mountain range, and draws thirty-two million visitors, more than any other national forest, because its spectacular scenery is easily accessible by roads (including the sixty-five-mile-long Angeles Crest Highway (Rte. 2), which has appropriately been named a national scenic byway). The sections of the forest east of San Gabriel Road (Rte. 39), which climbs from Azusa to Crystal Lake Recreation Area to the San Bernardino county line, crossing the 10,000-foot peak known as Mount Baldy, are described later in this chapter, just before the college town of Claremont. (Areas on the northern side of the mountains that are more accessible from the High Desert communities are described in Chapter IX.) There are several visitors centers in the forest, which provide local information; the Angeles National Forest Information Office (701 N. Santa Anita Ave., Arcadia 91006; 626-335-1251) is a central clearinghouse for maps and information because five ranger districts currently administer this resource.

The Angeles, the first forest preserve established in California, was given priority because it serves as a watershed for the region. Fire management plays an important role in maintaining the watershed because most of the Angeles forest land at lower elevations is cloaked in chaparral, an explosive mixture of dry brush with sycamore, cottonwoods, and mesquite. The Angeles Crest Highway climbs quickly and from it drivers can see a panoply of mountain peaks that support forests of juniper, piñon, fir, and ponderosa pine. On Mt. Baden-Powell—a 9,399-foot peak named for the founder of the Boy Scouts—there is an ancient grove of limber pines, including some specimens that are 2,000 years old.

Many day-trippers' final destination is the Mount Wilson Observatory, which is reached by turning onto Mount Wilson-Red Box Road from Angeles Crest Highway. The observatory (Sat.–Sun. 10 a.m.–4 p.m.; 626-793-3100) at the top of 5,710-foot Mount Wilson was funded in 1904 by astronomer George Ellery Hale, who a few years later would join the board of Throop Polytechnic Institute and lead its transformation into the world-class college of science and engineering that in 1920 was renamed California Institute of Technology. Hale continued to design larger and larger telescopes; he built the 200-inch model still used at Caltech's Palomar Observatory in San Diego County, until recently the most powerful optical telescope in the world. Edwin P. Hubble—whose own telescope design is not only the largest astronomical instrument ever placed in orbit but also so precise that it can track a dime-sized object from a distance of more than 300 miles—formulated his theories of an expanding universe and the existence of galaxies beyond the Milky Way while he was affiliated with Mount Wilson Observatory. A small museum at Mount Wilson features exhibits on Hale and Hubble, as well as photographs of heavenly bodies; Skyline Park has picnic tables with spectacular views across the L.A. basin to the Pacific.

By the time Caltech astronomers produced the first survey of the entire sky visible from the Northern Hemisphere—an atlas of the heavens which identified thousands of new stars, galaxies, and comets—they made their observations from Palomar because the lights of Los Angeles had already overwhelmed dim objects in the night sky. In the late 1970s Caltech stopped operating Mount Wilson Observatory, and in the mid-1980s the Carnegie Institute (who had also helped administer the site) shifted its support to a facility in Chile; supporters of the observatory, however, were not about to allow "arguably the most important site in the history of astronomy" to be mothballed. The Mount Wilson Institute, under the direction of Dr. Robert Jastrow, has retrofitted the 100-inch telescope with adaptive optics so it again delivers images as sharp as when Hubble used it in the 1930s. Research teams again utilize the facility for their projects, and through the Institute's Telescopes in Education program amateur astronomers and school groups can rent the twenty-four-inch telescope (along with sophisticated software to maximize results). To reserve a night under the Telescopes in Education program or to become a member of the Mount Wilson Institute, call 626-793-3100 or write to P.O. Box 70076, Pasadena 91117.

More intrepid visitors will push on to the **Chilao Visitor Center**, about twenty-seven miles east of Interstate 210 and at 5,280 feet, which presents exhibits on the history and management of the Angeles National Forest in a modern building (Fri.–Mon. 9–5) whose design recalls a wickiup, a structure built by native peoples. Bird walks are scheduled on

John Panatier Nature Center (2240 Highland Oaks Dr., Arcadia 91006; 626-355-5309) includes displays on the plant and animal life in 120-acre Wilderness Park and the adjacent Big Santa Anita Canyon.

Sundays at 10 a.m., as well as different family activities on Sundays at 1 p.m.. There are picnic sites with barbecue pits and one area that is clear of brush to provide a snow play area, with safe sledding and cross-country skiing. Hiking trails include short loops from the visitors center and the Chilao campground, as well as access to the Pacific Crest Trail.

The road climbs from here into mountain wilderness and finally to the small community of Wrightwood; we'll resume our tour from the San Gabriel Valley foothills, below.

Heninger Flats, named for the family that homesteaded this claim in the 1800s, is one of five forest tracts owned by the L.A. County Fire Department, but it is unique among them because it has a campground and a small museum (Sat.–Sun. 7 a.m.–5 p.m.; by appt. Mon.–Fri.). The museum includes displays on native animals—rattlesnakes as well as lots of birds—and plants—with a comprehensive survey of pinecones, catalogued by size and weight, and a cross-section of a 750-year-old redwood—as well as on some of the colorful characters and local history that came together in this spot. It is a three-mile hike from the pedestrian gate (2260 Pinecrest Dr., Altadena) to the visitors center at Heninger Flats (626-794-0675) by a roadway that was once the Mount Wilson Toll Road but is now a firebreak on which private vehicles are prohibited. Nonetheless, the cheerful ranger assured me, about 300 people make the trek most weekends during warm weather because this world apart, with 230 forested acres inhabited mainly by deer, bobcats, raccoons, and coyotes, is easily accessible from urban Pasadena. Since the 1920s the fire department has run an experimental nursery on the site, growing fire- and drought-tolerant plants; visitors are invited to take home a free tree.

In the 1890s Professor Thaddeus Lowe invested (and lost) a fortune building a cog railroad that ascended Mount Lowe. The tortuous journey entailed riding an electric trolley ride through Rubio Canyon, then boarding an incline cable car to the summit of Echo Mountain, where the complex of tourist facilities known as White City included a hotel, zoo, and observatory. The intrepid traveler transferred to a narrow-gauge cog railway that ascended the southwest flank of Mount Lowe to 4,400 feet; Lowe had originally planned to continue the railroad to Mount Wilson but had exhausted his funds by 1893.

Pasadena City College

1570 E. Colorado Blvd.
Pasadena 91105
626-585-7123

The extended campus program offers non-credit courses in decorative arts, horticulture, choral and instrumental music, and sponsors the Tuesday Evening Forum of lectures and films. Five student productions are staged each year in Sexson Auditorium or the Little Theatre, and the music department offers a wide range of concerts. The After-School Music Conservatory is a structured program (sixteen weeks in fall and spring, six-week summer session) that since 1973 has helped improve music literacy and offered instruction on a variety of instruments. The College Art Gallery supports an active studio program in visual arts with changing exhibitions.

El Molino Viejo

1120 Old Mill Rd.
San Marino 91108
626-449-5450
Tues.–Sun. 1–4 p.m.
Entry: free, donations welcomed

Site of the first water-powered gristmill in Southern California—el Molino Viejo means "the old mill"—this adobe structure was built circa 1816. It was a dependence of the San Gabriel Mission two miles to the south, but was considered too far away to be practical and was replaced in 1823 with a mill next to the mission; in 1846 it was sold as part of a 16,000-acre parcel of mission lands. The structure has served many functions over the past century, including as a clubhouse for the golf course at the nearby Huntington Hotel; today the California Historical Society maintains its Southern California headquarters here and maintains a small museum with exhibits on state history and a garden with drought-tolerant native plants.

If you were to ask the author of this book the question that everyone who knows her does pose—"What is the one place you would choose to show visitors or residents a great day in Los Angeles County?"—after inquiring about this hypothetical visitor's particular interests and redefining the question, she'd admit that the Huntington is her top pick. Why? It incorporates a sense of history, which few places in this young city do, of when this fertile valley was filled with citrus and avocado ranches, its landscape was identified with paradise, and humans indulged in grandiose landscaping intended to reveal and even improve upon the ideal. Its three distinct parts offer something for every visitor, and most visitors will enjoy a taste of all three specialties.

The Huntington's administrators have noted, with some dismay, that 80 percent of their patrons never enter the buildings—some visitors apparently think the architecture is intimidating, the collections arcane—and are drawn instead to the gardens. The gardens are magnificent and incredibly varied, with different theme gardens—Japanese, Australian, lily ponds—and the extraordinary collections that make this a unique botanical laboratory: roses, camellias, palms, cycads, bamboo, and the complete range of plants that will survive in a desert environment. It's the perfect place to push a stroller; look for early spring color in the camellia forest or Japanese garden.

But don't miss the library and art collections! A display of rare books is not usually considered the appropriate domain for a toddler, but when my son was three he accompanied me into the library for what I expected would be a short foray; he was drop-jaw impressed when I pointed out John Smith's own chronicle of life in the Virginia colony, which he later identified as "the real story of Pocahontas." Some of the most accessible books, selected for their dazzling beauty or historical importance, are on display in one gallery at the front of the library where you won't disturb scholars from their reading or feel obliged to speak in hushed tones.

The newest of the art collections is one that does not require a specialist's taste or knowledge to appreciate: the Virginia Steele Scott Gallery houses American paintings and decorative arts from the colonial period through the beginning of the twentieth century, including furniture by Charles and Henry Greene, the Pasadena architects who made this city a locus of the Arts and Crafts movement.

Huntington Library, Art Collections, and Botanical Gardens

1151 Oxford Rd.
San Marino 91108
General information: 626-405-2141
Special events and exhibitions: 626-405-2281
Botanical events and bloom highlights:
626-405-2282
www.huntington.org
Tues.–Fri. noon–4:30 p.m., Sat.–Sun. 10:30 a.m.–4:30 p.m.
Entry: adults $8.50, seniors $7, students $5.
children under 12 free

The Huntington comprises three entities—library, art collections, and botanical gardens—each of which merit the superlatives invariably used to describe this place. Henry Edwards Huntington amassed a fortune in the railroad business and developed the Pacific Electric line, an interurban rail system that efficiently linked the distant areas of the Los Angeles basin. That civic contribution was later destroyed, but the San Marino ranch he endowed with a great collection of books and art was protected in perpetuity by the trust he established in 1919.

In 1908 Huntington retired to the 600-acre ranch he had purchased in San Marino five years earlier, and he began to develop his collection in earnest; English and American history and literature were the focus of his book collections, and he began to purchase entire libraries. Today the Huntington Library holds about four million items—maps, prints, drawings, photographs and negatives, manuscripts, and historical records as well as half a million rare books that document British and American civilization from the Middle Ages to the present. Its early quartos and folios of Shakespeare's plays are unsurpassed by any other library, and it holds early editions of all major British writers. Its collection on the early history of America includes the

manuscript for Benjamin Franklin's *Autobiography* (written in his own hand); letters and writings of Washington and Jefferson; and Noah Webster's *American Dictionary*. Curators have drawn on these holdings to showcase thematic exhibitions of important figures in American history, including Abraham Lincoln and George Washington, as well as topics of more local interest, like water procurement and Southern California development.

Do not hesitate to enter the imposing library building, where changing displays of some 200 books and manuscripts are on view in the Exhibition Hall. The Ellesmere manuscript of Chaucer's *Canterbury Tales* (circa 1410) is the centerpiece of the medieval collection, which also has many illustrated Books of Hours and Bibles. The transition from the handwritten books of the Middle Ages to printed books is particularly well-documented at the Huntington: a Gutenberg Bible (1455), the first book composed with moveable type, is often displayed with books printed from wood blocks and typographic masterworks by William Caxton, the first English printer. The Huntington sometimes combines the strengths of its collections by, for instance, exhibiting books and manuscripts of William Blake's poems alongside his paintings, drawings, and prints from the gallery collection.

Each year more than 2,000 scholars from all over the world undertake research among the rare books, manuscripts, and art works in the Huntington's collections, and many participate in a program of conferences, seminars, and lectures. The research program awards nearly 100 grants annually to scholars in the fields of history, literature, art, and history of science; produces the *Huntington Library Quarterly* and several books each year; and serves 30,000 schoolchildren and thousands of adults through the education program.

The Huntington's art collections developed more slowly and reflect the influence of Henry's second wife, Arabella (the widow of his uncle, Collis P. Huntington), whom he married in 1913. The beaux-arts building that houses the art was designed by Myron Hunt and Elmer Grey, and it was the Huntingtons' residence as well as home to their art collections. In 1934 after Mrs. Huntington's death—Henry Huntington died in 1927—the main gallery wing was added, but the domestic setting has been retained throughout the gallery.

Arabella Huntington had already formed a collection of Old Masters during her first marriage, but the advice of noted art dealer Sir Joseph Duveen helped establish a focus for the new couple's collecting: British and French art of the eighteenth century. A set of Beauvais tapestries depicting courtiers gamboling in pastoral landscapes was their first notable acquisition in French decorative arts; these tapestries, designed by François Boucher, remain on view in the large living room (which also includes two Savonnerie carpets commissioned by Louis XIV for the Louvre). Some extraordinary pieces of French furniture embellish these rooms, which also feature contemporary paneling carved in popular eighteenth-century styles.

Starting with three portraits by Gainsborough, the Huntingtons amassed what has been called the finest collection of British full-length portraits in the world. The twenty paintings in the main gallery include Thomas Gainsborough's famous *Blue Boy, Mrs. Siddons as the Tragic Muse* (which some consider Sir Joshua Reynolds's finest work), and *Pinkie* by Sir Thomas Lawrence, which was purchased one month before Henry Huntington's death. Also displayed are great landscapes, including *Salisbury Cathedral* and *View on the Stour* by Constable and *Grand Canal, Venice* by Turner.

Although the most salient feature of the original art collection was its specialized character, the chronological and geographical bases have been widened since Mr. Huntington's death. The holdings now include approximately 17,000 British drawings, as well as British silver, sculpture, and decorative arts. A fine representative group of eighteenth-century French paintings enriches the collection of French decorative art, and the collection also features noteworthy examples of Renaissance paintings and bronzes, British miniatures, and ceramics.

The Virginia Steele Scott Gallery was funded by the Pasadena art patron of that name, and fifty paintings donated by the Virginia Steele Scott Foundation established the core of this collection. There are colonial portraits by Charles Willson Peale and John Singleton Copley, as well as one of Gilbert Stuart's famous renderings of George Washington (a second version is in the Huntington Gallery); mid-nineteenth-century still lifes by Peto and William Harnett; landscapes by John Frederick Kensett, Frederic Church, and Heade; and late nineteenth-century works by William Chase, Mary Cassatt, John Singer Sargent, and Childe Hassam which reflect both the influence of impressionism and the aesthetic movement upon their work. The

broad spectrum of social and aesthetic concerns expressed by American artists who worked in the first decades of the twentieth century can be seen in paintings by Maurice Prendergast, John Sloane, George Luks, George Bellows, and Edward Hopper (see photo, p. 132), while choice pieces of American decorative arts and sculpture complement the paintings from each period.

The Dorothy Collins Brown Wing of the Scott Gallery has been dedicated to the Arts and Crafts movement, which was closely identified with Pasadena during the first decades of the twentieth century. A long-term loan from the Gamble House of furniture designed by Charles and Henry Greene is installed with fine pieces of Arts and Crafts pottery and silver from the Huntington's holdings; works by California painters of the Arroyo school and American impressionists complete these extraordinary rooms. Another gallery is devoted to changing exhibitions that often feature works from the Huntington's fine collection of American drawings, prints, and photographs.

The 200 acres of gardens were developed by Huntington under the able direction of William Hertrich, who spent sixty-two years planning and planting the diverse schemes. The broad lawns bordered by mature specimen trees are a gracious setting for the buildings, and shaded benches—some of them beneath one of the 1,000 native oaks that were Huntington's personal favorites—allow visitors to enjoy the bucolic view. Among the princely elements of the mansion's landscaping is the formal environment of the North Vista, where Italian baroque stone statues and stately

palms line a 600-foot grass allée and frame a view of snow-covered peaks in the San Gabriels; more informal winding pathways are landscaped with azaleas and camellias to brighten the winter months. The three acres planted in roses are not pruned until early January to allow visitors to the Rose Parade to see one of this area's finest collections, but this garden is at its peak from April through October, the long hot season that these flowers prefer.

The twelve-acre desert garden—Huntington's first botanical collection—now contains more than 4,000 species; the collection is augmented during annual expeditions to Mexico. Within this garden is a conservatory providing the precise conditions some succulent plants need to survive in Southern California. Among the many curiosities here are lithops, called "living stones," which mimic the shapes and colors of rocks in their native environment, while stapeliads (succulents in the milkweed family) bear some of the showiest flowers in the desert garden.

Huntington had the lovely Japanese garden (see photo, p. 131) created in a wild canyon west of the mansion as a wedding present for his bride; to hasten its development he purchased all the plants and a traditional structure from a commercial tea garden operated by Pasadena resident George T. Marsh. The original garden, which was expanded in 1968 with a walled *karesansui*—"dry landscape"—environment, is laid out as a stroll garden. A weeping willow accents a moon bridge over ponds filled with koi; flowering trees, wisteria, and azaleas add early spring color, and maples brighten the fall landscape. From the reconstructed Japanese house, a zigzag bridge crosses a dry streambed to the raked gravel and rock garden; its designs derive from Zen Buddhism of the

Muromachi period, which drew inspiration from symbols rather than nature.

The scholarly enthusiasms of the botanist rather than Henry Huntington's particular interests led to the creation of the Australian, subtropical, and jungle gardens. Today the Australian garden includes 160 species of eucalyptus; Huntington, however, was not stirred as others were by the craze of planting eucalyptus for timber and railroad ties. He chose only a few, including a lemon-scented gum that he selected for his own mausoleum, and the rest—like the 1,000 planted by the U.S. Department of Agriculture—were experiments planted after his death. The multistory plantings of the jungle garden, growing beneath a high canopy, suggest natural tropical growth; huge stands of bamboo, with many rare species, mark this garden, and a waterfall-fed stream provides the moist environment needed by members of the banana family (including such flowering forms as heliconias and strelizias). The subtropical garden includes those plants that thrive in a Mediterranean climate—those that will survive a light frost but not prolonged freezing—so it acts as a test garden for plants that will adapt well to gardens in the San Gabriel Valley. Among the species tested in this garden which are now are found commonly in the landscape of Los Angeles are jacaranda and coral trees, the lovely flowering vine called angels' trumpet, and such South African bulbs as freesias and agapanthus.

The Huntington offers visitors a wide range of options for enhancing their museum experience. An elegant afternoon tea is served Tuesdays through Sundays in the Rose Garden Tea Room; it adds to the otherworldly experience of a day at the Huntington and is a festive treat when entertaining the in-laws or celebrating birthdays or Mother's Day (call 626-683-8131 for reservations). Light meals and refreshments in a casual indoor/outdoor setting are available at the Rose Garden Cafe. The bookstore offers a wide variety of books, posters, stationery, and gift items inspired by all of the Huntington's collections.

There are too many educational activities on the Huntington's calendar to list in this guide but call 626-405-2281 for schedules. Until a few years ago, admission to the Huntington was free, giving little incentive for people to become members; however, the cost of making the grounds and facilities accessible to large numbers of visitors—about 500,000 per year—was not anticipated by the trust Huntington established,

A group of small historical museums present displays of early life in the East San Gabriel Valley; their hours are very limited (usually on weekends), so call before visiting.

and these costs cut into the budget available for the scholarly agenda he had intended. An admission fee was imposed, and people are encouraged to join: membership (from $60, which covers two adults and children under the age of eighteen) not only encourages repeat visits, but also provides advance notice of docent-led garden tours, lectures, plant sales, book signings, and open-air concerts.

The Arboretum of Los Angeles County

301 N. Baldwin Ave.
Arcadia 91007
626-821-3222
Daily 9 a.m.–4:30 p.m.; grounds close at 3 p.m. (except when evening events are scheduled)
Entry: adults $5, seniors/students $3, children 5–12 $1.

Arcadia, which signified to the Greeks a place of rural simplicity, was the name E. J. "Lucky" Baldwin chose for the town surrounding his sprawling rancho in the San Gabriel Valley. A bucolic 127-acre parcel of his property is now the Arboretum, a living repository of plants from around the world which is administered by the Department of Recreation and Parks.

The wide-open landscapes composed of native Australian and African plants (which are compatible with the dry Southern California climate) are a good place to stretch your legs; water, including koi ponds and waterfalls, is abundant in the North and South American sections. Colonies of strolling peacocks seem to like the man-made waterfall; it recirculates 40,000 gallons per hour and leads to the riparian meadowbrook and Kallam Garden with colorful displays of annuals and perennials. In the tropical greenhouse—a refreshingly moist environment for people as well as the plants growing there—there are collections of orchids, bromeliads, and ferns; begonias and other shade-loving plants are in an adjacent structure. In the water-conservation garden, drought-tolerant plants, including many California natives, are identified. The herb garden contains plants mentioned by Shakespeare, as well as those used for medicines, dyes, fragrance, and cooking.

A shuttle ($1.50 per person) makes six stops within the garden—passengers can disembark to explore and reboard—and passes the historic buildings preserved on the grounds: the Santa Anita railroad depot (by tour only, Tues.–Wed. 10 a.m.–4 p.m., 1st Sun. of month 1–4 p.m.), Queen Anne cottage, and Hugo Reid adobe are clustered along the shores of Baldwin Lake. A collection of cycads and a redwood grove provide shelter for hungry waterfowl that live by the lake.

Science Adventures Day Camp (800-472-4362) and a concert series are special activities in summer months; the Los Angeles Garden show is held in the fall, providing local gardeners with ideas for the last planting season of the year.

Monrovia Historical Museum

742 E. Lemon Ave.
Monrovia 91016
626-357-9537
Wed., Thurs., Sun. 1–4 p.m.
Entry: free

Housed in a renovated 1925 Spanish colonial building that had formerly housed part of the municipal swimming pool, this historical museum has a striking collection of early telephones and illustrates the history of GTE, which began here in 1899 as the California Water and Telephone Company. There is a large collection of dolls—800 of them—which includes figures of all of the American presidents from Washington to Kennedy. In addition, the life of city founder William Monroe is documented with personal artifacts, and a collection of vintage photographs shows the early history of Monrovia.

Founded in 1915, **Citrus College** is the oldest community college in Los Angeles County; about 15,000 students attend day and evening classes on a 104-acre campus (100 W. Foothill Blvd., Glendora 91740; 626-963-0323). The Haugh Performing Arts Center offers a varied and professional performing arts series, as well as a monthly theater program for kids; it also serves as the venue for the college's music and drama departments. Right in the heart of the San Gabriel Valley, on a lovely campus, you'll find "perfect sightlines, ample legroom, free parking and dedicated staff," the brochure promises, and wouldn't every performance venue in the county be delighted to make such claims? The fare includes popular music—Big Band Salute to WWII, Irving Berlin and Cole Porter, Glenn Miller and the Kingston Trio—and more specialized programs, like the finalists from the Van Cliburn piano competition, taiko drummers from Japan, and Hal Holbrook as Mark Twain. The Theater for Young Audiences series comprises six classic tales staged by some of the best companies in the U.S., and if you buy the series, each performance costs just $3 per seat. To receive a season brochure or order tickets by phone, call 626-963-9411.

Heritage Park (5001 Via de Mansion Rd., La Verne) preserves a vestige of the citrus groves that once occupied 40,000 acres of the San Gabriel Valley; it is also the site of the century-old Weber House, which La Verne Heritage (909-593-2862) hopes to refurbish for public viewing soon. The public is welcome to harvest navel oranges and lemons (January to April or until fruit is gone) from the 300 trees in the orchard; the cost is about $4 for a ten-pound bag.

The eastern sector of the Angeles National Forest can be reached by turning onto circuitous East Fork Road, just after Highway 39 passes the San Gabriel reservoir; or try Glendora Mountain Road, which is called Glendora Ridge Road for the last mountainous miles before it enters Mount Baldy Village. Mills Avenue, which begins on the north side of the campus of the Claremont Colleges, becomes Mount Baldy Road, but stays just west of the San Bernardino county line until it reaches the little town at the base of Mount San Antonio.

Crystal Lake, located twenty-five miles north of Asuza, is the only natural lake in the San Gabriel Mountains and the only alpine lake in all of L.A. County. Rainwater and snowmelt from the mountains collect in this cedar- and pine-forested basin, but swimming is prohibited because of abundant plant growth. Crystal Lake is stocked with rainbow trout by the California Department of Fish and Game, and five fish per day can be taken by those with licenses; permits can be procured at Crystal Lake Visitors Center (2 mi. north of the intersection of Hwy. 39 and Crystal Lake Rd.). The center (Sat.–Sun. 8 a.m.–4:30 p.m.; 626-910-1149) also has exhibits on the natural features of the area and trail maps.

Nature trails meander through 100 acres of chaparral and riparian woodside at **San Dimas Canyon Park** (1628 N. Sycamore Canyon Rd., San Dimas 91773). Natural history exhibits are found in the nature center (daily 9 a.m.–5 p.m.; 909-599-7512); the on-site wildlife zoo is notable for its rehabilitation cage for rescued birds of prey.

Marshall Canyon Regional Park (6550 Stephens Ranch Rd., La Verne 91750), county parkland located on the outskirts of Los Angeles County—abutting the Angeles National Forest west of Mount Baldy—has slowly evolved from its func-tion as a tree nursery supplying other county parks into an equestrian center. Although thirty acres are being developed for this purpose (and many features are already in place), the lack of toilet facilities limits its use. The equestrian ring and corral and outdoor amphitheater with fire ring are utilized by different groups for various events, but making this an overnight layover spot for horses and riders trekking the 400 miles of trails within the county is still a dream. Dry camping in tents and RV camping is permitted, and there is plenty of space for horse trailers in the ample parking lot. A consignee just down the road offers pony rides and leases horses so riders can explore the five miles of trails within Marshall Canyon, as well as access many more within the Angeles National Forest. Call 909-596-5568 for information on this rapidly evolving site.

Mount Baldy is officially named Mount San Antonio, but the Forest Service now recognizes the gold prospectors' nickname for the mountain's rounded treeless summit (which tops the 10,000-foot mark). The county line that divides Los Angeles from San Bernardino bifurcates Mt. Baldy Village and crosses the mountain itself, however imperceptibly. The Mount Baldy visitors center is located in the village (Fri.–Sun. 8 a.m.–4:30 p.m.; 909-982-2829); it has trail maps and general information about this end of the Angeles National Forest, as well as a bookstore that also sells gift items. The Visitors Center building was constructed in 1920 as a one-room schoolhouse and was used for that purpose (with some additions over the years) for fifty-five years; it retains one room preserved as a country classroom, but there are also displays of animals that live in these mountains—squirrel and raccoon, mule deer and Nelson bighorn sheep, Steller's jay, redheaded woodpecker, and Coopers hawk—placed on a rocky backdrop with flowing water. That trickle of water symbolizes San Antonio Falls, a "three-tier, 100-foot, spring-fed, year-round, positively gorgeous waterfall," according to the enthusiastic ranger, which is accessible just three miles up the road. It is suggested that visitors stop there en route to the ski lift a mile farther (where the road ends); on weekends and holidays outside of ski season, the road transports visitors to Baldy Notch and the miles of hiking trails that stretch across seven mountains.

Monrovia Farmers Market
Library Park (at Myrtle and Lyme Aves.)
Fri., 5–9 p.m.

Monrovia Public Library
321 S. Myrtle Ave.
Monrovia 91016
626-358-0174

Artist Rod Baer was commissioned by MetroArt to create the playful large-scale concrete sculptures that mark the Claremont MetroLink station.

Rancho Santa Ana Botanic Garden
1500 N. College Ave.
Claremont 91711
909-625-8767
Daily 8 a.m.–5 p.m.
Entry: free, donations welcomed

Rancho Santa Ana Botanic Garden moved from Orange County to the far eastern edge of Los Angeles County in 1951. Its eighty-six acres, located in the foothills of the San Gabriels at the northern end of College Avenue in Claremont, are dedicated exclusively to a living collection of native California plants (especially those that flourish in the southern part of the state). The large desert garden includes all cactus species that live in our state, plus many succulents and hardy shrubs, and there are palms that flourish in oases. The garden is most spectacular during the peak blooming period (Mar.–May) when fragrant ceanothus (California lilac) scent the air and wildflowers carpet the mesa and desert gardens. Free wildflower walks are offered on Saturday and Sunday afternoons at 2 p.m. (Sept.–June); the local Audubon Society conducts bird walks in the garden on the first Sunday of each month.

The large area devoted to California flowering shrubs is also lovely in spring; a streamside garden and riparian trail create a fresh oasis that attracts both humans and birds. The Home Demonstration Garden displays attractive landscaping that requires minimum watering thanks to extensive use of drought-tolerant native species. In addition to its function in providing public enjoyment, this facility is dedicated to research in plant systematics and evolution, preserving native flora, and developing native cultivars suitable for landscaping use.

Children will learn about native plants at special workshops offered by the garden's education staff, which also conducts guided visits for school groups; in a recent program children made Native-American toys and games—including wooden bull-roarers and corn-husk shuttlecocks and paddles—from natural materials. The active program of special events for all ages is included in listings of events on the Claremont college campuses and also appears in the *Claremont Courier.*

Once part of the land owned by the Mission San Gabriel, the town of **Claremont** was incorporated in 1907, a decade after the Santa Fe railroad linking Chicago to Los Angeles was laid through the region. The citrus industry and the creation of the college complex (which began with the founding of Pomona College in 1887) dominated the town's first half-century; Claremont is a now college town in a big way, with five colleges, a large graduate program, and a school of theology. The landscaped campuses and solid academic architecture infuse the town—which nestles beneath the majestic San Gabriel Mountains at the eastern edge of Los Angeles County—with a New England atmosphere reinforced by street names borrowed from Ivy League schools. The town of "trees and Ph.Ds" celebrates the former with three itineraries throughout the older sections of town, where the most outstanding specimens are identified with their common and botanical names.

It is a fifty-minute trip from downtown L.A.'s Union Station to Claremont via MetroLink trains (call 213-808-5465 for information), which arrive at the old Santa Fe depot in the "village" (as the town's shopping district is known). Within walking distance are antique shops and bookstores for browsing and a restaurant row with both affordable eateries and upscale dining. The **visitors center** in the Chamber of Commerce (205 N. Yale Ave., 909-624-1681; Mon.–Fri. 9 a.m.–5 p.m.) has maps for self-guided walking tours of the colleges and the village, while Claremont Heritage (590 W. Bonita Ave.; 909-621-0848) leads guided downtown walks ($5 per person) at 10 a.m. on the first Saturday of each month, and two-hour walking tours ($8 per person) of the campus (quarterly: Jan., Mar., June, Oct.). **Claremont Heritage** also sponsors an annual house tour in October to showcase the diverse architectural styles in the town. And they are diverse: fourteen houses constructed in the 1930s entirely of reclaimed materials (along the 300 block of South Mills Ave.) have been called "as fine an example of folk architecture as you will find anywhere in the state"; "Claremont potatoes"—rocks cleared from fields as the citrus groves expanded—were used to construct residences on the north edge of town (at Baseline Rd.). Another way to experience the campus architecture is to follow the two-mile parcourse (start on Dartmouth Ave. between Ninth and Tenth Sts.); there are twenty-four stations with three levels of difficulty to exercise all muscle groups.

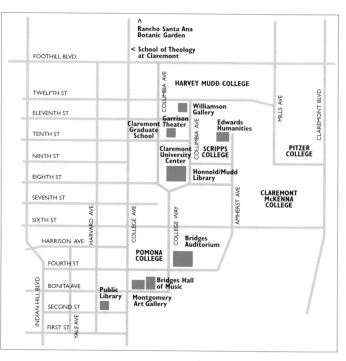

^
**Rancho Santa Ana
Botanic Garden**

< **School of Theology
at Claremont**

FOOTHILL BLVD.

HARVEY MUDD COLLEGE

TWELFTH ST

ELEVENTH ST

**Williamson
Gallery**

Garrison
Claremont Theater
Graduate
School

**Edwards
Humanities**

TENTH ST

NINTH ST

**Claremont
University
Center**

**SCRIPPS
COLLEGE**

**PITZER
COLLEGE**

EIGHTH ST

**Honnold/Mudd
Library**

SEVENTH ST

**CLAREMONT
McKENNA
COLLEGE**

SIXTH ST

HARRISON AVE

**Bridges
Auditorium**

FOURTH ST

**POMONA
COLLEGE**

COLUMBIA AVE

MILLS AVE

CLAREMONT BLVD

HARVARD AVE

COLLEGE AVE

COLLEGE WAY

AMHERST AVE

BONITA AVE

**Public
Library**

**Bridges Hall
of Music**

SECOND ST

**Montgomery
Art Gallery**

FIRST ST

INDIAN HILL BLVD

YALE AVE

Summer concerts are held
on Monday evenings at
7:30 p.m. at the Memorial
Park Bandshell
(840 N. Indian Hill Blvd.,
Claremont), and Rancho
Santa Ana Botanic Garden
(see p. 135) hosts musical
evenings on Thursdays at
6 p.m. with the garden
open for strolling.

The Claremont Colleges regularly schedule exhibitions at several libraries and galleries on campus; call 909-621-8000 for information. There is still an active and varied program of cultural events at **Bridges Auditorium** (450 N. College Ave.; 909-621-8032), but packaged series are no longer available; check the local paper and college calendar for event information. The Fiske Museum of Musical Instruments is located in the basement of Bridges Auditorium and can be viewed when that building is open for events or by appointment. Among the 750 American, European, and ethnic instruments on display are keyboards, winds, and mechanical and electronic instruments produced by various cultures over the past 300 years, but the brass section is the great strength of the collection: it includes the largest trumpet in the world—seven feet of brass cast in Cleveland in the 1920s—among flugelhorns, bugles, tubas, cornets, and saxhorns. Special tours for schools and groups with musical affiliations can be arranged; call 909-621-8307 for information or an appointment. **Honnold/Mudd Library** (Ninth St. and Dartmouth Ave.), which is the central library for all the colleges (and also issues library cards for town residents), holds special collections of material about Oxford University (the model for the college consortium); Californiana (especially wa-

ter resources development); music; and fine printing (with many early masterpieces). The 700-seat **Garrison Theater**, another facility shared by all the colleges, boasts a Millard Sheets-designed tile mural on the facade which depicts characters from Shakespeare's plays.

Pomona College was the first of the Claremont colleges (founded in 1887) and is still the largest with 1,400 undergraduates in equal proportions of men and women. It is considered one of the finest liberal arts colleges in the nation, and is part of the pantheon of colleges established by the Congregational Church; others include Harvard, Amherst, and Middlebury in New England, and Oberlin, Carleton, and Grinnell in the Midwest. During its first year of existence, classes were held in the Claremont Hotel—built as part of the land speculation accompanying the completion of the Santa Fe Railroad's line to Los Angeles—which was given to the fledgling college after the real estate boom collapsed.

The first mural painted in the United States by Mexican artist José Clemente Orozco, which depicts Prometheus stealing fire from the gods for the benefit of mankind, was realized on the ceiling of the dining room of **Frary Hall**; a black-and-white mural of Genesis by Rico LeBrun (one of the leading figures in California painting after World War II) is located in the portico outside the same building.

Montgomery Gallery (333 N. College Ave. at Bonita Ave., 909-621-8283; Tues.–Fri. noon–5 p.m., Sat.–Sun. 1–5 p.m.; free) serves as both museum and exhibition space at Pomona. The museum's exhibitions have been varied: in one exhibition, real objects could be compared with their depiction via image-access computer software; for another, a young curator made selections from the museum's permanent collection. The end of the academic year is dedicated to a juried show of student work and the culminating exhibition of the work of senior studio-art majors. The Rembrandt Club of Pomona College, founded in 1905 to support the arts in Claremont, sponsors monthly lectures (followed by teas) and excursions to area museums and collections; those interested in becoming members of the Rembrandt Club should call the Montgomery Gallery.

Myron Hunt, who designed many of the prominent buildings at Occidental College as well as the Huntington residence (now the Huntington Art Collections) and library, created the **Bridges Hall of Music** (1915), a Romanesque basilica with flexible seating and a coffered ceiling that reflects Southern California's Mexican heritage in its painted decoration. To receive information about musical events scheduled at Pomona, call 909-621-8155; the department of Theater and Dance schedules events at the Seaver Theater complex (909-621-8525).

Scripps College, founded in 1926, enrolls about 700 women in its degree program, which is noted for humanities, fine arts, and social sciences programs. Its pretty campus is Spanish in style, with white-washed walls and red tile roofs; architect Gordon Kaufmann (who also built Caltech's Athenaeum) considered the plan for Scripps College his finest work. Among Kaufmann's masterpieces is the **Denison Library** (1931), which emulates the cruciform shape of a Renaissance chapel and has stained-glass windows that pay tribute to the masters of early printing. Edward Huntsman-Trout planned the campus landscaping; there are walkways bordered by tulip and orange trees, and many campus architectural features are identified with prominent trees: there are courtyards named Sycamore, Eucalyptus, Olive, Persimmon, and Cypress. The last major work by Mexican muralist Alfredo Ramos Martínez is on view in the **Margaret Fowler**

Garden (Mon.–Fri. 9 a.m.–5 p.m.) —the 100-foot fresco entitled *The Flower Vendors* has recently been restored by a team of Getty conservators. (If you're in Claremont in March, don't miss the chance to see the Martínez mural framed by an ancient blooming wisteria that covers the arbor with lavender flowers and scents the air.) A smaller tile version of the mural is found in the courtyard of Balch Hall, which serves as the college administration building. Next to the Lang Art Building is a sunken Oriental garden designed in 1931 by former Scripps professor Millard Sheets. For musical events on the Scripps campus, call 909-607-3266.

The **Ruth Chandler Williamson Gallery** (Twelfth St. and Columbia Ave.; 909-607-3397; Wed.–Sun. 1–5 p.m.) presents the Scripps Ceramic Annual, which showcases cutting-edge works in clay; this exhibition can be credited in part with attracting the donation of the 1,000-piece ceramics collection amassed by Fred Marer. Its active program of exhibitions also features photography—exhibitions of the work of Julia Margaret Cameron, Eugène Atget, and Berenice Abbott, among others—prints, thematic exhibitions of the permanent collection, and contemporary art.

The Clark Museum (in Humanities Bldg., Tenth St. and Columbia Ave., 909-607-3606; Mon.-Fri. 8 a.m.-noon, 1-5 p.m., during school year) is known for book exhibits that complement and highlight the experimental typographic laboratory founded at Scripps in 1941, but the exhibition program is varied and includes shows of prints, drawings, and works in other media. Frederick W. Goudy designed a typeface used exclusively by the college, called Scripps Old Style, that has just been digitized a half-century after it was created, and will be licensed by the type lab in 1997.

One-quarter of the graduates of **Claremont- McKenna College** attend law school; this statistic reflects the undergraduate-level emphasis on economics and government. The college was founded in 1946 to provide for the education of veterans under the GI Bill. Since 1976 Claremont-McKenna has admitted women, who are as likely as the male students to be athletic and politically conservative; interestingly, the round shape of the landmark Bauer Center conforms to the donors' requirement that an ROTC rifle range be incorporated in the basement.

Claremont-McKenna students prepare food from their native countries and cultures for the weekly **International Place Lunch and Conversation,** which also features a speaker. Call 909-621-8344 or check the campus calendar for the schedule of this well-loved and long-lived program, which concludes with a weekend-long festival in late spring.

Harvey Mudd College, considered one of the top undergraduate engineering schools in the nation, is the only one of the Claremont Colleges to offer a bachelor of science degree. The school tolerates—or perhaps cultivates—the eccentricities of its 450 men and 150 women: one dorm is populated by unicycle riders, and campus parties are famous for their computerized special effects. Its president was a strong advocate of a proposal to create a graduate engineering school focusing on the life sciences—from biotechnology to environmental studies—and he resigned in 1997 to spearhead fundraising for the institution, the first to be added to the Claremont consortium in over thirty-five years.

The distinguished California landscape architect Thomas Church planned the grounds of this campus, grouping large trees to create a peaceful wooded environment; the mall stretching from Foothill Boulevard to Twelfth Street (where commencement is held) is lined with liquidambar trees that add colorful foliage to the autumn landscape.

Pitzer College—the most recent addition to the collegiate complex—was intended to redress the imbalance between male and female students; it initially admitted only women. The fact that it was founded during the 1960s is reflected in its interdisciplinary approach and willingness to allow its students (300 men and 400 women) to design their own majors. It was named for a 1900 graduate of Pomona College who owned more than 1,000 citrus-planted acres and was a major benefactor to many campus projects. On campus is the **Nichols Gallery,** located in the Broad Center, which has an eclectic program of exhibitions (909-621-8219; Mon.–Fri. 8 a.m.–5 p.m.; free).

Among the facilities shared by the colleges—and administered by Claremont University Center, which also directs the Graduate School—is Bridges Auditorium (450 N. College Way); the concert series Fridays at Noon is sponsored by the Claremont Graduate School. Call 909-621-8081 for program and ticket information. The Art Building (Tenth St. and Columbia Ave.) showcases works created by students in the highly rated Graduate School of Art, who define the cutting edge of contemporary art.

A variety of the events held on the Claremont campuses is broadcast on Channel 54 (Insight Communications System), where the schedule (usually Mon.–Thurs. 7–8 p.m.) appears between regular programs; check the *Claremont Courier* for the broadcast schedule, or call 909-626-3521, extension 271.

George C. Stone Center for Children's Books

131 E. Tenth St.
Claremont 91711
909-607-3670
Mon.–Thurs. 1:30–6 p.m.

This library, dedicated even more than most to helping children discover the joys of reading, hosts a special program of stories and crafts on the first Saturday of each month from 10 a.m. to noon. The collection of 20,000 titles can be borrowed by Friends of the Stone Library; membership costs $25 per year.

For more than thirty-five years, the annual Young People's Reading Conference has combined workshops with authors and illustrators and a book fair in a literary festival for kids in grades two to ten. This springtime event sells out every year—I couldn't even wrangle a place for the daughter of a Pulitzer-Prize winner—so advance registration is required; call 909-625-2391.

The largest display of fossil footprints in the United States can be found at the Raymond M. Alf Museum at the Webb School (1175 W. Baseline Dr., 909-624-2798; adults $1, children under 5 free); there are also geological exhibits. An open house on the first Sunday of the month helps elucidate the museum's mission: "to teach the history of the earth through fossil documentation."

Petterson Museum of Intercultural Arts

Pilgrim Place
730 Plymouth Rd.
Claremont 91711
909-621-9581 (switchboard) 399-5544 (museum)
Fri.–Sun. 2–4 p.m.
Entry: free, donations welcomed

Pilgrim Place was dedicated in 1915 as a home for returning missionaries. It is a community infused with a multicultural and spiritual atmosphere; more than 300 "Pilgrims," all retired from professions in Christian service, reside at the thirty-three-acre complex. Twice each year the Pilgrims stage public events for the community: the Pilgrim Festival in November includes children's activities and a bazaar, and the Celebration of International Arts in spring features the arts and cultures of countries in which residents served.

Those who proselytize in far corners of the globe often return with arts and crafts—precious mementos of their host culture; Alice and Richard Petterson decided to collect and preserve these artifacts, the core of the collection at the Museum of Intercultural Art, when they found an extraordinary object for $5 at the annual bazaar. An early pilgrim (who had been a tutor in the imperial household in Victorian-era Japan) returned with a cherished *obi* (sash) woven with gold threads, which was given to her by the sister of the Empress Dowager. This *obi* is now displayed in the museum along with costumes, textiles, and objects from various cultures; dolls from around the world and shells are on view in the noncirculating library. A third gallery containing ceramics reflects the interests of Petterson (a professor of that art at Scripps) and includes two pieces by world-renowned Japanese potter Shoji Hamada.

Woodworker **Sam Maloof**, who was recognized for his creative genius with a MacArthur Foundation grant in 1985, has been working since 1952 on his most complex and comprehensive project: the home where he and his wife Alfreda raised their family, entertained (with unique graciousness), and where Sam designed and built furniture. It is a treasure house, crammed with books, gifts from artist friends, and the collection of Native-American ceramics, basketry, and textiles that Alfreda began decades ago when she worked on reservations in the Southwest. But the house itself may be Sam's most astounding piece of work, on which he lavished the fastidious, unflagging attention of a craftsman more than a homeowner. Every door has a freeform latch, crafted from some branch that caught his eye; the beams in one room were from a fallen tree in the grove of citrus, avocado, fruit and nut trees that surround the house; the circular stairway in another was crafted from packing crates shipped from Taiwan.

Woodworkers (including President Jimmy Carter, who had ordered a Maloof rocker for the White House, but not soon enough—it was delivered during the Reagan administration) and art lovers fortunate enough to wrangle an invitation flocked to this bucolic site to savor the genial atmosphere of Sam's shop and the quiet beauty of the world that inspired his muse. But the site, not far from where Sam was raised, also lay right on the extension of the San Bernardino Freeway, and the demands of commuters in the burgeoning housing tracts all around finally forced an accommodation. The astounding house will be moved two miles north and one mile west to a site in the Alta Loma foothills, where it will be reconstructed as the Sam and Alfreda Maloof Foundation (expected to open in 1999). The legendary craftsman was already in his eighties when he designed another house, under construction on the same property, where he and Alfreda will live.

FINDING GOD IN THE CITY OF ANGELS

Mary Jane O'Donnell

* indicates area code that changes in 1998

In Nathanael West's acerbic novel of Hollywood, *The Day of the Locust* (1939), Tod Hackett, the book's main character, worships nightly at different local churches: "He visited the Church of Christ, Physical, where holiness was attained through the constant use of chest-weights and spring grips; the Church Invisible where fortunes were told and the dead made to find lost objects; the Tabernacle of the Third Coming where a woman in male clothing preached the Crusade Against Salt, and the Temple Modern under whose glass and chromium roof, Brain-Breathing, the Secret of the Aztecs, was taught."

Regrettably, there are those who believe that this is still an apt summation of the city's religious character. True, if Tod were to come back today, he would feel right at home in some of the city's more adventurous spiritual havens. Los Angeles has certainly had its rogue practices (after all, the Branch Davidians got their start here), and there are still movements that provoke heated debate. (The Church of Scientology International —which is headquartered in Los Angeles and has considerable real estate holdings in the city, primarily in Hollywood— comes to mind.) And a growing number of

practices may seem foreign to the more mainstream practitioner because, in fact, they are.

But to dismiss that which is spiritually unfamiliar as simply bizarre is to miss the whole point—and strength—of the city, which is that, even today, Los Angeles is a frontier town. Whether out of necessity or a desire for adventure, people come here—as they have from the city's very beginning— to start anew. They bring with them the comfort of their own ways as much as a desire to shed the baggage of the past. As a result, even mainstream religions have been forced to come to terms with the essential uniqueness of the city's faithful.

Though better known for its interest in the pleasures of the flesh, Los Angeles offers a richly diverse array of pleasures of the spirit. The city's churches, synagogues, temples, mosques, and shrines offer the visitor an intimate introduction to the many customs and traditions of the people who live here. These are living, breathing places full of people who attempt to reach beyond this world, where even ancient cultures come alive through contemporary practices. Some of these places may reveal the peace to be found in silence; others, passionate expression of faith. The music may be haunting, or it may knock your socks off. A handmade offering may open your eyes to a kind of beauty no architectural effort could match.

There are literally thousands of religious sites in the city. The list that follows is by no means inclusive; be assured, however, that each of these sites welcomes respectful visitors and offers a place to begin what could be a lifetime of exploration.

In the Beginning . . .

Mission San Gabriel Arcángel
537 W. Mission Dr.
San Gabriel 91776
626-457-3048
Daily 9 a.m.–4:30 p.m.
(Oct.–May), daily
10 a.m.–5:30 p.m. (June–Sept.)
Entry: adults $4, seniors $3, children 6–12 $1

Mission San Fernando Rey de España
15151 San Fernando
Mission Blvd.
Mission Hills 91345
818-361-0186
Daily 9 a.m.–4:30 p.m.
Entry: $4, seniors/children 7–15 $3, children under 7 free

The history of Los Angeles has its roots in the establishment of the Franciscan missions in San Gabriel in 1771 and in San Fernando in 1797. The group of settlers who founded El Pueblo de la Reyna de los Angeles came from the San Gabriel Mission. As with all European settlement of the New World and its effect upon native peoples, it is a mixed history. Prior to the arrival of the Spanish conquistadors and Franciscan clerics, native peoples—including the Tongva, Chumash, and Tataviam tribes—had lived in the area for centuries. Well intentioned as they may have been, the missionaries, in effect, greased the wheels of Spanish expansionism as they went about their business of claiming land and converting the natives, not only to their religion but to their way of life as well. Although the Franciscans respected the culture of the indigenous people enough to allow them to incorporate their rituals into Catholic worship, the Indians were in fact a conquered people and ultimately either died off or were assimilated. A cross at the San Gabriel Mission commemorates the 6,000 Indians buried at the site.

At its peak the San

Gabriel Mission had 1.5 million acres of land; the San Fernando Mission, a mere 121,542. The missions were enterprising ventures that included vineyards, orchards, livestock, and facilities for the production of such items as tallow, soap, and hides. Today each mission (both renovated, if not rebuilt, many times over) is open to the public and includes churches, museums, cemeteries (San Gabriel's is the oldest in the area), and gift shops. The archives of the Archdiocese of Los Angeles are located at the San Fernando Mission and are open to the public (Mon., Thurs., Fri. 1–3 p.m.). Each displays priestly artifacts, furnishings, and libraries that serve as a reminder, even in this remote outpost, of the glory that was Spain.

Our Lady, Queen of the Angels (La Placita)
535 N. Main St.
Los Angeles 90012
213-629-3101

La Placita, as this church is affectionately known, is the city's oldest church—and surely one of its liveliest. Established in 1784, the church was originally located at what is now the intersection of Sunset and Broadway but was destroyed by floods. Construction of the church at the present site was started in 1819 and completed in 1822; it has, however, been renovated and expanded extensively since then. There is both the old church, with its beautifully ornate altar, and the newer, more functional, but less architecturally interesting church adjacent to it. La Placita, like the San Fernando and San Gabriel missions, harks back to a time when Catholicism was the official religion of the area and when the flags of Spain, and later Mexico, flew over El Pueblo.

An especially delightful time to visit La Placita is early Sunday morning. Families from all over the city fill the adjacent patio, where vendors sell food and religious items and the faithful pray in makeshift shrines. Another festive time to visit is on Saturday mornings, when the *quinceañeras,* marking the coming of age of fifteen-year-old girls, are usually held. These high-spirited celebrations, which evolved from rites of passage of the indigenous peoples of the Americas, are strongly discouraged by the Catholic Church because of the considerable financial burden they place on families, but they remain popular.

Our Lady of Guadalupe

One of the most ubiquitous devotional images in the city is that of Our Lady of Guadalupe, the patroness of Mexico. Not only is this icon a centerpiece of worship in many churches, but it also appears on more worldly items such as costume jewelry, sweatshirts, and tire covers. The faithful believe that the image is the result of the miraculous appearances of the Virgin Mary to Juan Diego, a peasant, at Tepeyac in December 1531. Because church authorities were reluctant to believe such a story, the Virgin gave Juan Diego signs of her visits: a bed of Castilian roses growing in the frozen ground, which he picked and took to his bishop, and, even more astonishing, her image on the peasant's *tilma,* or cloak.

Today Juan Diego's *tilma* with the miraculous image is enshrined in the New Basilica of Guadalupe in Mexico City. The feast of Our Lady of Guadalupe is celebrated in *las mañanitas,* or the wee hours of the morning, on December 12, complete with serenades to the Virgin, processions,

the Mass, and, often, a re-creation of her appearance to Juan Diego, usually enacted by children. The biggest celebration takes place at La Placita; other especially interesting places to see this event are Our Lady of Soledad (4561 Cesar E. Chavez Ave.; *213-269-7248) and Santura rio de Neustra Señora de Guadalupe (4100 E. Second St.; *213-261-4365).

Cathedral of Our Lady of the Angels
Cathedral Square
  (Grand Ave. at Temple St.)
Los Angeles 90012

The Cathedral of Our Lady of the Angels will be consecrated on September 4, 2000. This date, like the choice of Spaniard José Rafael Moneo as the cathedral's architect, provides a symbolic link to the country that established Catholicism here (and in much of the Americas), for it is the anniversary of the date in 1781 when El Pueblo de la Reyna de los Angeles was first settled and claimed as a territory for Spain.

The new cathedral will replace the city's original cathedral, Saint Vibiana's (114 E. Second St.), which was designed by Ezra F. Kysor (who also designed the city's first synagogue, the B'nai B'rith Temple on Broadway, which is no longer standing) and completed in 1876. When Saint Vibiana's was built, it was, after La Placita, one of only two Catholic churches in Los Angeles, making it truly the focus of church life. (Ironically, just after Saint Vibiana's was dedicated, Catholic dominance of the area began to wane; the newly completed railroads would bring an influx of mostly Protestant settlers from the Midwest during the 1880s.) As the city grew, however, the Catholic population spread to the new parishes being built throughout the city. With the decline of downtown in

the middle of this century, Skid Row began to grow up around the cathedral, further diminishing its appeal to the faithful. By the time it closed in 1996, the cathedral's membership had dwindled to 100 parishioners. Damage to the structure caused by the 1994 Northridge earthquake left Cardinal Roger Mahony, archbishop of Los Angeles, with the choice of completely renovating the old cathedral or building a new one; to the considerable dismay of preservationists, he chose the latter. The fate of Saint Vibiana's, now optioned to a developer, is uncertain as of this writing. Artifacts from the cathedral—the marble catafalque containing the remains of Saint Vibiana (a third-century virgin and martyr), the stained-glass windows, the main altar, and the organ —will be incorporated into the new structure.

Saint Andrew's Abbey (31001 N. Valyermo Rd., Valyermo 93563; 805-944-2178), a Benedictine monastery on the edge of the Mojave Desert, offers a rejuvenating spiritual getaway. Organized group or private retreats are offered throughout the year, and one is also welcome to simply spend a few hours —or days—at the monastery, which is open to people of all faiths. Visitors are invited (but not required) to follow the monastic schedule, which begins at 6 a.m., and to share meals with the monks. An arts festival, which is held every fall; a ceramics studio; and a well-stocked bookstore provide much of the abbey's income. It was founded in 1956 by monks who were forced by the communist government of China to flee their monastery there. Its first prior, Father Raphael Vinciarelli, asked architect Louis Kahn to design a new

monastery. Unfortunately the monks did not have the resources to realize Kahn's plans, but the unassuming structures they were able to build or refurbish do very well in this arid but stunning setting.

Go Forth and Multiply

The completion of the Southern Pacific Railroad in 1786 and the Santa Fe line in 1886 opened Los Angeles to the rest of the country and resulted in the boom of the 1880s, the first great explosion of the city's population. Although Protestant clergy had ventured into the area as early as 1841, the boom brought the greatest variety of mostly mainstream Protestant denominations, many of which are still faithfully practiced to this day.

The first Protestant service in the city was led by Bishop William Money, who, according to historian Michael E. Engh, S.J., of Loyola Marymount University, was one of the first of a long line of spiritual eccentrics attracted to Southern California. Claiming to have been born with the likeness of a rainbow in his eye, he established the short-lived Reformed Church in 1841, which was followed by another brief foray into the area by the more conventional Methodists. It was not until 1865 that the city's first permanent Protestant congregation was established, Saint Athanasius Episcopal Church on Pudding Hill, where City Hall now stands. Unfortunately, few of the original places of worship of any denomination still stand; they have been brought down by earthquakes or by the even more formidable forces of urban development. There are still, however, interesting churches to visit.

A historic (and conveniently clustered) group of churches and temples may be found along Wilshire Boulevard in the Miracle Mile district. Many of these large, imposing structures were built in the 1920s in concert with the development of the then-glittering Miracle Mile. Some of the most fashionable Protestant congregations of the day were assembled here, including the **First Baptist Church of Los Angeles** (760 Westmoreland Ave.; 213-384-2151), **First Unitarian Church** (2936 W. Eighth St.; 213-389-1356), **Immanuel Presbyterian Church** (3300 Wilshire Blvd.; 213-389-3191), **Saint James Episcopal Church** (3903 Wilshire Blvd.; 213-388-3417), **Wilshire Christian Church** (634 S. Normandie Ave.; 213-382-6337), and the **Wilshire United Methodist Church** (4350 Wilshire Blvd.; *213-931-1085). They are joined by a Jewish place of worship, the **Wilshire Boulevard Temple** (3663 Wilshire Blvd.; 213-388-2401), as a testament not only to faith but also to the glamour of another era. The architecture of these buildings embodied a desire, probably more social than spiritual, to create an establishment for the new city. Their congregations were then almost exclusively Caucasian; now they serve many of the city's immigrant communities. Nearby is the **First Congregational Church** (540 S. Commonwealth Ave.; 213-385-1341), the oldest continuing Protestant congregation in the city. Established in 1867, it offers extensive music programming, including free organ recitals on Tuesdays and Thursdays.

L.A.'s Protestant churches reflect the diversity of the city's population. **Bel Air Presbyterian Church** (16221 Mulholland Dr.; 818-788-4200) draws its congregation from the San Fernando Valley as well as from West Los Angeles. When he was able, former President Ronald Reagan regularly attended services at Bel Air Presbyterian, which is one of two Westside churches designed by the late Charles Moore and the architectural firm of Moore Ruble Yudell. The other is **Saint Matthew's Episcopal Church** (1031 Bienveneda Ave., Los Angeles; 310-454-1358) in Pacific Palisades, which, in addition to its regular ministry, houses the Contemplative Outreach Program of Southern California, a center for contemplative prayer (a kind of meditation based on ancient monastic practices, which was revived for contemporary, primarily lay, audiences by Thomas Keating, a Trappist monk). The **Metropolitan Community Church of Los Angeles** (8714 Santa Monica Blvd., West Hollywood; 310-854-9110) ministers to the gay, lesbian, bisexual, and transgender communities in the city. It is a Christian church that was founded in Los Angeles by Rev. Troy D. Perry, who had been expelled from his former church because of his sexual preference. Since its founding, the church has developed more than 300 new congregations worldwide in more than eighteen countries, including Russia and South Africa. **Fuller Theological Seminary** (135 N. Oakland Ave., Pasadena; 626-584-5400) is an evangelical seminary that trains ministers, missionaries, and lay leaders for every major Protestant denomination. Founded in 1947, it is the largest multidenominational seminary and the second-largest theological seminary in the United States, with an enrollment of 3,000. The small prayer garden on the campus is especially inviting. Another local Protestant seminary, the **Claremont School of Theology** (1325 N. College Ave., Claremont; 909-626-3521), houses the Ancient Biblical Manuscript Center, which contains the only complete set of photographic copies of the Dead Sea Scrolls outside Israel.

Hollywood Beverly Christian Church (1717 N. Gramercy Pl.; *213-469-5107) exemplifies the changing role of churches. Led by Dr. Peggy Owen Clark, this seventy-five-year-old church was once a stately structure and home to a prosperous congregation. In recent years, however, changing demographics have led to the loss of its original congregation, and the church itself has been severely damaged by fire and several earthquakes. Many pastors would have folded their tent and moved on, but the choice was made to serve the many needs of the mostly poor and culturally dislocated people of the neighborhood, including Latinos, Armenians, African-Americans, and a variety of Asian immigrants. The church's leaders consider it as much an urban center as a church. Although the traditional worship services are still offered on Sundays, during the week the church is home to gang prevention programs, including an alternative high school run by Soledad Enrichment Action, Inc.; an adult school; health programs; youth programs; and substance abuse programs.

At the **Los Angeles Temple of the Church of Jesus Christ of Latter-day Saints** (10777 Santa Monica Blvd.; 310-474-1549), only the visitors center is open to the public (daily 9 a.m. to 9 p.m.). The large, imposing temple, which may be seen from Santa Monica Boulevard, is not. Only Mormons in good standing with the church may enter. The sole purpose of the visitors center is to introduce people to the faith, a task that is usually handled by missionaries. According to Mormon tradition, the faithful are encouraged to give one or two years of their lives to missionary work, usually during young adulthood. Also open to the public is the Family History Center for genealogical research. Mormons believe that even the dead may be saved, but they must be saved by name. Thus, a genealogical trace of ones ancestors is a must for the Mormon faithful.

A Joyful Sound

Many of the city's early black churches were originally clustered along Central Avenue, the city center for African-Americans in the early part of this century. Today Los Angeles has many churches that serve the African-American community; some are short-lived, located in tiny storefronts, others are large and enduring, but all are testaments to deeply held faith.

First African Methodist Episcopal (AME) Church
2270 S. Harvard Blvd.
Los Angeles 90018
*213-735-1251

This is the first and oldest African-American congregation in the city. (The AME Church was started in Philadelphia by a black Methodist minister who, along with his fellow black congregants, had been asked to sit in the balcony during a worship service.) Rev. Cecil Murray is the church's senior pastor and one of the city's most prominent religious figures. Rev. Murray and his church played an important role in ending the 1992 Los Angeles riots and in helping to heal the community afterward through its extensive social service ministries.

West Angeles Church of God in Christ
3045 Crenshaw Blvd.
Los Angeles 90016
*213-733-8300

This was the first and largest African-American Pentecostal church to come out of the city's Azusa Street Revival in 1906, when the Pentecostal movement began (see below). The church has more than 16,000 members, including such celebrities as Magic Johnson, Angela Bassett, and Denzel Washington. There are five services every Sunday (including one for Hispanic worship), which are characterized by dramatic preaching and glorious music from its world-class choir. (The church has its own record label, West A Music Corporation.)

Headed by Bishop Charles Blake, the church is as much an economic force in its Crenshaw community as it is a spiritual one. Construction will soon begin on a new 5,000-seat church—which, judging from the drawings, will resemble Orange County's Crystal Cathedral —at the corner of Crenshaw and Exposition Boulevards. The project, with an estimated cost of $50 million, is expected to stimulate the area's economy by some $100 million. The church's nonprofit development corporation was established to bring jobs to the community, particularly in high-tech industries.

Praises of Zion Missionary Baptist Church
8222 S. San Pedro St.
Los Angeles 90003
*213-750-1033

This African-American Baptist church is in the heart of South Central Los Angeles. Until just a few years ago this community was predominantly African-American, but now more than 60 percent of its population is Latino. Faced with such dramatic change, churches such as Praises of Zion must either adapt, move, or fade away. The church has chosen to expand its mission to accommodate the changes in its neighborhood and now provides spiritual and social services to the Latino community.

Praises of Zion was organized by Rev. J. Benjamin Hardwick in 1955 and now claims 5,600 members. The church provides extensive social services to the homeless, the elderly, at-risk children, and families in need in the area through its own social service agency, the Personal Involvement Center.

Suddenly from Heaven

One of the most important and powerful religious movements to emerge in Los Angeles is Pentecostalism. Now second only to Roman Catholicism in worldwide membership, the movement has almost 500 million adherents (Catholicism, almost a billion). Despite its size, however, the movement is viewed suspiciously, if not derided, by many in both the religious and the secular world. The Pentecostals fall into different groups, including denominational (Assemblies of God, Foursquare Gospel, Church of God in Christ, etc.), charismatic (denoting those adherents who give a Pentecostal cast to their practices in Catholic and Protestant mainstream churches), and independent churches. Prompted by what the faithful believe to be a baptism in the Spirit, its characteristics include speaking in tongues, divine healing, and a belief in the imminent coming of the Lord, which demands of the faithful a missionary zeal. Pentecostals see themselves in relation to the experiences of the apostles, as described in Acts 2 of the New Testament: "When the day of Pentecost had come, they were all together. . . . Suddenly from heaven there came a sound like the rush of a violent wind. . . . All of them were filled with the Holy Spirit and began to speak in other languages."

The roots of the movement can be traced to several charismatic movements that developed out of the nineteenth-century Holiness revival in various parts of the United States. But Pentecostalism didn't really take off until William J. Seymour, an African-American preacher from Texas, arrived in Los Angeles and established the Apostolic Faith Gospel Mission at 312 Azusa Street in 1906. According to Cecil M. Robeck Jr., a professor at Fuller Theological Seminary who is writing a biography of Seymour, attendance at the mission grew from an initial handful in April 1906 to 1,500 four months later. Within a year it was spread by missionaries throughout the United States and the world—first to Norway, Palestine, Canada, and India and then, later that year, to Sweden, Denmark, Finland, England, Germany, Holland, Mexico, Liberia, Angola, Egypt, the Philippines, China, and beyond. *The Apostolic Faith*, a publication put out by the mission, developed a worldwide subscription list of more than 50,000 during the mission's second year.

The Azusa Street Mission no longer exists. The Japanese American Cultural and Community Center (244 S. San Pedro St.) now stands on its former site. Only a street sign remains to commemorate the mission, but a mural depicting Seymour and the mission is planned. Prior to its use by Seymour, the church was home to the Stevens African Methodist Episcopal Church, which later became the First AME Church.

Asberry Home
216 N. Bonnie Brae St.
Los Angeles 90026

Before moving to Azusa Street, Elder Seymour conducted Bible classes at this house near downtown Los Angeles. It was here that he and his congregation first spoke in tongues, which in many ways signified the beginning of this movement. Blacks and whites alike flocked to the house and worshiped together, literally hand in hand. Almost immediately the congregation was denounced by both civic and religious leaders, as much for its integrated worship as for its unorthodox spirituality. The home still stands today and is open to the public on a limited basis (call 888-763-8624 for information). The house is now owned by the West Angeles Church of God in Christ, which is planning to restore it to its 1906 condition and to build a museum of Pentecostalism next door.

Angelus Temple
1100 Glendale Blvd.
Los Angeles 90026
213-484-1100

This is the home of the International Church of the Foursquare Gospel, founded in 1923 by the colorful Aimee Semple McPherson, the first to bring the principles of show business to the pulpit. If William Seymour planted the seeds of Pentecostalism, Sister Aimee added the Miracle-Gro. Through "The Sunshine Hour," her radio show on church-owned KFSG (still operating at 96.3 FM), she reached thousands, paving the way for today's televangelists.

Sister Aimee's church

continues to this day. She offered a welcoming spiritual home, especially to people on the margins of society, who were often overlooked by mainstream churches, but also to members of the Hollywood community. Today there are more than seventeen million followers worldwide. At the Angelus Temple, still the mother church of the faith, a brochure proudly boasts of fifty nations represented in its nine congregations— Armenian, Bulgarian, English-speaking, Filipino, Hispanic, Indonesian, Japanese, Korean, and Slavic, yet another reminder of the diversity that is Los Angeles.

I Will Make of You a Great Nation

Jews began to settle in Los Angeles in the middle of the last century. Joseph Newmark, the city's first Jewish religious leader, began conducting regular services in observance of the Sabbath in 1854. In that year the Hebrew Benevolent Society (now known as the Jewish Family Service of the Federation Council of Greater Los Angeles) was formed and is considered the city's first charitable organization. By 1862 **Congregation B'nai B'rith** was organized under the leadership of Rabbi Abraham Wolf Edelman, who built the city's first synagogue (no longer standing), which was completed in 1873.

From the beginning, Jews had been welcomed participants in the growth of this still-new city. Catholics made challah for Jewish families to use on the Sabbath, and the fundraising for the synagogue was an ecumenical affair (as it would be for Saint Vibiana's). Jews flourished, as did the rest of the city's population, in the boom of the 1880s. The influx of

newcomers, however, mostly Protestants from the Midwest, brought a new set of tensions for the Jewish community and inaugurated a period of social exclusion, which was to continue into the next century.

During this time the main branches of Judaism— Orthodox, Conservative, and Reform—began to emerge in the city. The congregation of the B'nai B'rith Temple, for a long time Los Angeles's only synagogue, was originally Orthodox. When Rabbi Emanuel Schreiber succeeded Rabbi Edelman, however, it became a Reform body. In response, the Orthodox community established **Congregation Beth Israel** and built a synagogue in downtown Los Angeles in 1892. (The congregation continues to this day, now at 8056 Beverly Blvd.; *213-651-4022). Founded in 1906, the **Sinai Congregation** (now at 10400 Wilshire Blvd. in Westwood; 310-474-1518) was the city's first Conservative assembly.

In 1929 Congregation B'nai B'rith moved to the **Wilshire Boulevard Temple** (3663 Wilshire Blvd.; 213-388-2401) on the fashionable Miracle Mile. It was led for more than sixty-five years by Rabbi Edgar F. Magnin, historically one of the city's most prominent religious leaders. Across town in Boyle Heights, a working-class Jewish community made up of mostly Eastern European immigrants emerged (and, with it, a resurgence of the Yiddish language). The Orthodox **Congregation Talmud Torah** was established in 1912 (in the now-abandoned Breed Street Shul, on Breed between First St. and Cesar E. Chavez Ave.) to serve this community.

Today the spiritual life of the city's Jewish community flourishes in a variety of ways. Rabbi Harold M.

Schulweis, who heads the Conservative congregation at **Valley Beth Shalom** (1539 Ventura Blvd., Encino; 818-788-6000) provides a particularly articulate voice for today's Jewish community. The Reform **Temple Emanuel** (8844 Burton Way; 310-274-6388) in Beverly Hills is now headed by Rabbi Laura Geller, the first woman to lead a major Jewish congregation in the United States. InWestwood, **Chabad** (741 Gayley Ave.; 310-208-7511) is the West Coast headquarters of the followers of the late Rabbi Menachem Mendel Schneerson, the charismatic spiritual leader of the Brooklyn-based Lubavitch Hasidic movement. One of the most important places in the city for learning about all aspects of Jewish culture is the **Skirball Cultural Center** (2701 N. Sepulveda Blvd., Los Angeles; 310-440-4500), which is addressed at length elsewhere in this publication. The **University of Judaism** (15600 Mulholland Dr.; 310-476-9777) in Bel Air was established in 1947. It houses an undergraduate college of arts and sciences; the Lieber School of Graduate Studies; the Fingerhut School of Education; the Ziegler School of Rabbinic Studies, which prepares Conservative rabbis for ordination; and the Center for Policy Options, which studies topics related to Judaism and Israel. Programs available to the public include an extensive continuing-education program (many classes explore aspects of Judaism), a sculpture garden, and the Platt Art Gallery. The **Home of Peace Memorial Park** in East Los Angeles (4334 Whittier Blvd.; *213-261-6135) is the city's oldest existing Jewish cemetery. (It replaced the first one, which was in Chavez Ravine, near what is now Dodger Stadium.)

There are two museums in Los Angeles that commemorate the Holocaust: the **Museum of Tolerance** at the Simon Wiesenthal Center (9086 W. Pico Blvd.; 310-553-8403) and the **Martyrs Memorial and Museum of the Holocaust** (6505 Wilshire Blvd.; *213-651-3175). **My Jewish Discovery Place Children's Museum,** for kids aged three to eleven, features interactive exhibits on Jewish life and history. It is located at the Westside Jewish Community Center (5870 W. Olympic Blvd., Los Angeles; *213-857-0036, ext. 2278).

Awaken ...

More than seventeen schools of Buddhism exist in Los Angeles today, brought here by their followers in the Asian immigrant communities. Despite the obvious differences in their practices, they share a devotion to the teachings of the Buddha, the former Siddhartha Gautama, who lived in India more than 2,500 years ago.

Buddhism was brought to Los Angeles primarily by the Japanese, most of whom practiced Jodo Shinshu, or Pure Land Buddhism. The sects represented by Asian-Americans in Los Angeles today have been carved out of centuries of practice in the countries and cultures to which the practice of Buddhism spread, including China, Tibet, Japan, Korea, Sri Lanka, Burma, Cambodia, Vietnam, Thailand, and Taiwan. The principles of Buddhism are found in dharma, its teachings, and in the sutras, its sacred scriptures.

Nishi (Hompa) Hongwangji (369 E. First St.) in Little Tokyo is the oldest Buddhist temple still standing in Los Angeles. Built in 1925, it now houses the Japanese American National Museum. One block away is the new **Nishi Hongwangji Temple**

(815 E. First St.; 213-680-9130), where Jodo Shinshu Buddhism is practiced. The **Zen Center of Los Angeles** (923 S. Normandie Ave.; 213-387-2351), which offers classes in the practice of Zen Buddhism, is especially accessible to the Western seeker. **Vipassana Support Institute** (4070 Albright Ave., Los Angeles; 310-915-1943) is a good place to find out about Vipassana, or mindfulness meditation, which comes from the Burmese Theravada school of Buddhism and is an increasingly popular practice in the United States. **Thubten Dhargye Ling** (3500 E. Fourth St., Long Beach; 562-621-9865), a small Tibetan monastery, arranged for His Holiness, the Dalai Lama, the spiritual head of Tibetan Buddhism as well as the temporal head of the Tibetan government (now in exile in Daramsala, India), to come to Los Angeles in 1997. More than 10,000 people attended his lectures and classes, attesting to the considerable interest in Buddhism in the United States, not only to those of Asian ancestry but to Westerners as well. The public is welcome to attend the teachings of the monastery's spiritual director, Geshe Tsultim Gyeltsen (Sun. 10:30 a.m., Wed. 7:30 p.m.). The **Wat Thai Temple** in North Hollywood (8225 Coldwater Canyon; 818-780-4200) serves not only as a place of worship but also as a cultural center for the Thai community in Los Angeles. Unlike the generally more modest Buddhist temples in the area, the **Hsi Lai Temple** (3456 S. Glenmark Dr.; 818-961-9697) in Hacienda Heights is an astonishing site. Built in 1988 as a Western adjunct of the Fo Kuan Shan monastery in Taiwan, it is the largest Buddhist temple in the Western Hemisphere. It

too is as much a cultural center for the Taiwanese community as it is a place where one can learn and practice Buddhism. Sundays are a wonderful time to visit the temple, which is filled with families who come to worship and socialize in its shrines, gardens, and tea and dining rooms.

Om . . .

Hindu Temple Society of Southern California
1600 Las Virgenes Canyon Rd.
Calabasas 91302
818-880-5552

Just as the rituals and ceremonies performed in any Hindu temple directly convey the principles of Hinduism, so too does its architecture. The Hindu Temple in Calabasas, one of the largest and most authentic in the Western Hemisphere, is no exception. Like all sacred spaces, the Hindu temple is believed to be the place where human beings go to interact with the divine and, in the case of the Hindus, the gods who manifest the divine: Brahma, Vishnu, and Shiva.

Historically the architecture of the temples in India developed along regional lines and according to the tastes of their patrons, usually the regional rulers. The brilliantly white, intricately carved temple in Calabasas is done in the the Chola style, which came from Chola kingdom in Southern India in the tenth and eleventh centuries. The temple's architect and its craftsmen were specially trained in the arts and sciences of temple construction, and the design of the temple followed strict codes known as Shastras.

This temple was built to honor the deity of Lord Venkateswara, an incarnation of Lord Vishnu. There are also shrines honoring other deities. In many ways Hinduism is considered a philosophy rather than

a religion. Its beliefs and practices come from its sacred scriptures, particularly the ancient Vedas. Other key texts are the epics: the *Mahabharata* (first brought to the attention of secular audiences in L.A. through Peter Brooks's nine-hour dramatization of its stories during the Olympic Arts Festival in 1984), which contains the *Bhagavadgita* (the most important religious text of Hinduism), and the *Ramayana*. The temple is open daily throughout the year (Mon.–Fri. 9 a.m.–noon, 5–7 p.m.; Sat.–Sun. 8 a.m.–7 p.m.; open until 8 p.m. in the summer), and visitors are welcome.

Vedanta Society of Southern California
1946 Vedanta Pl.
Los Angeles 90068
213-465-7114

Despite the din of the Hollywood Freeway, which cuts just below, the Vedanta Society manages to maintain an air of tranquillity in the midst of harried urban circumstances. Founded in 1930 by Swami Prabhavananda, the society is dedicated to the study of Vedanta, a philosophy based on the Vedic texts, the earliest sacred scriptures of India.

The society was particularly attractive to members of L.A.'s artistic and intellectual community in the 1930s and 1940s. The novelist Christopher Isherwood produced several works on Vedanta and wrote about his relationship with the swami in *My Guru and His Disciple* (1980). His fellow English expatriates Aldous Huxley and Gerald Heard were devotees as well.

The Vedanta Society is a lovely place to visit. A small, almost miniature, onion-domed temple stands in the middle of the property; the monastery,

a cozy Craftsman-style house now used for lectures, and the bookstore are nearby. In addition to services and classes, the society sponsors lectures and seminars on many aspects of spirituality. All are open to the public.

Something More

Self-Realization Fellowship Lake Shrine
17190 Sunset Blvd.
Los Angeles 90272
310-454-4114
Tues.–Sat. 9 a.m.–4:30 p.m., Sun. 12:30–4:30 p.m.

If Shangri-La or, perhaps, the Garden of Eden is your image of heaven, this is the place for you. Established in 1950 by Paramahansa Yogananda, the shrine boasts a spring-fed lake, waterfalls, lush tropical gardens, swans, tranquil paths, and, in an only in L.A. architectural moment, a reproduction of a sixteenth-century Dutch windmill which serves as a meditation chapel. A shrine to Mahatma Gandhi contains a portion of his ashes, and tributes to the world's major religions may be found in the Court of Religions.

The fellowship, which embraces all faiths, was founded by Sri Yogananda in 1920 and is not considered a religion. Rather it teaches a meditation technique known as Kriya Yoga, which "allows truth-seekers of all races, cultures, and creeds scientific techniques of meditation for attaining direct personal experience of God." Open to the public, the Lake Shrine is a beautiful spot to unwind, meditate, or pray. The Self-Realization Fellowship Temple is nearby. It too is open to the public for services and classes. Other temples are in Hollywood (4860 Sunset Blvd.; *213-661-8006) and Pasadena (150 N. El Molino Ave.; 626-578-9765).

Allah Is the Light of the Heavens and the Earth ...

Muslims refer to God as Allah and see themselves as descendants of the Old Testament's Abraham and Hagar (just as the Jews see themselves as descendants of Abraham and Sarah). They consider Muhammad their prophet and the Qur'an their sacred scripture. Los Angeles is home to the third-largest Muslim population in the United States.

Islamic Center of Southern California
434 S. Vermont Ave.
Los Angeles 90020
213-382-9200

It's ironic that in a nation of immigrants, immigrants —especially the newly arrived—are viewed with such suspicion. This is especially true in the Muslim communities, and the Islamic Center has therefore made it its mission to establish "an Islamic presence in the United States capable of effective interaction with American society." Its goal is to create a truly American Muslim community. Founded in 1977, the center serves as much as a meeting place for Muslims from all over the world as it does as a house of worship. The Muslim Public Affairs Council, which is housed at the center, offers a Muslim voice in the city's political affairs.

The Islamic Center serves Muslims not only from the Middle East but from countries all over the world, including Egypt, Pakistan, Indonesia, Malaysia, Iran, Turkey, and even China and Korea. Among the more recent arrivals are Bosnian Muslims fleeing the civil war in their county. The center is open for the traditional five daily prayers (at dawn, noon, afternoon, sunset, and night) and on Friday, the Muslim day of worship.

The center is housed in a former office building that bears little resemblance to a traditional mosque, except for one key detail of paramount importance in Muslim worship: a *mihrab*, or niche, which points the faithful in the direction of Mecca, Islam's most sacred city and specifically to the Ka'bah, the remains of the temple said by Muslims to have been built originally by Adam and amended by Abraham. Although the faithful are still called to prayer in a traditional manner, the structure lacks a minaret, the exterior tower from which the faithful are called to prayer, a key feature of a traditional mosque.

Non-Muslims are welcome to attend services, and except for the bookstore (open Tues.–Fri., Sun. 10 a.m.–4 p.m.), the center is open to the public only fifteen minutes before and after the daily prayers and for a longer period on Friday. For the non-Muslim the best way to visit the center is to attend the service on Friday with the lecture by the imam (prayer leader) at 1 p.m. (men and women are in different rooms; visitors sit in the chairs, the faithful on the floor). Lunch is available afterward in the cafeteria. In addition, the center offers many lectures and seminars on topics of interest to the community at large. Call for a schedule.

For an architecturally more traditional mosque, complete with dome and minaret, visit the **Masjid Omar Ibn Al Khattab** near the University of Southern California (1025 W. Exposition Blvd., Los Angeles; *213-733-9938). One of the area's newest mosques is the **Islamic Center Northridge** (11439 Encino Ave., Granada Hills; 818-360-9963), which serves a congregation from all over the world but has an especially large number of Pakistani and Indian members. Although its leaders sought to build a traditional mosque, local restrictions kept them from doing so.

According to Seyyed Hossein Nasr, author of *Islamic Art and Spirituality*, the architecture of the mosque symbolically represents a re-creation of nature, the ultimate Muslim place of worship. The Arabic word for mosque is *masjid*, which means a place for prostration (*sujud*), one of the key positions in ritual Muslim worship, when the faithful prostrate themselves and touch their heads to the floor. Therefore, the floor is a focal point of the structure. The dome reminds the faithful of heaven and, at its center, the One. To the Western observer more familiar with the (comparatively) busy furnishings of churches and synagogues, the mosque's interior will seem not only spare but empty. Again, this is a deliberate architectural device, meant to convey the glory of spiritual poverty (a favorite concept of the Prophet) and the invisibility of the spirit. Light is a key dimension of the mosque and considered to be the first creation of Allah. The Arabic word for the minaret is *al-manárah,* or the place of light. The crescent moon and star signify the beginning of Ramadan, the holy month of fasting for Muslims. Finally, the light is the Word, which to the Muslim is, of course, the Qur'an.

Strangers in a Strange Land

A key role religious institutions have played, and continue to play, in the city is to help millions of newcomers adjust to life in Los Angeles. Whatever the newcomer's denomination or whether they come from here or abroad, churches, synagogues, temples, and mosques offer comfort, solace, and community to people who are, more often than not, bewildered by the new culture, lonely and separated from family and friends, and longing for the familiar ways they have left behind. Many of these institutions, particularly the ethnic churches, help preserve the culture and traditions of the old countries for the new, American-born generations to come. Others give clues to the city's dynamic history of immigration and assimilation.

For those who appreciate the rich ethnic diversity of Los Angeles, visiting these places provides an ideal opportunity to see and enjoy the many cultures that make up Los Angeles today. Certainly, Islamic mosques and Buddhist and Hindu temples are rich in the cultures they represent and provide a good starting point. Other places to look are mainstream religious sites that cater to immigrant communities. For example, **Saint Peter's Italian Catholic Church** (1039 N. Broadway; *213-225-8119) in Chinatown offers the Mass in Italian and reflects a time in the city's history when Chinatown was, in effect, Little Italy. Nearby is **Saint Anthony's Croatian Catholic Church** (712 N. Grand Ave.; 213-628-2938). **Our Lady of the Bright Mount** (3424 W. Adams Blvd.; *213-734-5249) serves the Polish community, and **Saint Columban's** (125 S. Loma Dr.; 213-250-8818), the Filipino. The **Breed Street Shul** in Boyle Heights stands abandoned, the Eastern European Jewish congregation that once lived in the area long gone. New congregations of Russian Jewish immigrants have, however, sprung up in the West Hollywood and

Fairfax districts. **Saint Mary's Episcopal Church** (961 S. Mariposa Ave.; 213-387-1334) in Los Angeles has long served the Japanese and now Korean communities. The **Young Nak Presbyterian Church** (1721 N. Broadway; *213-227-4093) in Lincoln Heights, with 7,000 members, is the largest of the city's nearly 1,000 Korean Protestant churches. The church ministers to recent immigrants as well as to more established families with services on Sunday morning and Wednesday evenings, which are conducted in English and Korean. Koreans are the fastest-growing ethnic group in the city. The first Koreans to arrive here in the early part of this century did so because of prompting by Protestant missionaries, particularly Presbyterians, and although there are Korean Buddhist temples in the city, most Korean-Americans living in Los Angeles today are Protestants.

Saint Sophia Cathedral

1324 S. Normandie Ave.
Los Angeles 90006
*213-737-2424

As of the 1990 census, Los Angeles was home to more than 100,000 Greeks; this Greek Orthodox church serves as a spiritual centerpiece of Greek life in the city, even for those removed by several generations from their homeland. To walk into Saint Sophia's is to enter a queen's jewel box.

Completed in 1952, the Byzantine structure itself serves as an intersection between the promises of faith and the dreams—in this case, fulfilled—of the immigrant. The money to build this church was raised almost entirely through the efforts of Spyros and Charles Skouras, Greek immigrants who were the heads of 20th Century Fox Studios and the Fox theater chain, respectively. The massive Czechoslovakian crystal chandeliers were a gift from the Pepsi Cola Company, a prominent vendor in the Fox movie houses, and William Chavalas, the head of the 20th Century Fox art department, designed the cathedral's elaborate interior as well as its many icons, which were executed by his staff. (The figure of Moses in one mural looks like Charlton Heston because the actor served as the model for the painter; Heston, then under contract to 20th Century Fox, was about to make Cecil B. DeMille's *The Ten Commandments* for the studio at the time the cathedral was being built.)

The cathedral's name refers not to a patron saint, but to the Greek word for wisdom, in this case, "holy" wisdom. Architecturally it is divided by a small but elaborate gold altar screen, which separates the church militant (those in the pews) from the church triumphant (the priests). This symbolizes the primary aspiration of the Christian: to pass from this world through the

portals (death) to heaven. The altar where the divine worship takes place is enclosed in a sanctuary behind the altar screen and is much more physically removed from the faithful than in today's non-Orthodox Christian churches. The cathedral, which faces east (toward the light), welcomes visitors daily from 10 a.m. to 2 p.m. (except Thursday). The best time to visit, however, is when all of the chandeliers are lit, usually during a service such as the divine liturgy, which is said every Sunday at 10 a.m. Tours of the cathedral are led by the amiable George Bliziotis, the church's sexton.

Saint Garabed Armenian Apostolic Church of Hollywood

1614 N. Alexandria Ave.
Los Angeles 90027
*213-666-0507

This is one of approximately forty churches that serve the Armenian community of Los Angeles, the largest outside Armenia, with more than 250,000 people. (Other denominations that serve this community include **Our Lady Queen of Martyrs Armenian Catholic Church** [1339 Pleasant Ave.; *213-261-9898] in East Los Angeles and the **United Armenian Congregational Church** [3480 Cahuenga Blvd. West; *213-851-5265] in Los Angeles.) The majority of the Armenians living in Los Angeles today have arrived since the

1970s, although some families have been here since the turn of the century.

The term *apostolic* refers to the establishment of the roots of Christianity in Armenia sometime between A.D. 60 and 80 by two of Christ's apostles, Bartholomew and Thaddeus. In A.D. 301 Armenia became the first country to officially accept Christianity as the state religion, an event prompted by the healing and subsequent conversion of King Tiridates III by the monk who was to become Saint Gregory the Illuminator, the first bishop of Armenia. Grand celebrations are held every century to commemorate this date, which, according to more recent scholarship, is more likely A.D. 314. Nevertheless, the next celebration of the founding of the Armenian Apostolic Church is scheduled for 2001.

Saint Garabed's is located in the Hollywood community informally known as Little Armenia. Architecturally it is completely authentic in terms of the Armenian Apostolic tradition, a source of great pride for its parishioners. The church's most festive holiday is Christmas, which is celebrated on January 6. Visitors are welcome to visit the church, which is open daily, or to attend its Sunday Mass, which begins at 10:30 a.m. and lasts for two hours—a bit long by American standards, but one impressed visitor described it as a heavenly opera.

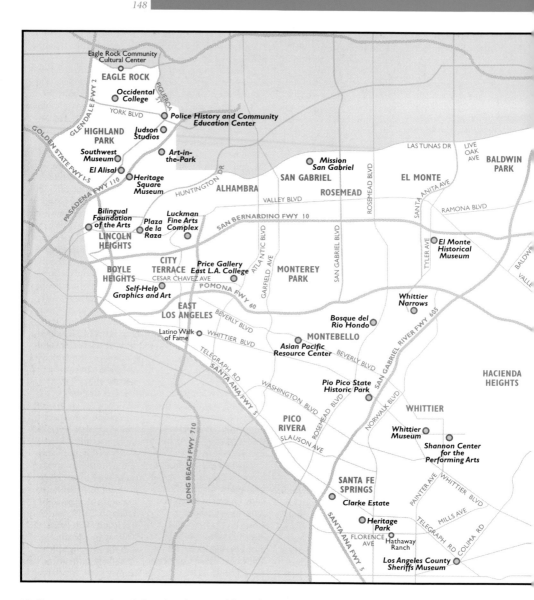

* indicates an area code that changes in 1998

As Los Angeles spread from downtown up the Arroyo Seco, neighborhoods were built in the Victorian style, which celebrated the technological advances of the Industrial Revolution with elaborate, machine-tooled decoration. Nearby, the Southwest Museum and the home of Charles F. Lummis represented a different aesthetic, which developed in appreciation of the area's natural landscape and its native and Hispanic cultures. This fascinating juxtaposition of aesthetics and architectural styles is still preserved in Highland Park, which may be reached from the oldest freeway in Los Angeles—the Pasadena (110)—which was (sadly) carved into the Arroyo.

Southwest Museum

234 Museum Dr.
Los Angeles 90065
*213-221-2164
Tues.-Sun. 10 a.m.-5 p.m.
Entry: adults $5, seniors/students $3, children 7-18 $2

Casa de Adobe

4605 N. Figueroa St.
Los Angeles 90065

All lovers of culture must hope that the oldest museum in Los Angeles has weathered the most difficult decade in its ninety-year history and will be ready by the time it reaches the century mark to take the place in the cultural fabric of the city that its extraordinary collection of the art and artifacts produced by native cultures

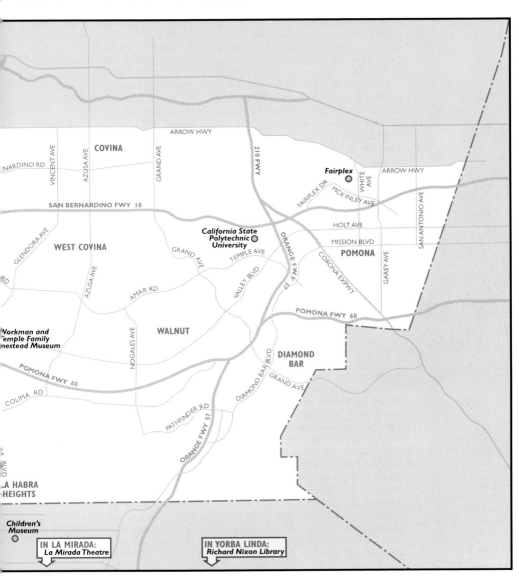

COVINA

NARDINO RD

VINCENT AVE

AZUSA AVE

GRAND AVE

ARROW HWY

210 FWY

Fairplex

WHITE AVE

ARROW HWY

FAIRPLEX DR

MCKINLEY AVE

SAN ANTONIO AVE

SAN BERNARDINO FWY 10

HOLT AVE

GLENDORA AVE

WEST COVINA

California State
Polytechnic
University

GRAND AVE

TEMPLE AVE

ORANGE FWY 57

MISSION BLVD

POMONA

GAREY AVE

RD

AZUSA AVE

AMAR RD

VALLEY BLVD

CORONA EXPWY

POMONA FWY 60

Workman and
Temple Family
Homestead Museum

WALNUT

NOGALES AVE

DIAMOND BAR BLVD

DIAMOND
BAR

POMONA FWY 60

GRAND AVE

COLIMA RD

DIAMOND BAR BLVD

PATHFINDER RD

ORANGE FWY 57

BLVD

LA HABRA
HEIGHTS

Children's
Museum

IN LA MIRADA:
La Mirada Theatre

IN YORBA LINDA:
Richard Nixon Library

of the Americas merits. Its new director, formerly at the Smithsonian, accepted this challenging assignment because he ranks its collection—the world's largest repository of California Indian culture and most extensive collection of Native-American textiles—as the best of its kind west of the Mississippi and among the top three in the nation. But he must create a productive administration after a decade of mismanagement that began with a criminal investigation (and conviction) of one former director of the museum for stealing and selling artifacts from the collection and ended with the resignation of another demoralized by the political pressures that derailed all plans to create a viable future for the museum.

The Southwest Museum still faces an uphill battle that stems in equal parts from its location—on a hilltop overlooking the Arroyo Seco in Highland Park, perceived by many Westsiders as too far from the beaten path—and its reliance on private funding, which provides a meager annual budget of $1.3 million. Dozens of scenarios for revitalizing the museum were explored, including relocating, a proposal angrily condemned by members of the city government whose promised support vanished once their will had been imposed. The administration now insists that it will never abandon the historic building it occupies in Highland Park, but serious problems exist: less than 2 percent of the collection can be displayed in the present building; temporary exhibits are crammed into wall cases in an auditorium that also serves as a classroom; fulfilling its didactic mission in such long-term exhibits as the California Hall allows little room for interpretive displays of the collection; and both the storage facilities and parking lot (located up a steep hill) are inadequate.

When he'd been at the museum for just a year the new director announced his strategy for bringing the museum's treasures out of storage and to the attention of a wider circle than can be lured to Highland Park: adding another exhibition venue within L.A. County. Less than a year after that he announced a new partnership with LACMA, in which the Southwest Museum will lease exhibition space within the newly renovated May Company building. The hundred masterpieces of Navajo textiles featured in the first exhibition should entice more Angelenos to visit the museum to see more of its collections. Because the initial phase of their tenancy will coincide with LACMA's 1999 Van Gogh exhibition, which is expected to draw one million visitors, that increased visibility—equivalent to about a decade of visitation to Highland Park!—should help the Southwest Museum build its membership (from less than 3,000 today). This is a win-win deal—it will also allow LACMA to fill the cavernous space of the May Company with high-quality programming at minimal expense—and a heartening display of intelligent cooperation among local institutions. In that regard, the financial support of the Getty Grant Program should also be acknowledged.

The museum's collections, and very existence, derive from the support of some of Los Angeles's most prominent citizens at the turn of the century. Charles Fletcher Lummis—who served as city editor of the *Los Angeles Times* and librarian of the city's fledgling library system while pursuing such interests as preserving the California missions (rescuing four through the Landmarks Club) and the native cultures of the Southwest—organized the museum to display artifacts collected during field expeditions for the Archaeological Society of America. In 1914 a mission revival–style building was grafted to the slopes of Mount Washington, a siting intended to recall the Alhambra; it was the first museum in Los Angeles to welcome the public. Four permanent exhibition halls with displays on the dominant Indian cultural groups of North America—Great Plains, Southwest, California, and Northwest Coast—occupy most of the building. Paintings and decorative art from the Spanish colonial period and folk arts of Mexico and Central America are also well represented in the collection. The museum offers guided tours for the general public (Sat.–Sun. 11 a.m., 1 p.m.).

Grace Nicholson was a plucky, self-educated art dealer who built the fanciful Chinese-style building that is today the Pacific Asia Museum and bequeathed it her Asian collection. She also worked tirelessly on behalf of the Southwest Museum, developing collections for its early major donors. Caroline Boeing Poole, whose legacy of 2,000 Indian-made baskets is featured in the open storage area that bears her name, bought 1,500 of these baskets from Nicholson in a single transaction in 1931. Anita Baldwin, whose family's ranch is today the County Arboretum, in 1921 loaned the museum 440 Native-American pieces purchased from Nicholson and continued to make acquisitions destined for its collection until her death. Homer Earl Sargent and George Wharton James were other committed Angelenos who worked with Nicholson to establish the museum's holdings. The focus of the collection has not changed as it has grown to 250,000 pieces documenting the earliest American cultures.

Original plans called for a tunnel to access the museum, but this feature was not built until the 1920s. The long, somewhat eerie tunnel (fitted with video surveillance today) features wall-mounted dioramas of important sites—Mesa Verde, the Hopi lands, Palenque—which provide a context for the collections. For many people, including the museum's director, the tunnel entrance is what they remember most about past visits to the museum; its restoration is evidence of the investment that the administration has made in this museum site. An ethnobotanical garden—planted and tended by kids from a local 4-H Club—has transformed the slope above the tunnel with native plants used by ancient cultures as medicine, food, and in making shelter, baskets, and other objects for everyday use.

Arroyo Day, in May each year, is a celebration hosted by the museums in this area.

The **Braun Research Library** (*213-221-2164, ext. 255; Wed.–Sat. 1–5 p.m.) contains 50,000 books and 120,000 photographs that document the anthropology, art, and archaeology of the New World; there are also 1,300 sound recordings as well as the personal papers and library of Lummis and other early scholars, covering the history of the western states, especially California, and documenting the culture of native populations. A grant has enabled the staff to computerize the holdings to make this important information more accessible to the public.

Henry O'Melveny, a prominent Los Angeles attorney, had support from members of the original ranching families in his drive to construct an adobe structure, which was intended to be a composite of all known adobes built in California before 1850 (rather than a replica of any single one). Plans to furnish the building, called Casa de Adobe, were not realized, and in 1925 it was deeded to the Southwest Museum, which installed period furniture and decorative arts. Earthquake damage and the expense of maintaining this separate building in the immediate neighborhood as gallery space have more recently limited its use to special events.

The Southwest Museum's programming celebrates the region's Native-American and Latino heritage. Indian Summer, highlighting Native-American traditions, includes such activities as pottery-making and storytelling for children; the Intertribal Marketplace, held each fall, features more than 100 American Indian artists in a weekend festival that includes art appraisals as well as craft sales. The museum's end-of-year celebrations are particularly festive and popular, and it kicks off the New Year with a festival of films created by or addressed to Latino and Native-American audiences that are rarely found in mainstream theaters. Members are kept abreast of events with a quarterly newsletter.

About 70,000 people visit the museum each year, including 45,000 schoolchildren, but public support for this important resource is needed to guarantee the security and interpretation of its collections. Like the prominent Angelenos who made this museum their first priority in developing cultural monuments in Los Angeles, today's movers and shakers need to rally round this institution that preserves the cultures of the original inhabitants of the Southwest. When was your last visit?

El Alisal (Lummis Home) Historical Society of Southern California

200 E. Avenue 43
Los Angeles 90031
*213-222-0546
Fri.–Sun. noon–4 p.m.
Entry: free

Charles Fletcher Lummis made an impression on Los Angeles before he ever reached the city. In 1885, during his 143-day trek on foot from Ohio, Lummis sent accounts of his journey to Harrison Gray Otis, who published them in the fledgling *Los Angeles Times*. Lummis became the first city editor of the paper, but even his enthusiasm for Los Angeles could not contain his restless spirit or assuage his interest in Native-American cultures, which led him to travel throughout the Southwest, Mexico, and Central America.

In 1898 Lummis began to build a home at the southern end of the Arroyo Seco about three miles from the city center, in what is now Highland Park. He wanted the structure to express the evolving spirit of the West, and it became a gathering place for all who shared his enthusiasm for the native and local culture of the city and the region. Named El Alisal—Spanish for the California sycamores that grow on the site—the house derives its eccentric style from the materials used in construction. The walls are constructed with boulders from the Arroyo; iron rails from the Santa Fe Railway reinforce the walls; and telegraph poles form the ceiling. The massive, hand-carved doors were designed by artist Maynard Dixon, and the windows are oriented to catch a breeze or frame a view of Lummis's beloved Southwest Museum just up the hill.

Lummis became a librarian in the then-developing city system, acquiring documents from the Spanish Colonial period and initiating its great Western history collection. He spearheaded the movement to establish the Southwest Museum and donated his own collections and library to it; he

also deeded El Alisal to the museum with the provision that his family be able to live there. Maintaining the house strained the museum's resources, and in 1971 it was acquired by the city of Los Angeles. The Historical Society of Southern California now has its offices and a bookstore at the property and has enhanced it with a waterwise garden. The landscape of water-conserving plants, including many California natives and annual wildflowers, is the inspiration for a garden fair, usually held in early April, which features technical demonstrations and a plant sale as well as tours. El Alisal remains a monument to the cultural ethos that Lummis helped to shape in this pioneer city, and the welcoming docents and resident members of the Historical Society of Southern California keep that history alive.

Arroyo Arts Collective (www.oversight. com/Arroyo; P.O. Box 42835, York Station, Highland Park 90050) was established in 1989 as a community of artists and writers who live in Northeast L.A. In addition to producing a quarterly newsletter that includes listings of cultural events in the community, the Arroyo Arts Collective sponsors a fall tour of artists' homes and studios in Highland Park; you can choose a tour that includes a luncheon and guided visit to the Judson Studios, or opt for a less expensive self- guided tour. Call *213-221-3225 for information; tickets may also be obtained at Random Gallery (6040 N. Figueroa St., *213-550-8000; Tues.–Sat. 11 a.m.–6 p.m.) or at El Alisal.

Juried exhibitions of work by Arroyo Arts Collective members have been held at Occidental College, Los Angeles City College, and Cal State L.A. Posters with multilingual poems have been hung in Figueroa Street shop windows as the public component of the Poetry in the Windows program (funded in part by the Lannan Foundation). The Arroyo Arts Collective has also worked with neighborhood youth to create Drive By Art Gallery, murals that decorate walls of public parking lots in Highland Park.

Eagle Rock Community Cultural Center

225 Colorado Blvd.
Los Angeles 90041
*213-226-1617

This new cultural center, which was formerly the Eagle Rock branch library, was built in 1914 with funds from the Carnegie Foundation. It now houses the Eagle Rock Valley historical society.

Heritage Square Museum

3800 Homer St.
Los Angeles 90031
818-449-0193
Sat.–Sun. (and some holidays) 11:30 a.m.–4:30 p.m.; guided tours on the hour noon to 3 p.m.; Fri. 10 a.m.–3 p.m. (grounds only)
Entry: adults $5, seniors/children 13–17 $4, children 7–12 $2, children under 7 free

Heritage Square, located in Highland Park near the Avenue 43 exit from the 110 Freeway, is an open-air museum of Victorian architecture; to date, eight endangered structures have been moved to the ten-acre park. Undergoing careful and gradual reconstruction as a Victorian environment, the museum will incorporate cobblestone streets, a trolley, gardens, and lighting appropriate to the period, as well as authentically restored architecture. Its mission is to preserve and interpret the architecture and culture that flourished in Southern California from 1865 to 1914, the period during which the village setting it reconstructs was the norm.

A visit to William H. Perry House (1876) and Hale House (1885), both listed on the National Register of Historic Places, would alone warrant making the trip to Highland Park. The formal Italianate facade of the Perry House is an interesting contrast to the exuberantly patterned and colored exterior of the Queen Anne/Eastlake-style Hale House. Terra-cotta and stained-glass panels, ornate brickwork, and elaborate carvings mark the exterior of the Hale House; the interior rooms, furnished with period antiques, are models of sensitive restoration.

Another architectural treasure preserved at Heritage Square is the Valley Knudsen Garden-Residence, named in honor of the founder of the Los Angeles Beautiful organization. This circa-1877 home was built by nineteenth-century craftsmen in the classical French Mansard style. The interior of the Ford House (1887) still awaits restoration, but from the front porch visitors may view its unusual wooden columns and elaborate ornamentation. The decorative elements, handcarved by John Ford, transformed an ordinary tract house into a showplace for this craftsman; his work also graces buildings at Stanford University, the California State Capitol, and Iolani Palace in Honolulu.

An example of the nineteenth-century fad for octagonal houses—by 1857, there were more than 1,000 of them in America—was one of only three left in Southern California when it was moved to the park. The Longfellow Hastings Octagon House, built in 1893, is a rare unaltered example that still awaits restoration, while a turn-of-the-century train depot, built circa 1887 for the Southern Pacific Railroad, is now the museum's ticket booth. The Lincoln Avenue Methodist Church (1897) is an excellent example of a so-called "Akron style" church, which is characterized by a diagonal axis. A bookstore and gift shop specializing in Victorian materials, and an 1899 carriage barn used as the restoration and maintenance shop currently complete the Heritage Square complex; future projects include installing a unique collection of turn-of-the-century apothecary equipment in a reconstructed Colonial Drugstore and adding a gallery for temporary exhibitions.

Much of the time-consuming labor to preserve these architectural treasures has been donated by volunteers, and the ongoing process of building Heritage Square is a great opportunity for community involvement. Information on membership, programs, and volunteer opportunities is available at Heritage Square, or call the administrative offices at 626-796-2898.

Tierra de la Culebra
240 S. Avenue 57
Los Angeles 90042
*213-223-3879

This neighborhood center and art park featuring sculpture fabricated by neighborhood kids was started as a response to the 1992 riots. A 450-foot-long sculpture of a serpent gave the art park its name— "la culebra" is a beneficial snake, not a venemous one. Some 150 trees have transformed once-abandoned land into an urban forest, with gardens, a pond, and an amphitheater. Tierra de la Culebra offers kids a place to gather and find assistance on their homework, other mentoring programs, as well as art and environmental workshops and performances. The park is administered by ARTCorpsLA, a group that works with low-income communities to effect neighborhood revitalization through art. **Spiraling Orchard** in the Temple-Beaudry area is another ARTCorpsLA park, with an installation reminiscent of the artworks by earth artist Robert Smithson.

Latino Heritage Month has been celebrated for more than twenty years during September and October; in 1997 it featured for the first time a month-long Latino Film Festival, which was produced by actor Edward James Olmos and held at the Universal Cineplex. Innovative programs—like 1997's tango festival—augment the always-full schedule of concerts and art exhibitions; call 562-403-2694 for a schedule of events.

Judson Studios
200 S. Avenue 66
Los Angeles 90042
*213-255-0131

For five generations the Judson family has fabricated stained glass, since 1919 in a studio building of eclectic design— Islamic revival overlaid on California bungalow— that originally housed the USC Art School, where founder William Lees Judson was dean. A fire in 1910 destroyed that building and many of Judson's plein-air paintings, but the structure was rebuilt on a foundation of boulders collected in the Arroyo, a technique also employed by his neighbor and friend, Charles Lummis, for his nearby home. The Judson Studio became the center of the local Arts and Crafts movement, which emulated the aesthetic of William Morris and Gustav Stickley, especially after William Lees Judson became president of the Guild of Arroyo Fellow Craftsmen.

During its early years, the studio produced as much secular as religious work, executing Frank Lloyd Wright's designs for the Barnsdall and Ennis Houses, as well as recreating the Gothic effect of European cathedrals. Among the local

glass monuments designed by Judson Studios are the Natural History Museum's rotunda, and the windows at St. James Episcopal Church and First Congregational Church, both on Wilshire Boulevard. Tours of the working studio, which celebrates its centennial in 1997, are offered on the third Thursday of each month at 2 p.m. and by appointment. A gallery of sacred and traditional art showcases work by contemporary practitioners of stained-glass art (Mon.–Fri. 9 a.m.–4:30 p.m., Sat. noon–4 p.m.; free) and is the site of monthly chamber music concerts and lectures.

Elyria Canyon Park, a thirty-five-acre tract of land on the slopes of Mount Washington, has been purchased with funds from 1992's Proposition A and preserved, bringing victory to the neighborhood residents who since 1979 have fought a planned condominium development on the site. A century earlier the Southern Pacific Railroad had purchased this land to build housing for its workers; by 1909 there was a 3,000-foot cable car up to the Mount Washington Hotel (now the Self-Realization Fellowship).

The plant life of Elyria Canyon Park, the easternmost tract of land in the Santa Monica Mountains, is predominantly California black walnut on cool, north-facing slopes and coastal sage scrub on the dry hills oriented to the south. The park, located at the end of Wollam Street (1550 Bridgeport Dr.) in Glassell Park offers hiking trails through an open wilderness in an urban area, as well as monthly guided nature walks and volunteer work days.

Los Angeles Police History and Community Education Center
6045 York Blvd.
Los Angeles 90041
*213-344-9445

This museum, expected to open in 1998 in a converted 1923 police station in Highland Park, will showcase "the proud history of the Los Angeles Police Department" and form a bridge of understanding between its officers and the public. Exhibits will be designed by Disney Imagineering "VoluntEars" and feature interactive displays on state-of-the-art police science, including fingerprinting, autopsies, and creating a composite sketch of a crime scene. Such special units as the SWAT Team, K-9 Corps, and Bomb Squad will be highlighted; tributes to fallen officers and exhibits on some of the LAPD's most famous cases will be featured. Facilities for such ongoing efforts as D.A.R.E., Neighborhood Watch, and antigang education will include a multimedia auditorium and outdoor amphitheater because the organizers expect the center to be a favorite destination of school groups.

Occidental College
1600 Campus Rd.
Los Angeles 90041
*213-259-2500

In 1887 Presbyterian ministers instructed Occidental College's first student body of twenty-seven men and thirteen women; a century later the enrollment in its non-sectarian four-year liberal arts curriculum is 1,600 students. The present campus was planned by architect Myron Hunt, who

also designed twenty-one of the buildings constructed from 1912 to 1940. In the view of architectural historian and Occidental professor Robert Winter, Hunt gave the trustees what they wanted, "a campus that looks like a college but also looks as if it had been founded on common sense." Beaux-arts-style buildings with red tile roofs and an axial plan with tree-lined walks fill the flat areas of the 120-acre campus, and those cat pawprints stenciled on the walkways are a reference to its founders' wish that this school become "the Princeton of the West." The art faculty organizes changing exhibitions in two galleries within the **Weingart Center** and around the central staircase of the Coons Administrative Center.

An outdoor amphitheater tucked into the hill above campus and a magnificent modern theater are the destination of most visitors to the campus. The **Keck Theater**, designed by Peter Kamnitzer and opened in 1989, is a flexible structure that can be converted from proscenium to thrust to arena stage by hydraulically altering the floor-level seating; a two-story horseshoe-shaped gallery encloses the space, with seating that envelops the stage. The behind-the-scene features were designed with equal care: a "fly gallery" (catwalk) above the stage allows enviable flexibility in lighting design; the dressing rooms and costume studio have state-of-the-art appointments and natural lighting. The surface of the stage is ideal for dance performances which—along with a Saturday series for families—are featured in the programming. All are welcome free of charge to the Sunday afternoon series Playwrights on the Verge, staged readings followed by a discussion and reception with the author. Musical performances are held in **Thorne Hall**, renowned for its acoustics. Call the box office at *213-259-2922 for program and ticket information.

The Hillside Amphitheater is the site of the summer theater festival, which has been offering savvy Angelenos an intimate alternative to the Hollywood Bowl for nearly forty years. Five hundred chairs are mounted on the terraced stone steps for reserved seating; 3,000 additional ticket-holders can bring cushions or folding chairs, and fill the amphitheater back to the line of live oaks on the horizon. A repertory troupe composed of professional headliners, emerging actors, and student interns mounts four thematically related plays that rotate throughout the two-month season. Tickets are reasonably priced and if you subscribe to the series, the fourth play costs just $1. Productions of the Children's Theater Project ($6 per adult, $4 per child) are presented on the more intimate grass stage (Wed., Fri.–Sat. 11 a.m. in the middle of the season); call the box office (*213-259-2922) for the summer program.

Art-in-the-Park
5568 Via Marisol
Los Angeles 90042
*213-259-0861
Mon.–Tues.,Thurs. 9 a.m.–2 p.m., Sat. 9 a.m.–3 p.m.

The Arroyo Seco Park clubhouse is the site of a new public/private partnership that plans to offer a program of inexpensive bilingual (English/Spanish) art classes, as well as stage festivals of interest to the local community, such as the annual Corn Festival of Northeast Los Angeles. The Summer Arts Program was initiated in 1997 with an eclectic mix of classes: (for children) photography, painting, mask-making, calligraphy, and Celtic dance, and (for adults) pre-Hispanic cooking, life drawing, paper marbleizing, folk art, and sculpture.

Plaza de la Raza
3540 N. Mission Rd.
Los Angeles 90031
*213-223-2475
Mon.–Fri. 9 a.m.–8 p.m., Sat. 9 a.m.–2 p.m.

Plaza de la Raza, a cultural center for the arts and education, occupies a complex of white buildings by the small lake in forty-six-acre Lincoln Park. Its facilities include a 175-seat dinner theater, a dance studio, a visual arts building, and music studios, as well as a small gallery located in a boathouse. The unaffiliated visitor most likely will experience this cultural center by viewing the occasional art exhibitions in the boathouse (call to confirm that an exhibition is on view) or attending a public performance like the concert series Con Sabor Latino…, which is presented on summer weekends at the 350-seat Willie Velasquez Outdoor Stage. A virtual museum of Plaza de la Raza's 2,000-piece collection of folk art and contemporary works is available on the Internet at www.plazaraza.org.

Plaza de la Raza is an important and well-loved educational force in the Latino community. Its after-school programs (Mon.–Fri. 4–8 p.m.) attract 500 kids each week and offer a stimulating curriculum of dance, music, theater, and visual arts. Annual registration costs $15 and the ten-week-long courses are $35. Classes are held in English, though most of the teachers are bilingual and can help a child who is more proficient in Spanish. Similar classes are scheduled on Saturday mornings.

Teenagers, who may have attended classes at this community center since they were youngsters, are offered intensive and imaginative training in theater and music through a Community Arts Partnership (CAP) with California Institute of the Arts. The theater program allows developing thespians to take the stage, while others work behind the scenes to mount full productions; dance and music training also continues for teens.

In summer Plaza de la Raza's School of Performing and Visual Arts sponsors bilingual classes ranging from the standard (piano, tap dance, guitar, drawing, and painting) to the unusual (folklorico dance, mask-making, Mexican folk songs). Many classes are free to children who live in certain areas of the city and who meet low-to-moderate income requirements; otherwise, tuition is $35 to $45 for ten-week, one-day-a-week classes. More intensive, five-week programs are sometimes offered as well. For further information, call *213-223-2475.

In the early twentieth-century the area around the **Lincoln Park Lake** was the site of the California Alligator Farm: in 1915 movie producer William Selig added a private zoo to his thirty-acre spread near the lake (where several of the *Tarzan* movies starring Johnny Weismuller were filmed). Visitors paid 25¢ to see hundreds of huge alligators, as well as iguanas and chuckwalla lizards. The gators, which had not always been contained by the chain-link fences surrounding the twenty ponds, were finally removed in 1953, an event commemorated by Bill Haley and the Comets in their song "See You Later, Alligator."

Mariachi Plaza (First and Boyle Sts.) is the site of an annual mariachi festival held in November (call 213-485-2437 for information); this site may become the first museum in the world to focus on this art form. Musician José Hernandez and L.A. city officials announced a fund-raising campaign in June 1997, with a benefit at the Greek Theater to raise funds for the construction of a Mariachi Heritage Museum that would house costumes, photographs, and recordings from the most respected practitioners of this traditional art. The Mariachi Heritage Society (626-279-1700) is spearheading the effort to fund the museum and welcomes inquiries and contributions.

Boyle Heights was founded as L.A.'s first suburb in 1876 and named for an Irishman, Andrew Boyle, who built a landmark brick home on a ridge overlooking downtown. By the 1920s it was known as the Lower East Side of Los Angeles because it was the destination of many Jewish immigrants from Russia and Eastern Europe. The community of Japanese-Americans in this area was disbanded by forced internment during World War II, but its presence is still recalled by the exotic form of the Rissho Kosei-Kai Buddhist Temple at 118 North Mott Street. This history and other information discovered by Roosevelt High School students who participated in a pilot project sponsored by the Getty Research Institute can be explored at a Web site (www.getty.edu/gri).

The Estrada Courts Housing Project (Lorena, Hunter, and Estrada Sts.) in Boyle Heights recently added six digitally produced murals to the more than fifty murals already on site. For more on this destination for outdoor and public art, see Murals, page 170.

Self-Help Graphics and Art

3802 Cesar E. Chavez Ave.
Los Angeles 90063
*213-264-1259

Since 1972 this community arts center in East Los Angeles has fostered the creation and promotion of Chicano art. Sister Karen Boccalero—the Franciscan nun who founded and directed Self-Help Graphics and Art—died in June 1997, but she left behind a generation of artists who share her belief in the transformative power of art. Self-Help Graphics did not invest its resources in a building, choosing instead to nurture the process of discovery, but their storefront on a principal commercial street in a Latino neighborhood has been transformed with multicolored pottery shards and paint, an eye-catching and festive decoration that suggests the spirit of the place.

Galería Otra Vez (Tues.–Sat. 10 a.m.–4 p.m.) is a showcase for colorful silkscreen prints, many of them produced in Self-Help's highly acclaimed atelier program, where advanced technical workshops are conducted by the resident master printer. More than 150 works created by artists in this program are circulated by the Exhibition Print Program to cultural centers throughout the United States and abroad, bringing this group of Chicano artists wider recognition.

Bilingual Foundation of the Arts (BFA)

421 N. Avenue 19
Los Angeles 90031
*213-225-4044

The Bilingual Foundation of the Arts presents three major theater productions each year at its ninety-nine-seat Equity-waiver theater just east of downtown. On alternate nights the play is produced in Spanish and English, allowing language students and the large Latino community in the vicinity to hear first-rate theater in Spanish; there are also performances on Sunday at 3 p.m. The group also presents two productions per year geared especially to young audiences, which tour statewide. For more on the history of this company, see Theater and Dance (p. 79).

The Sancho Show, hosted by Daniel Castro, provost of East Los Angeles College, on Saturday nights on KPCC (89.3 FM), and John Martinez's weekend show on KPFK (90.7 FM) give voice to concerns within the Latino community.

Vincent Price Gallery

East Los Angeles College
1301 Cesar E. Chavez Ave.
Monterey Park 91754
*213-265-8841
Daily noon–3 p.m., Thurs. 6–9 p.m.
Entry: free

The pride that East Los Angeles College takes in its fine art collection can be measured in the large and prominent space it occupies on the campus. A work of art from the collection is also featured on every bulletin of classes distributed to the 15,000 students enrolled in its two-year program.

Vincent Price was well known for playing suave villains during Hollywood's Golden Age; with the characters he portrayed in the film adaptations of Edgar

Allan Poe's works, he became identified forever with screen horror. His lifelong passion for the visual arts—which began with his study of art history at Yale, from which he graduated in 1933—has been given a permanent legacy in the teaching collection he established at East Los Angeles College. Price believed that art could play a humanizing role in every life, and in that spirit he acted as curator for Sears, Roebuck; he purchased 60,000 works of art which were then sold by mail order during his tenure in that position. Although he was a founding board member of the Los Angeles County Museum of Art, he selected East Los Angeles College as the beneficiary of his art collections, "because this is where it's needed." Invited in 1951 to lecture on the "Aesthetic Responsibilities of the Citizen," Price later recalled that while he was "speaking in a Quonset hut on a mud flat," the enthusiasm of the students overwhelmed him. He initially donated ninety works, and his support for establishing a collection that would span history and the globe attracted other donors; at the time of his death in 1993, East Los Angeles College had amassed 2,000 works of art.

Tom Silliman, the gallery director since 1957, has made exercising Price's vision for the collection his career; five shows each year are presented at the gallery, and many of them feature aspects of the Price legacy. For example, a recent exhibition at the Price Gallery presented a sampling of the collection (not a survey or thematic selection), which included several cases of pre-Columbian ceramics from Mexico and South America along with modern paintings by Mexican artists: Jesus Chucho Reyes, Rufino Tamayo, Rafael Coronel, José Luis Cuevas, and Francisco Zuniga. The selection of European art on view reflected an enthusiasm for the subject; the prints and paintings were stacked three deep in the traditional *cabinet* installation—as in some of the Louvre's galleries. Silliman calls Price "the inspiration of my life," but many students who first saw original works of art in the gallery credit him as an inspiring teacher. "He's a great custodian of culture," says artist Gronk, who—along with George Yepes, Patssi Valdez, Diana Gamboa, Kent Twitchell, and Gilbert "Magu" Lujan—is an alumnus of East Los Angeles College. Vincent Price would probably feel that their contributions to contemporary art are the most important legacy of his generosity.

The city library system includes three historic branches in East Los Angeles:

■ An Italian Renaissance-style building was constructed in 1916 with funds from the Carnegie grant to provide Lincoln Heights with more reliable service. Its design, modeled on a structure built for Pope Julius III in Rome, on which Michelangelo and Vasari are said to have worked, earned it a place on the National Register of Historic Places, among other accolades. The facility at 2530 Workman Street (*213-226-1692) was renamed Biblioteca del Pueblo de Lincoln Heights by a community vote in 1975.

■ Robert Louis Stevenson Branch (803 Spence St.; *213-268-4710) opened in 1914 on a street named for the author which later became Whittier Boulevard. The present facility, an L-shaped red-brick building designed to harmonize with the nearby public school, opened to the public in 1927. It was closed sixty years later to repair damage from the Whittier earthquake and reopened in 1991.

■ Construction of the Malabar Branch Library (2801 Wabash Ave.; *213-263-1497) was funded by a 1925 city bond issue, and a simple building of whitewashed brick with hand-hewn, exposed roof trusses in the large reading room opened in 1927. Damage from the Whittier earthquake also forced its closure, but the 6,000-foot facility was renovated and dedicated to the needs of patrons under the age of twenty.

Chicano Resource Center

East Los Angeles Public Library
4801 E. Third St.
Los Angeles 90022
*213-263-5087
Mon.–Thurs. 10 a.m.–9 p.m., Fri. 9 a.m.–5 p.m.,
Sat. 10 a.m.–5 p.m., Sun 1–5 p.m.

The Chicano Resource Center was the first of the county library system's special collections designed to meet the needs of specific communities; it was established in 1976 in response to the Chicano movement, which asserted the civil and educational rights of Mexican-Americans (who had suffered a disproportionate number of casualties in the Vietnam War). The word "Chicano" derives from *Mexicano,* which was used derogatively until it was reclaimed by activists, and it became the preferred name for university programs in Mexican studies. The history of East Los Angeles and of Mexico is one of the collection's strengths, and its resources in both Spanish and English include an excellent children's collection. The multimedia collection, with CDs, videos, cassettes, and protest posters, focuses on immigration, art, and fiction, and much of it circulates.

Cultural programs are scheduled at the Chicano Resource Center every month, and it also serves as an information center for other local events. Workshops on pre-Hispanic instruments, readings by authors, and celebrations of the Day of the Dead and other significant holidays are regular features of its programming. Storytelling for preschoolers is offered Tuesdays at 11:30 a.m.; a summer reading program for kids seven to twelve meets Tuesdays from 3 to 4:30 p.m.; and the Homework Help Center for high school students is open year round with computer stations and up-to-date software. Begin at the Beginning, a program for expectant mothers and new families, is held the first Tuesday of the month at 1 p.m.

The Latino Walk of Fame (Whittier Blvd. between Eastern Ave. and Atlantic Blvd.) was inaugurated in summer 1997 with a star honoring Cesar Chavez, founder of the United Farm Workers union. More than 300 plaques, in the form of a gold sun set in a burgundy granite tile, are envisioned to honor people who have contributed significantly to the Latino community. The Whittier Boulevard Merchants Association (*213-265-4321, *213-261-2591), which has initiated the effort, welcomes sponsors for this evolving community monument.

Harriet and Charles Luckman Fine Arts Complex

California State University, Los Angeles
5151 State University Dr.
Los Angeles 90032
*213-343-6610

Charles Luckman served on the board of the California State University system— the largest university system in the United States—for more than two decades, but that followed two distinct and equally distinguished careers. Unable to find work in his field when he graduated with a degree

in architecture from the University of Illinois in 1931, he took a temporary job in the advertising department of a large soap company. During his meteoric eighteen-year career at Lever Brothers, he became its president (at the age of thirty-seven) and oversaw construction of the company's landmark corporate headquarters, the glass-curtain Lever House that set the style for New York's Park Avenue in the 1950s. That experience rekindled his enthusiasm for architecture, and he left Lever Brothers to found the Luckman Partnership, which constructed Los Angeles International Airport, Madison Square Garden, Cape Canaveral Missile Test Center, and the Prudential Center in Boston. The Luckman Partnership also built the $22-million fine arts complex that opened on the campus of Cal State L.A. in 1994; its funders included the state of California as well as corporate donors—the Ahmanson Foundation, the J. Paul Getty Trust, the Kresge Foundation, the Times Mirror Foundation—and individuals, including Charles and Harriet Luckman.

A columned pathway marks the monumental entrance to the striped brick complex. The multi-use facility includes a flexible 500- to 1,200-seat theater, noted both for its acoustics and for the sprung stage floor that is especially well suited to dance performances. A gallery (Mon.–Thurs. noon–5 p.m. and one hour prior to performances in the adjacent theater) with 4,000 square feet of exhibition space features changing exhibitions of traditional and contemporary works that reflect the multicultural population of the campus and its environs. The Luckman Fine Arts Complex is the largest cultural facility on the Eastside, and its sophisticated and popular programming has attracted audiences from across the sprawling Los Angeles metropolis.

Dance Kaleidoscope, an annual festival of Southern California dance troupes, has made the Luckman one of its primary venues, and an eclectic group of local and international companies have also performed there, including: AVAZ International Dance Theatre of Central Asia; Ballet Hispanico; Lula Washington Dance Theatre; José Limon Dance Company; and the final performance of the Lewitsky Dance Company. Jazz is featured prominently on the schedule, with hometown boy Bobby Rodriguez drawing large audiences to hear the hot Latin sounds of the Hispanic Musicians Association Orchestra; tributes to Dizzy Gillespie, Duke Ellington, and Billy Strayhorn; and old favorites like the Carnegie Hall Jazz Band. A special Family Series ($5 per ticket) showcases theatrical classics like *The Velveteen Rabbit* and *Winnie-the-Pooh*, as well as magical puppetry, easily accessible musical groups, and energetic dance performances. An inexpensive ($2 per ticket) weekday series for school groups offers monthly performances from October to May. Call *213-343-6610 to receive the season brochure; tickets are available through TicketMaster outlets or the Luckman box office.

La Fiesta de San Gabriel has been celebrated at Mission San Gabriel on Labor Day weekend for more than sixty years. At Christmas, Las Posadas—the reenactment of Mary and Joseph's search for shelter in Bethlehem—is the focus of a holiday celebration.

Artist Terry Schoonhoven directed students from Cal State L.A. in the creation of a mural for the MetroLink station adjacent to the campus. The imagery represents the diversity of students and activities at the university, and includes the artist's signature trompe l'oeil elements: a man making a phone call is juxtaposed with a real phone booth, and there are three artists at work painting the mural—a painting within a painting that depicts its own creation.

Mission San Gabriel Arcángel

537 W. Mission Dr.
San Gabriel 91776
626-457-3048
Daily 9 a.m.–4:30 p.m. (Oct.–May);
daily 10 a.m.–5:30 p.m. (June–Sept.)
Entry: adults $4, seniors $3, children 6–12 $1

The "queen of the California missions" was badly shaken in the Whittier earthquake in October 1987 and closed for repairs. Following a $3-million restoration, it reopened in time for its 225th birthday in 1996. Mission San Gabriel Arcángel, constructed from 1775 to 1805 of cut stone, brick, and mortar, was also damaged by earthquakes in 1804 and 1812. Four-foot-thick walls with huge pillars buttress both sides, an unusual fortresslike design that historians think may derive from a Moorish church in Córdoba, Spain. A *campanario* (bell wall) with six huge bells—the lightest weighing 1,500 pounds—stands at the back of the church, separating it from the old cloister (now the museum).

Within the church is a domed baptistery that contains a hammered copper font, given to the mission in 1771 by King Carlos III of Spain and still used for celebrating the first of the seven sacraments that mark a Catholic life. The main altar, made in Mexico City in the 1790s, and reredos with six polychromed wooden statues—including Gabriel, the mission's patron saint at the top center—were damaged during the 1812 earthquake, but have been refurbished during the recent restoration.

The walled Campo Santo, the oldest cemetery in Los Angeles, includes a memorial to the 6,000 Indians buried there, along with the graves of the Christians who served at San Gabriel. Soap and tallow vats are evidence of how the community supported itself supplying candles and soap to the other California missions; a replica of a kitchen and five outdoor fireplaces stand

near the fountain that brought water to the mission via aqueduct. The museum contains the original redwood doors of the church, as well as Bibles, various other books, and priests' robes; among the Indian artifacts are paintings on canvas probably taken from ship sails.

■ **San Gabriel Historical Society** (546 W. Broadway, San Gabriel 91776; 626-308-3223; Wed., Sat.–Sun. 1–4 p.m.) displays artifacts of its earliest inhabitants, the Gabrielino Indians, along with photos of the town's evolution. Other exhibits include farming tools the Indians utilized to make the huge tracts of land owned by the San Gabriel Mission productive for agriculture, as well as plots of the first orange grove in California—400 trees planted at the San Gabriel Mission in 1804.

■ **Covina Valley Historical Society Museum** (125 E. College St., Covina 91723; 626-332-9523; Sun. 1–3 p.m.) displays artifacts from the citrus industry, including a colorful collection of crate labels, in a jail/firehouse built in 1911.

■ **Alhambra Historical Museum** (1550 W. Alhambra Rd., Alhambra 91802; 626-300-8845; Thurs., 2nd and 4th Sun. of month 2–4 p.m.) is a repository of artifacts and photographs on the history of Alhambra and the development of its city services.

■ The collection of the **Monterey Park Historical Museum** (781 S. Orange Ave., Monterey Park 91754; 626-307-1267; Sat.–Sun. 2–4 p.m.) includes twenty-one scale models of the California missions which were built by a local resident, as well as exhibits of Indian artifacts.

■ **Baldwin Park Museum** (14327 Ramona Blvd., Baldwin Park 91706; 626-338-7130; Tues., Thurs. 10 a.m.–noon, 2–4 p.m., Sat. 10 a.m.–noon) displays reconstructions of a blacksmith shop and schoolhouse, along with domestic interiors and artifacts on local history.

Juan Matias Sanchez Adobe (946 Adobe Ave., Montebello) is known today by the name of its second owner, who expanded the three-room house built on the site in 1845 and lived there until he lost his fortune in the 1876 crash of the Temple and Workman Bank. The city of Montebello opened the adobe as a history center in 1993, with domestic furnishings of the late 1800s and a display of the fourteen flags that flew over California before it entered the Union. Visitors are welcomed Sat.–Sun. 1–4 p.m.; *213-887-4592.

Asian Pacific Resource Center

Montebello Library
1550 W. Beverly Blvd.
Montebello 90640
*213-722-6551
Mon.–Tues. noon–8 p.m., Wed.–Thurs.
10 a.m.–5 p.m., Sat. noon–5 p.m.

This branch of the county library system has served the growing Asian population since 1979 with resources in Chinese, Japanese, Korean, and Vietnamese, as well as English, which describe the history, accomplishments, and cultural heritage of East Asia. In the 1990 census Asians and Pacific Islanders constituted more than 10 percent of the population of L.A. County and were one of the fastest-growing groups, a fact that is reflected in the modern Chinese commercial district that makes parts of Monterey Park look like Hong Kong and has transformed Garvey Avenue in Rosemead into a bustling Vietnamese neighborhood. The Asian Pacific Resource Center subscribes to five Chinese newspapers and one newspaper from Vietnam, as well as periodicals in those languages and Thai, Korean, Japanese, and English. The Center promotes cross-cultural understanding with bilingual brochures on important holidays, which are also celebrated with cultural programs.

San Gabriel Square houses forty Chinese stores and restaurants on a twelve-acre site at the corner of West Valley and Del Mar Blvds. that was dedicated to this purpose (instead of the park that some community members advocated) in order to generate sales-tax income to fund city services. The 22,000-square-foot shopping center with Spanish-style red-tile roofs and a 1,000-car parking lot has not only become a commercial success (it is being cloned in Las Vegas and Houston), it showcases the style and affluence of the contemporary Asian-immigrant community in a setting unburdened by the historic legacy of older Chinatowns.

Hsi Lai Temple (3456 S. Glenmark Dr., Hacienda Heights 91745; 626-961-9697) is the most imposing monument to the Asian cultures that have been transplanted to this part of L.A. County. The $25-million complex includes the largest Buddhist temple in the Western Hemisphere, built in the Chinese style of the Ming dynasty and reached by a monumental staircase bordered with white marble balustrades. In addition, an exhibition space (daily 9 a.m.–5 p.m.; free) has on view a pan-Asian collection of Buddhist sculpture.

El Monte Historical Museum

3150 N. Tyler Ave.
El Monte 91731
Museum: 626-444-3813
Tues.–Fri. 10 a.m.–4 p.m., Sun. 1–3 p.m.
Entry: donations welcome

A father-and-son team maintains 400 pieces of military equipment on a seven-acre site in El Monte (1918 N. Rosemead Blvd.; 626-442-1776; admission charged), loaning drivable tanks and such to the American Legion for use in parades, and inviting the public to inspect the displays on "dry weekends" (Sat.–Sun. noon–4:30 p.m.). This is the place to get a look at thirty-ton Sherman tanks, Jeeps and personnel carriers, self-propelled anti-tank guns, and uniforms, if that's your thing.

Outside this adobe-style building (built by the WPA in 1936) is a plaque announcing that this was the end of the Santa Fe Trail; the settlement on the banks of the San Gabriel River was the first town incorporated in Southern California. In the museum's archives are pioneer diaries, maps, and memorabilia of the trek west, but the history depicted in its displays is generally of a more recent and local nature, some of it quite colorful—for instance, from 1924 to 1942 Gay's Lion Farm, which occupied five acres in El Monte, raised African lions for use by the movie industry. Gay's proclaimed itself a major tourist attraction in its advertising of the 1930s— "To visit the great Southwest and not see Gay's Lion Farm is like going to Egypt and not seeing the pyramids"—and tourists (including Eleanor Roosevelt) flocked to see the great beasts, which were fed one ton of fresh meat daily (according to the ads).

Sketches and photographs recall the town's historic architecture, and several rooms of a turn-of-the-century home have been reconstructed and filled with period furniture and mannequins in Victorian dress. Artifacts of daily life are presented in replicas of a small town's main street: sheet music, gramophones, and instruments in the music shop; jars for storing herbs and scales for the druggist share space with the barber's chair, also used for pulling teeth. Period clothing, a dressmaker's model, lace piece goods, handbags, and other accessories illustrate the constant human desire for embellishment, while rows of simple wooden desks face a blackboard in the reconstructed schoolroom.

The entrance to El Monte's MetroLink station is surmounted by a metalwork sculpture that pays homage to Gay's Lion Farm; the artwork, funded by the MTA's Metro Art Program and created by Victor Henderson and Elizabeth Garrison, features silhouetted felines playing with a lion tamer's chair, and cutouts of movie-making apparatus.

Judy Baca's installation at the Baldwin Park MetroLink station incorporates the floor plans of the four California missions closest to the site. Text in five languages—Spanish and English, as well as those of three indigenous peoples: Gabrielino, Chumash, and Luiseño— provides factual evidence about the intermixing of different area populations, which had disastrous results for the native peoples. "I wanted to put memory into a piece of the land once owned by the American Indian cultures—memory and willpower are what any culture, the ones living then and those living now, has to have to preserve itself," Baca wrote of *Danza Indigenas* (Indigenous Dances).

Whittier Narrows Recreation Area and Nature Center

South El Monte 91733
626-575-5526
Daily 6 a.m.–sunset
Entry: free

At the intersection of the Pomona (60) Freeway and Rosemead Boulevard is Whittier Narrows Recreation Area, a sprawling natural area with an island-dotted lake, a golf course, areas dedicated to shooting practice and equestrian trails, and a Nature Center (1000 N. Durfee Ave.; 626-575-5523; free). The San Gabriel River circumscribes its southern edge and Rio Hondo divides the golf course from other parklands.

The small nature center is located within a 277-acre wildlife sanctuary bordering the San Gabriel River, where a network of self-guided trails loops through the riverside woodland; displays in the nature center identify plant and animal life that inhabit this environment. The flashy red cardinal is now naturalized in the area, thanks to the efforts of a homesick ex–West Virginian who imported the allowable quota of birds each year and released them in his yard. Bird walks (Sun. 8 a.m.) reveal this species as well as others native to the riparian environment.

Live animals—turtles, tortoises, fish, and snakes—fill tanks in the nature center building; stuffed birds are matched with their eggs and style of nest in another display. Other exhibits focus on the geology of the San Gabriel Mountains and the contemporary environment of the San Gabriel River. Hayrides are offered on Saturdays at 10 a.m. (adults $2, children $1).

A few blocks away, **Pioneer Park** (3537 Santa Anita Ave.) celebrates El Monte's association with the Santa Fe Trail. A covered wagon and a farmhouse from the 1890s evoke the lives of the early pioneers; the original El Monte jail, built in 1880, is evidence of the societal structure that had evolved within thirty years of the arrival of the first migrants.

Bosque del Rio Hondo Natural Area

San Gabriel and Rosemead Blvds.

A twelve-acre riverfront park wedged between Montebello and Whittier has reconstructed a popular swimming hole where many East Los Angeles residents congregated in the 1930s. It is the only freeflowing part of the Rio Hondo—the rest is lined with concrete—and stands on the 1,200-mile Anza Trail that Spanish colonists followed from Sonora, Mexico, to San Fran-

Whittier Public Library
7344 S. Washington Ave.
Whittier 90602
562-464-3450

Rio Hondo College (3600 Workman Mill Rd., Whittier) has a small art gallery with a school-year program of changing exhibitions and two venues on campus for performing arts events. Many cultural events are presented without charge, although reservations are required for the most popular offerings. Call the cultural events hotline (562-908-3492) for schedule and electronic ordering.

cisco. Before the freeways connected this part of L.A. with beaches on the Pacific, the riverside beach was a popular destination for Eastside families, who danced to mariachi music and picnicked along the river bank. Oil wells that sprang up along Rio Hondo polluted its waters and brush choked the pathways to the river, and the beach became only a piece of folklore, but the childhood memories of county supervisor Gloria Molina helped resurrect this unique locale with funding from a 1992 county parks measure. Now cottonwoods and sycamores line sandy paths to the boulder-studded river, where cranes and blue herons wade and little boys splash. A footbridge crosses the river and leads to hiking trails, which are dotted with picnic tables.

Pio Pico State Historic Park

6003 Pioneer Blvd.
Whittier 90606
562-695-1217
Park: Wed.–Sun. 10 a.m.–5 p.m.
House: by reservation
Entry: free

Pio de Jesús Pico, who served briefly as governor of Mexican California and, as a U.S. citizen, on the Los Angeles City Council, was born at the San Gabriel Mission in 1801; he was the son of a colonist from Sinaloa, Mexico, who came to El Pueblo de Los Angeles with the Anza expedition of 1775. He owned Pico House—the beautiful stone structure that was the city's first prestigious hotel and which now awaits restoration on the north side of the Plaza at Olvera Street—and in 1850 he purchased land fifteen miles east of downtown, where he built a country residence. **El Ranchito**, a two-story adobe beside the San Gabriel River, was deeded to the state in 1917 and became one of the earliest state historic parks in 1927. The fragile building, which has not been inhabited since before Pio Pico died in 1894, suffered structurally in both the Whittier and Northridge earthquakes.

The annual Coming Home to Pio Pico is celebrated around Cinco de Mayo. In the summer a junior ranger program in the park investigates the region's history with such activities as the construction of adobe bricks.

Ruth B. Shannon Center for the Performing Arts
Whittier College
13406 E. Philadelphia St.
Whittier 90601
562-907-4203

Since this state-of-the-art facility opened in 1990 it has offered ample incentive at least three weekends per month for local residents to venture onto campus. Low ticket prices are part of the draw: seats at

professionally staged theater classics cost $3 to $5 three nights a week and $4 to $8 on Fridays and Saturdays. Many music department offerings are free, and top-price tickets for the annual Bach Festival, which has been going strong for sixty years, are $5. Internationally recognized jazz and chamber music artists are featured, with most seats topping out at $20. On Sunday afternoons the center is often dedicated to fine performances for children—and I'm not going to mention ticket prices again, just note that they are made possible by local businesses, community organizations, and Whittier College. If you're anywhere in the area, patronize this place.

Center Theater (7630 Washington Ave., Whittier 90602) is a city-administered 400-seat theater that is rented to such groups as the seventy-five-year-old Community Theater (where Pat and Richard Nixon met) and the Junior Theater, which has been producing fine theater for kids for more than thirty-five years. Call the City of Whittier for schedules or booking information at 562-945-8205.

One of Whittier's oldest homes, the **Bailey House** (13421 E. Camilla St.; 562-698-3524), was actually built by another resident about ten years before the Baileys began to occupy it in 1887. The restored house is filled with furnishings from the last quarter of the nineteenth century, and is open to the public (Wed. 1–3 p.m., Sun. 1–4 p.m.; adults $.50, children $.25) except on rainy days.

Whittier Farmers Market
2000 block of Bailey St.
bet. Greenleaf and
Comstock Aves.
Fri. 8:30 a.m.–1 p.m.

The Santa Fe Springs
Library and Recreation
Services schedules
performing and visual
arts classes for children
at Heritage Park and
the nearby Clarke
Estate; call 562-946-
6476 for more
information.

Los Angeles County Sheriffs Museum

11515 S. Colima Rd.
Whittier 90604
562-946-7081
Mon.–Fri. 9 a.m.–4 p.m.
Entry: free

In the Hall of Sheriffs are documents on the men who've held the top position since the force was organized in 1850, as well as displays on the roles women have played since they were admitted to the force in 1912. An installation depicting a late-nineteenth-century jail and sheriff's office is animated: the prisoner explains his plight as the sheriff rocks in his chair. The exhibit of street weapons is sobering, with everything from simple kitchen implements to such purpose-designed weapons as brass knuckles and flying stars and the full panoply of guns, including modern assault weapons. The relative protection afforded by body armor is examined nearby, and there are examples of vehicles used on patrol: a 1938 Studebaker, Harley-Davidson motorcycles, and a Hughes helicopter.

Whittier Museum

6755 S. Newlin Ave.
Whittier 90601
562-945-3871
Entry: free

This museum of local history has a permanent installation depicting small-town life at the turn of the century. The town of Whittier, founded in 1887 and named for Quaker poet John Greenleaf Whittier, constructed a Quaker meetinghouse as one of its earliest buildings; it is the subject of one display. A re-created Main Street includes a Queen Anne cottage, which visitors may enter to see period rooms; a barn filled with tools and saddles; and the newspaper offices of the Whittier *Register*—every issue of the local newspaper is in the museum's archives.

Some of the museum's memorabilia documents local events and local luminaries: there is the desk ex-President Nixon used in his first law office and a revolver owned by Governor Pio Pico. Other exhibits highlight the importance of the citrus industry and the discovery of oil to the local economy.

Heritage Park

12100 Mora Dr.
Santa Fe Springs 90670
562-946-6476
Park: daily 7 a.m.–10 p.m.
Carriage Barn Museum: Tues., Fri.–Sun. noon–4 p.m.;
Wed.–Thurs. 9 a.m.–4 p.m.

The city of Santa Fe Springs has re-created many of the buildings that were once part of a citrus ranch located here a century ago, and they now form the centerpiece of a business complex, the Heritage Corporate Center. Photographs of the ranch revealed the Carpenter Gothic structures built around 1880 by a wealthy farmer named Hawkins; structures include a carriage barn, glass-roofed conservatory, and aviary that today has six large cages filled with 150 birds. Hawkins also created formal gardens modeled after English styles, which he adorned with concrete fountains and statuary; a picturesque tankhouse and windmill supplied water for the gardens, which featured such rare plantings as palms and such practical choices as carob trees (whose pods were fed to the ranch's cattle). The remains of an adobe home built circa 1815 by a Mexican citizen named Patricio Ontiveros were discovered during the reconstruction, and artifacts recovered from his family's trash pit are included in the historical displays in the **Carriage Barn.**

The Carriage Barn houses a local history museum. An Emerson surrey is the centerpiece of **Horse and Buggy Days**; artifacts from a turn-of-the century household are

featured in **Keeping a Home**; and farm implements demonstrate how to make **A Living from the Land**. Within a re-created train depot is a steam locomotive from the 1920s and a Santa Fe Railroad caboose, vintage 1955.

Clarke Estate

10211 Pioneer Blvd.
Santa Fe Springs 90670
562-863-4896
Tours: Tues., Fri., and 1st Sun. of month 11 a.m.– 2 p.m.

Until recently the country home on sixty acres of citrus groves designed by Irving Gill (circa 1920) for Chauncey and Marie Clarke had been overlooked by historians of the great modern architect. The Dodge House (1916) in West Hollywood, often cited as Gill's last large residential commission, was demolished in 1969, mobilizing an architectural preservation movement in Los Angeles, but the Clarke Estate survived, little altered but almost unknown. The discovery in 1921 of oil deposits in the Santa Fe Springs area, including on the Clarke property, transformed the area's rural character with the smells and noise of oil production. The Clarkes moved to the Coachella Valley but retained the house, which passed to heirs in Mrs. Clarke's will in 1948. Her cousin, James

Siemon, lived there until 1986; the site, adjacent to the town library and civic buildings, was then purchased by Santa Fe Springs.

The 8,000-square-foot structure is built of poured-in-place concrete, the slab-tilt construction technique pioneered by Gill. Its design reflects the architect's dictum, "to fling aside every device that distracts the eye from structural beauty." It is centered on an interior courtyard with Tuscan columns and simple arches, devices repeated at the front entrance. The unadorned exterior surfaces contribute to the building's cubist silhouette; Gill's minimalist approach is echoed in rounded corners and the absence of ornamentation—wainscoting, moldings, paneling—in the interior design.

This exceptional modernist structure is open for public tours and is rented for special events under the auspices of the Recreational Services Division of Santa Fe Springs. Much of the original land-

Children's Museum at La Habra

301 S. Euclid St.
La Habra 90631
562-905-9793
Mon.–Sat. 10 a.m.–5 p.m., Sun. 1–5 p.m.
Entry: adults, children 2 and up $4

La Habra is in northern Orange County, but its fine Children's Museum is accessible to families in this part of Los Angeles County. The playful environment, located in a 1923 Union Pacific railway depot in Portola Park, has tripled its space with a new wing. Its programming has been developing since 1977, when it opened as the first children's museum in the state; it now appeals to toddlers as well as school-age kids. Little ones enjoy climbing on bright, functional furniture in the shapes of trees, blocks, and bridges in the **Preschool Playpark** and enacting fantasies in the puppet theater; young parents will appreciate the shelf of books, periodicals, and clippings posted in the **Family Resource Center** in one corner of the Playpark. **Kids on Stage** is a fully equipped theater that includes backstage areas such as costume and scene shops, and sound and lighting booths. In the **Science Station** are a momentum machine, a pedal-operated generator, Jacob's Ladder, and other interactive displays that demonstrate scientific phenomena.

The **Model Train Village** and **Carousel** room are favorite permanent installations. Preserved animal specimens—raccoons, skunks, beavers, and deer—are installed along the **Nature Walk**, allowing children to understand the creatures' habitats and pet critters who would not submit so willingly in the wild. A space dedicated to changing exhibits often highlights a different part of the world: "Passport to Asia," for example, featured Japanese, Chinese, and Vietnamese cultures.

Richard Nixon Library and Birthplace

18001 Yorba Linda Blvd.
Yorba Linda 92886
714-993-5075
Mon.–Sat. 10 a.m.–5 p.m., Sun. 11 a.m.–5 p.m.
Entry: adults $5.95, active military $4.95, seniors $3.95, children 8–11 $2

Yorba Linda, in northern Orange County, is where Richard Nixon, the thirty-seventh president of the United States, was born in 1913. The Nixon Library and Birthplace, which opened in 1990, preserves the farmhouse Nixon's father built with his own hands and nine acres of a citrus grove that he hoped would support his growing family, but a museum that chronicle's Nixon's political life is the centerpiece of the complex. Although

"library" gets top billing in the institution's name, no original presidential documents are included in its collection because Nixon's records were seized by federal authorities shortly after he resigned the presidency in August 1974. Those documents remain in the custody of the National Archives, which also administers nine of the eleven centers dedicated to past presidents of the United States, at an annual cost to taxpayers of $25 million. The Nixon Library, which is run by a private foundation at no expense to taxpayers, does include his Congressional and vice-presidential papers, and the museum devotes a large part of its twenty-two galleries to his presidential years.

The perspective from which Nixon's controversial

scaping has survived, including part of the orange grove, stands of green bamboo, a lawn-bowling green, and California sycamores.

Hathaway Ranch (11901 E. Florence Ave., Santa Fe Springs 90670) welcomes visitors to tour its small museum only on the first Sunday of each month, from 2 to 4 p.m., but the grounds are open four weekdays (Mon.–Tues., Thurs.–Fri. 11 a.m.–4 p.m.) and the hay wagons, tractors and other farming and ranching equipment are installed there. This land supported 400 head of cattle and a business growing vegetables for an experimental seed company in the first two decades of the twentieth century, but the three Hathaway sons formed a business drilling for oil after it was discovered locally in 1921. The museum, housed in a residence the family built in 1935, displays period clothing and household goods. Call 562-944-7372 to schedule a special tour.

La Mirada Theater for the Performing Arts
14900 La Mirada Blvd.
La Mirada 90638
714-994-6150
Box office: 714-994-6310

The city of La Mirada converted an old movie house into a 1,274-seat performing-arts facility in 1977, and in 1994 it joined forces with producers Cathy Rigby and Tom McCoy, the Olympic gymnast-turned-actress and her husband, to add Broadway-style musicals to its repertoire: the public liked the innovation, with more than 80 percent renewing their subscriptions. La Mirada Symphony provides the classical musical component of the season. Two series for children ($6 per ticket) are also presented at this venue: La Mirada Theater's own Programs for Young Audiences includes such fine fare as Jim Gamble's enchanting marionettes, productions of such classic stories as *Curious George* and *Sleeping Beauty*, and kid-oriented perfor-

chapter in American history is presented is first enunciated in a film entitled *Never Give Up*, which is shown continually in the 293-seat theater, and elaborated in carefully crafted exhibits. Nixon not only overcomes the struggles and setbacks that marked his career, he seems reinvigorated by the process. The famous speech of 1952, in which he identifies the family's dog "Checkers" as the only politically motivated gift he's accepted, plays over and over on a monitor, but two later galleries are filled with less-tainted tokens he received from other world leaders and from American citizens. Visitors can sit in a 1960s-style living room and watch him debate John F. Kennedy on a vintage television set, then review how he occupied himself while out of public office, after his defeat in that campaign, in a gallery called The Wilderness Years.

Nixon takes his place among such world leaders as Mao Ze-dong, Charles de Gaulle, Golda Meir, and Anwar el-Sadat in a gallery where ten bronze statues are posed beneath their national flags. His explanation of their success is inscribed on the wall: "They are men who made a difference not because they wished it, but because they willed it." The Nixon administration's achievements in foreign affairs are chronicled in a gallery that includes a three-ton slab of the Berlin Wall and tributes from Chinese and Russian leaders. Pat Nixon is hailed as Ambassador of Goodwill in a gallery that documents her role as First Lady and includes the wedding dresses worn by her daughters. Nixon's favorite room in the White House, the Lincoln Sitting Room, is re-created, and the high points of his domestic agenda are evoked by a moon rock and the telephone

on which he talked with the Apollo XI astronauts.

The events that led the thirty-seventh president to resign his office, which were defined in the Congressional act that impounded Nixon's papers as "the abuses of governmental power popularly identified under the generic term Watergate," are redefined: "At the time commentators sought to portray Watergate strictly as a morality play, a struggle between right and wrong, truth and falsehood, good and evil. Given the benefit of time, it is now clear that Watergate was an open and bloody political battle fought for the highest stakes, with no holds barred." This revisionist history may satisfy those who believe Nixon took responsibility for action perpetrated by rogue members of his administration, and it is a fascinating display of the editorial and curatorial processes that shape perception.

The concern that Nixon "might not be a wholly reliable custodian" of his papers, which was stated as justification for the seizure, has been tempered by his death. In a precedent-setting agreement, the federal government has agreed to pay the Nixon estate $26 million in compensation for the forty-four million presidential documents that have been stored for a quarter-century at the National Archives. The monies received by the Nixon estate would be used to build a new library at the Yorba Linda facility, and the collection would be brought home to the site where Richard Nixon's life began and where he has been laid to rest: his grave and that of Mrs. Nixon are located among 1,400 rose bushes on the beautifully landscaped grounds.

Frank G. Bonelli Regional County Park (120 Via Verde Rd., San Dimas; 909-599-8411), bounded to the south and west by the 10 and 210 Freeways, encloses a golf course and the enormous Puddingstone Reservoir—although the aqueous features of the adjacent Raging Waters theme park, which leases this land from L.A. County, are better known.

The Los Angeles County Fairplex (1101 W. McKinley Ave., La Verne; 909-623-3111) has been the site of the County Fair for two weeks every September for seventy-five years. During the rest of the year the huge facility is leased to commercial vendors. A quarterly calendar listing the event schedule and organizers is available for an annual subscription of $15.

mances with lasers, juggling, and balloons. The Golden State Children's Theater has a youth theater troupe in addition to mounting three full productions yearly and offering acting workshops.

Within the Industry Hills Sheraton Resort is the Ralph W. Miller Golf Library and Museum (1 Industry Hills Pkwy., City of Industry 91744), proof positive that there is something for every taste within the confines of L.A. County. The collection amassed by a Los Angeles attorney contains more than 5,000 books compiled in an automated catalogue for easy access and 20,000 photographs, with a selection always on view. Displays chronicle the evolution of golf-ball design, as well as putters, clubs, and irons notable for innovations in design, special materials, or their owners; knickers worn by the first woman golf pro, scorecards, and scores of tees are among the offerings of this offbeat collection. The first manager of the city-owned resort, who had worked with Miller in youth sports programs, purchased the collection to help create an identity for the hotel and conference complex, which is surrounded by golf courses. The museum is open Tuesday to Friday 9 a.m. to 6 p.m., and Saturday to Sunday noon to 6 p.m.; call 626-854-2354 for more information.

Two historic homes in Pomona—La Casa Primera (1569 N. Park Ave.; 909-623-2198) and Adobe de Palomares (491 E. Arrow Hwy.; 909-620-0264)—evoke early rancho history at the eastern edge of L.A. County; they may be visited on Sunday afternoons (2–5 p.m.; free). The two structures, a mile apart, were on the 15,000-acre land grant acquired in the 1840s by Ignacio Palomares and Ricardo Vejar; a century later the city of Pomona reconstructed the adobes and furnished them with period pieces. The courtyard and gardens of the Palomares home have been refurbished, and its blacksmith shop contains horse-drawn carriages and tools.

Workman's original partner, John Rowland, built his own home (16021 Gale Ave., City of Industry 91745) in 1855 of fired brick, which has better withstood the passage of time than has adobe. The rooms contain some furnishings left by the three generations of the Rowland family who occupied the house, as well as Indian artifacts that are contained in the Dibble Museum. The house and its collections are open for public visitation on a limited schedule—the first and third Wednesday and Sunday of each month, 1 to 4 p.m.; call 626-336-2382.

Workman and Temple Family Homestead Museum

15415 E. Don Julian Rd.
City of Industry 91745
626-968-8492
www.homesteadmuseum.org
Guided tours on the hour: Tues.–Fri. 1–4 p.m., Sat.–Sun. 10 a.m.–4 p.m.; closed on the 4th weekend of the month
Entry: free

The six-acre Workman and Temple Homestead was once part of a 48,790-acre Mexican land grant owned from the mid-1840s by William Workman and a partner, John Rowland. Workman was born in England in 1799 but sought his fortune in the New World, settling in Missouri during the 1820s and later moving to Taos (which was then Mexican territory). The Englishman married a Mexican woman and so became a Mexican citizen (and thus gained the sobriquet Don Julian); he earned his living as a trader. In 1841 Workman and Rowland led about sixty-five settlers on the first overland expedition to Southern California. The emigrants settled in the east San Gabriel Valley, and with the labor of local Indians, built an adobe house and began raising cattle, the lifeblood of the California economy at that time.

He planted 5,000 acres in wheat and 60,000 grapevines that yielded about 100,000 gallons of wine each year. When the population of California swelled during the gold rush, established rancheros like Workman met the needs of this new population and profited handsomely from the rampant inflation in the new towns. A flood, followed by a drought from 1862 to 1864, ended the preeminence of cattle and devastated the local economy, but Workman's more diversified ranch survived.

Workman and his son-in-law F. P. F. Temple formed a short-lived bank during the 1870s, when Los Angeles experienced its first boom period. In 1872 the old adobe was expanded into a H-shaped plan with a steeply pitched roof, Victorian porches, and Gothic Revival decorations, a remodel directed by architect Ezra F. Kysor, who also designed Saint Vibiana's cathedral and the first Jewish synagogue in downtown L.A.

The Temple and Workman Bank was closed when the bubble burst in 1876, and Workman's lands and home were mortgaged and finally repossessed from his heirs in 1899.

That might have ended the tenure of the original family on this site, but in 1914 the nine-year-old great-grandson of William Workman found oil in the walnut grove his father farmed in the Montebello hills. The Temple family used its new fortune to repurchase seventy-five acres of the old homestead. Walter P. Temple commissioned architect Roy Seldon Price to build a new house in the Spanish colonial revival style next to the adobe-turned-Victorian manse. La Casa Nueva is a handsome residence embellished with antique elements that suggest a romantic view of early California—raised grape and wheat motifs surround the heavy, carved-oak door, a stained-glass window over the main stairway depicts a Spanish galleon in a storm, and a polar-bear rug fills the main hall.

The Temple family's occupation of their new home lasted only until the stock market crash, when Walter Temple lost the oil fortune that he had invested in local real estate and construction projects.

The two residences can be visited only by free guided tours, which docents animate with social history and local lore, but the public can tour a small gallery with displays on local history. The Campo Santo cemetery (see p. 159) is here; it's the final resting place of Pio Pico, the last governor of Mexican California, as well as members of the Workman and Temple families.

California State Polytechnic University, Pomona
3801 W. Temple Ave.
Pomona 91768
909-869-7659

The Kellogg Arabian Horse Center (located just off the San Bernardino [10] Fwy. at Kellogg Drive) is the last vestige of a huge ranch where the heir to the Kellogg's cereal fortune spent winters from the 1920s. The horses were Kellogg's passion, and in 1926 he initiated Sunday horse shows that in the first year attracted 14,000 visitors, including such celebrities as Ronald Reagan and Rudolph Valentino (who rode a Kellogg horse in *The Son of the Sheik*). At 2 p.m. on the first Sunday of each month during the academic year students put on a free, one-hour exhibition showcasing some of the ninety Arabian horses raised on the ranch and continuing the tradition begun by Mr. Kellogg; call 909-869-2224 to confirm the schedule.

The land was given to the University of California in 1932 and used as a cavalry remount station during World War II.

When the University of California decided not to develop the site as one of its campuses, Kellogg then gave it to the state university system, which developed it initially as an agriculture school. Today approximately 20,000 students are enrolled in seven colleges within this large university at the eastern edge of Los Angeles County. The agriculture school (909-869-2200) still exists and has become a model for environmentally sustainable and economically viable agriculture and landscaping in our dry climate. Its **LandLab**, created a decade ago, will in 1999 begin transforming the 339-acre site that was once the Spadra Landfill, utilizing $5.6 million from the Sanitation Districts of L.A. County to reclaim the degraded land with such features as a water-conserving golf course and a wildlife sanctuary. A visitor information center at the LandLab (3801 W. Temple Ave., Pomona) includes exhibits on food production, water use, and waste disposal; don't miss the farm store where produce—much of it unusual and organic—raised in fields and groves surrounding the campus can be purchased. **The Center for Regenerative Studies** is a living laboratory dedicated to creating sustainable systems and technologies; it includes a residential community where the buildings utilize active and passive solar technologies, wastes are recycled, and communal dinners are served nightly to teach interpersonal and organizational skills. Organic produce is harvested on site, and aquaculture from reclaimed water produces fish for human consumption and animal feed. Individuals and groups are welcome to tour the Center for Regenerative Studies (4105 W. University Dr., Pomona); call 909-468-1705 for information.

Art, often featuring student work, is exhibited weekdays (with some evening and weekend hours) at adjacent spaces within the University Union (Bldg. 35): **University Union Exhibit Gallery** (909-869-2850) and the **W. Keith and Janet Kellogg University Art Gallery**. The Theater department (909-869-3900) mounts one fully staged production each quarter in the 540-seat theater in Building 25. The music department has the largest faculty in the arts and offers commensurate programming, with a half dozen events each quarter (except in summer). Call 909-869-3554 for the schedule of musical events and tickets.

MURALS

Robin Dunitz

* indicates an area code that changes in 1998

Start with the region's mild climate, add inspiration from Mexican tradition, and it's easy to see why Los Angeles is home to nearly 2,000 murals. These varied and vibrant images appear everywhere—inside buildings and out, even along the area's infamous freeways. Local murals reveal striking contrasts of subject matter and attitudes, reflecting the persistence of this country's sharp class and racial divisions.

Before the grassroots appropriation of neighborhood walls for street art in the late 1960s, murals often conveyed a narrow, Eurocentric interpretation of beauty, history, and the American way of life. The social upheavals of the 1960s and 1970s empowered whole new segments of American society—those with little or no representation in history books, the media, or mainstream art venues. Murals were embraced by Chicano and African-American youth in particular. The result in some parts of Los Angeles was the transformation of neighborhoods into galleries showcasing cultural traditions, teaching a populist view of history, and exposing critical social problems.

The heart of L.A.'s mural movement is the Mexican-American Eastside. During the late 1960s the struggle for a better education and support for Cesar Chavez's United Farm Workers organiza-tion contributed to an explosion of wall art. In just a few short years the barrios of Boyle Heights, City Terrace, and other areas were ablaze with hundreds of murals created by local artist-activists.

Since about 1989 a new public art renaissance of sorts has been in progress in Los Angeles. Corporations, local government agencies, and community organizations have all sponsored murals, though with widely varying budgets. Korean, Chinese, Filipino, and Thai artists are beginning to participate more in the local mural scene, adding an exciting new dimension. Aerosol art is gaining wider respect and showing up (with permission) on the walls of businesses all over L.A.

Downtown Los Angeles

Olympic Freeway Murals

When the Summer Olympic Games were held in Los Angeles in 1984, the Olympic Organizing Committee commissioned ten artists of varied cultural backgrounds to paint murals on the freeways circling downtown. The original concept was the brainchild of **Alonzo Davis**, an African-American community artist and arts administrator. His mural, *Olympic Series* (also known as *Eyes on '84*), is a set of three abstract panels on the Harbor (110) Freeway at the Third Street on-ramp. At the Fourth Street off-ramp is **Judith Baca**'s tribute to women marathon runners, called *Hitting the Wall*. Two of the murals include elements from ancient architecture: **Terry Schoonhoven**'s *Cityscape*, combining ancient Greek and Roman structures with buildings from L.A.'s skyline, overlooks the 110 Freeway from the Sixth Street overpass. In **John Wehrle**'s *Galileo, Jupiter, Apollo*, on the Hollywood (101) Freeway at Spring Street, pieces of classical Greek sculpture and architecture float in a space landscape. Probably the two most popular Olympic murals are **Glenna Boltuch Avila**'s romping, fifteen-foot-tall children (*L.A. Freeway Kids*), on the 101 near Los Angeles Street, and **Frank Romero**'s tribute to the local car culture, *Going to the Olympics*, on the 101 between Alameda and San Pedro Streets.

Mural Tour

We start our tour at the main entrance to Union Station. Not as immediately visible as the elegant art deco architectural details are two outstanding murals, one painted and one in ceramic tile. Both are at the opposite side of the station from the main lobby. Head toward the trains and keep going through a long tunnel. Under the dome of the recently completed East Portal is *City of Dreams/ River of History* (1996), a collection of portraits of past and present Angelenos. This mural by **Richard Wyatt** is part of an environmental project made in collaboration with artist **May Sun**, architect **Paul Diez**, and fabricator **Oscar Weathersby**, which also includes an aquarium and a river bench. An escalator ride down from the East Portal is the southern end of the platform of the Metro Rail's Red Line station. **Terry Schoonhoven**'s clever ceramic *Traveler* (1991) is straight ahead. Its theme is travel—through time and via the imagination. Each section represents a different period of California history. The last scene is L.A. in the 1950s. Recognize the lady on the suitcase? She's actress Carole Lombard.

Return to the main entrance and Alameda Street. Drive south on Alameda (left from main exit). Cross the freeway and turn right on Third Street. After you cross Spring Street, look out your right window when you reach the middle of the block. Two large murals should be in view. Most sensational is a five-story-tall Anthony Quinn dancing à la Zorba (*The Pope of Broadway*), painted in 1983 by **Eloy Torrez**. The other mural, *Boy and Horse* by **Frank Romero** (also 1983), is partially obscured by the restaurant at the corner. Both murals are on the southwest-facing side of the Victor Clothing Company. This traditional men's clothing store, in business since 1920, sponsored most of the murals on the building as a thank-you to the Latino community. (Latinos make up 95 percent of the store's customers.) Five-story-high murals dominate the outside. **Kent Twitchell**'s *Bride and Groom* (1972–76) and **East Los Streetscapers**' *The New Fire* (1985) cover the building's northeast-facing wall. Murals also decorate the store's interior. On the left, as you enter, is **John Valadez**'s wonderfully realistic street scene, *The Broadway Mural* (1981). On the opposite wall is a less sophisticated work, *The Aztec Mural*, painted by a teenage artist, **Juan Garduño**, in 1977. Also noteworthy is Torrez's *Mural of Muralists*, a smaller work that depicts artists Twitchell, Betye Saar, and Carlos Almaraz and includes a self-portrait of Torrez painting on the sidewalk.

Travel south on Broadway to the middle of the next block. Reaching skyward from the front of the BBF Broadway Building (351 S. Broadway) is *Street of Eternity* (1993). San Francisco-based artist **Johanna Poethig** used symbols and artifacts from the ancient Americas as an homage to immigrants who frequent this busy shopping area. Reaching up to the heavens is a pre-Columbian Chimu-style metal sculpture from Peru.

Continue down Broadway. Turn right on Eighth Street. Turn left on Hill. Stop at the parking lot of 1031 South Hill to see **Kent Twitchell**'s amazing *Ed Ruscha Monument,* a tribute to the contemporary Los Angeles artist. Twitchell painted this mural between 1978 and 1987. He repainted parts of it several times, trying to get it exactly right. The shadow painted behind the image gives the figure a three-dimensionality, and you can almost feel the silkiness of the shirt.

You can get a close look at another Twitchell landmark by turning right on 11th Street. When you reach Figueroa, turn right again. Turn left on Eighth Street and then left again on a small street called Francisco. Park on this first block, if possible, and walk back to Eighth. Head toward the freeway. Directly in front of the freeway entrance, on the Citicorp Plaza parking garage, is *Harbor Freeway Overture* (1991–92), which portrays several members of the Los Angeles Chamber Orchestra. The mural was originally designed to include most of the orchestra's forty members, but funding limitations forced the artist to scale down. Unfortunately this highly detailed artwork is usually viewed at high speed from the 110 Freeway.

Return to your car. Continue south on Francisco. Take a left on Ninth Street; then turn left on Figueroa. Turn right on Temple and left on Broadway. Notice the unusual cylindrical mural at Broadway and Cesar E. Chavez Avenue (northeast corner). Called *Together: Working toward a Flourishing Society* (1995), it pays tribute to the Chinese immigration experience through various cultural icons, such as the Great Wall of China, the Golden Gate Bridge in San Francisco, the mythical Gold Mountain, and a phoenix (representing reincarnation). Artist **Christina Miguel Mullen** worked with students from four local high schools on the project.

Continue north on Broadway into Chinatown. Take a left on College Street, and drive two blocks. At the corner of College and Yale, on the exterior of the public library, is an unusual mural that shimmers in the sun. Embedded in the paint are jewels, eggshells, and colored glass. Chinese master lacquer painter **Shiyan Zhang** lived in Los Angeles from 1988 to 1993. Before coming to the United States, Zhang completed murals in China, Hong Kong, Switzerland, and the Netherlands. *The Party at Lan-T'ing* was painted in 1991 under the auspices of the Venice-based Social and Public Art Resource Center (SPARC). It showcases Chinese achievements in music, literature, and art by depicting a party of important artists organized by the famous calligrapher and poet Wang Xi-Zhi approximately 1,700 years ago.

This ends the downtown mural tour. To return to Union Station, take a left on Yale Street. Take another left on Vignes (the next street). Follow Vignes around to Cesar E. Chavez Avenue. Make a right. The next street is Alameda. One more left turn, and you're once again in front of Union Station (on your left).

Lincoln Heights, City Terrace, and Boyle Heights

In the mid-1960s the struggle of California farmworkers ignited a powerful Chicano civil rights movement. Anti–Vietnam War protests and local high school "blow-outs" for a better education also influenced artist-activists. While the intensity of that creative ferment has subsided, new images continue to appear regularly.

We begin our two-to-three-hour tour at Olvera Street, at the corner of Main Street and Cesar E. Chavez Avenue. There are three murals of note here. First, and most famous, is *America Tropical* by **David Alfaro Siqueiros,** one of the masters of the Mexican mural movement. Unfortunately this anticapitalist mural, painted above Italian Hall in 1932, was whitewashed almost immediately. It is currently covered with plywood, pending restoration by the Getty Conservation Institute. The mural will eventually become accessible to the public again. **Leo Politi**'s *Blessing of the Animals* (1978) commemorates an ancient ceremony that has been performed at Olvera Street since the 1780s. The mural overlooks the main plaza outside the Biscailuz Building. **Eduardo Carrillo**'s *Father Hidalgo Rang the Bell of Dolores* (1979) borders a fountain at Placita de Dolores. Made of tile, it complements a replica of the Bell of Dolores that was donated to the city of Los Angeles by the Mexican government in 1968. When Father Hidalgo rang the original bell in Dolores, Mexico, on September 16, 1810, his action became the opening salvo of the Mexican Wars of Independence from Spain.

From Olvera Street we drive north on Main Street, heading toward Lincoln Heights. At 1100 North Main (at Llewellyn) we find *A History of Los Angeles* by **Richard Jiminez**, a tribute to the contributions of the many cultures found in Los Angeles. More than a dozen nationalities are represented.

Continue north along Main to Daly Boulevard, and turn left. Stop after crossing North Broadway to see the first collaboration of **East Los Streetscapers** (David Botello and Wayne Healy), *Chicano Time Trip* (1977), on the bank at the corner. Hundreds of years of Chicano history are depicted in five panels. Continue on Daly, then turn right on Avenue 26, and right again on Workman. Pause at the Lincoln Heights Recreation Center (2303 Workman) to view another Streetscaper work—*Trucha! Vital Decisions Ahead!*—painted in 1988 for a TV special. Take a left at Manitou, a right on Griffin, and a left at Darwin. Stop just past Eastlake to see **Paul Botello**'s 1990 mural, *Combined Forces.* In this mural Paul (younger brother of David) addresses complex themes of family, technology, and the environment.

Turn right at the next corner, Gates, right again on North Main, and then left on Sichel. The neighborhood's changing composition is reflected in the next mural, *Golden Phoenix Is Flying* (1992). Located on a noodle factory and painted by a Chinese woman, **Hui-Xiang Xiao**, this eclectic painting combines pre-Columbian symbolism with Chinese imagery in an art deco style. Continue to the end of the block. Make a right on Alhambra Avenue, a right on Workman, a left on North Main, and another left on Marengo. Stop at Planned Parenthood (1920 Marengo Ave.) to see Jill Ansell's *Immaculate Perception* (1992). Dedicated to the strength of women, this surreal image explores the role of dream and imagination in the creative process.

At Soto Street turn right, then turn left on Wabash. In six blocks bear left onto City Terrace Avenue. Look for a church on the left with a blue tile roof. That is Saint Lucy's Catholic Church. On its facade is George Yepes's masterful *El Tepeyac de Los Angeles* (1993), a powerful contemporary interpretation of the Madonna and Child theme. Continue east along City Terrace for a block, then turn left on Miller. On the market at the corner is Willie Herrón's *La doliente de Hidalgo* (1976), and across the street, on the library, is Goez Studio's colorful tile mural, *Ofrenda Maya* (1978), designed by Robert Arenivar. Make a right turn into the alley behind the market. At the far end of the block, on the right, is a now-famous early self-sponsored piece of street art by Herrón, *The Wall That Cracked Open* (1972). He painted it after his brother was beaten at this spot by local gang members.

Turn right out of the alley onto Carmelita Avenue, then right onto City Terrace and left at Hazard (the first light). Stop just after crossing Hammel at the bottom of the hill. There, on your right, is Paul Botello's *Virgin's Seed* (1991), which reveals the artist's conflicting feelings about religion. This vibrant, complex work was sponsored by the church across the street, Our Lady of Guadalupe, to which the Botello clan belongs. Next, after a right turn at Cesar Chavez, pause to take a look at *Tree of Knowledge*,

a 1978 literacy mural designed and executed by a group of Chicana artists under the direction of Mexican muralist Josefina Quezada.

Continue west on Cesar Chavez until you reach Gage. The massive building on the left, decorated with pieces of broken tile and glass, is the home of Self-Help Graphics and Art (3802 Cesar E. Chavez Ave.), a community arts center that features a gallery with changing exhibitions, a small shop selling contemporary and folk art, and a highly regarded studio workshop where visiting artists produce amazing silkscreen prints. The center is worth a special stop. Notice the mural at the corner as you turn left on Gage. It's called *Respect What You See* and was painted by Bill Butler in 1979. Metal sculptor Michael Amescua has his studio in the center's parking lot. He welcomes visitors.

Head south on Gage (left out of the parking lot), then turn right on First Street. The First Street Store (3640 E. First St.) showcases Goez Studio's *A Story of Our Struggle* (1974), a nineteen-panel tile mural that traces Chicano heritage from ancient Mexico to the present-day United States. Across the street, on the Pan-American Bank (3626 E. First St.), is *Our Past, Our Present, and Our Future* by Mexican artist José Reyes Meza. This mosaic, unveiled in 1966, may be the earliest public mural in East Los Angeles.

Continue west on First Street for about a mile. Turn right on Soto Street, then stop at Cesar Chavez. This is one of the busiest intersections in Boyle Heights. There are four murals here. The earliest is Willie Herrón's *Advancements of Man* (1976), a

somewhat dark look at the downside of technological progress (on the northwest corner). When the artist returned in 1995 to repaint the badly graffitied mural, he added a small tribute to Cesar Chavez around the corner, called *No somos animales*. Directly north is East Los Streetscapers' *El corrido de Boyle Heights* (1984), a lively wedding scene. Paul Botello's *No Greater Love* is the most recent addition to this intersection. Painted in 1992, it is another of his intense meditations on science and religion, this time dominated by a portrait of Jesus.

Travel west one block on Cesar Chavez to Breed Street (southwest corner) to see Ernesto de la Loza's lovely *Resurrection of the Green Planet* (1991). It's about cherishing tradition and our planet. Drive south on Breed, turn right on First Street, then left on Saint Louis. On your left is another work by de la Loza, *Bridges to East L.A.* (1992), painted with both brush and spray can. He was assisted by young aerosol artists, who then did their own piece on the south-facing side wall. Continue south on Saint Louis to Fourth Street and turn left. Then go right on Soto and left on Whittier Boulevard. Two blocks past Lorena, turn right on Esperanza, where you'll discover *Tomé conciencia* (1987). Created by a group of artists from Mexico City, this iconographic montage expresses solidarity with the struggles of immigrants, especially the undocumented.

Stay on Esperanza and turn right on Eighth Street, left on Lorena, and right on Hunter. On the left is the Estrada Courts, a federally funded, locally run low-income apartment complex. In 1973 the late artist Charles "Cat" Felix started a mural project

here that involved hundreds of local youths and attracted international media attention. Between 1973 and 1980 about fifty murals were painted; during the 1990s several new ones have been added, and some of the original ones have been repainted. Among the artists represented here are Ernesto de la Loza (with the first new mural in more than a decade, *Los cuatros grandes* [1993], on Hunter near Lorena), Willie Herrón and Gronk (they collaborated on *Moratorium* [1973], at 3221 Olympic Blvd.), David Botello (*Dreams of Flight* [1973–78, repainted in 1996], at 3241 Olympic), Mario Torero and other San Diego artists (*We Are Not a Minority* [1973, repainted in 1996], at 3217 Olympic), and Frank Lopez (*Orale raza* [1974–79] at 1319 Lorena St.).

That ends the tour. To return to Olvera Street, take Olympic Boulevard west into downtown L.A. Turn right at Alameda Street. Continue for over a mile. Olvera Street will be on your left a block after you cross the 101 Freeway.

South Los Angeles

African-American artists have painted murals in many local communities, including Hollywood, Pacoima (in the San Fernando Valley), and East Los Angeles. An especially important body of work by black artists can be found in South Los Angeles, a traditionally African-American area. A two-to-three-hour tour showcases some of the best.

We begin our tour at Golden State Mutual Life Insurance Company, located at 1999 West Adams Boulevard, at Western Avenue. The company has one of the best private collections of African-American art in the United States. The centerpiece is a two-panel mural in the lobby called *The Negro in California History*. It was painted by two prominent New York artists and installed when the building was dedicated in 1949. The first panel, by **Charles Alston**, is on your left as you enter through the front door. Entitled *Exploration and Growth*, it covers California history from 1527 to 1850. The second panel, *Settlement and Development*, by **Hale Woodruff**, portrays important events after California achieved statehood. In 1985 local artist **Richard Wyatt** was commissioned by the city's Cultural Affairs Department to paint a mural in the auditorium in honor of the company's sixtieth anniversary. *The Insurance Man* is a life-size portrait, a tribute to the agents who serve in the trenches.

From Golden State, drive south on Western, then turn right on Jefferson Boulevard. Our next stop is *Black Seeds* (1991), at 2301 Jefferson (at Third Ave.). Designed by **David Mosley, Eddie Orr**, and others, the mural is a tree of life. Writhing human bodies emerge from the trunk and the branches. On each limb are portraits of important African-Americans. On the leaves are written the names of still others.

Continue west on Jefferson, then turn left on Sixth Avenue. *Genocidal Tendencies* (1990), an anti-nuclear mural by **Ian White**, is on the corner. Continue down Sixth to the first intersection (36th St.). Take a right, and go straight until you reach 11th Avenue. Take a right. Just before reaching Jefferson, stop to view *To Protect and Serve* (1996) by **Noni Olabisi**, a dramatic monochrome history of

the Black Panther Party. Fred Hampton, murdered by the Chicago police, is here. So is Bobby Seale, bound and gagged at the conspiracy trial of the Chicago Seven, with Judge Julius Hoffman looking down at him. Also making appearances are the Ku Klux Klan, Angela Davis, Huey P. Newton, and the Panthers' free breakfast program.

Turn left on Jefferson and then left on Crenshaw Boulevard. Turn left on 48th Street, and park. Walk to the Community Youth Sports and Arts Foundation, a small private school at 4828 Crenshaw. Located on the building's exterior is **Elliott Pinkney**'s *Visions and Motion* (1993), featuring vignettes on the themes of sports, performing arts, and education, with Malcolm X and Cesar Chavez as centerpieces.

Return to Crenshaw, continuing southbound. Turn right on 54th Street, then left on Mullen. Stop at the corner to see *Women Get Weary but They Don't Give Up*, a 1991 mural by **Alice Patrick**, on a wall of the National Council of Negro Women. The organization was founded by educator Mary McLeod Bethune, pictured in the mural seated and wearing a black dress. On her left is Dorothy Height, the group's former president. The other well-known figures, standing in back, are (from left to right) dancer Josephine Baker, TV personality Oprah Winfrey, singer Sarah Vaughan, and runner Florence Griffith-Joyner.

Return to 54th Street, and head in the direction from which you just came. Continue on 54th for a couple of miles, stopping just before Western. On the left side of the street is *Freedom Won't Wait*, an emotional powerhouse by **Noni Olabisi**. Painted in

1992, in the wake of the massive citywide upheaval following the acquittal of the policemen who beat Rodney King, the mural depicts a series of agonized faces. Incredibly enough, it was the artist's first mural.

That ends the tour. To return to Golden State Insurance Company, where we began, turn left on Western and continue north until you reach West Adams Boulevard.

Long Beach

Our two-hour walking and driving tour begins in the downtown area. Park your car in the Long Beach Plaza Mall parking structure on Third Street between Pine Street and Long Beach Boulevard. We will begin with two murals created in the 1930s under the auspices of the Federal Art Project (WPA). Nine murals from this era survive in Long Beach, more than in any other Los Angeles County community.

Just outside the parking garage, facing Third Street and the Promenade, is our first mural. This imposing forty-foot-high mosaic was created for the Long Beach Municipal Auditorium in 1938. Designed by **Henry Allen Nord, Stanton Macdonald Wright**, and **Albert Henry King**, *Typical Activities of a Beach and Harbor City* was executed by forty artisans. In 1979 a major community effort saved the mural from destruction when the municipal auditorium was demolished to make way for a new convention center complex. It was installed in its present location in 1982. Notice how each pattern is created using tiles of different shapes. This was an innovation of Wright's and can be seen in several other mosaics he designed around Southern California.

Cross Third Street, and

walk along the Promenade to Broadway. Turn right on Broadway, then left on Pacific Avenue. At the corner of Pacific and Ocean Boulevard is the Long Beach Public Library (101 Pacific Ave.). The entrance is in the Civic Center, off Pacific. Enter the library. On the wall of the periodicals section are the nine panels of **Suzanne Miller**'s 1937 oil-on-canvas mural, *Scenes from English Language Classics*. After you leave the library, walk back to Pacific Avenue. Return to your car by turning left on Pacific, right on Broadway, and left on the Promenade.

Turn right onto Third Street when you drive out of the garage. Take a left on Pine Avenue. Continue straight until Pine dead-ends at Shoreline Drive, where you will turn left. *Wyland's Planet Ocean (Whaling Wall XXXIII)* will be on your left. You can't miss it; this depiction of marine life off the Southern California coast wraps around the entire Long Beach Arena. It is listed in *The Guinness Book of World Records* as the largest mural ever created. It took **Wyland** just six weeks in 1992 to complete and required 7,000 gallons of paint.

Just past the convention center, Shoreline Drive changes to Alamitos Avenue. Take Alamitos past Fourth Street three blocks. Just about at Sixth Street, take a left fork in the road, which is Martin Luther King Avenue. Stop and pull over on the first block to view **Eva Cockcroft**'s ecological mural—*Oil, Life and Ecology* (1990)—across the street on the left side. Sponsored by a local parks department mural program, which involves youths as assistants, this was the first public artwork painted on a National Guard Armory. On the odd, triangular building on the right side of the street is **Art Mortimer's** clever, untitled trompe l'oeil decorative work (1995), which creates the illusion of doors and windows where none exist.

Continue north on Martin Luther King until Anaheim Street. Turn right, then left on Peterson Avenue. Stop at the neighborhood market at 14th and Peterson to examine **Elizabeth Garrison's** *Storytellers* (1991), a series of three panels that depict textiles and artifacts identified with African, Cambodian, and Mexican cultures, the ethnic roots of many of the people living in this area.

Stay on Peterson until it ends at 15th Street, where you will turn left. Take a right on Alamitos and a left on Pacific Coast Highway. Turn left on Pacific

Avenue. Drive past the school on your right, stopping in front of the mural on the school's facade, *Dancers of Life* (1995), by **Richard Brandt**. The Samoan dancer portrayed was modeled after a student at the school. The breakdancer is a self-portrait.

Turn right at the next corner (14th St.) and right again on Cedar to view the murals on the other side of Washington Middle School. The first mural we pass is *Expand Your Mind with Science*, also by Brandt and done right after *Dancers of Life*. At the corner of Cedar and 15th Street is a 1989 celebratory mural by **Ben Valenzuela** called *Community of Music*. It pays tribute to the universal language of music by depicting traditions

ranging from tribal music to contemporary jazz.

Go straight on Cedar to Pacific Coast Highway, where you turn left. Just before turning, be sure to notice *El sol naciente* (1990), a surrealistic landscape by **Georges Chevallier** at the Long Beach School for Adults (on the right side of the street). The artist credits Paul Gauguin as an important influence.

Take Pacific Coast Highway over the Long Beach (710) Freeway into West Long Beach, a more industrial part of town. About three blocks after crossing the freeway, take a left on Caspian. Drive six blocks. At the corner of Caspian and Cowles stop to see *Westside Montage* (1992), a well-executed urban landscape by **Ben Valenzuela**

and **Trace Tres Fukuhara**.

Stay on Caspian, then turn right on Anaheim. In four blocks turn right again onto Seabright. To conclude your tour, stop at the **Harbor District Japanese Community Center** (1766 Seabright Ave.) to enjoy Fukuhara's lovely and unique *Homage to the Harbor District Japanese American Pioneers* (1995). These nine panels showcase the story of Japanese immigration, little-known contributions of Japanese-Americans to local agriculture and industrial fishing, their internment during World War II, and their reassimilation into American society afterward. Other images allude to the cultural and martial arts classes offered at the community center.

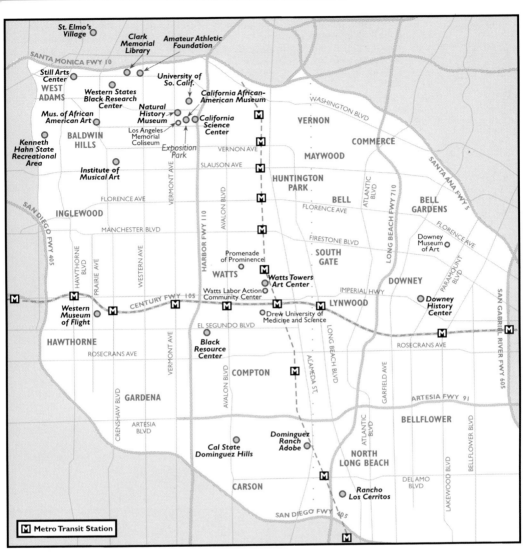

* indicates an area code that changes in 1998

Exposition Park—bounded to the north by Exposition Boulevard, to the west by Vermont Avenue, and to the east by Figueroa Street, just west of the Harbor (110) Freeway—stands on land designated in 1872 as an agricultural fairground for farmers to exhibit produce. It was transformed into a public park at the turn of the century through the efforts of a judge concerned that loiterers in the open area were having a negative effect on the morality of the neighborhood. Until recently its configuration derived from a 1913 plan inspired by the City Beautiful movement (whose ideas can better be seen today in the City Hall complex in Pasadena). The sunken garden, today the Rose Garden, was the central green courtyard connecting the red-brick National Guard Armory, an Exposition Building, and the Museum of History, Science, and Art that is today the Natural History Museum of Los Angeles County.

The new construction at the Museum of Science and Industry—now called the California Science Center—and damage to the Coliseum caused by the 1994 earthquake were the impetus for reviewing the entire plan for Exposition Park. Instead of simply focusing on the beautiful garden between the cultural institutions that are the park's primary tenants, the new plan seeks to better utilize the entire space, starting with the perimeter, which will be transformed into tree-lined promenades. Well-lighted pedestrian walks will link the California African-American Museum, Natural History Museum, and California Science Center, but it is the four corners of

Farmers Market
Adams Blvd. and
Vermont Ave.
Wed. 1–6 p.m.

Exposition Park that will be changed most significantly. Community parks—with such features as playground areas, picnic and barbecue facilities, and benches that reflect needs expressed by local residents—will become signature elements of the new plan. Although the state of California owns this land, Los Angeles County has invested $24 million from a bond issue to upgrade traffic flow and improve landscaping and recreational facilities. The master plan for the renovation of Exposition Park, which won the American Institute of Architects' 1993 Urban Design Award of Excellence, will be implemented in stages, but the first corner park (to debut in 1998 at Vermont and Exposition) will incorporate a pathway with pawprints of animals indigenous to California that leads to a central "watering hole" and playground equipment in the shape of other animals.

The seven-acre sunken **Rose Garden**, a still-viable and beautiful element of the 1913 plan for Exposition Park, features about 200 varieties of roses in the same number of beds. Open daily from 8 a.m. to sunset (except from January to March when the park is closed for pruning and maintenance), it is bright and fragrant, a lovely place to stroll or picnic between bouts in the museums. One of the most picturesque spots in town, it is a favorite for weddings, which allows visitors to a public peek at one of the most basic cultural rites.

An enlarged community center and additional recreational facilities will be located in the southeast quadrant of the park; current facilities include the **Sports Arena** and the **Swim Stadium**, which was built in 1984 for the Olympics.

Tours of the **Los Angeles Memorial Coliseum** (3911 S. Figueroa St.; 213-748-6131)—which its answering-machine tape identifies as "the most significant structure built by man in the twentieth century"—are offered on Tuesdays, Thursdays, and Saturdays at 10:30 a.m., noon, and 1:30 p.m. (adults $4, seniors $3, students $2, children under 12 $1; call 213-765-6347 for reservations). The Coliseum is a National Historic Landmark, the setting for such key twentieth-century events as the Summer Olympic Games in 1932 and 1984, the acceptance of the 1960 Democratic nomination by John F. Kennedy and Lyndon Johnson, and the public mass celebrated by Pope John Paul II during his 1987 American tour. The future of the aging structure was already under debate when it was struck a crippling blow by the 1994 earthquake. The cost of reconstruction and seismic upgrades, coupled with the structure's limited ability to generate sports revenue due to its fixed seating and lack of such high-priced amenities as enclosed boxes, may outweigh its historic and architectural value to commercial sports promoters. *The Olympic Arch*, one of the finest pieces of public sculpture in the city, was created by Los Angeles sculptor Robert Graham for the 1984 Olympics, and features a pair of headless bronze nudes.

Natural History Museum of Los Angeles County

900 Exposition Blvd.
Los Angeles 90007
213-763-DINO
www.nhm.org
Tues.–Sun. 10 a.m.–5 p.m.
Entry: adults $6, seniors/students $3.50,
children 5–12 $2

The museum, established in 1913 as the county's primary venue for exhibitions of history, science, and art, has maintained a hybrid identity that is reflected in the exhibits at its Exposition Park site and at the satellite facilities it administers. Two museums in the Miracle Mile/Museum Row section of Wilshire Boulevard and a historic home at the northern edge of L.A. County are all part of the Natural History Museum, whose members enjoy free admission to all of its sites. The newest addition is the Petersen Automotive Museum, which examines the dynamic relationship between the automobile and society; just down Wilshire, a spectacular collection of Ice Age fossils is on display at the George C. Page Museum of La Brea Discoveries in Hancock Park. Out in the Santa Clarita Valley, western art and memorabilia are shown at the William S. Hart Museum, the western film star's former home.

The museum's original building in Exposition Park is a Spanish Renaissance structure that was placed on the National Register of Historic Places in 1975; it boasts marble walls and domed rotundas, one rendered in stained glass by the local Judson Studios. The porch on the east side, fronting the Rose Garden, is no longer the museum's entrance, but it reveals this fine building's prominent place in the original plan for Exposition Park. Artist Charles R. Knight's 1926 mural depicting the Rancho La Brea tar pits—renowned as the foundation of modern knowledge of animals long extinct—has recently been restored. The two panels, which measure ten by fifty feet, are again displayed off the museum's rotunda, surrounded by skeletons of animals that lived in the L.A. basin 40,000 years ago. Docent-led tours of the building are offered daily at 1 p.m.

The Natural History Museum's collection is enormous (it's hard to quantify certain types of specimens, so I've seen statistics from fifteen to thirty-five million—you get the idea); only the Smithsonian Institution and New York City's American Museum of Natural History have larger collections. These artifacts reveal the 4.5 billion-year history of Earth and the evolution and diversity of its natural life and cultures. The museum's primary collections are organized in four departments: Life Sciences (birds, mammals, reptiles, fishes, mollusks, crustacea, worms, and insects); Earth Sciences (dinosaur bones, fossils, gems, and minerals); Anthropology (Native-American, pre-Columbian, and Pacific); and History (American and Southwest). Although the last two categories occupy almost half of the museum's permanent exhibition space, these collections are not as well known as they should be.

The museum's logo, derived from the saber-toothed cat that is California's state fossil, celebrates its excavation of the La Brea tar pits, which has yielded the more than 560 species of ancient plants and animals that can be seen at the Page Museum. Dinosaurs, however, remain the most popular mammal fossils and are the unofficial symbol of the Natural History Museum. In 1996 the museum embraced this identification by installing in its foyer **Dueling Dinosaurs**, a dramatic display of a *Tyrannosaurus rex* attacking the rhinolike *Triceratops*. The figures, standing eighteen feet high, were crafted from skeletons of the late Cretaceous period (about seventy million years ago), which were recovered by museum curators from digs at Hells Creek, Montana. The museum declined to incorporate its rare and complete *Tyrannosaurus* and *Triceratops* skulls into the installation, preferring to allow visitors a closer view of them in nearby cases. The museum's role in fostering the next generation of paleontologists produced the landmark exhibition "Dinosaurs Past and Present," which showed the evolution of new scientifically accurate images of dinosaurs; the exhibition also provided the museum with such state-of-the-art models constructed by Stephen Czerkas as *Carnotaurus* and *Allosaurus*. Don't miss these exhibits or the cast of a complete *Mamenchisaurus* skeleton found in the popular dinosaur gallery between the north entrance and the Discovery Center.

The Ralph M. Parsons Discovery Center (213-763-3238) is a 6,000-square-foot interactive environment especially well suited to four- to ten-year-olds, which encourages learning about natural science through tactile discovery. Educators help children select age-appropriate "discovery boxes," which may be filled with parts of a shark—teeth, skin, jawbone—to be touched and studied; the boxes may also contain a puzzle depicting the animals of the rainforest, or sensory games. There are foam building blocks, sandpits in which to dig for buried treasure, and puppets to put on performances, as well as books that offer parent and child a quiet respite from the excitement of a museum visit. Monthly Family FunDays, free with museum admission, explore such topics as bats, the rainforest, geology, natural camouflage, and sharks, in workshops geared for kids ages four and up; call 213-763-3239 for information.

Exhibits of live animals—fish and reptile tanks, for instance—were expanded when the Insect Zoo (213-763-3558) opened in 1992 on the mezzanine above the Discovery Center. Here's a fact that may drive you buggy: insects comprise more than half of the 1.4 million organisms that have been categorized, but scientists speculate that the known species may represent less than 10 percent of the actual number of insect species. Among some thirty live exhibits in the **Insect Zoo** is an ant farm that showcases some live specimens from North America's largest collection of ants, as well as local insects of all kinds and exotics like Madagascan hissing cockroaches and giant African tiger beetles, which live in terrariums. Southwestern butterflies and moths, another specialty of the collection, astound with their colors and beautiful patterns. The Insect Zoo's director, Dr. Art Evans, enhanced its collection recently by donating 40,000 scarab beetles he had personally collected, offering a glimpse of the passion great curators bring to their profession.

Nearly 100 dioramas that provide aesthetic backdrops for animal displays throughout the galleries also include detailed, scientifically accurate landscape paintings, such as elephants at a watering hole by Duncan Spencer and mule deer on the North Rim of the Grand Canyon by Hanson Puthuff, as well as masterful tableaux created by the current staff of scenic artists. The two large galleries on the main floor are filled with dioramas of African and North American mammals, giving them a timeless quality; they also provide the museum with one of the best party spaces in L.A. County.

More than 2,000 gems and mineral specimens, including a 212-carat emerald cabochon and a 3,106-carat diamond, glitter in another hall. A variety of gold-mining equipment and three hundred pounds of gold are displayed in exhibits that also chronicle gold rush cycles in the western states. Martian meteorites—rare scientific jewels that are 1.3 billion years old—are juxtaposed with information on the famous meteorite that scientists believe reveals the existence of microscopic living organisms on the Red Planet 4 billion years ago.

History was one of the focuses of the composite museum that was this institution's predecessor, and it has remained a core component of the collection. The Natural History Museum not only boasts the largest American and regional history halls in the western United States, it has dedicated space and resources to its fine pre-Columbian collection and to an appealing and informative new installation of American Indian artifacts in the **Times Mirror Hall of Native American Cultures**, which opened in 1993. The extraordinary Hearst Collection of 200 Navajo textiles and 4,000 baskets from California and the Great Basin is featured, along with a replica of a Pueblo cliff dwelling and encyclopedic displays of Southwestern pottery and jewelry. Three halls on the west side of the building are dedicated to American history: displays begin in 1492 with Columbus's arrival, examine in detail the fifty years preceding the Civil War and the development of the modern nation, and end with World War I. On the lower level, look for the renovated **Lando Hall of California and Southwest History**, which traces the modern development of the western states, one of the primary forces in the post–Civil War history of the United States; a section examining California's prehistory begins with another of the museum's signature dioramas, this one on native lifestyles. Exhibits on the era of Spanish exploration feature navigational instruments and ship models; the role of the

missions in the period of Mexican rule and in the mythology of early California is illustrated extensively by maps, manuscripts, and early photographs from the collections of the Seaver Center for Western History Research.

On the second floor is the **Schreiber Hall of Birds**, with its innovative exhibits. The ornithological collection has grown from 250 specimens in 1913 to more than 104,000 birds, including the world's largest collection of California condors. Their beautiful plumage and distinctive songs make birds among the most appealing of our natural neighbors, and visitors can acquire greater appreciation of their traits at twenty-seven interactive stations. In addition, three habitats can be walked through: one of the most enchanting is a marsh environment that is illuminated when a visitor enters; the exhibit cycles through a dawn-to-dusk scenario, as the light changes and different birds add their voices.

Marine-life exhibits are drawn from the second-largest collection of marine mammals in the world, and the ichthyology collection encompasses nearly half of the 25,000 known fish species and includes a rare megamouth shark (one of only nine specimens collected since the species was identified twenty-five years ago), and dioramas of California waters from the intertidal zone to the deep sea depict many plants and animals native to the Pacific. Whales, dolphins, and porpoises are the subject of other exhibits, and the curators play a central role in marine mammal research; they routinely investigate the phenomenon of cetacean stranding, for instance.

The museum has presented pioneering temporary exhibitions that have expanded the range of subjects traditionally associated with this institution. "Volcanoes," "Cats! Wild to Mild," and "Sharks! Fact and Fantasy" have deepened public understanding of natural history, while "Nomads of Eurasia," "Chinese Jade," and "Africa: One Continent, Many Worlds" revealed the wide-ranging expertise of its curatorial staff. Annual events include the popular Members' Open House and Family Day.

As participants in the Museum Research Apprenticeship Program, twenty high school students from around L.A. County spend their Saturdays at the Natural History Museum (Feb.–May, then eight weeks in summer) conducting research with museum curators. Students are trained in field- and collections-based research, undertaking projects in marine biology, paleontology, archeology, and molecular biology. There is no charge to the students; textbooks and other materials are provided, and they receive a stipend to cover transportation and other costs. The program is funded by the National Science Foundation and has launched many high school students on scientific careers. For more information and an application, call 213-763-3240.

Children (ages 3–13) explore many facets of science through hands-on exploration in week-long Adventures in Nature programs, offered winter and summer. My son gives an enthusiastic thumbs-up to Digging Dinosaurs, which helped fuel a new passion. Call the museum's Education Department at 213-763-3534 for the schedule.

More than 250,000 schoolchildren toured this museum last year; half of them were led by docents who train for a year and know the museum and its collections well. The most popular tour topics include dinosaurs, North American mammals, and American and California history. Tours of the Discovery Room and special exhibitions are also very well attended. Guided tours are offered Tuesday through Friday on the hour, 10 a.m.–noon; for a brochure detailing the full tour schedule, call 213-763-3535.

California Science Center

700 State Dr.
Los Angeles 90037
213-744-7400
Daily 10 a.m.–5 p.m.
Entry: free; admission to IMAX Theater

Its mission—to promote scientific and technological literacy through exhibits designed for participation on many levels—may sound a bit dry, but the all-new California Science Center defines itself in more popular terms, "245,000 square feet of fun, engaging ways to experience science learning." This is a major long-term redevelopment, intended to transform the northeast quadrant of Exposition Park into a statewide magnet for science education and a popular destination for tourists and residents alike. The crowds that flocked to see the first phase of the new Science Center when it opened in February 1998—more than 200,000 visitors in that month—indicate that it is a popular success. (To avoid sharing the galleries with the many school groups that have made this their destination of choice for field trips, individuals may want to schedule their visits in the afternoon: the big yellow school buses all depart by 2:00 p.m.) Changing the institution's name (from California Museum of Science and Industry to California Science Center) is one signal of its new purpose. Unlike other museums that draw on the artifacts in their collections (which the Science Center does not have) to develop their exhibits, the Science Center consists primarily of interactive exhibits, specially designed to be both durable and touchable.

In addition to the museum construction and renovation, the ten-year, three-phase development will include the Science Center School—a neighborhood science and math-focused elementary school—and the Science Education Resource Center. The project, budgeted at $265 million with funding from a variety of public and private sources, is a partnership among the California Museum of Science and Industry, the Los Angeles Unified School District (LAUSD), the University of Southern California (USC), and the NASA/Jet Propulsion Laboratory (JPL) of the California Institute of Technology, with different levels of funding and other support coming from each participant. The state of California, which owns the Exposition Park site, also committed $47 million for the Phase I building and $30 million for the school; the Science Center School—slated to begin enrollment in 2000—will be administered and staffed by LAUSD and utilized by the neighboring USC School of Education as a "professional practice site," or lab school. JPL provided initial funding to develop plans for the Science Education Resource Center, but that construction is slated for Phase III of the project, which will be the goal of a later fund-raising campaign.

The new California Science Center incorporates a historic brick-and-terra-cotta facade from the Howard F. Ahmanson Building, which has been stripped of layers of white paint. The newly revealed decorative roof pediment includes green-glazed elements, a color scheme repeated in the new green-glass, steel-framed structure that rises above it. Although visitors may enter the Science Center from the Rose Garden through a restored doorway (the 1960s-era glass-box entrance has been removed), the primary entrance is through a circular atrium with an 88-foot-high ceiling, which faces the south parking lot. A new $8-million IMAX Theater capable of projecting films in the standard format and in three dimensions occupies the large cube adjacent to the Science Center's south entrance; the entire renovation project was designed by the architectural firm of Zimmer Gunscul Frasca Partnership.

Science Plaza, the courtyard outside the main entrance, has been articulated with several large-scale artworks, including a pathway of paving stones etched with scientific riddles, inspirational quotes, and number games. **The California Gate** comprises two irregular blocks of granite, each thirteen feet tall, but the space between them, which reveals the outline of the state, conveys the meaning of the sculpture and is a witty demonstration of negative and positive imagery. **Water Story** is a dynamic fountain that depicts the human connection to water, especially as it pertains to California. A skylight of dichronic glass, which utilizes light refraction and color to evoke the beauty and inspiration of science, also draws the eye upward to *The Aerial,* a hanging sculpture comprising 1,578 gold and silver spheres by artist Larry Kirkland. A cross-section of a DNA strand, rendered in multicolored granite, forms a monumental bench engraved with thought-provoking quotations and images of living things.

Some of the most spectacular and engaging exhibits are suspended overhead in the Science Center's main lobby, a grand public space that soars 112 feet. The **"Hypar,"** or Hyperbolic Paraboloid (photo, p. 180), is a kinetic sculpture of aluminum links, connected by stainless steel pivots, which changes shape and size from fifteen to fifty feet; it elucidates such principles as minimal surfaces—natural forms that require the least amount of energy to maintain their shape. As it expands and contracts, the Hypar demonstrates that a structure can remain stable at all times while completely transforming itself and suggests the possibility of making buildings that change size and shape. Such phenom-

The large and well-stocked Explorastore off the lobby promises to provide revenues necessary to maintain the exhibits at this admission-free site. There are three places to eat within the building, from a McDonald's (sure to create friction between parent and child) to a cafe on the top floor that offers light fare with a panoramic view across the Rose Garden to the downtown skyline. (The latter space is available for rental, another important

ena have been documented in physics—the expanding universe—and biology—cell mutation—but how such minimal surfaces can be utilized in the built environment is a question that Hypar's designer, Chuck Hoberman, invites us all to ponder. A giant yo-yo makes a 200-foot automated circuit on the north side of the entry space, demonstrating how counterbalance is used to establish center of mass, which in plain English means that the smaller colored wheel inside the translucent circle acts as a counterweight to keep the yo-yo on the cable. The same principle keeps the **High Wire Bicycle** suspended on its cable forty-three feet above the floor, no matter how far the rider leans to the right or left. Visitors pay $3 to mount the little red bicycle and "experience the law of 'center of gravity' in dramatic fashion. They will learn firsthand that any force causing the system to tip will be offset by the force of gravity acting on an attached counterweight." My maternal trepidation over this exhibit was put to rest by the presence of a safety net and assurances that this net could only possibly be needed if the rider's weight exceeds 250 pounds and so overwhelms the torpedo-like counterweight that hangs beneath the bicycle.

source of income for the Science Center.)

Ultimately the exhibits will be organized in a four-part layout: **World of Life** and **Creative World** have been developed in Phase I of the construction. Only a small preview of the **World of the Pacific** and **Worlds Beyond** sections—respectively, a tank of jellyfish and a space-docking simulator (that costs $5 to try)—are included in Phase I, but the diverse ecosystems on the Pacific Rim, which range from icy Antarctic waters to coral reefs and tropical rainforests, will be fully developed in Phase II; in Phase III, exhibits in the Science Center will widen the window on the universe and human interaction with it, replacing the present Aerospace Hall. Each of these thematic sections incorporates a **Discovery Room,** where younger kids will find plenty of age-appropriate activities and even computer labs with terminals loaded for different age groups. Families can select from about thirty Discovery Boxes to play educational games and conduct simple experiments on picnic tables. The large **Weingart Special Exhibits Gallery** on the top floor will offer a changing focus on scientific topics, such as the engineering of toys, the very popular inaugural exhibition.

A reticulated tile mural leads to the

World of Life gallery, which explores how all living things function and compares human survival techniques with those of other animals. The cell is the common building block of life: human beings are each composed of 100 trillion cells, while some bacteria are single-celled. Visitors first encounter the five common functions of all living things—to take in energy and supplies; to get rid of waste; to react to the world; to defend oneself; and to reproduce—in a fifty-five-foot tunnel, where they are surrounded by a kaleidoscope of video images. Micro-

scopes in the **Cell Lab** allow visitors to perceive these building blocks of life, and in the **Cell Theater** both film and live demonstrations expand the understanding of cellular function in life. The five shared life processes are examined in each gallery with reference to a wide range of life forms: **Control Center** shows how different life forms react to stimulation with engaging displays on sensory systems, including one where people can get inside a bat head and attempt to "see" the world with sound. Even the youngest visitors will be able to see how fish react to currents and reorient themselves en masse when a button is pushed to reverse the flow of water through their tank. The various parts of the human nervous system are illuminated and described in another exhibit; the effects of alcohol on perception and reaction, with graphic statistics on drunk driving, comprise the human health aspect of this section.

Supply Network has many hands-on displays, including one that compares the pressure needed to get blood from the heart to the brain of both a boy and a giraffe, dynamically demonstrated by turning a crank and measuring the time and force needed to fill each neck with symbolic red. Another exhibit shows the relative size of the heart and the amount of blood in the circulatory systems of animals as varied as an elephant, a human, and a mouse. In

Defense Line, we discover how living things protect themselves against the elements, predators, and germs; visitors can employ these concepts by building a giant insect that can defend itself against almost anything (but is so loaded with apparatus that it may be unable to move!). The most striking exhibit allows visitors to witness open-heart and lung surgery, with a screen imbedded in the chest of the patient on which realistic images are projected; the surgical procedure is explained step-by-step on an audiotape.

Life Source incorporates EGGciting Beginnings, in which live animals demonstrate reproduction and genetics as baby chicks hatch and tadpoles metamorphose into frogs. The evolution of the human fetus is depicted in a dozen panels, with detailed explanations and warnings about the effects of smoking and alcohol and the benefits of good nutrition. The **Energy Factory** of the human body is graphically compared with that of other animals through thermal images. At the **Digestion Diner**, you do get to see Gertie's guts as well as a video on what animals eat. The centerpiece of **Body Works Theater** is Tess, a fifty-foot-tall transparent human figure with organ systems illuminated by fiber optics. During a fifteen-minute show in the 150-seat theater, Tess moves her head, blinks her eyes, and speaks, demonstrating with animatronics the internal teamwork required for a person to play soccer. The **World of Life Discovery Room** has a treehouse where kids can climb, live plants and animals, a puppet theater, and a well-stocked book nook where kids take a comfortable and quiet break from the intense stimulation of the exhibit floor.

Creative World allows visitors to marvel at the accomplishments of the human race, with displays of innovative responses to the basic needs for shelter, transportation, and communication. The three galleries of the Creative World are introduced by **Technoscapes**, a laser-animated, three-dimensional sculpture of a city street that captures the dynamic interplay of science and technology in contemporary life. The many possibilities for building things in these galleries are given real-life context by seeing how well the structure you've designed withstands an earthquake simulation. You can find out how well your nerves will fare in another simulated earthquake, experienced while taking a behind-the-scenes tour of the new Science Center, which shows the technological advances incorporated in its construction. The marathon through life's hazards continues as visitors

The Science Center's education staff spends some time recovering from the hectic summer schedule of classes, so the school-year program doesn't usually start until January. The catalogue is published in October (call 213-744-7444 to be added to the mailing list).

The California State Science Fair is an annual event coordinated by the Science Center. Winning projects are an inspiring display presented for a few weeks each spring. Teenagers compete for more than $30,000 in prizes and scholarships; science teachers at junior and senior high schools can tell interested students how to participate.

join dummies for a crash test to learn about driving safety. A planned exhibit on "smart highways" is one that local commuters should embrace.

Robotics and computer technology are utilized to allow visitors to play Virtual Volleyball and join in a Digital Jam Session on keyboard, drums, or guitar. Through a Video Periscope in the **Communications Gallery,** visitors to the Science Center can communicate audiovisually with people at the new Getty Center. Similar video cameras and display monitors create a child-sized TV studio in the **Creative World Discovery Room,** which features a city street with a construction zone and a transportation-themed play area for toddlers. In the tech lab, computers are loaded with the graphically stimulating program The Way Things Work and, for younger kids, Sammy's Science House. Seminars on how to navigate the Internet are planned.

A DC3 and DC8 parked at the corner of Figueroa Street and Exposition Boulevard announce one of the major themes of the Science Center. **Worlds Beyond** will be developed during Phase III of the construction to replace **Aerospace Hall,** designed by Frank Gehry in 1984 with an F-104 Starfighter pinned to its facade. The exhibits in this hall took a beating during the years when they provided the only public access to the Science Center, so when the new building opened, Aerospace Hall was closed for refurbishing. It is expected to reopen by Fall 1998. Until Phase III of the construction is complete, circa 2005, exhibits in Aerospace Hall will examine the technological innovations that have allowed humans to explore the universe, solar system, and their origins. The crafts that humans have developed to leave the surface of the earth and the ones they have sent aloft in their stead will be among the largest exhibits in this section. A Los Angeles Police Department helicopter hovers over the ground-floor exhibit space, where principles of flight—lift, control, thrust, and navigation—are explained in hands-on exhibits; nearby, visitors can design their own flying vehicles and test their knowledge of aeronautical principles in a computer game. The soaring open space is punctuated with a wide assortment of spacecraft, from a full-scale model of the Wright Brothers' 1902 glider to a 1986 Northrup F-20 Tigershark, one of the fastest fighter planes. There are replicas of *Sputnik I*, with which the Soviets launched the space race in 1957, and the first U.S. deep-space probe, *Pioneer 5*. The actual space capsules that were sent aloft

in 1961 *Mercury* and 1966 *Gemini 11* launches are displayed (along with spacesuits worn by American astronauts). Video feeds from NASA bring images of most NASA launches to a receptive crowd. In an open theater on the top level, *Windows on the Universe,* a slide show with a script by Ray Bradbury, chronicles manned and unmanned space missions.

At the **IMAX** ("image maximization") **Theater** film ten times larger than the standard 35mm is projected on a screen seven stories high and ninety feet wide. Like the former facility, the new Theater will be nonprofit, with income in excess of operating expenses contributed to the budget of the Science Center, and its films will be selected for their educational content. The overwhelming power of the imagery is enhanced by the enveloping six-channel sound. The Academy Award–nominated film *The Living Sea* featured golden jellyfish, humpback whales, and the inveterate surfers who share the California waves; the scale and complex natural forms of the Grand Canyon, Yellowstone, Alaska, and the Great Barrier Reef have also been beautifully elucidated in IMAX format. Different films are shown several times each day; for recorded show information and ticket prices, call 213-744-2014; for group reservations, 213-744-2019.

Each summer the Science Center offers a festival of exhibitions, classes, and events with a central theme. Thousands of kids attend during the six-week program, spending two hours at the museum for five days; there are also Saturday classes, with a different topic each week. Most of the ten-hour, five-day classes cost $61 for members and $68 for nonmembers, with some scholarships available. For the catalogue and application form, call 213-744-7440.

Colburn School of Performing Arts, which started in 1950 as the USC School of Music's Prep Division, had become an independent, nonprofit school whose activities had outgrown its facility on the USC campus. To continue training gifted musicians and other performing artists of every age, the Colburn School has built a new facility on downtown's Bunker Hill, where its proximity to the Music Center will create a campus akin to the Juilliard School at New York's Lincoln Center. Classes will take place at the new site starting in summer 1998, so the description of its programs has been listed in the downtown section (p. 16), but this reference is a memorial to its fine work in this community and is placed here to help residents find it again when it relocates.

The Exposition Park-Bethune branch of the Los Angeles Public Library (3665 S. Vermont Ave.; *213-732-0169) contains a mural painted in the early 1900s by African-American artist Charles S. White.

California African-American Museum (CAAM)

600 State Dr.
Los Angeles 90007
213-744-7432
Tues.–Sun. 10 a.m.–5 p.m.
Entry: free

Housed in a sleek building constructed for the 1984 Olympic Arts Festival at the southwest corner of Figueroa Street and State Drive, CAAM celebrates the achievements of people of African descent in history and art; the exhibition space begins in the forecourt, where large-scale sculpture is often on view. Changing exhibitions examine the contributions of African-Americans to athletics, education, and politics as well as to art, and a portion of its permanent collection is usually on view.

Because contemporary black artists often face continuing challenges in establishing their careers, CAAM has initiated a biennial exhibition of "Emerging Artists" selected from the slide files that the museum maintains; these exhibitions alternately feature artists working anywhere in the United States and those based in California. CAAM is also one venue for the biennial juried exhibition sponsored by the city's Cultural Affairs Department.

The museum's growing collection of historical artifacts will be featured in upcoming exhibitions and in a permanent gallery, slated to open in 1999, which will chronicle the westward migration of blacks from older urban centers and examine the communities they created in the western states. Guided student-oriented tours of the exhibitions (accommodating up to fifty students) can be arranged.

A ninety-nine-seat theater is used for lectures, storytelling, and other performances geared to kids, and the museum hosts a film series. Occaisional workshops for families explore different aspects of African-American culture and their historical antecedents. For instance, a lecture on the history of the West African Kente cloth was followed by a workshop in which looms were made and techniques for weaving Kente cloth were learned.

During the summer months CAAM transforms itself into a creative day camp that is dedicated to inspiring confidence, encouraging students to set higher goals, and teaching skills in a variety of disciplines. The six-week program utilizes all the resources of Exposition Park to explore selected themes; full-day sessions include a supervised lunch period and recreation in the park. Studio art workshops and story-

Glorious Repertory Players, which had produced its "message musicals" at the Odyssey Theater in West L.A., in late 1997 renovated a warehouse near USC as its new home, the 24th Street Theater (1117 W. 24th St.; 213-745-6516). It offers free workshops for youth, and neighborhood residents pay what they can for performances.

telling/performance groups are offered, along with programs in creative writing, genealogy, and black history; fees are very reasonable and some scholarships are available.

The Junior Docent Program, for students ages fifteen to eighteen, includes summer internships at the museum for those who complete a two-week course that surveys various elements of museum work, from exhibition preparation to writing labels and scripts for tours.

Amateur Athletic Foundation of Los Angeles

Paul Ziffren Sports Resource Center
2141 W. Adams Blvd.
Los Angeles 90018
*213-730-9696
Mon.–Fri. 10 a.m.–5 p.m., until 8:30 p.m. on Wed.; 1st and last Sat. of each month 10 a.m.–3 p.m.

This library—along with new and refurbished sports facilities built as event venues—is the legacy of the successful and imaginative management of the 1984 Olympic Games, which showed L.A. in its best light. Proceeds from the games were used to build a library to house Olympic memorabilia, including 50,000 photographs chronicling the event from the turn of the century and 30,000 books. Two or three thematic exhibits drawn from the collection of sports art and artifacts are mounted each year; boxing, baseball, historic graphics, and medallions from the Olympics were recent topics. The librarians suggest that individuals check the schedule of group tours to avoid noisy interludes at this popular destination for school groups.

University of Southern California (USC)

University Park
Los Angeles 90089
213-740-2311

USC calls itself the oldest—it was founded in 1880—and largest—with a student body of 28,000 (up from fifty-three in its inaugural class)—private research university in the American West. Its main campus, 150 acres bounded by Vermont Avenue, Jefferson Boulevard, and Figueroa Street north of Exposition Boulevard, encompasses more than 130 buildings, which have transformed its parklike setting into a discordant jumble in some sections, although the graceful pre–World War II plan of the campus is still evident in places. Free one-hour walking tours of the campus (Mon.–Fri. 10 a.m.–2 p.m.; call 213-740-6605 for reservations) leave from **Trojan Hall**, at the southeast corner of the campus where a new main entrance gate for the university is being created. Designed for prospective students, the tours also introduce the university and its facilities to the community, and individuals of all ages are welcome.

A campus map is posted at each of the entrance gates, but here are a few itineraries to orient visitors:

Libraries, the repositories of knowledge, are properly the focal point of any university, and USC recently dedicated almost $30 million to create a new state-of-the-art information complex in the **Leavey Library** (between 34th and 35th Sts. at Hoover), which opened in 1994. In addition to 115,000 books, Leavey has 500 electronic workstations and offers seminars on technologies—using the Internet efficiently, designing Web pages—which teach the information-management skills of the twenty-first century. **Doheny Memorial Library** (1932), designed by Samuel E. Lunden, stands on the central axis of the campus across Alumni Park from the 1921 Bovard Administration Building, designed by John Parkinson and his son Donald B. Parkinson (better known as architects of the nearby Memorial Coliseum, as well as Union Station and Bullocks-Wilshire) in Italian Renaissance style; Bovard includes the 1,600-seat, Gothic-style **Norris Auditorium**, used for various cultural events. The Doheny Library (Mon.–Thurs. 8:30 a.m.–10 p.m., Fri.–Sat. 8:30 a.m.–5 p.m., Sun. 1–10 p.m. when classes are in session; 213-740-6050) houses special collections in an environment characterized by a soaring marble rotunda with figured ceilings, mural paintings, and stained-glass windows. Among its holdings are

collections of American literature, especially first editions of post-1850 writers (including Henry James, Jack London, Herman Melville, and Mark Twain); Western history, including the archive of the Hearst-owned *Los Angeles Examiner* and the photographs of the California Historical Society; and examples of fine printing, with special emphasis on the works of California presses. Visitors might want to conclude this bookish tour at the USC Bookstore (open daily when

school is in session; 213-740-5200) adjacent to the Commons and Student Union, just west of the 1930 statue of Tommy Trojan, the USC mascot.

For art lovers: **Watt Hall of Architecture and Fine Arts** (located to the east of Watt Way, which begins at Gate #1 on Exposition Blvd.) houses the **Helen Lindhurst Gallery** (Mon.–Thurs. 9 a.m.–5 p.m., Fri. 9 a.m.–4 p.m.; 213-740-2723; free). The School of Architecture, one of USC's most renowned graduate programs, mounts exhibitions in this gallery. USC also maintains two off-site historic buildings that can be toured: see the **Freeman House** in chapter II (p. 50), and the **Gamble House** in chapter IV (p. 113). **Fisher Gallery** (Tues.–Fri. noon–5 p.m., Sat. 11 a.m.–3 p.m.; 213-740-4561; free), USC's primary space for art exhibitions, is next door in Harris Hall. Contemporary art and the emerging skills of students in the School of Fine Arts are featured in some of the six

Located on the USC campus, KUSC (91.5 FM) is a commercial-free classical music station that has been broadcasting for fifty years. Controversy about its music programming, which occupies 95 percent of air time, has been addressed with staff and format changes; the news and information programming has scored a hit with Marketplace, the nationally distributed daily program on business and economics.

shows Fisher Gallery presents each school year (the space is closed in summer). The permanent collection, established in 1939 with nineteenth-century American landscape paintings donated by Elizabeth Holmes Fisher and enriched by Armand Hammer and many other donors over the years, is regularly on view in the Quinn Wing.

Continuing east toward Trousdale Parkway, the **Mudd Hall of Philosophy** is a 1930 landmark with a 146-foot belltower modeled after a medieval Tuscan monastery; it features stained-glass windows, colorful tiles, and a second-floor library designed to foster contemplation. A block north on Trousdale is the Hancock Foundation Building, which reflects the myriad interests of its benefactor, Captain Allan Hancock, a long-time USC trustee; the woolly mammoth on the exterior refers to the prehistoric finds at the La Brea Tar Pits located on his property (now called Hancock Park in his honor). Inside, the **Hancock Memorial Museum** (by appt. only, call 213-740-5144; admission fee) incorporates four rooms from Hancock's mother's house (built in 1907 at Wilshire Boulevard and Vermont Avenue), and period furnishings, including some objects from the Mexico City palace of Emperor Maximilian which had been among her possessions.

USC's **School of Cinema–Television**, which pioneered such programs in 1929 and still ranks first in the nation, anchors a complex funded by (and named for) such entertainment luminaries as George Lucas, Steven Spielberg (who is also a trustee), and Johnny Carson. Free tours of the complex leave from 850 West 34th Street, at the loading dock (Fri. 2 p.m.; call ahead first, 213-740-2892). **Norris Cinema Theater** (213-740-1946) is a luxurious space with Dolby sound and 70mm capacity, but its free programs are so popular with students that the public, admitted last, may not be able to snag one of its 341 seats. Current films are shown on Wednesday and Friday evenings; the popular cinema class #466 also meets there and sessions are often followed by discussions with industry personnel. Retrospectives and thematic screenings are featured on many weekends; the schedule isn't well publicized off-campus, so call periodically for updated information.

The Spielberg Music Scoring Stage links the cinema complex with the adjacent music department buildings, and the grassy areas in between are often the site of impromptu concerts by rehearsing musicians. The **Bing Theater** is a 589-seat space used for stage performances, including works produced in the spring experimental theater class and productions of classic plays, with such musicals as *The Three-Penny Opera* or *Cabaret* in the annual offerings. The schedule of the Bing Theater is announced on the recorded message of the School of Theater (213-740-1285); tickets may be purchased from the USC Ticket Office (213-740-7111).

The Annenberg School of Communications includes the School of Journalism and is the new home of the Asia Pacific Media Center, which for the past fifteen years has toured to a dozen U.S. cities an annual festival of new works by Asian and Pacific Island filmmakers. Its programs, chosen for a cross-cultural approach that illuminates Asian societies, screen at the Norris Cinema Theater (call 213-743-1939 for a schedule).

Many Angelenos discover USC through its active sports program, and they'll probably relish the lobby of **Heritage Hall,** which our guide described as "basically a giant trophy case." There are four Heisman trophies on display, along with other artifacts of winning seasons and great athletes; that the first option on the automated USC Ticket Office line (213-740-7111) is for seats to football games must indicate the popularity of this offering. Sports facilities (mainly clustered in the northeast corner of the campus) include the swim stadium and diving pool built for the 1984 Olympics, and a fine tennis stadium, but these are reserved for student use.

Alumni House, a circa 1800 clapboard structure, was USC's first building; it was recently moved behind Doheny Memorial Library to allow for the construction of a new main campus entrance at the confluence of Hoover, Exposition, and Figueroa.

St. Elmo Village

4830 St. Elmo Dr.
Los Angeles 90019
*213-931-3409

Twenty-five years ago resident artists transformed a group of rundown bungalows into a community arts center, and they continue to teach free classes for adults on Friday evenings and for kids on Saturdays, thereby expressing the belief that all people can tap into their creative potential by sharing the artistic process.

Black Gallery

107 Santa Barbara Plaza
(adjacent to Baldwin Hills Crenshaw Plaza,
south of Martin Luther King Blvd.)
Los Angeles 90008
*213-294-9024
Wed., Fri., Sat. 1–6 p.m.
Entry: free

This community-based photo gallery is the public face of an educational organization, Black Photographers of California (BPC), which since 1983 has been dedicated to presenting and preserving the works of African-American photographers and other people of color. The group formed as an offshoot of the inaugural photography exhibition at the then-new California African-American Museum in Exposition Park and quickly became a permanent organization dedicated to presenting exhibitions that "preserve history and culture through photography and build bridges to other communities and cultures." Exhibitions have included "Life in a Day of Black L.A.: The Way We See It," which toured nationally, and "Collaborations," which teamed African-American and Korean-American artists to explore the issues underlying the civil disturbances of 1992.

Black Gallery sponsors Photographer's Roundtable, a monthly forum for critiquing work and presenting new technologies; they also present panel discussions and workshops. An exhibition of works from the annual photo contest, with cash and prizes to winners in youth and professional divisions, is a well-loved part of the gallery's schedule. BPC members also staff a workshop program to teach and mentor at-risk kids in L.A. public schools.

Paul Williams, the first African-American to attain prominence as an architect in Southern California, designed the structure of the Second Baptist Church (2412 Griffith Ave.) in 1925 in the subdued Romanesque style associated with Lombardy. The church remains a center of social and cultural activities, and all members of the community are invited to participate; call 213-748-0318 for more specific information on such annual events as: Martin Luther King Day celebrations (Jan.); Forums in Black for Black History Month (Feb.); the community service-oriented PREP—People Resource Participation program (June); and the Festival of Sacred Music, which invites choirs from all over the city (Sept.).

Pan-Africanist Marcus Garvey, one of the most dynamic African-American leaders of the twentieth century, is commemorated annually with a parade and festival at the Elegant Manor (3115 W. Adams Blvd.) on a weekend in August; call *213-735-9642 for information.

The Garvey-designed three-striped flag—red for the struggle for freedom, black for unity, and green for the future—has become an unofficial logo of this celebration as well as of Kwanzaa, the African-themed harvest festival conceived in the mid-1960s by a professor at Cal State Long Beach. Kwanzaa is celebrated at the end of the year for seven consecutive days, each of which is identified with a different value of Nguzo Saba (the principles of unity and a productive life). Kwanzaa has become a staple of public holiday celebrations, especially in the black community; the Watts Towers Arts Center hosts a free festival (310-412-1648), and Leimert Park Village is transformed by a marketplace and activities that span several days (call the African-American Unity Center, *213-789-7300).

Golden State Mutual Life Insurance Company, founded in 1925, has remained one of the country's leading minority-owned financial institutions. It celebrated the history of African-Americans in California in two murals commissioned in 1949 for its headquarters at 1999 West Adams Boulevard. The murals and 200 works by black artists that have since been accumulated in the collection may be viewed by appointment only. Call *213-731-1131 for information.

William Andrews Clark Memorial Library

2520 Cimarron St.
Los Angeles 90018
*213-731-8529

This has been a hidden treasure for too long: once an extraordinary destination reached only by invitation, the Clark Library, which is the flagship of UCLA's Center for Seventeenth- and Eighteenth-century Studies (310-206-8552), has expanded its public outreach in the past few years. Its Sunday-afternoon chamber

music series quickly became so popular that reservations are now awarded by lottery—get your application in during the autumn months—and its Poetry Afternoons are rapidly gaining a following. Symposia presenting recent scholarship on the early modern period are mainly for the initiated, but public programs and lectures on subjects of more general interest are occasionally offered.

Most importantly, the 1926 Italianate brick building, designed by Robert Farquhar and bequeathed to UCLA in 1934, is now open to the public (Mon.–Fri. 9 a.m.–4:45 p.m.). Neither an appointment nor a UCLA library card is required to use the on-site facilities, and librarians will conduct a building tour and show highlights of the collection to individuals or groups who call in advance. The collection strengths reflect the interests of William Andrews Clark Jr., who used the proceeds of his family's mining operations in Montana to compete with other monied bibliophiles like Huntington and Folger for prize acquisitions during the heyday of American book collecting. He focused on three areas that remain the core of the library's collection: English history and literature of the seventeenth and eigh-

teenth centuries (with special emphasis on the Restoration), and the works of Irish writer Oscar Wilde (1854–1900). Clark's personal interest in fine printing coincided with a turn-of-the-century revival of British production, which is documented in complete editions of books printed by the Doves and Kelmscott Presses. Clark librarians have continued to build this part of the collection, acquiring the archives of Eric Gill (whose typeface, Perpetua, we chose as the name for our press because its legibility makes it especially well suited to book typography). The library is a repository of fine American printing in the Arts and Crafts tradition, especially the fine presses of California, including those of Ward Ritchie, Saul and Lillian Marks (Plantin Press), and Patrick Reagh.

To spend a day reading in the gracious building, strolling its five acres of formal gardens and lawns, and rediscovering the West Adams neighborhood—one of the first and most sumptuous suburban developments in the relentless march of housing tracts west from downtown—this must be one of the great treasures of Southern California life.

Chamber Music in Historic Sites, a program of the Da Camera Society at Mount St. Mary's College, regularly holds events at the elegant Doheny Mansion on Chester Place. The doors open at 7:30 p.m., music begins at 8 p.m., and there is a catered reception following the performance; audiences are asked to dress compatibly with the formal elegance of the setting. Designed in 1900 by Theodore Eisen and Sumner Hunt as part of a sumptuous fifteen-acre residential development, the mansion is a French Gothic chateau complete with a Tiffany-designed glass ceiling. Call 310-440-1351 for the schedule of concerts at the Doheny Mansion and other historic sites.

The Doheny family funded construction of the neighborhood Saint Vincent Catholic Church (621 W. Adams Blvd.), an ornate 1925 design by Albert C. Martin with exterior decoration done in the Spanish baroque style called "Churrigueresque"; inside, there are painted ceilings and colorful tilework.

Vermont Square Branch Library (1201 W. 48th St.; *213-290-7405), built in 1913 with funds provided by the Carnegie Foundation, was the first branch library in the city system. The architecture is Italian Renaissance in style; the red tile roof and light-colored bricks frame an elaborate cream-colored terra-cotta frieze. The building was refurbished with funds from a 1989 library bond issue to comply with seismic codes and accommodate modern library technology. Through the patronage of Wells Fargo Bank, this branch has been made a "virtual electronic library," with computer workstations that link it to the resources of the Central Library as well as other databases. Functional library furniture created by artist Nobuho Nagasawa includes eleven stools scaled for preschoolers in the shape of letters that spell "imagination," and a glass table into which titles of books once banned from U.S. schools or libraries have been etched.

Leimert Park, a residential community in the Crenshaw district, was laid out by Olmsted and Olmsted. With its lovely curving, landscaped streets, Leimert Park has been one of Los Angeles's most pleasant places to live since it was developed in 1930; more recently it has become the center of a cultural renaissance in the African-American community.

A decade ago, Marla Gibbs, a successful television actress who got her professional start in free theater classes at a community center in Watts, spearheaded the community revitalization by purchasing the old Leimert Theater (3341 W. 43rd Pl. at Degnan Blvd.) and a large adjoining building. Renamed the **Vision Complex,** these facilities include a 1,000-seat theater, a ninety-nine-seat theater, and banquet and meeting rooms. At present, the complex is rented to a variety of organizations presenting live theater and musical productions (ranging from gospel, jazz, and R&B), and the Leimert Park Jazz Festival is held here in September. The **Crossroads Arts Academy and Steel Light Orchestra for Children** (310-301-4727), which provides art, theatre, and music training for kids, has already been relocated here, where it has room to expand its educational programming. **Marla's Memory Lane** (2323 Martin Luther King Blvd.; *213-294-8430) is another musical venue operated by the energetic woman who launched a neighborhood's renaissance.

World Stage Performance Space (4344 Degnan Blvd.) is managed by three musicians (including drummer Billy Higgins, honored in 1997 by the National Endowment for the Arts as an American Jazz Master), and it features some of the finest musicians in Southern California at its in-

expensive concerts on Friday and Saturday evenings. As a center for fine jazz, it is also a destination four times a year for the KLON (88.1 FM) Jazz Caravan; call 562-985-5566 for information. Free workshops for young musicians (Sat. noon–4 p.m.) offer a chance to play with and learn from masters; these began as a summer program but will be continued in ten-week sessions throughout the year. To counter the lack of music education provided by public schools, these workshops use ear training, sight reading, and harmonics to familiarize participants with the structure and sound of music; young people interested in participating, along with the general public, are invited to drop by, or call World Stage at *213-293-2451 for more information. Good music is also a regular feature of **Fifth Street Dick's Coffee Company** (3335 W. 43rd Pl.; *213-296-3970).

The two southernmost blocks of Degnan Boulevard are the heart of Leimert Park's commercial district: low-rise storefronts have attracted many merchants sympathetic to the cultural goals of the area. **Museum in Black** (4331 Degnan Blvd.; *213-292-9528; Mon.–Fri. noon–6 p.m.) is a gallery crowded with traditional African artifacts; drums and freestanding sculpture fill the floor space and the walls are covered with hundreds of masks. Upstairs, the owner displays his personal collection (which is not for sale) of advertising, signs, and dolls depicting black people. Across the street, the **Brockman Gallery** (4334 Degnan Blvd.; *213-294-3766) shows local and contemporary artists.

Leimert Park Fine Art Gallery (3351 W. 43rd St., *213-299-0319; daily 10 a.m.–8 p.m.), presents changing exhibitions and offers classes for kids and art workshops—including reverse painting on glass—for adults. **The Dance Collective** (4327 Degnan Blvd.; *213-292-1538) teaches various forms of West African dance, with separate classes for adults and children, as well as jazz and modern dance, drumming, and kung fu; the cost is about $10 per class. **KAOS Network** (4343 Degnan Blvd.; *213-293-4303) is a multimedia arts center; its programs and activities range from poetry readings and concerts to a studio where young people can record music and make videos and films.

Leimert Park Festivals maintains a hotline with information on its community events, including the springtime Family Fest and the weekend of great jazz at the Jazz Festival in September; call *213-960-1625.

Eso Won Books
is an established center of
African-American literary
life, but at a new address
(3655 S. La Brea Ave.,
*213-294-0324;
Mon.–Sat. 10 a.m.–7 p.m.,
Sun. noon–5 p.m.).

Bright Lights,
a multicultural children's
bookstore, stands out
for its stock and service
(phone orders accepted
twenty-four hours a day
and processed promptly),
as well as such popular
programs as storytelling.
Drop by 8461 S. Van Ness
Avenue, Inglewood 90305,
or call *213-971-1296.

Kenneth Hahn State Recreation Area

4100 S. La Cienega Blvd.
(Enter from La Cienega between
Rodeo Rd. and Stocker St.)
*213-298-3660

A reservoir at one end, a lake near the entry kiosk, and the Olympic Forest and Pond at the other end are major features of this large recreation area, which includes seven picnic areas (that can be rented for parties), a large playground, a separate swing area, and a community center.

Museum of African American Art

Robinsons-May Dept. Store, 3rd Fl.
Baldwin Hills Crenshaw Plaza
4005 S. Crenshaw Blvd.
Los Angeles 90008
*213-294-7071
Thurs.–Sat. 11 a.m.–6 p.m., Sun. noon–5 p.m.
Entry: free

Baldwin Hills Crenshaw Plaza hosts many performances of interest to the large black community in the surrounding residential area, and it also contains the Museum of African American Art, which gives this retail center an important cultural function. The museum hosts four changing exhibitions each year and offers educational programs on related themes. Unfortunately the museum has little space to display the art of African-descended people that it has conserved; its collections include African objects, as well as art produced in the Caribbean, South America, and the United States. Palmer Hayden, one of the leading artists of the Harlem Renaissance, left many of his works and his personal papers to the Museum of African American Art, making it a center for the study of that very creative period of black art in America. School groups are welcomed enthusiastically at the museum and treated to docent-led tours.

There are three separate organizations offering library services to the residents of Los Angeles County: the city library system is described along with its flagship Central Branch in the Downtown chapter of this book (pp. 13–14); the Metropolitan Community Library System is a consortium of independent cities throughout the county which provide library services within their areas. The county of Los Angeles also operates library facilities in unincorporated sections of the city. In addition to fulfilling the basic needs of these communities, the county system has assembled special collections that reflect each area's particular interests and ethnic makeup.

Black Resource Center, at A.C. Bilbrew Library (150 E. El Segundo Blvd., Los Angeles 90061; 310-538-3350) was established within the county library system in 1978 to support research on the unique social, historical, musical, and cultural aspects of the black experience in America. The collection includes primary sources and biographical information on African-American leaders, and maintains current information from a wide range of periodicals and newspapers on contemporary issues.

The Huntington Park Library (6518 Miles Ave.; *213-583-1461) has become the repository of a 10,000-piece collection on Native-Americans, which forms the nucleus of the county's American Indian Resource Center. In addition to books and newspapers, the collection has records, cassettes, films, and videos covering many aspects of traditional culture and current concerns, and much of it can be borrowed. Among the categories represented in the collection: tribal cultural histories, covering spiritual values and ceremonies; history, including biographies of leaders and relations with the U.S. government; art, featuring traditions in beadwork, pottery, jewelry, and basketry; and literary traditions, both oral and written. There are approximately 45,000 Native-Americans in L.A. County, but the population has routinely been undercounted, a condition the American Indian Resource Center tries to correct with an annual seminar on genealogy; it is offered in November, which is Native-American Heritage Month. Using census rolls on microfilm, the librarian shows participants how to legitimize claims to being Native-American.

William Grant Still Community Arts Center

2520 W. View St.
Los Angeles 90016
*213-734-1164
Tues.–Fri. noon–5 p.m., Sat.–Sun. noon–4 p.m.
Entry: free

First African Methodist Episcopalian (AME) Church (2270 Harvard Walk; *213-735-1251) has a mural in the sanctuary entitled God and Us by artist Eddie Edwards.

This small facility tucked between Adams Boulevard and the Santa Monica (10) Freeway is funded by the City of Los Angeles Cultural Affairs Department and acts as an information and arts center for the African-American community. It hosts an annual exhibition of black dolls during the holiday season, as well as changing displays of fine arts, historical exhibitions, and crafts in its galleries throughout the year.

The center is named for William Grant Still (1898–1978), a former resident of the West Adams area who rose from poverty in Mississippi to study at Oberlin University in Ohio. He became one of the most acclaimed and prolific American composers of all time, working in opera, symphonic, and popular styles. He established the precedent for black achievement in many areas of music: he was the first African-American to conduct an American symphony orchestra, leading the Los Angeles Philharmonic in a 1936 concert at the Hollywood Bowl, and the first to have an opera of his composition performed at the New York Opera Company. In Still's memory, the center sponsors music education and presents concerts as part of its annual programming.

Work by Southern California artists selected for the biennial juried exhibition held by the Cultural Affairs Department is featured on the summer exhibition schedule during odd-numbered years. Workshops tied in with exhibitions are aimed at all ages, from toddlers to junior high school students, and this busy arts center serves the African-American community with children's programs in fall, spring, and summer sessions lasting from six to twelve weeks. The low-fee classes, held after school and on Saturdays, include music (such as piano and voice), visual arts, and storytelling. The Creative After-school Alternatives Latchkey program is a model project that engages children living near the center in fun and educational activities, offered free of charge. Call *213-734-1164 for a class schedule and enrollment information.

The African Marketplace and Cultural Faire—which started more than a decade ago as a small festival on the patio at William Grant Still Community Arts Center—today is incorporated as one of the most popular events in the black community. The three-weekend event, held from mid-August through Labor Day at Rancho Cienega Park (5001 Rodeo Rd.) features more than 200 hours of live music on six concert stages and a 5,000-seat amphitheater, with performances of jazz, reggae, blues, soca, salsa, and gospel. Many community-based and local organizations, including the Still Arts Center, the California African-American Museum, and UCLA's Fowler Museum mount temporary exhibitions that reach a wide audience at this fair; the Medicine Tree addresses health issues and highlights services that exist in the community; more than 300 vendors display their crafts; and the food festival offers cuisines from the African diaspora. The Children's Village schedules performances and interactive workshops for kids—face painting, mask-making, mural painting, and building musical instruments—in a festive atmosphere with strolling clowns, storytellers, and drummers. There are pony rides, a petting zoo, and carnival diversions. General admission is $3 and children under ten are free. Call the Still Arts Center at *213-734-1164 for more information.

Western States Black Research Center

3617 Montclair St.
Los Angeles 90018
*213-737-3292
By appt. only

In assembling the extraordinary collection of books, films, music, documents, and memorabilia, Mayme Clayton, a professional librarian, has saved precious information on the history and cultural heritage of Americans of African descent for future generations. Most of the archives are stored at Clayton's home, which is open only by appointment, but the film holdings were transferred to climate-controlled vaults at PRO-TEK. Dr. Clayton is happy to assist teachers or researchers in using the collections.

Among the center's community outreach programs is the **Black American Cinema Society** (BACS), which programs an annual two-week marathon of films featuring African-Americans, including silent films, early talkies, and more recent productions. Dr. Clayton can provide a schedule of the film festival, which is also sent to members. Another annual activity is the BACS awards, which are presented to African American filmmakers in a judged competition. For membership information, application, and guidelines for BACS awards, write to the center.

A hyperrealistic portrait of Cecil Fergerson (an arts activist and curator), painted by Richard Wyatt as a tribute to his mentor on the exterior wall of the Watts Towers Arts Center, was recently restored. A sculpture by John Outterbridge— a concrete pyramid embedded with tile shards—pays homage to Rodia's monumental work.

The Dunbar Hotel (4225 S. Central Ave.; *213-234-7882) was the locus of much of the finest jazz produced in Los Angeles as well as the accommodation of choice for many black performers. After facing demolition in 1988, the hotel was converted to senior-citizen housing, and many of its residents have personal memories of Central Avenue in its heyday. The rest of us can revisit that era through the images and artifacts collected for the Vernon Central Community History Exhibit, installed in the old lobby.

Central Avenue, about fifteen blocks east of Exposition Park, is again animated with sounds of jazz on the first weekend in August when the Central Avenue Jazz Festival showcases well-known performers and schedules jam sessions. Call 213-485-2437 for information on this free event, which is sponsored by the City of Los Angeles Cultural Affairs Department.

Watts Towers Arts Center

1727 E. 107th St.
Los Angeles 90002
213-847-4646
Towers: always visible from the street
Arts Center: Tues.–Sat. 10 a.m.–4 p.m.,
Sun. noon–4 p.m.

The Cultural Affairs Department now administers this monumental piece of folk art, which was constructed single-handedly by Simon Rodia over the course of thirty-three years. Rodia, an Italian immigrant, began working in 1921 on a sculptural environment in his yard that soon dominated his home (which burned down in 1955). His comment, "I had in mind to do something big, and I did it," is often quoted, perhaps because Rodia generally refused to explain his creation. "Big" is accurate—the tallest of the spires is built of 100-foot-tall, reinforced concrete columns—but "magical" is a more telling description: stepping into Rodia's walled compound is like entering the human imagination

BLUE LINE

The artwork on this line begins between stations: in the tunnel between the **Seventh Street Metro Center** station and the **Pico** station, artist Thomas Eatherton's 1993 *Unity*—eighty-two fiber-optic "light paintings" of blue and white light—symbolizes the always-changing experience of life in L.A. Moving south from downtown to the **Pico** station, *Time and Presence* (1993) by Robin Brailsford is a work about the smallness of humans compared to the vast spaces of earth and the cosmos. At the **Grand Street** station, Mark Lere's *Who, What, Where?* (1994) contains images and texts sandblasted into the platform pavement, with travel used as a metaphor for the pursuit of dreams and goals. *Hope, Dream*—stainless steel portraits of neighborhood residents—and *Path, Focus, Belief* (both 1993) by Sandra Rowe at the **San Pedro** station are intended to honor the community's many immigrant populations and their aspirations. The **Washington** station is painted in bright primary colors and has colorful banners throughout, as well as painted steel panels attached to the track fences; all of these elements make up Elliott Pinkney's *Running for the Blue Line* (1997). The area around the **Vernon** station has been a mainstay of manufacturing in Southern California for more than one hundred years, and Horace Washington's 1994 *A Tribute to Industry* salutes the businesses that surround the station. The collaborative team of East Los Streetscapers has installed *South Central Codex* and

Slauson Serenade (both 1995) at the **Slauson** station; four ceramic/concrete panels at street level celebrate the shared values of church, school, and family, while the platform level boasts 96 porcelain enameled steel panels surveying the history of the South Central area. In the shadow of the Watts Towers at the **103rd Street** station, *Blue Line Totems in Red* (1994) by Roberto Salas salutes the much-beloved "red cars" of the defunct Pacific Electric Railway that served L.A. until the fifties. Eva Cockcroft's six dual-sided ceramic tile murals entitled *Compton: Past, Present and Future* (1995) for the **Compton** station feature historic local scenes with a particular emphasis on the arrival of ethnic groups (African-American, Latino, and Samoan) that have made important contributions to the city's character. At the **Artesia** station—artesia meaning "a place with a

Blue Line map:
UNION STATION
CIVIC CENTER
PERSHING SQ.
PICO
METRO CENTER
GRAND
SAN PEDRO
WASHINGTON
VERNON
SLAUSON
FLORENCE
FIRESTONE
103RD STREET
IMPERIAL/ WILMINGTON
COMPTON
ARTESIA
DEL AMO
WARDLOW
WILLOW
PACIFIC COAST HWY
ANAHEIM
PACIFIC
TRANSIT MALL
5TH STREET
1ST STREET

Unfortunately, few people have had that experience since the towers were shaken in the 1994 earthquake; tours were temporarily suspended and of this writing have yet to be resumed.

The towers are not massive, solid piles of masonry: they are open structures of frets and supports built with salvaged steel rods and pipes that were covered with cement. Every surface on the sculptures—as well as the ground below and the walls that surround them—is embellished: tiles, glass bottles, rocks, corncobs, horseshoes, and pottery fragments encrust the structures, and wild patterns of hearts and scrolls and imprints of hammers and other tools cover the concrete floor. Although Rodia built his structure without scaffolds—using only a window-washer's belt to climb the towers as he built—they are today obscured by metal scaffolding as extensive repairs and restoration continue.

Watts Towers Arts Center offers free workshops for children and adults year round. Its summer schedule includes a Sunday-afternoon adults-only class in West African dance, as well as a half-dozen choices for kids aged six to seventeen, Tuesday through Saturday. Acting/drama workshops, understanding architecture, handcrafted books, comic-book art, drumming/percussion, and black-and-white photography are among the subjects taught in the free eight-week-long classes; no preregistration is permitted for these sessions, and because enrollment is limited, groups are not welcome. School groups can visit the Watts Towers site and enjoy participatory workshops in the adjacent Arts Center; call 213-485-1795 for information about workshops, classes, and programs for school groups. A small gallery (Tues.–Sat. 10 a.m.–4 p.m., Sun. noon–4 p.m.; free) in the Arts Center offers

Compton

well where water rises to the surface"—Lynn Aldrich created *Blue Line Oasis* (1996) where, in addition to soothing respites evoked by oases, two symbols recur: wishes and longings (in the form of a wishing well/circular bench with trompe l'oeil coins, and in ceramic "wishes" from members of the community) and water (evoked through poetic metaphors and mosaic tile images of waves). *Del Amo Wheel* (1997) at the **Del Amo** station is a cast-stone cartwheel in the center of the platform, and it contains puzzles inspired by local history; artist Colin Gray was inspired by ornate designs on Indian temples. Jacqueline Dreager has created *Great Gathering Place* (1992) for the **Wardlow** station, taking the name of the work from the translation of the Chumash word for the area—puvunga; elements of the work include a sundial (symbol of home as the center of one's universe) inscribed with a Wallace Stevens poem, an etched glass disk, and a three-piece sculpture group. Twelve concrete, tile, and aluminum discs—representing principles deemed by various Long Beach community residents as important in a well-rounded person (faith, family, honesty, education, and hope, among others)—make up Joe Lewis's *Twelve Principles* (1994) installed

at the **Pacific Coast Highway** station. At the **Anaheim** station in Long Beach, fourteen photomontages were fabricated in porcelain-enamel panels; entitled *Local Odysseys,* Terry Braunstein's 1994 work recognizes local heroes who have made unique contributions. Jim Isermann's *Failed Ideals* (1995), at the **Fifth Street** station, creates in stained-glass architectural details from buildings (both extant and demolished) that make Long Beach unique. *Breezy and Delightful* (1994) at the **First Street** station reflects the diverse cultural heritage of Long Beach; Paul Tzanetopoulos uses textile designs—with influences from such sources as Cambodian shadow puppets and modern graphics—on wind-driven kinetic sculptures installed on the platform. At the **Transit Mall** station, *Angel Train* (1995) by Patrick Mohr acts as a metaphor for the journeys of life, realized in the artwork as a dialogue between two children as they make their way through their lives. At the last stop before the train heads north again, the **Pacific** station has twelve Venetian glass mosaic panels entitled *We Know Who We Are* (1995); artist June Edmonds made sketches of community residents and distinct symbols representing the cultural histories of Long Beach's diverse groups. If funding is secured, the Blue Line will be extended north from Union Station, with twelve more stations.

—*Sherri Schottlaender*

Free art workshops for families, Sunday Open Sunday, are a regular feature of programming at the Arts Center.

The Watts Towers are the site of many musical events, including a winter and summer series of free concerts in a variety of styles, and the annual festival celebrating jazz, gospel, and rhythm and blues which coincides with Day of the Drum celebrations in late September.

changing exhibitions of contemporary art, including the works of Southern California artists selected for the biennial juried exhibition held by the Cultural Affairs Department. Pieces from the Art Center's large collection of ethnic musical instruments are often on display.

The Promenade of Prominence, located at 103rd Street and Success Avenue, was founded in 1988 by community leader Edna Aliewine, one of the forces behind the Watts Christmas parade (an annual event for over thirty years). The Promenade honors individuals who have made a lasting contribution to the betterment of the community; it is a "walk of fame" that provides inspiration and hope to local residents as well as visitors. The first inductee was the late Kenneth Hahn, then a county supervisor, and there are now over thirty-five leaders who have their names enshrined on the heart-shaped markers that make up the Promenade of Prominence. Politicians, community activists, religious leaders, and prominent professionals are among those honored; some of the names on the walk are Danny J. Bakewell, Sybil Brand, Willie R. Brown, Jr., Ron Burkel, Barbara Butler, Rev. Toney Chisum, Johnnie L. Cochran, Alice Harris, Celes King, and Maxine Waters, among others.

Watts Labor Community Action Center (WLCAC)

10950 S. Central Ave.
Los Angeles 90059
*213-563-5600

A peaceful seven-acre enclosed site in the heart of Los Angeles, the WCLAC welcomes visitors: it encourages community residents to participate in the center's activities and find a refuge from the noise and other environmental hazards that plague this neighborhood; a visit by those who don't live in the area will help to dispel the negative stereotypes too often associated with Watts. An important goal of the center is to reveal the community as it defines itself through artistic and cultural expression.

Outside the center's complex, two works are on view. *The Mother of Humanity*, a bronze sculpture by Nigel Binns, celebrates the contributions of women to civilization; the monument is set in a tranquil water garden. Painted on the main building's 330-foot-long facade is *Mudtown Flats*, a mural of historic sites on Central Avenue, which provides a rich backdrop for outdoor events.

The Civil Rights Museum is an important focal point of the center's programming, with docent-led tours available to individuals and groups by appointment (call *213-563-5639). The museum tour includes a reconstructed film set that realistically depicts the hold of a slave ship; WLCAC commissioned artist Charles Dickson to produce additional sculptures of human forms—made from body casts of local students—which are crammed into the space to evoke the deplorable treatment of those exiled into slavery. This searing image is intended to be so revolting that its history can never be forgotten. The tour continues with a re-created Mississippi Delta dirt road, meant to evoke one aspect of life in the deep South in the 1960s.

Freedom Hall contains an exhibition entitled "Countdown to Eternity," which focuses on the Civil Rights movement of the 1960s and the life of Dr. Martin Luther King Jr.; the award-winning photographs were taken by Benjamin Fernandez. A complementary exhibition of works by photojournalist David Bacon is also on view, depicting the working and living conditions of Mexican workers in California. In adjacent Meridian Hall, a gallery space presents thematic exhibitions featuring emerging and midcareer artists four times per year (Tues.–Sat. 10 a.m.–5 p.m., Sun. 1–5 p.m.; adults $5, seniors/students $3, children under 12 free).

The center hosts a variety of programs in its three performance venues (which include the Tell-It Theater, a ninety-nine-seat theater-in-the-round), including Bones and Blues, an evening entertainment of dominoes and music. Plans are currently underway for the Watts Central Marketplace, which will house art studios, a restaurant, and retail facilities.

Charles R. Drew University of Medicine and Science (1730 E. 118th St., Los Angeles 90059; *213-563-4800), one of only four African-American colleges recognized by the U.S. Congress, not only educates physicians in its graduate school but also staffs twenty-three Head Start centers and a magnet high school for medical studies. Saturday Science Academy is an activity-based enrichment program that meets for two eight-week sessions (Oct. and Mar.) each year; kids can only enroll when they are between the ages of six and eight, but then can participate all the way through high school. Each eight-week session costs $150, but scholarships are available for all students in need; call *213-563-4926 to get information on this long-term learning activity beloved by kids.

One of Drew University's more accessible and popular events is the Jazz at Drew Legacy Music Series, which showcases about fifteen performances in a garden setting on the campus. The proceeds from the annual jazz weekend benefit the scholarship fund. Call *213-563-9395 for a roster of performers at this October event or for tickets (general admission per day, noon–10 p.m.: $25 in advance, $30 at gate).

California State University, Dominguez Hills

1000 E. Victoria St.
Carson 90747
310-243-3300

This campus of the State University system enrolled its first students in 1965, became a full university in 1977, and today enrolls 12,500 students on its 346-acre campus that was once part of the Spanish land grant Rancho San Pedro, located today northeast of the intersection of the San Diego (405) and Harbor (110) Freeways. It is home to the largest nursing degree program in California, and to the California Academy of Mathematics and Science, a public high school whose students are chosen from eleven school districts.

Allied-Signal Challenger Learning Center (310-243-2627)—funded by the Torrance-based aerospace company and the families of astronauts who died when the *Challenger*

space shuttle exploded in 1986—is a permanent learning center that simulates a futuristic space station. Its hands-on exhibits involve middle school students (grades five through eight) in the applications of science, math, and technology. More than 12,000 students from Southern California school districts visit the center each year.

The Olympic Velodrome (310-516-4000), a track built for cycling events of the 1984 Summer Games, offers many programs for cycling enthusiasts. It is open to those members of the larger community who complete a training program or can document prior track-cycling experience on Mondays and Wednesdays (5:30–9:30 p.m. or by appt.). The Velodrome also offers classes for adults and hosts races on Friday nights from March to September.

Dominguez Ranch Adobe

18127 S. Alameda St.
Downey 90242
310-631-5981
Tues.–Wed., 2nd and 3rd Sun. of month 1–3 p.m.
Entry: free

For his years of service to Father Junípero Serra, Juan José Dominguez was rewarded with the first Spanish land grant, 75,000 acres deeded to him in 1784. The Dominguez family remained involved in local politics and civic affairs and lived until 1922 in the adobe that was built in 1826; with no male heirs, they gave the property to a religious seminary.

The six original rooms of the adobe have been furnished with pieces from the Dominguez family and other objects that evoke the period of their occupation. In addition, rooms are dedicated to other pioneering families from the area—Carson, Del Amo, and Watson—and to the railroad and aviation industries. Dioramas of the 1910 Dominguez air show, the first international air event in the U.S., and photos and models that identify this area as the birthplace of California aerospace are in one room; small-scale steam trains occupy another.

The city of Norwalk maintains two buildings linked to local history: the Eastlake-style cottage built in the 1870s by Gilbert Sproul, the founder of Norwalk, has been moved to a city park at 12237 East Sproul Street, where displays on events in the community's evolution are installed. The house that the organizer of the Norwalk school system built for himself at 12432 Mapledale Street has been restored and that period in the town's evolution evoked with vintage furniture and photographs. Both sites are open Tuesday to Saturday 1 to 4 p.m.; free admission.

194

**Compton Farmers Market
"Hub City," east side of
Alameda St. at
Compton Blvd.
Fri. 10 a.m.–5 p.m.**

**South Gate Farmers
Market
South Gate Park at
Tweedy Blvd. and
Walnut Ave.
Mon. 9 a.m.–1 p.m.**

**Gardena Farmers Market
13000 S. Van Ness Ave.
Sat. 6:30 a.m.–noon**

**Downey City Library
11121 Brookshire Ave
Downey 90241
562-923-3256**

**Norwalk Farmers Market
Alondra Blvd. west of
Pioneer Blvd.
Tues. 10 a.m.–1 p.m.**

**Bellflower Farmers
Market
John Simms Park,
Oak and Clark Aves.
Mon. 10 a.m.–2 p.m.**

The oldest surviving **McDonald's** (vintage 1953) still stands on Florence Avenue in Downey, thanks to vigilance by the National Trust for Historic Preservation and the Los Angeles Conservancy. The golden arches may not have been introduced here, but these are their earliest form; combined with the flying wedge roof they define fast-food architecture of the 1950s.

Downey was also the site of **Rockwell International**'s Space Systems Division, which built the ships for the Apollo missions and the space shuttles *Columbia*, *Challenger*, *Discovery*, *Atlantis*, and *Endeavor*. It's been downsized and rebadged as Boeing, but the city of Downey has acquired sixty-eight acres of the former site, with no money down and twenty years to pay. Will this bit of history be recycled as an office park? Or, as some visionaries hope, will it become Space City: a museum, technocenter, and virtual reality space theme park? The Aerospace Legacy Foundation is working with the city government and Boeing administration to prevent the cultural heritage of this community from being obliterated. Call the Foundation (562-927-5236) to join the effort.

Western Museum of Flight
**Jack Northrop Field
at Hawthorne Municipal Airport**
12016 S. Prairie Ave.
Hawthorne 90250
310-332-6228
Tues.–Sat. 10 a.m.–3 p.m.
Entry: free

Unless the Downey visionaries realize their dream, this 1950 Quonset hut filled with restoration-projects-in-process is the closest thing to a local monument to the aviation industry that once employed so many citizens in this area. There are aircraft designed and built by Douglas and Lockheed on display, but the Bat—a manned glider with an unusual wing structure, a secret project designed by Jack Northrop during World War II—attracts the most attention.

Downey History Center (12548 Rives Ave.; 562-862-2777) features exhibits on John Gately Downey, the seventh governor of California, who gave his name to this area, but local aviation history is the museum's primary focus (Wed.–Thurs. 9 a.m.–2 p.m., 3rd Sat. of month 10 a.m.–3 p.m.)

Downey Museum of Art (10419 Rives Ave.; 562-861-0419) features twentieth-century art, primarily made by local artists, with four annual exhibitions that showcase developments in glass, ceramics, metal sculpture, and jewelry. The annual exhibition of art by local schoolchildren attracts an enthusiastic audience (Wed.–Sun. noon–5 p.m.).

Artesia, south of the Artesia (91) Freeway and east of the 605 Freeway, has become the commercial center for the growing population of immigrants of Indian descent. Merchants along a few blocks of Pioneer Boulevard, which has become known as Little India, service more than 50,000 Indians within a ten-mile radius; another 200,000 people whose ancestors came from the subcontinent now make their homes in Southern California. Word of mouth leads consumers to beauty shops where hands are stained with intricate designs rendered in henna, an ancient practice called *mehndi* that has been adopted by Hollywood trendsetters, and stores sell saris, samosas, and spices for curry.

Cerritos acknowledges that it is the birthplace of Pat Nixon, the former president's wife, with a permanent First Ladies Display in the Cerritos Public Library, adjacent to the City Hall at the intersection of Bloomfield Avenue and 183rd Street (562-924-5776). The library was built in the 1960s, then expanded and extensively remodeled in the late 1980s with a new children's library and theater and an arts and crafts room.

The city of Cerritos also operates a state-of-the-art Swim Center, with an Olympic-size (fifty-meter-wide) pool, at 13150 East 166th Street. Lap swimming and classes for different ages and levels of proficiency are offered to all, but a few hours each day are dedicated to recreational swim times that are open only to residents of Cerritos and their guests. Call 562-407-2600 for schedule and fees.

Cerritos Center for the Performing Arts (12700 Center Court Dr.; 562-916-8500/800-300-4345) is a brand new, beautifully designed theater at the outer edge of L.A. County, equidistant to Long Beach and Anaheim. It is drawing crowds, becoming within five years of presenting its first season the top-grossing venue of less than 3,000 seats in California, although it produces none of its own shows. See Theater and Dance, page 77.

THE GREEN LINE

In the westernmost station of this line, in Redondo Beach at the **Marine/Redondo** station, Carl Cheng's *Space Information Station* (1995) refers to two important aspects of the area: the coastal area is represented by an imaginary sea bottom that moves upward to a wavelike canopy on the platform; the significance of the aerospace industry on the local economy is evoked by geodes, "satellite" sculptures, and an imprint of the first footstep on the moon. Renee Petropoulos's untitled work at the **Douglas/Rosecrans** station explores the idea of "location"—physical places, a person's location in a place, and personal relationships. *For Your Intellectual Entertainment* (1995) is a thirty-foot-tall wire hand launching a "paper" airplane into the community that surrounds the **El Segundo/Nash** station; artist Daniel J. Martinez also designed seating, handrail patterns, stairwells that reference local red-and-white smokestacks, and terrazzo paving. The **Mariposa/Nash** station—"mariposa" means butterfly in Spanish—contains many references to this insect because the community was instrumental in efforts to save the rare local El Segundo blue butterfly; *Divine Order: The Manifestation of the Soaring Spirit* (n.d.) by Charles Dickson incorporates the butterfly motif. Passengers at the **Aviation/I-105** station experience the 1950s through Richard Turner's untitled work, which references the landscaping and furniture of a mid-century American home. *Companions* (1995), by Mineko Grimmer, is a series of bronze sculptures intended to bring a human scale to the sometimes overwhelming architecture of the **Hawthorne/I-105** station. At the **Crenshaw/I-105** station, Buzz Spector's 1995 *Crenshaw Stories* incorporates seventy-two stories from members of the surrounding community— in Spanish, Korean, Japanese,

Chinese, Thai, Arabic, Russian, and Tagalog—hand-painted onto tile; seventy-two of the most commonly spoken languages in Los Angeles public schools are embedded in the platform, each paired with the word "American." The agricultural legacy of the area adjacent to the **Vermont/I-105** station is evoked in *real green* (n.d.) by Kim Yasuda and Torgen Johnson, who worked to save a large tree that had been scheduled for removal. *Locus: City Imprint* (n.d.) located at the **Harbor Freeway/I-105** station (a very complicated freeway intersection point) seeks to tie South Central L.A.—to heal fractures—to the rest of the city; artist Steve Appleton worked with students from nearby Locke High School, creating entry tiles that have images of their makers' hands. Three artists created works for the **Avalon/I-105** station: Willie Middlebrook's 1995 *Portrait of My People #619* translates images of the area's artistic community into a porcelain-enamel photo-mural intended to honor unsung heroes; John Outterbridge's *Pyramid* (1995), a reinforced-concrete form chosen for its universal appeal and architectural integrity, is embedded with tile mosaics in homage to the nearby Watts Towers; in *Bridge of Culture* (1995) Stanley Wilson's ceramic-tile floor murals (and windscreen and bench designs) incorporate icons from African and Native-American cultures. At the **Wilmington/Imperial** station, where the Green and Blue Lines intersect—artist JoeSam. worked with local children to create *Hide-N-Seek* (1995), which features colorful cut-out figures of children engaged in the classic childhood game. *Celestial Chance* (n.d.) by Sally Weber, installed at the **Long Beach-I 105** station, was inspired by ideas about the sky and stars, in particular by Chumash and Gabrielino-Tongva native pictographs and legends. Erika Rothenberg's *Wall of (Un)Fame* (1995) at the **Lakewood/I-105** station creates a monument to ordinary people, with terra-cotta-colored concrete panels embedded with foot- and handprints and signatures of more than 650 residents of Downey, Bellflower, and Paramount. Meg Cranston's *Suka: Place of the Bees* (1995) at the Green Line's eastern terminus at the **I-605/I-105** station, refers to the Sejat people's name for the area that is now the city of Norwalk and uses a bee motif—in sculptures, silkscreened elevator designs, wall tiles, and pavers— to suggest that the commuters who use the station are as industrious and productive as worker bees.

—*Sherri Schottlaender*

MUSIC

René Engel and
Jason Martin

* indicates an area code
that changes in 1998

The music scene in Los Angeles is incredibly rich and equally eclectic. In addition to the more familiar places to experience music, be sure to check out the lesser-known venues; they often provide the most interesting musical experience, whether because of their creative, nontraditional programming or because of their ambiance and energy. In addition to offering great music, many of these venues reflect Los Angeles's rich artistic, architectural, and cultural heritage.

Discovering the Obvious

Although much of this section is dedicated to the hidden gems available to music lovers, there are certain well-known resources that cannot be overlooked. If you haven't yet sampled these world-class venues, take the next available opportunity.

Dorothy Chandler Pavilion
Music Center
of Los Angeles County
135 N. Grand Ave.
Los Angeles 90012
213-972-7211

The Music Center's Dorothy Chandler Pavilion is home to the Los Angeles Philharmonic Orchestra and the Los Angeles Opera, with other world-class classical performers and ensembles visiting throughout the year. The demise of Pasadena's Ambassador Auditorium left the Pavilion as the county's only central orchestra concert hall. But with the re-

turn of UCLA's Royce Hall in 1998, the eventual opening of Disney Hall right across the street, and orchestras such as the Royal Philharmonic visiting Cerritos, the Music Center's preeminence is open for serious challenge.

Departing managing director Ernest Fleischmann had the wisdom to leave the Philharmonic in the young, energetic, and ultimately capable hands of dashing and talented music director Esa-Pekka Salonen and newly appointed managing director Willem Wijnbergen. The Philharmonic is now poised to become *the* orchestra of the new millennium. In fact, it could be persuasively argued that under Salonen's leadership L.A. may be home to the best orchestra in the world. While some things have changed (Salonen brought in a new concertmaster), others remain the same—the wind sections have always been second to none and they continue to impress. The Phil's audience has become decidedly hip and younger, with the cognoscenti generally assembling for the Sunday matinee performances. Dress down for these afternoon concerts, and go when the orchestra already has a few performances under its belt.

John Anson Ford Amphitheater
2580 Cahuenga Blvd.
Los Angeles 90068
213-974-1396

Some in L.A. may still have a memory of this venue when it was the Pilgrimage Theater, with the cross overlooking this gorgeous outdoor amphitheater carved out of the Hollywood Hills; they may even remember free Sunday afternoon jazz concerts or a particularly hot performance by Doc Watson (guitar), David Grisman

(mandolin), Jerry Garcia (on banjo!), and bluesman Taj Mahal (on bass) in a bluegrass supergroup. The Ford continues to bring exciting popular artists—from Elvis Costello to barefoot diva Cesária Evora of the Cape Verde Islands—as well as numerous chamber music performances to this uniquely intimate venue (with less than 100 feet from the back row to the stage).

Greek Theater
2700 N. Vermont Ave.
Los Angeles 90027
*213-665-1927

Nestled into the base of Griffith Park, the Greek is an outdoor theater that presents the hottest popular performers in a season that generally runs from May until October. Often the final stop for musicians before embarking on a stadium tour, this 7,000-seat space saw the genesis of Neil Diamond's Hot August Nights and hosts Los Lobos's annual homecoming party. Like the Hollywood Bowl (though with only a third of the seating capacity), the Greek combines L.A.'s famous climate with a lovely performance space and ceiling of stars.

Hollywood Bowl
2301 N. Highland Ave.
Los Angeles 90068
*213-850-2000

It's hard to believe that there are still some people who have never been to the Hollywood Bowl. More than a place to hear music, the open-air Bowl is one of the quintessential L.A. experiences, which includes picnicking, balmy weather, stargazing, a view of the Hollywood sign, occasional pyrotechnics, and top-rate performers. The Bowl is the summer home of the L.A. Philharmonic and the Hollywood Bowl Orchestra, which is composed of a fine group of studio musicians and has a recording contract; it is

also the best place to hear Samuel Barber's *Adagio for Strings* punctuated by the occasional obbligato of a wine bottle rolling down the aisle. If you hate people—this venue seats 18,000—and traffic, you may want to stay home with your CDs. The Bowl seems to breed a communal energy, however, and the search for a corkscrew can bring together a surprisingly diverse group of people. While most performances are symphonic, the season includes jazz (for example, the Playboy Jazz Festival), mariachi, and occasionally popular music (such as the landmark performance by the Beatles in 1965). The main drawback is the truly horrific stacked parking, but you can easily avoid this by using a special shuttle; call *213-850-2000 for information.

Universal Amphitheater
100 Universal City Plaza
Universal City 91608
818-622-4440

One of the largest indoor venues (6,200 seats) in Los Angeles, the Universal Amphitheater has played host to many popular acts, from Cheap Trick and the Who to Latino superstar Luis Miguel and leading Filipino singer Lea Salonga. Unremarkable in its architecture, the Amphitheater lost whatever ambiance it had when they added a roof and made it an indoor venue—the powers that be put a lid on the place, literally and figuratively. But the music's the thing, and this is the place to find the hottest contemporary performers.

Free for All

Mounting a direct challenge to the cliché "you get what you pay for," Los Angeles County has seen the rise of a remarkable number of free series. While most people expect free performances to consist of bad barbershop quartets and junior high school jazz ensembles, some of the best live music in town is free to those who will search it out. Some of the most notable free music series are listed below, and they share certain characteristics: they are creatively programmed, held in attractive settings, and often manage to evoke a sense of spontaneity and fun, and most are held in outdoor venues that take advantage of fresh air and incredible views. There are countless festivals and fairs as well as coffeehouses, bars, and restaurants that lure customers with performances that would headline almost anywhere else in the world.

California Plaza Presents
350 S. Grand Ave.
Los Angeles 90012
213-687-2159

Set within a spectacular 1.5-acre urban garden anchored by a 100,000-gallon high-tech fountain, California Plaza's ongoing series epitomizes diversity, with performances ranging from Russia's internationally renowned Kirov Orchestra to the Tejano accordion of Mingo Saldivar y Los Quatro Espadas to the legendary intergalactic big-band jazz of the Sun Ra Arkestra. The highest concentration of performances is found during the summer, with noontime performances midweek, evening performances on weekends, and early afternoon performances on Sundays. The ambiance is open and relaxed, with audience members of all demographics dancing on a side dance floor provided for most concerts.

CITY OF WEST HOLLY-WOOD'S SUMMER SOUNDS

Pacific Design Center Outdoor Amphitheater
8687 Melrose Ave.
West Hollywood 90069
*213-848-6308

Exemplifying the eclectic entertainment opportunities available in Southern California, West Hollywood's Summer Sounds Concert Series has offered everything from edgy alternative rock to traditional Jewish klezmer music. The series takes place on Sunday afternoons from 6 to 7:30 p.m. between June and August.

CONCERTS IN THE PARK

Valley Cultural Center
Warner Park
Woodland Hills 91367
818-704-1547

From local symphonies to international folk groups, the Valley Cultural Center's Concerts in the Park series offers families an excellent Sunday afternoon entertainment option. Performances, scheduled Sundays from June through the end of August (call to confirm dates), begin at 4 p.m. with a local artist or family-oriented entertainment and continue through 7:30 p.m. with an established headliner. Seating is on the lawn, so bring chairs or blankets. Many of the regulars take advantage of the Valley's balmy summer evenings and bring a picnic.

CULVER CITY SUMMER SUNSET MUSIC FESTIVAL

City Hall Courtyard
(9770 Culver Blvd.)
Ivy Substation's Media Park
(9070 Venice Blvd.)
Culver City
310-253-6640

Founded in 1995, this young series, staged two early evenings a week from June through the end of August, draws modest crowds of a few hundred per show. This relatively low-budget operation, which is affiliated with Culver City, has pulled together a strong collection of performers from around Southern California; the eclectic series often manages to book artists who are performing at clubs or other venues around town.

Los Angeles County Museum of Art
5905 Wilshire Blvd.
Los Angeles 90036
*213-857-6000

LACMA presents two year-round free performance series. The Friday Night Jazz Concert Series is performed on the museum's plaza from 5:30 to 8:30 p.m. In addition, the only indoor series in this section, Sundays at Four, presents chamber music in the Bing Theater every week from 4 to 5 p.m. The museum is open during, and for a period after, these performances (though you must pay for admission if not a member). Additional free music festivals are presented throughout the year; call for specific information.

SANTA MONICA PIER TWILIGHT DANCE SERIES

Santa Monica Pier
End of Colorado Ave.
Santa Monica 90401
310-458-8900

With hot performances and a lack of seating that are guaranteed to bring audiences to their feet, this series features exciting music from all cultures. In what has become an ongoing programming coup, the Twilight Dance Series has managed to present the L.A. premiere of a top international artist nearly every summer. There is something magical about going to the literal end of the earth to hear reggae pioneer Toots and the Maytals cooled by an ocean breeze and backed by the sun setting on the Pacific. Performances are held each Thursday, 7:30 to 9:30 p.m., beginning in early July and continuing into early September.

STARLIGHT BOWL SUMMER CONCERT SEASON
1249 Lockheed View Dr.
Burbank 91504
818-238-5400

This is not a free series, but it comes really close, with a negligible ticket price of a few bucks. Nestled in the Burbank hills, the Starlight Bowl affords the audience incredible views of the L.A. basin. This open-air amphitheater is arranged with seats in the front and lawn seating in the back, so you can bring a picnic. Blankets are suggested. The early evening Sunday concerts have included top international performers like Queen Ida, Pacquito d'Rivera, and Christopher Cross, but community and nostalgia acts are more typical fare.

SUMMER NIGHTS AT MOCA

The Museum of Contemporary Art (250 S. Grand Ave.)
Geffen Contemporary at MOCA
(152 N. Central Ave.)
Los Angeles 90012
213-621-1749

Focusing on jazz, these performances are held each Thursday, 5 to 8 p.m., from June through September. Audiences are invited to enjoy both the performances and the museum free of charge. At the California Plaza location the sight lines and sound suffer from the plaza setting, but the skyline and the relaxed energy of hundreds of downtowners gleefully avoiding rush-hour traffic can give you the feeling that you're at the best of all possible cocktail parties.

WHITTIER CONCERTS IN THE PARK

Central Park (13200 Bailey St.)
Parnell Park (10711 Scott Ave.)
Whittier
562-464-3430

The concerts—presented Mondays (Central Park) and Thursdays (Parnell Park), July through August, from 7 to 8:30 p.m.—focus largely on local talent, but all performers are professionals with an interesting array of musical styles. While neither location was designed for performances and seating is on the lawn, picnicking is an option, and Parnell Park includes a dance floor to allow audience members to get into the act.

Performing Arts Centers and Performance Series

The large concentration of performing artists in Southern California—including musicians, dancers, and actors—has led to the growth of performing arts centers and performance series meant to bring all of these art forms into the individual communities. While many of these venues and series attempt to reflect the eclectic nature of the region, each is unique in its musical programming. Sample a few performances from the many series to see which best suits your tastes.

Alex Theater
216 N. Brand Blvd.
Glendale 91203
818-243-2539

Concerts at the Alex span all forms of music, from contemporary to classical and country to klezmer. Once a grand motion picture palace, the 1,450-seat theater retains all of the splendor of golden-era Hollywood, though from the mezzanine and balcony this remarkably deep house has a tendency to dwarf performers, and something about the layout of the balcony or rake of the seats makes the stage seem especially remote.

California State University, Long Beach (CSULB)
Carpenter Performing Arts Center
6200 Atherton St.
Long Beach 90840
562-985-7000

Built in 1994 and located on the campus of California State University, Long Beach, the exceptionally well-designed Carpenter Center blends a strong lineup of renowned American performers with a smattering of international artists. In addition to the center's concerts, there are numerous other performances presented at CSULB, such as college ensembles, which are not under the auspices of the Carpenter; for information on these events, call 562-985-5128. The Long Beach Opera also performs here; see SoCal Opera below.

California State University, Los Angeles
Harriet and Charles Luckman Fine Arts Complex
5151 State University Dr.
Los Angeles 90032
*213-343-6610

The 1,175-seat Luckman, which opened in 1994, has already gained a reputation for its extensive dance programming, including the annual Dance Kaleidoscope. It also programs some great jazz and big band concerts as well as a sampling of opera, world music, and classical.

California State University, Northridge
New Performing Arts Center
18111 Nordhoff St.
Northridge 91330
818-677-3943

This 500-seat state-of-the-art theater is a jewel nestled in the University Student Union complex. Though unimaginatively named and somewhat difficult to find (pay close attention to signs), it is definitely worth seeking out. The two-year-old center gives the Valley a quality performing arts venue and has already hosted several internationally known performers, such as South African pianist Abdullah Ibrahim and legendary Cuban band leader Chuco Valdés, in their only Southern California engagements.

Cerritos Center for the Performing Arts
12700 Center Court Dr.
Cerritos 90703
562-916-8500; 800-300-4345

Cerritos Center has been phenomenally successful since its opening in 1993, and has broken California revenue records for theaters with fewer than 3,000 seats (its flexible configuration allows for anywhere from 900 to 1,800 seats). The majority of the performers here are American or European, including such legendary musicians as Itzhak Perlman and Frederica von Stade, not to mention Steve and Edie. Most Angelenos would never expect to see such luminaries in Cerritos, but one need only enter the lobby and see the lavish, ultramodern space to understand that Cerritos doesn't do anything halfway.

El Camino Community College
El Camino Center for the Arts
16007 Crenshaw Blvd.
Torrance 90506
800-832-ARTS

This thirty-year-old performing arts series is presented in two theaters: the expansive (and somewhat barnlike) Marsee Auditorium, which seats 2,000 patrons, and the more intimate 360-seat Campus Theater. The program focuses on world music, jazz, and classical, with a bit of theater and dance. Performers range from top local mariachis to international taiko drummers, from the San Francisco Opera to the Peking Opera, and from legendary jazzman Charlie Haden to Van Cliburn Competition winner Jon Nakamatsu.

Japan America Theater
Japanese American Cultural and Community Center (JACCC)
244 S. San Pedro St.
Los Angeles 90012
213-680-3700

The complexion of downtown Los Angeles wouldn't be complete without this often-overlooked gem in Little Tokyo. A beautifully designed courtyard welcomes you to the Japanese American Cultural and Community Center as well as the Japan America Theater. The theater is a thoughtfully designed hall, which creates a very close connection between performer and audience, with a remarkable intimacy despite its 880-seat capacity. In addition to traditional and contemporary Japanese music, dance, and theater, the Japan American Theater hosts the Los Angeles Philharmonic New Music Group's Green Umbrella Series, presenting new, cutting-edge orchestral, chamber, and ensemble compositions.

Pepperdine University
Smothers Theater
24255 Pacific Coast Hwy.
Malibu 90263
310-456-4522

While a drive up the coast can be either relaxing or tortuous, depending on the traffic and weather conditions, take the time to attend a concert in the state-of-the-art Smothers Theater on the Pepperdine campus. Its diverse season features jazz, orchestral, musical theater, and cabaret. The programming here includes such contemporary acts as the Kingston Trio, an annual visit from songwriter David Wilcox, and a remarkable guitar series.

Plaza de la Raza Cultural Center
3540 N. Mission Rd.
Los Angeles 90031
*213-223-2475

Located in the Lincoln Park neighborhood, Plaza de la Raza's focus is on Latino arts and culture. The center hosts a summer music series but there are always additional performances scheduled throughout the year; presented on the Willie Velazquez Outdoor Stage, such area favorites as Dr. Loco's Rockin' Jalapeños and East L.A. Taiko can be heard.

Torrance Cultural Arts Center
3330 Civic Center Dr.
Torrance 90503
310-781-7171

The most community based of the performing arts venues listed here, Torrance Cultural Arts Center features several local groups—including orchestras, ensembles, and chorales—with a few international acts mixed in to spice up the season. Shrewd patrons can find many undervalued gems in this and other community theaters.

UCLA Center for the Performing Arts
310-825-2101

Offering more than 100 performances each year throughout L.A. (at venues ranging from several on-campus theaters to the Veterans Wadsworth to the Wiltern), UCLA Center for the Performing Arts is truly the granddaddy of local performing arts presenters, with world-class artists from L.A. and around the world. While the center generally stays away from rock and country, UCLA is a great source for the very best in classical, jazz, world music, and virtually every other genre. Performers have included internationally acclaimed cellist Yo-Yo Ma, leading South African township singer Mzwakhe Mbuli, and jazz legend Marcus Roberts. The series benefits from the reopening in 1998 of Royce Hall (closed for several years for earthquake repairs and seismic retrofitting), long the centerpiece and defining landmark of the performance series and of UCLA as a whole.

Wilshire Ebell Theater
4401 W. Eighth St.
Los Angeles 90005
*213-939-1128

The Wilshire Ebell is the home court of the Los Angeles Mozart Orchestra and first home of the Music Guild Chamber Music and has hosted many Shony Alex Braun concerts over the years. Even if Gypsy fiddling is not your cup of tea, this intimate, comfortable landmark is always worth a visit. Recommendation: sit with the cognoscenti in the balcony; you feel as if you're right on top of the stage, the sound is good, and the sight lines are top-notch.

Feast of Festivals

The Los Angeles Cultural Affairs Department lists more than 150 annual festivals in L.A. County alone. Arising from the many cultures and communities that make up the region, these festivals, most of which include a musical component, are an excellent, generally low-cost way to sample music you may be unfamiliar with or mingle with fellow fans of your favorite genre. For a comprehensive list, call the Los Angeles Cultural Affairs Department at 213-485-2433.

Cabaret L.A.

Anyone in Los Angeles will tell you that cabaret is an East Coast phenomenon. But if you are a cabaret lover, you can still find a stage to fit your needs. Though it presents cabaret only once a week, **Atlas Bar & Grill** (3760 Wilshire Blvd., Los Angeles; *213-466-4600) defines the cabaret image. The atmosphere seems somewhat manufactured, but the Atlas is located in a classic building (the Wiltern), serves excellent food, and has that Cary-Grant-may-arrive-at-any-time ambi-

ance. The music is a little more eclectic than you would expect of cabaret, but if it's the scene that you are looking for, this may be the place. The **Cinegrill** (7000 Sunset Blvd., Los Angeles; *213-466-7000), located in the historic Hollywood Roosevelt Hotel (home of the first Academy Awards and countless star trysts), is drenched in Glittertown mystique; only drinks are served. At the **Gardenia** in Hollywood (7066 Santa Monica Blvd., Los Angeles; *213-467-7444), the stage is small, and the food leaves something to be desired, but this is a classic venue for supper and a show. **Lunapark** (665 N. Robertson Blvd., West Hollywood; 310-652-0611) is a newer space that combines a top restaurant with two performance venues, including the downstairs cabaret.

Mariachi L.A.

Utilizing strings and brass, and often more than a dozen musicians and vocalists, this energetic Mexican music is now universally recognizable. With its large Mexican-American population and wealth of musicians, Los Angeles is considered by some the adoptive home of mariachi, with more local and touring ensembles performing here than anywhere else in the world. World-class artists can be found in all kinds of venues, from community clubs and restaurants to the Hollywood Bowl.

For example, two local restaurants are home to a couple of the world's most renowned mariachi bands. Located east of the Mid-Wilshire district is **La Fonda** (2501 Wilshire Blvd., Los Angeles; 213-380-5055), whose resident ensemble, internationally acclaimed Los Camperos de Nati Cano, performs several sets nightly, draw-

ing near-capacity crowds on the weekends. The influx of tourists from around the globe has led the band members to become multilingual, and they endeavor to converse with audience members in their native languages. To enjoy the music and margaritas with the regulars, slip in late on a weeknight. Or you can head to the outskirts of L.A. for **Cielito Lindo** (1612 N. Santa Ana Ave., South El Monte; 626-442-1254). Band leader José Hernandez's Mariachi Sol de México continues to test the boundaries of mariachi with innovative arrangements and unexpected repertoire. With enough music and energy for a space three times the size, this is not a place for the timid.

Mariachi USA, at the Hollywood Bowl, is an excellent series exploring all aspects of mariachi music. Any doubts about the Bowl's larger, less intimate space are laid to rest by the quality and sheer variety of the performances; call 213-848-7717 for information. Also meant to heighten awareness of mariachi as an art form, **Viva El Mariachi** is a one-day festival at the Greek Theatre which brings together many of the world's top performers; call *213-480-3232. For information on the **Los Angeles Mariachi Festival**, call the Cultural Affairs Department at 213-485-2437.

Jazz L.A.

Home of countless legends —such as Dexter Gordon, Hadda Brooks, and Charles Mingus—Los Angeles has a storied yet often overlooked jazz history. Recently much has been made of the Central Avenue tradition, and Leimert Park has emerged as the local seat of the new jazz explosion, but the rest of L.A. still thrives as a vibrant jazz city, and there a variety of great free venues (see Free for All, above).

There are three small paid venues that merit mention from the extensive list of Southland clubs. **Catalina Bar and Grill** (1640 N. Cahuenga Blvd., Los Angeles; *213-466-2210)—located in Hollywood, home to much of L.A.'s fabled jazz past—has never wavered from its commitment to presenting the major exponents of this American genre. The **Jazz Bakery** (3233 Helms Ave., Los Angeles; 310-271-9039) has displayed the same devotion to the advancement of the art form. (Its name derives from its location in the historic Helms Bakery building, near Culver City, former home of the "Award-Winning Bread of the Olympics.") And the jazz story isn't complete without a mention of **Chadney's** (3000 W. Olive Ave.; 818-843-5333) in Burbank. This club, the direct descendant of Shelley's Manne Hole and Donte's, remains the place where the Valley's musicians congregate, and many bring along their instruments for impromptu jam sessions. For information on these and other venues, consult the *Los Angeles Times* Sunday Calendar Section, the *L.A. Weekly*, or *New Times*. These publications have some excellent jazz writers who will highlight the most notable events of the following week.

CATALINA ISLAND JAZZ TRAX FESTIVAL
Casino Ballroom
1 Casino Way
Avalon (on Catalina Island)
90704
619-295-0396, 619-458-9586, 1-800-866-TRAX
(for tickets)
Scheduled for the first two weekends of October, this six-day festival features twenty concerts presented

in Avalon's historic 1929 casino. With a variety of jazz styles and performers on stage, this festival might be an extra incentive to get a few miles—eighteen nautical, to be precise—away from it all and visit this picturesque island.

JAZZ AT THE WADSWORTH
Veterans Wadsworth Theater
West Los Angeles Veterans Administration Grounds (at Wilshire and San Vicente Blvds.)
310-825-5706
Presented the first Sunday of each month (except when they're not), these ninety-minute free evening performances may be difficult to find in local listings; the 1,400-seat Wadsworth, which lacks an actual street address, is even harder to find. Call the number above to find out what's happening: the search is worthwhile, because these performances, programmed by the UCLA Student Committee for the Arts, provide a more traditional concert setting at which the jazz community can come together.

SoCal Opera

Opera trends seem to run in cycles, and Los Angeles County companies have mounted some remarkably innovative productions over the last several years; local opera buffs are also quite willing to travel to Orange County, home of Opera Pacific.

LOS ANGELES OPERA
(at the Dorothy Chandler Pavilion)
213-972-8001
Over the past several years the L.A. Opera has been both hailed and criticized for an adventurous spirit, with exciting new designers and directors and some in-your-face programming. From such rarely performed pieces as Janáček's *Cunning Little*

Vixen, to David Hockney's boldly colorful sets for *Tristan und Isolde* and *The Magic Flute,* to Maria Ewing's revealing Dance of the Seven Veils in Strauss's *Salomé,* L.A. Opera continues to push opera into the next millennium. Another critically questioned but audience-approved practice, the use of supertitles, now here to stay, allows patrons to read English translations projected above the stage. Beyond innovation, however, L.A. Opera continues to bring in top performers and classic productions that keep the devotees coming back.

LONG BEACH OPERA
(at the Carpenter Performing Arts Center)
562-439-2580
The oldest opera company in Los Angeles County, Long Beach Opera now forgoes the standard season, opting instead for a two-weekend festival of new or rarely performed works. If L.A. Opera occasionally pushes the genre, Long Beach is giving it a swift kick. Its recent premiere production of the American opera *Hopper's Wife* one-upped L.A.'s production of *Salomé* with an all-nude, all-the-time Ava Gardner. With modest resources, this company focuses on opera as modern theater. All performances are in English, so there is no need for supertitles here.

OPERA PACIFIC
Segerstrom Hall
Orange County Performing Arts Center
600 Town Center Dr.
Costa Mesa 92626
800-34-OPERA
When you think of Orange County, you are more likely to think of Mickey Mouse than *Die Fledermaus,* but that may be changing. Based at the Orange County Performing Arts Center, Opera Pacific is considered one of

the nation's top fifteen opera companies and has drawn more than a half million opera lovers from throughout Southern California with performances by such superstars as Placido Domingo and Luciano Pavarotti.

Notable Clubs

Scattered throughout the region are countless clubs offering every kind of music, ambiance, and price range. You can listen to acid rock in a coffeehouse or opera in a bar, so there is truly no good way to categorize these venues. That problem is compounded by the constantly changing nature of the club scene—not just here today, gone tomorrow, but country today, big-band swing tomorrow. For that reason, it's important to keep an eye on the local papers—most notably the *Los Angeles Times* (particularly the Sunday and Thursday Calendar sections), *L.A. Weekly,* and *New Times*—to find the clubs that fit your taste. One word to the wise: expensive doesn't necessarily mean better. Many of the smaller clubs get the same quality artists as big-name clubs, and for the price of one major concert ticket you can explore several fine smaller venues.

Dancing the Net

Some of the region's most interesting dance locales led former lives as motion picture palaces, upscale meeting places, or other establishments with ties to Los Angeles's golden era, and many of them seem to be infused with the ambiance of a bygone age. In searching out your destinations, be sure to investigate their history and architecture.

Since clubs and dance halls go in and out of fashion (and business) on a monthly basis, perhaps it is wise to bear in mind a very loosely paraphrased Peace Corps philosophy: "Give a man a list of dance clubs, and he dances for a month. Teach him to find the hot dance spots, and he dances for a lifetime." Therefore, the usefulness of the *L.A. Weekly*, *New Times*, and the *Los Angeles Times* Calendar listings of local dance spots cannot be overemphasized. What follows is a little information on specific dance scenes and a few hotlines and Web sites to help put you on the right track.

Country/Contra Dance/Cajun and Zydeco

Much of the dancing in town comes from American musical traditions. Contra dances, zydeco and Cajun, country dancing, and even swing are part of this country's musical heritage. The most traditional of these is the folk-based contra dance. One can get information on contra dances from the California Dance Cooperative; begin by consulting the dance hotline at 818-951-2003. Through the cooperative you will also be able to find information on Cajun and zydeco performances \and dances in Southern California.

Los Angeles has one of the largest expatriate populations from Louisiana, leading some to consider L.A. LA west (the hotline for Cajun music—626-793-4333—is known as the "LA LA Line"). With its mix of fiddles and accordions, the music is so infectious that you won't need any instruction to fall in with the seasoned two-steppers. But if you are having a hard time picking up the steps, many of these dance gatherings provide instruction for the uninitiated.

One facet of Cajun culture, zydeco music, has developed a more blues-rich flavor, with drums, amplified instruments, and full keyboard accordions. Check the Southern California Zydeco Hotline (*213-344-4044) for upcoming zydeco and Cajun events throughout the Southland. Many of the dances on the hotline are community fund-raisers taking place at unexpected spaces such as the Monrovia Knights of Columbus Hall and Saint Albert the Great Catholic Church on Compton Avenue in Gardena. One of the greatest pleasures of these dances is the chance to experience regional cuisine and hospitality. There are also several Cajun and zydeco festivals in Southern California.

Country music has reached two zeniths through the last two decades, its success in the 1990s (see Garth Brooks, the return of cowboy hats, and the "Achy-Breaky" phenomenon) surpassing even the Travolta-driven *Urban Cowboy* craze of the 1980s. As these trends cycle, so does the saloon saturation, but to keep your finger on the pulse, aim your Web browser at www.concentric.net/~ddprieto. For those without a modem, check in at some of L.A.'s storied dance halls, such as the **Foothill** in Long Beach (1922 Cherry Ave.; 562-494-5196), the **Cowboy Palace** in Chatsworth (21635 Devonshire St.; 818-341-0166), and—if you care to venture into the Inland Empire, where country and western still reigns supreme—the **Western Connection** in San Dimas (657 W. Arrow Hwy.; 909-592-2211).

Swing and Salsa

The same personal contact and structured steps that have kept people coming back to country dance can be found in swing dancing. This big-band sound has always been a staple for devoted "Lindy-hoppers," but it is now seeing a meteoric resurgence. This movement is based on a combination of nostalgia for the aesthetics of lounge music, early rock and roll and rhythm and blues, and the spirit of a bygone era.

A few nightspots have carried the torch of swing dance to its current heights. Among them are the same **Foothill** that has continued to host country and swing dance bands since the late 1940s (see above) and the epicenter of L.A.'s current swing resurgence, the **Derby** in Los Feliz (4500 Los Feliz Blvd., Los Angeles; *213-663-8979). Radio personality Chuck Cecil and his long-running radio program "The Swingin' Years" on KPCC (89.3 FM) have also kept swing music alive on the local airwaves. Now swing is taking hold more widely, on special nights at top venues throughout the region—from the Sunset Strip's Viper Room to the Miracle Mile's art deco El Rey Theater to the cool scene at Nicholby's in Ventura. Find out where and when over the Internet at www.SwingSet.net.

The lovers of salsa have been a prominent dance community in L.A. for many years. Like swing dancing, salsa has recently attained an unparalleled popularity. One can learn where and how to dance (and dress, for that matter) at the Web site www.salsaweb.com.

Among the most notable spots for lovers of Afro-Cuban, Caribbean, and Central American dance are **El Floridita** in Hollywood (1253 Vine St.; *213-871-8612), the **Mayan Theater** (once a grand motion picture palace) in downtown Los Angeles (1038 S. Hill St.; 213-746-4287), and other clubs from the Santa Monica Pier to the San Fernando and San Gabriel Valleys.

Busking L.A.

Wherever there's a street scene in L.A. (Old Town Pasadena, Santa Monica's Third Street Promenade, downtown Long Beach), you can rest assured street musicians will pop up. This is one of the oldest and simplest entertainment arrangements, with no producers, no publicists, just an overturned hat or open instrument case and entertainers offering a pay-what-you-can show. Just as it does at other venues throughout Los Angeles, the quality of performance varies—from a man who wails along to a portable karaoke machine to the groups that have, as urban legend would have it, won recording deals after being discovered streetside. (The only one of these stories that can be confirmed is that of the Red Elvises (formerly Limpopo), who were Santa Monica street performers and now perform at venues all over the Southland.) So when you wander by a street performer, give a listen; you might have to pay next time.

Destination L.A.: Leimert Park

One of L.A.'s oldest communities, Leimert Park is reestablishing itself as a center of jazz music, where legends train a lineup of tomorrow's stars and innovators. At the heart of this renaissance is the **World Stage Performance Space** (4344 Degnan Blvd.; *213-293-2451), a training and performance space founded and run by American Jazz Masters fellow Billy Higgins. This small indoor space features jam sessions that include legends of the genre as well as some of the hottest young performers. Thursday night jazz jam sessions run from 9:30 p.m. to 2 a.m., with Friday and Saturday night performances beginning at 9:45 and 11:30 p.m. Other performances and workshops are scheduled throughout the week. Often open to the public with no cover charge, **Fifth Street Dick's Coffee Company** (3347 W. 43rd Pl.; *213-296-3970) has become a mecca for performers who want to hone their set in an extended engagement or just let loose with a late-night jam session. This is an excellent place for patrons to begin their first exploration of the Leimert Park scene. The **Leimert Park Jazz Festival** (43d Pl. and Crenshaw Blvd.; *213-960-1625), a free festival founded in 1996, solidifies Leimert Park as a center of jazz on the West Coast, with past performances from the likes of Horace Tapscott and Black/Note. The multiday festival takes place in September.

Destination L.A.: Long Beach

On the southwest boundary of Los Angeles County, Long Beach has recently been revitalized. The downtown area has become a hot spot, with several clubs and coffeehouses offering music; in addition, there are a variety of festivals and outdoor series. Pine Avenue has become the center of this scene, with restaurants, bars, clubs, cafés, and coffeehouses all within walking distance, and the area

now attracts considerable evening and weekend foot traffic. The following are a couple of key clubs; if they are not offering something you are interested in, take a stroll up Pine, and let your ears lead you.

Located half a block off Pine Avenue, **Blue Cafe** (210 The Promenade; 562-983-7111) offers blues (obviously) as well as a sampling of rock and jazz. With a cover that is generally below $10, this multilevel club features top performers from Los Angeles and beyond as well as some outdoor seating and pool tables. Truly a dance club, **Cohiba** (110 Broadway; 562-437-7700) presents live acts on a raised stage. The dance floor is directly in front of the stage, so sight lines are obstructed at best. With multiple bars, an outdoor patio, Sinatraesque lounge, and combination pool and cigar room, however, this upstairs space offers the complete club experience. With no cover on most weeknights and a maximum of $10 on the weekend (generally only $5), **M Bar/Grill** (213A Pine Ave.; 562-435-2525) is an excellent place to enjoy trademark jazz performances as well as occasional rock and blues acts. Solving the sight-line problems endemic to clubs, the stage is set approximately ten feet up, in a nook above the restrooms. Whether from the tables or the bar, patrons are promised a great view, not to mention a good, reasonably priced menu.

Destination L.A.: Up on the Hill

The topography of L.A.'s cultural life shifts from lo-

cale to locale seemingly on a generational cycle. One of the significant centers that has been developing—and is still years from reaching its cultural apex—is the area referred to by many as "up on the hill." This clustering of institutions at the top of the Sepulveda Pass, which connects the San Fernando Valley with West Los Angeles, may well become the most important centrally located cultural destination for many Angelenos. It is uniquely accessible to a remarkably large population base, minutes from the expanse of the Valley and equally close to West L.A. The sites "up on the hill" are museums; educational and community centers; and presenters of music, lectures, readings, and other performances.

Getty Center
1200 Getty Center Dr.
Los Angeles 90049
310-440-7300

Beginning in early 1998, the new Getty Center will offer free performances, bringing together a variety of genres: music, spoken word, dance, and theater. Performed in two spaces (one indoors and one outdoors), both with approximately 500 seats, these programs for adults, young adults, and family audiences will draw on diverse cultural traditions. Many events will relate to the museum's permanent collection, changing exhibitions, or to collections and activities at other programs of the Getty Trust.

Skirball Cultural Center
Hebrew Union College– Jewish Institute of America
2701 N. Sepulveda Blvd.
Los Angeles 90049
310-440-4666

The opening of the Skirball in 1996 heralded the development of this hilltop as a cultural hub. A growing series of programs is presented year-round in an inviting, well-situated setting. The Cultural Center houses a 350-seat auditorium, and the outdoor plaza is an appealing concert environment for both free and paid performances. In addition to multiple performances of the Los Angeles Mozart Orchestra, the center's concert series features a fifty-fifty split of jazz and classical music.

Stephen S. Wise Temple
15500 Stephen S. Wise Dr.
Los Angeles 90077
310-476-8561

Before the arrival of the new Getty Center and the Skirball, Stephen S. Wise Temple provided—and continues to provide—a wide range of programming to the surrounding community. Events are scheduled year-round and most center on Jewish arts and culture such as performances by cantors.

University of Judaism
15600 Mulholland Dr.
Los Angeles 90077
310-476-9777

The university is the home of Gindi Auditorium, which seats 479. The hall presents chamber concerts with members of the L.A. Philharmonic, visits from other local ensembles, and the university's own season of events, which encompass theater, flamenco dance, comedy, and musical performances. *Judaism* is the operative word here, however, and the Gindi attracts top local and touring Jewish performers.

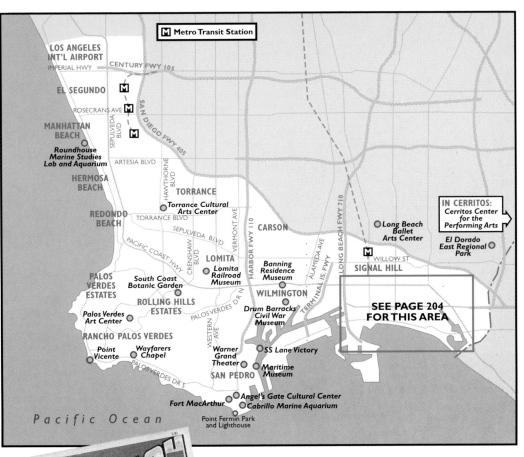

M Metro Transit Station

LOS ANGELES INT'L AIRPORT

IMPERIAL HWY CENTURY FWY 105

EL SEGUNDO

ROSECRANS AVE

MANHATTAN BEACH

Roundhouse Marine Studies Lab and Aquarium

ARTESIA BLVD

HERMOSA BEACH

SEPULVEDA BLVD

SAN DIEGO FWY 405

HAWTHORNE BLVD

TORRANCE

Torrance Cultural Arts Center

REDONDO BEACH

TORRANCE BLVD

SEPULVEDA BLVD

PACIFIC COAST HWY

CRENSHAW BLVD

VERMONT AVE

HARBOR FWY 110

CARSON

LOMITA

Lomita Railroad Museum

Banning Residence Museum

WILMINGTON

PALOS VERDES ESTATES

South Coast Botanic Garden

ROLLING HILLS ESTATES

PALOS VERDES DR N

Drum Barracks Civil War Museum

Palos Verdes Art Center

RANCHO PALOS VERDES

WESTERN AVE

Point Vicente

Wayfarers Chapel

PALOS VERDES DR S

Warner Grand Theater

SAN PEDRO

SS Lane Victory

Maritime Museum

Fort MacArthur

Angel's Gate Cultural Center
Cabrillo Marine Aquarium

Point Fermin Park and Lighthouse

Pacific   Ocean

ALAMEDA AVE

TERMINAL IS. FWY

LONG BEACH FWY 710

Long Beach Ballet Arts Center

WILLOW ST

SIGNAL HILL

IN CERRITOS:
Cerritos Center for the Performing Arts

El Dorado East Regional Park

SEE PAGE 204 FOR THIS AREA

Greetings from LONG BEACH CALIFORNIA

The sprawling estuary of mud flats and salt marshes that is now Los Angeles's harbor, officially called Worldport L.A., was first discovered by João Rodrigues Cabrillo, a Portuguese navigator dispatched by the Spanish viceroy of Mexico in 1542 to explore the Pacific Coast. Richard Henry Dana didn't see the commercial promise of San Pedro Bay; he described it more than a century ago in his novel *Two Years Before the Mast* as a rather useless area of marshland, sandbars, and small islands. But General Phineas Banning worked to con- vince other civic leaders that it—not Santa Monica Bay—should be developed as the port. Since the 1870s, dredging and the construction of a series of breakwaters has transformed adjacent sections of San Pedro and Long Beach into the most active cargo-handling port in the United States and the busiest passenger port on the West Coast.

The volume of trade income has quadrupled in the past twenty years, even after inflation adjustment, to $165 billion per annum (according to a University of Southern California report).

San Pedro and Wilmington were annexed by the city of Los Angeles in 1909 and consolidated as the Harbor District. The **Port of Los Angeles** encompasses 7,400 acres of land and water along twenty-eight miles of waterfront. Commercial fishing and canning operations are centered on Terminal Island, where supertankers unload oil. Long Beach, the fifth largest city in California, also has port facilities: an artificial deep-water port was dredged in 1910 to complement (and sometimes compete with) the sprawling industrial port complex. Development of the port boomed during World War II when naval facilities were built on Terminal Island and the shipyards built and repaired thousands of ships. In 1991 the Pentagon voted to decommission the Long Beach Naval Station (once the headquarters of the Pacific fleet), compounding the economic havoc wreaked by the massive loss of aerospace

Long Beach Farmers Market
Promenade North
(between Third St.
and Broadway)
Fri. 10 a.m.–4 p.m.

The interior of the historic First Congregational Church (241 Cedar Ave.; 562-436-2256) boasts stained glass and many decorative details. It also has an organ that features prominently in a spring and fall concert series, although a variety of musical styles is also presented.

Long Beach Public Library and Information Center (101 Pacific Ave.; 562-570-7500) is the flagship of a system with eleven branches throughout the city.

For information on the artworks installed at the Blue Line stations in Long Beach, see pp. 190–191.

jobs. The 145-acre site was offered in 1995 to the semi-autonomous Port of Long Beach, which signed a lease with Cosco (the shipping line owned by the Chinese government) to build a new terminal, thus beating out competitors in the adjacent port of Los Angeles. That agreement was voided in May 1997 by a judge who ruled in a lawsuit filed by Long Beach Heritage that port officials had been predisposed to approve the project without evaluating environmental impact studies.

Much of Long Beach Heritage's efforts recently have been devoted to publicizing (and reversing) the plight of the 1940 Roosevelt Base, which includes eleven buildings designed by Paul Williams, the first African-American member of the American Institute of Architects (who also designed the iconic elevated, circular building at LAX). These buildings include a gymnasium with such facilities as a basketball court, fifty-lane bowling alley, and Olympic-sized swimming pool, and an officers' club, which members of Long Beach Heritage (and others) hope are renovated to create a recreational center for the area.

Between 1900 and 1910 **Long Beach** was the fastest-growing city in the United States; its development, like that of Pasadena, was fueled by the transcontinental railroads bringing vacationing visitors to the beachfront town. The boom continued through the 1920s with the discovery of oil at Signal Hill, north of town. During this decade most of downtown Long Beach was built, with about $1 million poured into construction costs each month! Many structures did not survive the 1933 Long Beach earthquake; those that did were modified to meet new building codes using the prevailing art moderne style that still

characterizes downtown Long Beach today. The Office of Neighborhood and Historic Preservation (562-570-6684) offers free maps and an informational brochure for self-guided tours of the newly refurbished streets near Pine Avenue in the old downtown, and Long Beach Heritage (562-493-7019) leads guided tours on a regular schedule.

The long-term pumping of oil deposits in the harbor caused nearby land to sink as much as twenty-seven feet and thus jettisoned the downtown's development. Not until the 1960s was a solution for the sinking land devised, when water was pumped into depleted cavities to repressurize the land. Redevelopment of the downtown area continues today, and Long Beach is once again linked to downtown Los Angeles by public transportation: the Blue Line whisks passengers from one end of the line to the other in about fifty-five minutes. Commuters are offered free valet parking for their bikes at the Long Beach Commuter Bike Station (105 Promenade North; 562-436-2453); visitors coming from the opposite direction can rent two-wheeled transportation to explore the area ($5 per hour or $25 per day; join the bicycle club for $50 per year and get T-shirts, water bottles, and rates for bike rentals as low as $1 per day if you arrive by 9 a.m.)

The harbor and beachfront still form most visitors' first impression of Long Beach, although the huge city stretches inland for several miles. The **Convention and Entertainment Center** (300 E. Ocean Ave.) hosts many general-interest events and schedules cultural performances in its Terrace Theater (562-436-3636). The largest mural in the world—122,000 square feet of life-sized gray whales and dolphins, painted by Wyland—decorates the curving walls of the **Long Beach Arena** (Ocean Blvd. at Pine St.). The *Queen Mary* and *Spruce Goose* anchored an amusement complex in the port district throughout the 1980s; it was managed by Disney until the entertainment conglomerate abandoned plans for a 300-acre theme park at the harbor. By the mid-1990s the *Goose* had been sold to an aeronautics museum in the Pacific Northwest, the Japanese were bidding considerable sums to anchor the *Queen Mary* as a floating hotel in the Tokyo harbor, and a major new development was underway at the site. The multimillion-dollar development along Shoreline Park is intended to become the "premier waterfront attraction for Southern California" and is scheduled for opening in June 1998. Like other recent urban developments—Old Town Pasadena, CityWalk, and Third Street Promenade—this is planned as a family attraction and will be anchored by the Aquarium of the Pacific. The parkland south of the aquarium will be relandscaped and kept as open space; 225,000 square feet of commercial development will feature theme restaurants, large-screen (possibly IMAX) theaters, and shops.

The tall ship *Californian*, a full-scale recreation of an 1848 cutter, will be another focal point of the new development, anchored at a $2-million pier. Nautical Heritage (800-432-2201) will continue to offer individuals and school groups hands-on sailing experiences on the vintage ship; these last from a few hours to five days. Shoreline Village (Shoreline Village Dr. at Pine St.)—with its restored carousel— and several marinas offer cruises to Catalina, boats for sportfishing (and in winter, whale watching), plus shops and restaurants.

The **Historical Society of Long Beach** operates a small Gallery and Research Center at 418 Pine Ave (open Tues., Thurs. 10 a.m.–3 p.m., Wed., Fri. 10 a.m.–5 p.m.; entry: free; tel. 562-495-1210) with both long-term and changing exhibits that recall local history, including such lost landmarks as The Zone (a beachfront amusement park that closed in the 1970s), and Balboa Studios, a pioneer in movie-making. Long Beach Heritage conducts neighborhood walking tours ($5) that depart from the Historical Society on the third and fourth Saturday of each month; on Friday evenings, Twilight Tours ($4) meet at the WPA-era mosaic mural at the north end of the Promenade. Reservations required: call 562-493-7019.

The Camerata Singers of Long Beach is a fifty-member community-based choral group with a twenty-five-year history in the Long Beach/South Bay area. Led by music director Dr. David Wilson, the group presents the Long Beach Bach Festival, held annually in October; with guest artists, creative staging, and some contemporary adaptations, the festival celebrates J. S. Bach and his contemporaries. For information and performance schedules, call 562-986-2710.

The Firefighters Museum (1465 Peterson Ave., Long Beach 90815) houses a collection of vintage firefighting apparatus—ladders, breathing equipment, life nets, as well as wagons dating back to the 1890s—which are displayed in a building that served as Station 10 from 1925 to 1968. Open on the second Sat. of the month, 9 a.m.–3 p.m. Entry: free, donations welcomed.

Long Beach Aquarium of the Pacific

100 Aquarium Way
Long Beach 90802
562-590-3100
www.aquariumof pacific.org
Daily 10 a.m.-6 p.m.
Entry: adults $13, seniors $11.50, children 3-11 $6.50

The Long Beach Aquarium of the Pacific, destined to become one of the premier tourist attractions of Southern California with attendance projected at more than 1.6 million each year, is a huge structure with curved glass walls beneath an undulating wavelike roofline. Built on a prime five-acre waterfront site at a cost of $117 million, the aquarium was funded by the 1995 sale of tax-exempt private revenue bonds and is the most visible symbol of the Queensway Bay redevelopment in a community left reeling by closure of its signature naval base. The pride and excitement of its staff were palpable on the bright spring morning when I was offered a hard-hat tour of the nearly completed structure, scheduled to open in June 1988. That the public has embraced this new development was evident in both the size of the donors' walkway and the nearly 10,000 local families who have signed on as charter members.

The building, whose design—a collaboration between the L.A. office of Hellmuth, Obata & Kassabaum and Esherick Homsey Dodge Davis of San Francisco, the architects of the Monterey Bay Aquarium—expresses the fluid and dynamic nature of water, is divided into dry and wet zones. Steel frames glass walls on the dry side, offering panoramic vistas of the ocean that covers nearly half of our planet and is the focus of the exhibits. Concrete is used both to support the enormous weight of the tanks on the structure's wet side and defines the ample outdoor spaces, which include open-air amphitheaters and interactive discovery centers for kids as well as nearly 20 percent of the exhibits.

Nearly one million gallons of sea water will be enclosed in the seventeen major habitats and the thirty smaller installations called "focus tanks." Special design features include wave and

Long Beach
Farmers Market
Dooley's parking lot
(51st St., west of
Long Beach Blvd.)
Sat. 7:30–11:30 a.m.

surge machinery to replicate the natural marine environment of the 550 species represented in the aquarium's 10,000 specimens, and life-support systems installed on a floating raft to minimize danger to the exhibits in case of an earthquake.

The Great Hall of the Pacific is a soaring space, defined by my guide in that most American measurement, "the size of a football field," with a full-size (88-foot) model of a giant blue whale overhead. An enormous globe, donated by McDonald Douglas, will allow visitors to localize the three areas of the Pacific Ocean that are the focus of the exhibits. Preview tanks within the Great Hall introduce the diverse marine ecosystems, starting with the Tropical Pacific, a 10,000-gallon tank filled with colorful fish and artificial coral, and cool gray walls surrounding the denizens of the icy waters of the Northern Pacific.

At the far end of the Great Hall, a three-story, 142,000-gallon tank filled with "Predators" is a dramatic introduction to the local waters of Southern California and Baja. These specimens from the top of the food chain include sharks and rays, yellowtails, and wrasses; the unusual ability of the latter species to change sex during its lifetime is featured in a separate focus exhibit. The Amber Forest tank showcases the kelp that dominates the temperate coastal waters of California and is animated by schooling silver sardines. A

nearby exhibit, and touch tanks monitored by educators. A large open tank permits visitors to stroke rays and skates, a sensation my son likens to touching wet Gummi Bears!

The exhibits on the second floor highlight the extremes of the Pacific's marine habitats—from a tropical coral reef in Micronesia to the frigid but flourishing ecosystems of the Alaskan archipelago. Among the more engaging creatures of Northern Pacific waters are sea otters, whose voracious appetites create an environmental challenge for the aquarium: the waters in this large exhibit must be filtered every thirty to ninety minutes to eliminate animal wastes. Diving birds are featured in a cleverly designed exhibit with rocky ledges for nesting surrounding a deep pool where they fish. Anemones, urchins, and crabs will be featured in the Discovery Lab touch tanks in this section.

In the Tropical Pacific exhibits, visitors are led on a simulated diving trip to Palau, encountering first the top of a coral reef, populated by smaller fish— splotched, striped, irridescent, and shockingly bright colored. Focus tanks feature live coral exhibits and monitors that explain the propogation program the aquarium has already begun in the hopes of one day supplementing the artificial coral used in most exhibits. Volunteer divers descend regularly into the 350,000-gallon tank

to clean the coral, which is viewed from a tunnel, with soft species arrayed at left and hard species at right. Ultimately some 1,000 fish will populate this largest of the aquarium's exhibits, with giant grouper and zebra sharks as well as such colorful critters as racoon butterfly fish.

frolicking harbor seal was an irrepressible greeter in the tunnel passage that allows an underwater view of a large tank filled with seals and sea lions; when we reached the upper level, a pair of sea lions, just united in their future home, swam in circles, sunning themselves in the open air, surrounded by a rock-studded deck. Patrons at Cafe Scuba, the indoor-outdoor restaurant, will be able to survey both the sea lions' antics and a wide view of the Pacific.

Kids Cove is a playground environment that will appeal to the youngest visitors, with a concrete skeleton of a gray whale that kids can climb on, a full-size model of the endangered sea turtles featured in a

In addition to the large corps of docents who assist in the Discovery Labs, staff curators will offer a regular program of talks, and other educational programs will be presented in the Honda Theater, a 190-seat auditorium off the Great Hall. Revenues from the gift shop, which will be stocked with marine-related souvenirs, games, and educational toys, will help retire the public bonds that funded the aquarium's construction. The challenge of creating a popular and educational facility has been brilliantly realized in the Aquarium of the Pacific, which is a welcome addition to the cultural venues of L.A. County.

Queen Mary Seaport

1126 Queens Hwy.
Pier J, Long Beach Harbor
Long Beach 90802
562-435-3511
Daily 10 a.m.–6 p.m.; in summer,
Sat. 9 a.m.–9 p.m., with fireworks display
Entry: adults $12, seniors/military $10,
children 4–11 $6
Additional fee for behind-the-scenes tour
(10 a.m.–6 p.m. on the half-hour); discount
for combination admission/tour

The *Queen Mary* was the fastest and biggest of the North Atlantic luxury liners, acknowledged as the "Reigning Queen of the Atlantic" in 1,001 transatlantic crossings. Built in the 1930s, its architectural features are sumptuous art deco, and period furnishings still decorate some of its 365 original staterooms. It has been

owned by the city of Long Beach and operated (by various parties, including Disney) as a hotel, restaurant, and shopping complex since arriving in

port in 1967. Its fabled elegance has not made it profitable for the city, although its value as an icon jettisoned a recent plan to lease it to Japanese entrepreneurs who intended to tow it to Tokyo Bay for use as a floating hotel. It was paired with the *Spruce Goose* to create an offbeat theme park of transportation wonders that were technologically ahead of their time; however, the 200-ton, all-wood aircraft, which flew only once (for one minute in 1947) was sold and taken to Oregon, leaving the *Queen* to find its own audience. Occupancy in the hotel hovers around 50 percent, with room rates from $80 to $170 depending upon the view and decor.

A self-guided tour of the 81,000-ton vessel is included in the admission fee or hotel room rate. The guided tour of the *Queen Mary* takes you from its guts to its perfectly restored glitter, from the bowels of the immense boiler room to the art deco splendor of the spacious royal suites where the high-powered were pampered during the amazingly speedy four-day Atlantic crossing. The history of transatlantic travel, including the World War II years when the *Queen Mary* transported 15,000 troops per crossing—regular passenger capacity was 1,957—comes vividly to life as you tour the ship from bow to stern, top to bottom.

PUBLIC ART IN LONG BEACH

The public art program in Long Beach was established in 1989 as a partnership between the Public Corporation for the Arts (PCA) and the Long Beach Redevelopment Agency. The PCA works with developers and community groups to facilitate projects that help to create identity for the city through sculptures, murals, architectural restorations, and light works.

At Los Altos Market Center (Bellflower Blvd. and Stearns St.), **Jud Fine** designed *Puvungna Plaza*, an outdoor environment featuring artist-designed landscape elements and sculptures.

Rockne Krebs's *The Majic Wand* is a laser beam of intense green light that projects from the theater marquee in Pine Square (245 Pine Ave.). The light aims at a series of mirrors above Pine Avenue, crisscrosses the downtown area, and beams south toward Catalina Island. *Serendipity,* also by Krebs, is a brilliantly colored neon sculpture that arches over the open courtyard and accents the theater marquee.

Eric Orr uses light as a sculptural medium, projecting eight thousand feet of light from the roof of the Landmark Square building (111 W. Ocean Blvd.) into the night sky. **Richard Haas** created a five-panel mural in the building's main lobby, which depicts the history and development of Long Beach. The mural features aircraft manufacturing, the Port of Long Beach, the oil industry, the Southern Pacific Red Car, and its successor, the Metro Blue Line.

Using mirrors and columns, artist **Craig Cree Stone** successfully created the illusion of a floating ceiling inside a lobby of the Krinsky Building (140 Pine Ave.). The black granite on the floor is etched with cast shadows, further enhancing the sensation of weightlessness.

Shadow Casting on the Shore, by **Craig Cree Stone,** includes more than one hundred images of shadows that originate around parking meters along a fourteen-block stretch of Belmont Shore (Second St. between Bayshore Ave. and Livingston Dr.). Camouflaged among the real shadows on the sidewalks and walls, there are quirky shadows created by the artist: images of fish, a cup of coffee, a raven perched on a tree, a dog, and a carousel horse.

The PCA publishes informative guides and sponsors walking tours of public art; call 562-570-5250. The City of Long Beach Mural and Cultural Arts Program sponsors *Street Voices* as a joint project with the Long Beach Area Convention and Visitors Bureau and the PCA. Launched in 1985, the program has brought in professional artists to collaborate with neighborhood residents, organizations, schools, businesses, and youth in creating site-specific murals; see Murals (pp. 171–72) for more information.

—Noriko Fujinami

Long Beach Museum of Art

2300 E. Ocean Blvd.
Long Beach 90803
562-439-2119
Wed.–Sun. 10 a.m.–5 p.m., Fri. until 8 p.m.
Entry: adults $2, seniors/students $1,
children under 12 free

Long Beach Arts,
founded in 1924, is one
of the oldest artist-
member organizations
in California. Its gallery
(447 Long Beach Blvd.,
562-435-5995; daily
noon–4 p.m.; free)
features monthly
competitions for new
and emerging artists.

Situated on a bluff overlooking the Pacific, the cedar-shingled Craftsman-style building that houses the Long Beach Museum of Art was originally a private residence built in 1912. Today its galleries are filled with contemporary art, much of it by California artists, whose works form a large part of the permanent collection. Although the transitions between galleries remind visitors that this building had a previous function, the rooms are well-fixtured for an active program of changing installations. Because the building is small, only a little of its permanent collection can be displayed at a given time, which makes each visit a different experience, but has also frustrated the administration's efforts to expand its programming. In late 1997 the museum submitted plans to the city to double its exhibition space and offered them for public review. To add a two-story, 12,000-square-foot addition for the new galleries, the plan calls for the carriage house (which houses the bookstore) to be moved from the back lawn to the parking lot on the east side of the building.

The Long Beach Museum of Art has become identified with artistic experimentation in video through numerous installations and through its post-production studio (5373 E. Second St.) and large collection of video art. The museum offers workshops, tours of exhibitions for groups (including schoolchildren), and programs for teachers.

Casa de la Cultura de Long Beach

629 Atlantic Ave.
Long Beach 90802
562-435-3144

In July 1993 the Community Hispanic Association initiated public programming in a 1906 Victorian house; their mission is to celebrate all the cultures of Latin America. There's an annual poetry contest, a Posada at Christmastime, as well as a yearly Ecuadorian fiesta to celebrate the founding of the city of Quito. There are English and citizenship classes, as well as instruction in computers, folk dancing, and yoga.

Museum of Latin American Art

628 Alamitos Ave.
Long Beach 90802
562-437-1689
Tues.–Sat. 11:30 a.m.–7:30 p.m., Sun. noon–6 p.m.
Entry: adults $3, children under 12 free

The art of our own hemisphere is too infrequently celebrated and its influence is too often obscured by the dominance of European traditions in standard art historical presentations, but the new Museum of Latin American Art intends to change that. Its founder, Dr. Robert Gumbiner, who also started the first large-scale HMO, has been an active participant in defining its role not merely as a museum but as a cultural center in which the community is actively engaged. Its mission is broadening the view of Latin American art (a view still dominated by Mexico) and bringing it up to date: the emphasis will be on contemporary art, in changing exhibitions as well as in the permanent collection. Gumbiner established the museum's permanent collection with about 200 pieces that reflect his practice of purchasing works directly from artists; more than half of the pieces were created after 1980 when Gumbiner accelerated the pace of his collecting.

Historic buildings house the new museum: a 1920s roller-skating rink called the Hippodrome and an adjacent building once part of Balboa Studios, a pioneer in movie-making. A preview gallery opened in November 1996, but the renovation of the buildings will offer a much larger facility (including a 199-seat theater) for exhibitions and other programming. The museum is intended to be the nucleus of a cultural center offering lectures, films, and other educational activities (such as tours of L.A.'s murals). Family Sundays feature special events and workshops, and kids also benefited from a low-fee art camp initiated during the museum's first summer, with five two-week sessions devoted to different aspects of making art with paper. The morning session (10 a.m.–1 p.m.) is for kids six to ten years, and the afternoons (2–5 p.m.) for junior high-and high school students.

Membership and single-admission fees have been kept very low to encourage the broadest community participation. There is a well-stocked shop with a good selection of books and craft objects, as well as a restaurant on the site.

The beachfront city sure knows how to party: summer kicks off with a Beach Fest and Chili Cook-Off in May (562-436-7727), continues with Hot Summer Nights and such special events as the Cajun and Zydeco Festival in June (562-427-3713) and the Long Beach Jazz Festival in August (562-436-7794). Information on arts events in Long Beach is available from the Public Corporation for the Arts, which not only supports great programming but does an exemplary job at providing information (562-570-5250).

City Beach stretches from First Place to 72nd Place. Between 20th and 35th Place, the beach is surmounted by Bluff Park, which is popular with joggers and pedestrians who can enjoy the ocean views on one side and the fine residences (many in the Craftsman style) on the other. At 39th Place is **Belmont Pier**, which caters to sportfishing and offers whale-watching trips (call 562-434-6781 or 562-434-4434); the Belmont Plaza Olympic Pool is at the foot of the pier. Belmont Shore's Second Street offers a lively street scene as well as some witty public art.

The residential community of **Naples**, bounded by the Orange County line, was developed from 1903 to 1906—by building up marshland in Alamitos Bay to form three islands—then purchased by railroad tycoon Henry E. Huntington. The neighborhood is a pedestrian's dream, with waterfront walkways that offer peeks into the cheerful gardens of the eclectic homes. One distinctive residence (5576 Vesuvian Way), was designed in 1962 as part of the Case Study House program, which sponsored the creation of well-designed, affordable residences during the Southland's postwar housing boom. Gondola rides and an annual Christmas boat parade are featured events in the Naples marina.

The presence of KLON (88.1 FM) on campus has helped develop a loyal following for jazz and blues, and the Carpenter Performing Arts Center presents a strong program of both musical styles.

Long Beach Ballet Arts Center
1122 E. Wardlow Rd.
Long Beach 90807
562-426-4112

The non-profit Long Beach Ballet Arts Center has for forty years trained aspiring dancers, many of whom were among the founding members of the Long Beach Ballet in 1982. Kids fill the studios for after-school classes, and in the summer, students from the ages of ten to nineteen come from across the Western states for the intensive, five-week Dance Camp. Admission is by audition, or applicants may send a tape for consideration. Call for information about audition schedules, tuition, and housing (available at nearby Cal State Long Beach).

California State University, Long Beach (CSULB)
1250 Bellflower Blvd.
Long Beach 90840-1901
562-985-4111
Arts Events Hotline: 562-985-5128

Established in 1949 during the postwar boom in Southern California, Cal State Long Beach now educates more than 30,000 students each year. The campus has a collection of modern sculpture that dots the 320-acre campus, stretching for two miles along landscaped pathways; eight of these pieces were created in 1965 during a summer-long symposium that paired artists with industrial sponsors who provided technological assistance, materials, and tools. The University has continued to collect and commission art, including a mural that Terry Schoonhoven painted on the north wall of Fine Arts 4. In addition to the sculpture walk, the **Earl Burns Miller Japanese Garden** adjacent to Earl Warren Drive provides a quiet spot for rest and reflection (Tues.–Fri. 8 a.m.–3:30 p.m., Sun. noon–4 p.m.).

Although the **University Art Museum** (North Campus Library, 5th Fl., 562-985-5761; Tues.–Thurs. noon–8 p.m., Fri.–Sun. noon–5 p.m.; free) is small, the professional standards of its exhibition program have been recognized as "a model for university museums" by the California Arts Council. An active outreach program addresses the needs of teachers in a Summer Institute and helps members access sites of interest in the area and the U. S. through its Museum Tours and Travel Program.

The **Carpenter Performing Arts Center** (6200 Atherton St.; 562-985-7000), which opened in 1994 and is named for alumni donors Richard and Karen Carpenter, has made the northeastern corner of the campus a destination for culture. Because its programming is funded in part by student fees, the Center seeks to satisfy the needs and tastes of those enrolled and working on campus as well as provide programming not available anywhere else in the community. Its administration reports to the dean of the College of Arts, a decision it hopes will encourage a personality and point of view that reflect the student body and its diverse cultural heritage. The facility is exceptional (if not unique) in its compatibility with 70mm film projection, a fact that has piqued the interest of industry professionals and led the Carpenter Center to expand its annual WideScreen Film Festival to three fall weekends. Call for current schedule of cultural events on campus; see also Film and Video (p. 106) and Music (p. 198).

Rancho los Alamitos

6400 Bixby Hill Rd.
Long Beach 90815
562-431-3541
Wed.–Sun. 1–5 p.m.
Entry: free

Signal Hill Public Library
1770 E. Hill St.
Signal Hill 90806
562-989-7323

Today four acres of beautifully landscaped gardens and lawns surround this graceful, sprawling ranch house, which was built in 1806 when the 300,000-acre land grant given to Manuel Nieto, a member of Portola's expedition, was divided among his heirs. The property, then reduced to 26,000 acres, was acquired in 1881 by the Bixby family, who lived there until the 1960s when they gave it to the city of Long Beach. In the early part of this century, Rancho los Alamitos (Ranch of the Little Cottonwoods) was a flourishing ranch and citrus farm. The old ranch house, listed on the National Register of Historic Places as the oldest domestic building in California, contains much of the Bixby's original furnishings and is so perfectly maintained, cozy, and family-friendly that it seems hard to believe no one currently lives there. The historic site also features several barns and a blacksmith's shop, all well preserved and stocked with authentic equipment. Docent-guided tours of the house and barns bring back early California life, as do such annual events as Citrus Days (June), Hispanic Heritage Day (September), Fall Harvest Festival (which features agricultural games), and Christmas celebrations.

Generations of Bixbys spent nearly 100 years transforming their piece of California into an Eden-like ranch, and enlisted some of the finest landscape architects—including the Olmsted Brothers, Paul J. Howard, and Florence Yoch—to create its special atmosphere. Two enormous Moreton Bay fig trees and a walkway lined with jacarandas are notable features of the landscaping, which also includes gardens of cactus, native plants, herbs, and hybrid roses of the 1920s. The grounds may be enjoyed on self-guided tours.

El Dorado East Regional Park

7550 E. Spring St.
Long Beach 90815
562-570-1771
Park: daily 7 a.m.–5 p.m. (winter),
7 a.m.–8 p.m. (summer)
Nature Center: Tues.–Fri. 10 a.m.–4 p.m., Sat.–
Sun. 8:30 a.m.–4 p.m.; trails open 8 a.m.–4 p.m.
Entry: free

This eighty-five-acre park just west of the Orange County line is characterized by two lakes inhabited by ducks, geese, and other birds; its facilities include camping areas and an archery range (site of the 1984 Olympic competition in that sport). The nature center, located on an island in the northern lake, includes displays on small urban animals who inhabit the area. Younger children can touch different natural packaging—pinecones, feathers, and snake skin—while older kids investigate geological evolution, ecosystems, and recycling. The park's hiking trails are landscaped with 500 varieties of trees and plants, and a native-plant demonstration garden showcases the hardy species that have adapted to our hot, dry climate. Naturalist-led programs for children and families examine the park's habitat, including insects, seashore animals, and the wildlife of the ponds; call 562-570-1745.

Arts of Apsara Gallery and Cultural Center

United Cambodian Community Plaza
2338 E. Anaheim St., Ste. 105
Long Beach 90813
562-438-3932
Tues.–Sat. 10 a.m.–5 p.m.
Entry: free

Southern California, now home to more foreign-born residents than any other area of the country, has the largest expatriate Cambodian community in the world, centered in Little Phnom Penh along Anaheim Street in Long Beach. Some 40,000 people have found refuge here from the killing fields of Southeast Asia, drawn, like earlier seafaring immigrants—Greeks, Italians, Portuguese, Scandinavians, and Japanese—to the fishing and maritime industries.

The Arts of Apsara Gallery has relied on grants to establish its exhibition program of four shows per year. The gallery is working toward self-sufficiency through its sale of art; the sales are intended as an outlet for artists still working in Cambodia as well as for residents of the Long Beach area. The center offers classes in traditional Cambodian arts, ranging from fabric-making and embroidery to ceramics and dance.

Homeland Neighborhood Cultural Center

1321 E. Anaheim St.
Long Beach 90813
562-570-1740

Located in a multiracial neighborhood known as the Anaheim Corridor, Homeland is a cultural center and a civic experiment, offering both art exhibitions and innovative community outreach programs. Its mission is the recognition and celebration of the neighborhood's ethnic diversity, which the four languages—English, Spanish, Vietnamese, and Khmer—in which the word *library* is rendered at the local branch only begin to suggest.

The city-funded center, which moved to MacArthur Park's recreation building in 1996, offers workshops in painting and writing, and has plans for future programs in graphic arts and video. In a sometimes racially troubled area, Homeland Neighborhood Cultural Center is a flickering hope for ethnic pride and fruitful coexistence.

Rancho los Cerritos

4600 Virginia Rd.
Long Beach 90807
562-570-1755
Wed.–Sun. 1–5 p.m.; guided tours Sat.–Sun. only, on the hour
Entry: free

Rancho los Cerritos, once part of the same Spanish land grant as Rancho los Alamitos, owes its preservation, as does that site, to the Bixby family. The home that Jonathan Temple built for himself when he purchased the ranch in 1843 had been abandoned for fifty years when Llewellyn Bixby began to remodel the structure in 1931. He converted the simple working ranch to a two-story adobe in the Monterey style, with red-tile roof and rows of wooden doors opening to a covered arcade. Listed since 1970 as a National Historic Landmark, the adobe house conjures up Old California both by its appearance and in the exhibits that preserve the rancho lifestyle. Most of the furnishings are heavy, Victorian pieces that Bixby acquired from family members.

The visitor center features changing exhibits drawn from the collections of period costumes, photographs, and archival materials on Southern California's rich ranching history. The well-stocked research library, with 5,500 volumes, is noncirculating but available for public use during the museum's operating hours.

Banning Residence Museum

401 E. M St.
Wilmington 90748
310-548-7777
Tours: Tues.–Thurs. 12:30, 1:30, 2:30 p.m.;
Sat.–Sun. 12:30, 1:30, 2:30, 3:30 p.m.
Entry: $3 donation requested

Los Angeles had been incorporated as a city and California had become a state only one year before the 1851 arrival of twenty-one-year-old Phineas Banning at San Pedro. Banning sailed from the East Coast to Panama, made his way overland to the Pacific, and then sailed 3,000 miles north to reach San Pedro Bay, where he went into business providing horse-drawn transportation for people and freight from the muddy estuary that served as a boat landing to the dusty urban center twenty miles north. Within six years he had founded a new town at the point where the Los Angeles River met the estuary—he gave it the name of his birthplace in Delaware: Wilmington.

Banning championed the creation of a sophisticated communications and transportation infrastructure that would allow Los Angeles to develop into a major commercial center. Although he is often called "the father of the Port of Los Angeles," he was also instrumental in developing railway lines between Los Angeles and San Francisco and linking the two cities by telegraph. He saw the development of Southern California as part of the evolution of the nation and was a staunch Union supporter during the Civil War. Banning pressed for development of the port upon his election to the state senate in 1865, and he successfully secured legislative funding for the Los Angeles–San Pedro railroad in 1869 and for the San Pedro breakwater in 1873.

Tours of the Greek Revival home that Banning built on his 640-acre ranch are docent led and on a fixed schedule, but displays in a first-floor gallery offer an engaging way to pass the wait. More than 100 historic photographs recording the development of the harbor are on view, along with early photos of Catalina Island, which Banning's sons owned from 1892 to 1919 and developed as a resort. The island was then linked by steamer service with the mainland and offered glass-bottomed boats for recreation and a tent city for accommodations.

The handsome white clapboard structure, built in 1864 with a double-deck porch topped by a triangular pediment on the front, could serve as an ideogram for the word *house*. The cupola that straddles the gable roof, called a lantern, allowed Banning to survey the harbor. In seafaring towns on

Averill Park (1300 Dodson Ave.) is a local favorite for its lovely landscaped hills, and the tidepools at Royal Palms State Beach (Western Ave. at Paseo del Mar) are a sure kid-pleaser.

the New England coast, residences with this element and in this upright and proper style are common, but the Banning residence was rare in its day and remains the finest example of Greek Revival architecture in Southern California. The twenty-three-room house was the most elegant and commodious in the area, with its English patterned wallpapers and Empire-style furniture (many pieces original to the house were donated by the Banning family). The rooms have been carefully restored and embellished with everyday objects that suggest family life during the sixty years that the Bannings resided there. School tours are very popular, especially with students studying California history; docent-led tours are embellished on a regular schedule with a program called A Taste of History, in which Victorian-era foods are prepared and served to visitors in the period kitchen. Other special events and programs in this lovely, historic home include Tasteful Interlude, a Friday luncheon served to groups with advance reservations and followed by a special tour; and a two-day Christmas celebration that features elaborate Victorian-era decorations.

In the twenty-acre park that surrounds the house today are mature shade trees, a pergola with an ancient and enormous wisteria vine, and rose gardens, as well as one of the original barns. Seven horse-drawn vehicles—of the sort used for short runs on city streets rather than for the longer routes that Banning plied in his first local job—and a wheelwright's shop are displayed in the barn.

Drum Barracks Civil War Museum

1052 Banning Blvd.
Wilmington 90744
310-548-7509
By guided tour only: Tues.–Fri. on the hour, 10 a.m.–1 p.m.; Sat.–Sun. on the half-hour, 11:30 a.m.–2:30 p.m.; reservations necessary for groups of 8 or more
Entry: $2.50 donation requested

Drum Barracks is the only intact U.S. Army building from the Civil War-era in Southern California, and one of the rare military structures from that period to survive west of the Mississippi. The sixteen-room, clapboard Greek Revival building originally served as officers' quarters at Camp Drum, which in 1862 consisted of nineteen buildings on sixty acres. The land for this base had been donated by two Union supporters and civic leaders, D. D. Wilson (the first mayor of Los Angeles, whose grandson made military history as General George Patton) and Phineas Banning (whose own residence is preserved as a museum nearby). It was the primary training, staging, and supply area for military operations in the western United States during the 1860s, housing as many as 7,000 Union Army soldiers. It was decommissioned in 1871 and, nearly a century later, saved from demolition and converted to a Civil War museum. Along with such historical artifacts as furniture, clothes, photos, and portraits, the museum includes several displays of period weapons, and a rare thirty-four-star Union flag. Its noncirculating research library welcomes the public, especially teachers, to consult its resources, which include a reprint set of *The Official Records of the Union and the Confederate Armies*.

The Drum Barracks hosts a special independence celebration around the Fourth of July with food, entertainment, and tours of the Civil War museum.

The Federal Building and Post Office (839 S. Beacon St.) was built by the Works Progress Administration in 1936 in the art deco style now known as WPA Modern; it contains a mural depicting the harbor area's heritage.

The YWCA (437 W. Ninth St.) was designed by Julia Morgan—the first woman to be licensed as an architect in California—who is best known for the commissions she executed for William Randolph Hearst, including Hearst Castle on the Central Coast.

Muller House Museum (1542 S. Beacon St.; 310-548-3208), an 1899 home built by a Wilmington shipbuilder and occupied by his family until they donated it to the San Pedro Bay Historical Society in 1983, offers a glimpse of turn-of-the-century life in this area. It is open 1 to 4 p.m. on the first three Sundays of each month.

Although the harbor facilities hum day and night, **San Pedro** itself is a pleasantly situated, rather placid coastal town on the bluffs; it boasts spectacular views of the harbor, the ocean, Catalina Island, and the Palos Verdes Peninsula.

The San Pedro Peninsula Chamber of Commerce (P.O. Box 167, 390 W. Seventh St., San Pedro 90733, 310-832-7272; Mon.–Fri. 9 a.m.–5 p.m.) is happy to provide information for visitors. Their number-one recommendation is to ride the trolley: it costs just twenty-five cents, and one fare entitles passengers to get off and visit attractions at any stop, then reboard. The route extends from the beach at Cabrillo Marine Aquarium, around the Marina (with a stop at the 22nd Street Landing, where sportfishing and diving boats are docked), to the SS *Lane Victory*, then follows the main channel north to Ports O'Call Village and the Maritime Museum. It then turns west to Old San Pedro (bounded by Fifth and Tenth Sts. from Grand Ave. to the harbor), which has retained some architectural gems from the 1920s and 1930s and attracts visitors to its many ethnic restaurants, bookstores, and shops. The trolley plys this route, which terminates at the World Cruise Center and Catalina Terminal, every forty-five minutes (daily 9 a.m.–7 p.m. in summer; Thurs.–Mon. 9 a.m.–5 p.m. in winter).

The three "villages"—Fisherman's Village, Ports O'Call, and Whaler's Village—on this largest man-made harbor in the Western Hemisphere add to its atmosphere and offer shops and restaurants. They are the point of departure for boat charters, rentals, and cruises, and all kinds of ships are visible from the cobblestone walkways and dockside boardwalks. At Berth 78, the offerings include two-hour coastline cruises on Saturday and Sunday, daily narrated harbor cruises, and whale-watching excursions from January through March. Call Los Angeles Harbor Cruises (310-831-0996) for information.

Warner Grand Theater

478 W. Sixth St.
San Pedro 90731
310-548-2493

The marquee of this 1931 movie palace glows again for the first time in twenty years, symbolizing the rebirth of the 1,500-seat theater that Warner Bros. built to premiere their feature films: in 1996 the city of Los Angeles purchased it for use as a performing arts center to be managed by the Cultural Affairs Department. The facility retains the charm of a bygone era—from its neon moderne sign and marquee to the art deco opulence of its lobby and auditorium—but funds will be needed to make the theater's original technical systems compatible with contemporary performance requirements. The facility is rented out year round for a variety of programming; film, musical, and community-based productions, as well as touring shows fill the Warner, which, it is hoped, will become a centerpiece to the revitalization of downtown San Pedro.

Warner Kids is an arts education program held in a building adjacent to the theater (464 W. Sixth St.); it is administered by the Junior Arts Center (located in Hollywood's Barnsdall Park). Visual and performing arts workshops ranging from drama and dance to painting and stage production are offered for young people ages three to seventeen; call 310-548-2496 for a class schedule.

Los Angeles Maritime Museum

Berth 84, at the foot of Sixth St.
San Pedro 90731
310-548-7618
Tues.–Sun. 10 a.m.–5 p.m.
Entry: $1 donation requested

There's playground equipment at the flat, sandy beach that stretches on both the channel and ocean sides of the San Pedro breakwater, which was built continuously from 1899 to the 1940s to protect the port. Out by Angel's Gate Lighthouse, windsurfers catch steady breezes. North of the Cabrillo Marine Aquarium, a salt marsh has been planted with pickleweed and saltgrass to provide a habitat for seabirds.

Formerly the Municipal Ferry Building, this 75,000-square-foot facility is the largest maritime museum on the West Coast. Located on the waterfront at the Port of Los Angeles, it offers an overview of contemporary harbor activity as well as a fascinating window on the nautical past. More than 700 models document the vessels in which humans have gone to sea over the years, whether for transportation, recreation, military, or commercial purposes.

The centerpiece of the model collection is the eighteen-foot-long exact replica of the *Titanic*, with a highly detailed cutaway view of the interior. Also featured is the twenty-two-foot-long model of the so-called *Poseidon* (actually the *Queen Mary*), which was used in the 1972 film *The Poseidon Adventure*. Other highlights of the museum's vast collection are models of the *Bounty* (*Mutiny on the Bounty*, starring Clark Gable, was filmed near San Pedro), Teddy Roosevelt's Great White Fleet of Battleships, and the USS *Constitution* ("Old Ironsides").

Exhibits chronicle maritime arts and crafts, nautical lore, and the development of the Los Angeles Harbor. Various seaman's knots are displayed, along with rope to try your hand at duplicating them. Scrimshaw, the sailor's pastime of ivory-carving, and ships in bottles are well represented; there are displays on the elegant designs of the tall ships and even an authentic Thai fishing boat, and a ham radio station communicates with posts all around the world. There is also a sixteen-inch naval gun from

the USS *New Jersey* in the Naval Memorial adjacent to the museum.

Various nautical items—a giant torpedo, nine-ton and twenty-one-ton propellers, a life-size mock-up of the flying bridge of the USS *Los Angeles*—enliven the museum grounds and invite both adults and children to explore (and actually climb) onto the exhibits. Docked next to the museum is the *Ralph J. Scott*, a firefighting boat built in 1926 which has been designated a National Historic Landmark. Although boarding is prohibited, there is often a friendly port firefighter from the adjacent headquarters who will explain the workings of the boat and the harbor to curious school groups. A sailing replica of a revolutionary privateer, the *Swift*, is at the museum dock; sailing classes for at-risk youth are offered through various local agencies.

SS *Lane Victory*

Berth 94, Los Angeles Harbor
(Next to the World Cruise Center)
San Pedro 90733
310-519-9545
Daily 9 a.m.–4 p.m.
Entry: adults $3, children 5–15 $1

One of more than 500 Victory ships built during World War II to transport cargo and war materiel for the Allied troops, the *Lane Victory* is a Southern California native, built in 1945 at Terminal Island. The U.S. Merchant Marine ship also served in Korea and Vietnam, then was mothballed from 1971 to 1988, when Ronald Reagan approved the petition of a group of veterans and conveyed the ship to them. Towed to Los Angeles and lovingly restored to working order, the ship is often rented as a set for TV and film productions. A National Historic Landmark, the ship is itself a museum piece, and collections of photographs and other documents on its wartime service, as well as Jeeps and other vehicles (including a fire engine from an Air Force station) are displayed in a museum aboard the ship.

The *Lane Victory* is also authorized to offer six trips per year to the public, who are invited to journey back in history to the ship's heyday. These Memorial Cruises simulate a WWII battle, with the guns of the *Lane Victory* firing back at "Nazi" warplanes in the Catalina Channel. The full-day cruise (boarding 7:30–8:30 a.m.; no wheelchair access) is offered one weekend in July, August, and September, with breakfast, buffet lunch, and a band playing vintage music included in the fee (adults $100, children 15 and under $60).

Cabrillo Marine Aquarium

3720 Stephen White Dr. (off Pacific Ave.)
San Pedro 90731
310-548-7562
Tues.–Fri. noon–5 p.m., Sat.–Sun. 10 a.m.–5 p.m.
Entry: free; parking $6.50

Once you've paid the steep fee to park at Cabrillo Beach, leave the car in the lot and jump on the trolley—for just 25¢—to visit the rest of San Pedro.

The Cabrillo Marine Aquarium (formerly Museum) moved in 1981 from the Spanish-style bathhouse near the San Pedro breakwater, which it had occupied since 1934, to a cluster of indoor and outdoor spaces designed by Frank Gehry and enveloped with his signature chain-link. In the courtyard is a whale graveyard with a massive jawbone that, like the full-scale silhouette drawing on the floor, suggests the enormous size of these extraordinary creatures. A text panel explains that the leatherback turtle suspended overhead is the largest marine turtle, well adapted to cold northern waters, and consumes enough jellyfish to achieve a weight of 1,500 pounds. The visitor is in a different world even before entering the building.

Inside, the jagged spaces are defined by different habitats. In the open ocean are whales and dolphins, sea birds and seals, schooling fish, sharks, and rays; hardy creatures that tolerate pounding surf live in aquaria—some complete with wave effects—which simulate rocky shores; and in gentle waves rolling onto a sandy beach, halibut and turbot, barely distinguishable from the sand, flop in the current. The Aquarium recently added a 3,600-gallon kelp tank to showcase that majestic plant and the fish that live in and around it. Kelp forests are the preferred habitat of many sea creatures, and the plant itself is used in products from dog biscuits to Cool Whip, onion rings to vitamin pills.

The daily diet of the sea otter—which consumes 25 percent of its body weight every day—includes three abalone, seven rock crabs, four Pismo clams, seven sea urchins, and a few clusters of mussels. (This seafood lover began to dream of being reincarnated as a sea otter, but fishermen are often less tolerant of its voracious appetite.) The Mantis shrimp, with its fluorescent blue flippers and sleek tropical pink-gold body, is certainly too pretty to eat, but humans are among the predators of the diverse crustaceans in nearby tanks.

At the Touch Tank out back, which is open for twenty-minute sessions throughout the day as announced on the loudspeaker, kids poke at billowing sea anemone, retreat from prickly sea urchins, and pat colorful starfish. The staff answers questions, and a shark and giant lobster can be seen—but not touched—moving about the deep-water pool.

Tidepool walks at nearby Point Fermin Marine Life Refuge are regularly conducted by Aquarium staff. From March to July, the Aquarium hosts its ever-popular Meet the Grunion program, which features a nighttime excursion to the shoreline to wait for the silvery sardinelike grunion—the only species of fish that lives in the sea but lays its eggs on land—to make an appearance. The grunion come ashore in masses to spawn, just after the highest high tide (which coincides with the full moon, making them easier to spot), and each female burrows into the sand to deposit 1,000 to 3,000 eggs, which will hatch fourteen days later when the newborns will be swept out to sea by the next high tide.

The Aquarium cosponsors a whale-watching program with the American Cetacean Society. These popular boat trips promote the safe observation of whales; on-board naturalists share their knowledge about the Pacific gray whale as well as dolphins, sea lions, and marine birds. Volunteers train for six months to become guides on Cabrillo whale-watch vessels, earning this program high praise from veteran whale watchers. Reserve early for weekends and check for individual seats on weekday cruises (which are largely booked with school groups); call 310-832-4444.

Educational programs for five- to twelve-year-olds expand the opportunities for visitors to make the close acquaintance of many sea creatures. Family classes feature in-depth scrutiny of tidepool creatures, the study of whales and other marine mammals, and many marine-oriented craft projects such as printing T-shirts inspired by the sea's colors. Summer programs include reasonably priced week-long day-camp programs (Mon.–Fri. 9 a.m.–noon) for school-age children, which feature marine biology, with excursions to the nearby beach and tidepools. Special events, such as seafaring storytelling, are offered in one-day summer workshops open to children and their parents. Call 310-548-7562 for details.

Angel's Gate Cultural Center (AGCC)

3601 S. Gaffey St.
San Pedro 90731
310-519-0936
Wed.–Sun. 11 a.m.–4 p.m.

The Marine Mammal Care Center (3601 S. Gaffey St., San Pedro; 310-547-9888) allows wounded and sick pinnipeds and other animals to recover with specialized care. Its facilities are primarily utilized by the L. A. Unified School District and San Pedro High School as an educational center in marine science, but other school groups (from kindergarten through college) may book tours, which will be tailored to their interests and abilities, and the public is invited for regular open-house events.

Ranchos Palos Verdes Farmers Market Peninsula Center parking lot (Hawthorne Blvd. and Silver Spur Rd.) Sun. 9 a.m.–1 p.m.

Angel's Gate Cultural Center, located in the former Army barracks of Fort MacArthur Upper Reservation, was started in 1981 to provide cultural arts programming for San Pedro and adjacent South Bay communities. AGCC is a nonprofit, multicultural, and multidisciplinary arts center, which encourages participation and experimentation in contemporary art by supporting a dynamic group of serious emerging and midcareer artists. Exhibitions, performances, open studio tours, and film and video screenings invite the public to experience the center's unique atmosphere.

AGCC has continued to increase the number of classes and public events it sponsors, with contemporary music concerts, mask-making workshops, modern-dance classes, and outdoor jazz festivals. The creative energy at AGCC should inspire anyone's muse.

The Bell of Friendship, located in 160-acre Angel's Gate Park (3601 S. Gaffey St.; daily 8 a.m.–4 p.m.), was a Bicentennial gift from the people of South Korea to the people of the United States. It represents Korea's rich cultural heritage and testifies to the myriad contributions that Koreans have made to Los Angeles. It is the largest Oriental bell in existence. Suspended in a pagoda-style belfry on a windswept bluff, its design features the Statue of Liberty and a Korean spirit holding Korea's national flower, the Rose of Sharon. The bell is hung very low to the ground, which makes the sound reverberate against the earth and move through a sound tube. Due to the unique design of the bell and the scooped-out, tile-lined hollow just below it, the sound is heard and felt as a low rumble over a wide area for five minutes after it is struck.

Fort MacArthur Military Museum
Battery Osgood-Farley

3601 Gaffey St.
San Pedro 90731
310-548-2631
Tues.–Thurs., Sat.–Sun. noon–5 p.m.
Entry: free

The Fort MacArthur Military Museum, located in the historic Battery Osgood, overlooks the Pacific Ocean from one of the most scenic points in San Pedro. Battery Osgood was constructed in 1916 as part of the Fort MacArthur and Los Angeles Harbor defense system: the batteries housed fourteen-inch retractable guns that could fire a projectile seventeen miles, farther than the biggest weapon on any battleship at that time. By World War II new developments in weaponry and aviation had rendered these guns obsolete, so they were deactivated and dismantled, but the batteries at Fort MacArthur remained active and were rearmed with the latest weaponry.

Photos and exhibits on the defense of the Los Angeles Harbor from 1916 to 1945, World War I and II history, and memorabilia and dramatic displays documenting local civilian war-defense efforts are featured in the museum. A walking tour of the Battery Osgood-Farley facility includes a look at the plotting room, the "brains" of the battery; the commander's station, from which the still-working speaking tubes emanate; the decontamination room, built to "wash off" poison gas; and the gun pit. Restoration is ongoing, but there is much to see here that brings our military past vividly to life.

The museum holds its annual artillery show (admission $3) in early July in Angel's Gate Park. The show features artillery demonstrations, reenactments, and drills; displays of historical uniforms and encampments; and a diverse array of vehicles representing American military units from 1776 through 1946.

Point Fermin Park and Lighthouse (Paseo del Mar and Gaffey St.) is named for Father Fermin Francisco de Lasuén, who founded nine of the Alta California missions. The white-clapboard, Eastlake-style lighthouse was built in 1874 and is the last of the wooden lighthouses that once guided navigators along the California coast. The surrounding thirty-seven-acre park is landscaped with palms and Moreton Bay fig trees and offers an unobstructed view of Catalina and Palos Verdes Peninsula.

The spectacularly beautiful coastline of the **Palos Verdes Peninsula** remains unspoiled, in part because nature seems to rebuke all efforts to develop it. Attempts to grade the land at Portuguese Bend in order to extend Crenshaw Boulevard triggered landslides in 1956 and permanently destabilized a 270-acre tract that creeps toward Palos Verdes Drive South at the rate of a few inches each year, keeping the roadway under constant repair. The facilities at **Friendship County Regional Park** (off Western Ave. and Ninth St.) include the **San Pedro Recreation Center**, with playground and baseball diamonds, but a proposed $4.4-million nature center has become mired in controversy over the role played by County Supervisor Deane Dana, for whom it would be named, in planning the project.

Resort hotels marked the south coast—at Abalone Cove, Royal Palms, and White Point—from the turn of the century to the 1930s, but none survived the geological activity and fierce storms that can pound the coastline. By 1900 Japanese fishermen had developed abalone beds at White Point, utilizing underwater hot springs (which are still active) to nourish these mollusks with chemosynthesis; the springs later fed a Japanese bathhouse at White Point Hot Springs, a resort built on land since reclaimed by the ocean. Today Abalone Cove is an eighty-acre ecological reserve with extensive tidepools at Portuguese Point and Inspiration Point, and sandy beaches at East Beach and Smuggler's Cove. Royal Palms and White Point are state beaches popular with surfers and scuba divers, respectively. Marineland, once an oceanside destination for area families, closed years ago, but access to the rocky shore and free public parking are permitted daily 8:30 a.m.–4:00 p.m. at the site just south of Point Vicente.

The Wayfarers' Chapel

Wayfarers Chapel

5755 Palos Verdes Dr. S.
Rancho Palos Verdes 90274
310-377-1650

Architect Lloyd Wright surrounded the glass and Palos Verdes-stone chapel he built in 1951 with redwood trees, which have since grown to envelop the structure as he intended: "I want the trees and their trunks to be seen, and the space beyond, so that those who worship in the sanctuary will perceive the grandeur of the world around them and beyond them." More than 600 marriages a year are celebrated at Wayfarer's Chapel, and memorial services are held regularly in keeping with the Swedenborgian tenet that life is ongoing after death. The front lawn and landscaped gardens afford spectacular views and quiet places for meditation.

Palos Verdes Peninsula not only has lavish estates from the 1920s and 1930s in a community landscaped by Olmsted and Olmsted, but also some of the most spectacular oceanfront land in Southern California. The entire 4.5-mile shoreline of **Palos Verdes Estates** was preserved as a 130-acre blufftop park, but the rocky beaches can only be reached (with difficulty) on steep and hazardous trails. Malaga Cove, the only sandy beach on the peninsula, can be reached by an access road from the parking lot at the end of Via Arroyo, off Paseo del Mar.

Hermosa Beach
Farmers Market
Thirteenth St. and
Hermosa Ave.
Fri. noon–4 p.m.

Point Vicente Interpretative Center

31501 Palos Verdes Dr. W.
Rancho Palos Verdes 90275
310-377-5370
Daily 10 a.m.–5 p.m.; 10 a.m.–7 p.m. (summer)
Entry (to Interpretative Center): adults $2, seniors/children 4–14 $1

I'd have been happy to spend my visit to the Point Vicente Interpretive Center just watching dusk transform the wintry seascape and peering through binoculars in hopes of spotting migrating whales, but seeing my notebook, a docent volunteered to give me a tour and plied me with lots of interesting facts that are also the subject of displays. Palos Verdes Peninsula was an island created by uplift on the ocean floor during the Pleistocene, and was then gradually linked to the mainland by sedimentation from the Los Angeles basin. This extraordinarily beautiful piece of real estate had only four owners between the days of the Gabrielino Indians and World War II, but its promise was not realized until the postwar population boom caused people to consider living in areas formerly thought too remote.

Displays explain the history of Palos Verdes Peninsula and its development, including exhibits on its first inhabitants, the Gabrielino Indians. The Pacific gray whale—which passes by the promontory on its annual 11,000-mile round-trip migration from the Arctic to Baja Mexico between December and May—is one of the subjects of exhibits on marine life. A botanic trail along the bluff has markers identifying the plantings, chosen for their ability to survive in the salt air. Because the bluff trails overlook extensive kelp beds and the open ocean, they are a good spot to view marine life. Volunteers from Whalewatch conduct a census of the annual whale migration with data collected from the observation center at Point Vicente.

Torrance offers special recreational facilities through its Parks and Recreation Department (310-618-2930); proof of residency is required for the low-fee Las Canchas Tennis Facility (25942 Rolling Hills Rd.; 310-530-8212) and Sea-Aire Golf Course (22730 Lupine Dr.; 310-316-9779). The Plunge, a fifty-by-twenty-meter heated pool (3331 Torrance Blvd.; 310-781-7113), offers an extensive program of swimming instruction in summer months. Roller-hockey rinks are located at Columbia Park (4045 190th St.) and Wilson Park (2200 Crenshaw Blvd.); for more information on this sport, call the Torrance Skate Association (310-320-9529). More than half of the forty parks in Torrance have great playground equipment, including La Romeria Park (19501 Inglewood Ave.).

Four historical museums in this area together give a comprehensive look at these South Bay communities and how they have evolved:

Manhattan Beach Historical Society

1601 Manhattan Beach Blvd.
Manhattan Beach 90266
310-374-7575
Sat.–Sun. noon–3 p.m.

A circa-1905 beach cottage houses a timeline that marks important dates pertaining to the pier; there are also artifacts of the Gabrielino Indians.

Hermosa Beach Historical Society

710 Pier Ave.
Hermosa Beach 90254
310-318-9421
Sat.–Sun. 2–4 p.m.

Hermosa Beach claims to have been the birthplace of surfing in the 1920s—maybe they mean on the mainland—and this museum displays surfing paraphernalia and photos from that era, as well as examples of tile and glass produced in local factories. Downtown got a facelift in 1997, with new sparkle-flecked sidewalks and nautical-looking streetlights; funds from 1992's Proposition A are earmarked for work on the ailing pier.

Torrance Historical Museum

1345 Post Ave.
Torrance 90501
310-328-5392
Tues.–Thurs., Sun. 1–4 p.m.

Located in the former city library—a classic example of WPA Moderne architecture—the museum has exhibits on how the model city developed, including a display on the role of women in the South Bay.

Redondo Beach Historical Museum

302 Flagler Ln. (Dominguez Park)
Redondo Beach 90277
310-318-0684
Sat.–Sun. 1–4 p.m.

A Queen Anne Victorian cottage contains exhibits on the evolution of the surfboard, as well the development of piers and playgrounds along the beach.

South Coast Botanic Garden

26300 Crenshaw Blvd.
Palos Verdes Peninsula 90274
310-544-6815
Daily 9 a.m.–5 p.m.
Entry: adults $5, seniors/students $3,
children 5–12 $1

Mined for diatomite until 1956, then used as a landfill until 1960, the South Coast Botanic Garden began development in 1961 as a highly innovative eighty-seven-acre land-reclamation project. A three-foot layer of topsoil covers more than 100 feet of garbage—3.5 million tons of trash seethe and settle beneath the tranquil and diverse botanical gardens. Heat and gases caused by the decomposition of organic matter dissipate through pipes; scientists at a nearby landfill are experimenting with using these gases as an energy source.

The transformation of debased land into such horticultural health and abundance is an inspiration that brings visitors from all over the world to see this extraordinary and pioneering example of land recycling. A man-made stream and a two-acre lake support diverse animal and fish populations. Many plants from South Africa, the Mediterranean, and Australia, whose climates resemble that of Southern California, are included among 150,000 plants representing 140 families, 700 genera, and 2,000 species. It is an astonishing rebirth where once there was once only a man-made wasteland.

The South Coast Botanic Garden is a place of great beauty and a living laboratory of horticultural study that's well worth a visit for all ages. Special programs are scheduled every Sunday, including a bird walk at 8 a.m. on the first Sunday of every month; there are plant sales throughout the year, and a Shakespeare Festival is held every summer (call 310-265-0627).

Palos Verdes Art Center

5504 W. Crestridge Rd.
Rancho Palos Verdes 90274
310-541-2479
Mon.–Sat. 10 a.m.–4 p.m.; Beckstrand Gallery,
daily 1–4 p.m.

Founded in 1931, the Palos Verdes Art Center promotes the appreciation and expression of the arts in the peninsula community through exhibitions, professionally taught studio classes, and active school outreach programs. The multiuse facility has four gallery spaces (which present about twenty changing exhibitions each year) and an art sales space called the Artists' Studio Gallery. There is a ceramics workshop, a print workshop, an audiovisual film gallery, a darkroom, and art-filled classrooms where year-round classes and summer arts programs for children and adults are offered in visual art, performance, and music. About 300 local artist/members provide support for the center's programs; funds have been raised with an October arts fair since 1962.

Lomita Railroad Museum

Woodard and 250th Sts.
Lomita 90717
310-326-6255
Wed.–Sun. 10 a.m.–5 p.m.
Entry: adults $1, children $.50

Dedicated to the era of the steam engine, the Lomita Railroad Museum is the vision of Irene Lewis, a rail fan who built an exact replica of the Boston and Maine Railroad's turn-of-the-century station at Wakefield, Massachusetts, after researching many such extant structures. The station agent's office and the ticket booth have also been realistically re-created.

Details of the plans used to construct this gleaming, handcut-hardwood storehouse of colorful memorabilia are displayed in some exhibits, while railroad lore and history are recalled by the collected artifacts —semaphore signals, locomotive whistles, marker lights, and mileposts. Outside stands a Southern Pacific steam locomotive built in 1902, and nearby is a 1910-vintage Union Pacific caboose; kids and adults are encouraged to climb aboard to get a feel for what it was like to work and live on the rails of yesteryear.

A park opposite the museum entrance is a favorite spot for picnics and can be rented for birthday parties; a 1923 Union Oil tank car, a 1913 outside-braced wooden boxcar, and an all-metal Santa Fe caboose extend the railroad atmosphere.

Torrance Cultural Arts Center

3330 Civic Center Dr.
Torrance 90503
310-781-7150

The Old Town Music Hall (140 Richmond St., El Segundo; 310-322-2592) presents live concerts and classic movies; perhaps most notable is its programming of great Hollywood silent films, which are accompanied on "the Mighty Wurlitzer." For information about other silent movie screenings in Southern California, check out the Silents Majority Southern California Silent Calendar at www.mdle.com/classic films/scsc.

The dramatic glass-fronted buildings anchored by the 500-seat James R. Armstrong Theater (and linked by the Pine Wind Japanese Garden and the 14,000-square-foot Torino Festival Plaza) have been a source of civic pride since the $12-million facility opened in 1991. Programming at the Center is scheduled by several organizations, including Torrance Parks and Recreation Department (310-618-2930), South Bay Conservatory (310-618-6364), and the Torrance Cultural Arts Center Foundation (310-781-7194). The wide variety of classes—music, theater, studio arts, dance, and computer—is publicized in the quarterly Recreation Roundabout, available in local libraries.

The Joslyn Fine Arts Gallery (Tues.–Sat. noon–5 p.m.) features changing exhibitions of works by local artists, and the facility is rented by such local arts organizations as the Torrance Symphony and South Bay Ballet. Wild Wednesdays! are free noontime concerts staged in the Torino Festival Plaza during summer months. Administrators believe that the Center's flexible partnership with organizations throughout the community will result in rich and diverse programming; the schedule can be fluid, so those in the area should check the local papers for information.

The irregular rocky coastline of Palos Verdes gives way to wide, flat, sandy beaches at Redondo that continue all around Santa Monica Bay. The Pacific shoreline has been pretty solidly built up from Monstad Pier—which juts 300 feet into the Pacific (from the end of Torrance Blvd.) and is one of the best fishing spots on the coast—to King Harbor, a small-boat harbor with three basins accommodating more than 1,400 boats. **Seaside Lagoon**, a 2.5-acre saltwater park (between King Harbor's basins 2 and 3) that receives about 90,000 visitors between Memorial Day and September, is scheduled for a $2-million renovation. A new pumping system and water slides will be installed, picnic areas with barbecue pits will be expanded around the perimeter, and new playground equipment and grassy areas will make the park more usable after the swimming season ends.

Roundhouse Marine Studies Lab and Aquarium

Manhattan Beach Pier
Manhattan Beach 90266
310-379-8117
www.commpages.com/roundhouse/
Mon.–Fri. 3 p.m.–sunset, Sat.–Sun. 10 a.m.–sunset
Entry: donations welcomed

When the pier (at end of Manhattan Blvd.) was remodeled in 1993, the city of Manhattan Beach leased this space to Oceanographic Teaching Stations, a nonprofit educational group that had been working with local schools for fifteen years. They've installed live animal exhibits and tanks in the small Roundhouse—but they caution that their space is not on the same scale as Cabrillo's, for instance—and offer programs to supplement the exhibits, including beach walks with naturalists to collect specimens, and plankton labs. Call about information regarding three-hour workshops for up to thirty-five kids in grades K–12.

Santa Catalina Island lies eighteen nautical miles southwest of San Pedro, not "twenty-six miles across the sea," as the song says. Its hulking silhouette and fifty-four miles of untouched coastline have beckoned pleasure-seekers from Southern California ever since it was developed as a resort, before the turn of the century. Avalon—named for the refuge of blessed souls in Celtic mythology—is the island's only town, and most visitors disembark at its ferry terminal (although during the summer daily boats also link the village of Two Harbors with the mainland). Most of the island's 40,000 acres have been preserved in a natural state, crisscrossed only by unpaved trails for hikers, bicyclists, or equestrians. There is a small, sandy, and

From July to October there are tours of the 1889 Holly Hill House, a distinctive historic residence on Avalon Bay, and in December, an open house at William Wrigley's home on Mount Ada is a fund-raiser for Catalina's museum.

crowded beach in the center of Avalon, but it's only a short walk in almost any direction to less congested parts of the shore. Santa Catalina Conservancy (P.O. Box 2739, Avalon 90704; 310-510-2595), a nonprofit foundation established in 1972, owns 88 percent of the island's seventy-six square miles and continues the tradition of protecting the island's natural resources begun by William Wrigley Jr. A thirty-acre hillside botanical garden (1400 Avalon Canyon Rd., 1.7 miles from downtown Avalon; adults $1, children free), another Wrigley legacy, is now administered by the Conservancy. Eight plants endemic to Catalina are featured along with many other California native species.

Permits for hiking are required; they are free and can be attained from the Conservancy, which will provide a map of the trails that crisscross much of the wilderness area, some accessible to mountain bikes (which require a separate permit for a small fee that includes insurance). Jeep-Eco-Tours (from $65, proceeds benefit Conservancy programs) visit the inland wilderness, which is complete with a resident buffalo herd, left behind after an early movie shoot. Other outfitters offer bus tours in season, and bicycles are rented in Avalon.

Wrigley, scion of the chewing-gum fortune, purchased the island in 1919 from the sons of Phineas Banning—the "Father of Los Angeles Harbor"—who had introduced glass-bottomed boats and erected a tent city for accommodations. Wrigley made Catalina the winter training ground of his ballclub, the Chicago Cubs, and built the circular casino with a 1,000-seat, acoustically advanced cinema and ballroom; big-band music was broadcast from the casino in its heyday, bringing the little resort national prominence. Today the 1929-vintage casino houses a small museum (daily 10:30 a.m.–4 p.m., with summer evening hours 7–9 p.m. Fri.–Sat.; adults $1, children free). Exhibits on human history include the lives of the first inhabitants, photographs of Avalon's evolving landscape during its first fifty years, and displays on the tile and pottery that were manufactured locally from the 1920s until World War II. Maritime history features the famous glass-bottomed boats, sport fishing, and models

of the ships that ferry people to the island. Other exhibits explore the natural history of the island and ranching and mining. The museum also schedules events in the casino's theater, including the popular annual silent film festival in early June which kicks off the summer and the October jazz festival. See Music (p. 200) for more information.

Although Catalina is only twenty miles from Los Angeles, it seems as remote and lovely as an island in the Adriatic. The recreational possibilities are many: viewing kelp beds from glass-bottomed boats, scuba diving, and snorkeling are just the beginning. Bring a mask and snorkel and you can get up close to the local marine life at Avalon Underwater Park, which extends seventy-five yards out from Casino Point and 250 yards along the coast. The reef is artificial, but the water is the clearest on the West Coast, dropping off to ninety feet in depth. The golden garibaldi (state fish), lots of playful sea lions and seals, and several nautical wrecks can be seen underwater. Diving at this site is free, and there's a van nearby to refill diver's tanks. Avalon Aquatics (310-510-1225) and Catalina Divers Supply (310-510-0330) offer diver certification classes in the park. More recently, two sixty-foot, fifty-ton submarines began plying Catalina's waters, carrying up to thirty-six passengers on forty-minute underwater tours (adults $21, children $14; call Discovery Tours at 310-510-2500).

Catalina Express (310-519-7957) schedules daily ferries from Long Beach (adjacent to the Queen Mary) and San Pedro (Berth 95); Catalina Cruises (800-228-2546) advertises the lowest fares and leaves from 320 Golden Shore Boulevard in Long Beach. The Avalon Visitors Bureau provides information on accommodations and activities; call 310-510-1520. Hermit Gulch Campground, adjacent to the Botanical Garden, offers inexpensive teepee and tent cabins and simple amenities for campers with their own equipment; for reservations, call 310-510-8363. For information on Two Harbors, a small village located on the other side of the island, call 310-510-1550; there is a kayaking and diving center, a safari bus linking this isolated cove with Avalon, and facilities (including rentals) are available for camping.

LITERARY L.A.

Ellen Krout-Hasegawa

* indicates an area code that changes in 1998

The health of any city's literary landscape can usually be gauged by the number and diversity of its bookstores. It's a testament to Los Angeles and its book lovers that so many independent bookstores can survive alongside such chains as **Barnes & Noble, Bookstar, Borders, Brentano's,** and **Rizzoli.** Many of the chains do attempt to offer something different: Barnes & Noble and its affiliate Bookstar energetically promote more popular trade titles and best-selling authors in stores often outfitted with easy chairs and reading tables. Borders Books and Music tends to have a better selection of more serious titles. Its stores usually feature coffee bars and also sell CDs and videos. Rizzoli, whose elegant flagship store in New York was once a mecca for art book buyers, operates a group of stores that still feature coffee-table editions on art and architecture. Brentano's Bookstores, associated with Waldenbooks, offer a range of titles from the very popular to the more serious. Waldenbooks, B. Dalton, and Crown Books also have outlets in the area. The chain stores can be found readily through telephone directory assistance.

Los Angeles Public Library System

With six million books, the L.A. Public Library System has the largest collection of any public library in the western United States.

While the majority of its special collections is stored in its downtown headquarters, several of them are scattered among its sixty-six branches throughout the city. They include a Chinese-language collection, a Korean-language collection, a Chicano and Spanish-language collection, and a Japanese-American and Japanese-language collection. There is also an archive of film and TV scripts and signed biographies and scripts. Items from these collections can be summoned to any of the branch libraries within three days and are listed on the online catalogue, which is available at any branch or through the Internet (www.lapl.org). Requests can be faxed to 213-623-6455.

Asian American Writers' Workshop

Los Angeles hotline: 213-960-1615

The New York-based organization, devoted to "the creation, publication and dissemination of Asian American literature," sponsors a series of literary readings that spotlight Asian-American writers of local or national stature. Readings are held in different venues across the city. Call for the schedule.

Downtown/ Exposition Park

L.A. Public Library/ Museum of Contemporary Art (MOCA) Reading Series ("Racing toward the Millennium: Voices from the American West")
213-228-7025

This joint effort between two downtown organizations, the L.A. Public Library and MOCA, has drawn countless Angelenos downtown on Sunday afternoons. Modeled on the Lannan series (see below), in which an author reads and then is interviewed,

the series celebrates the wealth of writing that is unique to the West, focusing on writers who either live in the western United States or write about its people or landscape. The readings alternate between the two sponsoring organizations. Some of the authors who have taken part in the series either as readers or interviewers are essayist and novelist Bernard Cooper, humorist Cynthia Heimel, fruit grower David Mas Masumoto, and naturalist and nature writer Terry Tempest Williams. (Note: Even on a Sunday afternoon, parking is tough in downtown.) Sundays at 2 p.m. at one of two venues: **Mark Taper Auditorium,** Central Library, 630 W. Fifth Street, or **MOCA at California Plaza,** 250 S. Grand Avenue.

Japanese American National Museum
369 E. First St.
Los Angeles 90012
213-625-0414

The museum hosts readings by new and established voices within the Asian-Pacific-American community. Notable readings in the past have featured Frank Chin, David Wong Louie, Sesshu Foster, Shawn Wong, Gerrit Hongo, and Kimiko Hahn. Call for programming.

Kinokuniya Bookstore
Weller Court
123 Onizuka St.
Los Angeles 90012
213-687-4447
Daily 10 a.m.–8 p.m.

Ten to 20 percent of Kinokuniya's stock (10,000 books) is in English, but the rest is in hiragana, katakana, and kanji. Most of what is in English are translations of Japanese fiction, classical and modern. There's also a selection of books on Japanese language, culture, history, and the Japanese-American internment camps.

Instituto Cultural Mexicano
125 Paseo de la Plaza
Los Angeles 90012
213-624-3660
Mon.–Fri. 9 a.m.–5 p.m.

This store near Olvera Street stocks 2,000 *libros en español* on Mexican history, culture, and literature, as well as the better-known Latin-American authors.

Libros Revolución
312 W. Eighth St.
Los Angeles 90014
213-488-1303
Wed. 2–6 p.m.,
Thurs.–Sat. 10:30 a.m.–6 p.m.,
Sun. noon–5 p.m.

The bilingual version of Revolution Books in Berkeley, the store is staffed by volunteers, mostly supporters of the Revolutionary Communist Party. Copies of Mumia Abu-Jamal's *Live from Death Row* can be found in both Spanish and English; the same with *The Red Book of Mao.* Half of the 750 titles are in Spanish. Here *revolución* is in the air, and so is the smell of free coffee.

USC SPECTRUM READING SERIES
University Park Campus
University of Southern California
3551 University Ave.
Los Angeles 90089
213-740-2176, 213-740-1111

In 1997 USC's Division of Student Affairs played host to Native-American novelist and poet Sherman Alexie, the award-winning science fiction writer and Pasadena resident Octavia Butler, and such international authors as the African poet, novelist, and playwright Wole Soyinka. Call for tickets and programming.

Librería Azteca
1429 W. Adams Blvd.
Los Angeles 90007
*213-733-4040
Mon.–Fri. 9 a.m.–6 p.m.,
Sat. 9 a.m.–3 p.m.

The *Los Angeles Times* described this little-known family-owned business near USC as a bookstore that "offers Spanish-speaking lovers of literature a way to feed their passion without leaving the country." I couldn't have said it better. Azteca's shelves bulge with the poetry, plays, and novels of the Spanish-speaking world.

South Los Angeles/ Mid-City

Southern California Library for Social Studies and Research
6120 S. Vermont Ave.
Los Angeles 90044
*213-759-6063
Tues.–Sat. 10 a.m.–4 p.m.

Founded by political activist Emil Freed in 1963, the library is the only thing of its kind, billing itself as "Southern California's archive for radicalism and social change." Interviews, personal papers, and clippings related to the Civil Rights movement, the Spanish Civil War, McCarthyism and the Hollywood blacklist, and L.A.'s labor movement are among its holdings.

William Andrews Clark Memorial Library
2520 Cimarron St.
Los Angeles 90018
*213-731-8529
Mon.–Fri. 9 a.m.–4:45 p.m.

The Clark is home to UCLA's Center for Seventeenth- and Eighteenth-Century Studies, and visiting the library is a little like visiting prison. You are let in and out by a staff member (in addition to signing in and out) and required to store your handbag or backpack in a locker. Manuscripts and books can be perused only under supervision in the reading room. The beauty of the taxpayer-supported Clark is that you needn't be a scholar to gain access to its first-rate collection of Restoration literature (England, 1640–1800) or its collection of Oscar Wilde material (by and about), the most compre-

hensive in the world. You must apply in person to obtain a reader's card and demonstrate "a serious interest in the collection," however, in order to handle rarities that privately funded research libraries would deem too valuable to grace public hands. Also the site of chamber concerts and readings, the eighty-three-year-old Clark is one of the best-kept secrets in the literary Southland. A catalogue of its holdings can be viewed via the Internet (www.humnet.ucla.edu/humnet/clarklib).

World Stage Anansi Writers Workshop
World Stage
Performance Space
4344 Degnan Blvd.
Los Angeles 90008
*213-293-2451

This program allows young writers, particularly from the African-American community, to mature in their craft. The workshop portion is followed by a reading by an established writer. An open reading then closes the long evening, which sometimes goes on without much of a break. Writers like Pulitzer prize winner Yusef Komunyakaa, Wanda Coleman, Peter J. Harris, Keith Antar Mason, and Kamau Daaood (one of the original members of the Watts Writers Workshop) read and give critiques. Poet Ruth Forman, winner of the Barnard New Women Poets Prize in 1992 and a product of the workshop, has also read. As readings go in L.A., there isn't one more intimate and emotionally charged. Every Wednesday; workshop at 7:30 p.m., featured reader at 8 p.m., open reading at 9 p.m.

Eso Won
3655 S. La Brea Ave.
Los Angeles 90016
*213-294-0324
Mon.–Sat. 10 a.m.–7 p.m.,
Sun. noon–5 p.m.

Although its name sounds more Chinese than African,

this African-American specialty bookstore bears the name of Egypt's Aswan Dam, which was once called Eso Won in the indigenous tongue, meaning "water over rocks." "It's a way of taking people back to Africa," says co-owner James Fugate. The store stocks not only books on ancient and present-day Africa but anything that speaks to the African-American experience on this continent as well, from Sojourner Truth's biography to Caryl Phillips's *Crossing the River*. The selection is so vast and varied—with particular emphasis on history, politics, culture, memoir, literature, and children's books—that spies from chain stores trying to beef up their own African-American sections have been caught taking notes here.

Pathfinder Bookstore
2546 Pico Blvd.
Los Angeles 90006
213-380-9460
Mon.–Fri. noon–7 p.m.,
Sat. 10 a.m.–9:30 p.m.,
Sun. 10 a.m.–7 p.m.

Like Libros Revolución, which is staffed by supporters of the Revolutionary Communist Party, Pathfinder is run by volunteers from the Socialist Workers Party. The store—whose press publishes the words of Malcolm X, Karl Marx, Leon Trotsky, Fidel Castro, Che Guevara, Eugene Debs, and Nelson Mandela in both Spanish and English—carries these catalogue titles as well as books on the U.S. labor movement, socialism, communism, women's issues, and immigrant rights.

Hollywood/Los Feliz

No trip through literary L.A. would be complete without at least a cocktail at **Musso & Frank's** (at seventy-eight, it's Hollywood's oldest restaurant, where Brecht lit up and Faulkner and Fitzgerald slugged them down (6667

Hollywood Blvd.; *213-467-7788; Tues.–Sat. 11 a.m.–11 p.m.). Be prepared to tip well and often. Dress code. Park in the back (two hours for $2 with ticket validation).

Barnsdall Art Center Municipal Art Gallery and Gallery Theater
4800 Hollywood Blvd.
Los Angeles 90027
213-485-4581, 213-485-0709

Overseen by the city's Cultural Affairs Department, the Barnsdall Art Center is the site of readings, lectures, performances, salons, exhibitions, and even a free biweekly poetry workshop that has no instructor but is led by workshop members in rotation. Call for programming. For the poetry workshop, call 213-485-2116.

Poetry Society of America (PSA) in Los Angeles
310-669-2369

On Sunday afternoons PSA presents well-known local and nationally recognized poets in the lobby of the Château Marmont hotel (8221 Sunset Blvd.). Convenient parking is practically nonexistent; arrive early.

Book City
6627 Hollywood Blvd.
Los Angeles 90028
*213-466-2525
Mon.–Thurs. 10 a.m.–10 p.m.,
Fri.–Sat. 9 a.m.–9 p.m., Sun.
10 a.m.–8 p.m.

This is the only bookstore left on the boulevard that carries used, rare, and out-of-print books. Book City places its stock at 250,000. Hollywood collectibles (celebrity autographs and letters) are available at **Hollywood Legends** (6621A Hollywood Blvd.; *213-466-0120; by appointment only).

Dawson's Book Shop
535 N. Larchmont Blvd.
Los Angeles 90004
*213-469-2186
Wed.–Sat. 9 a.m.–5 p.m.,
Mon.–Tues. by appointment only

Founded in 1909, Dawson's

is the oldest antiquarian store in L.A. It remains family owned. Dawson's specializes in rare and out-of-print books on photography and the regional history of L.A. and Southern California.

Koma Bookstore/Amok Publishing
1764 N. Vermont Ave.
Los Angeles 90027
*213-665-0956
Mon.–Sun. noon–8 p.m.

After ten years of goosing the public by selling books that transgressed sexual and societal boundaries, Amok (then under Stuart Swezey's ownership) was about to close its doors on Vermont—that is, until Dan Wininger, the bookstore's former manager, stepped in as owner. (Swezey's Amok has now returned to its humbler mail order origins in an effort to concentrate on publishing.) Save for a change in name (the addition of *Koma*, which is *amok* spelled backward), the store is essentially the same, offering, as its motto dictates, "extremes of information in print." Places like the Soap Plant in Los Feliz (4633 Hollywood Blvd.; *213-663-0122), and now even a few chains, stock coffee-table books on taboo subjects that at one time nobody else but Amok would carry. Still there are things that can't readily be found elsewhere—like copies of Georges Bataille's *The Trial of Gilles de Rais*, George Lincoln Rockwell's *White Power*, and shelves devoted to autoerotic fatalities, self-amputation, and "the dark arts"—all of which can be found at Koma or obtained through Amok's cyberspace address (www.amokbooks.com). Or look for the *Amok Sourcebook,* put out by Random House.

Skylight Books
1818 N. Vermont Ave.
Los Angeles 90027
*213-660-1175
Daily 10 a.m.–10 p.m.

Less committed to the literary than it was in its first incarnation, as Chatterton's, Skylight strives to serve the general needs of the ethnically and sexually divergent bohemian neighborhoods of Los Feliz and nearby Silverlake. By building its stock slowly over time, the still-emerging Skylight has managed to avoid the claustrophobic oppressiveness that plagues many bookstores. Will Self and Gary Indiana are among the out-of-town authors who come to read here.

The Miracle Mile

WRITERS IN FOCUS POETRY SERIES
Los Angeles County Museum of Art
5905 Wilshire Blvd.
Los Angeles 90036
*213-857-6512

The best of the Southland's poets come and read here, from Eloise Klein Healy to Richard Garcia. The museum's public address system makes reading, as one featured reader described it, "effortless." Sometimes, however, the poet must compete with the live jazz that drifts in whenever the door to the courtyard swings open.

New Mastodon International Books
5820 Wilshire Blvd., #101
Los Angeles 90036
*213-525-1948
Tues.–Fri. 11 a.m.–6 p.m.,
 Sat. 11 a.m.–5 p.m.

Situated across the street from the La Brea Tar Pits, this small but comfortable bookstore stocks contemporary and classic German fiction and philosophy in its original tongue.

Sun & Moon Press
6026 Wilshire Blvd.
Los Angeles 90036
*213-857-1115
Mon.–Fri. 9 a.m.–5 p.m.,
 Sat. 9 a.m.–4 p.m.

One of the busiest small presses in the country, with more than 400 books in print, Sun & Moon averages forty to fifty new books a year. It's not the volume that makes this press special, however, but the exceptionally sophisticated work it publishes, by the likes of Lyn Hejinian, Nathaniel Mackey, Gertrude Stein, and Mac Wellman—poets, writers, and playwrights who challenge the conventions of language. Sun & Moon's offices include shelves of new and hard-to-find books for purchase, as well as a bargain bin.

Third Street (between Fairfax Ave. and La Cienega Blvd.)

Stop at **The Farmer's Market** at Third and Fairfax, where Christopher Isherwood and Thomas Mann routinely met other exiles and émigrés for tea and talk.

Traveler's Bookcase
8375 W. Third St.
Los Angeles 90048
*213-655-0575
Mon.–Sat. 10 a.m.–6 p.m.,
 Sun. 11 a.m.–5 p.m.

Staffed by intrepid travelers whose collective wanderings have covered the planet, the store offers the more timid a running start in the world of travel. Whether you're escaping to or from Los Angeles, the Traveler's Bookcase can ignite your wanderlust or dampen the anxiety associated with crossing several time zones in a single bound. Aside from the standard array of travel guides (from Lonely Planet to Zagat), the store carries guidebooks for women globe-trotting by their lonesome, pocket-size world atlases, travel videos (to rent or buy), foreign-language tapes and dictionaries, and books on how to teach yourself Zulu. For those who like to travel but hate stepping outside their front door, this store has a special section just for you: international fiction and nonfiction under the header "Armchair Travel."

Cook's Library
8373 W. Third St.
Los Angeles 90048
*213-655-3141
Mon. 1–5 p.m.,
 Tues.–Sat. 11 a.m.–6 p.m.

All one needs to appreciate any of the 3,800 titles here is an interest in eating. Like its next-door neighbor, the Traveler's Bookcase, this store has a couch that beckons the browser to stay an hour or two. Anything in print related to cooking or entertaining is here, from gourmet vegan to Indochinese cuisine to the libation rituals of martini sophisticates. Also available are books like *The Lord's Table: The Meaning of Food in Early Judaism and Christianity*, which provides nourishment for the soul as well as the mind.

West Hollywood and Vicinity

Bodhi Tree Bookstore
8585 Melrose Ave.
West Hollywood 90069
310-659-1733,
 800-825-9798
Daily 10 a.m.–11 p.m.;
 used-book section:
 daily 10 a.m.–7 p.m.

Here, in what is the county's largest bookstore devoted to religious and New Age spirituality, you'll find the Gay and Lesbian Studies section peacefully coexisting on the same shelf as Sex/Marriage. Neatly housed under one roof (note: the used-book section, which carries duplicate titles and out-of-print books, has an entire building to itself) is a daunting range of subject matter—from Egyptology to eating disorders, from Jung to yoga—most of which relates to the more mystical aspects of human experience. Even if you're in a rush on the road to enlightenment, your dharma in this neighborhood is to focus on the earthly task of parking. Read all signs, and make hourly offerings to the meter.

Book Soup

8818 Sunset Blvd.
West Hollywood 90069
310-659-3110
Daily 9 a.m.–midnight

If you're looking for a bookstore with attitude, this is it. I mean, where else would they stock an entire shelf with literary criticism on the work of Anne Rice? Where else would you find *The Journal of Lesbian and Gay Studies* smack-dab in the porn section, between *Spurs* and *Lusty Letters*? Devoted customers haven't just grown to accept 'tude as part of its charm, they've come to expect it from this brainy West Hollywood bookstore. Its newsstand is tops. This is a major stop for authors, and the more glamorous types—glitterati like Brett Easton Ellis and David Foster Wallace—seem to blow through here with greater frequency than anywhere else in town.

Heritage Bookshop

8540 Melrose Ave.
Los Angeles 90069
310-659-3674
Tues.–Fri. 9:30 a.m.–5:30 p.m.,
Sat. 10 a.m.–4:30 p.m.

This is L.A.'s leading antiquarian store and one of the finest in the world. It has an on-site bindery and an autograph gallery where you can gaze at Oscar Wilde's penmanship or read Hemingway's small, cramped, rolling script in a 1959 letter to a New York book dealer.

A Different Light

8853 Santa Monica Blvd.
West Hollywood 90069
310-854-6601
Daily 10 a.m.–midnight

In the heart of WeHo, as it is sometimes unkindly referred to by outsiders, the bookstore caters to the city's gay, lesbian, bisexual, queer, and trans-gender communities by offering the county's largest array of fiction and nonfiction by and for folks who understand the ins and outs

of closets better than most architects. With events almost nightly, the flagship, which has stores in New York and San Francisco, plays host to some of the country's best—not just in gay and lesbian fiction but in literary fiction period. When touring, Michael Cunningham, David Leavitt, and Edmund White make a point of stopping here.

SportsBooks

8302 Melrose Ave.
Los Angeles 90069
*213-651-2334, 800-626-0158
Tues.–Sat. 10 a.m.–5 p.m.

This is one of a tiny handful of stores in the world that specialize in books and magazines on sports and related topics. Books on baseball and golf are the biggest sellers, but here you'll find pages on anything that works up a sweat, from football to falconry, rugby to rowing. The store also stocks collectibles, from old issues of *Sports Illustrated* to signed copies of Muhammad Ali's biography.

Beverly Hills/ West Los Angeles

Beverly Hills Public Library

444 N. Rexford Dr.
Beverly Hills 90210
310-288-2201

This has become one of the busiest venues for community literary events, from storytelling festivals to play readings to PEN West's informative panel discussions. Unfortunately, every time I sit in its Y-shaped auditorium, I can never quite shake that feeling of being back in high school.

SELECTED SHORTS

The Getty Center

1200 Getty Center Dr.
Los Angeles 90049
310-440-7300

There is nothing like having a story read to you, es-

pecially if the one doing the reading is adroit at drawing the listener into the realm of make-believe. Actors are just such experts, and Selected Shorts, billed as "a celebration of the short story," is a program, taped to be aired over National Public Radio, that pairs well-known actors with stories by well-known and not-so-well-known authors. Each evening carries a theme selected by the program's director and host, Isaiah Sheffer, artistic director of New York City's Symphony Space (which produces the series). One program, titled "Nighttime Travelers," featured stories by Margaret Atwood, James Thurber, Guy de Maupassant, and Ethan Canin, read by, respectively, Christina Pickles, Leonard Nimoy, René Auberjonois, and Harold Gould. The series, which began at the Getty Villa in Malibu, resumes at the new Getty Center. Look for announcements in the *Los Angeles Times* or *L.A. Weekly*, or call the Getty for information.

LOS ANGELES TIMES FESTIVAL OF BOOKS

University of California, Los Angeles (UCLA)
405 Hilgard Ave.
800-LA-TIMES,ext. 2665
One weekend each spring

While this weekend of book-buying, readings, and literary panels is a bookworm's dream-come-true, it is a nightmare for the perpetually disorganized. Usually held on the third weekend in April on the UCLA campus, where the process of parking alone can induce a sense of helplessness and defeat of epic proportions, the festival attracts more than 100,000 book lovers from all over Southern

California. In the past panelists have ranged from critics' favorites David Foster Wallace and Jorie Graham to best-selling author Michael Crichton and self-help guru Marianne Williamson. In order to avoid having to turn away long lines of people, last year the organizers began requiring tickets for admittance to the panels, which were free but had to be obtained in advance through selected ticket agencies. Look for the schedule in the *Los Angeles Times Book Review* the Sunday before the festival weekend.

SKIRBALL CULTURAL CENTER READING SERIES

Skirball Cultural Center
2701 N. Sepulveda Blvd.
Los Angeles 90049
310-440-4500

Working with the Unterberg Poetry Center of New York's Ninety-second Street Y, the Skirball launched its reading series in 1996. Each event consists of a reading by a well-known poet or writer, followed by questions from the audience. Past authors have included Larry McMurtry, Mona Simpson, Gary Soto, and Tobias Wolff.

UCLA AT THE ARMAND HAMMER POETRY READING SERIES

UCLA at the Armand Hammer Museum of Art and Cultural Center
10899 Wilshire Blvd.
Los Angeles 90024
310-443-7000

Nationally recognized poets and those up-and-coming are presented in a museum setting that's ceremonious and stiff, a perfect training ground for future laureates. Poets who have read in the past include Jorie Graham, Richard Howard, W. S. Merwin, Harryette Mullen, and Robert Pinsky.

Bernard Hamill
Spanish Books
10977 Santa Monica Blvd.
Los Angeles 90025
310-475-0453
Mon.–Sat. 10 a.m.–5:30 p.m.

This bookstore carries literary and popular fiction in Spanish, from Cervantes to James Ellroy.

La Cité des Livres
2306 Westwood Blvd.
Los Angeles 90064
310-475-0658
Tues.–Sat. 10 a.m.–6 p.m.

This bookstore offers news-stand fare, fiction, and children's books in French.

Dutton's
Brentwood Books
11975 San Vicente Blvd.
Los Angeles 90049
310-476-6263
Mon.–Fri. 9 a.m.–9 p.m., Sat. 9 a.m.– 6 p.m., Sun. 11 a.m.–5 p.m.

Dutton's is the Westside book lover's paradise. Like Vroman's in Pasadena, it has all the amenities of a chain store, including a café and an outdoor courtyard, without being one. The store holds literary readings (indoors or out, depending on the weather) practically every day, making it a popular West Coast stop for writers on tour. The staff is courteous and friendly, like owner Doug Dutton, the younger brother of Davis Dutton, who owns Dutton's in North Hollywood (see below).

Sisterhood Bookstore
1351 Westwood Blvd.
Los Angeles 90024
310-477-7300
Daily 10 a.m.–8 p.m.

Housed in a Tudor-style building, Sisterhood stocks the county's largest selection of books for and by women, including titles that Sports-Books should have but doesn't, like Susan Fox Rogers's *Sportsdykes: Stories from on and off the Field*. This is one of the few women's bookstores where men can feel comfortable, provided they can put up with some gentle ribbing

from the outgoing staff. In fact, it's the one sure bet for men shopping for their girlfriend, wife, daughter, or lesbian sister. Sisterhood also conducts monthly reading groups and hosts readings that reflect feminism's multifaceted nature, featuring authors such as antiporn crusader Andrea Dworkin, poet-essayist June Jordan, and screenwriter Robin Swicord.

Vagabond Books
11706 San Vicente Blvd.
Los Angeles 90049
310-442-BOOK
Mon.–Sat. 11 a.m.–6 p.m.

As far as used books go, Vagabond (which also deals in rare books) might not have the best prices in town, but it certainly has the best selection, from a collection of F. Scott Fitzgerald's notebooks and letters to *The Book of Irish Weirdness: An Anthology of Horror, Tragic, and Odd Stories*. People don't seem to mind paying a little extra, especially since owner Craig Graham gives out what he calls "free analysis": the prescribing of books or passages for regulars and walk-ins. He jokingly refers to his store as "a couch with books." In some ways he's right. The day I was there, I noticed that everyone left slightly more relaxed than they were when they came in.

Venice

Sponto Gallery (7 Dudley Ave.) now occupies the former site of **Venice West**, the coffeehouse that hosted readings by Gregory Corso, Robert Creeley, Diane di Prima, Lawrence Ferlinghetti, Allen Ginsberg, Jack Hirschmann, Stuart Z. Perkoff, and Gary Snyder during the heyday of the Beats. (Some say Jack Kerouac read here too, but poet and Venice West regular Frank T. Rios disputes

that, saying, "Nah, Kerouac didn't read, but he sat and listened.") Years later it became a place that Jim Morrison frequented.

Beyond Baroque
Literary Arts Center
681 Venice Blvd.
Venice 90291
310-822-3006
Bookstore hours: daily, except Wed., 2–6 p.m.; Wed. 5–9:30 p.m.

For any writer interested in *not* churning out the next best-seller, Beyond Baroque is an oasis. The site of readings, classes, year–round workshops, a bookstore, and a priceless archive of small-press publications, the center is committed to providing a home for literary experimentation. Founded in 1968 by a coalition of avant-garde poets, Beyond Baroque has nurtured countless writers through its various workshops and classes. Among them are Exene Cervenkova, Dennis Cooper, John Doe, Bob Flanagan, Amy Gerstler, David Trinidad, Tom Waits, and Benjamin Weissman. Among the readers featured over the years have been Dorothy Allison, Harold Brodkey, Raymond Carver, Allen Ginsberg, Bob Holman, Christopher Isherwood, Li–Young Lee, Philip Levine, Grace Paley, Ishmael Reed, Anne Waldman, Fay Weldon, and Edmund White. As the oldest literary arts center in Southern California, it's one of the main arteries that keeps literary L.A. alive.

Small World Books
and the Mystery Annex
1407 Ocean Front Walk
Venice 90291
310–399–2360
Daily 10 a.m.–8 p.m.

Right on the boardwalk, this is the perfect place to pick up summer reading, whether it be the latest fiction or true crime, or poetry at bargain rates.

Santa Monica

Midnight Special
1318 Third St. Promenade
Santa Monica 90401
310-393-2923
Mon.–Thurs. 10:30 a.m.–11 p.m., Fri.–Sat. 10:30 a.m.–11:30 p.m., Sun. 11 a.m.–11 p.m.

Named after a train in a Leadbelly song, the store responds to the needs of L.A.'s divergent communities. Well known for its politics (its bookmark sports a quote from Brecht: "Hungry man reach for the book, it is a weapon"), the handsome red-brick space serves as bookstore and gathering place for intellectuals, activists, and writers of differing classes and ethnicities. Its wide and varied selection gives it the most cosmopolitan feel of any bookstore in the Southland.

Hennessey & Ingalls Art
and Architecture Books
1254 Third St. Promenade
Santa Monica 90401
310-458-9074
Daily 10 a.m.–6 p.m.

Hennessey & Ingalls has the largest selection of new and out-of-print books in art and architecture outside of Manhattan. In this atmosphere of almost over-abundance, art lovers and art historians act like kids in a candy store, combing through stacks of oversized books in search of a buy.

Form Zero Architectural
Books + Gallery
2433 Main St.
   (Edgemar Complex)
Santa Monica 90405
310-450-0222
Tues.–Thurs. 10:30 a.m.–7 p.m., Fri.–Sat. 10:30 a.m.–9 p.m., Sun. 11:30 a.m.–6 p.m.

This store is itself an architectural statement. With the interior sleeked down to I-beams and concrete, Form Zero looks as intimidating as its postmodernist, theory-laden stock. Here you'll find not only books on Rem Koolhaas, "queer space," and the English hospital

(1070–1570) but books on the poetics of light and on gardens as well.

Novel Café
212 Pier Ave.
Santa Monica 90405
310-396-8566
Mon.–Fri. 7 a.m.–1 a.m.,
Sat.–Sun. 8 a.m.–1 a.m.

At the outside tables you can sit in the sun, ply yourself with caffeine and nicotine, and read to your heart's content. Don't forget the sun block. (A $10 purchase of used books gets you a free cup of java.)

North Hollywood

Dutton's Books (New, Used, and Rare)
5146 Laurel Canyon Blvd.
North Hollywood 91607
818-769-3866
Mon.–Fri. 9:30 a.m.–9 p.m.,
Sat. 9:30 p.m.–6 p.m.,
Sun. 10 a.m.–6 p.m.

Opened in 1960 by Davis Dutton, whose family's name is the best known in L.A. bookselling (see Dutton's Brentwood), this modest-looking storefront is an abridged version of Acres of Books in Long Beach (see below)—just neater, cleaner, and lots closer to L.A. It sits next to the corner where Johnny's Drive-in (one of the film locales in *Mildred Pierce)* used to stand.

Sam's Book City
5245 Lankershim Blvd.
North Hollywood 91601
818-985-6911
Daily 10 a.m.–10 p.m.
(Tues. until 8 p.m.)

Friend to the local poet and micro press, Sam's is a cozy place as long as you're not a cat. (Sam, the store's namesake, is a dog belonging to owner Craig Klapman.) It's apparent from the store's selection that when it comes to used books, Sam is eclectic in her tastes, from Danielle Steele's supermarket sellers to Charles Bukowski's *Love Is a Dog from Hell.* Sam's got a little bit of everything

here, including poetry readings on weekends, organized by Lorca the Poetry Dog, who belongs to poet Rafael F. J. Alvarado.

Glendale/Eagle Rock

Brand Bookshop
231 N. Brand Blvd.
Glendale 91203
818-507-5943
Sun.–Thurs. 10 a.m.–9 p.m.,
Fri.–Sat. 10 a.m.–11 p.m.

This is one of those bookshops that you don't want anyone to know about. In fact, there are too many books to want here. Turn your back on a book for a moment, and it's gone. It's just not fair. So many books (100,000), so little time.

Occidental College Bookstore
1600 Campus Rd.
Eagle Rock 90041
*213-259-2630
Mon.–Wed. 8:30 a.m.–6 p.m.,
Thurs. 8:30 a.m.–9 p.m.,
Fri. 8:30 a.m.–5 p.m.,
Sat. 10 a.m.–2 p.m.
(call for summer hours)

The smartest little bookstore in the county. Academics and students come from as far as CalArts to riffle through its critical theory and gender studies sections, which are well tended, as is the rest of the store. In addition, Oxy's tiny bookstore somehow manages to give a 20 percent markdown on the *New York Times* bestseller list.

San Gabriel Valley

Huntington Library, Art Collections, and Botanical Gardens
1151 Oxford Rd.
San Marino 91108
626-405-2124
See main entry, p. 130, for hours

Although the Huntington is first and foremost a research library and allows only scholars access to its vast collections, the library offers the public a viewing of some of the rarest and oldest printed manuscripts

in the English-speaking world, accompanied by insightful commentary. Tracing the history of publishing from the earliest uses of movable type in Western Europe (the Gutenberg Bible) to the groundbreaking publication of James Joyce's *Ulysses* in 1922, the display, heavily culled from the Huntington's Anglo-American collection, demonstrates how advances in technology fostered the literary arts by making it economically feasible for books to become "a part of our everyday lives." A must-see for any book lover, the Huntington also offers a notable reading series, which in recent years has brought literary heavyweights like John Barth and A. S. Byatt to the Southland. (The grounds include a Shakespeare Garden, planted with species mentioned by the Bard.)

Along the portion of Route 66 that runs through **Pasadena,** you'll find five bookstores within walking distance of one another, each of which has a distinct character. Either begin or end your walking tour at **Vroman's Bookstore,** Southern California's oldest and largest bookstore (695 E. Colorado Blvd.; 626-449-5320, 800-769-BOOK; Mon.–Fri. 9 a.m.–9 p.m., Sat. 9 a.m.–7 p.m., Sun. 10 a.m.–7 p.m.). Although it has been in existence since 1894, Vroman's refuses to look any older than its newly renovated space, which was completed in 1996. Newsletters, charge accounts, story time for the kids, 100,000 new titles in stock, readings and signings almost every day of the week, parking, staff recommendations, a coffee bar, and one of the Southland's two best storefront newsstands (the other belongs to Book Soup in West Hollywood) make book buying all the

more habit-forming.

Just to the west of Vroman's on the same side of the street is **The House of Fiction** (663 E. Colorado Blvd.; 626-449-9861; Mon.–Sat. 10 a.m.–9 p.m., Sun. noon–5 p.m.), which deals primarily in used books (with an emphasis on history, literature, and baseball) and a few rarities like the British first edition of Zelda Fitzgerald's *Save Me the Waltz* or John Lennon and Yoko Ono's songbook *Some Time in New York City,* which includes the music and lyrics to "Woman Is the Nigger of the World." Its bohemian tone and modest prices attract mostly students and more than a few regulars.

Next to the House of Fiction is the **Browser's Bookstore** (659 E. Colorado Blvd.; 626-585-8308; Mon.–Sat. 10 a.m.–9 p.m., Sun. 10 a.m.–5 p.m.), which is air-conditioned (not a minor detail on hot, smoggy days) and, in contrast to its next-door neighbor, obsessively neat. Every section is fastidiously alphabetized. Though not outstanding, the selection is fair. You've hit pay dirt if you're into *Star Trek* or John F. Kennedy; they each have an entire section.

Across the street and farther west on Colorado is **Cliff's Books** (630 E. Colorado Blvd.; 626-449-9541; Mon.–Sat. 10 a.m.–midnight, Sun. 11 a.m.–midnight), which has the largest selection of used books in the immediate area (170,000 titles). Its poetry section is excellent, and so is its fiction. An hour or two passes quickly in this place.

Staying on the same side of the street as Cliff's, travel east until you're standing directly across the street from Vroman's. Now duck into a courtyard surrounded by shops, and look for **Prufrock Books &**

Etc. (696 E. Colorado Blvd., #2; 626-795-0818; Wed.–Thurs. noon–5 p.m., Fri. noon–8 p.m., Sat. noon–5 p.m.). Here you'll find a small but collectible stash of photography books, African-American fiction and nonfiction (some of which dates to the turn of the century), and women's literature.

Alexandria II
567 S. Lake Ave.
Pasadena 91101
626-792-7885
Mon.–Thurs. 10 a.m.–9 p.m.,
  Fri.–Sat. 10 a.m.–10 p.m.,
Sun. 10 a.m.–7 p.m.

This is the San Gabriel Valley's purveyor of new and used books on New Age spirituality, science, metaphysics, mythology, world religions, psychology, "ufology," and just your everyday paranormal phenomena. Like its L.A. cousin, the Bodhi Tree (see above), the store stocks New Age music, subliminal tapes, tarot decks, and mood-enhancing incense.

American Friends Service Committee Bookstore
980 N. Fair Oaks Ave.
Pasadena 91103
626-791-1978
Mon.–Fri. 11 a.m.–5 p.m.

Of its 3,000 titles, a third are devoted to history, multicultural perspectives, civil and economic rights, gay and lesbian rights, and Chicano studies. The rest are about Quakerism and related topics such as pacifism and conflict resolution.

Distant Lands: A Traveler's Bookstore
62 S. Raymond Ave.
Pasadena 91105
626-449-3220
Tues.–Thurs. 10:30 a.m.–7 p.m.,
  Fri.–Sat. 10:30 a.m.–9 p.m.,
Sun.–Mon. 11 a.m.–6 p.m.

Like Traveler's Bookcase in L.A. (see above), Distant Lands has an "Armchair Travel" section and hosts

slide lectures and author signings.

Oriental Bookstore
1713 E. Colorado Blvd.
Pasadena 91106
626-577-2413
Mon.–Sat. 11 a.m.–5:30 p.m.

If you can get past the name, you'll find the world's largest selection of new and used books in English on the Middle East, Asia, and the Pacific (about 60,000). A favorite among collectors and academics who specialize in dead languages like Sanskrit or Sumerian, the store is the best place to find anything related to Asian-American history or literature.

Long Beach

Acres of Books
240 Long Beach Blvd.
Long Beach 90802
562-437-6980
Tues.–Sat. 9:15 a.m.–5 p.m.

Welcome to what must be the largest used bookstore in California: 750,000 titles, 250,000 more in stock, and miles of shelving (six and a half, to be exact). Originally a western bar and dance hall, the seventy-three-year-old site still exudes an air of mystery and excitement. Sections devoted to various subjects are laid out at random, and the only existing maps are tattooed on the inside of staff members' skulls. On cloudy days the customers are given flashlights to help them weed through the fiction stacks. With a little patience, a thirst for adventure, and a high tolerance for dust, there's no telling what a determined browser will sniff out. The store carries books on almost any subject, from fur farming to funerals. Reserve at least half a day to browse. If you're taking the Blue Line, which we recommend, get off at Broadway and First Street.

Cultura Latina Bookstore
4125 Norse Way
Long Beach 90808
562-982-1515
Mon.–Fri. 11 a.m.–7 p.m.,
  Sat. 10 a.m.–5 p.m., Sun.
  11 a.m.–5 p.m.

Cultura Latina has a small but varied stock (about 4,000 new titles) of Chicano and Latin American literature, literary criticism, history, politics, and reference books in Spanish and English. The store has a reputation for hosting the leading writers of the day (in a single month Argentina's Juan Gelman and American Book Award winner Victor Martinez visited). Cultura Latina's readings (by authors such as Rudolfo Anaya) have been known to draw hundreds from all over the Southland.

Pearls Booksellers
224 Redondo Ave.
Long Beach 90803
562-438-8875
Mon.–Fri. 11 a.m.–7 p.m.,
  Sat.–Sun. noon–5 p.m.

Lesbian fiction and nonfiction is featured here, along with books on abuse and recovery.

Both Sides of the Equator
12909 Philadelphia St.
Whittier 90601
562-907-2526
Mon.–Sat. 11 a.m.–9 p.m.,
  Sun. noon–8 p.m.

This gallery-bookstore-stationery store is only two years old yet already stocks 10,000 new and used titles in literature, contemporary fiction, and multicultural politics in Spanish and English.

Premier Aztlán Bookstore
2008 Montebello Town Center
Montebello 90640
*213-722-9350
Mon.–Fri. 10 a.m.–9 p.m.,
  Sat. 10 a.m.–8 p.m.,
  Sun. 11 a.m.–7 p.m.

This store has 1,000 titles, primarily Chicano authors in paperback.

Claremont

George C. Stone Center for Children's Books
131 E. 10th St.
Claremont 91711
909-607-3670
Mon.–Thurs. 1:30–6 p.m.,
  summer hours:
  Mon.–Thurs. noon–4 p.m.

Housed in an unassuming California Craftsman bungalow on the outskirts of the Claremont Colleges, the Stone Center has quietly amassed a treasure trove of literature to delight readers young and old. Primarily established for the use of Claremont Graduate School students conducting research in children's literature, the library happily extends lending privileges (for an annual family fee of $25) to those outside the gated walls of academe. The Stone carries several decades worth of folk tales and myths, biographies, and nonfiction written for children of all ages (from toddler to young adult) and diverse cultural backgrounds. For any parent in need of a break from at bedtime, this is a godsend. The shelves are stocked with Virginia Hamilton, Maira Kalman, Arthur Say, Maurice Sendak, Laurence Yep, and even Richard Scarry in Spanish. The Brothers Grimm might not be surprised to learn that the demands of modernization have turned *Cinderella* into an urban tale by the name of *Cinder-Elly*.

Huntley Bookstore (of the Claremont Colleges)
175 E. Eighth St.
Claremont 91711
909-607-1502, 909-607-1509, 909-607-1510
Mon.–Thurs. 8:30 a.m.–5:30 p.m.,
  Fri. 8:30 a.m.–5 p.m.,
  Sat. 10 a.m.–5 p.m.
  (call for summer hours)

This is the only place east of Eagle Rock where you'll find anything remotely resembling a book on cultural studies or French feminism. The store takes special orders and carries some fiction and a fair number of academic journals.

Charles Goldschmid's Bookstore
128 Yale Ave. (upstairs)
Claremont 91711
909-624-0757
Tues.–Sat. 10:30 a.m.–5:30 p.m.

The walls are covered with bags from other bookstores around the country and, in some cases, around the world. Goldschmid's carries a fair amount of rare and used fiction and some poetry, but its heart lies in Californiana and other Western Americana. In one glass case there's a touching exhibit dedicated to local printer Ruth Thomson Saunder (1901–52) and her work.

More Reading on Readings
Next magazine, the Southland's monthly guide to the local poetry and coffeehouse scene, can be trusted for insider gossip, strong opinions, and outright eccentricity. Check your local indie coffeehouse, ask an independent bookseller, or pick one up at Beyond Baroque in Venice. *Poetry Flash*, a monthly published in Berkeley, covers Northern and Southern California reading events in its listings. People pick it up not only for its listings but also for its insightful reviews of poetry and inter-

views with major and emerging poets.

The *Los Angeles Times Book Review*, which comes in the paper's Sunday edition, lists readings in the Southland, as far south as Laguna Beach.

The *L.A. Weekly*, West Coast cousin to the *Village Voice*, has a listing (compiled by this writer) devoted to literary events in L.A. and a "Reading Pick of the Week," which highlights a reading by a visiting or local poet or writer.

Each week from Santa Monica, host Michael Silverblatt, "the written word's most compassionate evangelist," is heard across the country on *Bookworm*, interviewing the top writers working in the field of literature today. On KCRW (89.9 FM), Thursdays, 2:30–3 p.m.; check out the Web site at www.kcrw.org /c/ bookworm.html.

Bookstores for Young Readers
Parents already know how valuable these bookstores are: they offer a wide selection (including parenting books and whole shelves devoted to topics like the birth of a

new sibling or divorce) and well-informed salespeople whose suggestions are often based on firsthand experience. For those of us not fluent in baby talk, these places can save hours of agonizing over what's age-appropriate for a young reader. Many offer extras like regularly scheduled story hours, author visits, and other special events. Some will even gift-wrap books at no extra charge—a godsend when you and your child are en route to that birthday party that started twenty minutes ago.

All of the stores listed here are members of the Southern California Children's Booksellers Association.

Catch Our Rainbow Books
3148 Pacific Coast Hwy.
Torrance 90505
310-325-1081
Mon.–Fri. 10 a.m.–5:30 p.m.,
Sat. 10 a.m.–4:30 p.m.

Chevalier's Books
126 N. Larchmont Blvd.
Los Angeles 90004
*213-465-1334
Mon.–Sat. 10 a.m.–6 p.m.,
Sun. 11 a.m.–2 p.m.

Children's Book World
10580 W. Pico Blvd.
Los Angeles 90064
310-559-BOOK
Mon.–Fri. 10 a.m.–5:30 p.m.,
Sat. 10 a.m.–5 p.m.

Creative Play Resources
9420 Reseda Blvd.
Northridge 91324
818-886-4150
Mon.–Fri. 9:30 a.m.–6 p.m.,
Sat. 10 a.m.–5 p.m.

Mrs. Nelson's Toy and Book Shop
1030 Bonita Ave.
La Verne 91750
909-599-4558
Mon.–Sat. 9 a.m.–6 p.m.
(Fri. until 7 p.m.),
Sun. 11 a.m.–5 p.m.

Once upon a Story
3740 E. Fourth St.
Long Beach 90814
562-433-6856
Tues.–Fri. 10 a.m.–6 p.m.,
Sat. 9 a.m.–5 p.m.,
Sun. 9 a.m.–3 p.m.

Pages: Books for Children and Young Adults
18399 Ventura Blvd., #15
Tarzana 91356
818-342-6657
Mon.–Fri. 9:30 a.m.–7 p.m.,
Sat. 9:30 a.m.–5:30 p.m.,
Sun. 11 a.m.–4 p.m.

San Marino Toy and Book Shoppe
2424 Huntington Dr.
San Marino 91108
626-309-0222
Mon.–Sat. 10 a.m.–6 p.m.,
Sun. 11 a.m.–5 p.m.

Through a Child's Eyes
7827 Florence Ave.
Downey 90240
562-806-6490
Mon.–Fri. 10 a.m.–6 p.m.,
Sat. 10 a.m.–5 p.m.

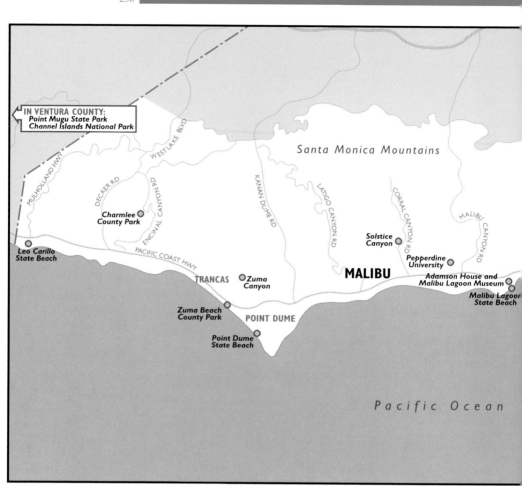

In the map:

IN VENTURA COUNTY:
Point Mugu State Park
Channel Islands National Park

MULHOLLAND HWY
WESTLAKE BLVD
DECKER RD
ENCINAL CANYON RD
KANAN DUME RD
LATIGO CANYON RD
CORRAL CANYON RD
MALIBU CANYON RD

Santa Monica Mountains

Charmlee
County Park

Leo Carillo
State Beach

PACIFIC COAST HWY

Solstice
Canyon

Pepperdine
University

MALIBU

Adamson House and
Malibu Lagoon Museum

Malibu Lagoon
State Beach

TRANCAS Zuma
Canyon

Zuma Beach
County Park

POINT DUME

Point Dume
State Beach

Pacific Ocean

The area between the San Diego (405) Freeway and the Pacific Ocean was, until recently, defined not by great cultural institutions but by a great climate and topography. The relocation of the Skirball Cultural Center and the construction of the new Getty Center within sight of the 405 have changed that, so this chapter highlights the new cultural corridor, bordered on the east by UCLA and extending from the crest of the Santa Monica Mountains south to the new center for creative filmmaking envisioned for Playa Vista. Los Angeles city officials pledged $70 million in tax credits to lure DreamWorks SKG to this site in the hope of securing thousands of high-paying, high-tech jobs and the region's dominance in the burgeoning multimedia industry.

Skirball Cultural Center

Hebrew Union College–
Jewish Institute of America
2701 N. Sepulveda Blvd.
Los Angeles 90049
310-440-4500
Mon.–Fri. 10 a.m.–4 p.m., Sat. noon–5 p.m.,
Sun. 10 a.m.–5 p.m.
Entry: adults $7, seniors/students $5,
children under 12 free

Among the institutions that have relocated along the 405 Freeway between the Valley and LAX and transformed this area into a new cultural destination is the Skirball Cultural Center, which encompasses a museum that has been part of Los Angeles's cultural life for more than twenty-five years and includes rich collections that have evolved for more than a century since its parent institution, Hebrew Union College, began accumulating art and artifacts of Jewish heritage at its Cincinnati campus.

Only a small fraction of the Skirball collections could be exhibited in its former

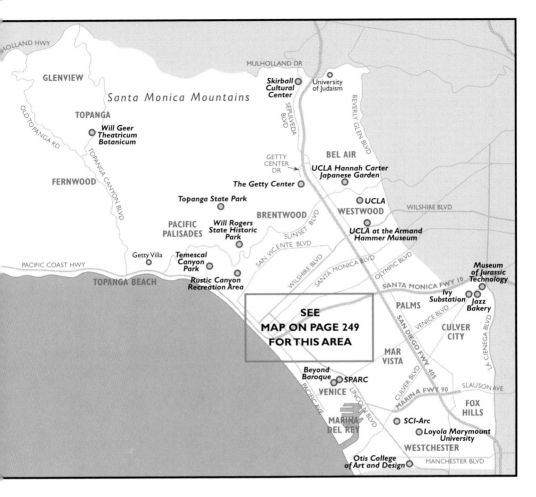

create an oasis, enunciated by the interplay of mass (concrete and stone walls) and light (stainless steel and glass roofs). "The fusion of archaeology and invention," which these materials represent to the architect, "is not an inappropriate concept for American Judaism," Safdie concludes. The oasis theme is most evident in the ample, beautifully landscaped courtyards, open to the surrounding hillsides and warmed by the sun, but enclosed within the center's powerful striated walls. Because all visitors are expected to arrive by car, the architect faced the challenge of providing sufficient parking that is convenient but does not dominate the site. His solution to this problem is not as well realized: Cars are relegated to two lots north and south of the building, so most visitors follow circuitous routes through side entrances and

location on the campus of Hebrew Union College, near USC and Exposition Park. Its new fifteen-acre site, tucked beneath the crest of the Santa Monica Mountains, is at the geographical center of Jewish communities in L.A., midway between the San Fernando Valley and the Westside. In his architectural plan, Moshe Safdie wanted to never see the welcoming front entrance with its broad stone staircase; the number of spaces is also insufficient for the crowds that flock to the Skirball's holiday festivals.

The 4,000-year history of the Jewish people is the subject of the museum's long-term inaugural exhibition, "Visions and Values," and special emphasis is placed on the American experience, one of the happiest and most recent chapters of this chronicle as Jews have flourished in the open society of the United States. The biblical command to Abraham—"Go forth . . . and be a blessing" (Genesis 12:1–3)—is a reminder of the long exile that the Jews have endured and the moral responsibilities inherent in the gift of faith.

The first galleries present the ancient civilization of the Israelites and follow the journeys of the Jewish people from the conquest of their Middle Eastern homeland 2,500 years ago to the far-flung communities of the Diaspora. By the Middle Ages these communities stretched from China to Europe, with especially vibrant centers circling the Mediterranean. A Golden Age of Jewish culture in Spain (called *Sepharad* in Hebrew), which flourished from the beginning of Muslim rule in 711 C.E., ended with the Inquisition and the expulsion of the Jews in 1492. The Spanish exiles formed a network of Sephardic communities that ultimately stretched from Turkey to Colonial America and retained cultural forms that can be traced to their Spanish period.

In the next suite of galleries the visitor discovers the ways that Jewish ritual renders time sacred. The **Holidays** gallery features ceremonial objects that mark the rich calendar of celebrations in Jewish life. Star-shaped oil lamps, traditionally lit to inaugurate the Sabbath, kiddush cups, and an embroidered challah cover are mounted in a tableaux with Moritz Oppenheim's painting *Sabbath Afternoon*, a nineteenth-century depiction of an Eastern European family's weekly observance. Ceremonial objects used in observing the High Holy Days, from Rosh Hashanah (New Year) to Yom Kippur (the Day of Atonement), include the shofar, or ram's horn, that is sounded in the synagogue. Many different menorah, the candelabra used during the eight-day celebration of Hanukkah, make a fascinating display in one alcove. Contemporary home movies of holiday celebrations, shown continuously in another alcove, display the vitality of tradition in the new customs and interpretations added by each generation. An interactive computer station provides information

about celebrating each holiday, as well as the history and symbolism of the objects associated with each ceremony.

The varied rituals that mark events in the cycle of human life and connect individuals to the Jewish community are seen in a video at the center of the **Life Cycle** gallery. Photographs, including an exceptional series of black-and-white prints from L.A.'s own Bill Aron, of life-cycle events—circumcision, coming of age, marriage, death—are displayed with objects used in celebrating each life passage. *Ketubbot*, illustrated marriage contracts, are mounted on pull-out panels, allowing visitors to view a dozen examples from the Skirball's extraordinary collection of documents dating from the medieval to the modern era.

A replica of Berlin's New Synagogue, an architectural landmark from its dedication in 1866 and symbol of German-Jewish civilization prior to the Holocaust, is the backdrop for objects used in temple services. Different traditions for displaying the Torah scroll, which contains the first five books of the Hebrew Bible, evolved in Jewish communities around the world, and these are seen together in this gallery, accompanied by historic recordings of cantorial music.

The focus then shifts to the New World, with posters advertising steamship passage, a turn-of-the-century photomural of the New York skyline, and a replica of the Statue of Liberty's torch setting the scene for the flourishing of Jewish culture in twentieth-century America. **Project Americana**, an ongoing campaign by the museum to collect and preserve artifacts of everyday life that document the Jewish experience in America, has yielded a rich repository that is incorporated into such exhibits as a Lower East Side kitchen and a newsstand stocked with Jewish-American publications. The synagogue arks that Marcus Illions carved in Europe are displayed alongside the wooden carousel horses for which he became famous in America. A film highlights the Jewish composers (Irving Berlin, George Gershwin, Jerome Kern), writers (Clifford Odets, Gertrude Stein, Nathanael West), entertainers (Fanny Brice, Eddie Cantor, Harry Houdini), and movie producers (Metro Goldwyn Mayer, Warner Bros.) who transformed American popular culture.

The cruel reality of the Holocaust is evoked by six portraits representing the six million European Jews who perished in Nazi death camps, which lead visitors to a quiet space illuminated by an eternal flame for a moment of remembrance. The effort to reestablish a Jewish state in Palestine gained momentum in the period following World War II, and its existence, realized in May 1948, is celebrated in a monumental photomontage of Israel's diverse peoples and transformed landscape.

The exhibition culminates in a kaleidoscopic multimedia presentation that surrounds visitors with the marvelous accomplishments of Jews in the modern era, then sends them out into the world with the biblical challenge renewed: "Go forth . . . and be a blessing." Check the daily schedule for free docent-led tours of both "Visions and Values" and temporary exhibitions.

Programming at the Cultural Center, even in its inaugural phase, expands the offerings of the museum. Holiday festivals, where families explore a rich heritage through hands-on activities and popular performances, have been particularly well received. Film series are presented Sundays at 2 p.m. in the beautiful auditorium, and a monthly series of literary readings was one of the highlights of the Skirball's first year. Free concerts at Zeidler's Café on Thursday evenings and more formal presentations in an ambitious spring series brought Jewish musical traditions to the Skirball campus. Family days are featured monthly, with art and music workshops geared to seasonal celebrations.

The Jewish community's enthusiastic response to the Skirball Cultural Center has made it a choice location for weddings and bar/bat mitzvahs. The demand for this revenue-producing service has led the Skirball to undertake another building project to accommodate such receptions without tenting one of the courtyards. Architect Moshe Safdie has already designed a wing at the north side of the site for such functions, and he is working on better solutions to parking requirements.

University of Judaism

15600 Mulholland Dr.
Los Angeles 90077
310-476-9777

The mission of University of Judaism, which was founded in 1947, is to educate the future leaders of American Jewish life, including the next generation of Conservative rabbis. Its lovely twenty-six-acre campus, situated just across the San Diego (405) freeway from the Skirball Cultural Center and just up the hill from UCLA, was inaugurated in 1977.

Visitors to the University of Judaism enter the third level of the main building; stacked terraces on the other side of the building face the south lawn where a small but choice collection of sculpture is displayed. The Smalley Sculpture Garden contains contemporary works by many well-known artists, but my guide pointed out that the brushed aluminum triangles in *Two Open Triangles Up Gyratory* by George Rickey sometimes align to form the Star of David. Because I couldn't imagine an open-air piece by Jenny Holzer, I asked to see her 1988 work *Action Causes More Trouble…*, which takes the form of a bench. Also within the main building is the Platt Gallery (Sun.–Thurs. 10 a.m.–4 p.m., Fri. 10 a.m.– 2 p.m.; free), which is run by the volunteer fine arts council, a group of artists and collectors who use their access to the local art scene to stretch a limited budget and produce about six thoughtful exhibitions per year. Lita Albuquerque, Frank and Nancy Romero, and Peter Shire are local artists whose work has been profiled, along with internationally known figures like Robert Rauschenberg.

From November to March, the 479-seat Gindi Auditorium hosts a performing arts series that showcases six artists who represent a variety of styles in music, dance, theater, and comedy. Lectures and book signings are offered through the adult education program, which has a broad range—from Talmud study to yoga—and a large number of classes, both day and evening. Call to request the season brochure for Continuing Education or the International Festival of Performing Arts (see Music, page 202, for more information).

The Getty Center

1200 Getty Center Dr.
Los Angeles 90049
310-440-7300
Sat.–Sun. 10 a.m.–6 p.m., Tues.–Wed. 11 a.m.–7 p.m.,
Thurs.–Fri. 11 a.m.–9 p.m.
School groups with reservations (310-440-7300)
have exclusive access to the museum on
weekdays 9–11 a.m.
Entry: free, parking $5/car

The Getty, as the seven entities funded by the J. Paul Getty Trust are known collectively, includes a museum, five institutes, and a grant program, which are now physically united for the first time on the 110-acre mountaintop campus along the San Diego (405) Freeway in West Los Angeles. The statistics are compelling: it is the largest single-phase construction project ever undertaken, costing about a billion dollars, and comprises six buildings designed by Pritzker Prize–winning architect Richard Meier, with a combined area of one million square feet. The buildings occupy only about five acres of the site, with 105 acres devoted to gardens and public spaces that encourage visitors to enjoy the panoramic view; 600 acres of surrounding land, preserved in its natural state, further insulate the complex. Its elevated siting evoked now-familiar criticism that this rich, Eurocentric, elitist institution had little concern or connection with Los Angeles, but the spirit of the new complex, which opens on all sides to panoramic vistas— of untouched chaparral-covered mountains and distant islands floating in the blue Pacific, as well as the ribbon of cars on the freeways and the urban grid of the man-made landscape—seems instead to embrace and celebrate its surroundings, to rejoice in the intertwined destinies that will make this city a cultural destination in the twenty-first century.

That it is expected to become a destina-

tion for residents and visitors to Los Angeles alike is revealed by the size of the parking garage with space for 1,200 cars. Advance parking reservations are the only sure way to visit the Getty Center because the fire code limits the number of people on site to 4,500. Although city buses also stop at the Getty Center, and visitors may arrive by taxi, bicycle, or on foot, those with reservations are given priority and other visitors might find delays or lines when the site's quota is already filled. In its first year the Getty Center now expects to receive 2 million visitors—up from 1.3 million projected before it opened—but administrators expect visitation to level off at about 1.5 million annually.

Silent white electric trams whisk visitors to the eastern edge of the huge Arrival Plaza, whose size was dictated in part by the requirement that a fire truck be capable of making a 360-degree turn in the space and racing up a broad ramp (hidden behind a stone wall) to the front door of the museum. The three-tiered flight of monumental stone steps and terraces— which makes the transition from the plaza level to the museum entrance—recalls the entrance to New York's Metropolitan Museum or Rome's Spanish Steps, where people congregate to bask in glorious public space; but alas, the fire code prohibits its use for performances. Beyond a shocking lavender trellis—the color a witty reference to the wisteria vine it supports—is a building that houses two restaurants: a formal room upstairs, and on the lower level, a café with glass walls and an ample west-facing terrace banked in sunset bougainvillea, for outdoor dining.

The three-acre Central Garden, designed by light-and-space artist Robert Irwin, occupies a natural ravine between the museum and the Research Institute, a circular structure with a glass-walled library (housing 700,000 volumes) as its primary feature. The three buildings on the northeast sector are punctuated with glass walls and clad in light-colored aluminum panels. These modern materials are more in keeping with the architect's signature style and are ones that he thinks are appropriate to the institutes of the Getty devoted to science—conservation, education, and information—which are housed there, along with the Trust offices and the grant program.

But this assignment will forever alter the public perception of Meier's architecture, which will henceforth be identified with his masterly use of natural stone. Travertine was quarried in Tivoli, Italy, and cut with a guillotine blade to produce cleft panels with an uneven surface that reveals the stone's internal structure, including many small fossils. The heavy panels are mounted with a four-point bolting system, so they appear to float; and the complex textured surfaces, which suggest past worlds and the vast flow of time, present a natural range of coloration that is continually altered by environmental conditions. Neither the

stone nor the aluminum panels can accurately be summarized as white, so Meier has modified the canon of modernism and mollified the critics who predicted that the design of the Getty Center would be simply an expanded version of the High Museum in Atlanta. Nearly 300,000 of the travertine panels are incorporated in the complex, forming the perimeter walls and grounding each of the buildings to the site, but they only dominate in the museum building.

The museum's entrance foyer is strikingly modern, with three pairs of glass doors on one side and walls of glass that slide open on the other; the elliptical space is defined by metallic ramps, railings, and *brise-soleils*—partitioned overhangs that fracture the incessant sunlight into appealing patterns of shadow. Off the lobby are two small theaters, where eight-minute museum orientation videos play continuously, and a large store that allows the Getty to enter the arena of museum merchandising, a move that was precluded by the cramped quarters at the Getty Villa in Malibu. A deep courtyard stretches ahead, enclosed by the five stone-clad pavilions of the museum and punctuated by long troughs of water lined with London plane trees and large basins where water cascades off boulders of native California greenstone marble. Ample seating, both inviting and ingenious—a smooth stone seat cantilevered from a rough-cut wall, a chunk of travertine that forms a natural bench—conveys the invitation to relax, to take a moment in this oasis to refresh your spirit. A protected stage and seating for 500 are subtly incorporated into this space, which will be used for such performances as the Friday Night at the Getty series and summer-evening concerts.

The new museum offers almost three times the gallery space of the Getty Villa, and unlike that re-creation of period architecture (which was only marginally

compatible with the display of art other than antiquities), this museum combines the finest elements of traditional exhibition design with state-of-the-art technology to create ideal environments for viewing each type of art in the Getty's major collections. In addition to the antiquities and French decorative arts that reflect J. Paul Getty's personal collecting interests (and remain among the museum's strengths) and the paintings collection that has been developing for several decades since he began it, the museum has more recently focused its unmatched financial resources on assembling new collections of sculpture, drawings, illuminated manuscripts, and photographs. What was once a spotty collection of European paintings has been augmented with savvy acquisitions and shaped into a pleasing survey that begins with late medieval paintings on gold-leaf grounds and concludes with Cézanne's *Still Life with Apples* of 1893, which the museum acquired in 1996 for a reported $30 million.

"The main purpose of the new museum is to show visitors works of art in a setting where they look their best," says director John Walsh, and for paintings that means being illuminated with the same natural light in which they were painted. Twenty galleries of paintings therefore occupy the top floor of four of the five museum pavilions, each illuminated from forty feet overhead by louvered skylights, computerized to adjust to daily fluctuations in light. The huge volume of ceiling may be spatially inefficient, but it allows diffuse light to flood the space, in a way that reminds Walsh of the Dulwich Picture Gallery outside London, which was designed in 1811 by Sir John Soane. The finishing in these galleries seems both luxurious and classical, but it is revealed to be efficient and spare as well, with dark wood flooring that climbs eighteen inches up the wall, ending in a notched band mirrored by the picture-hanging rail halfway up the wall—both devices that disguise the vent and return for the heat and air-conditioning. Such technology can only be so seamlessly integrated into new construction, which is why this has been such a challenging and satisfying assignment for the architect and the museum professionals who had the resources and the opportunity to design ideal environments for viewing and conserving art. When the building was still in the initial phases of construction, my guide described the marvelous innovations in the miles of cable and conduit then revealed overhead, and raved about the loading dock, an enthusiasm best understood from the perspective of the rocky road that artworks had to follow into the Getty Villa.

The popular program, Selected Shorts, is expected to resume at the Getty Center (see Literary L.A., p. 225). Musical events will be held in the 450-seat auditorium, and in outdoor sites on campus (see Music, p. 202)

So what art is there to see? I asked the director to highlight works in each gallery, and his selections, not surprisingly, were all acquisitions made since the Getty Trust received a $700-million endowment following Getty's death in 1976. That fortune has ballooned under the shrewd management of the Trust's first president and CEO, former chairman of the U.S. Securities and Exchange Commission Harold M. Williams, to more than $4 billion today, and by law 4.25 percent of it, or $170 million, must be spent every three of four years. In the first gallery, Walsh pointed to a panel painted circa 1330 by Bernardo Daddi, which depicts the Virgin Mary between Saints Thomas Aquinas and Paul. The conservator who examined it prior to its purchase in 1993 declared that he had never seen a trecento picture so well preserved, its glazes still intact to modulate the bright colors of the drapery, its punched gold background glowing softly. By contrast he motioned across the room to a work that had suffered later restoration: its colors seemed stripped and harsh, its gold too bright. In the second gallery we stopped by a two-sided panel, mounted perpendicular to the wall so both sides are visible, on which a German artist had painted a complex scene of the Three Magi, burdened with an entourage and all the accoutrements of travel, being greeted by the prophets who had foretold their arrival. Andrea Mantegna's *Adoration of the Magi* (ca. 1495–1505) is a very different version of this sacred story, a close-up scheme that focuses on the psychological interactions among the principal characters. The star of the third gallery is the Florentine Renaissance altarpiece by Fra Bartolomeo for which the museum paid $22.5 million in 1996. It is shown in the context of many other works of the period in the collection which had either been kept in storage or not hung under ideal light conditions or with sufficient space, including *Triptych with Madonna and Child* by Bernardo Daddi. A portrait by Pontormo (illustrated at right), whose subject was identified as the eighteen-year-old Cosimo I de' Medici during the years it hung in Malibu, is called *Portrait of a Halberdier (Francesco Guardi?)* in a recent publication; this is one example of how the additions to and study of the collection in recent years have revealed new thematic and historical connections.

The golden age of Venetian painting is represented by Titian's *Venus and Adonis* (1555–60) and many other works, but Walsh points out *Mythological Scene*, painted in the early 1520s by Dosso Dossi,

because such magical landscapes embody the idealized image of classical antiquity that is the lasting legacy of Venetian painters. In the seventeenth-century Italian gallery, he directed my attention to a "great portrait, subtle and complicated, by someone you've never heard of"—he's right, Domenico Fetti is not a name that will spring to many visitors' minds—because he hopes viewers will be drawn by the searching gaze of the young man holding a musical instrument and remember the painting for its own qualities, not its price tag.

Mr. Getty's own collecting did not extend much beyond religious and mythological subjects, so virtually all of the paintings in the next four galleries, dedicated to Dutch, French, and Flemish painting of the seventeenth century, are works acquired since his death. Memorable works in the Dutch gallery include: *The Drawing Lesson* (1665) by Jan Steen; a luminous seascape, *Shipping in a Calm at Flushing* (1649) by Jan van de Cappelle, acquired in 1996; and Paulus Potter's *The Piebald Horse*, a loving depiction that reflects the value of such property in seventeenth-century Holland. Just weeks before the opening of the Getty Center, the British government granted an export license for *Landscape with Calm* by Nicholas Poussin, which will be featured in the French gallery along with *Holy Family* (ca. 1651) by the same artist (a work jointly owned with the Norton Simon Museum but shown at the new Getty Museum). Georges de la Tour's *Musicians' Brawl* (1625–30) is an enigmatic composition—the title has been changed, substituting *musicians* for *beggars* since the museum's collection catalogue was revised in 1991—but the expressive detail of the faces is engrossing even if the meaning of the work eludes us. Recent acquisitions in the Flemish gallery include Anthony Van Dyck's *Portrait of Agostino Pallavicini* (ca. 1621) and *The Entombment* (ca. 1612) by Peter Paul Rubens.

The corner gallery showcases works by Rembrandt, an artist Mr. Getty appreciated enough to violate his own ban of 1957 on painting acquisitions—"I think the JPG museum has enough pictures. We have no space for any more"—with the purchase of a 1661 portrait, now identified as *Saint Bartholomew* because the subject holds a knife, the instrument of his martyrdom. That image and *An Old Man in Military Costume* (ca. 1631) are Rembrandt working in a familiar style, but Walsh directed our attention to a small composition of

1632, *The Abduction of Europa*, which illustrates a mythological scene from Ovid and reveals the young artist, still in his twenties, "in full stride and about to overtake his teacher," Pieter Lastman, whose *The Resurrection* (1612) hangs next to it. (He did not mention that this work by Rembrandt cost the museum an estimated $35 million in 1995, but I will.)

The bright sunlight flooding the corridor adjacent to the Rembrandt gallery on the day of my visit made it difficult to focus on these dark paintings, but translucent scrims now cover this glass wall and other places that form the transition between enclosed galleries and exterior terraces. The amount of space dedicated to such outdoor rooms, which offer ample seating as well as refreshment stands, reflects the administration's hope that visitors will not attempt a marathon through the museum. The southeast-facing terrace, which an early guide prophesied will become *the* place to propose in Los Angeles, has such a commanding view that visitors may be able to see their futures stretched before them. The spiky cactus ranged on the south promontory drew an appreciative chuckle from many visitors, but the bird's-eye view from the west-facing terrace (between galleries for temporary exhibitions) into the Central Garden commands more serious attention. Robert Irwin calls it "a sculpture in the form of a garden aspiring to be a work of art," and his masterly plan not only gracefully accommodates such technical requirements as wheelchair access—in a ramped pathway of herringbone-patterned slate slabs that zigzags across the stream and down the slope—but incorporates elements of Paradise garden design, like the *chadar,* a cobbled stone wall that fragments the smooth water as it plunges into a pool surrounding a maze of azaleas.

Perhaps it was the refreshing pause on the southeast terrace, but I found strolling through the galleries in the West Pavilion, which bring the survey of painting through the end of the nineteenth century, to be an exhilarating experience. There were so many views of the Grand Canal in the first gallery that I temporarily enjoyed a fantasy break in eighteenth-century Venice. Goya's 1804 *Portrait of the Marquesa de Santiago* is annotated with an English contemporary's not-so-flattering opinion of the subject as "very profligate and loose in her manners, and scarcely admitted into female society," which concludes with "she is immensely rich." Jacques-Louis David is more sympathetic to the erotic parting of the nymph Eucharis and Telemachus, the son of Homeric hero Odysseus, in a painting that epitomizes late neoclassicism. Géricault's portrait of a black man may represent the professional model who posed for his 1819 masterpiece *The Raft of the Medusa,* which hangs in the Louvre.

The next two galleries contain an eclectic group of paintings that reveal various attempts to create a modern style in the latter half of the nineteenth century. I'm not familiar with the Belgian artist Fernand Khnopff, but his 1885 *Portrait of Jeanne Kefer,* a little girl standing by a closed doorway, is spellbinding. *A Walk at Dusk* (ca. 1832–35) is a small composition by Caspar David Friedrich that combines all the elements of German romanticism. As a young artist, Jean-François Millet replaced the conventional stylization of bourgeois portraiture with a humane vision that infuses his 1841 image of *Louise-Antoinette Feuardent*, the young wife of a friend in his hometown of Cherbourg, and is evident in such later depictions of peasants as *Man with Hoe* (1860–62).

In the final gallery filled with large paintings, visitors' attention is grabbed by *The Entry of Christ into Brussels in 1889* by James Ensor, which hangs on the far wall. This huge, boldly colored canvas, which depicts Christ astride a small gray donkey and surrounded by a raucous procession of masked Mardi Gras revelers, remained in the artist's studio for forty years after it was painted in 1888 because its technique and subject matter shocked contemporary sensibilities. Viewers had to stand within six feet of this masterpiece at the Getty Villa, so for the first decade that the Getty owned this work it could never really be seen; to my eye, it so dominates the gallery where it now hangs that it makes many important works in this seminal transitional period appear timid and small. Manet's *Rue Mosnier with Flags* (1878) is small, but it is a gutsy work, its center occupied by a deserted street with a distant vanishing point painted with virtuoso brushwork and a restrained palette. The one-legged man who hobbles into the left foreground "suggests the inequities of life in the new

urban environment," according to the label copy. Vivid color and powerful brushwork characterize Vincent van Gogh's *Irises* (illustrated, p. 235), which the museum acquired in 1990 after the Australian tycoon who had purchased it at Sotheby's for $53.9 million (then the highest price ever paid for a painting) suffered financial reverses. Monet's first series paintings, thirty images of wheatstacks composed during a nine-month period in 1891, included *Wheatstacks, Snow Effect, Morning,* which entered the Getty collection in 1995.

Antiquities, one of the central holdings of the Getty, will be featured in the museum's temporary exhibition galleries during its inaugural year, but this presentation, entitled "Beyond Beauty: Antiquities as Evidence," will use new ideas in archaeology, conservation, and scholarship to reveal the cultural, historical, and technological information embedded in these works. Digital technology will allow visitors to take a virtual-reality tour of the Forum of Trajan in Rome. This exhibition is intended as a preview of the center for comparative archaeology that will occupy the Getty Villa in Malibu when it reopens in 2001 (see p. 254). "Making Architecture: The Getty Center from Concept through Construction," which will also remain on view throughout the inaugural year, will feature a fifteen-year time-line of the project as well as a thirty-nine-foot model. An illustrated guide, intended as the map for a walking tour, points out the architectural features of the Getty Center campus. A sixty-minute film, *The Making of the Getty Center,* and a twenty-minute film that explores the full range of international programs initiated and funded by the institutes and grant program is shown daily in the auditorium.

Fourteen galleries on the lower level contain what Walsh unabashedly calls, "the greatest collection of eighteenth-century French furniture and decorative arts in the world." This is the legacy of J. Paul Getty's personal collection, which he began in the 1930s and described in a 1949 publication entitled *Europe in the Eighteenth Century.* With the prospect of filling the new Malibu museum in 1974, he and the curatorial staff began to build a representative collection of French decorative arts from the reign of Louis XIV (1643–1715) through the Revolution of 1789. New York architect Thierry Despont was hired to work with long-time curator Gillian Wilson and conservator Brian Considine in designing this "museum

within the museum" at the Getty Center, installing original eighteenth-century carved wood paneling in four period rooms—two of them Régence, the others rococo and neoclassical—then reinventing such elements as carved and gilded plaster ceilings (the originals could not be transported) and selecting appropriate flooring and furnishings from the collection. Pale blue Régence panels constructed in 1719 for a library in a townhouse on the Plâce Vendome had been moved to a country residence in 1841 and altered, but two sections not used in the later installation provided clues on how to restore the ensemble, now installed here in its original state. Panels from the neoclassical room designed in 1793 by the architect Ledoux were later installed elsewhere in the Hôtel Hosten. But the original plan has been faithfully restored in an installation that features the gilded and polychromed panels with floral and mythological designs; mirrored arcades opposite each other create a false gallery in reflection.

The most outstanding pieces in this extraordinary collection are by André-Charles Boulle (1642–1732), who crafted monumental cabinets and coffers of wood marquetry and veneers in brass, pewter, tortoiseshell, and ebony. The dazzling virtuosity of his huge cabinet-on-stand was intended as a fitting tribute to Louis XIV's victories. His Majesty reveals no remorse for his vanity in a portrait, after Rigaud, which hangs at the entrance to this suite of galleries where he can overlook his treasures. The bombastic style of the last gallery, with red brocade walls and *faux-marbre* paneling, leaves no doubt that this was not an era of modest good taste, but it is a daring installation of a set of six tapestries depicting the Emperor of China, whom none of the artisans at the Beauvais Manufactory had ever seen.

These galleries and another eight dedicated to the fine collection of sculpture that has been accumulated by curator Peter Fusco are intended, according to Walsh, "to give three-dimensional art the prominence it has been denied since impressionism usurped public interest." The installation of these galleries eschews modern display furniture; the curator has instead "hoarded" old pedestals so the works can be seen as they would have been in the period of their creation. The neoclassical gallery features works by Antonio Canova, the most famous working artist of his day (1757–1822), hailed as the true heir to the artists of classical

An open-air café, tucked beneath the museum's special exhibitions pavilion and overlooking the Central Garden, serves lunch and other light fare.

Greece. A full figure of *Apollo* (1781), in which Canova articulated the heroic type of male beauty based on ancient models, is called a statuette because the human figure is not rendered at full scale; its detail and visual impact belie that term, and a marble column (of the period) raises the figure to eye level. Separate figures of the *Three Graces*, and a *Vestal Virgin* are also by Canova. Francesco Franzoni, the great animal sculptor who is best known for the *Sala degli Animali* in the Vatican, crafted white marble supports in the form of rams' heads as the base of a monumental table; its surface is a four-inch-thick slab of dark, figured Brecia Medicea marble, a type that the Medici family had quarried in the Alpuan Alps beginning in the late sixteenth century. (It sits on an isolator base, a shock-absorbing mount designed to roll with any seismic waves and prevent the heavy marble top from crushing the sculptured base, which demonstrates the prudent use of modern technology, even in period installation.) The noble bust of a black man by the artist Francis Harwood is not the stereotypical rendition, like a blackamoor, that might be expected of such a subject in this era, but is instead a loving study of an expressive visage and a regal bearing. Late eighteenth- and nineteenth-century sculpture is showcased in an unusual display, with several *modellos* and terra-cottas casually arrayed on pedestals and tables as they might have been in an artist's studio. The pieces together demonstrate the various uses of terra-cotta: as sketches for ideas and presentation models for works that would ultimately be rendered in larger scale and different media, and as finished works. The room itself is also unusual, not large but with a double-height ceiling; the spacious volumes and subdued coloration allow the sculptures to dominate, revealing architect Meier's mastery and the wisdom of curator Fusco's confidence in his art.

A description of the online networking initiative, L.A. Culture Net, which launched the Getty Information Institute in 1997, can be found in Virtual L.A., p. 260.

Other galleries on the lower level will hold changing exhibitions from the collections of Old Master drawings, illuminated manuscripts of the Middle Ages and Renaissance, and 65,000 photographs—all media that can tolerate only limited light exposure and so must be rotated often. A collection of drawings, the most universal of all art forms, was started in 1981 and has since grown to about 500 works by the most brilliant draftsmen from the fifteenth through nineteenth centuries. With the 1983 purchase of 144 richly painted manuscripts collected in Germany by Dr. Peter and Irene Ludwig, the Getty Museum established itself as an important repository for the most elaborately crafted examples of the medium by which the tenets of Western civilization—its history, law, religious scriptures, literature, and science—were conveyed. It continues to acquire examples that extend the historical and artistic range of the collection and displays its treasures in a half dozen thematic and spotlight exhibitions each year.

The photographs collection, unique among the museum's holdings because it contains contemporary works (although pieces by contemporary artists have been commissioned for public spaces at the Getty Center and purchased for the interior decoration of the administrative offices), was likewise established with the purchase of several of the most important private photo collections in the world. The collection, particularly rich in works by the pioneers of the new medium in the 1840s, is international in scope and includes representative examples by the master photographers of the twentieth century. The inaugural photography show, "Capturing Time: A Celebration of Photography," will feature one of the museum's most recent acquisitions, a landmark photocollage by David Hockney entitled *Pearblossom Hwy., 11–18th April 1986, #2*, which incorporates 750 color prints of a Mojave desert road disappearing into snowcapped mountains. The purchase (for an undisclosed sum) culminated a decade-long effort by curator Weston Naef to convince the artist to part with this piece; Hockney was persuaded by the center's state-of-the-art conservation facilities, where the collage will be kept in cold storage when not on display, and he donated his negatives and preparatory maquette to the museum.

Four multimedia Art Information Rooms—each with a different theme and one designated specifically as a Family Resource Center—will be located within the museum's four permanent collection pavilions. "Visitors tell us they enjoy looking at art when they can learn something about it, so we've attempted to create centers that will be engaging, informative, and fun for the museum's diverse audiences," explains Diane Brigham, head of education. That includes audioguides on CD-ROM for self-guided examinations of aspects of the collections, as well as a special audio tour for families. Computer stations within each room will allow visitors to explore different topics that interest them, but people will also staff these rooms to introduce visitors to the Getty's resources and lead hands-on activities and educational programs.

University of California, Los Angeles (UCLA)

405 Hilgard Ave.
Los Angeles 90024
310-825-4321

Mount St. Mary's College (12001 Chalon Rd., Los Angeles 90049) is home to the Da Camera Society, which sponsors the popular annual concert series Chamber Music in Historic Sites. Call 310-954-4300 for information.

UCLA has the largest enrollment of the nine campuses of the prestigious University of California system. The campus, which was established in 1919, began with four buildings on Royce Quad. Today it includes more than 100 buildings on 419 beautifully landscaped acres south of Sunset Boulevard, sandwiched between the Bel-Air and Brentwood neighborhoods. Visitors may want to pick up a map at any of the information booths or take a campus tour (weekdays at 10:30 a.m. and 2:30 p.m.; call 310-206-0616 to make a reservation

and to check the tour schedule; if there are students in your group, call 310-825-8764). The public can enjoy and use facilities at UCLA, including libraries, galleries, sculpture and botanical gardens, and cafes. The university's museums of art and cultural history are reasons for repeat visits to the lovely Westwood campus. Parking is available for $5; stop at the information kiosk at a campus entrance for instructions. For a complete schedule of arts and cultural events, call 310-UCLA-ART. Or check the university's Web site (www.ucla.edu) or the School of the Arts and Architecture's Web site (www.soaa.ucla.edu).

The **Mildred E. Mathias Botanical Garden**, 7.5 acres at the southeast corner of the campus, is bounded by Hilgard and Le Conte Avenues and accessible from walk-in entrances at the southeast and northwest corners. This quiet spot (open Mon.–Fri. 8 a.m.–5 p.m., Sat.–Sun. 8 a.m.–4 p.m.; free) is a haven for nature lovers, who can take a seat along the stream leading to a koi pond surrounded by a bamboo grove where lovers have carved their names. The grassy slopes planted with palms are a nice place to read, and for those curious about botany, all the trees along the walkways are identified. "The Nest"—an open, outdoor facility for classes, meetings, and events—is available at no cost to

schools, community organizations, and clubs. The garden contains 4,000 types of plants, including a large selection of subtropical and tropical plants that cannot be grown elsewhere in the United States except in greenhouses. For information, call 310-825-3620.

The **UCLA library system**, which is ranked among the top five in North America, includes the University Research Library, the College Library, and eleven other specialized libraries. Total holdings of more than 6.6 million items include extensive collections of government publications, computer-based information, manuscripts, maps, music scores, recordings, photographs, and slides. Perhaps the most interesting of the library buildings is Powell Library, one of UCLA's four original buildings, which are grouped around the main "quad" at the center of the campus. All four of these buildings, constructed in 1929, are built in the red-brick Romanesque style of Northern Italy and are richly decorated with engravings, sculpture, and stained glass. Powell Library, which was recently restored to its original 1929 splendor, contains one of UCLA's architectural treasures: the ceiling of the central reading room, which was rebuilt piece-by-piece during the restoration. A guide to the library system at UCLA is available at the University Research Library, in the northeast corner of the campus, or at Powell Library.

UCLA's Center for the Performing Arts is your ticket to enjoying music, dance, and theater performed by such artists as the Alvin Ailey American Dance Theater, cellist Yo-Yo Ma, Stomp, the Royal National Theatre with Ian McKellen, or the Grand Kabuki Theater of Japan. In 1997 the Family Series of four special events included tap dancing, Vietnamese puppetry, and a storyteller who uses vintage folk instruments in an engaging act. Some 200 events each year are sponsored by UCLA Center for the Performing Arts, which returns in 1998 to Royce Hall, another of the original quad buildings, closed since the 1994 Northridge earthquake. The

1,828-seat hall benefits from technical improvements in acoustics and stage machinery, in addition to a complete seismic retrofit, during the renovation, whose cost has been pegged at $68 million. Performances are also held at various venues on campus and nearby. Except for the free monthly jazz concerts on the first Sunday of the month at Veterans Wadsworth Theater, prices for events are similar to those at commercial theaters, although students, seniors, and UCLA faculty and staff are eligible for discounted seats. For the season brochure, call 310-825-2101; to purchase tickets, call the UCLA Arts Line, 310-UCLA-ART, or the UCLA Central Ticket Office, 310-825-2101. You can also visit their Web site (www.performingarts.ucla.edu). See Theater and Dance, page 82, and Music, page 199.

The UCLA Center for the Performing Arts outreach program, **Design for Sharing**, sponsors free demonstration performances for public school students, provides thousands of free tickets annually through community organizations, presents music master classes, and sponsors My Special World, an audience-participation program for youngsters aged five to seven; call 310-825-7681 for information.

UCLA's **American Youth Symphony** and **Young Musicians Foundation** perform several free children's concerts a year, both at UCLA and in Los Angeles–area schools. The foundation also offers a few scholarships to gifted young musicians. Call 310-859-7668 for a concert schedule or scholarship information.

Fowler Museum of Cultural History

(Wed.–Sun. noon–5 p.m., Thurs. until 8 p.m.; 310-825-4361), just down the Janss Steps from Powell, focuses on non-Western art and material cultures from around the world, emphasizing art and anthropology. The collections of ethnic arts, which had been accumulating in campus museums since the 1960s, were installed in a brick building surrounding a peaceful inner courtyard in 1992. Masquerade regalia, ceramic wares, and textiles from the Americas, Africa, Asia, and Oceania, as well as a large collection of South American folk art, are important aspects of its holdings. But the Fowler immediately distinguished itself with a landmark exhibition on the pre-Columbian people of Peru and has continued to mount the results of scholarly research revealing little-known aspects of cultural history. Lectures, family workshops, and dance and music festivals are regular features of its programming. Admission: $5 adults; $3 seniors, non-UCLA students, UCLA faculty, staff, and alumni; $1 for UCLA students.

More than seventy pieces of sculpture are displayed in the five-acre **Franklin D. Murphy Sculpture Garden**, named for a former UCLA chancellor. This open area east of the University Research Library is shaded by mature trees, including the purple haze of jacaranda in the spring. With works by fifty-one artists—including Auguste Rodin, Henry Moore, Alexander Calder, Joan Miró, Isamu Noguchi, and David Smith—it is the largest outdoor sculpture garden on the West Coast and one of the most distinguished collections in the country.

The **UCLA Film and Television Archive** offers a diverse year-round calendar of film, television, and video series, ranging from Hollywood treasures to contemporary international cinema and classic television. Annual film festivals include the Festival of Preservation—dedicated to screening rescued, preserved, and restored film, television, and animation—and the **Asian Pacific Film and Video Festival**. Programs from television's golden age have been donated by the Hallmark Hall of Fame, ABC, Jack Benny, and Milton Berle. Attendance of 60,000 at 500 local programs each year attests to the strong interest of the Los Angeles community in film and media. Most films are shown in the **James Bridges Theater** (formerly the Melnitz Theater), at the northwest corner of campus. Tickets are generally $6 for adults and $4 for students and senior citizens, and sometimes include multiple films. For film screening schedules, call 310-206-FILM; see Film and Video, p. 106.

The Westwood Playhouse reopened its doors in October 1995 with a new name (which recognizes a $5-million donation from the Geffen Foundation) and a new affiliation with UCLA. West Coast premieres of shows originated elsewhere, as well as a few productions mounted at the **Geffen Playhouse**, have already built audiences for this Westside venue, which may become more adventuresome with its success. Tickets are available at the Geffen Playhouse box office (10886 Le Conte Ave.; 310-208-5454) or through Telecharge (800-233-3123).

UCLA Extension offers continuing education for the public, with more than 1,500 stimulating and innovative arts seminars, lecture series, and special programs each year, along with courses for arts professionals. Courses cover writing, literature, film, music, architecture, graphic arts, multimedia, design, and cultural enrichment. In addition to campus sites, UCLA Extension offers programs in other locations throughout the L.A. basin: art and design at two sites in Santa Monica; business, management, engineering, computer science, and English as a second language at the World Trade Center in downtown L.A.; and an eclectic mix,

from screenwriting to computers, at Universal CityWalk. Call 800-554-UCLA to learn more.

UCLA Summer Session Expanding Horizons is a program for academically motivated high school students, who are eligible to attend UCLA's summer sessions based on transcripts, PSAT/SAT scores, and recommendations from their schools. Grades become a permanent part of the student's academic record, so students should consider seriously whether they are prepared for this level of intellectual challenge before enrolling in the program. All lower-division classes with course numbers 99 and below may be taken. Housing for high school students is available. For more information, contact UCLA Extension's Department of Education, Room 514, 10995 Le Conte Avenue., Los Angeles 90024, or call 310-206-7229.

Diverse groups on campus, not university sponsored, offer other cultural activities. The **International Student Center** (1045 Gayley Ave.; 310-208-4587) hosts many such events. Among the offerings are English conversation classes open to the community and an international speakers bureau, which invites speakers of international stature to speak to community groups and high schools.

UCLA at the Armand Hammer Museum of Art and Cultural Center

10899 Wilshire Blvd.
Los Angeles 90024
310-443-7000
Tues.–Sat. 11 a.m.–7 p.m., Thurs. until 9 p.m., Sun. 11 a.m.–5 p.m.
Entry: adults $4.50, senior citizens/non-UCLA students/UCLA faculty and staff/Alumni Association members $3, UCLA students $1; children under 17 free

A few blocks south of the campus in Westwood is UCLA at the Armand Hammer Museum of Art and Cultural Center. The black-and-white-striped marble building, designed by Edward Larrabee Barnes at the headquarters of Occidental Petroleum Company, opened in 1990, just two weeks before the death of Armand Hammer, who had formed its collections and strong-armed the company's board into funding the museum building. The controversy was not laid to rest with Dr. Hammer, but in 1994 UCLA signed a ninety-nine-year agreement to operate the museum, without committing university funds. To supplement the existing operating budgets from the Wight Art Gallery and the Grunwald Center for Graphic Arts, Leonardo da Vinci's Codex Hammer was put on the auction block (and snapped up by software billionaire Bill Gates, who restored its name to the Codex Leicester).

The European and American Old Masters and impressionist paintings that Hammer had collected (and pledged to LACMA, where they were displayed for decades, before he reneged on that commitment) include masterworks by Mary Cassatt, Vincent van Gogh, and Claude Monet. Hammer had formed the largest collection in the U.S. of works by the French caricaturist Honoré Daumier, which complements the collections of UCLA's Grunwald Center for the Graphic Arts, which is now housed in the Hammer complex, with its works on paper by Albrecht Dürer, English satirist George Cruikshank, Henri Matisse, Jasper Johns, and Picasso.

Henry Hopkins, who had directed the San Francisco Museum of Modern Art through the 1980s, agreed to lead UCLA's administration of the Hammer (along with continuing his teaching commitments on campus). He hired a competent staff, which promptly began presenting a diverse schedule of historical and contemporary art exhibitions—many of which focus on California art—offering museumgoers more incentive to visit Westwood than the still-weak collection does.

The cultural programs—musical per-

Westwood Farmers Market
Weyburn Ave. and Westwood Blvd.
Thurs. 3–7 p.m.

Westwood Park, tucked behind the Veterans Administration Building along Sepulveda Boulevard (1350 Sepulveda Blvd.; 310-473-3610), has great playground equipment, a recreation center with tennis courts, and playing fields.

Los Angeles Temple Visitors Center (10777 Santa Monica Blvd.; 310-474-1549) is the Southland headquarters of the Mormons (Church of Jesus Christ of Latter-Day Saints). See Finding God in the City of Angels, p. 142, for information on its facilities, which include a genealogical research center.

formances, poetry readings, artist talks, and guided exhibition tours—fulfill the Hammer's educational mission. Its art history classes (on Saturday mornings) reveal the academic grounding that its UCLA affiliation has brought. The free series designed for children (ages three to ten), offered several Saturdays each month, include professional storytellers in Draw Me a Story and kids performing for their peers in Children for Children. More ambitious Saturdays for Families, scheduled about once a month, cumulatively reveal the rich cultural diversity of Los Angeles.

UCLA Hannah Carter Japanese Garden

10619 Bellagio Rd.
Bel Air 90024
310-825-4574
By appointment only
(generally Tues. a.m. and Wed. p.m.)

This traditional Japanese garden is located on two acres in Stone Canyon, north of the UCLA campus. The garden was donated by Edward Carter, a former University of California regent and merchant known for establishing the Broadway department store chain, who died in 1996, and named for his wife, former Olympic skier Hannah Carter. All trees and plants—except the live oaks, which antedate the Japanese garden, and the exotics in the separate Hawaiian garden—are found in Japan: pine trees with distinctive forms and Japanese maples with red and purple foliage surround the koi pond. The main structures in the garden —teahouse, family shrine, bridges, and main gate—were built in Japan and reassembled at the garden by Japanese artisans. A bathhouse, moon-viewing deck, and five-tiered pagoda are also discovered during a stroll along the steep paths and stone bridges of this tranquil enclave. Behind the teahouse is the Hawaiian garden, which contains ferns, orchids, and tropical flowering vines.

Museum of Jurassic Technology

9341 Venice Blvd.
Los Angeles 90232
310-836-6131
Thurs. 2–8 p.m., Fri.–Sun. noon–6 p.m.
Entry: adults $4

The name is an oxymoron intended to convey the subtle mysteries of the displays, which are devoted to the history of science and natural history, according to David Wilson, a CalArts graduate and the museum's founder. This is a museum in the original sense of the term, "a spot dedicated to the muses," with exhibits intended to engage the visitor in the learning process. "The learner must always be led from familiar objects toward the unfamiliar . . . guided along, as it were, a chain of flowers into the

mysteries of life," is the enigmatic aphorism that has become the museum's unofficial motto. Something about the place captures the public imagination: when *New Yorker* editor Tina Brown killed Lawrence Weschler's piece on the place, he turned it into a book that met with great reviews and good sales; when other local institutions saw NEA funding slashed, this little museum got its grant. Its ardent supporters represent the full spectrum of L.A.'s cultural life—from magician Ricky Jay to Getty Museum director John Walsh to theater maven Steve Martin. Because financial management does not seem to be the administration's strength, the *L.A. Times* predicted it "could go the way of the dinosaurs," when the building in which it is housed was put up for sale. Instead, the Lannan Foundation, which had just closed its own gallery space and disbanded its art collections, funded the building purchase.

The staff describes its goals as fostering a "somewhat different, more eclectic contemplation about science and art." The displays emphasize unusual qualities of nature and technology, documenting the now-extinct European mole; interesting characteristics of the Deprong Mori, or "piercing devil" (a tiny white bat); and early holographic experiments. One section is devoted to a neurophysiology professor's encounter with an opera singer, which produced groundbreaking theories about memory. More recently the curators have ventured into sociological studies, displaying collections formed by the denizens of area trailer parks, for instance.

Exploration Station

3909 Sepulveda Blvd.
Culver City 90230
310- 445-1428
Sat. 10 a.m.–5 p.m., Mon.–Fri. 9:30–11:30 a.m., 1–3 p.m.
Entry: adults and children $5, school groups $3.50

Lindberg Park (Rhonda Way and Studio Dr., near Jefferson and Overland in Culver City) is a playground with climbing equipment so challenging and cleverly designed it's worth a trek across town.

This new children's museum, run by S.T.A.R. Inc., a nonprofit educational company (whose acronym abbreviates Sports, Theater, Arts, Recreation) which for the past decade has offered after-school and vacation-time programming, opened in July 1997. The museum was a labor of love for S.T.A.R.'s founder, who lost a battle with Lou Gehrig's disease shortly after it opened. But his legacy endures in the renovated florist's shop that now houses tropical animals in installations created by Hollywood set designers. Each environment is a separate ecosystem: a walk-in aviary for birds, including cockatoos and a double yellow Amazon parrot; **Lost City** has reptiles—lizards, snakes, bearded dragons, and iguanas; **Treasure Reef**, a marine biology lab, has beautiful fish in wood-framed aquariums. Most of the animals had been brought in illegally and were donated by the U. S. Fish and Wildlife Department. The mission here is preservation through education: to replace the need for exotic pets with an environmental museum and wildlife sanctuary.

Education rooms are set aside for hands-on programs that develop the themes of the installations and exhibits. Expect to find projects that explore Native-American cultures, the rainforest ecosystems, and recycled art on a weekend visit, or request a special focus for a group tour. Proceeds from admissions fund scholarships for S.T.A.R.'s enrichment programs, which have been adopted by thirty-five schools on the Westside and in Sacramento.

Culver City Ice Arena (4545 Sepulveda Blvd., Culver City 90230; 310-398-5719) Mon.-Sat. 12:30–5 p.m., Sun. 1:30–5 p.m., Wed.–Sun. 8–10:30 p.m. Entry: adults $6, children under 12 $5; skate rental $2

Ivy Substation

9070 Venice Blvd.
Culver City 90230
310-253-6640

Built as a power station for the Red Line trolleys from downtown to Venice, Ivy Substation is now a performance venue rented by such top performance groups for kids as We Tell Stories. It is also one of venues for the Culver City Summer Sunset Music Festival, a series of informal concerts with a diverse range. The free concerts are held from 6 to 7 p.m. on Thursdays, at City Hall's Courtyard (9779 Culver Blvd.); on Saturdays, at Ivy Substation. Call 310-253-6640 for information and schedule. (See Music, p. 197.)

Culver City Redevelopment Agency has approved an initial plan submitted by the **Center Theater Group**, which operates the Ahmanson Theater and Mark Taper Forum at downtown's Music Center, to renovate the **Culver Theater** at the intersection of Washington Boulevard and Hughes Avenue. The building, constructed in the 1940s with a distinctive marquee and tower, would be converted to two theaters, with a 420-seat theater in the main auditorium and a ninety-nine-seat space created from its balcony. Although the Center Theater Group remains committed to its Music Center site, luring Westsiders downtown for experimental productions has been difficult, and success in a more convenient venue might build audiences ready to venture further afield.

Jazz Bakery

3233 Helms Ave.
Culver City 90034
310-271-9039

For the past five years the nonprofit Jazz Bakery has been presenting concerts, primarily mainstream jazz, and other events in a relaxed atmosphere, which is neither a club nor a formal concert hall. There's a café in the lobby, but there's no smoking, no cover or minimum; just buy a ticket ($16–$20) and enjoy the music. Student rush seats ($10) are available as soon as the audience has been seated. There are no age restrictions at the concerts, and on Sunday afternoons—usually at 12:30, sometimes at 4 p.m.—there is a special interactive performance just for kids. Those under the age of ten are welcome free of charge, but a parent or paying adult must accompany them. There are art supplies to interpret the music, dancing is encouraged, and techniques for playing various instruments are explained. (See Music, p. 200.)

Otis College of Art and Design

9045 Lincoln Blvd.
Los Angeles 90045
310-665-6800

Culver City Public Library (4975 Overland Ave.) has story time for preschoolers twice a week (Tues. 7–7:30 p.m., Thurs. 10–10:30 a.m.). Call 310-559-1676 for information on this and other programs.

Otis, which has offered superior education in the fine and applied arts since 1918, was a county-funded institution until the passage of Proposition 13 forced it to seek support elsewhere and it merged with New York–based Parsons School of Design. By 1993, having outgrown its facility in the urban MacArthur Park neighborhood (which General Harrison Gray Otis, founder of the *Los Angeles Times,* had donated to the county) and severed its relationship with Parsons, Otis sought to reestablish itself as an independent school at a new site. It backed out of a plan to lease space in the May Company building at Wilshire and Fairfax, which LACMA purchased in 1994, citing the high costs of renovating that structure, and purchased instead a seven-story building on a 4.5-acre site in Westchester, which had served as IBM's regional headquarters for twenty years. Otis has also opened a branch within the California Mart (110 E. Ninth St., Ste. C201) in the downtown garment district, where most classes in fashion design are held.

The new campus headquarters includes the Otis Gallery (Tues.–Sat. 10 a.m.–5 p.m.; free), which was established in 1953 to support the college's curriculum by mounting professional exhibitions of contemporary art and design. It continues that tradition by presenting works of emerging and established artists in a half-dozen exhibitions each year. Call 310-665-6905 for a schedule of exhibitions.

Otis's continuing-education department offers a wide range of courses in fashion design (including textile/surface, jewelry, and shoe design), as well as photography, computer graphics, book arts (including typography and illustration), drawing, painting, and sculpture. Courses in portfolio preparation enable students to apply for professional degree programs in the arts.

Public Art Tour

Culver City

The building of a new **city hall** (9770 Culver Blvd.) led to the selection of four artists to complete public art projects for Culver City. In 1995 **Nobuho Nagasawa** created a luminescent sculpture called *Truth or Fiction* in a small park two blocks east of City Hall. In response to the citizens' request to create artworks that reflect the history of the city, the three-piece triangular columns cast images that allude to the film industry, which can be seen at night. Recently, when vandals broke one of the panels, a local councilman began a petition to remove the sculpture.

In front of City Hall, in Heritage Park, a reflecting pool by **May Sun** is called *La Ballona,* a tribute to the Ballona Creek, which runs through Culver City, and to the Gabrielino Indians, who once made their homes along the creek. A few steps from the pool is **Barbara McCarren's** *Panoramic,* a sculpture of a movie camera and thirty-three historical images of Culver City.

Inside the building are twenty-seven paintings by **Blue McRight,** which portray various aspects of Culver City's history, including Harry Culver, the city's founder.

At Culver Boulevard and Main Street, in Town Square, **Renee Petropoulos** has summarized movie making with ten pieces of sculpture that are strewn about like movie props.

The 175 feet of fencing surrounding Sony Pictures Entertainment's Child Development Center on Clarington Avenue were designed by **John Okulick** with colorful geometric forms.

Soon after the above projects were completed, however, the Public Arts Program in Culver City came to an abrupt halt when the city council, pressured by an influential developer, decided that good architecture was sufficient to satisfy the percent-for-art requirement, thus eliminating the need for artists to create works of art for public spaces.

Venice

At the corner of Main Street and Rose Avenue, *Ballerina Clown,* a cartoonish thirty-foot-tall figure by **Jonathan Borofsky,** is hard to miss. Commissioned by a private developer in 1989, the brightly painted figure of a ballet dancer with huge, oversized gloves and the head of a circus clown has become a landmark.

Santa Monica

The entry to the city of Santa Monica along Wilshire Boulevard is marked by **Tony DeLap's** 1989 arch, entitled *The Big Wave,* which spans Wilshire at Franklin. Along the **Third Street Promenade** from Wilshire Boulevard to Broadway, artists **Claude and François LaLanne** created the *Dinosaurs of Santa Monica* in 1989, a series of steel dinosaur topiaries now covered in ivy. At the State Beach, north of the Santa Monica Pier, **Carl Cheng** has created *Santa Monica Art Tool "Walk on L.A."*—a large rolling pin that can be pulled over the sand to create an instant L.A. cityscape. First installed in 1988, it used to be rolled by a bulldozer about once a month, but due to budget cutbacks the work has remained inactive and unavailable. Also at the beach, north of Pico Boulevard, **Doug Hollis** created a sound sculpture called *Singing Beach Chairs* in 1987 as a homage to the lifeguard's chair; one can sit and experience its sound and the ocean. Near Hollis's *Chairs,* artists **Helen Mayer** and **Newton Harrison** created *California Wash: From the Mountains to the Sea* in 1993.

Several murals from the WPA era, particularly by **Stanton Macdonald Wright,** survive in Santa Monica: *Landing of the Vikings in Vinland* (1936), at Santa Monica High School, and *Colonial Spanish—Restoration* (1939), at Santa Monica City Hall.

—*Noriko Fujinami*

In the summer of 1997 Otis began offering classes for children, focused workshops that met for six long sessions in a two-week period.

Summer of Art is a four-week summer program in the visual arts, which is open to high school students but also attracts older students already pursuing training in art and design. The daily regime includes a required Foundation Studio in the morning, which focuses on drawing, design, and art history; for the afternoon sessions students may elect from ceramics, cartoon illustration, computer-based graphic design, environmental arts, toy design, video, and photography. The four-week program earns three units of college-level credit and costs $750 (or $1,450 with housing on the nearby campus of Loyola Marymount University).

Marina del Rey Harbor comprises 780 acres, more than half of them underwater, making it one of the largest artificial harbors in the world. Since the 1960s the marina's private holdings have been developed with sixty-year leases on county-owned land. Although the leases bring $23 million in annual revenues, most of that is used to service bond debt incurred in 1993, when the County Board of Supervisors mortgaged it to raise operating funds. Some marina leaseholders are pressing for extensions on their leases, which begin expiring in 2020, to enable them to finance a more lucrative and contemporary development, like those that have revitalized Santa Monica's Third Street Promenade and Universal CityWalk. Although the marina includes slips for 10,000 boats, cars still dominate the maritime landscape, but the new plan would be linked with walkways to provide public access to the docks and encourage pedestrians to enjoy the activities of the pleasure port. Harbor cruises are offered from the boathouse at Fisherman's Village (13755 Fiji Way; 310-823-5411), where visitors will also find many shops and restaurants; free concerts (Sun. 2–5 p.m.) are offered there at the Lighthouse Plaza year round (weather permitting).

Loyola Marymount University

7900 Loyola Blvd.
Los Angeles 90045
310-338-2700

Loyola Marymount, the oldest college in Los Angeles, was founded in 1865 and is the only one of the prestigious Catholic universities administered by the Society of Jesus in the Southwest. There are twenty-eight stained-glass windows that depict other Jesuit universities in Loyola's Sacred Heart Chapel, which is used for organ recitals and other musical performances, including the Gala Christmas Concert, as well as for daily celebration of Catholic Mass. Students lead tours of the campus Monday through Friday at 10 a.m. and 1 p.m.; during the academic year a tour is also offered on Saturdays at 11 a.m.

Laband Gallery is a more recent addition to the campus, part of the 1984 Burns Fine Arts Center. Wedge-shaped skylights illuminate the 2,300-square-foot gallery (Wed.–Fri. 11 a.m.–4 p.m., Sat. noon–4 p.m. during academic year; closed June–late Aug.; free, donations welcomed). Exhibitions selected for Laband Gallery must feature traditional or nontraditional spirituality, explore social or political issues, or present ethnological or anthropological concerns. The biennial exhibition of the Los Angeles Printmaking Society and an annual exhibition of student work are also regular features of the calendar. Call 310-338-2880 for information.

Murphy Hall, which seats more than 200, is the site of musical events, many of them free. Theater and dance performances are held in the Strub Theater at 8 p.m., and most tickets cost $5 or less. For the calendar of events on the LMU campus, contact the Office of Fine Art Productions (310-338-7439) or the Central Ticket Agency (310-338-7588).

One of the largest private real-estate developments in the country, touted as transforming sleepy little Playa Vista into the center of the region's important and growing multimedia industry, is still on the drawing boards, but the projected start of construction has been delayed for more than a year. Los Angeles city officials pledged $70 million in tax credits to lure DreamWorks SKG to this site, which is being developed by Maguire Thomas Partners, in hopes of securing thousands of high-paying, high-tech jobs.

The **Lannan Foundation**, named for J. Patrick Lannan, whose career as director of International Telephone and Telegraph funded a $100-million endowment and the purchase of a large collection of contemporary art, enhanced Los Angeles's standing in the art world when it chose to open a public exhibition space in this city in July 1990. For five years it presented provocative exhibitions at a facility near the marina, which included an artist-designed garden, but the foundation changed course under the direction of the founder's son, who pledged more of its support to Native-American communities. In 1997 its collections were disbanded, with MOCA receiving the largest share locally of its treasures; the exhibition space was closed; and its garden, enclosed within high-backed benches inscribed with Wallace Stevens's poem "Anecdote of the Jar," was donated to a Midwestern college. Even the extraordinary literary programs, which the Lannan Foundation had vowed would continue to include an L.A. venue, were abruptly terminated in Spring 1998 and this program was relocated to the Santa Fe headquarters.

Sunset Magazine in 1997 named **Mothers' Beach** (at the intersection of Via Marina and Admiralty Way, Marina del Rey) one of the best on the West Coast. Beach Art, Inc., a Culver City organization that calls itself "the official open-air art museum of L.A. County beaches," chose Mothers' Beach for the first of thirty artist-designed lifeguard stations it has sponsored. This design by Rip Cronk features alphabet blocks in primary colors; artists Lita Albuquerque, William Crutchfield, Sergio Premoli, Sandra Rubin, and Terry Schoonhoven are preparing designs for five more lifeguard stations, which will debut in Venice in 1998.

Beginning in 1904, **Venice** was developed with a grand canal and a network of smaller canals drawn from the Ballona Wetlands, but the engineering plan was faulty—in sewage drainage and circulation—which led to a rapid decline of the area. Within twenty-five years the amusement park had been dismantled, and all but four canals (south of Venice Blvd. at Canal St.) were paved over. The three-mile stretch of Venice City Beach and Ocean Front Walk known as the **Venice Boardwalk** is not just a place, it is a symbol—of counterculture and California beach life—and so is one of Southern California's premier tourist attractions. It is also the beachfront community's playground, with joggers, skaters, cyclists, bodybuilders, and beachgoers jostling for space on the 1.7-mile asphalt walkway. The Recreation and Parks Department began a multimillion-dollar renovation in 1997, which includes a new surface for the walkway, an additional bike path to separate cyclists from skaters, an area designated for skate dancers, more bathrooms, and new benches. A children's playground and a basketball court will be added, but the funky, feisty spirit of the place will be unchanged. The 1,500-foot **Venice Pier** (at the end of Washington Blvd.) was closed in 1987, but after a $3-million renovation it again welcomed fishermen a decade later.

Arts Mecca (310-281-6188), which for five years has served low-income kids with free art workshops on everything from pops orchestra to architecture, petitioned the L.A. Recreation and Parks Department for a permit to convert the long-vacant 18,000-square-foot Venice Pavilion into a permanent community arts facility, but it failed to meet its initial fund-raising goals. Arts Mecca will continue to offer classes at the local library, churches, SPARC (see p. 248), and other community centers, but its administrative headquarters will be in the renovated former library at 610 California Street, along with other social service agencies.

The **Venice Art Walk**, a May weekend of activities, has for the past twenty years been a fund-raising benefit for the Venice Family Clinic (310-392-8630). It now raises a half-million dollars annually for that organization, drawing about 5,000 people (adults, Sun. only, $45) to the Westminster School (1010 Abbott Kinney Blvd.) where a silent auction of 250 original works, music and food, and a children's art center (storytelling, crafts, and building projects) whet the appetite for self-guided tours to the studios and homes of fifty contemporary artists. Patrons who pay $100 per ticket take architectural tours on Saturday and docent-led visits to the artists' studios. Call 310-392-9255 for recorded information.

Beyond Baroque

681 Venice Blvd.
Venice 90291
310-822-3006

This center for literary arts, located in the old Venice City Hall, features programs that encourage writers and artists to explore and experiment. Fiction, poetry, and nonfiction are featured in its reading and performance series, many of which offer free admission. A long-running poetry workshop on Wednesday nights is another free event, and a rite of passage for many Los Angeles poets; a variety of other writing workshops (ranging from $85 to $150 for an eight-to-ten-week course) are also offered. Beyond Baroque's bookstore (Tues.–Sat. 2–6 p.m.) features hard-to-find small-press titles and poetry. See Literary L.A., p. 226.

Social and Public Art Resource Center (SPARC)

685 Venice Blvd.
Venice 90291
310-822-9560

One of the first projects undertaken by this multiethnic arts center, founded in 1976 by three women artists, was *The Great Wall of Los Angeles,* a half-mile-long mural in the Tujunga Flood Control Channel. Since 1988 SPARC has created more than seventy murals that celebrate the ethnic heritage of communities throughout Los Angeles through its neighborhood pride program called Great Walls Unlimited, cosponsored by the Cultural Affairs Department. Its purpose is to examine what society chooses to memorialize through its public art and to develop alternative processes for its creation. In

Southern California Institute of Architecture (SCI-Arc)

5454 Beethoven St.
Los Angeles 90066
310-574-1123

This five-year degree program, taught by some of the most prestigious and progressive local architects, attracts some 400 students from around the world. A fall and spring lecture series on Wednesday evenings is open free to the public, and artwork created as student projects is displayed throughout the nondescript commercial building that was recently converted to classrooms and labs. A short summer program, Making and Meaning, is intended to help high school students and others evaluate whether architecture is a field they should pursue.

seeking to express the aspirations and concerns of individual communities, it has trained hundred of young residents, who apprentice with its established muralists and artists.

At its headquarters, a 1929 art deco building that once served as the Venice police station and city jail, SPARC maintains the Mural Resource and Education Center, which includes a slide library with 30,000 images of murals around the world. Slide sets and classroom curriculums on this form of popular art are available to educators. With the Mural Conservancy of Los Angeles, SPARC offers almost monthly thematic bus tours of mural art in Southern California; call 310-822-9560 or 310-470-8864 for information and reservations.

Frank Gehry's own
residence (1002 22nd
Street) is one of Santa
Monica's architectural
landmarks.

Horatio West Court
(140 Hollister Ave.) was
designed by Irving Gill
(1919–21).

Along three miles of beach in wealthy Santa Monica, business is booming, and tourists and locals flock to the renovated pier and the Third Street Promenade, an outdoor mall where topiary dinosaurs prance, which has become a national model for downtown revitalization. A double row of Washington palms lends the cliffs of Palisades Park a tropical flair, framing the views of the sunset above wide, sandy Santa Monica Beach. A camera obscura, built in 1889, is maintained by the city in the Senior Recreation Center in Palisades Park (1450 Ocean Ave; Mon.–Fri. 9 a.m.–4 p.m., Sat.–Sun. 11 a.m.–4 p.m.). Cirque du Soleil regularly encamps at the foot of Colorado Boulevard by the Santa Monica Pier. Children of all ages twirl to the infectious sound of the Wurlitzer organ on a vintage carousel; its animals, hand-carved in 1922, have been lovingly restored. The deck around the carousel was rebuilt in 1986, with bench seating overlooking the beach below, and a Children's Park at the south end of the site includes a concrete ship and a dragon that emits mist.

There's no charge to enter **Pacific Park**, but it's pay-as-you-go ($1 to $3 per ride), or you can purchase a day pass (price varies with the season, about $15). Call 310-260-8744 for hours of operation, which vary seasonally. There are rides suitable for small children, and the West Coast's biggest ferris wheel moves gently through its rotation and affords spectacular views of the coastline. By the weather station at the end of the pier are terraced seats for enjoying a snack and cool ocean breezes, as well as a photo chronology of the pier's evolution.

UCLA Ocean Discovery Center

UCLA's Ocean Discovery Center, tucked underneath the carousel pavilion, is a small facility that was built primarily to give its teacher-training program a hands-on site, but it welcomes the public on weekends throughout the year and several weekday afternoons during summer months. There are three large aquariums—with moon jellies in one and the animals that prefer the habitats of a rocky reef and the intertidal zone beneath the pier in the others—plus a shallow, open box filled with small sharks and rays, and two large touch tanks. Activity boxes fill shelves by the entry ramp, and knowledgeable and patient volunteers happily engage kids in exploring whatever interests them. Other activities are already laid out on tables within the center and on the patio outside, again with volunteers ready to facilitate such hands-on activities as making a sea otter puppet, fishing with magnetic poles, and comparing models of sharks and whales. We dropped in for a few minutes on our way to Pacific Park, and the kids were instantly engaged in activities both restful and educational, a pleasant respite from the frenzied carnival atmosphere above. School groups are offered age-appropriate classroom instruction in the fifty-seat multimedia auditorium, but advance reservations are required.

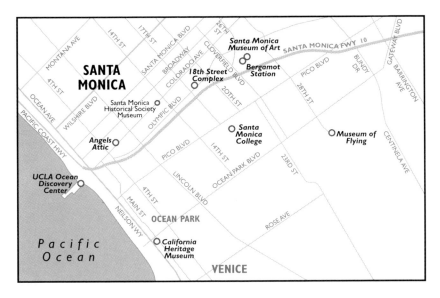

Santa Monica Playhouse, housed in a landmark building (1211 Fourth St.), has celebrated its thirty-fifth anniversary and is especially known for producing great theater for kids. It also offers drama classes. Call 310-394-9779.

The annual **Santa Monica Festival,** sponsored by the City of Santa Monica Arts Commission and the Cultural Affairs Division, kicks off with a daylong performing-arts celebration in Clover Park (2600 Ocean Park Blvd.) and continues for ten days with events, installations, and exhibitions at locations throughout the city; call 310-458-8350 for the schedule. Cultural Affairs also schedules a free dance and music series on the Santa Monica Pier, Thursdays at 7:30 p.m. Call 310-458-8900 for schedule.

There are thirty-one murals and fourteen public sculptures in Santa Monica—from the arch that marks the city's eastern border on Wilshire Boulevard to art on the beach. See Public Art Tour, page 245, for more information.

Community concern over the pollution in Santa Monica Bay is expressed by **Heal the Bay,** a volunteer organization that offers educational outreach programs. Heal the Bay has organized many activities to press for a "swimmable, fishable ocean" and issues a Monthly Beach Report Card, now posted on its Web site (www.healthebay.org/healthebay). Rock the Bay is a fund-raising concert on a weekend just after Labor Day at the Santa Monica Beach. Coastal Cleanup Day follows soon after: last year 8,500 volunteers were mobilized to pick up trash along the county's beaches. Adopt-a-Beach is a year-round program of groups that monitor a small stretch of the coastline. Memberships cost $25, a small price to pay to reclaim one of the natural treasures of Southern California; write to 2701 Ocean Park Blvd., #150, Santa Monica 90405, or call 310-581-4188 or 800-HEALBAY for more information.

Angels Attic

516 Colorado Ave.
Santa Monica 90401
310-394-8331
Thurs.–Sun. 12:30–4:30 p.m.
Entry: adults $6.50, seniors $4, children under 12 $3.50

Angels Attic, a museum of antique dollhouses, is a delightful surprise, a fascinating collection of architectural miniatures crammed into a lovingly restored Victorian house. The small scale of the buildings allows children to appreciate architectural features that are overwhelming on full-scale buildings. The furnishings and figures enhance the historic reality of the structures, evoking the lives led in such buildings in times past.

About fifty miniature models are on view at any time, and some exhibits are changed every few months. Among the Victorian houses is a replica of an Eastlake-style row house that is still standing in San Francisco. A nineteenth-century carved-wood Noah's Ark, which was called the "Sunday toy" because children were allowed to play with it on the Sabbath, when more secular games were deemed inappropriate, and a rare and elaborate Schoenhut Circus demonstrate changing ideas about children's toys. Dolls, a perennial favorite, include fragile antiques as well as many that were popular in the 1930s and 1940s.

The collection and displays are tended by an energetic pair of women who donate part of their profits to support the Brentwood Center for Educational Therapy, a school for autistic and developmentally impaired children. To raise money, they serve afternoon tea ($7.50, reservations required) to museum visitors on the front porch or rent the back garden for parties—although they caution that the crowded galleries require close supervision of kids to prevent damage. Groups can tour by appointment during regular museum hours, but one adult must accompany each group of five children.

Los Angeles Baroque Orchestra (310-578-7698), headquartered in Santa Monica, produces a series of orchestral, chamber, and vocal concerts on period instruments, often performing at the Water Garden (1620 26th St.); the all-volunteer Santa Monica Symphony (310-996-3260) presents free concerts at the Santa Monica Civic Auditorium.

California Heritage Museum

2612 Main St.
Santa Monica 90405
310-392-8537
Docent-led tours only:
Wed.–Sat. 11 a.m.–4 p.m., Sun. 10 a.m.–4 p.m.
Entry: adults $3, seniors/students $2,
children under 12 free

Santa Monica Library, Ocean Park Branch (2601 Main St.) was built in the Greek Revival style in 1917 with funds provided by the Carnegie grant.

The house was built in 1894 by renowned architect Sumner P. Hunt for Senator John Jones, the founder of Santa Monica, and moved to its present location in 1977. Its permanent displays of vintage residential interiors do not attempt to re-create the building as it existed when it was occupied by the Jones family but instead reflect the area's history in a more eclectic way. The kitchen and dining room are brightened by displays of colorfully glazed pottery, produced locally by Catalina, Pacific, and Bauer. The living room has a hand-carved brick fireplace and domestic furnishings from the 1890s. The entry parlor is now a museum store with historic postcards, books on Santa Monica, and California pottery.

The second-floor gallery features changing exhibitions, which have included "Aloha Spirit," showing Hawaii's influence on California lifestyle; a retrospective on the California Arts and Crafts movement; and collections of toy cars and boats. Lecture series are organized to coincide with major exhibitions, and musical events are scheduled as funding permits. The museum's growing collection of historic photographs is being made computer-accessible.

The Santa Monica Historical Society Museum (1539 Euclid St., Santa Monica; 310-394-2605) is open for a few hours on the second and fourth Sunday of each month so that visitors can browse through this attic of local history. The most interesting exhibits are the illustrated chronology of Santa Monica with vintage photographs of such businesses as Douglas Aircraft and maps of the early ranchos.

The Institute of Cultural Inquiry has a small gallery (1708 Berkeley St., Santa Monica 90404; 310-828-5622) where groups of artists explore how visual imagery reflects and shapes cultural concerns. Many of its initial events involved AIDS: "Chronicles," compilations of news items from the front pages of the daily New York Times and Los Angeles Times which include references to AIDS, are displayed annually on December 1. "The Bottle Project" began as a memorial to a victim of AIDS, but was later expanded to include vessels that those afflicted have created as personal legacies. Call to confirm gallery hours, which are irregular, or visit their Web site (www.culturalinquiry.org).

Santa Monica College

1900 Pico Blvd.
Santa Monica 90405
310-450-5150

Two planetarium shows are offered on Friday nights at the new John Drescher Digistar Planetarium, on the second floor of the Technology Building. A general look at the night sky at 7 p.m. is followed by a more specialized program—on supernovas or the Comet Hale-Bopp, for instance—at 8 p.m. ($4 for one show, $7 for two shows). The programs are offered regularly during the extended academic year (Sept.–July), but call 310-452-9396 to check the current schedule or visit the Web site (www.smc.edu).

The college's art gallery shows contemporary work by Southern California artists (call 310-452-9231 for schedule). A gallery in the library shows work by contemporary photographers (310-450-5150).

KCRW (89.9 FM), which broadcasts from the Santa Monica College campus, provides National Public Radio to much of Southern California. Its music programming, once known for its eclectic, even quirky, style, has had a more narrow range in recent years. Its excellent informational programming on local issues has been expanded: Which Way L.A.?, a community forum hosted by Warren Olney, began as the station's effort to address issues raised by the Los Angeles riots but has become a valued fixture of its programming; the well-researched series, United States of Los Angeles, is worth checking out whenever it is offered. The Internet, which allows this nonprofit station to offer its broadcasts to the entire world, is KCRW's new frontier. Listeners can check out favorite programs on their own schedules at www.kcrw.org.

Bergamot Station

2525 Michigan Ave.
Santa Monica 90404

Bergamot, a wildflower in the mint family, gave its name to a trolley car station that was developed with support from the city of Santa Monica into a destination arts complex. The industrial buildings on the 5.5-acre site were unified by architect Fred Fisher with railings, stair treads, and columns painted a vibrant yellow. Since it opened in September 1994 with a handful of galleries and architectural offices, it has attracted thousands of visitors on weekends and lured dealers from areas hard hit by the urban turmoil of 1992. For more information on this complex, see Art Galleries, pages 43–44.

Santa Monica Museum of Art

Bergamot Station
2525 Michigan Ave., Building G1
Santa Monica 90404
310-586-6488
Wed.–Sun. 11 a.m.–6 p.m., Fri. til 10 p.m.
Entry: suggested $3; seniors, students, artists $2

The Santa Monica Museum of Art in 1988 began to present contemporary art exhibitions and performances in a small space at Edgemar, a Frank Gehry–designed commercial development on Main Street, where it enjoyed five rent-free years granted it by developer Abby Sher, who is also a member of the museum's board. When the time came to exercise its option to purchase the space, at the agreed price of half of its then-market value, the Westside art scene had coalesced at a different location. In April 1997 the museum left Edgemar, but its plans to resume

its programming in a former ice-packing plant at Bergamot Station were delayed for a year by litigation between the partners of that complex. In May 1998 the new museum space, designed by Narduli/Grinstein, was inaugurated with a 10,000-square-foot gallery, a bookstore, and dedicated space for its education programs.

The Santa Monica Museum of Art functions as a *Kunsthalle*, or artist's space, rather than anything as formal as a "museum of art" (despite its name), eschewing the formation of a permanent collection to "forge a participatory, interpretive link between artists, their work, and the viewer." More than 1,000 artists—most of them emerging or midcareer professionals from Southern California—have been showcased at the museum in curated shows in the Main Gallery or Focus Gallery series or through original works commissioned by the museum for its Artist Projects series. Friday Evening Salons—thought-provoking discussions, films, and performances that constitute a "field guide to the world" and offer the community a "cultural living room" to inaugurate the weekend—and Kids' Art Station—an artist-led, hands-on introduction to art making, art appreciation, and art history—will resume at the new site.

18th Street Arts Complex

1639 18th St.
Santa Monica 90404
310-453-3711

This cultural complex, which "promotes the development of innovative art forms and critical dialogue among artists concerned with social issues and the communities they serve," may, by its own design, always be a work-in-progress. It is perhaps best known for Highways Performance Space, which has become a financially separate institution but remains on site; financial difficulties forced the closure of its exhibition space, New Gallery, which has been renovated as studio space by artist Lita Albuquerque. Other artists occupy its subsidized studio, living, rehearsal, and exhibition spaces, and arts-related enterprises occupy parts of the complex.

Highways Performance Space (1651 18th St.) features cutting-edge theatrical performances, and its gallery space offers about a dozen changing exhibitions each year exploring the boundaries between performing and visual art forms. To develop the skills of artists, Highways offers workshops, some free, on dance, performance, and writing. Its constituency, "culturally marginalized communities—communities of color, women, the physically challenged, lesbians and gays, abuse victims, and people with HIV," will find some of their specific concerns addressed in such annual events as the two-month Ecce Lesbo/Ecce Homo and Women's Festivals; Asian-American artists are showcased in the series Treasure in the House. Call Tickets LA (*213-660-8587) for information and reservations.

Museum of Flying

Santa Monica Airport
2772 Donald Douglas Loop N.
Santa Monica 90405
310-392-8822
Wed.–Sun. 10 a.m.–5 p.m.
Entry: adults $7, seniors/students $5, children 3–17 $3

The Museum of Flying tries to keep its aircraft in flying condition, as if they could be rolled out on an adjacent runway of the Santa Monica Airport and taken for a spin. That would be a dream come true for the enthusiastic docents, many of whom flew aircraft like those on display during World War II, but meanwhile they're content to give animated tours of the museum. If your participation in aviation has been solely as a passenger, taking the tour with a docent will greatly enhance your enjoyment of the collection.

The museum is located on the site where Douglas Aircraft Company (founded in 1922) moved in 1928: an airstrip then called Clover Field, where many pioneering flights embarked. The company's role in making Southern California a cradle of the aviation industry is evoked by artifacts from its collection, including the round table with an inset globe that was designed for its original boardroom, but the still-airworthy craft designed by Douglas are its greatest legacy. A DC-3, one of the 13,000 built by Douglas after the first one flew in 1935, is parked just outside. About thirty vintage planes are displayed inside the lofty, open museum, which occupies one wing of the very modern Supermarine building. The configuration of the aircraft on display suggests planes circling a racing pylon, and the museum's central pillar is appropriately painted with large red and white blocks. The Douglas-built *New Orleans*, one of four planes that in 1924 completed a seventy-one-day round-the-world rally, is the museum's oldest artifact from aviation's short history.

Displays of World War II–era planes feature the trio that brought victory to the Allies—the P-51 Mustang (which was the fastest prop plane of that era), the British Spitfire, and a Hawker Hurricane —as well as a plane used by the Blue Angels to showcase naval flying skills, and a DC-3 like General Eisenhower's command plane. Other Douglas-built planes in the collection in- clude a 1951 Navy Ad-6 Skyraider and a Douglas A-4 Skyhawk, designed for combat. More than one hundred wood and metal production models show both concept airplanes and the evolution of Douglas's passenger aircraft.

Video terminals in the galleries show short films on various planes and on aviation history and its pioneers.

A theater regularly screens longer films re- lated to aviation; recent topics included the Blue Angels and the Stealth bomber. For an additional $2, visitors can take a four-minute ride in a flight simulator.

The interactive children's wing— Airventure—is a more recent addition, an open space with aircraft suspended overhead that allows kids to sit at the controls of a helicopter and climb into an old-fashioned cockpit. The museum offers free educational workshops for families (every other Sun. noon–2 p.m.) which explain fundamental concepts like the three axes of rotation and the four forces of flight and how they are used in aircraft design. On Tuesday through Thursday evenings DC-3 Restaurant uses this space to offer free child care for parents who have reservations to dine upstairs. Our playgroup feted the end of a neighbor's pregnancy this way: the kids enjoyed a supervised spaghetti supper and came home with paper airplanes and aviation- themed coloring books, and the ladies had a good dinner and uninterrupted conversa- tion—within calling distance if we were needed. I recommend it.

The live-action scenery of the Santa Monica Airport can be enjoyed from the observation area on the museum's upper level; when the weather cooperates, the view extends to the busy flight path into LAX as well as the distant silhouette of the Palos Verdes Peninsula and Catalina. There are also two free and accessible viewing areas: at the Airport Administration Building (3223 Donald Douglas Loop S.); and in Clover Park (25th St. and Ocean Park Blvd.), where there's a viewing area with a telescope focused on the airport runway. With advance reservations (310-397-3755), groups may visit the air traffic control tower, but only if they can climb the nine flights of stairs to the "cab" itself.

Rustic Canyon Recreation Area

601 Latimer Rd.
Santa Monica 90402
310-454-5734

National and state parks are generally open from 8 a.m. to sunset every day.

This lovely facility in a tree-shaded canyon offers swimming, tennis, and yoga, as well as classes in dance, crafts, guitar, and piano. The line forms early to get one of the coveted spots in its summer camp program, and it organizes a week of fun activities for kids during other school breaks. Call to request the schedule for this center, operated by the L. A. Department of Recreation and Parks.

Temescal Gateway Park

Sunset Blvd. at Temescal Canyon Rd.
Pacific Palisades
310-459-5931

From Sunset Boulevard south to the Pacific Coast Highway, Temescal Canyon Road is one of the prettiest streets in Pacific Palisades. A broad area on both sides of the roadway is landscaped with native plants, and picnic tables are available. North of Sunset the park is less well manicured, but its trails give hikers access to Topanga State Park and Will Rogers State Historic Park. The Temescal Canyon Association leads hikes on the park's trails.

Nursery Nature Walks (310-364-3591) organizes forty family walks per month and other educational programs at many area parks, including Temescal and Santa Ynez Canyons, Will Rogers, and Sullivan Canyon in Pacific Palisades, and Malibu Lagoon and Solstice Canyon, a bit farther up the coast.

Will Rogers State Historic Park

14253 Sunset Blvd.
Pacific Palisades 90290
Park: 8 a.m.–sunset
Tours of house: 10 a.m.–5 p.m.
310-454-8212

The state has owned Will Rogers's 186-acre ranch since 1944, nine years after the popular actor and newspaper columnist was killed in a plane crash in Alaska. The ranch may be visited on a self-guided tour, and guided tours of the house are offered on the half-hour from 10:30 a.m. to 4:30 p.m. A short film on Rogers's life and accomplishments is shown regularly in the visitors center. Rogers first became famous for his roping skills, and his stables, riding arena, and polo fields are still used. The Loop Trail to Inspiration Point, well named for its panoramic sunset views, intersects the Backbone Trail, which will, on completion, connect Pacific Palisades with Point Mugu.

Some of the finest and best-preserved Case Study Houses are private residences clustered along Chautauqua Boulevard near the intersection with Pacific Coast Highway, including the house that Charles and Ray Eames designed for themselves in 1947 at 203 Chautauqua Boulevard. The aim of the Case Study House Program (1945–60), sponsored by *Arts & Architecture* magazine, was to develop prototypes for affordable housing using modern building techniques and materials. But these are private residences, so please respect posted No Trespassing signs.

After the J. Paul Getty Museum vacated its Malibu building to move to the Getty Center in Brentwood, the re-creation of an ancient Roman country villa and peristyle gardens was closed for renovation. When the Getty Villa (as it is now known to differentiate it from the new Getty Center) reopens, anticipated in 2001, only the Greek and Roman antiquities will be installed in the building, whose design J. Paul Getty chose for its compatibility with this type of art. The facility (17985 Pacific Coast Hwy., Malibu) will also house a center for comparative archaeology and cultures, dedicated to exploring the information about the ancient world that is embedded in artifacts from those times. The use of new technologies to interpret ancient art will also be the subject of "Beyond Beauty: Antiquities as Evidence," one of the inaugural exhibitions at the Getty Center. The challenge of creating this new research and exhibition facility at the Getty Villa has been entrusted to long-time curator Marion True.

Getty, who spent part of his youth in Los Angeles but lived mainly in Europe from the 1930s, purchased the Malibu ranch for his retirement. He never lived there, but in 1953 part of the house was opened as a museum to display his art collections. By 1971 he had commissioned a separate museum building, whose plan is based on that of the Villa dei Papiri, which was buried (along with Pompeii and Herculaneum) by the eruption of Vesuvius in A.D. 79. The Villa dei Papiri was known only from notes and plans drawn in the eighteenth century until it was accidentally rediscovered and explored (before it was deemed unsafe and sealed up again sixty feet underground). A walled garden, decorated with illusionistic wall paintings in the Pompeian style, encloses manicured shrubbery and trees that could have grown two thousand years ago in southern Italy.

Adamson House and Malibu Lagoon Museum

23200 Pacific Coast Hwy.
Malibu 90265
310-456-8432
By guided tour only: Wed.–Sat. 11 a.m.–3 p.m. (last tour 2 p.m.)
Entry: adults $2, children over 6 $1

It is no accident that the Adamson House is situated on what may be the finest Malibu beach property: the Moorish-Spanish colonial-style house was built in 1928 for Rhoda Rindge Adamson, the daughter of the last owner of the Spanish land grant for Rancho Malibu, and her husband. The couple had the first pick of the territory, and they chose well. Bounded by Malibu Creek (where steelhead trout still spawn) and its lagoon (where 200 species of birds have been observed among the migrating flocks), and Surfrider State Beach, which offers some of the best surfing in Southern California, the site is extraordinary, and the house, designed by Stiles Clements, is gracious and extravagant. It is lavishly decorated with Malibu tile, which was manufactured by the Rindge family near the site from 1926 to 1932, when a fire and financial difficulties forced them to halt production. The pool and bathhouse also feature colorful Malibu tile. The grounds are beautifully landscaped with pines shaped by the wind and flowering trees and shrubs that attract hummingbirds. Picnic tables, shaded by gnarled old trees, offer panoramic ocean views and a perspective on the now-shuttered Malibu Pier.

Docents give a spirited tour of the house during limited hours, but the larger history of the area is presented in displays in the adjacent Malibu Lagoon Museum (Wed.–Sat. 11 a.m.–3 p.m.; free); the museum also offers nature tours of the lagoon (call 310-457-8142 for information). The presence of the Chumash Indians is recalled by a mural and artifacts found in the area. The 17,000-acre parcel was largely undeveloped by the first four owners of the Spanish deed, and in 1892 it was sold to Rindge for $10 an acre. From 1905, when she was widowed, May Knight Rindge fought in the courts to keep her ranch intact, without the incursion of a public road. In 1923 the U.S. Supreme Court forced her to grant an easement to the State of California, and the construction of Pacific Coast Highway (CA 1) was begun.

Rindge also undertook the construction of a castle containing some fifty rooms on the steep cliff overlooking Adamson House. It too was lavishly embellished with tile from the Malibu Potteries, but the project proved too grandiose when her fortune suffered in the 1929 crash. By 1932 construction had been abandoned; ten years later the massive structure was sold for $50,000 to the Catholic Church, which has since operated it as a retreat. The mansion and its tilework were damaged by a fire on September 5, 1970, and it has been rebuilt to serve its present purposes.

Other displays in the museum depict the history of Malibu surfing and the genesis of the Malibu Colony, on land that Rindge leased to developers in 1926 to create hideaway retreats for Hollywood stars. Comparative resale values for Malibu Colony houses in the 1920s and 1980s are already outdated but nonetheless staggering. The colony is visible across Malibu Lagoon—the lavish houses crowded on the beautiful white beach are a startling contrast to the flocks of seabirds in the foreground.

While its weekend hours aren't too convenient, this site offers a combination

of scenery, local crafts, and history that definitely merits a visit, and always wows out-of-town guests. School groups and groups of more than twelve people can be accommodated at other times with advance reservations; bus tours on Tuesdays only.

Malibu Lagoon State Beach

Pacific Coast Highway at Cross Creek Rd.
Daily 8 a.m.–sunset
California State Parks: 818-880-0350

Adventures on Horseback (818-706-0888) rents horses for every level of expertise ($25 an hour) and leads trail rides through the Santa Monica Mountains, including two-hour sunset rides and full-moon jaunts.

Where it spills into the Pacific Ocean, Malibu Creek forms a brackish lagoon that supports some 200 species of migratory birds, commuting along the Pacific Flyway, and a large colony of fish. The thirty-five sandy acres of adjacent Surfrider State Beach, popularized in surfing movies of the 1950s and 1960s, still draw surfers. The first Malibu Pier was built to unload supplies for the Rindge ranch (see Adamson House). In 1980 the state acquired the pier, but it has continued to deteriorate since; recently the city of Malibu declined to refurbish the pier, anticipating that it may not may not withstand the storms of the next El Niño winter.

The Malibu Bluffs, as part of the Malibu Lagoon State Beach, are isolated from the rest of the site. Located west of Malibu Colony, between Pacific Coast Highway and Malibu Road near the intersection of Malibu Canyon Road, the Bluffs comprise ninety acres devoted to playing fields for baseball and soccer. Public stairways at 24500, 24400, and 24300 Malibu Road provide beach access, but be careful not to trespass on adjacent private property.

Will Geer Theatricum Botanicum

1419 N. Topanga Canyon Blvd.
Topanga 90290
Business office: 310-455-2322
Box office: 310-455-3723
Kid's Koncert series: 310-455-1140

In 1953 actor Will Geer and some colleagues, who were all blacklisted in Hollywood, found refuge on a few acres in bucolic Topanga Canyon. They created an outdoor theater that flourished for a few summers before Geer moved on. He returned in 1973 and spent the last five years of his life realizing his dream of a theater in the woods. His daughter, Ellen Geer, is now the artistic director of an active program offering three plays, including at least one by Shakespeare, in repertory through the summer months, Friday night cabaret concerts ($10), and Sunday morning concerts for kids ($6). The nonprofit group offers low-priced tickets (general admission $15, seniors/students/Equity members $8.50, children 6–12 $4), and children under five are admitted free. During the summer of 1997 the amphitheater was renovated to improve seating and acoustics, but it still retains its rustic atmosphere.

Pepperdine University

24255 Pacific Coast Hwy.
Malibu 90263
310-456-4000
Center for the Arts: 310-317-EVNT, 310-456-4594
Box office: 310-456-4522
Museum: 310-456-4851, 310-456-4055

On the western edge of L.A. County, on a hillside with a panoramic view of the Pacific Coast—including a startling perspective on the high-rise buildings in Santa Monica—in an area known for natural disasters and natural beauty, Pepperdine University offers the beauty of the performing arts at

the **Smothers Theater** and a fine exhibition program at the **Frederick R. Weisman Museum of Art.**

As with other university-based performing arts programs, ticket prices at Smothers Theater represent good value, especially for series subscribers, and there are free events ranging from campus musical groups and seats for less than $10 to plays mounted by the local theater troupe. Many Saturdays are devoted to family programming, with shows at 11 a.m. and 1 p.m., and Sunday afternoons alternate between the jazz series and classical music recitals.

Part of the collection formed by Frederick R. Weisman was put on exhibit at Pepperdine in September 1992 and can be seen year-round on the second floor of the museum. Each fall a broader survey of this international collection of modern and contemporary art is installed to inaugurate the year's exhibition program. Weisman personally chose Pepperdine as recipient of his art collection, although the donation has not yet been finalized, to commemorate the years he lived in this community. Private tours of the Weisman Art Foundation, at the collector's Westside home, are available by appointment only; call 310-277-5321 for information and reservations.

Point Mugu State Park

9000 W. Pacific Coast Hwy. at Sycamore Cove
Malibu 90265
California State Parks: 818-880-0350
Daily 8 a.m.–sunset

The westernmost park in the Santa
Monica Mountains National Recreation
Area comprises 13,360 acres, with five
miles of shoreline in Ventura County.
The park's name derives from a Chumash
word for beach, *muwu*, and the beach is
the focus of most visitors' activities.
There are two campgrounds and a large
picnic and barbecue area near the shore.
In the winter this park is a perfect place
for whale watching or viewing flocks of
monarch butterflies. Some 6,000 acres of
parkland in the interior have been set
aside as a wilderness area, accessible only
by foot or on horseback.

The La Jolla Trail at Point Mugu provides the only coastal access along the
Backbone Trail, and is an excellent introduction to the diverse ecologies and topography of the largest tract of land in
the Santa Monica Mountains.

Leo Carrillo State Beach

35000 Pacific Coast Hwy.
Malibu 90265
Daily 8 a.m.–sunset
California State Parks: 818-880-0350

Leo Carrillo was an actor who played the
Cisco Kid's sidekick, Pancho, in the famous
television series; the great-grandson of a
governor of California during the last years
of Mexican rule; and a commissioner for
the state parks and beaches for fourteen
years. This spectacularly beautiful 2,000-
acre beachfront park is named to honor
him for the latter role. Caves and tunnels
have been sculpted in the cliffs along 6,600
feet of the Pacific Ocean; tidepools are clustered at the Arroyo Sequit, a rocky intertidal
area. Diving, surfing, ocean fishing, hiking,
and camping (tent sites and parking for
RVs are available) are popular activities.

Point Dume State Beach

Westward Beach Rd. and Pacific Coast Hwy.
Malibu 90265
California State Parks: 818-880-0350
Daily 8 a.m.–sunset

The peninsula of Point Dume juts into the
Pacific, forming the northwestern end of
the Santa Monica Bay. The shore beneath
the 200-foot-high lava bluffs is rocky, but a
thirty-four-acre sandy beach to the west of
the headlands may be reached from Westward Beach Road.

Charmlee Natural Area

2577 South Encinal Canyon Rd.
Malibu 90265
310-457-7247
Daily 8 a.m.–sunset

This little-known park stretches between
Encinal Canyon (where its main entrance is
located) and Decker Roads. Trails through
with 524 acres of meadowland are brightened
by wildflowers from February through June
and lead to coastal vistas. Picnicking and kite
flying are popular activities. A small nature
center (open on Sunday afternoons), has a
large mural of local flora and fauna, examples
of which can also be seen in the exhibits.

Zuma Beach County Park

30050 Pacific Coast Hwy.
(west of Kanan Dume Rd.)
Malibu 90265
Daily 8 a.m.–sunset

The first sight of Zuma Beach, heading north
on Pacific Coast Highway, is breathtaking.
Rolling surf hits the 105 acres of white sand,
which are often crowded with surfers and
families enjoying the beach and playground
in this well-equipped county park. Volleyball is
a popular sport, reinforcing the quintessential
Southern California look of the site. In the
spring and summer months grunion spawn
on the beach for several nights following the
full moon. Surf fishing, scuba diving, and surfing (at a designated area near lifeguard stand
#11) attract many enthusiasts.

Zuma Canyon

Busch Dr. and Pacific Coast Hwy.
Malibu 90265
National Park Service: 818-597-9192, ext. 201
Daily 8 a.m.–sunset

Where the residential development gives way
to a dirt road, the equestrians and dog walkers
enjoy the promenade that overlooks Point
Dume and leads into Rancho Topanga and its
miles of open space. In 1989 the Santa Monica
Mountains Conservancy transferred 768 acres
in the southernmost section of Zuma Canyon
to the care of the National Park Service, which
already administered parts of Zuma and
Trancas Canyons.

Solstice Canyon

Corral Canyon Rd. at Pacific Coast Hwy.
Malibu 90265
Mountains Conservancy Foundation: 310-589-2400

Enter the canyon through the heavy white
gate a few feet up Corral Canyon Road from
Pacific Coast Highway. This huge parcel of
land is tranquil and fragrant, with a stream
spilling across the access road, which lures
walkers to keep on exploring.

Channel Islands National Park

1901 Spinnaker Dr.
Ventura 93001
805-644-8157

In 1980 five of the eight islands off the Southern California coast were designated as a new national park, one of about 350 sites throughout the United States which represent the nation's natural and cultural history. Anacapa, Santa Cruz, Santa Rosa, San Miguel, and Santa Barbara Islands are preserved as parklands, and an area extending six nautical miles around each island in the park was also set aside as the Channel Islands National Marine Sanctuary, creating a 125,000-acre underwater zone to protect the habitat of indigenous marine life.

Visitors gain access to the parklands through the park headquarters for the Channel Islands, which is located on Ventura Harbor (1901 Spinnaker Dr., Ventura 93001); there is a pleasant small museum at that address, and next door is Island Packers, the authorized concessionaire for the Channel Islands, which operates excursion boats. Island Packers offers a variety of trips, including a four-hour cruise with no landings (adults $19, children $12) and a seven- to eight-hour trip to Anacapa Island with a landing for nature walks or snorkeling (adults $34, children $18). Drop by the Island Packers office adjacent to park headquarters; write to them at 1867 Spinnaker Drive, Ventura 93001; or call 805-642-1393.

Displays in the museum at park headquarters include topographical maps of the five islands—which range in size from Santa Cruz Island, the largest at 62,000 acres, to Santa Barbara Island, the smallest at 640 acres—plus exhibits on the marine and bird life and the ecology of the islands. A tidepool is inhabited by small crabs, starfish, abalone, burrowing anemone, mussels, and sea urchins. Cormorants, pelicans, and gulls float above eerie displays of the caliche forest of San Miguel. The chemical reaction between plants and the calcium carbonate in the sand and shells has created a naturally occurring but unique phenomenon: the "ghost forests," called caliche. The caliche retains the form of the plant it covered, making this section of San Miguel look like a lunar landscape. Visitors are invited to pick up a piece of caliche, which is heavy and has a gritty surface, and compare it with a bird skeleton, which is hollow and very light.

An observation tower surmounts the museum building, and photographic displays along the steps and landings to the summit simulate the ocean environment—from the darkest, coldest, least-inhabited depths to sun-filled kelp forests near the surface, which teem with marine life. There are telescopes on the observation deck to enhance the panoramic view of the harbor and the islands in the distance. A twenty-five-minute narrated film on the islands is shown hourly, and rangers conduct special programs on Saturday and Sunday at 2 p.m. Picnic tables along the harbor and sand dunes adjacent to the parking lot are other special features of this site. Even without taking a boat excursion to the Channel Islands, visitors can learn a lot about the islands and have a very pleasant day at the park headquarters in Ventura Harbor.

VIRTUAL L.A.

Margaret Trumbull Nash

If you've got a computer with a connection to the Internet and a World Wide Web browser, you can tour Los Angeles without ever getting into a car. You can obtain information about community events and projects, find historical data about Los Angeles, view museum collections, or locate books or articles at the library. No more traffic to worry about. You can travel as far as you can click your mouse.

First off, see what's shaking. The United States Geological Survey's Pasadena Field Office—**www.socal. wr.usgs.gov**—links you to maps of recent earthquake activity as well as to the Southern California Earthquake Center and California Institute of Technology's Seismological Laboratory for the latest data on seismic activity in Southern California.

A good place to start is **www.californiasedge.com,** the site developed by the Convention and Visitors Bureau (see also, p. 23). This virtual guidebook was designed to promote California cultural diversity by offering a series of tours representing the Asian, African, Latino, Gay, and Jewish communities as well as topics such as Jazz and Blues, Art to Architecture, Performance and history in San Francisco, Los Angeles and San Diego. The city tours are not grouped strictly by category, but offer an amalgam of opportunities from museums to restaurants to

clubs. Click on the Tour de Force section, then click on 'Los Angeles' to get six different tours of the city, ranging from downtown Los Angeles to the Los Angeles Gallery scene. The web designers have used banner and frame technology to keep the pages visually stimulating while at the same time keeping the main text frame easy to read. The footer on every page allows you to change the tour at any time by clicking on a drop-down list of tour options. The site was created by a coalition of California tourism and arts groups, prominent among which is the Los Angeles County Arts Commission.

Another good place to continue your tour is "Los Angeles: Past, Present, and Future"—**www.usc.edu/ Library/Ref/LA**—which has enough information on L.A. history and culture to keep you busy for hours. Maintained by the University of Southern California's Doheny Reference Center, the site has a straightforward layout, without a lot of fancy graphics, but is easy to navigate. The home page allows you to search for related topics, then lists where those topics can be found within the site. The "Cultural L.A." section takes you to "Landmarks of Ethnic Communities," which includes a page on Japanese landmarks with links to information about the World War II–era detention camps and a copy of President Roosevelt's 1942 Relocation Order. (Los Angeles's ethnic communities are generally well represented on the Web. A place to start browsing is **www.at-la.com/@la-min.htm**.) The "Tour of the Great Wall of Los Angeles Mural" takes you to SPARC's mural page. The section on public art lets you explore the city neigh-

borhood by neighborhood, breaking downtown into many sections. Each area provides background information on the site, biographical notes about artists, and graphic images of the artworks. The "Garment District" page links to an exhibition called "Hidden Labor: Uncovering L.A.'s Garment Industry," a project of the Common Threads Artist Group, which documents the history of the garment industry in Los Angeles in photographs and text. The "Los Angeles Literature" section includes bibliographies on the city.

Return to the home page, and head in the direction of "Documenting L.A." for a wealth of resources for researchers of Los Angeles history. The USC Regional History Center displays sample photographs from the Hearst, California Historical Society, and Whittington collections. "Photographic Images On-Line" points to other resources, such as the California Museum of Photography's historical photographs of Los Angeles. Return to the home page again, and go to the "Historic L.A." area to learn more about "Murders, Scandals, and Other Crimes in L.A. History." The story of William Mulholland and the St. Francis Dam scandal is documented in detail. The site's fourth area, "Other L.A. Web Sites," has a link to the Downtown Los Angeles Walking Tour site, created by the USC Geography Department. There's a clickable map that takes you to a specific location, then gives you a list of sites within that area. There's also a link to the Metropolitan Transportation Authority home page — **www.mta.net**—for the latest Hollywood subway tunnel progress report.

(The area devoted to the Hollywood extension of the Metro Red Line also includes "Station Profiles" describing the art and architecture at each of the stations.) The link to the Parkinson Archives contains a collection of drawings of Los Angeles landmarks.

Most Los Angeles museums and galleries have a Web presence; indeed, they are too numerous to list here. The art magazine *ArtScene's* Internet edition —**artscenecal.com**—is a good place to go for an extensive listing of art galleries and museums, with area maps, reviews, and articles. Clicking on an image in the virtual gallery takes you to a review of a current exhibition in which the work appears. Each review contains a link to a page describing the exhibition venue. The gallery also contains links to pages about individual artists featured in current solo exhibitions, where you will find biographical information and images of works.

While all museum sites are good resources for information about museum hours, exhibition offerings, and special events, a few sites are being developed specifically with the Internet in mind. The Natural History Museum of Los Angeles County— **www. lam.mus.ca.us**—offers plenty of scientific information, from an "Exotic Entomology" section displaying nineteenth-century scientific illustrations to a slide show on DNA. Go to the On-Line Exhibits page for a list of viewable collections. The QuickTime Virtual Reality Tours of the George C. Page Museum and the Mammal Hall of the Natural History Museum are particularly interesting, although the files take a while to download if you don't have a high-speed connection. Once you have downloaded the file, you can take a three-dimensional tour of the exhibits by clicking the mouse. This site also has links to the other institutions administered by the Natural History Museum: the George C. Page Museum of La Brea Discoveries, the Petersen Automotive Museum, and the William S. Hart Museum.

The USC Interactive Art Museum at the Fisher Gallery—digimuse. usc. edu/museum.html—has been designed as an interactive art museum. A remote telerobotic device, on loan from the Jet Propulsion Laboratory, allows you to view Ernst Wench's sculpture *Drinking Maiden* from various angles by clicking on the robot's arm. The "Romance with Nature" exhibition page features works by twelve nineteenth-century American landscape artists, accompanied by text. There are also audio selections describing the exhibit.

The Museum of Contemporary Art's site—www.moca-la.org/mocamain.htm—is easy to navigate. The permanent collection section includes general text about the col- lections and thumbnail graphic images of artworks, which you can save to your computer. LACMAWeb, the Los Angeles County Museum of Art's site—at www.lacma.org—allows you to view items from the permanent collection and temporary exhibitions. The page for the 1995 exhibition "P.L.A.N.: Photography Los Angeles Now" has a graphic compass that points you to different areas of the exhibition and includes a gallery-by-gallery tour. There are also links to sites about artists and to other museums where their works are displayed. At the Huntington Gallery—www.huntington. org—you can stroll the gardens or stop by the art collections. The Norton

Simon Museum of Art—www.citycent.com/CCC/Pasadena/nsmuseum. htm—features simple-to-navigate text and graphics documenting the permanent collections. The UCLA/Armand Hammer Museum's site—www.arts. ucla.edu/hammer/main. html—offers primarily text-based descriptions of exhibitions.

The Getty site—www.getty. edu/getty.htm —is a gateway to the Getty's museum, five institutes, and grant program. Graphic images representing the different Getty institutions spread across the screen. The Getty Information Institute, an organization dedicated to bringing cultural organizations together to collaborate on projects, sponsors Los Angeles Culture Net, home.lacn.org/lacn. The "Community Properties" page allows you to search for online cultural resources. The "Culture Lab" section has a link to the "Faces of L.A." project, another collaborative effort to develop digital access to cultural resources. Links to the participating organizations are also available. The "Neighborhood Views" section records conversations with graffiti artists. The "Tour Bus" takes you to a clickable map of Los Angeles. If you have Shockwave, you can drive the bus over the area you want to visit. Otherwise, you can click on the link for a graphic picture and Web address of the selection.

Several online arts magazines focus solely on Los Angeles. At the *Los Angeles Contemporary Arts Magazine*—www.artcommotion.com—you will find an eclectic mixture of art, literature, interviews, and reviews. One of the best features of this site is the ability to listen to a performance

artist while reading the artist's text. Another online arts magazine is *Oversight: The Magazine of Community and Alternative Arts in Los Angeles*—www.oversight. com. In the "Hot Platters" area, special old records are auctioned, annual "Artists Discovery Tours" allow you to visit local artists' studios, and a musical history tour features Los Angeles locations made famous in songs. There's also a link to the home page of the Arroyo Arts Collective.

For a look at Los Angeles architecture, go to www.cf.ac.uk/uwcc/archi/jonesmd/la. Matt Jones combined his photographs of Los Angeles with text from Reyner Banham's 1971 *Los Angeles: The Architecture of Four Ecologies* to create an architectural photo digest of Los Angeles, which travels through downtown, "surfurbia," foothills, and autopia. The UCLA Department of Architecture and Urban Design's Virtual L.A. project—www.gsaup. ucla.edu/proj/vla.htm—is a site to watch as it develops. The project is designed to simulate urban environments in the Los Angeles basin, combining three-dimensional models with aerial photographs and street-level video.

It would be impossible to see Los Angeles murals in one day by car, but the L.A. Murals Home Page—latino.sscnet.ucla. edu/murals/index1.html —gives you a head start. The site is sponsored by CLNet at UCLA, the Mural Resource Center of the Social and Public Art Resource Center (SPARC) in Venice, the Los Angeles Mural Conservancy, and Social Sciences Computing at UCLA. From there you can browse over to SPARC's tour of Chicano

murals in L.A., a history of Chicano murals, and Robin J. Dunitz's *Street Gallery: Guide to 1,000 Los Angeles Murals*. The Mural Conservancy of Los Angeles, an organization helping to preserve Los Angeles murals, can be located at artscenecal. com/MCLA. html.

Listen to radio during your virtual tour by pointing your browser at KRCW's page: www.kcrw.org. You'll need a sound program, RealAudio, to hear the program, but links to RealAudio are provided. Click on the "Which Way, L.A.?" graphic to listen to one of Warren Olney's radio programs focusing on current Los Angeles topics.

Find a book or an article in a library near you by going to the Los Angeles Public Library site: www.lapl. org. The catalogue can be accessed through the Web using the CarlWeb system. There's a list of local branches and Electronic Information Resources at LAPL, such as Virtual Electronic Branch Libraries and Homework Centers or the Los Angeles Times Literacy Center. The Los Angeles Public Library can also be accessed via Telnet at 213-237-0974.

The large universities also offer access to their library systems. You need permission to enter Orion, UCLA's internal library system, but Melvyl, a catalogue accessing all the libraries in the UC system, can be found at www. melvyl.ucop.edu. The University of Southern California's library system, Homer, can be found at library.usc.edu. Many of the community libraries have access as well, such as Santa Monica—www.ci.santa-monica. ca.us/ cityhall/library/—and Pasadena—www.ci. pasadena.ca. us/library.

If you're interested in Los Angeles theater, make

a stop at L.A. Onstage—
www.laonstage.com/
ticket.html—for a com-
prehensive listing of
Southern California the-
aters, complete with ad-
dresses. If you're still not
sure how to get there, the
site links you to Vicinity's
Map Blast, where you can
locate the street address on
a map. The L.A. Onstage
"Floor Plans" page displays
seating charts for some of
the larger venues around
town. Another site for theater listings is the *Los Angeles Times* Theater Calendar:
www.latimes.com/ HOME/
ENT/THEATER. This site
links to a critic's choice list
as well as a calendar of de-
buts and openings. Playbill
also links to Los Angeles
theaters. Start at the home
page—www.piano. symgrp.
com/playbill—then use
the search box to get a list
of local theaters. The Actors Interactive site—ac-
tors-interactive. com/1/
theatresLosAngeles.html—
is yet another resource for
Los Angeles theater.

Or perhaps you'd prefer
a little music. You can
drop by the Los Angeles
Opera's home page—www.
laopera.org—to find out
about upcoming opera
events in Los Angeles. The
Los Angeles Philharmonic
page— www.laphil.org—
gives information about
neighborhood concerts
and lets you learn about
the orchestra's musicians.

Both the city and county
of Los Angeles have Web
sites with useful govern-
ment information as well
as cultural links. The L.A.
County Online site—
www.co.la.ca.us—links to
the Los Angeles County
Arts Commission home
page—located at www.
lacountyarts.org—which
has a directory of more
than 1,000 arts organiza-
tions, a schedule of performances at the John Anson
Ford Amphitheater, and
lists of grants and funding
resources for artists. From
the City of Los Angeles
site—www.ci.la.ca.us—
click on the "Departments"
section to go to the Cul-
tural Affairs Department,
where you can find out
about the public art pro-
gram and access the calendar of events and
the festival guide. These
documents are kept in

Adobe Acrobat format, so
you'll need to download
the program to read the
contents. From the city's
"Department" section you
can also visit the Los Angeles
Zoo: www.lazoo.org. The
zoo's home page is
visually splashy and very
inviting, a great site for
children. There are photographs of the animals and
videos of animals feeding.

After a long day of tour-
ing the city by modem, gaze
at the stars by going to the
Griffith Observatory:
www.griffithobs.org. You
can look at the planets in
the Hall of Science. For
those of you getting ready
for the millennium, there's
a link to planetary align-
ments in 2000.

The Jet Propulsion
Laboratory site—www.jpl.
nasa.gov—offers more in-
formation online than you
would get if you drove to

Pasadena. The latest astronomical events are at
www.jpl.nasa. gov/news,
the planets can be viewed
at pds.jpl. nasa.gov/plan-
ets, and the Imaging Radar
Home Page—southport.
jpl.nasa.gov—has infor-
mation about the work
NASA and JPL are conduct-
ing in radar remote sensing
of the earth's surface with
radar data and images.

Now that you've got a
wealth of information
about cultural events in
Los Angeles, you're probably
eager to go out and visit a
few real places. First, check
out the traffic situation—
at www.scubed.com/
caltrans/la/la_small_map.
—for a map of current Los
Angeles–area freeway
speeds, updated every few
minutes. At "In Our Path:
History of LA Freeways,"
—www.tmn.com/iop—
you can view a photo-
graphic essay by Jeff Gate
on the impact of the development of the Century
Freeway on L.A. neighbor-
hoods . There's an interactive map, essays,
introduction, and photo-
graphs as well as a link to
live freeway conditions.

Before you log off, make
sure to keep a few good addresses tucked away in
your favorites list for your
next outing. Cyberspace is
ever-changing, but one thing
is a given: every time you
take a virtual tour of Los
Angeles, it will be different.

Here are some additional addresses that you may want to keep handy.

Sponsor	Address
@LA	www.at-la.com
L.A. Weekly: "Picks of the Week"	www.laweekly.com/picks/index.html
Los Angeles Times: "Calendar Live!"	www.calendarlive.com
Yahoo Los Angeles	la.yahoo.com/
The Boulevards Guide to Los Angeles	www.losangeles.com
Fountainhead's Los Angeles Superstation	www.fountainhead.com/super/super.html
USA CityLink	usacitylink.com/ca.html
Excite CITY NET	www.city.net/countries/united_states/california/los_angeles/

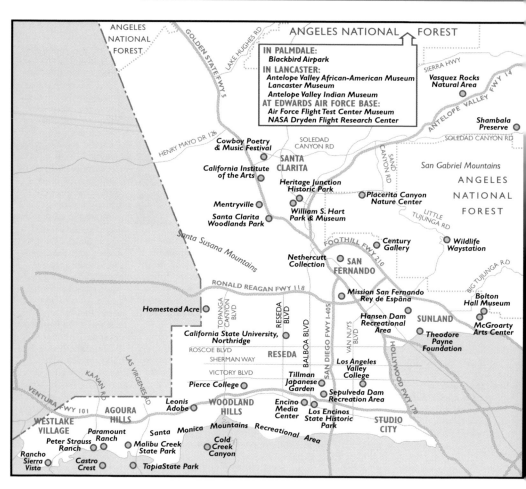

ANGELES NATIONAL FOREST

ANGELES NATIONAL FOREST

IN PALMDALE:
Blackbird Airpark
IN LANCASTER:
Antelope Valley African-American Museum
Lancaster Museum
Antelope Valley Indian Museum
AT EDWARDS AIR FORCE BASE:
Air Force Flight Test Center Museum
NASA Dryden Flight Research Center

Vasquez Rocks Natural Area

Shambala Preserve

Cowboy Poetry & Music Festival

SOLEDAD CANYON RD

San Gabriel Mountains

ANGELES NATIONAL FOREST

SANTA CLARITA

California Institute of the Arts

Heritage Junction Historic Park

Placerita Canyon Nature Center

Mentryville

William S. Hart Park & Museum

Santa Clarita Woodlands Park

Century Gallery

Wildlife Waystation

Santa Susana Mountains

Nethercutt Collection

SAN FERNANDO

Bolton Hall Museum

RONALD REAGAN FWY 118

Mission San Fernando Rey de España

McGroarty Arts Center

Homestead Acre

Hansen Dam Recreational Area

SUNLAND

Theodore Payne Foundation

California State University, Northridge

ROSCOE BLVD

RESEDA

SHERMAN WAY

VICTORY BLVD

Los Angeles Valley College

Pierce College

Tillman Japanese Garden

Leonis Adobe

WOODLAND HILLS

Encino Media Center

Sepulveda Dam Recreation Area

Los Encinos State Historic Park

STUDIO CITY

WESTLAKE VILLAGE

AGOURA HILLS

Santa Monica Mountains Recreational Area

Paramount Ranch

Peter Strauss Ranch

Santa Monica

Cold Creek Canyon

Rancho Sierra Vista

Castro Crest

Malibu Creek State Park

Tapia State Park

Three valleys ringed by mountains define the northern sector of Los Angeles County. Although the valleys—San Fernando, Santa Clarita, and Antelope—are flat, the mountains—Santa Monica, Santa Susana, and San Gabriel—which form their borders afford more than just a view of the sprawling suburbs. They are the entire county's backyard, but their proximity to the valleys gives its residents special access to this recreational resource. The mountains are also an important environmental resource, essential to air quality and as a watershed.

In 1769, more than 200 years after Spain had claimed and mapped the California coastline, the first group of Spaniards to explore California by land described the San Fernando Valley, which they first viewed from the Sepulveda Pass, as "a very spacious and pleasant valley." Its wide-open spaces created a buffer zone

for the developing urban metropolis: annexing the San Fernando Valley in May 1915 more than doubled Los Angeles's size, adding 177.19 square miles to the 107.62 square miles previously incorporated. The aqueduct from the Owens Valley to L.A. was completed in 1913, bringing enough water for the arid valley to someday support a large population. Today more than one million people live in the San Fernando Valley; its demographics, although changing, do not reflect the ethnic mix of Los Angeles's urban areas. "America's suburb" is still being developed: almost half of the new homes constructed in Los Angeles County during the past decade were built in the Valley, which periodically threatens to secede from the larger city that governs it.

The **Santa Monica Mountains**—the southernmost chain crossing California and one of the few east-west mountain ranges in America—divide the city basin from the San Fernando Valley. Along Mulholland Scenic Parkway (the ridge road that stretches from the Hollywood [101] Freeway to Leo Carrillo State Beach), the mountains east of the San Diego (405) Freeway are assimilated into the canyon communities and are cloaked in domesticated plants. West of the freeway, the mountains continue in rugged splendor, rising in places to an elevation of 3,000 feet until they drop into the Pacific Ocean at Point Mugu in Ventura County. A long section of Mulholland west of the 405 to Topanga Canyon is unpaved, but thereafter it is a navigable and scenic route to the northern boundary of Los Angeles County.

Santa Monica Mountains National Recreation Area (SMMNRA)

National Park Service Visitor Center
30401 Agoura Rd., Ste. 100
Agoura Hills 91301
818-597-9192, ext. 201
www.nps.gov/samo/
Visitor center: Mon.–Fri. 8 a.m.–5 p.m.,
Sat.–Sun. 9 a.m.–5 p.m.
Entry: free

More than 150,000 acres are preserved within the Santa Monica Mountains National Recreation Area, which was set aside by Congress in 1978 for "its scenic, natural, and historic setting and its public health value as an airshed for the Southern California metropolitan area." The southern and western boundary, stretching forty-six miles from Point Mugu to the Santa Monica Pier, is the Pacific Ocean; this coastline—characterized by sandy beaches interspersed with rocky bluffs, with two of the few remaining lagoons on the Pacific—is described in Chapter VIII. The major inland parks of the SMMNRA are listed below, starting from Point Mugu in Ventura Country and proceeding southeast along the mountain ridges. The scenic and recreational facilities of the northwestern districts of the Angeles National Forest and the desert parks of the Antelope Valley are described later in this chapter.

The parklands are administered by a coalition of public agencies, and the National Park Service provides a general map showing all park facilities, a free quarterly calendar of events, and brochures for individual sites. Hiking, horseback-riding, tidepooling, bicycling, whale-watching, camping, swimming, scenic drives, and ranger-led programs are listed as recreational activities offered in Los Angeles's own national park. The different parks within the recreation area have many characters, terrains, and attractions: they are

a wilderness to be experienced at different seasons and best appreciated with different activities. Much more than a day trip is required—this is a resource to enjoy again and again until it becomes part of the fabric of your life.

The Mountains Conservancy Foundation (5775 Ramirez Canyon Rd., Malibu 90265; 310-589-2400) is a private organization that is raising funds to complete the seventy miles of the Backbone Trail, which runs northwest along the mountain spine through Los Angeles County. All but six miles of the trail—those just east of the Ventura County line—are now complete, but state and federal funding for the project has been exhausted; Proposition A, passed by L.A. County voters in 1996, will match funds raised by the Mountain Conservancy's efforts. Ultimately the Backbone Trail will be administered by the National Park Service as part of the Santa Monica Mountains National Recreation Area. The serpentine route along the crest of the Santa Monica Mountains has in the past decade filled gaps in the California Coastal Trail, part of the proposed 1,600-mile patchwork of beach and coastal trails that will connect Mexico to Oregon and allow hikers to trek through this area as they may, for instance, along the Appalachian Trail in the eastern seaboard states.

The Mountains Conservancy has recently opened the Mountains to the Sea Gallery in donated space at Point Dume Plaza (29169 Heathercliff Rd., Ste. 4; Mon.–Fri. 10 a.m.–5 p.m., Sat. 10 a.m.–4 p.m.; free) in which paintings produced by the Allied Artists of the Santa Monica Mountains are displayed; the images help to raise awareness of the beauty of the local mountains and 20 percent of the sale proceeds revert to the foundation.

Weekly garden tours of the Streisand Center for Conservancy Studies—the former Barbra Streisand estate in Malibu, which the actress donated to the agencies seeking to preserve the Santa Monica Mountains—are offered by the Mountains Conservancy Foundation. The two-hour tour (by reservation only: 310-589-2850) costs $30; the tour includes discussion of the agency's conservation goals, compares native plants with landscaping imposed on the site, and concludes with tea. Members of the Mountains Conservancy (memberships start at $25 per year) receive the quarterly magazine L.A. Wild and a monthly newsletter that lists events, including such perennial activities as those in the month of November dedicated to raising awareness of the Backbone Trail.

Rim of the Valley Trail Corridor, an extension of the Santa Monica Mountain Zone, was defined and approved in 1990 legislation, but little funding was provided to realize its goals. The trail system linking the Simi, Santa Susana, and Verdugo mountains surrounding the San Fernando Valley will provide wildlife corridors, a watershed, a viewshed, and an airshed, but because much of the land is still in private hands, many of the connecting trails have not been built. To learn more about the open lands north of the Ventura (101) Freeway, request the calendar of hikes (published six times per year) from the Northern division staff at 310-589-3200.

Rancho Sierra Vista/Satwiwa Site

Potrero Rd. and Pinehill Rd.
Newbury Park
National Park Service: 818-597-9192, ext. 201
Friends of Satwiwa: 805-499-2837
Daily 8 a.m.–sunset
Entry: free

This park conserves 839 mountainous acres; its name, Satwiwa—"the bluffs"—is derived from the Chumash village of the same name which historians believe was located near here, along the route Native-American people traveled from the inland valley to the sea. Rancho Sierra Vista was the name given to it in 1937 by Carl Beal, who constructed the buildings (including his own home in Sycamore Canyon) when he converted the land for modern ranching. The site was purchased by the National Park Service in 1980 and is now dedicated to the Chumash Indians. A Native-American Indian culture center (Sat.-Sun. 10 a.m.-5 p.m.) is one of the new features of this evolving park. Every week the park hosts Satwiwa Sundays, at which Native-American guests share traditional knowledge with visitors; on the last Saturday of each month at 10 a.m. rangers lead visitors in a program of American Indian games and stories. The hiking trails (accessible daily 8 a.m.–sunset) include easy 1.2-1.5 mile routes through the park, as well as a strenuous eight-mile-long path through Big Sycamore Canyon down to the beach at Point Mugu.

Arroyo Sequit (34138 Mulholland Hwy., Malibu) and Rocky Oaks (Mulholland Hwy. at Kanan Rd., Agoura) are smaller mountain parks (155 and 198 acres, respectively); call 818-597-9192 for information on ranger-led hikes and other activities scheduled at these parks.

Peter Strauss Ranch

30000 Mulholland Hwy. at Troutdale Rd.
Agoura 91301
National Park Service: 818-597-9192, ext. 201
Daily 8 a.m.–5 p.m.
Entry: free

This sixty-five-acre ranch was first developed in 1936 as Lake Encanto, a lakeside resort with a star-shaped dance floor paved in terrazzo, an outdoor amphitheater, and a circular swimming pool. It prospered for twenty-five years, then passed through various hands until it was acquired by actor/producer Peter Strauss in the late 1970s. Now the open land, sheltered by sycamores and eucalyptus, invites hikers and picnickers, and open-air performances are staged in the amphitheater during the summer months.

Paramount Ranch

Kanan Rd. at Cornell Way
Agoura Hills 91301
National Park Service: 818-597-9192, ext. 201
Daily 8 a.m.–sunset
Entry: free

Paramount Pictures filmed its earliest westerns on 4,000 acres; the area boasts wide-open space with a variety of scenery. The ranch was sold during the lean war years, but in the 1950s another owner developed another film lot in the area and constructed a "western mining town" where made-for-TV westerns like *The Cisco Kid, Bat Masterson, Zane Grey Theater,* and *Have Gun, Will Travel* were shot. Today the set is best known as the site where *Dr. Quinn, Medicine Woman* is filmed (except during the summer hiatus in July and August). Visitors may walk through the town or ride horses on trails throughout the 760-acre site. Rangers lead history walks at 9:30 a.m. on the first and third Saturday of each month, and in late spring Paramount Ranch hosts a banjo and fiddle contest—the great country music gives the artificial town a wonderful new life.

Malibu Creek State Park

1925 Las Virgenes Rd.
Calabasas 91302
California State Parks: 818-880-0350
Ranger station: 818-880-0367
Daily 8 a.m.–sunset
Entry: free

Three large parks mark the Santa Monica Mountains National Recreation Area west of the 405 Freeway: Point Mugu and Topanga State Parks occupy its northwestern sections, and Malibu Creek State Park occupies some 5,000 acres in the

Remember the
Sierra Club motto:
take only pictures,
leave only footprints!

central portion in the mountains along Malibu Canyon–Las Virgenes Road. Malibu Creek forms rocky swimming holes as it falls through the gorge, and two-acre Century Lake lures fishermen in search of trout. The park's vast size and varied terrain support a diverse system of animals and plants, including huge live oak trees that are more than 500 years old. Chumash Indians lived here until the mid-1800s, and the area has been used as a film site in this century: Twentieth-Century Fox filmed the movie *South Pacific*, as well as *M*A*S*H** and other television series on some 2,000 acres it owned in Malibu Canyon.

A small nature center (open only on weekends) is located .8 mile from the parking lot entrance at Las Virgenes-Malibu Canyon Road; picnic areas are maintained in the western entrance to the park, near Cornell Road on Mulholland Highway. Each spring the docents at Malibu Creek offer a series of lectures and hikes designed to lure new recruits and teach them basic information about the park, but others are welcome to join in most of the activities. Call 818-880-0350 or the National Park Service (818-597-9192, ext. 201) for schedules or information.

Tapia State Park

844 N. Las Virgenes Canyon Rd.
Calabasas 91302
California State Parks: 818-880-0350
Ranger station: 818-880-0367
Daily 8 a.m.–sunset
Entry: free

Only ninety-five acres and a subunit of Malibu Creek State Park, this is one of the smallest parks in the SMMNRA, but it is very popular. The striking setting, access to water in Malibu Creek, and well-fixtured picnic and barbecue facilities draw crowds on weekends, when it's easy to get involved in some game on the playing field.

The Mountains Conservancy Foundation (310-589-2400) developed a self-guided nature trail in Solstice Canyon (Corral Canyon Rd. at Pacific Coast Hwy.), which was badly burned in the 1996 Malibu fires. The three ecosystems within the 556-acre park—riparian, coastal sage, and chaparral—are described on markers and in a pamphlet (translated into five languages) available at the visitors center.

Castro Crest

End of Corral Canyon Rd. in Malibu
Latigo Canyon Rd. in Calabasas
National Park Service: 818-597-9192, ext. 201
Daily 8 a.m.–sunset
Entry: free

Drivers who enjoy roads that squiggle from here to eternity will be in heaven if they continue up Corral Canyon Road—as long as they aren't bothered by changes in elevation. Driving to Castro Crest may be half the fun, but its 800 acres include many hiking and equestrian trails with panoramic views across the mountains to the Channel Islands.

This is an area where the patchwork of public and private land has not yet taken its final form, while the Santa Monica Mountains Conservancy negotiates with landowners and developers (whose presence is already evident along the serpentine route) to realize individual investments while completing the public park for the benefit of all.

Cold Creek Canyon/ Valley Preserve

Stunt Rd.
Calabasas 91302
By appt. only: 818-346-9675

This 820-acre preserve on the north edge of the Santa Monica Mountains contains a year-round stream, so it supports a complete cross-section of lifeforms native to this mountain range. The Preserve is administered by the Mountains Restoration Trust in Canoga Park; call for permission to make an independent visit to the preserve or to arrange for group visits. Cold Creek Docents (818-346-9620) offers school programs and guided walks.

Stunt Ranch (off Stunt Rd., 1.3 mi. south of Mulholland Hwy. in Calabasas) includes 243 acres that are open to the public, while sixty-seven acres are managed by UCLA and accessible only by permit: call 310-206-3887 for information about the UCLA Stunt Ranch Santa Monica Mountains Reserve.

Cheeseboro Canyon/Palo Comado Canyon Site is the northernmost park in the Santa Monica Mountains National Recreation Area. To secure some 5,700 acres of undeveloped mountain land owned by Bob Hope, fifty-nine acres of Cheeseboro Canyon were transferred from national parkland to build an access road for an adjacent development. This segment of the Simi Hills, which lies north of the 101

Freeway (Chesebro [sic] Rd. exit) and crosses the Ventura County line, was heavily grazed by cattle for 150 years; because many native plant and animal species had been displaced by the cattle, the Park Service is hastening the natural recolonization with techniques—prescribed fire, habitat restoration—designed to re-create the original ecology. A natural pathway, Cheeseboro Canyon is used as a corridor for wildlife migrating between the Santa Monica Mountains to the south and the Simi Mountains to the north. Call the Park Service (818-597-9192, ext. 201) for more information.

There are two long hiking trails within the parkland: Sulphur Springs Trail is an easy 4.6-mile hike through valley oak savannah and a streamside live oak zone to the springs that lend their distinctive aroma to the area. Palo Comado Trail, at 4.4 miles, is more strenuous: it follows a creek to the old ranch center, then climbs dramatically 2,140 feet to the canyon headwall, scenic China Flat.

Juan Bautista de Anza Park (3701 Lost Hills Rd. at Las Virgenes Rd.) is the first park built by the city of Calabasas. Spanning eight acres, it has three playgrounds with age-specific apparatus—including one with exercise equipment for teens and adults—and fountains where visitors are encouraged to cool off. Open-air concerts take place in the open area where trails lead into the Santa Monica Mountains; call 818-880-6461 for information about park programs and activities.

Just over the Ventura County line

Moorpark College (7075 Campus Park Dr., Moorpark; 805-378-1441), located at the west end of the Simi Valley (CA 118) Freeway in Ventura County, prepares students in its Exotic Animal Program to be zookeepers and animal trainers. A self-guided tour around the four-acre zoo—with camels, sea lions, parrots, and baboons among its 150 animals—is included in the modest admission charge to the animal shows that are offered every weekend (Sat.–Sun., gates open 11 a.m., shows at noon, 1, 2, and 3 p.m.; adults $4, children over 12 $2, children 12 and under free).

Circle X Ranch (on Yerba Buena Rd., 5.4 mi. north of Pacific Coast Hwy., Malibu; 818-597-9192, ext. 201 [National Park Service]), is a 1,655-acre park that includes the highest point in the Santa Monica Mountains: Sandstone Peak, at 3,111 feet. A nature center, picnic area with barbecue pits, and thirty miles of hiking and equestrian trails are within its borders; most of the park lies within Ventura County.

Bottle Village (4595 Cochran St., Simi Valley) is a landmark folk art environment built by Tressa "Grandma" Prisbrey from thousands of scavenged bottles. There are no public visiting hours because of earthquake damage and safety hazards, but the complex is visible from the street; for more information or to contribute to its preservation, send a self-addressed, stamped envelope to P.O. Box 1412, Simi Valley 93062, or call 805-583-1627.

Tierra Rejada Family Farm (3370 Moorpark Rd., Moorpark; 805-529-3690) offers sixty acres of pick-your-own produce from artichokes to zucchini, and there is lots of fruit, including apples, apricots, blackberries, and strawberries.

Groups of twenty-five or more can request a guided tour to learn about the cultivation of various fruits.

Ronald Reagan Presidential Library and Museum

40 Presidential Dr.
Simi Valley 93065
800-410-8354
Daily 10 a.m.–5 p.m.
Entry: adults $4, seniors $2, children under 15 free

The museum at the Ronald Reagan Presidential Library has photographs and memorabilia from all stages of Reagan's life, not only after he was elected to our nation's highest office. A section of the Berlin Wall, which was dismantled during Reagan's term in office, is on display along with mementos from world leaders and the citizens of the United States. "Gifts to U.S. Presidents," an exhibition culled from collections throughout the U.S. and mounted by the National Archives, made a six-month stop in Simi Valley as its only venue outside the nation's capital. The library has presented an eclectic series of changing exhibitions —from Civil War artifacts to watercolors by the Prince of Wales, and artworks by Grandma Moses to photographs of presidential families—and mounts an active program of special events. For the annual Christmas festival, the halls are decked out with some thirty trees festooned in styles from around the globe and an exhibition with a seasonal theme is featured, like "Seasons Greetings from the White House," with cards and gifts given by and to First Ladies and Presidents.

Club Disney, billed as an "imagination-powered playsite," includes a dozen play environments based on Disney characters in a 25,000-square-foot site at the Westlake Promenade Shopping Plaza (120 S. Westlake Blvd., Thousand Oaks; 805-777-8000). The interactive multimedia center is designed for children ten and younger (who must be accompanied by an adult); it is open six days a week (Tues.–Sun. 10 a.m.–7 p.m., Fri.–Sat. until 8 p.m.) and admission is $8 for all ages.

Calabasas Farmers Market
Calabasas Rd.
and El Cañon Ave.
Sat. 8 a.m.–noon

Calabasas got its name— "squash" in Spanish—from an overturned wagonload of pumpkins that grew rampant for generations in the surrounding fields.

Plummer House— the "oldest house in Hollywood"—was moved in 1983 from Plummer Park (in present-day West Hollywood) to this site in far-off Calabasas, where it serves as the visitors center on the Leonis Adobe grounds.

Topanga State Park
20825 Entrada Rd.
Topanga 90290
California State Parks: 818-880-0350
Ranger station: 310-455-2465
Daily 8 a.m.–sunset
Entry: free

Topanga Canyon Boulevard twists upward from Pacific Coast Highway through a rocky canyon on a spectacular road reminiscent of the Route Napoleon in the south of France (with which it shares a Mediterranean-type ecosystem) to the entrance to Topanga State Park. At 9,000 acres, Topanga State Park is the largest park within the Los Angeles city limits: its vast and steep acreage runs from Mulholland Drive to Sunset Boulevard to Will Rogers State Historic Park in Pacific Palisades, and includes deep canyons as well as some of the highest summits in the Santa Monica Mountains; it boasts spectacular views and almost untouched wilderness in close proximity to densely populated urban areas. Hikers can enjoy thirty-five miles of trails, including three that begin at Trippet Ranch (the Entrada Road entrance to the parklands). A nine-mile trail of moderate difficulty may be accessed from the south end of the park (via Palisades Drive), but it is best traversed starting at Topanga and heading toward Will Rogers so that the 1,800-foot drop in elevation works in the hiker's favor. The brave and fit can hike across chaparral-covered slopes and rocky ridges on some of the highest points in the Santa Monica chain; those feeling less vigorous can follow the one-mile nature loop from park headquarters (which has maps) or walk the three-mile round-trip Santa Ynez Trail to a waterfall. Call Topanga Canyon Docents at 818-888-6856 for information on scheduled hikes or events.

Leonis Adobe
Plummer House Museum
23537 Calabasas Rd.
Calabasas 91302
818-222-6511
Wed.–Sun. 1–4 p.m.
Entry: adults $1, children 25¢

Miguel Leonis, a Basque, was born in the French Pyrenees; he came to the California frontier in the mid-1800s while still in his twenties. His marriage to an Indian widow, Espíritu Chijulla, gave him title to the 1,100-acre El Escorpión ranch in Calabasas and to large herds of livestock. Because of his extensive land holdings and shrewd trading skills, he became famous as "the King of Calabasas"; his litigious nature

made him infamous, and the Leonis name filled court records until Miguel died in 1889. Espíritu lived at the adobe until she died in 1906, and she is buried at the Mission San Fernando.

The Leonis adobe retains the structure of a working ranch. A 600-year-old white oak tree dominates the yard separating the main house—dating from 1844, with major additions in the 1880s—from the barn, blacksmith shop, and beehive oven; children are welcome to climb on the old farm equipment, and cattle, horses, sheep, and goats still graze in the pasture. Leonis family portraits still hang in their original positions in the living room, and the house is furnished much as it would have been when the family occupied it.

California State University, Northridge
18111 Nordhoff St.
Northridge 91330
818-677-2285

The **New Performing Arts Center**, part of a $16-million expansion of the University Student Union, opened in 1995 with a 500-seat theater. It has presented a varied series of musical events (by guest artists and from the resident music department groups), as well as programs of jazz and world music, dance, distinguished speakers, and various ethnic cultural events; call the events hotline (818-677-3943) for the season brochure.

The **Art Dome** (Music Lawn 236, 818-677-2226; Mon., Sat. noon–4 p.m., Tues.–Fri. 10 a.m.–4 p.m.; free) is the primary exhibition space on campus, presenting historical and contemporary, thematic and media-oriented exhibitions that reflect the broad spectrum of art in the global society. Australian aboriginal art, Mexican folk art, textiles from Thailand, Laos, and India, and solo exhibitions by contemporary artists have been featured. **North Gallery** (818-677-3024; Mon.–Thurs. 11 a.m.–4 p.m.; Sat. 3–7 p.m.; free) presents weekly exhibitions of student work.

Four greenhouses and a one-acre botanical garden with a redwood grove are more traditional uses of campus land, but the university recently withdrew a controversial request to lease eleven of its acres to developers for a shopping mall, which it had projected could add $1 million to its budget each year.

Pierce College
6201 Winnetka Ave.
Woodland Hills 91371
818-719-6401

Pierce College was founded in 1947 as the Clarence W. Pierce School for Agriculture and is among the largest of the nine Los Angeles Community Colleges. Though Pierce still maintains animal husbandry and horticulture departments, the land reserved for the beef and dairy cattle, sheep, horses, and pigs on its 427-acre campus has been valued at $1 million an acre, which must put financial pressure on its long-term survival.

Weekly public tours of the working farm ceased five years ago and were replaced with seasonal Farm Walks in fall, winter, and spring (call 818-703-0826 for a schedule). Guides manage to ply adults with facts about commercial agriculture while

allowing children to see farm animals in a natural environment; while adults consider statistics on water and feed consumption per pound of beef produced, kids push sheaves of hay through the fence to contented calves, and view pink pigs (who are always busy at the feeding troughs and water spigots). The horses are most obliging, allowing little hands to caress and explore their soft muzzles, and low-fee riding classes are available for children over twelve through various community organizations. A self-guided walk through a fifteen-acre nature center, which has seven different ecosystems, is particularly interesting in the winter when migrating Canadian geese and ducks find sanctuary there.

The Life Science Museum and Nature Center (Rm. 1711, Life Science Bldg.) includes a dinosaur replica, wildlife specimens, and natural history exhibits. The displays may be visited when department personnel are working or by appointment (818-710-6465).

Orcutt Ranch Horticultural Center
23600 Roscoe Blvd.
West Hills 91304
818-883-6641
Gardens: daily 8 a.m.–5 p.m.
House tours: last Sun. of month 2–5 p.m. (except in summer)
Entry: free

William Orcutt—considered by some contemporaries to be the father of modern geology for his role in excavating the La Brea Tar Pits—was really searching for oil (which was his profession) when he discovered an extinct giant ground sloth in Hancock Park; while scientists catalogued the fossil finds from the tar pits, Orcutt went to work for Union Oil Company, becoming its vice-president.

In 1920 C. G. Knipe designed a 3,000-square-foot adobe house, finished with Mexican tilework and carved wooden mantels and moldings, at the Orcutts' weekend retreat in Canoga Park (present-day West Hills). Rancho Sombra del Roble (Ranch of the Shaded Oak) is still cooled by large oaks, but the ranch has been planted with citrus for more than fifty years. The gardens surrounding the ranch house are bright and fragrant with flowering trees and wisteria; stone statues of historic figures (including a fine image of Father Junípero Serra) were carved in the 1930s by Frank Knapp, a local mason.

Each year in early July the public is invited to pick fruit in the citrus groves at Orcutt Ranch. Grapefruit and oranges may be picked for $1 a bag or $2 per bushel box.

The 1994 Northridge earthquake severely damaged Canoga Park's downtown business area, and the Madrid Theater (built in 1926 and showing X-rated movies in 1994) was damaged beyond repair and was demolished. Federal and state earthquake-recovery funds have been dedicated to building a new community arts center on the site, which will include a 499-seat multiuse auditorium equipped for musical, theatrical, and dance performances, as well as film screenings. The development of the new Madrid Theater (21626 Sherman Way, Canoga Park 91303) is expected to be a catalyst for reinvigorating the downtown area by providing families with affordable, high-quality entertainment in a local center; it is scheduled to open in December 1997. Call the City of Los Angeles Department of Cultural Affairs (213-485-2437) for an update on this facility, under construction when this book went to press.

Homestead Acre and Hill-Palmer House

Chatsworth History Museum
10385 Shadow Oaks Dr.
Chatsworth 91311
818-882-5614
1st Sun. of month 1–4 p.m.
Entry: free

The last San Fernando Valley homestead cottage with acreage dedicated to citrus and a kitchen garden was occupied for ninety years by members of the family that originally built it. Now it is a museum whose collections depict the nineteenth-century lifestyle of the Valley; artifacts such as a period kitchen and vintage sewing machine highlight women's roles. In addition, Indian and pioneer artifacts are displayed in the Hill-Palmer House, a 1911 California bungalow filled with period furniture. Special tours for school groups may be scheduled.

The Canoga Owensworth Historical Museum (7248 Owensworth Ave., Canoga Park 91303; 818-884-4222) is open the second Sunday of each month from 2 to 4 p.m.; there is no admission charge.

Shadow Ranch (22633 Vanowen St., Canoga Park; 818-883-3637) is reputed to be the site where Australian eucalyptus was first introduced locally; it is used today as a community center.

Santa Susana Mountain Parks Association (818-704-9304) organizes hikes exploring various historic sites in these mountains, including the rugged pass called Devils Slide that was a vital link in the 1850s stagecoach trail to points north. Land that has been set aside as a State Historic Park—but as yet has no official designation—surrounds Chatsworth Park South on three sides, in rugged open terrain with rock formations and the vestiges of an Indian village site.

Los Encinos State Historic Park

16756 Moorpark St.
Encino 91435
818-784-4849
Wed.–Sun. 10 a.m.–5 p.m.
Entry: free; adobe tour, adults $1, children 6-17 $.50

Spanish explorers in 1769 named this part of the valley Los Encinos (the Oaks) for the plentiful groves in the area. The first private landowner in the Valley, Francisco Reyes, owned 4,460 acres (one square league) in what is today Encino; this one-term mayor of Los Angeles was run off his property for alleged mistreatment of his Indian workers, to whom title of his land

passed. The adobe building was constructed on the site by a later owner, and it became a carriage stop on the principal route to the north because it offered the only reliable source of water between the Cahuenga Pass and Calabasas. The main building in the present five-acre park is preserved as a museum that illustrates early ranching life in the San Fernando Valley. Spring-fed Encino Lake supports an abundant population of ducks and geese, and bird food is available for a small fee at the ranger station.

Encino Media Center

16953 Ventura Blvd.
Encino 91316
818-784-7266

This facility, previously operated by the Los Angeles Cultural Affairs Department as a photography center, was reborn in October 1996 as a partnership between the San Fernando Valley Arts Council (818-784-7266) and California Institute of the Arts (CalArts). Ten-week classes in animation are taught by CalArts faculty and are open to teenagers and adults, symbolizing the management's recognition of the high-tech media companies that have recently provided new good-paying jobs in the entertainment sector of the local economy.

The low-fee photography classes (for which the Encino facility was well known) will continue with classes for kids as young as eight, as well as instruction for adults. Members aged eighteen and over may rent darkroom space ($4 per hour) in the newly renovated lab.

Japanese Garden at Tillman Water Reclamation Plant

6100 Woodley Ave.
Van Nuys 91406
818-756-8166
Grounds: Mon.–Thurs. noon–4 p.m.
Tours by appt. only, adults $3, seniors and children $2

This 6.5-acre site is an oasis whose prominent water features—lake, stream, and waterfall—are all fed by reclaimed water. Reservations are required for a full tour of the gardens, which are offered only on weekday mornings, but the garden is now open for strolling during office hours so that those who pay for municipal water services can also enjoy this beautiful environment. A dry garden near the entrance features stone arrangements and gravel raked into symbolic water patterns, but the basic plan is a stroll garden like those built in the eighteenth century on the vast estates of feudal lords.

Van Nuys Farmers Market
City Hall parking lot,
(Van Nuys Blvd.
and Sylvan St.,)
Sat. 8 a.m.–noon

Sepulveda Dam Recreation Area

6335 Woodley Ave.
Van Nuys 91406
Parks and Recreation Dept.: 818-756-8891
Daily, sunrise–sunset
Entry: free

The Sepulveda Dam Recreation Area (bounded south and east by the Ventura [101] and San Diego [405] Freeways and north and west by Victory Blvd. and White Oak Ave.) includes many specialized facilities for recreational activities within a 2,000-acre flood control basin. Facilities include three eighteen-hole golf courses, as well as lighted tennis courts, an archery range, and a ten-mile bicycle path that is rated among the best of its kind in L.A. County. Twenty acres are fixtured for picnics with tables and barbecue facilities, and children's playgrounds are nearby. A plan to develop a cultural center in the Sepulveda Basin has progressed little in the past decade, but Jazz on the Lake has become a popular annual summer music festival.

Sixteen acres, divided into 420 plots, are rented yearly ($20 for a ten-by-twenty-foot plot) to allow urban gardeners to exercise their green thumbs at the Sepulveda Garden Center (16633 Magnolia Blvd., Encino). Call 818-784-5180 to get on the list for a plot; at the annual fair vendors sell plant material and offer information on recycling and water conservation.

The Great Wall of Los Angeles (Coldwater Canyon Ave. between Burbank Blvd. and Oxnard St.), a half-mile-long mural depicting the history of ethnic groups in Los Angeles, was painted over the course of five summers (beginning in 1976). Two hundred volunteers, many of them students, were led by forty artists under the direction of Judy Baca (who founded the Social and Public Art Resource Center [SPARC]); the panels include prehistoric landscapes dotted with dinosaurs as well as little-known incidents in California's history. (See Murals. pp. 168–72 for more on this art form.)

Everywoman's Village (5650 Sepulveda Blvd., Van Nuys 91411) also welcomes men, teenagers, and children to its interesting roster of classes, which include fine arts and crafts, languages, personal development, and computers, among others; there are six semesters a year, with sessions lasting eight to nine weeks. For classes and schedules, call 818-787-5100.

Los Angeles Valley College

5800 Fulton Ave.
Van Nuys 91401
818-781-1200

To celebrate the twenty-fifth anniversary of Los Angeles Valley College, the administration pledged to begin accumulating artifacts and oral history that would prevent "the history of our Valley, rich in great people and replete with a variety of accomplishments, from passing into oblivion." The collections that resulted from that promise— early maps and real estate plots, lithographs, paintings, and photographs of the Valley from the nineteenth century, as well as exhibits of native plants and tools used by its prehistoric residents— fill ten rooms of a historic bungalow (located adjacent to parking lot H) on campus. The Historical Museum is open Monday to Friday 1 to 4 p.m. when school is in session, and admission is free; for information, call 818-781-1200, ext. 373.

A gallery in the fine arts building presents changing exhibitions (Mon.–Thurs. 11 a.m.–2 p.m., 7–9 p.m.; free); call 818-781-1200, ext. 356 for current program information.

The only air show in L.A. County has been held each July since 1963 at the Van Nuys Airport (6950 Hayvenhurst Ave., Van Nuys). The Aviation Expo drew 150,000 spectators in 1997.

San Fernando Valley Historical Society

Andrés Pico Adobe
10940 Sepulveda Blvd.
Mission Hills 91346
818-365-7810
Mon. 10 a.m.–3 p.m.
Entry: free

Begun in 1834, this adobe residence is identified with Andrés Pico, who added on to it and then gave it to his two adopted children (who married each other) to live in. The house fell into disrepair in the 1920s but was saved and restored in the 1930s by Mark Harrington, a curator at the Southwest Museum. Currently the headquarters of the San Fernando Valley Historical Society, the adobe's rooms are filled with a variety of period furnishings. Severely damaged by the 1994 Northridge earthquake, the house is once again open to the public, though only for limited hours.

Mission San Fernando Rey de España

15151 San Fernando Mission Blvd.
Mission Hills 91345
818-361-0186
Daily 9 a.m.–4:30 p.m.
Entry: adults $4, seniors/children 7–15 $3, children under 7 free

The first church at San Fernando—dedicated in 1797, replaced in 1806 with a larger structure—was the seventeenth in the California mission system; never an architecturally distinguished building, it was demolished and rebuilt after being severely damaged in the Sylmar earthquake in 1971. The nearby convent with its long exterior portico of Roman arches (which today front on San Fernando Mission Boulevard) is the most distinctive feature of the mission complex, constructed from 1810 to 1822. The walls of both the church and the convent have been painted with decorative Indian motifs that recall the builders of the complex, who also formed its earliest congregations, and many of the early parishioners are buried in the flower-filled graveyard behind the church.

A collection of Hispanic *santos* and an ornate baroque altarpiece from the Ezcaray chapel in Spain have been installed in the convent. The museum houses Native-American artifacts, as well as historical displays on this mission complex and the role of the missions in California's development; dioramas of the complex's workshops evoke the economic life of the mission community. Peacocks wander in the pleasant gardens linking the buildings, birds splash in the fountain (modeled on one in Córdoba, Spain), and chickens scratch in the patio in front of the majordomo's house, but otherwise the complex is quiet and peaceful.

**Sunland-Tujunga
Branch Library**
7771 Foothill Blvd.
Tujunga 91402
818-352-4481

The Ararat Home (15105 Mission Hills Rd.), founded in 1949 as a retirement community for Armenians, built a lovely new residential facility in Mission Hills a few years ago. Recently it transformed a tree-shaded walkway into a 350-foot time line of Armenian history, where red, blue, and orange tiles—the colors of the Armenian flag—surround graphics commemorating religious events, battles, and scientific discoveries. There is also a small museum and a traditional chapel on site.

McGroarty Arts Center

7570 McGroarty Terrace
Tujunga 91042
818-352-5285

John Steven McGroarty was a journalist for the *Los Angeles Times* for forty years; he was also poet laureate of California and author of eleven books and seven plays. His most famous dramatic work was the *Mission Play*, which depicted the early history of California and set a world performance record with its long run at the Mission Playhouse in San Gabriel.

Located on twelve acres in the Verdugo Hills, Rancho Chupa Rosa (McGroarty's residence for the last two decades of his life) retains many of his personal effects as part of a memorial archive and library; docents recount the rancho's colorful history during guided tours offered on the second Friday afternoon of each month (call ahead). Owned since 1953 by the Los Angeles Department of Recreation and Parks, it is operated as the McGroarty Arts Center by the city's Cultural Affairs Department; student art is often exhibited at the house, which periodically hosts concerts and other performances. There is an active year-round program of classes for adults and youth: classes include Preschool Art Potpourri (art, music, ceramics, stories), ballet, yoga, tai chi, film animation, and ceramics. The modest fees for classes at this city of Los Angeles facility range from $30 to $45; call for more information.

Bolton Hall Museum

10110 Commerce Ave.
Tujunga 91402
818-352-3420
Tues., Sun. 1–4 p.m.
Entry: free

This small building, constructed in 1913 of local stones left in a near-natural state, served as Tujunga's city hall and jail before being named to the original roster of historical monuments in Los Angeles. It now houses a museum of local history.

Theodore Payne Foundation

10459 Tuxford St.
Sun Valley 91352
818-768-1802
Events hotline: 818-768-3533
Wed.–Sun. 8:30 a.m.–4:30 p.m.
Entry: free

Where drab industrial developments give way to residences that retain a rustic and rural look—surrounded by old fruit trees and sheltering a few horses in the yard— the Theodore Payne Foundation has created a preserve for wildflowers and native plants. The twenty-three-acre site includes a rambling trail system with displays of wildflowers and a well-stocked nursery and seed room that reveal the beauty and diversity of native plants. The bookstore and library contain many references on how to create landscapes that feature such plants, and seminars featuring how-to information are offered regularly. Thematic plant sales—desert and riparian plants in August, California natives best planted in October—are offered bimonthly.

There are presently about 140,000 acres of the **Angeles National Forest** within the Tujunga Ranger District (818-899-1900). A planned reorganization will eliminate this administrative district entirely, but that should not affect public access to the spectacular mountain scenery or adversely affect recreational opportunities. This is one of the best areas for mountain biking, and both equestrian and hiking trails are numerous; **Big Tujunga Canyon** has many aquatic sites, which are affected by the amount of water running from the mountains. An education center is planned for Wildwood Recreation Center. Although **Earthquake Picnic Grounds** (more than 5 mi. up Little Tujunga Canyon Rd. from Foothill Blvd., past Wildlife Waystation) has a name that could kill the appetite of the seismic-phobic, it appropriately celebrates the telltale natural features created by past events. Bring champagne and celebrate living on the edge!

Wildlife Waystation

14831 Little Tujunga Rd.
San Fernando 91342
818-899-5201
By appt. only: 1st and 3rd Sun. of month, tours on the hour 10 a.m.–3 p.m.

Since 1968 this 160-acre ranch purchased with personal funds by founder Martine Colette has served as a refuge for animals in need: whether abandoned, injured, or abused, wild and exotic animals are offered veterinary care, food, and protection by this volunteer-supported organization. Rescue and rehabilitation success stories— related by guides on the Sunday afternoon tours offered twice each month—include an orphaned and blind baby deer given shelter and a raccoon nicknamed Voltage for the jolt he survived after stepping into a main transformer at the Jet Propulsion Laboratories.

Exotic animals are often illegally owned and suffer malnutrition and other abuse from owners who don't understand their needs; for instance, the Fish and Game Department confiscated a pair of pygmy marmosets covered with urine burns because these arboreal primates were caged without branches or perches—but they recuperated at Wildlife Waystation with an appropriate environment and all the finely chopped food their tiny bodies could absorb. Many exotic animals are placed in zoos or other controlled facilities when they have regained their health; other aging specimens are retired from zoos to live out the remainder of their days in these tranquil surroundings.

The crowds of visitors who bumped down the dirt road on the fine spring day I visited seemed to somewhat overwhelm the staff and facilities. We passed the hour-long wait for a tour by visiting the petting zoo and drinking lemonade in the hot sun: at least 200 adults and children had traveled to this remote and beautiful location, and the dedicated volunteers, pleased with the turnout, used the opportunity to campaign for animal rights.

Hansen Dam Recreational Area

11770 Foothill Blvd.
Lakeview Terrace 91342
818-899-8587
Daily, sunrise–sunset
Entry: free

A 130-acre body of water called Holiday Lake—the focal point of the 1,437-acre flood-control basin at the east end of the San Fernando Valley from the 1950s—was ironically closed in 1982 due to flooding, which filled the lake with silt. By 1994 restoration of the park had begun, but not until funding was provided from Proposition A (a county bond issue passed in 1996) did reconstruction of the park's water features begin in earnest. Two lakes are now planned, to separate swimming—in filtered, chlorinated water—from fishing and boating. There is a nineteen-hole par 72 golf course with clubhouse, children's playgrounds, softball field, and a picnic area with barbecue facilities.

Century Gallery

Los Angeles County Veteran's Memorial Park
13000 Sayre St.
Sylmar 91342
818-367-8561
Mon.–Fri. 10 a.m.–5 p.m., Sat. noon–4 p.m.
Entry: free

For twenty years L.A. County has owned this small gallery, which is operated by staff from Mission College and located in a beautiful woodlands park. An active exhibition program showcases works by contemporary artists working in Southern California. Mission College is the newest of the nine colleges that make up the Los Angeles Community College District; its campus (13356 Eldridge Ave., Sylmar 91342) was completed in 1991 and includes an $8-million library and learning resource center with more than 200 computer stations among its facilities.

Nethercutt Collection

San Sylmar
15180 Bledsoe St.
Sylmar 91342
818-367-2251
Tours by appt. only: Tues.–Sat. 10 a.m. and 1:30 p.m.; children under 12 not allowed
Entry: free

San Sylmar is "not a museum but a treasure house of functional fine art," announces the guide as the tour enters the building where J. B. Nethercutt, chairman of the board and co-founder of Merle Norman Cosmetics, exhibits his collections of antique cars, mechanical musical instruments, and decorative arts. San Sylmar is located next door to the container division of Merle Norman Cosmetics in Sylmar, epicenter of the 1971 earthquake, which damaged the collection and delayed its public opening; since 1974 nearly a million "guests" have taken the tightly scripted, two-hour tour, which is offered free to those who reserve several weeks in advance.

Visitors wait for the tour group to form in a gallery crammed with Rolls-Royces, from the 1913 Silver Ghost used by the Edwardian elite to all six models of the Phantom series, including a two-tone green 1956 Phantom IV Saloon and an almost contemporary 1979 limousine. The group is escorted through bronze doors "designed in a fifteenth-century Italian style but cast in Burbank," according to the guide, who stresses that one aim of the collection is to foster craftsmanship; the Grand Salon, "built in a composite period style of architecture," has marble floors and columns, a coffered and gilded ceiling, and crystal chandeliers that must have kept many craftsmen occupied during their construction.

More than thirty hand-built luxury cars from the 1920s and 1930s fill the mirrored Grand Salon, suggesting a palatial showroom. Few of the manufacturers of these luxurious motor vehicles survived the Great Depression, but all of the cars are presented in impeccable condition (employing another group of craftsmen in their continual restoration); indeed, keeping hundreds of luxury cars in running condition requires an entire corps of able mechanics. Following a short introduction, visitors are allowed to wander among the cars for a close-up look, while a 1927 Knabe "reproducing piano" plays a song that was recorded on a paper tape. When the music stops, the group is directed up the staircase.

The mezzanine contains ornate French furniture in the eighteenth-century style, both originals—a stand-up butler's desk with rich marquetry—and reproductions—

**Santa Clarita
Farmers Market**
College of the Canyons
(Rockwell Canyon Rd.
and Valencia Blvd.)
Sun. 8:30 a.m.–noon

a copy of a desk used by Louis XV at Versailles. An extraordinarily large and varied collection of hood ornaments includes many fanciful motifs and period designs, and there is one case of crystal sculptures that survived the 1971 earthquake (half of the collection was destroyed).

The group then climbs a spiral staircase to Cloud 99, the dramatic room housing most of the musical instrument collection. Mechanically produced music enjoyed its greatest popularity from 1880 to 1930; it was then supplanted by other recording systems that could reproduce the human voice. The collection includes "reproducing pianos," which have an electric motor that can play ten songs from a paper recording; nickelodeons, a commercial version of the same concept, often used lights and gaudy decoration to attract customers. There are also huge installations of organ pipes, pianos, and percussion instruments that bounced off a ceiling or wall, used in German beer gardens and the like to play oompah music for dancing. During the last half of the tour the guide describes the mechanical system of each instrument and plays a sample piece from several.

Santa Clarita, a community of forty-three square miles on the northern edge of L.A. County, was only incorporated as a city in December 1987, and it subsumed four existing communities: Valencia, a master-planned, 1960s development named for the oranges grown locally; Newhall and Saugus, nineteenth-century towns (named, respectively, for the man who in 1875 bought 48,000 acres in the valley and the town in Massachusetts where he was raised); and Canyon Country, a community that included both horse and hog ranches and condominiums. Planning commissioners are considering a proposal to develop Newhall Ranch, a city of nearly 25,000 new houses and ten schools on nineteen square miles, but the project is opposed by some groups who contend that local water resources are too scarce to support an additional 70,000 people. Newhall Land has included construction of a $7-million water treatment plant to supply reclaimed water for one-third of the projected consumption and is willing to phase in the development over time so its impact on services, traffic, and resources can be monitored.

**The Western Walk of
Fame** (San Fernando Rd.
bet. Fifth and Ninth
Sts., Santa Clarita)
recalls this area's role
in filmmaking.

Santa Clarita Woodlands Park

24255 The Old Road (Park Headquarters)
Newhall 91321
Various entry points;
trailhead parking is available at several locations
Santa Monica Mountains Conservancy:
310-589-3200
Ranger station: 805-255-2974
Daily, sunrise–sunset
Entry: free

Santa Clarita Woodlands Park, encompassing more than 4,000 acres of open space on the north slopes of the Santa Susana Mountains, is an extraordinary mosaic of forests, canyons, year-round streams, meadows, and oak woodlands within view of Interstate 5. The Santa Monica Mountains Conservancy acquired and manages most of the land; additional acquisitions are planned to ensure trail connections and wildlife survival. Each canyon in the park has its own special features: mixed deciduous and big-cone Douglas fir forests characterize Rice and East Canyons; Wiley Canyon is known for natural oil seep, and the vistas from its trails; Towsley Canyon houses the visitors center and a sandstone gorge; and Pico Canyon has the ghost town Mentryville (see p. 275). Trails for hiking, bicycling, and horseback riding are available in each of the canyons.

In Towsley Canyon, Ed Davis Park—named for the former state senator who authored legislation that added the Santa Clarita Woodlands to the Conservancy's Rim of the Valley Trail Corridor and provided funding for the first parkland land purchase —has picnic facilities, an overnight lodge available for group rentals, and a small nature center with exhibits on the natural and cultural history of the Woodlands. Volunteer docents lead weekend hikes.

The geology of the Woodlands became its destiny: petroleum seeps attracted early mammoth hunters as well as latter-day Tataviam Indians, who used the asphalt for medicinal purposes and to waterproof their baskets; Spanish settlers later used the tar to cover the roofs of their adobe homes. Darius Towsley, Alex Mentry, and H. C. Wiley (son-in-law of General Andrés Pico) were early oil explorers and pioneers in the fledgling California oil industry. The last owner of this land was Chevron, which sold or donated all of its historic holdings to the Conservancy in 1995.

Towsley Canyon was the scene of some of the finest horse shows in the West at the Rivendale Ranch Rodeo, and a mecca for early filmmakers: Clayton (Lone Ranger) Moore, Gene Autry, and Roy Rogers rode through the canyons.

Mentryville

27201 Pico Canyon Rd.
Newhall 91321
Santa Monica Mountains Conservancy:
310-589-3200
Ranger station: 805-255-2974
1st and 3rd Sun. of month, noon to 4 p.m.;
docent tours are available; plans are underway
to expand park hours for general trail use;
call first for information
Entry: free

Deep within Pico Canyon, on September 26, 1876, oil gushed from California Star Oil No. 4, marking the debut of the first commercially successful oil well in the West. Charles Alexander Mentry, a French immigrant by way of the Pennsylvania oil fields, drilled out the well and supervised the subsequent oil boom in Pico Canyon; he also established the company town of Mentryville, where as many as 100 families lived in the 1880s and 1890s. California Star Oil Company was bought out by Pacific Coast Oil, which was itself absorbed by the giant Standard Oil Company near the turn of the century, and still later became Chevron USA. As part of a landmark deal with the Santa Monica Mountains Conservancy, Chevron donated all 851 acres of Pico Canyon for public parkland, including the historic remnants of the company town.

During Mentryville's halcyon days, bachelor oil workers lived in bunkhouses while those with families erected cottages along Pico Creek, and a community hall was built for dances and socials. A one-room schoolhouse, named after Charles N. Felton (a future senator and financial backer), was erected in 1885 to serve the children of the area, and a thriving bakery operated by the Cochem family turned out bread and macaroons (for which they became famous) for the canyon workers and for "export" into Newhall. Mentry built himself a spacious Pennsylvania-style two-story home worthy of a prosperous oil field superintendent; wellhead natural gas provided lighting and heating for all the Pico Canyon residents.

Mentry died from a bee sting on October 4, 1900. His untimely demise and competition from other oil fields gradually left Mentryville a ghost town, even though a number of wells continued to produce until old No. 4 was finally plugged and abandoned in 1990: the site of the well is on the National Register of Historic Places as the longest-producing oil well in the world.

Only a few structures still remain from the oil boomtown days: Felton School; Mentry's beautiful superintendent's house (which was severely damaged in the 1994 Northridge earthquake); and the blacksmith's barn, a mule barn, pig sheds, and a tin garage. The Friends of Mentryville provide docent-led interpretive walks around the town, while a moderate stroll up the canyon brings visitors to Johnson Park—a picnic ground built by Chevron for its workers—with rugged sandstone outcrops, an oak-lined year-round stream, luxuriant spring wildflowers, valleywide vistas, and the site of California Star Oil No 4.

Every year in March, the **Cowboy Poetry and Music Festival** celebrates the western heritage of the Santa Clarita area—its cowboys, ranchers, pioneers, *vaqueros*, and Native-Americans—with a three-day, city-sponsored festival at three historic venues: Melody Ranch, William S. Hart Regional Park and Museum, and Mentryville, California's pioneer oil town. This annual gathering highlights the cowboy tradition with performances by some of the finest poets, musicians, and balladeers in the country. Melody Ranch, once owned by legendary cowboy Gene Autry, is the main venue for the festival with performances in the Melody Ranch Theater and Music Hall. Continuous street entertainment animates the western street, and festival-goers can shop along Main Street or in tents in Mercantile Row, choosing from a wide array of western art, gear and tack, clothing, jewelry, and artifacts. There's an authentic chuckwagon and other options in the food court when hunger pains strike.

A special performance of music and poetry is held in silent film star William S. Hart's Spanish colonial mansion (see p. 276). For the adventurous, there is a trail ride through Pico Canyon ending in the old town of Mentryville, and the Santa Clarita Valley Historical Society offers a motor-coach tour that highlights the history of this beautiful valley. Call or write the Santa Clarita Cultural Affairs Office (23920 Valencia Blvd., Ste. 120, Santa Clarita 91355; 805-255-4910) for the schedule of events and ticketing information.

The **Santa Clarita Valley** was the site of the first discovery of gold in California, at Placerita Canyon in 1842, and the place where the railroad lines linking northern and southern California were joined, with a golden spike driven at Lang in 1876. In that same year, oil was discovered in Newhall, which contains the oldest continuously producing oil well in the world.

William S. Hart Regional Park and Museum

24151 San Fernando Rd.
Newhall 91321
Park: 805-259-0855
House tours: 805-254-4584
Park: daily 7 a.m.-sunset
House (by guided tour only):
Wed.–Fri. 10 a.m.–12:30, Sat.–Sun. 11 a.m.–3:30
p.m.; tours on hour and half-hour
Entry: free

William S. Hart was born in New York in 1864 but spent much of his childhood in the Dakota Territory; his pioneer experience in the American West became the basis of his later creative output of western movies and books and gave him a love for Native-American peoples and culture. As a teenager Hart returned with his family to New York, and he eventually developed a successful stage career there. Only in 1914, when he was in his fifties, did Hart move to California and establish a permanent legacy of nearly seventy westerns made during his eleven-year career in silent films. He was an excellent horseman who performed his own stuntwork, and he hoped to convey an authentic vision of the Old West to correct the "impossibilities or libels of the West" that he thought characterized early efforts.

"Two-Gun Bill" became one of the founding partners at Famous Players-Lasky (later Paramount) and one of the biggest money-makers in Hollywood, commanding $150,000 per film plus a share of the profits. In 1925 Hart retired and built his home, La Loma de los Vientos (Hill of the Winds), on the Newhall ranch. The Spanish colonial house is filled with Indian artifacts—including great Navajo textiles —and western paintings and sculpture. Memorabilia of films and prominent people—including western personalities Will Rogers and Wyatt Earp, and aviator Amelia Earhart—suggest the rich life Hart lived here in his later years. He wrote a dozen western novels and short stories and an autobiography, *My Life East and West;* several of his books and videos of his films are available in the gift shop.

On his death in 1946 Hart left his estate to Los Angeles County for a museum, which is administered by the Natural History Museum, and a park, which is operated by the Recreation and Parks Department. The grounds include an exhibit of farm equipment, live animals, a large grassy picnic area, and hiking trails (posted with rattlesnake warnings) through the 155 acres of wilderness.

Heritage Junction Historic Park

Santa Clarita Valley Historical Society
24107 San Fernando Rd.
Newhall 91322
805-254-1275
Grounds: daily 7 a.m.–sunset
Museum: Sat.-Sun. 1–4 p.m.
Entry: free, donations welcomed

In 1876 a golden spike—connecting the tracks of the Southern Pacific Railroad running north from Los Angeles and south from San Francisco—was driven at Lang in the Santa Clarita Valley. The railroad brought development to the pastoral area, and it also brought day-trippers from Los Angeles for rodeos or hunting; the Presidential Special of Benjamin Harrison visited in 1891, and Teddy Roosevelt stepped off the train in 1903. Train stations were central to life in the Santa Clarita Valley at the beginning of the century, but in 1971 all service was discontinued. Only one station has survived: the Saugus train station, built in 1886 of California redwood, was moved in 1980 to its present location in Hart Park, where it serves as the centerpiece of a collection of historic buildings and as the headquarters of the Santa Clarita Valley Historical Society. Permanent exhibits within the museum document local oil and mining industries, the discovery of gold at Placerita Canyon, and westerns filmed in the area; an annotated map identifies such points of interest as the site of the 1928 dam collapse in San Francisquito Canyon—a disaster equaled in property damage and loss of life only by the 1906 San Francisco earthquake and fire—and the Saugus Speedway, which was built in 1924 as a rodeo stadium.

In 1982 the Society was given a circa 1900 Mogul locomotive, which is being restored on tracks next to the station. In 1986 Society members literally took a stand around the Mitchell Adobe Schoolhouse, which was threatened by bulldozers; the adobe was removed, brick by brick, and reassembled and restored at Heritage Junction. In 1987 the Junction received three new structures: Kingsbury House, a circa-1878 residence from downtown Newhall, and a schoolhouse and chapel from Mission Park (a tourist attraction located in Culver City until 1963, then moved to Mint Canyon). The 1927 schoolhouse was constructed as a movie set and was later converted to hold desks, a blackboard, and a lectern from a small school in Vallejo (which had served from 1858 as a mining camp and frontier settlement not unlike those in this area during the nineteenth century). The 1926 Ramona Chapel, named after the famous novel by Helen Hunt Jackson, was designed by tourist-attraction operator Robert E. Callahan after one at Rancho Camulos, where the novel was written; he used bits and pieces of old churches in his construction and created the altar with materials salvaged from a 200-year-old mission. It was used as a movie set by western stars (including John Wayne), and Gary Cooper was inducted into the Sioux Nation on its front steps.

In 1989 the Edison House—a residence of Swiss-Germanic design that had been built in 1919 by Southern California Edison to house employees—joined the collection; it had been the home of Patrolman Raymond Starbard, who alerted his neighbors to the 1928 collapse of the St. Francis Dam, which took more than 450 lives. The Newhall Ranch House (ca. 1861) is an example of Victorian stick architecture, with a gabled roof and veranda on three sides; purchased by town founder Henry Mayo Newhall in 1875, it was ranch headquarters for his land holdings near the present site of the Six Flags Magic Mountain theme park. Pardee House, also known as the Good Templars Hall, was built circa 1890 by Henry Clay Needham, who ran for the U.S. Senate on the Prohibition ticket and was a favorite-son candidate for the presidency in 1920—it derives its name from a later owner, Ed Pardee, a pioneer oil man, local constable, and owner of a livery stable. It too was featured in cowboy movies, and it has been fixtured as a visitors center for the city and its historical society. Walkways constructed of recycled bricks link the various structures, leading to picnic tables and a rose garden featuring 300 varieties popular between 1850 and 1950.

Olde Towne Days is an annual springtime event at Heritage Junction that features hay rides, music, old-fashioned games, and craft demonstrations.

An expedition to the **Roy Rogers –Dale Evans Museum** is offered as part of the Cowboy Music and Poetry Festival. Although it is not in L.A. County, this treasure trove of memorabilia collected by the most famous cowboy couple of all time is easily accessible from Highway 15 in eastern San Bernardino County (15650 Seneca Rd., Victorville 92392; 619-243-4547). Two videos are presented continuously, but the highlight is Trigger, who still looks great after all these years, perhaps because he has been mounted (not stuffed) with loving care. This museum is open daily from 9 a.m. to 5 p.m. (adults $5, children $3).

Placerita Canyon Nature Center

19152 W. Placerita Canyon Rd.
Newhall 91321
805-259-7721
Daily 9 a.m.–5 p.m.
Entry: free

Local historians assert that Placerita Canyon is the spot where gold was *first* discovered in California, six years before the strike at Sutter's Mill that began the Gold Rush. Legend holds that on March 9, 1842, Francisco Lopez, the majordomo of the Mission San Fernando, pulled a wild onion from the ground beneath an ancient, majestic oak tree and found a gold nugget clinging to its roots; the Heritage Trail is an easy (and wheelchair accessible) walk leading from the Nature Center in Placerita Canyon to this site, California Historical Landmark #168, which is still shaded by the Oak of the Golden Dream.

Other, more rigorous trails can be followed through the 350 dramatic acres of Placerita Park, and easy self-guided nature trails depart from the nature center. Printed guides "written for primary level ecologists" help identify plants, characteristic geological formations, and animal habitats, and well-designed displays in the nature center building elucidate similar concepts, such as the biotic communities, geological formation, microclimates, and the food chain of the canyon. There are live animal exhibits indoors and out on the enclosed patio, and three huge stuffed birds are suspended overhead—a California condor, great horned owl, and golden eagle. Families enjoy the nature walks (Sat. 11 a.m.) and the animal shows presented at the nature center (Sat. 1 p.m.). The flat grassland near the building has a playground and picnic tables under the oaks near the stream.

Location scouts brought early moviemakers into Placerita Canyon: *Robin Hood* (with Errol Flynn) and *The Cisco Kid* and *Hopalong Cassidy* serials were filmed here, and Disney still maintains a 691-acre ranch nearby with a western town set that can be glimpsed from the road (the working facility is not open to the public).

Eight-day summer camp sessions for children six to twelve concentrate on specific topics such as ecology, geology, botany, reptiles, and amphibians. The three- and five-day sessions include lots of nature walks through the park, along with hands-on encounters with plants and animals; for more information, call 805-259-7721.

California Institute of the Arts (CalArts)

24700 McBean Pkwy.
Valencia 91355
805-255-1050
www.calarts.edu
Tours: Mon.–Fri. 1:30 p.m.
(when school is in session)

CalArts, which Walt Disney, a founding board member and principal financial supporter, dreamt would be the "Caltech of the arts," incorporated two existing professional schools—the Los Angeles Conservatory of Music and Chouinard Art Institute—and in 1961 became the first degree-granting institution in the U.S. created specifically for students in both visual and performing arts. Conceived as a community unrestrained by traditional boundaries, where student creativity was to be nurtured by professional artists, CalArts offers degrees in dance, film, video, and theater, as well as art and music. In 1971 it established its campus on sixty hilly acres overlooking the Santa Clarita Valley; within a single building that covers eleven acres, its faculty (225 professional artists) and 1,000 students explore the process of making art together. The proximity of the departments fosters a cross-fertilization of the arts and makes the CalArts campus a creative hotbed.

CalArts points with pride to the success of its graduates: playwright James Lapine has been awarded Tony and Pulitzer prizes; two CalArts grads have won the coveted MacArthur "genius" grants (performance artist Guillermo Gomez-Peña and actor-vaudevillian Bill Irwin); and Oscars have gone to animator John Lasseter and special-effects wizard Robert Blalack. Many of its graduates have become productive filmmakers, and CalArts continues to invest in state-of-the art equipment to train the next generation in cutting-edge technologies.

The School of Art has programs in art, photography, and graphic design, and a separate school, Critical Studies, complements students' art training by teaching the humanities, sciences, and social sciences, and offers graduate degrees in writing.

CalArts has no rivals for cultural programming in the Santa Clarita Valley, and more than 500 performances, art exhibitions, films, poetry readings, and special events held each year on the campus are open to the public. Musical performances are offered on a regular schedule: every Tuesday at noon a free concert is presented by a faculty-student group in the Main Gallery, and on Wednesdays and Fridays a noon jazz concert is held in the same location. For information on evening events that showcase young artists who are learning art by making art, call the ticket office (805-253-7800 or 818-362-2315; Mon.–Fri. noon–6 p.m.).

High school students can participate in a variety of workshops and classes presented through the Community Arts Partnership (CAP): call 805-222-2710 for information.

The **Ridge Route**, thirty miles of twisting, rutted roadway between Castaic and Gorman, had been cut by horse-drawn dirt-scrapers in 1914 through the intersection of three mountain ranges, the San Gabriels to the east, the Sierra Madre to the west, and the Tehachapis to the north. But by 1933 an alternative route was opened, and that second pass eventually became the steep five-mile grade that motorists today know as the Grapevine. The Ridge Route was all but forgotten, but some of those who had survived early car trips to northern California remembered this engineering feat, and one sought the assistance of administrators at the Angeles National Forest in preserving this piece of local history. In 1997, they were successful in having the Ridge Road added to the National Register of Historic Places, seeking a federal (rather than local) designation because most of the route passes through U.S. Forest Service land.

The **Saugus Ranger District** of the Angeles National Forest separates the Santa Clarita Valley from the Antelope Valley and provides residents of both areas with recreational opportunities in a land of strange and wonderful scenery. This northernmost stretch of L.A. County climbs towards the Grapevine and shelters three lakes—Pyramid (805-257-2986), Elizabeth (805-296-9710), and Castaic (805-257-4050)—which draw boating and fishing enthusiasts from throughout Southern California. Contact the Ranger office (30800 Bouquet Canyon Rd., Saugus 91350; 805-296-9710) for information on camping, as well as maps of 145 miles of hiking and equestrian trails (including 100 miles along the Pacific Crest Trail); mountain bikers will find 7.5 miles of trails that welcome them along the Warm Springs Mountain and Artisan trails. A Place to Shoot (9 mi. up San Francisquito Rd.; 805-296-5552) offers archery and riflery ranges, and is the only authorized area for these activities.

Vasquez Rocks Regional Park

10700 W. Escondido Canyon Rd.
Agua Dulce 91350
805-268-0840
Daily 8 a.m.–sunset
Entry: free

This 745-acre park in the high desert was named for Tiburcio Vasquez, a nineteenth-century horse thief and robber who hid out among its unusual rock formations (until he was hanged for his misdeeds). Giant slabs of sandstone—tilted by movements of the San Andreas Fault—create hidden canyons that can be traversed on horseback, and caves lure intrepid explorers.

Shambala Preserve

6867 Soledad Canyon Rd.
Acton 93510
805-268-0380
One weekend per month by advance appt.; guests must be over 18
Entry: $35 per person

Actress Tippi Hedren is the force behind the nonprofit Roar Foundation, which maintains sixty acres along Soledad Canyon Road (off the Antelope Valley [CA 14] Fwy.) for the shelter of exotic animals, mainly wild cats and a few elephants; Shambala, from the ancient Sanskrit, means "a meeting place of peace and harmony for all beings, animal and human."

Some 800 trees have been planted to create a high canopy above the Santa Clara River, which is lined with native cottonwoods. The waterway, ponds, and lakes create a stopover on the Pacific Flyway, where white egrets and gray herons have created a habitat, and many migrating ducks can be seen.

The "safaris" are four-hour visits that include both guided tours and free time to picnic or stroll through the beautiful site. The seventy cats (large and small, exotic and native) are the focus of most visitors' attention: there are African lions, Bengal and Siberian tigers, African and Asian leopards, cheetahs, servals, and American mountain lions, but none of these "wild ones" were born in the wild, nor could they survive there. Shambala Preserve, which relies on donations to the Roar Foundation to supply expert veterinary care and appropriate diets, has created a safe haven for these magnificent animals.

The **Antelope Valley**, geographically part of the Mojave Desert, is said by some to have derived its name from herds of those animals which once roamed there, but author Mike Davis asserts in *City of Quartz* that there is no evidence for that derivation, that pronghorns were only "introduced in the Space Age, partially to allow the Valley to live up to its name!" This isolated area of Los Angeles County certainly identifies itself with the Space Age. It boasts two specialized museums on flight testing and is the home of Edwards Air Force Base (though Edwards is no longer the primary site of space shuttle launches or landings), which straddles the L.A.-Kern county line. Bright fields of California poppies and other spring wildflowers, and strange desert formations preserved in its parks—Saddleback Butte, Red Rock Canyon, and Devil's Punchbowl —attract other visitors more willing to remain on earth (even if it does resemble the moon here).

The odd outline of Los Angeles County includes Lancaster and Palmdale, remote desert towns that are an anomaly in the county. A plaque located southwest of Palmdale on the Antelope Valley (CA 14) Freeway describes features of the San Andreas Fault; the fault is visible in rock formations caused by tectonic compression, which can be seen along the highway and in the immediate vicinity.

A wildflower information line (818-768-3533), operated in the spring during peak wildflower season, directs visitors to the most scenic vistas.

The **Antelope Valley California Poppy Reserve** (15101 W. Lancaster Rd. near 160th St., Lancaster (15 mi. west of town); 805-942-0662) encompasses 1,700 acres reserved for viewing California's official state flower. The fields of orange flowers can be viewed from about seven miles of easy trails, each about 1.5 miles round-trip, and are spectacular in spring—if climatic conditions have been favorable and if the desert wind isn't blowing too hard. Exhibits in the visitors center (daily 9 a.m.–4 p.m. mid-March to mid-May; 805-724-1180) explain how the building's passive solar design demonstrates state-of-the-art techniques for energy conservation.

The state park system includes a 566-acre forest of Joshua trees (located just west of Lancaster) named for Archie Ripley, an Antelope Valley rancher who bequeathed it for use as a public park. Like most desert plants, the Joshua tree, which is actually a giant lily, grows slowly—about three inches per year—but specimens with the proportions of trees are not unusual; in spring Joshua trees are covered with creamy white blooms that grow larger and larger for about three months. Mormon settlers gave the plant its name because its strange silhouette suggested the prophet pointing the way.

Red Rock Canyon State Park (off Hwy. 14, 23 mi. northeast of Mojave in Cantil; 805-942-0662) also preserves stands of Joshua trees, but it is better known for the unique rock formations that have earned it the nickname "Little Grand Canyon of California": accordionlike folds of red and white sediments are capped with a harder layer of black basaltic rock or pink volcanic tuff. Creosote bushes, which scientists think may be one of the oldest forms of plant life, are abundant. Desert-dwelling animals emerge during the cooler hours of the day, and birds—migrating and resident populations—make this a prime destination for bird watchers. During the nesting season (Feb.–May) access to Scenic Canyon is restricted to permit new families of birds of prey to form in the cliffs, but the visitors center (Sat.–Sun. 8 a.m.–4 p.m. mid-Sept.–Memorial Day) contains exhibits on birdlife, as well as geology, paleontology, and the human history of the area (which was home to the Kawaiisu people). Nature hikes are scheduled on Sunday mornings at 9 a.m. (Feb.–May, Oct.–Nov.).

Tomo-Kahni, the winter home of the Kawaiisu people, is the newest state park in the Mojave; the site, just outside the town of Tehachapi, is accessible only by guided tours, which are scheduled in spring and fall. Call the Mojave Sector office (805-942-0662) or the Tehachapi Heritage League (805-822-3937) for more information.

Devil's Punchbowl Park (28000 Devil's Punchbowl Rd., Pearblossom), a county park, may upset those who fear earthquakes, which formed its unusual landscape: rock slabs jumbled in the bowl-like depression at the center of the 1,300-acre park reflect the active geological faults in our area. The garden of ancient, fossilized rocks is three miles long and up to a mile wide; there are groves of manzanita, juniper, and piñon, and a seasonal stream. A small visitors center (Sat.–Sun. 9 a.m.–4 p.m.; 805-944-2743) near the rim has displays on the natural history of this area, which lies within the Angeles National Forest.

Antelope Valley Indian Museum

15701 E. Avenue M
Lancaster 93584
805-946-3055
Sat.–Sun. 11 a.m.–4 p.m. (closed July 1–Oct. 1)
Entry: adults $3, children 6-12 $1.50

A half-mile nature trail surrounding the Antelope Valley Indian Museum identifies plants and animals of the desert environment and allows visitors a closer view of the butte's unusual rock formation.

The Antelope Valley Indian Museum incorporates three distinct elements, which have bonded over time in a curious symbiosis that makes it unique. The site itself is characterized by a butte—a natural rock formation—onto which a structure in the unlikely Swiss-chalet style was grafted in the 1930s. Since 1940, the unusual building has been used as a museum of Native-American and Southwestern artifacts, some left by the first owner, others added and installed by the second owner.

Howard Edwards, who built the fanciful stone structure with seven roof elevations and two gabled turrets, had homesteaded a claim near Piute Butte (about seventeen miles east of the center of Lancaster) and intended the building to serve as his family home and to house his extensive collections; the second-story room known today as the California Hall, whose floor is the top of a rock structure, was designed specifically for artifact display. He furnished the house with pieces fashioned from redwood planks and Joshua-tree branches, and he built dioramas that depicted his understanding of Indian life. Within a decade of constructing the building, the Edwardses tired of its remote location, but its unique structure and isolation appealed to Grace Oliver, a student of anthropology researching Piute Butte—she purchased the building and operated it as a private museum for almost forty years. Displaying California Indian artifacts in the upstairs California Hall, as Edwards had intended, she transformed the former living and dining rooms on the lower level with large panels of kachina dolls painted on the pitched ceiling, and

added displays about Southwestern Indian groups, which include many Native-American textiles.

When the state of California acquired the property in 1979, the style of the exhibits reflected the spirit of the founders more than they did contemporary scholarship. With state ownership, the museum for the first time was staffed by a professional administration, who began to sort and catalogue the collections and confront the environmental problems inherent in the building. It is a difficult, ongoing task —compounded by the loss of all collection records—but aided by a National Endowment for the Arts grant in 1992, more than half of the museum's nearly 10,000 objects have been catalogued and photographed to create a modern database on CD-ROM. Some artifacts were discovered to be fakes, while the unique value of others was revealed. Researchers were puzzled by some of the kachinas—some had odd painted motifs and were constructed from balsa wood rather than the traditional root of the water-seeking cottonwood tree—and they discovered that Mr. Edwards had in fact crafted them; these items are now identified as "pseudo-kachinas" on interpretive panels prepared to aid visitors on self-guided tours. Docents, who undergo rigorous training, lead groups of ten or more on a more insightful visit; tour reservations are required (805-942-0662).

The California Hall showcases objects from coastal indigenous peoples of Southern California and the Channel Islands; there are woven sea-grass specimens that are 2,500 years old, as well as fishing equipment and stone animal effigies. The downstairs rooms were reinstalled in 1991 with displays on the people of the western Great Basin—lands east and southeast of the Sierra Nevada, including the Mojave Desert.

Saddleback Butte State Park (3,000 acres just east of the intersection of E. Ave. J and N. 170th St., Lancaster) was created in 1960 to preserve native Joshua tree woodland and the butte itself, a flat-top rocky outcropping that is a vestige of a long-ago larger mountain. A two-mile trail to the top of 3,650-foot Saddleback Butte offers a panoramic view of the desert and the San Gabriel Mountains that divide it from the L.A. basin. A nature trail provides information on rare Mojave ground squirrels, desert tortoises, Mojave rattlesnakes, roadrunners, kangaroo rats, and other native wildlife; call Mojave Desert State Parks (805-942-0662) for information about regional parks.

Air Force Flight
Test Center Museum

1100 Kincheloe St., Bldg. 7211
Edwards Air Force Base 93523
805-277-8050
Tues.–Sat. 9 a.m.–5 p.m.
Entry: free

Within just a few years of World War II, aerospace science evolved from the prop plane to the space shuttle, which was tested and first landed on the baked earth of Rogers Dry Lake—"nature's finest landing field"—at the northernmost edge of L.A. County. The legacy of the test pilots and research personnel of Edwards AFB who contributed to this technological leap forward is preserved in a small museum that includes the "First Flights Wall," a model display of more than 100 aircraft that completed their maiden flights here. Other exhibits document the base's role in supersonic flight: after Chuck Yeager's blast

was changed a few years back. Californians will again be able to witness a pioneering space program when the X-33 begins testing in 1999. This half-scale prototype of a new unmanned shuttle is part of NASA's effort to scale back costs: because the space vehicle is unmanned, it is expected to deliver a payload of the same size as the current shuttle at 10 percent of the cost. When the bugs have been worked out of the X-33 prototype, the full-size *VentureStar* space vehicle will launch and land from the California desert in the next millennium; call 805-258-3449 for program information.

Dryden Space Shuttle Update (805-258-3520) is a hotline with recorded information, but the launches themselves take place from Florida. Until X-33 testing begins, Angelenos can no longer pack binoculars and a thermos to witness aeronautical history dawning at one of the sites where so much has happened in the past.

through the sound barrier in October 1947, successive barriers of time and space—to Mach 6 and above 300,000 feet —were conquered by flight pioneers in the sky above the high desert. Films on flight testing and Edwards are shown in the museum's theater.

Part of the collection of sixty-five historic aircraft is on view, and more will be displayed when a new museum is constructed at a site on Rosamond Boulevard. Entry to the base is restricted, so visitors (who are advised to telephone before driving there) request a map to the museum at one of the three entry gates.

Edwards Air Force Base, which straddles the L.A.-Kern county line, is now only the secondary landing site of the space shuttle, and because the vehicle must be transported at great expense across the U.S. to the Kennedy Space Center in Florida for launch, it is rarely used. There have been no launches or landings at this site in the past two years, and only ninety-minutes' advance warning was given for those that were made in the desert since the policy

NASA Dryden
Flight Research Center

TR-42, Edwards Air Force Base 93523
805-258-3446, 805-258-3460
By guided tour only:
Mon.Fri. 10:15 a.m. and 1:15 p.m.;
reservations advisable
Entry: free

This facility was built in the postwar years to develop the first vehicles to fly at or beyond the speed of sound. There is a small room with models and gear used by pilots and astronauts on display, but you need reservations (805-258-3446, 805-258-3460) for the ninety-minute tours offered twice each weekday. Then you can: stroll to a spot overlooking the dry lakebed used for shuttle landings; enter a few hangars and see the F-18 collection of jet aircraft used as chase planes, as well as aerial photography; and get a close look at static displays that are parked outside the museum. While waiting for the tour, peruse the exhibits on the aeronautical research conducted at Dryden, which includes many of the operating systems of the space shuttle—from flight control software to thermal shields.

Blackbird Airpark

U.S. Air Force Plant 42
25th St. E. at Ave. P
Palmdale 93550
Edwards Air Force Base: 805-272-6700
Fri.–Sun. 10 a.m.–5 p.m.
Entry: free

The Lancaster Performing Arts Center (750 W. Lancaster Blvd., Lancaster; 805-723-5950) is a 759-seat, city-run venue.

Three acres of the Air Force's Production Flight Test Installation at Palmdale have been dedicated to "preserve the proud heritage of the entire Blackbird family," including the first Blackbird ever built—an A-12 that completed its maiden flight on April 26, 1962. The Lockheed SR-71A, a once ultrasecret drone on loan from NASA, performed operational duties for twenty years at Beale Air Force Base.

A microclimate in the high desert allows luscious summer fruit to flourish in one valley (between Palmdale and Lake Hughes) dubbed **Cherry Valley**, although its formal name is the Leona Valley. There are fifteen or twenty ranches with varieties from Bing to Royal Ann ready for picking in June along Leona Avenue and 87th and 90th Streets. Call the Leona Valley Cherry Association Hotline (805-266-7116 or 805-724-1732) or the chambers of commerce in Littlerock (805-944-6990) or Pearblossom (805-261-3308) for more information.

The Benedictine monks at **Saint Andrew's Abbey** (31001 N. Valyermo Rd., Valyermo; 805-944-2178) in the northeastern corner of L.A. County, invite the public to an old-fashioned country fair during one fall weekend at the ranch they converted to their headquarters after they were kicked out of China in 1952. Admission is free, but parking costs $4, and there are modest charges for the petting zoo ($1) and pony rides ($2). Local 4-H kids display prized animals, pumpkins and ceramics made at the monastary are for sale, and on the entertainment stage, Nuns for Fun are the headliners.

City of Lancaster Museum and Art Gallery

44801 N. Sierra Hwy.
Lancaster 93534
805-723-6250
Tues.–Sat. 11 a.m.–4 p.m., Sun. 1–4 p.m.
(closed bet. exhibits; call ahead)
Entry: free, donations welcomed

This city-owned facility was inaugurated in 1986 so that locals don't have to go "down below"—into Los Angeles—to get a cultural fix. Seven or more exhibitions each year, range from an annual juried art show, surveys of early California missions, Antelope Valley history, and ethnic art. The museum also administers Lancaster's oldest building, the 1889 **Western Hotel/Museum** (557 W. Lancaster Blvd., Lancaster; 805-723-6260), which is generally open Friday to Saturday noon to 4 p.m. (call to confirm).

Antelope Valley African-American Museum

416 Lumber St.
Lancaster 93534
805-723-0811
Tues., Thurs., Fri.–Sat. 10 a.m.–3 p.m.
Entry: donations welcomed

In 1993 an entrepreneur who had been a resident of the Antelope Valley since 1962 spearheaded the effort to create a museum dedicated to the history of people of African descent. The displays start with the Book of Genesis and feature historical exhibits on African kings, including Hannibal (237–183 B.C.), the master strategist who crossed the Alps and came close to defeating the Roman empire. The process of weaving Kente cloth is explained and some fine examples are displayed. In a a section dedicated to American history there are photographs of 180 African-Americans who have made important contributions, underlining its founders' belief that only when our history is viewed as shared by all people can it be understood and appreciated.

Photo Credits

I. Downtown

p. 13: Central Library, courtesy Foad Farah; p. 15 top: by permission of the Music Center Operating Company; p. 15 bottom: Robert Graham sculpture, photo © 1982 David Randle; p. 16 left: model of Walt Disney Concert Hall, Frank O. Gehry and Associates, photo by Joshua White; p. 16 right: sketch of Colburn School of the Performing Arts, courtesy Colburn School of Performing Arts; p. 17: class at Colburn School, photo by Dana Levy; p. 18: MOCA at California Plaza, photo by Tim Street-Porter, courtesy The Museum of Contemporary Art; p. 19: Pershing Square following its 1994 redesign by Ricardo Legoretta and Laurie Olin, photo by Erhard Pfeiffer, courtesy Maguire Thomas Partners; p. 20: interior of the Bradbury Building, photo by Bruce Boehner, courtesy Los Angeles Conservancy p. 22 bottom; Union Station, photo courtesy Catellus Development Corporation; p22 top:entrance to Gateway Transit Center showing *City of Dreams/River of History* (with mural by Richard Wyatt), photo courtesy MTA Metro Art; p. 26: courtesy Los Angeles Children's Museum; facade of the Los Angeles Theater Center, photo by Thomas K. Meyer, courtesy City of Los Angeles Cultural Affairs Department; p. 29 top: lobby of the Los Angeles Times building, courtesy Los Angeles Times; p. 29 bottom: courtesy Latino Museum of History, Art and Culture; p. 31: model of the addition to the Japanese American National Museum, designed by Gyo Obata, Hellmuth, Obata and Kassabaum, St. Louis; p. 32: entrance to the former Nishi Hongwanji Temple, now the Japanese American National Museum, photo by Norman H. Sugimoto; p. 33: MONA logo, designed by Lili Lakich, courtesy Museum of Neon Art; p. 35: Victorian residences on Carroll Avenue, photo by Robert Brennan, courtesy Los Angeles Conservancy.

II. Hollywood, Miracle Mile, Beverly Hills

p. 48: 1944 War Bond benefit concert at the Hollywood Bowl, photo courtesy Music Center Operating Company Archives, Otto Rothschild Collection; p. 49 top: Ford Amphitheater, photo courtesy Los Angeles County Arts Commission; p. 49 bottom: the Hollywood sign, photo by Dana Levy; p. 50: Freeman House, photo by Julius Shulman, courtesy USC School of Architecture; p. 52:; model for the American Cinematheque at the Egyptian Theater, photo courtesy Hodgetts + Fung Design Associates; p. 54 left: sign announcing many small shops and businesses at Olympic Plaza in Los Angeles's Koreatown, photo courtesy Korean Cultural Center, Los Angeles; p. 54: interior view of the Korean American Museum of Art and Cultural Center, courtesy Korean American Museum of Art and Cultural Center; p. 55: Bullocks-Wilshire building, photo by Julius Shulman, courtesy Los Angeles Conservancy; p. 56: George C. Page Museum of La Brea Discoveries; p. 57: four 1931 vehicles in the opulent setting of an Auburn/Cord dealership, photo courtesy Petersen Automotive Museum; p. 58: Jamm's Diner is modeled after a typical drive-in coffee shop of the 1950s, photo courtesy Petersen Automotive Museum; p. 59: Japanese folk toys, courtesy Craft and Folk Art Museum; p. 60: Henry Kupjack, *Small Roman Triclinium (Banquet Hall),* 1989 photo by Jay Kupjack, courtesy Carole and Barry Kaye Museum of Miniatures; p. 61 top: Anderson Building, Los Angeles County Museum of Art; Rembrandt Harmensz van Rijn, *Portrait of Marten Looten,* 1632, photos courtesy Los Angeles County Museum of Art; p. 61: Diego Rivera, *Flower Day,* courtesy Los Angeles County Museum of Art; p. 64: *Dancing Shiva,* tenth century, courtesy Los Angeles County Museum of Art; p. 67: exterior detail of the Museum of Tolerance, and p. 68: installation in the Tolerancenter, both photos by J. Mendenhall, courtesy Museum of Tolerance at the Simon Wiesenthal Center for Holocaust Studies; p. 70: interior of the Pauline Schindler studio in the 1921—22 Kings Road house/studio by R. M. Schindler, photo by Gerald Zugmann, Vienna, courtesy MAK Center for Art and Architecture, L.A.; p. 73: poster for *Tarantula,* courtesy Universal Studios; p. 75: interior of Greystone Mansion, courtesy Beverly Hills Recreation and Parks Department.

III. Los Feliz, Burbank, Glendale

p. 86: Griffith Observatory, photo by E. C. Krupp; p. 87: Travel Town Museum, photo by Dana Levy; p. 88: Sunday morning at Live Steamers, photo by Dana Levy; p. 89 top: photo by Taud Motoyama; p. 89 bottom: Adventure Island, photo by Dana Levy; p. 90: cover image from *Independent Spirits* catalogue, published by the University of California Press to document a special exhibition at the Autry Museum of Western Heritage; p. 92: American Film Institute's Warner Communications building on the Los Feliz campus, photo by Lee Salem, courtesy AFI; p. 93: Hollyhock House, courtesy Barnsdall Art Park, City of Los Angeles Cultural Affairs Department; p. 97: top and bottom, courtesy Universal Studios; p. 101: exhibits in the Warner Bros. Museum, courtesy Warner Bros.; p. 103: exterior view of the Brand Library and Art Center, photo courtesy City of Glendale; p. 105: Japanese teahouse and garden, courtesy Descanso Gardens.

IV. Pasadena, San Gabriel Valley, Claremont

p. 111: the Rose Bowl; dome of Pasadena's City Hall, both photos courtesy Pasadena Convention and Visitors Bureau; p. 113: staircase and art-glass front door of the Gamble House, courtesy USC School of Architecture; p. 114: exterior rear view of the Gamble House, photo by Tim Street-Porter, courtesy USC School of Architecture; p. 116: gallery in the Norton Simon Museum, courtesy Norton Simon Museum, Pasadena, CA; p. 117: Francisco de Zurbarán, *Still Life with Lemons, Oranges, and a Rose,* 1633, courtesy the Norton Simon Foundation, Pasadena, CA; p. 119 top: 1977 building by Craig Ellwood, courtesy Art Center College of Design; p. 119 bottom Grace Nicholson Chinese Treasure House, now home to the Pacific Asia Museum, Pasadena, which supplied the photo; p. 121: logo for Kidspace Museum, courtesy Kidspace; p. 123: Caltech building, Beckman Laboratory of Chemical Synthesis, courtesy Caltech; p. 125: Deep Space One spacecraft, courtesy Jet Propulsion Laboratory; p. 129: illuminated book, courtesy The Huntington; p. 130: exterior view of the Huntington Mansion (now Art Gallery), designed by Myron Hunt and Elmer Grey, courtesy The Huntington; p. 131: spring in the Japanese garden, photo by Dana Levy; p. 132: Edward Hopper, *The Long Leg,* 1935, courtesy The Huntington; p. 137: Peter Voulkos, ceramic vessel, 1956, from the Marer Collection of Contemporary Ceramics, courtesy Ruth Chandler Williamson Gallery, Scripps College, Claremont; p. 139: rocking chair by Sam Maloof, photo courtesy the artist.

V. Highland Park, East Los Angeles, Pomona

p. 150: Lucy M. Lewis, Lightning pot, photo by Dana Levy, courtesy the artist's estate; p. 151: rendering by John Feeley of El Alisal, former home of Charles F. Lummis, courtesy the Historical Society of Southern California, whose offices are there today; p. 153: crest of the Arroyo Guild over the main entrance of the Judson Studios, which supplied this photo by Tom M. Apostol; p. 154 top: photo © Occidental College; p. 154 bottom: the Los Angeles Police Museum on Wheels, photo courtesy Archives of the Los Angeles Police Historical Society; p. 156: the late Sister Karen Boccalero, founder of Self-Help Graphics and Art; p. 157: Rico Lebrun, *Portrait of Vincent Price,* ca. 1950, photo by Thomas Silliman, courtesy Vincent Price Art Gallery Foundation, East Los Angeles College; p. 158: the Harriet and Charles Luckman Fine Arts Complex, courtesy California State University, Los Angeles; p. 159: drawing of the newly restored San Gabriel Mission, ca.

1993, courtesy Helen Nelson; p. 162: interior view of the Ruth B. Shannon Center for the Performing Arts, courtesy Whittier College; p. 163: Heritage Park, courtesy City of Santa Fe Springs; p. 164: Richard Nixon's birthplace, courtesy Richard Nixon Library and Birthplace; p. 165: Richard Nixon and Elvis Presley, photo ca. 1971, courtesy Richard Nixon Library and Birthplace.

VI. Exposition Park, Crenshaw, South Central L.A.

p. 174: aerial view of the Los Angeles Memorial Coliseum, ca. 1984, photo by Kevin Miller © Bernstein Assoc., Inc., courtesy Los Angeles Memorial Coliseum and Sports Arena; p. 175: Rose Garden entrance of the Natural History Museum of Los Angeles County; p. 176: some actual-size bug specimens from the Insect Zoo collection; Dueling Dinosaurs, photo by Dick Meier and Dan Watson, all photos courtesy Natural History Museum of Los Angeles County; pp. 178–179: view of the new California Science Center; p. 180: "Hypar" sculpture by Chuck Hoberman, photos courtesy California Science Center; p. 182: Jacob Lawrence, *Toussaint Captured Marmalade*, 1987, courtesy California African-American Museum; p. 183: Mudd Hall of Philosophy on the campus of the University of Southern California, courtesy USC; p. 185: music and arts program, courtesy Second Baptist Church; p. 186: William Andrews Clark Memorial Library, courtesy UCLA's William Andrews Clark Memorial Library; p. 188: courtesy Museum of African American Art; p. 190: Terry Braunstein, *Local Odyssey*, installed at the Anaheim station on the MTA Blue Line; p. 191: Eva Cockcroft, *Compton: Past, Present and Future*, installed at the Compton station on the Blue Line, photos courtesy MTA Metro Art; p. 192: Watts Towers, courtesy Watts Towers Arts Center; p. 195: Carl Cheng, *Space Information*, installed at the Marine station on the MTA Green Line, photo courtesy MTA Metro Art.

VII. Long Beach, Harbor District, South Bay

p. 204: historic postcard of Long Beach, Ruthann Lehrer, City of Long Beach; p. 206: architects's rendering of the new Long Beach Aquarium of the Pacific; p.

207: Alexej Jawlensky, *Dreaming Head*, 1916, from the Milton Wichner Collection, courtesy Long Beach Museum of Art; p. 208: Esau Andrade, *Jugando al Pueblito*, 1996; p. 209: Javier de la Garza, *Estructuras*, 1990, both works from the Robert Gumbiner Foundation, courtesy Museum of Latin American Art, Long Beach; p. 210: The Long Beach Public Corporation for the Arts supports arts, culture, and heritage in the local Cambodian community (the largest outside Cambodia) and the many rich cultural traditions in Long Beach; p. 212: Greek Revival homestead built in 1864 at the General Phineas Banning Residence Museum, photo courtesy Dale Berman; p. 213: Vincent Thomas Bridge, courtesy San Pedro Chamber of Commerce; p. 214: a water-cannon salute for the SS *Lane Victory* as it departs Worldport Los Angeles, courtesy SS *Lane Victory*; p. 215: model of an Orca whale in the courtyard of the Cabrillo Marine Aquarium, courtesy Cabrillo Marine Aquarium; p. 216: Point Fermin Park and Lighthouse, photo by Steve Bush, courtesy San Pedro Chamber of Commerce; p. 217 top: wedding at Wayfarers Chapel, designed in 1951 by Lloyd Wright, photo by Dennis DiDomenico; bottom: postcard showing construction, 1951, courtesy Wayfarers Chapel; p. 217 bottom: artist's rendering of the tropical environments at the Long Beach Aquarium of the Pacific, which supplied this photo; p. 219: Lomita Railroad Museum, courtesy Lomita Railroad Museum; p. 220: rendering of Catalina Live-Forever (*Dudleya Hassei*), a plant endemic to Santa Catalina Island, and a native fox, both images courtesy Santa Catalina Conservancy.

VIII. Along the 405 (from the Sepulveda Pass to LAX) and West to the Pacific

p. 231: Skirball Cultural Center, designed by Moshe Safdie, photo by Timothy Hursley; p. 233: Torch of Liberty, photo by Grant Mudford, both photos courtesy Skirball Cultural Center; p. 234: aerial view of the new Getty Center, photo taken in April 1997, by Warren Aenal © J. Paul Getty Trust; p. 235: Vincent van Gogh, *Irises*, 1889; p. 237: Pontormo, *Portrait of a Halberdier (Francesco Guardi?)*, 1528–30; p. 238: Johan Gregor van der Schardt, *Mercury*, ca. 1570–80, all photos courtesy

the J. Paul Getty Trust; p. 240: the recently renovated Royce Hall is a well-known symbol of UCLA and has featured many major performing artists since its opening in 1929; p. 241: David Smith, *Cubi XX*, 1964, in the Franklin D. Murphy Sculpture Garden on the UCLA campus in Westwood; exterior view of UCLA at the Armand Hammer Museum of Art and Cultural Center, designed by Edward Larrabee Barnes; p. 242 bottom: traditional gate at the UCLA Hannah Carter Japanese Garden, all photos courtesy UCLA; p. 243 top: *Duck's Breath*, from "Tell the Bees" exhibition at the Museum of Jurassic Technology; p. 246: Sacred Heart Chapel on the campus of Loyola Marymount University, photo by Glenn Marzano, courtesy the university; p. 248: courtesy Social and Public Art Resource Center; p. 250: *Para los Niños*; p. 252: computer-generated rendering of the new Santa Monica Museum of Art, exterior view from Michigan Avenue, by Narduli/Grinstein Architects, courtesy Santa Monica Museum of Art; p. 253: courtesy Museum of Flying; p. 255: Malibu Tile fountain at the Adamson House, photo courtesy Malibu Lagoon Museum; p. 256: a performance at the Smothers Theater on the campus of Pepperdine University, Malibu.

IX. Three Valleys: San Fernando, Santa Clarita, Antelope

p. 267: The New Performing Arts Center at California State University, Northridge; p. 271 top: a contemporary view of the *convento* at the Mission San Fernando Rey de España; p. 271 bottom: drawing of the Tujunga home of John Steven McGroarty, which is now the McGroarty Art Center; p. 273: this lion is one of the exotic animals that has found shelter at Wildlife Waystation, courtesy Wildlife Waystation; p. 278 top: main building of California Institute of the Arts, and bottom: Frank Terry, director of character animation working, with students in the 2D Computer Animation Lab, photo by Steven A. Gunther, courtesy California Institute of the Arts; p. 279: animals from the Shambala Preserve, courtesy Shambala Preserve; p. 281: Antelope Valley Indian Museum, photo by Nancy Geary, courtesy State of California Department of Parks and Recreation; p. 283: courtesy NASA Dryden Flight Research Center.

Index